Sad, Mad and Bad

SAD, MAD AND BAD

Women and the Mind-Doctors from 1800

LISA APPIGNANESI

McArthur & Company

Toronto

First published in Canada in 2007 by
McArthur & Company
322 King St. West, Suite 402
Toronto, ON
M5V 1J2
www.mcarthur-co.com

Library and Archives Canada Cataloguing in Publication

Appignanesi, Lisa   Sad, mad and bad : women and the mind-doctors from 1800 / Lisa Appignanesi.

Includes bibliographical references and index. ISBN 978-1-55278-6765

1. Women—Mental health--History. 2. Women—Mental health services—History.
3. Mentally ill women—Rehabilitation—History. 4. Mental illness—Treatment—History. I. Title.
RC451.4.W6A66 2007   362.2082'09   C2007-905160-X

Cover Design by Tania Craan
Typeset by M Rules
Printed in Canada by Friesens

The publisher would like to acknowledge the financial support of the Government
of Canada through the Book Publishing Industry Development Program (BPIDP) and
the Canada Council for our publishing activities. The publisher further wishes to acknowledge
the financial support of the Ontario Arts Council for our publishing program.

10 9 8 7 6 5 4 3 2 1

For John, Josh and Katrina
who drive me mad
and make me sane

CONTENTS

PART FOUR

INTO THE PRESENT

ACKNOWLEDGEMENTS

This book owes a great debt to all the researchers, historians, thinkers, doctors – indeed patients, biographers, memoirists, writers and poets – who have ploughed this rich terrain before me. In particular I am grateful to the late, brilliant and indefatigable Roy Porter, who has served as inspiration to so many and who was also a friend. Something of an unattached outsider in the history of psychiatry and psychoanalysis, my debt extends across the divisions in what is nothing if not a contested field. Historians such as Edward Shorter, Andrew Scull, Sander L. Gilman, Richard Hunter and Ida Macalpine have shown the way; but so, too, have Jan Goldstein and Elisabeth Roudinesco in France, Nathan G. Hale, Nancy Tomes, and the anthropologist Tanya Luhrman in America, and Elaine Showalter. Attention needs to be drawn to the maker of one particular and superbly abundant website, Andrew Roberts of Middlesex University.

Over the years I have had conversations with more 'mind doctors' across the psy fields, patients and clients, than I can name or than might wish to be named here; they will find their ideas dotted, transmuted, sometimes argued with, across the coming pages. I also owe a particular debt to Cyril Cannon for a case he pointed me to; to Alison Gardener, Assistant Archivist of the Lothian Health Services Archive, Edinburgh University Library, and Dr Michael Neve of the Department of the History of Medicine at University College London, as well as Andreas Meyer of the Max Planck Institute in Berlin and Jacqueline Carroy, Director of the Centre Alexandre Koyré in Paris. Maria Duggan kindly supplied me with health policy papers, while Jonathan Grey scrutinized and collated all the end matter. Elise Dillsworth, editor, and Sue Phillpott, copy-editor are owed special thanks for their assiduous attention.

I have been honoured by a grant from the Authors' Foundation which helped me see my way to the end of this book. I am very grateful to the Foundation and to their awards committee.

I owe particular thanks to my agent, Clare Alexander, who sparked my writing of this book, and my editor and publisher at Virago/Little, Brown, Lennie Goodings, two extraordinary women, who listened to my occasional moans and encouraged on the way.

The closer to home I get, the greater my debts grow. I could not have written this book without heated arguments, support, constant help and the occasional, usefully pedantic, vigilance of John Forrester, Professor of History and Philosophy of Science at the University of Cambridge, with whom some years ago I co-authored *Freud's Women*. If the final product perhaps bears little relation to what he might himself have written, it nonetheless bears traces of our vigorous discussions. Finally, I thank my children, Josh Appignanesi, who while I was writing this book managed to make an astonishingly fine feature film, and Katrina Forrester, who somehow made her way through Cambridge University. Without their curiosity and energy, little seems worthwhile.

Lisa Appignanesi January 2007

Much madness is divinest sense
To a discerning eye;
Much sense the starkest madness.
'T is the majority
In this, as all, prevails.
Assent, and you are sane;
Demur, — you're straightway dangerous,
And handled with a chain.

From *Life* by Emily Dickinson

INTRODUCTION

The simplest way to begin is to say that this is the story of madness, badness and sadness and the ways in which we have understood them over the last two hundred years. Some of that understanding has to do with how the dividing lines between them were conceived and patrolled, in particular by a growing group of professionals or 'mind doctors', who came to be known, as the nineteenth century turned into the twentieth, as 'alienists', psychiatrists, psychologists, psycho-analysts and psychotherapists. They were also sometimes neurologists, pathologists and latterly neuroscientists and psy-chopharmacologists. All of them thought they were in one way or another illuminating the dark corners of the mind and amassing crucial knowledge. In that sense, and appropriately, they thought of themselves as scientists. They were helped along the way by crimi-nologists, judges, statisticians and epidemiologists. Crucially, they were also helped by patients.

So this is also the story of the way in which madness, badness and sadness — and all the names or diagnoses these states of mind and being have been given as time went on — were lived by various women. Frenzies, possessions, manias, melancholy, nerves, delusions, aberrant acts, dramatic tics, passionate loves and hates, sex, visual and auditory hallucinations, fears, phobias, fantasies, disturbances of sleep, dissocia-tions, communication with spirits and imaginary friends, addictions, self-harm, self-starvation, depression — are all characters in the story this book tells. So too are the Latinate and Greek designations they took on as diagnoses — monomania, melancholia, hysteria, dementia praecox, schizophrenia, anorexia — and their often casual, but scientiz-ing shorthand today, MPD, ADHD, OCD and so on.

Since mind-doctoring, for better or worse, is not only about under-standing and exploring the mind or psyche, emotions and acts, but also sometimes about making them work better together, treatments are also players in this book, whether they are 'moral', surgical, galvanic, electrical, pharmaceutical or talking – sometimes even writing.

I have long been aware of the shallowness of sanity. Most of us are, in one way or another. Madness, certainly a leap of the irrational, is ever close. We have all been children and can remember a parent's or sib-ling's sudden rage – even, though less well, our own explosions. We all sleep and wake and sometimes the dream lingers, won't be shaken off, incomprehensible with its ruptures of time, space and sometimes shape, so that we're as small as Alice confronted by the caterpillar, let alone party to the languorous visions of that opium pipe. We drive along in our cars and suddenly emerge from a trance in which we can't remem-ber who we were. At other times, our dead won't let go of us and shadow our days, as if they were there, in the room, too close. Or we or a partner wakes and simply can't rise. The light has suddenly gone out on the world. It feels as if it will never go on again. Everything is too big, too difficult, too miserable. No pulling up of the socks will fix things. Those negative, persecuting screams of all that is wrong in our lives are so loud only suicide feels as if it might blot them out.

All this is common enough – as are physical symptoms for which the doctor can find no organic base. If any of this persists, or grows exag-gerated, in partners, children or ourselves, we feel fear and perhaps shame. The fear that our minds have grown alien to us, the shame that our acts, words or emotions can slip from our control, are often com-bined with a wish to disguise both states if at all possible, or to find a simple physical reason at their base. In our therapeutic society, we may equally feel that a trip to GP or mind doctor will provide us with a pill that cures.

One of the things that propelled me to start out on the journey that this book became was a sudden rush of blinding information, complete with statistics, of the sort: 'Half of Americans May Meet *DSM-IV* [The Diagnostic and Statistical Manual of Mental Disorders] Criteria for a Mental Disorder During Their Lifetime.' 'One in five women develop Clinical Depression.' 'In a recent 14-country study on disability associated with physical and mental conditions, active psychosis was ranked the third most disabling condition, higher than paraplegia and blindness, by the general population.' Between 1992 and 2002, the use of antidepressants went up by 234 per cent.[1] Three-quarters of the female prison population in Britain suffer from mental health problems.[2]

Such statistics are startling. They made me want to know whether we had entered a century where sadness and madness, let alone attendant badness, had really grown to terrifying proportions. Or whether we had begun to count things we hadn't counted before and certainly not in the same way. In other words, had what we now term a mental disorder come to encompass something more than, or different from, what it had while I was growing up in what now seems like a distant last century, let alone in the century before? Since the business of history, like novel-writing, makes one distrust present certainties, I also wanted to know whether this incessant growth in illness might be linked to the unstoppable growth in potential cures. There is nothing like the discovery of a much publicized set of pills to invoke a mirroring illness. To put this another way, the shape of our unhappiness or discontent can, proteus-like, be morphed to fit the prevalent diagnoses. Sometimes the pills, like other cures, work. At other times, they can make things worse – no matter what the scientific imprimatur they wear. This, too, is part of the matter of this book.

There is a battle being waged in the area of mental health. As more and more of our unhappiness is medicalized, as diagnoses are increasingly attached to conditions or aspects of behaviour and the number of sufferers grows, people want more service – either more pills or more therapy, even of the kind that comes as a computer program. They want doctors to cope with their wild, inattentive (ADHD), suicidal or self-starving children. They want some kind of control or overseeing of those who may be 'perverted', dangerous to others or themselves when in the midst of a frenzy which is also an inner anguish. Or they want help to see them through what they can't get through alone.

At the same time, there's a rising disenchantment with our mind doctors, from within their own ranks, too. The medical imperializing of all parts of our mental, emotional and psychic lives, the pills that promised to make us 'better than well', may now, it seems, have overreached. To assume that sadness, even in its malignant form, is *caused* by a chemical imbalance may not be an altogether useful hypothesis or a particularly true one. I feel sad when my dog dies. That causes a change in my brain. The emotion isn't caused by the brain. Everything animate beings do or feel – from watching a football match, to kissing, to eating – causes complicated chemical change. But no amount of serotonin will bring Mr Darcy to the door, make England win the World Cup, bring peace to warring neighbours or end global warming. Nor – any more than God – may the latest much publicized cure-all: cognitive behaviour therapy. There are many aspects of our lives which have ended up within the terrain of the mind doctors when they might more aptly belong in a social or political sphere either of action or of interpretation.

Exploring the history of madness and mind-doctoring brings all this into focus. Putting historical periods, old diagnoses and symptoms side by side might, some would imagine, give us a bright sense of the rise and rise of science and of our present medical and pharmaceutical miracles. We certainly know far more about our neural and biochemical make-up than Pinel, the founder of 'alienism', or Freud dreamt of. We have more efficient drugs and more elaborate hypotheses. But where we have what may arguably be more sophisticated, certainly more ordered diagnoses, disorders proliferate and also grow in complexity. Therapeutic ideals have so penetrated our Western world that there is sometimes a sense that the 'psy' professions can fix everything. What much of the ensuing history puts into relief is that cures are rarely absolute or for ever.

In one of his pithy, throw-away remarks, the philosopher Ian Hacking noted: 'In every generation there are quite firm rules on how to behave when you are crazy.' Anthropologists have long charted the different expressions of madness and the forms cure may take in unfamiliar cultures. Nor are modern cultures, however globalized, altogether homogeneous where disorder is in question. A BBC programme about Japan, where the population is ageing, recently explored a prevalent and debilitating form of 'stress' characterized by medics as 'retired husband syndrome', an illness that could turn a wife's repressed worry about a salaryman-husband's imminent return to the home, where habits of obedience and servitude would have to be reinforced, into a round of skin rashes, ulcers, asthma and high blood pressure.[3]

As I was amassing material for this book, I realized that symptoms and diagnoses in any given period played into one another in the kind of collaborative work that all doctoring inevitably entails. Often enough, extreme expressions of the culture's malaise, symptoms and disorders mirrored the time's order — its worries, limits, border problems, fears. Anorexia is usually an illness of plenty, not of famine, as depression is one of times of peace and prosperity, not of war. It is perhaps no surprise that an age in which the sum of information available in any given minute is larger than it has ever been in history should find a condition in which attention is at a deficit. This is not a simple matter of mind doctors spotting, shaping, naming — in a word, 'diagnosing' — or even suggesting an illness, though all that happens too. People, and it is people who become patients, are not utterly passive. We are talking here of mental or psychic illness, and, mad or sane, patients are as susceptible to knowledge as doctors and often know how to hide from or use it.

As historians of medicine have increasingly argued, illness is the product of a subtle interplay between cultural perspectives and what is also a shifting biological reality. This is particularly the case with mental illness. In the 1820s and 1830s George Man Burrows was as certain that he had proof of the links between the uterine system and the disordered brain as some doctors and drug companies are today that what is known in the psychiatric manuals as 'Female Sexual Dysfunction' is a question of specific hormones.[4] There was a sense during the last years of the twentieth century that certainty had been arrived at and that the causes of mental illness had been located in brain chemistry, or so the pharmaceutical companies had led us to believe. The new century has brought altered perceptions about biology itself.

If symptoms or disorders can sometimes have aspects of a collaborative production between patients and doctors, this does not make the torment, the anguish of a mind gone awry, any the less real. And intervention by mind doctors can make illness better, though the kind of intervention — care or pill or talk or time away from the family — may not always be as instrumental in the process as is sometimes thought. I was surprised to discover that — in so far as people might be counting the same thing — the percentage of cures through care or time does not seem to have changed all that much over the two hundred or so years that this book's story charts. But our managing of the most extreme forms of mania or delirium has.

I decided to focus on women as a way into this history of symptoms, diagnoses and mind-doctoring for various reasons. Perhaps the first is simply that there are so many riveting cases of women, and through them a large part of what we recognize as the psy professions was constructed. With John Forrester, I had explored some of this terrain in *Freud's Women*.

There is more. Contemporary statistics always emphasize women's greater propensity to suffer from the 'sadness' end of madness. Go to any hundred websites and this will be reiterated, and perhaps not only because women buy more self-improving drugs:

Women are twice as likely to experience depression as men.
Depression is the leading cause of disability in women.
Almost 15 per cent of women suffering from severe depression
 will commit suicide.
Approximately 7 million women in the United States are
 clinically depressed. In Britain, one out of every nine seek
 help for a mixture of anxiety and depression.[5]
Forty per cent of those claiming incapacity benefit in the UK do
 so on grounds of mental illness: the majority are women.[6]

These figures may be true enough. Certainly if they aren't 'true', the cultural illusion prevails. A magazine like *Psychologies*, which looks at the softer side of psychic order and disturbance, always carries a woman's face on its cover, as if psychology, that whole business of understanding the (troubled) mind and relations, were uniquely a feminine undertaking, whatever the gender of the doctors. Hardly surprising to find that two out of three clients for the talking cures offered by Cambridge University's Staff Counselling Service are women.[7]

The study of women, madness and mind doctors has its own history, and one which has gone through several shifts since Simone de Beauvoir first explored the terrain in *The Second Sex*. What came clear in that major study was that a particular period's definitions of appropriate femininity or masculinity were closely linked to definitions of madness. Not conforming to a norm risks the label of deviance or madness, and is sometimes attended by confinement. For Friedan, Millett, Greer, the great feminists of the second wave, mind doctors constituted the enemy, agents of patriarchy who trapped women in a psychology they attributed to her, stupefied her with pills or therapy, and confined her either to the 'madhouse' or the restricted life of conventional roles. The promise was held out that women's rise in the professions would change all this.

Historians of the 1980s and '90s showed us that not only were there hidden prejudices in the way in which women were conceived of and treated, but that easy notions of historical progress and objectivity were themselves to be interrogated. It became clear that disease as much as gender and biology were hardly fixed universals, free of their time's, or our, ways of seeing. The history of psychiatry was not just the history of a great march down the Boulevard of Science towards immutable scientific laws and better drugs for everything. Today, we might want to question whether brain scans and neurochemistry, whatever else they may teach us, really do hold the keys to an ultimate knowledge of the mind and its disorders.

One of the questions I set out to explore in writing this book was how the growing number of women on all sides of the mental health professions had reshaped the practice; whether, indeed, they had made things better for women and in the process redefined the 'female malady'. My findings, which make up the last section of this book, did not always live up to my own hopes; but the habit of interrogating history or the present doesn't stop because its actors change gender. Alternatively, whatever my own wish to separate biology altogether from destiny, my exploration did make me think again that certain events in a woman's life, whether childbirth or menopause, could well in some cases bring with them a susceptibility to disorder.

Clifford Geertz, the great anthropologist, once talked of 'blurred genres', a kind of thinking and writing which drew on any number of mixed, cross-disciplinary sources to arrive at a thick texture of descriptions. I make no apology for using what may at first seem like a random assortment of materials, from philosophy or text book to hospital notes, memoir, letters, biography and popular magazines. I have also plundered the work of more specialist historians who over these last decades have done so much to fill in the gaps of a riveting set of practices and ways of thinking about the human. I have made my way through this wealth of material by focusing in on individual cases. Cases illuminate. They allow us to tease out the intersections and interactions of culture, psychiatric practice and illness in a given historical moment. They show us how disorders are suffered, but also lived over time. What they clearly reveal is that lives can be both productive *and* punctured or punctuated by madness and sadness, let alone badness.

I have been drawn by two kinds of cases. There are those which retrospectively divulge the various threads that go into the thinking of their time and so exemplify a condition. Such, for example, are Mary Lamb, Alice James, Celia Brandon, Sylvia Plath and Marilyn Monroe. Others, like those of Henriette Cornier, Miss Beauchamp, Charcot's Augustine and Freud and Breuer's Anna O, are cases which were important in moving the profession and the understanding of mental disorder forward in their own time. Narrated or exhibited to a wide public, these cases also played into the mimicry and diffusion of symptoms and diagnosis. Because I am also interested in the whole protean process of symptom-shaping, I have deliberately not steered away from the famous cases. After all, Sylvia Plath's iconic marriage of great talent, depression and suicide made her into an influential model of one way of being woman.

The book begins in 1796 with Mary Lamb because that turn of the century marked a moment before mind-doctoring in any modern sense had begun, though some of the philosophical currents which would shape it were under way. Her story provides a useful point of comparison for what comes after. The next three sections chart the rise of the new science, particularly in Britain, France and then America, up into the present. Each chapter coalesces around a dominant cultural interest, or form of understanding, which also marks prevalent sets of diagnoses and symptoms. My 'theory', such as it is, is all in this structure, which is also a means of selection.

It became clearer and clearer to me, as my research went on, that particular periods for whatever reason threw certain expressions of mental illness into view and that diagnoses or explanations clustered around these. Deep historical forces, it would seem, sometimes bring to the surface certain crystallizations of disorder and its antidote, though the second can occasionally come first: passions, nerves, sleep, sex, food, abuse have all had their moment as symptom and point of scientific interrogation.

As for solutions, human care (and what is good doctoring, at its root, but that, plus a useful placebo effect!) may often be more effective than scientific cure, as some of the odd partnerships in the history of mental suffering show – whether between sister and brother, wife and husband, or even patient and therapist, though the latter would probably prefer to call this care 'science'. Policy makers might also find it worth noting that on the whole when asylum populations go up, prison populations go down, and vice versa. And whichever form of *confinement* period and place decide on, humane care, attentiveness and occupation help. Few people are mad, bad or sad continually and for ever: if the pain endured by the sufferer is frightening, unbearable and damaging, often to those around her as well, it can dissipate, too. There are no firm rules where sadness and madness are concerned. But there can be, as this history shows, full and intriguing lives with heroes on both sides of that doctor–patient divide which has for the last hundred years been increasingly permeable.

Finally, people have asked me why, after writing fiction, I have chosen to immerse myself in the history of a science and practice which has so many of its own writing professionals. Have I been a practitioner? Am I a patient?

I could answer that, as a writer, I simply have a faith in the outsider's view and have always had a fascination for the vagaries of the human mind. Or, since there are many ways of tracing one's trajectory, I could say that an interest in madness was also a form of survival. My early family life – which I evoked in *Losing the Dead* – amongst people chased by the Holocaust to peaceful Canadian shores had its own strangeness, one that was hardly reflected in television sitcoms. Retrospectively, it makes sense that I wrote an MA thesis on Edgar Allan Poe and his hauntings by the dead and undead; and that I worked part-time for a psychoanalytic publishing house in New York, turning what was often expert babble into prose. My doctorate, though in literature, already contains some of the strands of this book: how femininity was constructed and understood by the great writers of the turn of the nineteenth century, in particular, Henry James, brother of Alice, who features in these pages; Proust, still the greatest literary psychologist, and Robert Musil, a near-neighbour of Freud's, who also came into that modernist literary picture with its everyday psychopathologies.

Freud's Women is, of course, part of this trajectory, as are several of my novels, from *Memory and Desire* to *Sanctuary* and *Paris Requiem*, where mind doctors somehow seem to intervene to strut their stuff. Finally, my mother's Alzheimer's vividly reminded me both how fragile and how extraordinary the human mind is. It sent me on a journey into the harder side of the brain sciences. I spent two years shadowing the world of the Brain and Behaviour Lab of the Open University. Here, neuro-scientist Steven Rose led research into memory. I was forced, through what sometimes felt like supervisions, alongside reading and confer-ences, to confront a biochemical approach to brain and mind. All this is partly reconfigured in my novel *The Memory Man*. Of course, it also pre-pared me for the work in these pages.

In a way, *Sad, Mad and Bad* is a book I have been writing all my life.

PART ONE

A TIME BEFORE . . .

1

MAD AND BAD

On Saturday 24 September, 1796, *The Times* of London carried the following report of a matricide.

> On Friday afternoon the Coroner and Jury sat on the body of a Lady, in the neighbourhood of Holborn, who died in consequence of a wound from her daughter the preceding day.
>
> It appeared by the evidence adduced, that while the family were preparing for dinner, the young lady seized a case-knife laying on the table, and in a menacing manner pursued a little girl, her apprentice, round the room. On the calls of her infirm mother to forbear, she renounced her first object, and with loud shrieks approached her parent. The child, by her cries, quickly brought up the landlord of the house, but too late. The dreadful scene presented to him the mother lifeless, pierced to the heart, on a chair, her daughter yet wildly standing over her with the fatal knife, and the old man her father weeping by her side, himself bleeding at the forehead from the effects of a severe blow he received from one of the forks she had been madly hurling about the room.
>
> For a few days prior to this, the family had observed some symptoms of insanity in her, which had so much increased on the Wednesday evening, that her brother, early the next morning, went to Dr. Pitcairn, but that gentleman was not at home. It seems the young lady had been once before deranged. The Jury of course brought in their verdict, Lunacy.

The unnamed 'young lady' who stabbed her paralysed mother several times, and wounded her senile father, was Mary Lamb, then thirty-one years old and named by the *Morning Chronicle*, which carried the story two days later, as a mantua maker. This is the same Mary Lamb who with her more renowned brother, Charles, was to write *Tales from Shakespeare,* a much loved volume, continuously in print since its first appearance in 1807. Charles was ten years younger than her. His close friendship with Coleridge, together with his poetry, essays and articles, a proportion of which – not unlike Wordsworth's sister, Dorothy – she had some share in, put the two of them at the urban epicentre of the Romantic movement. Together Mary and Charles ran something of a salon in the early years of the nineteenth century, hosting a 'ragged regiment' of poets, scholars, critics, actors, musicians and the occasional sea captain. With her warm, kindly, intelligent face, now forever framed by a frilly bonnet,[8] Mary welcomed the turn of the century's greatest. Adjectives such as calm, judicious, rational, serene and cheerful were regularly used about her, even by those who knew her history. The close friendships she and her brother enjoyed, the love the pair elicited, are evident in the vast correspondence which chronicles their lives and that of their wide circle.

Today Mary Lamb might very well find herself incarcerated in the psychiatric wing of a prison. How then was she able two centuries ago to live a free, productive, if difficult life after committing a murder and being designated mad?

The family was poor, and Mary at the time of the violent outburst coroner and jury described as 'lunacy', its only breadwinner. The father, John Lamb, had been servant and clerk to the lawyer Samuel Salt. His wife Elizabeth Field had served as Salt's housekeeper. This arrangement allowed the family lodgings in the quiet, leafy enclave of London's Inner Temple where they shared Salt's double chambers. It also meant the children had ready access to Salt's library and benefited from his exemplary generosity.

Mary went to a local day school and studied English composition and arithmetic, before being apprenticed at the age of fourteen to a dressmaker. Salt assured Charles a place at the prestigious Christ's Hospital school, where he met fellow 'bluecoat' Coleridge and developed the love of literature he shared with his sister. At the age of fourteen, again with Salt's help, Charles trained in a counting house, moved to a post at the South Sea Company, and then to an apprenticeship at the East India Company. Of the seven Lamb children only three survived into adulthood: the eldest, John, was Mrs Lamb's favourite. He was tall and blond, unlike the next sibling, Mary, and the youngest, Charles. Brother and sister, both dark and small, the former afflicted with a limping gait and a worse stammer, were bonded from the first, in part by their mother's coldness, in part by their love of books. They were also bonded by an experience of madness, which in Charles's case was characterized by what he called melancholy, and in Mary's by repeated bouts of mania.

Samuel Salt had been dead three years by the time of the murder. His death had precipitated a run of ill-fortune. The family had had to move from their home in the Temple. Grandmother Field, housekeeper to a large country house complete with grounds the children adored and visited regularly, had also died, and with her the link to this second home. The Lambs' new quarters in Holborn were cramped and made more so by the live-in presence of a grumpy, aged aunt. The father, though only fifty-eight, suffered from progressive dementia. The mother, at fifty-six, lay paralysed from a series of strokes. John had had a serious accident, was delirious with the subsequent infection and also living at home. Mary had the Sisyphean task of looking after all the infirm and catering to their needs. Since Charles was still serving his apprenticeship, Mary was also the family's principal earner. She sewed cloaks all day and often into the night, when the only bed awaiting her was one shared with the paralysed mother who had never shown her any affection.

The punishing routine had already helped to bring on one stretch of delirium in the winter of 1794–5. This was probably the prior period of derangement referred to by the coroner and noted in the *Morning Chronicle*: 'the young Lady had been once before . . . deranged, from the harassing fatigues of too much business'.[9] A worried and perhaps guilty Charles had then written about his 'guardian angel' Mary's illness to Coleridge, always his intimate, who had commiserated in a poem. Coleridge, too, knew what it was to love and in Coleridge's case permanently lose a sister to whom all those 'hidden maladies' of the heart could be communicated. In the poem, Coleridge also praises the Mary he already admired: her affection, wisdom and mildness are features other friends commented on throughout her life.

> Her Soul affectionate, yet wise,
> Her polish'd wit as mild as lambent glories
> That play around a holy infant's head.[10]

At the time of Mary's first recorded illness, Charles was tormented by an intense but unrequitable love, the most acute passion of his life. Mary took the brunt of frustration he couldn't air elsewhere. 'To My Sister', written a little later, underscores Charles's guilt.

> If from my lips some angry accents fell:
>   Peevish complaint, or harsh reproof unkind,
> Twas but the error of a sickly mind,
> And troubled thoughts, clouding the purer well,
>   And waters clear, of Reason . . .

If Mary's illness was precipitated by the fact that the attentions of the brother she had effectively raised now lay elsewhere, her delirium, alongside his searing disappointment in love, played into the serious bout of 'melancholy' or 'temporary frenzy' Charles himself suffered at the end of 1795. Describing the illness in a letter to Coleridge (11 June 1796), he writes that a 'tide of melancholy rushed in again, and did its worst mischief by overwhelming my reason'. Charles voluntarily confined himself to the Hoxton madhouse for six weeks, only coming out for his twenty-first birthday.

At play in Charles's bout of illness were not only a hopeless love and the family's straitened circumstances, but the prospect, hardly attractive to a budding poet, of an interminable office life in the accounts section of the East India Company. Like some perspicacious contemporary adolescent, Charles in talking about his illness was also aware that weeks of high excitement, drinking and talking with the unstoppable Coleridge resulted, after his friend's departure, in an uncontrollable descent. Indeed, Coleridge's heady influence combined with heavy drinking remained a salient fact of Charles's life. The later nineteenth century or our own time might well have medicalized the drinking and linked

Charles's recurring cyclical depression to alcoholism: he often needed drink to write; drink also lubricated his alarming stammer into what many considered charming wit.

But Charles's 'hidden maladies' were never again to take him to a madhouse – except when he was accompanying his sister. It could almost be said that Mary bore the madness for the entire family. Arguably, she had learned a little of its attractions and, one might speculate, its 'behaviours' from her favourite brother. Madness had, as many mind doctors were to note, its secondary gains. It had an enviable quality of escape about it, as Charles underlined to Coleridge, who was himself hardly immune to its charms as well as its horror:

> At some future time I will amuse you with an account as full as my memory will permit of the strange turn my frenzy took. I look back upon it at times with a gloomy kind of envy; for, while it lasted, I had many, many, hours of pure happiness. Dream not, Coleridge, of having tasted all the grandeur and wildness of fancy till you have gone mad! All now seems to me vapid; comparatively so. [11 June 1796]

Mary's murderous madness came some three months later. On 21 September 1796, the evening before the event, her state already so worried Charles that he rushed out first thing in the morning to find the doctor. But Dr Pitcairn, whose uncle had been the Christ's Hospital school medic, was not at home and when Charles returned he found the bloody scene which was to colour the rest of their lives. On 27 September, he communicated the ordeal to Coleridge: 'I will only give you the outlines: – My poor dear, dearest sister, in a fit of insanity, has been the death of our own mother. I was at hand only time enough to snatch the knife out of her grasp. She is at present in a madhouse, from whence I fear she must be moved to an hospital.' Charles's directness in naming Mary's condition, his fear that she might be moved from a private madhouse to a public hospital, indeed the entire way in which her condition is described, interpreted and managed, pinpoints this period as a key transitional moment in the understanding of madness and the institutions and legislation which surround it.

Little, of course, is as unstable as the ways in which madness is viewed in any given cut through its history. Competing definitions, causations, symptoms, treatments and cures seem ever to be at hand. There are, however, dominant trends to which loose dates can be put. This turn of the century in England, where madness was writ large in the fate of George III, could be said to mark the move from one era into another.

MADNESS AND THE LAW

Until the end of the eighteenth century, Common Law – the system of traditional law in Britain built up case by case out of individual judges' rulings – dealt with criminal insanity in two interrelated ways. Either the subject was deemed 'unfit to plead' – which could, nonetheless, result in a judge asking for her to be confined. Or the subject could be tried, deemed insane at the time of the crime and then acquitted on grounds of that insanity. The great jurist Sir William Blackstone in his *Commentaries on the Laws of England* (1765–9) supplied the broad guidelines: those who suffered from a 'defect of understanding' such as children, or a deficiency of will such as lunatics, could not be held accountable for their own acts, not even treason.

In the summer of 1786, Margaret Nicholson had tried to stab George III with a blunt dessert knife. Like Mary Lamb, she was never brought to trial. Indeed the King had shouted out to his guards, 'Take care of the woman – do not hurt her, for she is mad.'[11] The Privy Council committed her to Bethlem after examination by Drs John and Thomas Monro, two of the family of four physicians associated with the hospital who ran it over a period of 128 years.

Bethlem Hospital, the Bedlam Charles Lamb feared his beloved sister might end up in, was one of the oldest asylums in Europe. Founded in the thirteenth century, the City of London took on the running of it in 1547 and continued to do so until 1948.[12] Although there were several other charity-run asylums by the late eighteenth century, Bedlam remained the sole public institution – one with both paupers' and private quarters. It loomed large in the popular imagination and was a regular haunt for Sunday pleasure-seekers avid for the spectacle Hogarth so sensationally portrayed in the final tableau of his *Rake's Progress*, where the ranting and raving, chained and maniacal Bedlamites stand in for all Britons.

In 1758, thirty-eight years before Mary Lamb's crime, Bethlem was
attacked by the founder of the competing St Luke's, William Battie. His
influential *Treatise on Madness*, the first tract to call for a proper study of
a field which had been left too long to stagnate amongst untrained
'empiricks', or quacks, attacked the 'shocking' and therapeutically stag-
nant techniques of the Monros – the repeated bloodletting, vomiting
and blistering they administered.[13] The Monros defended themselves
but had no real therapeutic programme with which to counter Battie.
Bedlam was a chamber of horrors where the Georgian mad were no
better treated than chained, raving beasts. The great painter J.M.W.
Turner's mother, admitted in 1800, died here four years later. As an
anonymous poet wrote:

> Within the Chambers which this Dome contains
> In all her 'frantic' forms, Distraction reigns . . .
> Rattling his chains, the wretch all raving lies
> And roars and foams, and Earth and Heaven defies.[14]

This was not the place Charles Lamb wanted his dear sister Mary confined to. Indeed, she had expressed a fear, even before the murder, that
she might end her days here. The gallows at Newgate, which had shadowed both their childhoods, now also loomed uncomfortably close.

Directly after he found his mother dead, his father wounded and
his Mary blood-spattered and with the tell-tale knife in her hand,
Charles acted with admirable quickness. Mary was taken to an Islington
madhouse. Coroner and jury – who did not constitute a court, but
came to establish the facts – followed his lead and deemed her insane.
According to the existing legislation, a lunatic charged on a criminal
offence could 'be liberated on security being given that he should properly be taken care of as a lunatic'.[15] In other words, Mary's freedom
depended on the responsible presence of someone who could guarantee
care either in a private madhouse or by a custodian.

The discretionary nature of the coroner's ruling must have provided
Charles with an additional challenge: would he, at his young age of
twenty-one, be able to reassure the coroner that he was sufficient 'security', particularly in circumstances as financially restricted as his own?
His speedy removal of Mary to the madhouse was a way of pre-empting

an unfavourable ruling: his prior experience of the madhouse system was of undoubted use here. It was certainly Charles who also informed the coroner of Mary's earlier madness: the mention of this in the *Times* report underlines its importance in the verdict of lunacy. This was a society and a family which shared a certain sophistication about what madness meant, and the patterns it took. Recurrence was already one of these.

The law which allowed Mary's release into a 'care system' would change and harden in 1800 when the king whom Shelley termed 'old, mad, blind, despised' was once more subject to an assassination attempt. This time George III was shot at during the opening night of *Figaro*, ironically an opera in which traditional hierarchies are in question. James Hadfield, a former soldier, had taken good aim with two pistols and missed his target by inches. Hadfield's attorney, Thomas Erskine, who had also defended the revolutionary Thomas Paine, put forward an early distinction between madness which was ever and always a form of manic raving and a more nuanced version. He argued that although Hadfield wasn't mad by what became known as the 'wild beast test' — far too simple a definition of insanity in that it called for total deprivation of memory and understanding — he was nevertheless insane: 'insane persons frequently appear in the utmost state of ability and composure, even in the highest paroxysms of insanity'.[16] Hadfield had shot at the King because he suffered from *delusion* — which was the true character of insanity, when there was no frenzy or raving madness. Erskine's language was borrowed from John Locke's psychology. When his insanity plea held, despite the greatness of the crime, it enshrined a new, subtler definition of madness, both in law and in the public imagination.

In one sense it is remarkable that Hadfield was acquitted and saved from being hung, drawn and quartered, the ultimate penalty for treason. After all, these were times of Terror: revolutionary wars were being fought, a neighbouring monarchy had recently been overthrown, and a king sent to the guillotine. On the other hand, given the very excess of a historical moment in which extreme acts were part of the political landscape, perhaps it was better and expedient logic to label an attempt on a king's life as insane rather than revolutionary. Madness, it must be said, was a condition George III was not unfamiliar with.

The ruling Erskine attained for the assassin pointed out a serious gap in the law – the very one which had allowed Mary Lamb her relative freedom. The man, deemed insane, who had shot at George III could soon be at liberty. An 'Act for the Safe Keeping of Insane Persons Charged with Offences' was rushed through Parliament. This guaranteed that any person charged with 'Treason, Murder, Felony' and acquitted on grounds of insanity would be kept in strict custody until His Majesty saw fit to release him. Hadfield was promptly incarcerated for life in Bedlam. Here the man who, during his trial, had a residual head wound so severe that the jury were invited to inspect the membrane of the brain itself, murdered another patient. Hadfield was indeed dangerous.

Under the new legislation of 1800, Mary Lamb, who never attempted a violent act again, would not have been permitted the freedom she had, whether or not there was a brother to hand to act as her carer and an assortment of private madhouses ready to take her in when need became evident.

THE GEORGIAN MADHOUSE

The private madhouse, small or sizeable, was a particularly English institution, one which thrived in the largely unregulated eighteenth century economy. In its smaller configuration, the madhouse often grew out of an informal boarding arrangement. A local doctor, pastor or widow might take in a lunatic or two who couldn't be housed at home because of danger, shame, disruption or the fear of publicity. Slightly larger premises, serving between a dozen and twenty boarders, could mean a profitable business. These dotted the countryside. Even the most substantial houses – Hoxton House, where Mary would eventually go, was one such – rarely numbered over two hundred patients. Indeed in 1826, when national statistics began to be available, under five thousand[17] people were confined throughout England out of a population of some eleven million. This is a mere handful if one considers that by 1900 the beds in just two London asylums, Colney Hatch and Hanwell, numbered 4800, and the figure for public asylums nationwide was 74,000.[18]

Partly because of relatives' wish for secrecy, records were rarely kept until an act of 1774 turned madhouses into 'licensed' establishments with some form of minimal regulation. The business of the houses was confinement rather than cure: some had no medical presence at all. This largely continued even after 1796 and the establishment of the influential 'moral treatment' at the Quaker tea merchant and philanthropist, William Tuke's, famous York Retreat. Madness became pre-eminently a *medical* concern in Britain only gradually.

Promise of therapy or not, the conditions in madhouses did worry people and, eventually, the government. Throughout the eighteenth century advertisements seeking custom for private madhouses hold out the promise of something better than the usual chains and brutality. Champions of the new-wave public asylums such as William Battie, founder of St Luke's in London, stress the importance of care and the need for gentleness. They abhor the use of violence.[19] In a competitive market, selling a madhouse to the better rank of patient and her family meant living up to an ideal. From these ads and writings, the contours of the period's utopian asylum are clear: clean, temperate air, pleasant gardens, good fires, meat and drink, privacy as well as entertainment, and above all kindness, accompanied by visits from a private physician.

Existing conditions rarely lived up to this ideal. Chains and various forms of restraint, brutality, theft by vicious carers, were all too common. So were dirt, filthy accommodation and worse sanitation, not to mention rape and beatings by carers. Paupers, needless to say, whose weekly payment was made by the parish, were treated far worse than private patients. These could expect regular visitors for whom appearances needed to be maintained.

Profiteering by keepers was also rife. A little bribe could have patients confined well beyond any period of madness, if indeed any madness had ever existed. There were cases where keepers collaborated with siblings or partners in abducting and confining troublesome, though sane, members of families whose fortunes were worth stealing. Rebellious women like Maria, the heroine of Mary Wollstonecraft's unfinished novel *The Wrongs of Woman*, who escapes the sexual captivity of marriage to a lewd, drunken husband, might also find themselves imprisoned in a madhouse so frightening it made them doubt their own sanity.

*

Forced to take over his sister's role as the person principally responsible for his family and its welfare, Charles Lamb managed to assuage an elder brother who would have preferred a pauper's ward for Mary, and find the sizeable £50–£60 annual fee necessary for a private room and nurse at an Islington madhouse. It is most likely that the one Mary was taken to was Fisher House on what is now the Essex Road.

Charles writes to Coleridge that the women looking after his sister were 'vastly indulgent' to her, that they treated her as 'one of the family, rather than one of the patients'. 'The good lady of the mad house and her daughter, an elegant sweet behaved young lady, love her and are taken with her amazingly, and I know from her own mouth she loves them, and longs to be with them as much.' The lady of the madhouse also told him he could drop doctor and apothecary and save some money in the process.

It is uncertain what kind of treatment, if any, Mary actually received. At the time there was a variety of available options, most of them aimed at calming frenzy or mania, 'cooling' the patient, as the left-over humoral understanding of the mind–body relationship dictated. Cold baths followed by hot, cropped hair to cool the head, digitalis or opium, purging and bleeding – any or all might have been used on Mary. Whatever the actual treatment regime, her 'reason' returned quickly.

'My poor dear dearest sister, the unhappy and unconscious instrument of the Almighty's judgments to our house, is restored to her senses,' Charles writes to Coleridge on 3 October 1796, less than two weeks after the murder. As if suddenly aware that this was almost too speedy a return to reason for someone who has committed murder, he adds that it is also a return

to a dreadful sense and recollection of what has past, awful to her mind and impressive (as it must be to the end of life) but tempered with religious resignation, and the reasonings of a sound judgment, which in this early stage knows how to distinguish between a deed committed in a transient fit of frenzy, and the terrible guilt of a mother's murder. I have seen her. I found her this morning calm and serene, far very very far from an indecent forgetful serenity; she has a most affectionate and tender concern for what has happened. Indeed from the beginning, frightful and hopeless as her disorder seemed, I had confidence enough

in her strength of mind, and religious principle, to look forward to a
time when even she might recover tranquillity.

CHILDHOOD AND ITS DEFORMATIONS

Two weeks after this letter, Charles writes to Coleridge again about his
sister. This time in describing Mary's, one particular feature of his letter
evokes an eerily contemporary conception of her condition. Like some
proto Freud or Winnicott, Charles distinctly places the genesis of Mary's
illness in childhood. Mary does, too. He quotes her as hoping that her
mother and grandmother will understand her better in heaven. It was
the latter woman who plagued Mary with a repeated and self-fulfilling
condemnation of her 'poor, crazy, moyther'd [muddled]' brains.
Charles underlines their own mother's lack of affection as a precipitating factor in her daughter's madness, coupled with the burden of
Mary's own sense of overarching filial duty.

> Poor Mary, my mother indeed never understood her right. She loved
> her, as she loved us all with a mother's love, but in opinion, in feeling,
> and sentiment, and disposition, bore so distant a resemblance to her
> daughter, that she never understood her right. Never could believe how
> much she loved her – but met her caresses, her protestations of filial
> affection, too frequently with coldness and repulse . . . she would always
> love my brother above Mary, who was not worthy of one tenth of that
> affection, which Mary had a right to claim. But it is my sister's gratifying
> recollection, that every act of duty and of love she could pay, every
> kindness (and I speak true, when I saw to the hurting of her health, and
> most probably in great part to the derangement of her senses) through
> a long course of infirmities and sickness, she could show her, she ever
> did. [17 October 76]

The cold, uncaring mother, the repulsed daughter, the childhood
which shapes a predisposition to considering oneself deranged, the
inner conflict – all this was part of the backdrop to Mary's recurring
adult illness. What is surprising is how easily the self-same reading of
her illness could have been offered within the frame of a Freudian or

post-Freudian understanding of the aetiology of mental illness, though of course Charles doesn't mention the enacted Oedipal rage.

There is more. Although during her lifetime and because of the murder, none of her writings could appear under her own name, Mary collaborated with Charles not only on the *Tales from Shakespeare*, but on the collection of children's stories *Mrs Leicester's School: or, The history of several young ladies, related by themselves* of 1808. All but three of the stories here come from Mary's pen, though each bears a different pseudonym. It is clear from these stories that Mary was particularly adept at entering into the voice of childhood; and mother–child relations, with all of the child's frustrations, anger and disappointed hopes, are a recurring theme.

In the story 'Mahomet Explained', published under the pseudonym Margaret Green, Mary seems to be reinvoking and examining a particular sequence from her own childhood, part of which was spent in the large country-house, complete with library, which her grandmother looked after.

The little girl in the tale is a lonely creature. Apart from a word exchanged over breakfast, neither her mother nor the lady of the house ever speak to her, so engaged are they with their 'needlework'. This leaves the child to her own devices and to the discovery of the locked and forbidden library with its strange tome, *Mahomet Explained*. She immerses herself in the story of Abraham, Ishmael and Mahomet, secretly reads it over and over. 'It must have been because I was never spoken to at all that I forgot what was right and what was wrong,' the narrator comments. The thrall of the tale, the repetitive, forbidden reading, her abandonment and loneliness make her susceptible to transforming the imaginary into the real. She is consumed by a fear that anyone who is not a True Mahometan Believer, as she has become through her reading, will be unable to cross the 'silken thread' of a bridge that leads to the afterlife. The unconverted will tumble into a 'bottomless gulf'. She longs to tell her mother and the woman of the house, but to do so is to admit her trespass.

Trapped between the desire to save her mother by converting her and the panic of self-revelation, she falls into a fever. When need finally forces the story from a mouth no longer accustomed to speech, her mother, who is now sleeping in the child's room, thinks she is 'delirious' and sends for a physician. Madness here is both real and a misunderstanding: it comes from an inexpressible wish and the tantalizing desire, which Mary Lamb makes us alert to, for revenge. Delirium is the only action the trapped child can take.

The kindly doctor extracts the admission that the child has read herself into a 'Mahometan' fever. He gives her medicine and recommends rest. Once the temperature has subsided, he takes the girl away to his wife, who he says has experience in such cases. The wife is a better mother. In this early version of a cure through love and innocent talk therapy, she engages the child in conversation. She then recommends, instead of medication, a visit to Harlow Fair. Here cheerful human faces and a little spoiling work wonders on the child. After a month with these new parents who bring friends to the house for games and amusement, she is returned home completely cured.

'Mahomet Explained' is redolent with echoes of Mary's childhood and her adult assessment of its lacks, the part played by an inattentive mother in bringing on her 'delirious' state. It can hardly be coincidental that the obsessive labour which keeps the two women in the story from ever engaging with the child is needlework — the very needlework which was to drive the adult Mary to the 'delirium' in which she killed her mother and which flung her into the 'bottomless gulf'.

In her essay 'On Needlework', published in *The British Lady's Magazine* in 1815 under the name Sempronia — a character out of Addison and Steele's *The Tatler* who is a shark amidst matchmakers, marrying women off with no attention to their future well-being — the fifty-year-old Mary Lamb condemns an activity which keeps middle-class women falsely busy, where in fact their intelligence would benefit from the kind of leisure which is men's natural right. The busy-ness of needlework is also at the expense of the working-class woman who has few other means of earning her keep. The activity, which is meant to keep the devil who loves idle hands at bay, in fact keeps women chained. 'Needle-work and intellectual improvement are naturally in a state of warfare,' Mary writes, as fervent in her analysis of women's condition as her near-contemporary Mary Wollstonecraft, and foreshadowing Virginia Woolf's later analysis. There were no seventeenth-century women poets, Woolf wrote, because 'Shakespeare's sister' was too busy mending stockings or tending to the stew. From Mary's point of view, her mother had even given the needlework precedence over her daughter.

Mary Lamb's account of her childhood state and the fall into delirium is interesting on several counts. It builds up an experience of the child's madness as a misassociation of ideas. The little girl generalizes from her book, a kind of primer about Mahomet complete with missing pages, to build up a mistaken notion of the real. This is a picture of madness clearly based on the ideas of John Locke, whose probing of mental states was so to influence the rise of the first 'theoretical' psychiatry in France. Locke's ideas about madness moved away from earlier religious conceptions and classical paradigms reinvigorated in the Renaissance. Madness was no longer either possession or retribution for sin. Nor was it the overthrow of reason by an excess of passion, whether beastly or holy. Nor was it hereditary or biological. Rather, madness, as the eighteenth century progressed and took on an increasingly Lockean hue, became a matter of the false association of ideas.

In his *Essay Concerning Human Understanding* of 1690, Locke differentiates the mad from what he calls 'idiots', or 'naturals', the congenitally damaged, and argues that the first 'do not appear to have lost the faculty of reasoning but having joined together some ideas very wrongly, they mistake them for truths, and they err as men do that argue right from wrong principles'.[20] This is an optimistic view of madness: it leaves open the possibility of cure and introduces a commonality of reasoning — from false to true — between the sane and the mad and within the same person.

Mary's little girl in this story has, one might say, a Lockean experience of madness. But the fact that the adult Mary Lamb, the writer who developed from this child, thinks it worthwhile to remember this girlhood experience and in a sense show its genesis and 'cure' casts it into a different register. The idea of a formative link between childhood experience and the deformations of the adult is so familiar to us now that it seems natural, altogether self-evident. Conceptually, however, this pairing is new to the late eighteenth century and the Romantic movement. Richard Burton in the several volumes of his encyclopaedic disquisition on madness, *The Anatomy of Melancholy* (1652) — an early exploration of all the many factors that play into the humour of melancholy — has nothing to say of the subtle ways in which the child is father to the adult.

Nor does Burton search for the roots of melancholy in childhood experience.

Once Jean-Jacques Rousseau and the Romantics burst on the scene, everything shifts. Childhood, the importance of education, of relations between parents and children, become paramount. Given this and their personal experience, it is perhaps not surprising that childless Charles and Mary not only take on godchildren and enjoy their company above much else, but also engage in the writing of stories for children. They translate Shakespeare with an eye to education, and in Charles's case are adamant that children need their imaginations educated as much as their minds. Deforming pasts can be formed anew in the next generation.

MADNESS, NERVES AND SENSIBILITY

In his essay 'Christ's Hospital Five and Thirty Years Ago', Charles Lamb, in the guise of his most popular persona Elia, reminisces about his schooldays and remembers how their games 'would have made the souls of Rousseau and John Locke chuckle to have seen us'. The pairing is important. The period derived a vocabulary of sensation from Locke and mixed it with Rousseau's language of imagination and memory: that faculty through which childhood is recovered. To experience feeling, its extremes in passion, became important; so too did the analysis of feeling. Within this new language of the emotions, madness is transformed. Extremes of passion are states people see they have in common. Outbursts of passion, from revolutionary fervour to assassination attempts on the King, are manifestations worthy of intellectual interest. They are cultivated and indeed fascinate the young, radical intelligentsia.

Byron, in *Childe Harold*, had hailed 'wild Rousseau', the 'self-torturing sophist', as 'The apostle of affliction, he who threw Enchantment over passion' and knew 'How to make madness beautiful'. In 1766, Rousseau, exiled from France and Switzerland, had been brought to England by David Hume. Given a house at Wootton in Staffordshire, not to mention a pension of £100 a year by George III – which Rousseau drew for only one year – he wrote the first six volumes of his confessions. It is in the first part of *The Confessions* that, remembering his early facility for reading, Rousseau notes how he acquired – not unlike the young heroine in 'Mahomet Explained' – 'a too intimate acquaintance with the passions. An infinity of sensations . . . without possessing any precise idea of the objects to which they related.'

It is also in the opening chapter of his *Confessions* that Rousseau analyses the way in which childhood punishment shaped his life. In the first instance, the spanking he received at the age of eight from a woman of thirty influenced 'my propensities, my desires, my passions for the rest of my life, and that in quite a contrary sense from what might naturally have been expected'. Rousseau sought out humiliation, and was, as he explicitly confesses, roused by it because of this childhood punishment which had a disciplinary intent.

The second punishment, a beating inflicted by his uncle, had a different if equally formative impact. Intended as chastisement for a theft of which Rousseau says he was innocent, it turned him into a champion of justice, so deeply did it engrave itself on his being:

> Even while I write this I feel my pulse quicken, and should I live a hundred thousand years, the agitation of that moment would still be fresh in my memory. The first instance of violence and oppression is so deeply engraved on my soul, that every relative idea renews my emotion: the sentiment of indignation, which in its origin had reference only to myself, has acquired such strength, and is at present so completely detached from personal motives, that my heart is as much inflamed at the sight or relation of any act of injustice.

Childhood shapes the adult irrevocably in Rousseau's analysis, shapes him sexually, too.

Charles and Mary's understanding of madness and its precipitating childhood experience falls into this new culture of Rousseauian Romanticism. We might speculate that Charles is not only tolerant towards his sister's 'lunacy'. He respects it and, given his own bouts of melancholia and their lifelong proximity, also identifies with it. So, judging from the tone of Coleridge and Hazlitt's comments on Mary, not to mention her correspondence with Dorothy Wordsworth, do the others in their circle. They are compassionate. Despite the enormity of her crime, they are prepared to accept her into their society as an equal.

It would be wrong to generalize across the whole of the period from a single example from the writing classes. However, certain things are clear. With the eighteenth century, the age of reason, a change of sensibility had made a certain nervous susceptibility a sign of class. Not the dullards, but those 'of the liveliest and quickest natural parts, whose Faculties are the brightest and most spiritual, and whose Genius is most keen and penetrating', are prone to nervous disorders from melancholy to hypochondria.[21] According to Dr George Cheyne, author of *The English Malady* (1733), it was the most refined and sensitive amongst the rising middle classes, those with the most leisure, who succumbed to spleen, to the vagaries of imagination, to various maladies of the *nerves*, those newcomers on the medical scene – mysterious messengers between body and mind and somehow responsible for a host of imprecise ailments. In the moist, vaporous climate of Britain, where cities had grown 'populous and consequently unhealthy', where there are 'Efforts to go beyond former Times in all the Arts of Ingenuity, Invention, Study, Learning, and all the Contemplative and Sedentary Professions', nerves were particularly susceptible to 'distemper'.

Only in the eighteenth century does it become possible to 'suffer from nerves'. The expression doesn't appear in Shakespeare, for whom 'nervy' is a cognate for 'strong'. Beginning with Cheyne, weak nerves become a marker for sensitivity and, indeed, a cultural superiority. Dr Johnson, with a tinge of disapproval and under the label of 'medical cant', nonetheless notes this new meaning of 'nervous' in his *Dictionary*: 'having weak or diseased nerves'. Casual allusions occur in the Lambs' *Letters*. Mary Lamb refers to her 'weak nerves'; Charles talks of 'a sad depression of spirits, a most unaccountable nervousness'; of his and Mary's 'nervous minds'.[22]

For Cheyne, a successful London and Bath doctor, as for Freud over a century and a half later, civilization comes at the price of certain discontents. The times give rise to a proliferation of difficult-to-diagnose illnesses – prominent amongst sensitive women – for which patients and their families want to find a physical cause, where none except perhaps the activity of the nerves, so elusive in their determinable function, may be to hand to provide a somatic substratum. Yet insist on that bodily base, Cheyne does – it is something which separates him radically from the understandings of madness that had come from seventeenth-century doctors and thinkers: nervous distempers for him have nothing to do with 'Witchcraft, Enchantment, Sorcery and Possession', which are the 'Resource of Ignorance'.[23]

George Cheyne (1691/3–1743) was a remarkable doctor, one in a series who were their own most illuminating patients. In his twenties, he suffered a breakdown. He pulled himself together with a blend of mysticism, based on Jakob Boehme and the quietist asceticism of such women mystics as Antoinette Bourignon and Jeanne Guyon, and a milk-based diet. Rebuilding his practice in the spa town of Bath and in London, he gathered around him a fashionable clientele including Robert Walpole's daughter Catherine, and the novelist/printer Samuel Richardson whose *Sir Charles Grandison* would become a key text in the later establishment of French psychiatry. He also began to write a series of what could be called the first medical self-help books: bestsellers which had what we would now call a holistic underpinning, linking mind, body and spirit in a whole marked by commonsensical advice and moral exhortation. 'Learned, philosophical and pious' were the adjectives Samuel Johnson used to describe the good doctor, who called for moderation in all things. His *Essay on Gout* (1720) was followed by *An Essay on Health and Long Life* (1724), which ran to nine editions in his own lifetime and was translated into several European languages.

Cheyne himself was enormously fat, his weight in the late 1720s reaching a record 32 stone (448 pounds, 200 kilos) – which brought in its train many of the symptoms he set out to cure: melancholy, biliousness, nausea, spleen (or a kind of aggravated, near- metaphysical lethargy), anxiety, distemper. These were the by-products of affluence and civilized life, Cheyne noted. The cure was dietary moderation, vegetarianism, exercise, emetics and forays to the spa in Bath. Prevention, however, was better than any cure.

For Cheyne, mental distempers had their origins in the body, and primarily in the nerves. Nerves, those conveyors of sensation and motion, like the strings of a musical instrument, had to be kept well tuned. They needed to vibrate at a proper pitch when struck; if they lost their tone, grew weak and inelastic, or were obstructed through the excesses of civilized life, pain, sluggishness, gloom, resulted, perhaps even chronically – not to mention fevers, 'cholick's, gouts, 'wandering and delusory images on the brain', paroxysms, and convulsions which could be accompanied by raving and incoherence. Since the quickest thinkers, those of greatest sensibility, had this weakness of the nerves, it was all the more important to prevent breakdown: a balanced life had to be led, a golden mean kept to.

Cheyne was not a mind doctor in the sense that the specialization was to emerge in the next century, though he could be seen as an early neurologist, a medical tradition that sometimes coincided with, sometimes strayed away from, what became psychiatry. Patients, however, often presented similar symptoms to both kinds of doctors, particularly when it came to the 'functional' diseases, to use the later term. Vaporous mental states running the gamut from instability and unsettledness to hysterical fits and even paralysis and apoplexy were not, according to Cheyne, psychological phenomena, produced by mind and emotions. They were the product of obstructed nerves and vessels, clearly the province of bodily malfunction. Many from the mid-eighteenth through to the nineteenth century followed his cue.

Dr William Cullen (1710–90), one of the great figures in that bastion of Enlightenment thinking, Edinburgh University, provided something of a physiology to underpin Locke's philosophy of associationism – how ideas combine in the mind out of representations of experience. Cullen's influential *First Lines of the Practice of Physik*, published between 1778 and '84, gives great prominence to the underlying role played by the nerves in disease. He coined the term 'neurosis' to refer to all motor and sensory afflictions which are not linked to a 'topical affection of the organs, but a more general affection of the nervous system'. Importantly, in terms of future psychiatric research, he also linked mania and melancholy to fluctuations in the flow of nervous impulse or 'excitement' to the brain, noting that since intellectual operations require orderly and exact recollection, abnormal or unequal excitement in the brain may give false perceptions, associations and judgement.[24] He also gave an explanation for hysteria and linked it to sexual overactivity, a 'turgescence of blood' in the female genitalia. In 1807 Thomas Trotter (1760–1832), a Scottish doctor, published his *View of the Nervous Temperament*, in which he claimed that 'nervous disorders have now taken the place of fevers, and may be justly reckoned two thirds of the whole, with which civilized society is afflicted'.[25] Two thirds of all ailments, suffered particularly in the city where nervousness is rife, implicates a great many sufferers.

What Cheyne and his like helped to produce was a time which, as Roy Porter[26] has argued, grew more sympathetic to madness and oddities of mood and behaviour. Even if many of Cheyne's quoted cases of distemper – and he provides eighteen histories plus his own far longer and more detailed one – are arguably at the milder end of the 'madness' spectrum, their fashionable prevalence, together with his insistence on the good character and often high birth of his patients, made even more extreme states seem less threatening. The 'vapours', various forms of derangement, could come and go like so many cycles of the moon, which had kindly lent its name to the state of 'lunacy'.

By the time Mary Lamb murdered her mother and wounded her father, this sympathy was in full play and married to a Romantic sensibility open to greater extremes of behaviour. The climate, however, was soon to shift and we see this through the course of Mary's own lifetime. The very ideas surrounding madness which were to allow her a life within society – that is, its periodic nature; its invisibility within periods of sanity – were increasingly to combine with the growing profession of mind doctors, or alienists, to transform her and her kin into 'dangerous individuals'. Such newly invented types[27] could erupt into 'homicidal mania', which was what the 'dangerous frenzy' attributed to Mary became – its very invisibility and unpredictability determining that danger.

But to say that such catalogued, categorizable and confined individuals were the creation of state powers working in some kind of collusion with the courts and a nascent psychiatric profession in Britain – as Michel Foucault, the great French historian and philosopher, claims for France and tangentially the rest of Europe – would be wrong. It is not quite accurate – and not only because of the laissez-faire nature of the state and the liberal economy in confinement which allowed both state and private care, and prevailed until mid-century in Britain. What Mary's case shows us is that she and her brother, along with their peers, the literature and modes of life they championed, the new understanding of childhood they put into play with its impact on the nature of remembering and imagination, its quest for sensitivity and feeling, also turned the desired new individual into one in whom the invisible inner life was a priority and its remarkable nature something of an asset. Multiple forces played on and into each other to create this new being who sometimes preferred to be the exceptional case the doctors diagnosed.

This did not happen all at once.

MADNESS AND EVERYDAY LIFE

Returned to reasonableness some six weeks after the events, Mary stayed on in the Islington madhouse, in part because her elder brother John wanted her to be kept in confinement, in part because Charles could not keep her at home while their senile father — who had witnessed the terrible events and was afraid of his daughter — was still alive. By April of 1797, however, Charles had moved her into lodgings of her own, as his letter to Coleridge explains:

> I have taken her out of her confinement, and taken a room for her at Hackney, and spend my Sundays, holiday, etc, with her. She boards herself. In one little half year's illness, and in such an illness of such a nature and of such consequences! to get her out into the world again, with a prospect of her never being so ill again — this is to be ranked not among the common blessings of Providence . . . Congratulate me on an ever-present and never-alienable friend like her. [7 April 1797]

Mary may have remained Charles's 'never-alienable' friend. She may never again have been ill enough to commit murder. But she suffered from recurrences of her condition almost annually, sometimes more frequently.

In April 1799, after the death of their father, brother and sister set up house together, first in Chapel Street in Pentonville. Some return of Mary's madness, or perhaps simply the suspicion of neighbours which distressed her and might have exacerbated her condition, forced a move to Holborn and then for some years back to the childhood haunts of the Temple, which they both adored. 'It is a great object to me to live in town,' Charles wrote in a letter of 20 May 1800 to Thomas Manning, 'where we shall be much more private; and to quit a house and a neighbourhood where poor Mary's disorder, so frequently recurring, has made us a sort of marked people. We can be no where private except in the midst of London.'

The bustling city, with its anonymous crowds and rampant eccentricities, seemed more conducive to ordinary life than the quiet of village or countryside. When she was well, Mary helped Charles with his writing, did her own — including all the comedies in their *Tales from Shakespeare* — kept house for him, entertained. From what we know, fatigue, overexcitement, occasioned by a run of visitors or travel, the report of deaths, or something to remind her of her mother, all singly or together, might spark a new bout of illness. At each bout, in the early years, Charles brought her to one of the Hoxton madhouses. Mary and Charles both learned to recognize the gathering symptoms. They took pre-emptive action. As did Coleridge. Staying with them in late March and April 1803, he writes to his wife Sara:

> I had purposed not to speak of Mary Lamb — but I had better write it than tell it. The Thursday before last she met at Rickman's a Mr Babb [or Babbs?], an old friend and admirer of her mother.
>
> The next day she smiled in an ominous way — on Sunday she told her brother that she was getting bad, with great agony — on Tuesday morning she layed hold of me with violent agitation, and talked wildly about George Dyer [a friend of the Lambs]. I told Charles, there was not a moment to lose/and I did not lose a moment — but went for a Hackney Coach, and took her to the private Madhouse at Hogsden/She was quite calm, and said — it was the best to do so — but she wept bitterly two or three times, yet all in a calm way. Charles is cut to the heart. [4 April 1803]

In this description, Mary is resigned to her need to be confined until the 'violent agitation', which often also expressed itself in a rush of language, a galloping imagination uncontrolled by judgement, subsides. Friends talk of the poignant spectacle of brother and sister walking hand in hand to the madhouse carrying a straitjacket between them, the tears rolling down their faces.

Brother and sister were deeply upset both by Mary's 'breakdowns' and by the difficulty of emerging from them. 'I strive against low spirits all I can, but it is a very hard thing to get the better of,' she writes to Dorothy Wordsworth on 9 July 1803. Charles often fell into 'low spirits' too, sometimes in tandem with his sister's explosions: one might speculate that they set each other off, though it is difficult to know who lit the spark on any given occasion.

Melancholy was a 'fashionable' condition for Georgians of sensibility. For a condition to be fashionable means that its symptoms are known to many and in some sense aspired to. To put it the other way round, the malaise of everyday life, unhappiness, suffering, can be cast into the shape of the 'fashionable' disease. Others, including doctors, recognize its existence. Recognition can help the unconscious shoe-horning of free-floating symptoms into the given shape. A little like Pascal's wager – in which to live the rituals which attend the possible existence of God eventually makes of one a believer – the wearer of that particular condition's shoes may eventually find the fit so perfect, the shoes no longer come off. Amongst many others, James Boswell (1740–95), Samuel Johnson's biographer, suffered from melancholy, and did so flamboyantly. He gave the column he wrote in *The London Magazine* (to which Lamb also later contributed) the title 'Hypochondriacus', reflecting one of the period's alternative names for that mixture of lethargic low spirits, mood swings and unplaceable and misplaced fears and anxieties that make up melancholy. But the lability of imagination and temperament in which Boswell indulged, Johnson warned him – and he knew from his own experience – was always shadowed by the possibility that it would topple into uncontrolled madness. There are some suggestions that Boswell's playing with melancholy, enacting its tropes, did finally topple his hold and sped the collapse of his last years.[28] The fact that any of this can be observed rarely means that it is willed or wilful.

Around 1800, when Coleridge asked Charles Lamb to write a pastiche of Burton's *Melancholy*, Charles also produced the poem 'Hypochondriacus'. This galloping doggerel enacts the fashionable, tolerable sides of melancholy. It spoofs them. At the same time, it is redolent of the threat that melancholy with its persecutory sides poses.

> Black thoughts continually
> Crowding my privacy;
> They come unbidden,

Like foes at a wedding,
Thrusting their faces
In better guests' places,

. . .

In my ears whispering,
'Thy friends are treacherous,
'Thy foes are dangerous,
'Thy dreams ominous.'

It is tempting to think of Charles and Mary Lamb as living out the two possibilities that madness in Georgian England presented. Charles, the melancholic; Mary, the passionate revolutionary, who explodes to kill off the oppressive elders and is perpetually burdened by the fear that violence will return. The later essays Charles wrote in the person of Elia, with their digressive flow of free and imaginative association – an outpouring which mirrors self-confession, always slipping out of control and being ushered humorously back into its confines – are the apogee of early Romantic sensibility. Mary lives out the darker side, where judgement goes awry, control is lost, and the 'perturbed conversation' which signals and accompanies mania returns almost annually 'in the most wretched desponding way conceivable'.

Charles's continuing and assiduous care of her feels like part of a devil's bargain. There can be no partner other than Mary, since she enacts what he fears most and drinks increasingly to escape.[29] On her side, one senses, she is so grateful to him, she has to escape his presence via the only route she increasingly knows: madness. And though she talks of the madhouse as her 'banishment', she keeps the straitjacket by her side, packs it on travels, and goes willingly to the nearest asylum when she feels her condition coming on.

In one of her rare letters about the condition, Mary writes to her friend Sarah Stoddart about her mother, who has 'gone out of her mind':

. . . do not I conjure you let her unhappy malady afflict you too deeply –
I speak from experience and from the opportunity I have had of much
observation in such cases that insane people in the fancy's they take
into their heads do not feel as one in a sane state of mind does under the

real evil of poverty the perception of having done wrong or any such thing that runs in their heads.

Think as little as you can, and let your whole care be to be certain that she is treated with tenderness. I lay a stress upon this, because it is a thing of which people in her state are uncommonly susceptible, and which hardly any one is at all aware of, a hired nurse never, even though in all other respects they are good kind of people. [November 1805]

The insane can not be held accountable for the fancies that leap into their heads: nor should their near ones take these to heart. But tenderness is important. In fact, kind treatment is everything.

It is unclear whether Charles, for all his lifelong loyalty (and who would blame him!), always provided tenderness: there are reports of teasing behaviour which many, and even Mary herself, sometimes found insulting, certainly discomfiting. Then there was his alcoholism, which worried Mary and which she attempted, with little success, to control. Then, too, there was Charles's inability either to get on with his writing or to finish projects he had started.

But Charles cared for his sister to the point of misery – certainly giving up any realistic hope of a married life that might exclude her. In a letter to Dorothy Wordsworth, written just after Mary has been confined, he notes: 'when she begins to discover symptoms of approaching illness, it is not easy to say what is best to do. Being by ourselves is bad, and going out is bad. I get so irritable and wretched with fear, that I constantly hasten on the disorder. You cannot conceive the misery of such a foresight' (16 June 1805).

The guilt Charles expresses in letters to friends is a perennial aspect of this cycle of illness and care, in which his depressions or passions provoke hers, and round again, until in one sense the spectre of insanity encompasses them both. As Mary's periods of madness grew longer – three months of agitation followed by two of deep depression – and her needs greater, Charles simply moved into a private `madhouse' with her. It seemed more straightforward. After all, he couldn't live in any way, and certainly not happily, without her. Walking in Edmonton just before Christmas 1834, not far from the custodial house they lived in, Charles, more than likely drunk, fell over, contracted blood poisoning and died of erysipelas a week later. He had been mourning Coleridge's death since July that year. Mary lived on for another twelve years. Surprisingly perhaps, for the first three years after Charles's death she was remarkably well, almost, one could say, released into good health. After that her periods of madness lengthened. She died in May 1847 at the ripe age of eighty-two.

CRIMES AND DOCTORS

It may be that one reason Mary stressed the mad person's need for tenderness of treatment is that she had experienced or at least witnessed, the brutality the confined could encounter within the madhouse. Sarah Burton, Charles and Mary's most recent biographer, states that Mary spent time in the Whitmore madhouse or at Warburton's, about which an anonymously published report of 1825[30] – found to be by John Mitford, a journalist and former inmate – catalogued a range of horrors that keepers perpetrated on even the better class of inmates. A young married lady was 'so forcefully fed that her teeth were falling out and her gums were putrid'. She died in great misery. Another, named as the daughter of the Chief Clerk to the Secretary of State, was beaten on the breast with a broomstick and 'prostituted on the steps leading to the lodge by more than one keeper'. When complaints were lodged, the head of the madhouse, Warburton himself, said, 'It is no matter, she don't know what is done to her.' Flogging, stealing of clothes and then reporting to family that these had been ripped by 'the great destroyers of apparel' the mad were known to be, refusing to allow the patient to see family alone so that she might report on mistreatment – all this was commonplace, according to Mitford.

A report by John Wilson Rogers, a visiting physician at Warburton's paupers' asylum in Bethnal Green, ten years earlier, was equally damning. The catalogue of abuses he lists includes chaining to bedposts for hours, and simultaneous beating; filthy infected sores brought on by chaining, the inability to move, the general filth, gagging or bandaging of the whole head to prevent talk, force-feeding of such brutality that spoon handles punctured the mouth; suffocation, blinding.

According to Andrew Roberts, whose Middlesex University website is a remarkable and detailed source of data on the history of madness and asylums in Britain,[31] Mary Lamb was certainly never a pauper patient at Warburton's in Bethnal Green; nor would her and Charles's finances have permitted confinement at the expensive Whitmore's. Roberts argues that the madhouse Mary was regularly confined in was Hoxton. Following this line would mean Charles Lamb's assertions that his sister was on the whole well treated by her keepers are based neither on his ignorance, nor on his guilt. Equally this would mean that Mary reported no terrible abuses, not because she was frightened or failed to remember them, but simply because she experienced relatively good care.

Good care did not mean cure. There was no therapeutic intent linked to the institutions where Mary stayed. They were simply places of confinement: a way of removing her from the danger she posed to others and herself and perhaps 'calming' her. Of the two doctors who make an appearance in Mary's case, one, however, does seem to have done her some good. This is Dr George Leman Tuthill (1772–1835), who applied around the time he was treating Mary for a post at St Luke's, the large private asylum founded by the reformer Battie. He was unsuccessful but in 1816 was appointed joint physician to Bethlem and Bridewell. So he had more than a passing interest in madness.

'I was then so ill as to alarm him [Charles] exceedingly,' Mary writes to Dorothy Wordsworth on 13 November 1810, 'and he thought me quite incapable of any kind of business . . . I am at present under the care of Dr Tuthill. I think I have derived great benefit from his medicines. He has also made a water drinker of me, which, contrary to my expectations, seems to agree with me very well. '

Tuthill, who had been imprisoned by Napoleon and had his attractive wife to thank for his release, was, in 1810, only at the beginning of his career, but his rise was meteoric. He was a chemist, a popular lecturer in physic, and was knighted in 1820. Part of the Lambs' social circle (Charles mentions his imprisonment in France in a letter of 1806), he was the doctor who wrote the letter which obtained for Charles his long-awaited retirement from the East India Company in 1825. Tuthill was active in producing the new edition of the *Pharmacopoeia Londiniensis* of 1824, the original of which had appeared in 1618 and was the basic treatise for apothecaries in their preparation of medicines. Compound remedies arranged by class – waters, ointments, lozenges – were listed, many of them as old as Galen and Avicenna. Tuthill, with a committee, brought the whole up to date and he was largely responsible for its appearance in English. According to one source, Tuthill 'spoke in quick, short sentences, seldom uttering a word more than the occasion required, or omitting one that was necessary'.[32]

It is not clear what Tuthill prescribed for Mary from his pharmacopoeia, aside from water. Opium and laudanum were both used at the time to still fits, but there is no record of Mary taking either. Tuthill did, however, seem to calm her through an enforced regime of rest, or what she thought of as 'idleness': she was to do no work, see friends as little as possible and go to bed early – a set of prescriptions which were to attend women diagnosed with hysteria or neurasthenia throughout the latter part of the century and into the next. Under Tuthill's care, Mary's bouts of mania moved more rapidly towards recovery than when she was confined to Hoxton. Perhaps the singleness of his attention helped. Nor is it clear what Tuthill prescribed for Charles, whose controllable depressions were not infrequent, but the waters may have done him good as well, particularly as a relief from alcohol. This dietary management follows a direct line from Cheyne. Indeed, taking the waters of various kinds remained one form of treatment for both sadness and madness throughout the nineteenth century across Europe. From our chemical twenty-first, we may look back sceptically, but these mineral waters often enough contained the basis of some of our contemporary drugs, for example lithium.

For all his work with Mary and patients in Bridewell and Bethlem, Tuthill nowhere appears as a specialist in madness. There is as yet no such established discipline. Those whom the period names as specialists in madness are largely 'managers' of the insane. Dr Francis Willis, whose authority was such as to make George III fear him enough to become 'manageable' in his lunacy, was initially a Reverend, unrecognized by the medical fraternity. His model asylum, Greatford Hall, in Greatford, Lincolnshire, which opened in 1776, as well as his treatment of the King, made him famous. With Maria I of Portugal, Willis was less successful. The Queen, who came from a family in which insanity claimed a number of members, suffered from what was diagnosed as melancholia and religious mania. A sequence of deaths and misfortunes, not to mention fears sparked by neighbouring revolutions, exacerbated her

condition. When Willis came to her bedside in 1792, she believed herself
eternally damned, had hideous nightmares, prolonged insomnia and
stomach problems alongside delirious outbursts, often lewd in content,
and melancholia. Willis's moral management calmed her a little at first,
but relapse was quick.

Nonetheless, this new form of dealing with the mad began to take
hold. Willis's therapy – in so far as it was one – shunned physical brutality and replaced it with moral authority. Willis would, the accounts
go, pierce patients with his powerful eye – like the early continental
mesmerists with whom he was contemporary – and make them obedi-
ent to his will. As Michel Foucault has pointed out, with moral
management, the manacles, chains, handcuffs, strong chairs and scold's
bridles – the whole apparatus of physical coercion – gradually went, to
be replaced by the moral tools of talk, observation and judgement. The
control of the mad moves inward and works through regimentation
and an instilling of discipline.

Dr Willis's asylum and William Tuke's famous York Retreat provide the
models for what becomes asylum life in the first and more optimistic
part of the nineteenth century. Willis's fame spread, in part because his
reports to Parliament on the King's health were widely reprinted in
cheap editions. Hardly a revolutionary himself, Willis ended up by profoundly influencing the founders of French revolutionary psychiatry.
This description originally appeared in a French source:

> As the unprepared traveller approached the town, he was astonished to
> find almost all the surrounding ploughmen, gardeners, threshers,
> thatchers and other labourers attired in black coats, white waistcoats,
> black silk breeches and stockings, and the head of each 'bien poudré,
> frisé, et arrangé'. These were the doctor's patients, and dress, neatness of
> person, and exercise being the principal features of his admirable system,
> health and cheerfulness conjoined to aid recovery of every person
> attached to that most valuable asylum.[33]

At the York Retreat, run along Quaker principles and best described
by its founder's grandson Samuel Tuke in his 1813 account, all physical
restraints were put aside in favour of a system of rewards and moral

punishments which encouraged self-restraint in the inmates. The keepers effectively became stern but kind parents eliciting good behaviour from unruly children, who needed to be kept busy and orderly. Work, with its regular hours, its obligations and requirements of attention, served, with talk, as an exemplary treatment which could contain ravings, instil self-esteem and mould the mad into a semblance of good citizenship.[34]

The Willis family, the Quaker Tukes and the English practice of moral management were to help shape the field that grew into a specialism and became known first as alienism and later as psychiatry. When moral management crossed the Channel to meet the Revolution, it abandoned its religious hue altogether: madness and its French medics and managers were at first emphatically secular. Indeed, with the application of a little theory and more state regulation, the English Malady became a French Science.

BEING A WOMAN

In 1801 the Lamb's friend George Dyer wrote what became a popular poem evoking the plight of a fetching young Ophelia-like innocent in Bedlam:

> If moon-struck horrors haunt thy restless head,
> All-hopeless Pity here shall take her stand . . .

In 1815 the two writhing, brutish and chained male personifications of madness in front of Bedlam were replaced by figures of women — a 'youthful, beautiful, female insanity'.[35] Madness, at least in representation, it would seem, was becoming feminized and tamed, no longer wild, raving and dangerous, but pathetic.

Elaine Showalter in *The Female Malady* has persuasively argued that nineteenth-century cultural ideas about women — their supposed irrationality at a time when Reason was male, their weakness and lability occasioned by a biology which includes the coming of menses at puberty, then pregnancy and lactation, then menopause, together with notions about 'proper' feminine behaviour — shaped the time's definitions and treatment of women's insanity. Pretty, victimized Ophelia, Lucia di Lammermoor who on her wedding night murdered the bridegroom chosen by her parents, and the servant girl Crazy Jane, abandoned by her lover, are the three iconic figures around whom she sees understanding of female madness coalesce. All link women's madness in one way or another to their sexual relationships to men.

Does this help us to understand Mary Lamb's case?

One could say about Mary that her brother's falling in love with another precipitated her sense of being entombed in a family from which, like Lucia, she had to break free. Donning Freud-tinted spectacles, we could even suggest that the needlework Mary herself singles out as oppressive signals not only her madness-inducing enslavement in drudgery, but also that (masturbatory) repression of sexual urges which leads to her fatal Oedipal act. Or we could stretch the Ophelia/victim line into our own time's favourite psy narrative. This would entail examining her childhood not only for instances of maternal deprivation and lapses in thought, that Lockean cementing of incoherent ideas, but also for instances of sexual abuse bringing in their train dissociation and fears which make her younger, limping brother the only safe male in her life.

Such accounts or stories shed some light on Mary's case, though not quite the one she or her time would have chosen. In Mary's own writing, apart from her complaints about needlework and the way it prevents women from indulging in the 'idleness' which might be renamed education, her only other emphasis on women's condition has to do with a wish to warn a friend against romantic illusions and about the difficulties marriage may bring, not least amongst them the dangers of childbirth. Though one could rush to interpret this as Mary's own unconscious sexual fears, it would be a mistake not to take her comments at face value, as well.

What emerges from Mary's and indeed Charles's letters, is the sense that her feminine identity is tied up with being 'useful', ever busy in household tasks or indeed, needlework, or ever seeing friends, being serviceable to them, entertaining. Throughout the nineteenth century, talented, middle-class women were to shake off the chains of their socially restricted forms of usefulness by unconsciously choosing invalidism as a preferable form of life. The poet and political radical Elizabeth Barrett Browning, eldest of twelve children, developed an ailment at the age of fourteen which saved her from the drudgery of looking after her siblings and an autocratic father, and allowed her to take to the studious writing life she preferred. Wooed from her bed-chamber by the poet Robert Browning, whom she loved 'freely as men strive for right', she was proud, invalid that she had been, to be able to give birth to his child at the age of forty.

For Mary Lamb, the very feminine usefulness she prides herself on is also the agitation which leads to her exhaustion, which in turn brings on her mania. During these bouts of mania, the conversation she engages in to give friends pleasure takes on a speeded-up and elaborate mantle, full of descriptive detail, 'like the jewelled speeches of Congreve only shaken from their setting . . . It was as if the finest elements of mind had been shaken into fantastic combinations like those of a kaleidoscope.'[36]

Mary's culture, the possibilities, habits, restrictions of behaviour her time endorses for women, inflect her mania. But does her femaleness affect the way her peers understand her madness and the treatment she receives for it? The response here is hardly a straightforward one, and historians over the last thirty years might differ in their assessment. Feminist challenges to more traditional history in the 1980s and '90s stressed that women were more likely than men to be institutionalized as mad and indeed to have their dissatisfactions with their condition read as madness by their time. More recent historians have shown that asylum statistics do not altogether bear this out.[37]

The later nineteenth century may have enshrined women as the weaker vessel, frailer by constitution, and thus more easily susceptible to madness. But Mary Lamb's brother and friends in their voluminous correspondence – which comprises most of the prominent members of the Romantic movement up until Charles's death in 1834 – rarely mention anything that would make a tender, vulnerable Ophelia of Mary. What they most often comment on is how surprising madness is in a person with so great a hold on good sense as hers. She is 'the last woman in the world whom you could have suspected, under any cir-cumstances, of becoming insane, so calm, so judicious, so rational was she.' As William Hazlitt used to say, 'Mary Lamb is the only truly sensi-ble woman I ever met with.'[38]

Cheyne, too, in his case histories of young women, even when he is describing what seem to be extreme psychosomatic symptoms, 'histerick fits and collicks' that can leave the sufferer crippled in hands and feet, rarely links these directly to a female condition or a weakness of mind or will. Then, too, his male cases outnumber those of women, just as during the Georgian period male admissions to asylums outstripped those of women.[39]

In 1845, the York Retreat showed men outnumbering women by about 30 per cent.[40] The pattern changed after mid-century with the rise of the vast public asylums. The Lunacy and County Asylums Act of 1845 not only brought asylums more closely under medical inspection: it also required provision of public asylums for all pauper lunatics by local authorities. The mad and those thought to be mad by their families, the incapable, the troublesome, the geriatric, no longer had to be kept at home or be paid for where possible in private madhouses, but could be housed at government expense. This increased the asylum population and along with it that of women: according to the census of 1871, for every 1000 male pauper lunatics there were 1242 women pauper lunatics, a number somewhat in excess of the proportion of women in the general population, which was 1056 to 1000.[41] But historians have recently argued that, important as gender was to psychiatric and psychological theory at the turn of the nineteenth century and in the early twentieth, this did not translate into asylum figures or practice in any simple way. The figures for admission and release do not vary greatly enough between the sexes in Britain: if anything, single men are over-represented amongst the mad in the nineteenth-century asylum.[42]

If within the madhouses of the turn of the eighteenth century woman's fate seems to be no worse than man's, there are nonetheless some abuses which – through their repetition in various reports – do add up to a pattern particularly suffered by women. Accounts of rape and sexual assault, sometimes occasioned by a woman keeper who is out to gain, occur frequently. Even more frequent are accounts of force-feeding. John Haslam, the apothecary at Bethlem, in his *Observations on Madness and Melancholy* of 1809, writes: 'It is a painful recollection to refer to the number of interesting females I have seen, who, after having suffered a temporary disarrangement of mind, and undergone the brutal operation of spouting [force-feeding] in private receptacles for the insane, have been restored to their friends without a front tooth in either jaw.'[43] One is left wondering whether the violent impatience of this particular form of assault is an indication that there were greater numbers of women 'starving' themselves than men: and whether this might be a particularly feminine response to an illness one aspect of which is later specialized into anorexia.

SYMPTOMS OF THE TIME

In 1810, the London physician William Black prepared a table detailing the causes of insanity of patients admitted to Bethlem. The everydayness of these categories underlines the lack of a specific psychiatric language. The copious first category might be rewritten simply as 'life drives you mad'. To compare this list with *DSM IV*, today's most widely used and American-based diagnostic manual, is to see how far the mind doctors have moved in creating a 'scientific' discipline. Instead of the dozens of finely differentiated psychotic, cognitive, mood and substance-related disorders, the eating and anxiety disorders, the personality, sleep, adjustment, impulse control and intermittent explosive disorders, Bethlem registered the following categories and causes:

Misfortunes, Troubles, Disappointments

Grief	206
Religion and Methodism	90
Love	74
Jealousy	9
Pride	8
Study	15
Fright	31
Drink and Intoxication	58
Fevers	110
Childbed	79
Obstruction	10
Family and Heredity	115
Contusions and Fractures of the Skull	12
Venereal	14
Small Pox	7
Ulcers and Scabs dried up	5[44]

It is worth noting that this list shows an interest in the causes of madness, unlike the *DSM* which focuses only on the fine-tuning of diagnoses based on visible signs and behaviours – on symptoms. The Bethlem table points to a wide set of explanations for insanity, ranging from the organic to the hereditary, from circumstances of environment or emotion, travails of life, to character defects. Interestingly, religion and Methodism appear as *causes* of insanity: we have entered a world where a secular medical discourse is beginning to nudge against and displace a religious one. Divine madness – and it was a time of great religious enthusiasm – is no longer simply a tolerable matter of holy fools, but one of intolerable extremes which lead to confinement.

The table also points out that a substantial number of inmates are there because of insanity occasioned by 'childbed' – that is, by giving birth or nursing. The figure is larger than that for drink which, as the condition of 'alcoholism', was to help fill the asylums of the second half of the nineteenth century. Mary Lamb had killed her mother. At the opposite generational pole were women who killed their children or who grew mad when they appeared. The specifically female diagnosis of puerperal madness was to remain an important one. French doctors, who from the Revolution on were interested in population politics and hence the welfare of mothers, were perhaps even more preoccupied than their British kin with the ramifications of this particular aspect of women's experience.

In Britain, until the First World War, despite Lunacy Acts and the implacable growth in the number and size of asylums and a rising profession of alienists, there is no generalized change in the way in which the causes of mental illness are categorized. A highly reputable, large private asylum like St Andrew's in Northampton in the period up until 1907 differentiates mental illness along 'Moral' (by which is meant psychological) and 'Physical' lines. The first include anxiety, trouble, disappointment in love, fright, jealousy, pecuniary difficulties, religion, novel-reading and spiritualism. Life, it seems, causes madness. Reading may be even worse. For women, as the century goes on, certain activities are particularly dangerous, as the Victorians warn. Physical causes of insanity seem hardly more medicalized. Yes, there is apoplexy, brain disease, heredity, syphilis and, for women, change of life; but physical causes still also include over-study, overwork, self-indulgence and the Victorian category of masturbation.[45]

Generalizing across the spectrum of mental illness and its treatment is hazardous. All changes in theory and practice come slowly and piece-meal, like long-term negotiations towards a treaty which would somehow reconcile the ongoing battle between sanity and insanity. The borders keep shifting, so does the terrain. Hospitals far from the front line carry out one set of practices. Those closer spell out treaty rules which some, but only some, follow. Patients may be more aware than doctors, particularly if they've travelled either from one institu-tion to another or from one country or doctor to another. This said, however, certain trends emerge. Historians agree that a medical spe-cialization to do with mental health took place first in France and the German-speaking countries. The practice of asylum management, however, was greatly influenced by the British experience, even if, in the first instance, asylum keepers were themselves hardly mind doctors.

PART TWO

THE RISE AND RISE OF THE NEW SCIENCE

2

PASSIONS

Revolution engenders revolutionary enthusiasms. In Napoleonic France and through the first part of the nineteenth century, medicine takes on a new momentum as a tool both of social good and of what can begin to be called scientific inquiry. First-hand clinical observation – the development of what Michel Foucault calls the medical gaze[46] – is married to a new sense that medicine can encompass both a knowledge of nature *and* a knowledge of man in society. Where the mad are concerned, the new breed of doctors suppose that it is worth both managing them *and* acquiring knowledge of how their minds and emotions work. Such knowledge, it is presumed, is not only part of the wider practice of detailed medical observation which comes to be known as *la clinique*: it will also help to effect cures. The inner experience of madness, madness from the point of view of the sufferer, thus becomes the object of an intense curiosity. In turn this intense curiosity about the mind and the various forms of medical practice that come along with it inevitably have a shaping effect on mind itself and on those descriptions of subjective experience that people bring to doctors and to each other. The files and records that the new science keeps increasingly confine the individual in illness categories, even when she is not confined in an asylum.

A growing willingness to assume a continuity of sensations between the mad and the sane also marks the moment. The mad are not in any way simply 'wild beasts' raging, like Bertha in the Brontë attic, and poised to bite. They are interesting, perhaps subtle. J.E.D Esquirol – with Philippe Pinel, his teacher, the most important pioneer in the new field – traces a long and honourable history for mania and gives it a Greek and biblical pedigree, which includes Oedipus and Orestes.

The most important term in what would become the French mind sciences, le délire, suggests an experience which encompasses the ecstatic joy of the poet, the hashish smoker and the revolutionary rioter, as well as the more medicalized fever of an English 'delirium'. Esquirol gives delirium its broad, foundational definition. A man 'is in delirium when his sensations are not at all in agreement with external objects, when his ideas are not at all in agreement with his sensations, when his judgements and his resolutions are not at all in agreement with his ideas, when his ideas, judgements and resolutions are independent of his volition'.[47] For Esquirol, delirium is a sickness of the soul. Uncontrollable passion and imagination are of its essence: in fact, madness is simply imagination gone awry. Delirium, like the altered states which mesmerism induces, can be experienced by the sane, while the mad are not always deliriously so.

With this kind of understanding, making distinctions between the undelirious mad and the deliriously sane becomes a subtle business and one necessitating expertise. This had several effects. It helped engender the new profession of alienism – a forerunner of psychiatry – and gave it a certain social power. The status of the mad improved, at least marginally, and certainly in the eyes of urban progressives. Conversely, under the power of the new professionals, claims of madness were now more difficult to reverse: for those with less social power, like women, this could make unwanted confinement difficult to resist or escape.

While English 'moral management', with its private or charitable asylums, had substantially influenced pioneering French doctors, in France the revolutionary state was early invoked to take on responsibility for the mad. A rising profession of medics, keen to carve out their niche in this brave new world of growing 'specialisms', did the invoking. They would seek whatever expertise could be garnered from the untrained custodians of the mad, as well as from the travelling charlatans with their magical, mesmeric or faith cures.[48] Each had something to teach – certainly as much as the antiquated pre-revolutionary medics steeped in arcane theories with little observational base. And the new professionals were ready to learn in order to take over. They were also keen to assume the burden of care that the clergy, those retrograde collaborators with the *ancien régime*, had previously held. Under the aegis of these new enterprising medics, demon possession would give way to scientific diagnoses, though the boundaries of what constituted science remained fluid and permeable. One thing, however, was clear: if the Revolution had freed the people from their metaphorical chains, it must also free the mad from fetters that were all too real.

This new medical passion for public health went arm in arm with a need to gather what we now call statistics. Freed from manacles, the mad began to be fixed in the categories and paper chains of the new state apparatus with its growing medical bureaucracy. Already on the eve of the Revolution, the surgeon Jacques Tenon, preparing a report on the Paris hospital system for a reforming government minister, found that the best information available lay with the Lieutenant General of the Paris police[49] – an expert on hospital admissions.

Statistics – still an unnamed science though a term used in Germany for 'state-knowledge', deriving from the word *Staat*, but there in germ in the new wave of fact-gathering – were needed for shaping policy. They also influenced theoretical speculation. Tenon's researches led to interesting questions and to a novel field of inquiry: 'It is certain that among furious lunatics, there are more women than men. A new subject for research. Does this difference originate in the sequelae of childbearing, in the nervous sensations accompanying lactation?' Though he cannot yet answer his own question, Tenon is keen to arrest the 'deterioration' of the sex that 'perpetuates society'. The new Sainte-Anne hospital, he determines, must have more facilities for mad women than for men, unlike the Hôtel-Dieu where the ratio went the other way. This hospital, Tenon asserts, emphasizing the hopes of the times, will be a *machine à guérir*[50], a machine for cures.

For the new alienism's key pioneers, Philippe Pinel, author of the seminal *Traité médico-philosophique sur l'aliénation mentale, ou la manie* (1801; expanded, 1809), and his pupil, Jean-Etienne-Dominique Esquirol, puerperal madness continued to be a strand of diagnosis, just as the size of the population and care for mothers continued to be a preoccupation for the French state. However, unlike their later progeny, both doctors tended to give more weight to social and environmental determinants of madness than to specifically biological ones. In their vision, the biological might act as a trigger, or occasion a susceptibility, but already-existing passionate conflicts or life crises were the weightier determining 'cause' of mental illness.

French psychiatry, born with the Revolution, is initially closely bound up with a cultural and social, rather than a biological or hereditary, imperative. Environmental forces occasion madness, just as they occasion revolution. Interestingly, symptoms, too, express the times. Pinel, Esquirol and their growing number of students are alert to the fact that the mad to some extent choose the shape their symptoms will take: they learn 'mad' behaviour from those around them, and in their agitation enact the passions the culture provides. 'Other illnesses . . . reveal themselves to us by constant signs, as invariable as their causes . . . Only madness [la folie], a kind of morbid Proteus, is the transitory and changing image of the interests that govern men, of the emotions that agitate them; and, like the world, a lunatic asylum is a mosaic of the passions.'51

Mimicking Napoleon's rise and rise to imperial status, the condition of *manie ambitieuse* – ambitious mania – finds its way into the madhouses. This is the socially-propelled malaise of the soul both Stendhal and Balzac identify in their heroes. It is the 'dark ambition' which drives Julien Sorel, the hero of *The Red and the Black*, on to a path of glory that ultimately ends in crime. Indeed, the two novelists were fascinated by the new science. Convinced of the importance of character expressed through physiognomy, Balzac gives the same detailed, almost clinical attention to his characters as the new 'moral' medics give to their patients, enshrining them in the rising naturalistic genre of the 'case history' and classifying them by diagnostic kind.

There is a growing sense through the first part of the century that clues to character, to the workings of the mind itself, are visible on the surface of the body and can be read by the trained eye. This sense gives rise to the study of physiognomy and to phrenology, the reading of character by the tapping of the skull, on the basis that psychic traits are the expression of particular organs of the brain.

Citizen Pinel (1745–1826): liberator of the insane

Philippe Pinel, the doctor in charge of the Parisian madhouses during the Revolution, took on a legendary status through his act of ordering the mad to be liberated from their chains. It was a scene much depicted in popular prints of the time and reinvoked in the writings of his son Scipion as well as in a much reproduced painting of 1887 by Tony Robert-Fleury. This last shows a compassionate Pinel 'freeing the insane' (the painting's title) – symbolized by a beautiful Marianne-like maiden in loosely flowing dress and unleashed hair. While her chains are unlocked, Pinel looks on with a beneficent scientific curiosity.

The man who was to make a medical science out of the treatment of madness was born to a poor family in a small town in south-west France. In love with the great illuminating *philosophes* of the *Encyclopédie*, with literature and mathematics, he felt the limitations of his first medical degree from the Faculty in Toulouse and went on to the renowned medical school in Montpelier. Here he frequented the city's several hospitals and already began to develop the medical technique he later encouraged in his own students: he observed the patient carefully, translated what he saw into written notes while at the sickbed, and eventually recorded the entire course of a severe illness. He also talked and listened to the patient. Pinel's lasting contribution to the new medicine was to underline the importance of observation and of the doctor–patient relationship in fostering a cure.

From Montpelier, like so many of the heroes of French literature, Pinel felt irresistibly drawn to the capital. Here, although he made medical friends, he was unable to practise: the all-powerful and conservative Faculty of Medicine twice refused him a much needed scholarship and entry to its ranks. The seeds of later rebellion against a powerful medical orthodoxy were sown at this time. The young provincial fell into a depression and dreamt of fleeing the baseness and intrigues of Paris by journeying to America. Instead, in 1784 he accepted the post of editor of the *Gazette de Santé*, and wrote articles, many of them on hygiene, 'moral' treatment and mental disorders. Pinel's considerable talents as a writer are certainly not inconsequential in the shaping of his reputation and indeed of French medicine. The success of the later *Traité*, sought out by Stendhal, must in part be due to the brilliance of its prose, the narrative impetus of its case studies, as well as Pinel's interest in the philosophical underpinnings of medicine.

In 1785, Pinel translated some important texts of Scottish and English medicine: William Cullen's *First Lines of the Practice of Physik* and three volumes of the *Philosophical Transactions* of the Royal Society of London. He also became a regular at the influential salon of the beautiful Madame Helvétius, wife of the philosopher who is known as the father of utilitarianism. Influenced by Locke and Condillac, Helvétius believed that human behaviour is determined by education and environment, that actions and judgements are generated by the natural desire to maximize pleasure and minimize pain. All this was to inform Pinel's later writing on the mad and his attempt to create better environments for them.

The tragedy suffered by a close friend sparked his interest in madness. A shy provincial like himself, the friend had fallen into despair and then 'mania' when his legal aspirations failed to materialize. Unable to help the younger man once he had all but ceased to eat, Pinel had brought him to the Hôtel-Dieu where a treatment of baths and food seemed to restore him. But his worried family intervened and took him home before he was quite well. The youth escaped their hold, fled to the woods and was found dead only after the wolves had got at him.

Pinel sought out work at a private madhouse. For five years the *maison de santé* owned by a former cabinetmaker, Belhomme, served as his observational training ground and allowed him to hone ideas and therapeutic technique. With the Revolution, Citizen Pinel's star rose. The Comité de Mendicité (Committee for the Welfare of the Poor) wanted to make madhouses centres for cure. In 1793, Pinel was appointed to run the hospice at Bicêtre, which had never had a medical head. (The Marquis de Sade was brought there in 1803.) It was here that Pinel first freed madmen who had been chained for twenty years or more and protected them from the jeering crowds who came to gawk. During his nineteen months at Bicêtre, Pinel listened to each inmate's life story and carefully tracked symptoms in order to build a sense of the 'natural history of the disease'.

Next came a Chair in Hygiene – the equivalent of public health – at the newly formed Ecole de Médécine in Paris where the training emphasis was now on 'seeing' and doing, rather than reading and accepting old 'theoretical' visions of the body and disease which could so easily occlude the visible. In 1795 Pinel not only became Professor of Pathology, a post he kept for twenty years, but was transferred to the Salpêtrière, the facility for 'incurably' mad women. It is to the Salpêtrière – a hospice which numbered some 5000–7000 inmates, about

600 of them mentally ill — that his name has become indissolubly attached. With the help of the General Council of Paris Hospitals which accorded Citizen Pinel two paid medical students to help him with his research into madness, the foundations of the new medical science of alienism were laid, here amidst the women. Freud was later to say that the most humane of all revolutions was launched at the Salpêtrière by Pinel when he freed the mad from their chains.[52]

Alienism was only one of Pinel's undertakings. His contemporaries knew him equally well as a great medical diagnostician classifier, and in particular through his *Nosographie Philosophique* of 1798. The book makes thorough use of the new practice of *la clinique*, that observation and taking of histories which allows the doctor coolly to delineate the whole course of a disease, its symptoms and progress through to its internal appearance *post-mortem*. A vast hospital also provided ready access to a large number of corpses for autopsy. This is the moment when medicine begins to acquire the systemized status of a science.

Such was Pinel's distinction that for a time he served as Napoleon's physician — a post which must have attuned him to the nature of ambition. It is clear from Pinel's seminal *Traité* that his goals are already those of a man intent on setting up a profession that straddles the medical, the scientific and the philosophical.

The *Traité* investigates the field of 'mental alienation' systematically, drawing together a wide range of those Pinel wants to designate as precursors in the field and setting out best practice. It begins with a section on causes of mental illness. Pinel names five general areas that can play a role in mental alienation: heredity, 'irregularities' in the environment, the role of sudden or oppressive or excessive passions, a melancholic constitution; and lastly, physical causes. The second section describes 'lesions', or abnormalities, of perception, thought, memory, association and judgement. The third provides Pinel's classification system with its four main groupings: the many kinds of mania, melancholy, dementia and finally imbecility. Section four moves from observation to best practice: Pinel is intent on advocating the kind of morally managed and enlightened therapeutic institution he believes in, as well as on disseminating the kind of teaching and research that is necessary to the new medicine.

It is clear that doctors are to take over the burden of care from priests and that religious mania can be contagious and must be carefully restrained. His anticlericalism is both part of Pinel's revolutionary stance and marks the rise of a competing caring, but now scientific, profession. He also underlines that the most effective treatment, if it is to be repeated successfully across the nation, cannot be based only on personal experience. For the truths of alienation to emerge, research must be carried out across a sufficient population, by regular, detailed observation over many years. In that sense, he is a *modern* doctor.

Pinel's contribution to medical theory lay in his certainty that many kinds of madness were *partial* and therefore curable: the patient's reason, in abeyance but reachable, had to be engaged so that she became an accomplice in her cure. This was married to his insistence on the careful observation of symptoms. Such *external* manifestations of illness were the basis for disease classification.

Pinel's empirical bent made him particularly open to English medical management, as well as to the experience of the non-medical guardians in the mental institutions, both male and female. He was alert to the tacit skills of experience, the way the *concierges*, or guardians – in particular the superintendent at Bicêtre, then at Salpêtrière, Jean-Baptiste Pussin and his wife – managed the mad by appearing to be party to their imaginary ideas, or by diverting them with laughter and trickery until they were calmed or fed. A populist who was also interested in philosophy, Pinel had no compunctions about inviting mesmerists into the Salpêtrière to see what effect their brand of treatment might have on the patients. Such popular forms of mind control and suggestion could all be tapped in the shaping of a field which was still porous.

Strangely, for a practitioner of that new clinical method which in its non-alienist manifestations liked to localize disease in body parts, Pinel was less interested in the search for any physical and brain-related causes of madness. He believed that brain lesions might produce idiocy, but not the kind of mental alienation so many suffered from. Although he admired anatomical studies of brain lesions and glands, he was sceptical about their usefulness. 'Can one establish any link between physical appearances manifested after death and lesions in intellectual function observed during life?' he asked. A lesion in the brain, a swelling of the meninges or brain tissue, after all, does not easily translate into 'ambitious monomania', a patient believing she is Queen. Since lesions are unlocatable during a patient's lifetime, they hold out little use for treatment. Then, too, there is the underlying problem about the similarity of the post-mortem brains of the normal to those who have been mentally ill. This poses a grave obstacle to any theory which wants to make a wholesale link between insanity and brain disease.[53]

Pinel's followers – Esquirol to a certain extent, Etienne-Jean Georget, and the institution of alienism that grew up around them – were similarly critical of those who, like the brilliant young pathologist Antoine-Laurent Bayle, set out to find a physiological and anatomical base for mental illness through post-mortem research. The search for physical causes and, even more so, the certainty that they would eventually be found, had to wait for subsequent generations.

If brain lesions as causes of mental illness were not of primary importance to Pinel, the imagination was. Already in his early journalism he was well aware of the way imagination could produce physical ills and in turn help to speed their cure. He was convinced of the happy effects 'consoling and reassuring words'[54] had on patients in general medicine – in other words, of bedside manner. His founding principle was *la douceur*, a winning gentleness. The 'moral treatment', in today's terms a psychological treatment, proceeded from these grounds.

Whatever distance our theories and knowledge of brain chemistry may have travelled, Pinel's procedure once more seems eminently sensible, practical and humane. Through *douceur* and an attentive listening, the doctor won the patient's trust and made her tractable to the authority that had to be established from the first. If force ever had to be used, it must be clear that it was used against the grain of the doctor's wishes and only in a difficult moment when gentleness was impossible – such as in the first, highly agitated states of mania when restraints were to everyone's benefit.

Pinel distinguished two main kinds of alienation – the word he prefers to *folie*, or madness. The first was caused by erroneous ideas or pathological reasoning, a very Lockean form of madness. He treated this by attempting to divert the patient, through a kind of theatrical ploy – an *appareil* – which would shift the patient's mind on to a new track or demonstrate the error of the thinking he or she was trapped in. In this way a tailor, driven mad by his worry that his fellow revolutionaries would punish him for a momentary expression of sympathy for the guillotined King, was prescribed a staged trial in which the judges ruled his sentiments of the most patriotic. A temporary cure was thus effected.

The second and far more prevalent form of alienation, according to Pinel and his growing school of followers, particularly his favourite and successor Esquirol, was caused by pathological passions – extreme emotions stirred by the traumas of life. Pinel cites the cases of three girls driven mad by fear: one by a ghost 'introduced' at night into her room, another by a violent clap of thunder experienced at that certain time of month, the last by the horror inspired when she was tricked into a particular place.

Amongst the overwhelming and oppressive passions capable of driving an individual mad he lists hatred, envy, jealousy, grief and remorse. He notes that these are passions that also serve art. However, when overly strong or in conflict with each other, they can derail reason or send the subject into a melancholy stupor. Sufferers are characterized by external signs such as paleness, loss of appetite, loss of muscular force, laborious breathing interspersed by sobs and either the most violent delirium or a profound passivity. He describes the case of a woman who watched her family being butchered in war, another who lost everything after the death of her father and couldn't earn her keep; one who had dedicated herself to God and chastity at the age of fourteen, then decided on marriage and, though seemingly happy, her scruples resurfaced after the birth of her fourth child, and the ensuing inner conflict produced delirium. Another young woman, driven mad by the tug of war between God and temptation, refused to eat for a month.

Such diseased passions – so potently part of that pivotal Romantic philosopher Rousseau's thinking – can not and should not be entirely removed, according to Pinel. Passion is crucial to the revolutionary personality, after all. However, in the interests of good health, the diseased passion needs to be 'counterbalanced'. In Rousseau's *La Nouvelle Héloïse*, the mentor performs this function. A doctor can do the counterbalancing for a patient with the help of various theatrical ruses. Treatment is most effective when coupled with confinement away from the corruptions and hurly-burly of the city.

Therapeutic confinement, kindness which entails listening to the patient, and constructive occupation are thus the key features of Pinel's treatment. The confinement is important. Pinel is emphatic, as Freud and Laing were later, that his patients suffer from their families and need to be removed from them. In the asylum those traditional treatments for lowering or raising a patient's 'state' – such as bleeding, purging, immersion in freezing water and blistering – gave way to talk and occupation therapies. As well as regular purposeful work, physical exercise and understanding are the keys to cure. The last might include placing the patient in an invented family group – something of a rehearsal for non-institutional life. In this Pinel feels thoroughly modern, as he does in his radical departure of suggesting that convalescent or cured patients be hired as nurses. This would help their re-integration into ordinary working life and also serve as an example of hope to patients who had known them on the other side of that wavering divide between sanity and madness.

All this, needless to say, was an ideal. Throughout France, and even in the capital, far more primitive conditions often prevailed. Then, too, that seemingly salutary idea of partial madness, which linked the mad and the sane in a family of behaviours and imaginings, could equally be used as a way of labelling the more or less sane as 'mad' and in need of confinement. From the beginning, what would become psychiatric science wore a Janus face.

Jean-Etienne-Dominique Esquirol (1772–1840)

If Pinel laid the basis for French alienism in the nineteenth century, it was his pupil Esquirol who disseminated his ideas and consolidated the relationship between the new medical expertise and the state.

Born into a wealthy merchant family in Toulouse, Esquirol's bourgeois background facilitated his dealings with power, especially after 1815 when a reactionary Restoration bureaucracy grew suspicious of the preceding regime's favourites. Comfortable with those in power, he was nonetheless committed to helping the helpless insane, whose plight he described in rhetoric vivid enough to provoke the most dry-eyed of government ministers into ultimately passing the law of 1838 which was intended to provide departmental asylums for the mad poor throughout France. 'I have seen them at the mercy of veritable jailers, victims of their brutal supervision. I have seen them in narrow, dirty, infested dungeons without air or light, chained in caverns where one would fear to lock up the wild beasts that luxury-loving governments keep at great expense in their capitals.'[55]

Armed with a medical degree and two years as a public health official in the southern town of Narbonne, Esquirol first arrived in Paris in 1799. At the Salpêtrière, he quickly became Pinel's favourite student. In order to further the research on madness they were both so interested in, Pinel apparently put up the security for the private asylum Esquirol ran on the rue de Buffon. It became one of the three best in Paris and provided the case work for Esquirol's thesis of 1805, *Des Passions considérées comme causes, symptomes et moyens curatifs de l'aliénation mentale*. Aberrant, extreme or insufficient passion is, for Esquirol, at once cause, symptom and means of cure.

Following the death of the Salpêtrière's *concierge*, or guardian, the very Pussin from whom Pinel had learned so much about the mad, Esquirol was made the medical head of the asylum. He thus effectively became, as Pinel underlined, the first doctor devoted wholly to the study of insanity. The patients in the Salpêtrière were of course women, and it was in observing and listening to them that Esquirol like Pinel honed the specialization that would become psychiatry.

Pinel's choice of a second was a good one for the growth of alienism. Esquirol had a talent for public affairs: he inspected facilities for the mad throughout France, produced reports for government as well as books and, in 1817 – still a *médecin ordinaire*, not a professor – he instituted the first formal and highly popular course in *maladies mentales*. His students were many and dedicated. The number of alienists grew and, with them, the use of what was Esquirol's most popular diagnosis – monomania. This became the mental illness of the times, arguably the first culturally engendered diagnostic fashion, breeding copycat sufferers who, nonetheless, in that symbiosis between mind and symptom so common in the history of mental alienation, really suffered from the named condition. Monomania was also the diagnosis which took psychiatry emphatically into the courts, making doctors expert witnesses in criminal trials where the line between responsibility, free will and extenuating madness was not immediately visible to the 'lay' eye.

Astute, dedicated, diplomatic enough to distance himself slightly from Pinel and the liberals who were forced into the sidelines by the Restoration government, Esquirol was appointed Inspector General of the Paris Medical Faculty in 1822. In 1825 he became the director of the Charenton Hospice. He was also the architect of the Natural Law of 1938 that created an asylum in every French *département*. His monomania flourished during the period of the constitutional monarchy, while the bourgeoisie, like the new alienists, rose and rose, and France enriched itself. By the 1870s when theories of degeneration and hysteria took over, the diagnosis had virtually vanished.[56]

MONOMANIA

In order to establish the new science of alienism, Esquirol wanted to cut off links to any ancient humoral classifications. Contemporary scientific thinking needed to be reflected in new names. For melancholy, he proposed 'lypemania', which never quite caught on as a term. What did was the newly minted condition of monomania, 'that partial madness dependent on exciting, expansive and buoyant [*gaies*] passions'.[57] He saw monomania as being 'intermediate' between lypemania, or depression, and mania. With the first it shared 'fixity and concentration' on a single set of ideas, though the lypemaniac in his partial madness was morose, fearful, and suffered from prolonged sadness. With mania, it shared an exalted nature and excessive moral and physical agitation. In advanced societies, he noted, monomania was caused and characterized by pride, by an abnegation of all belief, by ambition, despair and suicide.[58] In older societies, or in the country, it could as well be characterized by erotic or religious passions.

Esquirol, like his teacher, made copious observations of his patients: physiognomy, minute details of behaviour over time as well as past history, come into play in his notes and, later, in his books with their summaries of cases, treatments, their success and failure. So important was this 'documentary' evidence to Esquirol that he called in artists to draw his patients, just as a natural historian might have delicately copied a rare plant in the wild. Esquirol's physiognomy of the monomaniac has all the elements of a Balzacian portrait: monomaniacs are 'animated, expansive, hypermobile; the eyes are lively, sometimes shining and look 'injected', their walk has an energetic gait. They're noisy, garrulous, petulant, brave, overcome all obstacles', unlike the lypemaniac, whose gaze is anxious, whose features are drawn and immobile and who is prey to miserable ideas and a listless sadness and may often refuse food. Excited by ideas of grandeur, wealth and happiness, individuals who are subject to monomania are often impatient and irascible, suspicious of near ones, prone to hallucinations which topple them into delirium, sometimes suicidal. A crisis of failed hopes, transforms them into princes, noblemen, empresses, distinguished scholars and inventors, poets and orators whose disquisitions must be listened to.

Amongst his patients at the Salpêtrière, Esquirol notes a young woman who has had some 'instructions from above' and thinks she orders the sun, the moon and the clouds. She threatens staff with rain or sun when she grows impatient with her stay at the hospice. Esquirol also mentions an empress, a dauphin, an Apollo Caesar, a sufferer from what came popularly to be known as 'ambitious monomania'. He identified this as the primary madness of the age of 'new kings'. Revolutionary upheavals had destroyed traditional hierarchies, dismantled structures of authority and introduced a mobility which crossed over into madness, one in which patients imagined themselves kings and queens. Though on the whole Esquirol and his followers were less likely to diagnose an 'ambitious monomania' in women than in men, and in the poor than in the rich, it was nonetheless the disease of the times, and could be caused by an incident of overwhelming passion. People were tipped into monomania, Esquirol notes, when the King, Queen or Danton were guillotined.

That rather porous dividing line between the monomaniac and the ordinary radically single-minded person is not always easy to see. Only when the subject of the monomaniac's delirium comes into focus does the mania grip him and become visible. When Abraham hears an angel telling him to sacrifice Isaac, Esquirol notes, he is in the grip of a hallucinatory monomania, akin to that suffered by patients he calls religious monomaniacs. Indeed, religious delusions and the classification of these as madness play a substantial part in the building of this new scientific and adamantly secular discipline. In the acute phase of the illness, he states, the partiality of the monomania – when the sufferer is able to reason well across a range of thought unrelated to the driving *idée fixe* – disappears.

Théroigne de Méricourt

One of Esquirol's most famous cases of monomania was that of the
revolutionary 'Amazon', Théroigne de Méricourt, a woman of many
sobriquets who was also known as the panther and *la belle Liegeoise* after
the principality where she was born in 1762. The poet Baudelaire later
immortalized her in his *Fleurs du Mal*, comparing her to Diana:

> Have you seen Théroigne, that lover of carnage,
> Exciting a barefoot mob to the attack?
> Her eyes and cheeks aflame, she plays her part . . .
> But the sweet Amazon's soul
> Is as charitable as it is murderous;
> . . . And her heart, ravaged by passion, has always
> Held a reservoir of tears for the worthy.

The daughter of well-off peasants, Anne-Josèphe Terwagne, as she
first was, had a difficult childhood and left home early to become companion to a lady of Anvers who taught her the ways of polite society.
Soon thereafter, this reportedly beautiful and adventurous young
woman lived as a courtesan and singer, a demi-mondaine courted by a
variety of men, one of whom was a jealous marquis, another a castrato
who worked in the Sistine Chapel. She travelled widely, went to London
and worked as a singer in Paris. With the Revolution, she threw herself
into activism. She hosted a political salon frequented by the radical
greats of the day – Desmoulins, Brissot, Danton and Mirabeau. Dressed
as an Amazon and carrying pistol and sword, she addressed crowds on
the rights of women. The Club des Amis de la Loi, which she founded,
became the famous Cordelier Club.

Targeted by the royalist press as a Sadean libertine, accused of plotting to kill Marie Antoinette, de Méricourt was forced to flee Paris. In
her case history, Esquirol states that she was sent to Liège to foment
uprisings amongst the people and that at the time she held a military
rank. She was noticed amidst the 'savage' crowd that attacked Versailles
on 5–6 October 1790. Back in Liège the Austrians arrested her in January
1791. Detention took her to Vienna, where Emperor Leopold asked to

see her. So convincing or, as some have said, so 'seductive' was Théroigne that he had her set free. By the end of '91 she was back in Paris and in the thick of revolutionary activity once more, this time heading a 'bonneted women's brigade' on behalf of the radical Jacobins. Esquirol, basing his statements as much on rumour as on fact, says that she played a leading role in the events of September 1792 and that though she may not have taken an actual part in the massacres of the royalists, stories circulated of her having, in good castrating fashion, sliced off the head of a man who was purported to be an ex-lover.

Whatever the truth of this rather conventionally misogynistic attribution conflating radicalism and debauchery, what is generally agreed is that like so many other early leaders, de Méricourt was trapped in the escalating rage of the revolutionaries during that phase of events when the 'people' rose against the very bourgeoisie which had initiated the Revolution. In May 1793, during the uprising of the Paris Commune against the ruling Convention, a crowd of women turned on de Méricourt and whipped her to nakedness. Marat, who was himself to be assassinated in just two months' time, stepped out of the crowd to save her from the women of his own party and led her away. It was the end of her political life. The public flogging by the very women she had battled for was to haunt the rest of her life and play itself out in the nakedness on which she later insisted.

Feminist commentators have suggested that de Méricourt's flight into madness after this incident was her way of saying that the Revolution itself had gone mad. Others say her mental imbalance was already long in evidence, but her manic bouts of frenzy which dipped into depression had been masked by the Revolution's own roller-coaster-like excesses.[59]

Just before the fall of Robespierre in July 1794, one of de Méricourt's brothers reported her 'insane', perhaps to prevent her being lost to the Terror and arrested in the general round-up of Jacobin supporters. When she finally was, the authorities found her to be suffering from persecutory delusions – hardly a surprising condition for the times. Freed, she was committed once more and sent to the Hôtel-Dieu.

From then on, de Méricourt's life is a story of confinement. In his case history, which falls into the passionate register Pinel and he are so fond of, Esquirol dates her madness from the end of her revolutionary hopes with the establishment of Napoleon's Directorate. He also mentions that the letter she wrote to Robespierre's lieutenant Saint-Just, found amongst his papers and dated 26 July 1794, in other words at the time her brother first sought her confinement, already shows signs of a 'deranged mind'. This fluidity, where deranged thoughts need not be, but, as in de Méricourt's case, are propelled by external shocks into wholesale madness, is common enough to Esquirol's case histories.

In December 1799, de Méricourt was amongst the women transferred to the Salpêtrière where Pinel had taken over and begun to establish his therapeutic regime. De Méricourt, however, protested at whatever treatment it was that she received, and was soon sent to the Petites-Maisons hospital. In 1807 she was returned to La Salpêtrière, where Esquirol was now in charge of the patients. In *Des Maladies Mentales*, the drawing of her that Esquirol commissioned from the former guillotine artist Georges-François Gabriel shows a fierce, ravaged beauty, with short spiky hair and an expression of great intensity. Esquirol himself – fully aware that he has a 'curiosity', a relic from the Reign of Terror, amongst his patients – describes her as a woman of middle height, with chestnut hair, large blue eyes, mobile physiognomy and a quick, casual, even elegant demeanour. By the time he writes his case history, he has taken on the conservative tone of a man of the Restoration. He is quick to blame the revolution for de Méricourt's madness. He deplores her 'loose' actions at the time. 'She gave herself to various heads of the popular party whom she served during various disturbances', and 'especially contributed, during 5–6 October 1789, to corrupting the Flanders regiment by bringing prostitutes into the ranks and distributing money to the soldiers'.[60] He disapproves not only of Théroigne's revolutionary activism but also of her sexual activity, let alone her current monomania about people's degrees of radicalism and political affiliation.

> She was very agitated, swearing, threatening everyone, talking of liberty and committees of public safety, revolutionaries, etc., accusing everyone who approached her of being a moderate, a royalist, etc.
>
> In 1808, when an important man, who had been head of a political party, came to see her at the Salpêtrière, Teroenne [sic] recognized him, rose from her straw bed, swore at him roundly and accused him of

having abandoned the party of the people, of being a moderate, whom an arrest warrant from the Committee of Public Safety would soon bring justice to.

Esquirol's disapproval, however, fades into sympathy as de Méricourt's condition is aggravated and she falls into a state of dementia, in which 'traces of her dominant ideas' are still visible. Interestingly, no Pinel-like *appareil*, or ploys or bits of stage management, are used to rupture the cycle of her delusional thinking and fixed ideas. Perhaps she was already considered to be too far gone. For the rest of her life, she remained trapped in the tumultuous years of the Revolution.

Whatever improvements 'moral management' may have brought to the care of patients, de Méricourt's living conditions are barely adequate. Esquirol continues:

She can hardly bear to wear any clothes, not even a chemise. Every day, morning and night and at regular intervals through the day, she pours several buckets full of water over her straw bed, lies down in it and covers herself with a sheet in summer and a sheet and blanket in winter. She likes to walk around bare-foot on the wet stone floor . . .

Despite the small dark humid room without furniture, she seems happy enough. She pretends to be busy with important things, she smiles at people who come up to her . . . in a low voice, she repeats phrases in which the words fortune, freedom, committee, revolution, decree, idiot, arrest warrant repeat themselves. She hates the moderates . . .

She hardly leaves her cell and is normally lying down. If she comes out, it is naked or wearing only a chemise. She only takes a few steps, more often, she walks on all fours or stretches out on the ground. Her eyes fixed, she picks up whatever morsels she can find and eats them. I've seen her devour straw or feathers or dry leaves, pieces of meat that have been dragged through mud. She drinks the water from the gutters while the courtyard is being cleaned; though the water is foul and full of excrement, she prefers it to all other drink . . . All sense of modesty has left her and she doesn't blush to find herself naked in the full view of men . . .

De Méricourt died at the age of fifty-seven on 9 June 1817, having spent the last ten years of her tumultuous life in Esquirol's Salpêtrière. Describing the post-mortem – post-mortems were carried out on most patients – Esquirol comes full circle to where he began his case history to note that de Méricourt's colon had moved out of its proper place and was close to her pubic bone. It is something he has observed in other monomaniacs who also suffer from depression. The observation apart, he proposes no causal links from the physical to the mental.

Despite the case of Théroigne de Méricourt and others like her, Esquirol is generally optimistic about the possibility of cure. He offers little new, however, apart from *douceur* and the ploys that never seem to have been used on de Méricourt. Lukewarm baths, antispasmodics, together with the moral treatment in which understanding is combined with ingenious subterfuges devised by a doctor of experience and talent, are the chosen therapies. There is no attempt to mask the fact that patients often suffer a relapse.

Under his classification of mania, Esquirol includes cases which within a contemporary diagnostic regime would be reclassified under obsessive-compulsive disorder or manic depression. It is interesting to note that these cases – from both the upper and the working class and monitored over years – meet with no more or less success than those treated by contemporary psychiatry. Esquirol's patients go home, sometimes permanently. Others return six months or two years later. The asylum renders them 'better', but life often seems to shunt them straight back into care. Monomania in its emphasis on partial madness may be a diagnosis that offers hope, yet the hope is never much more than modest.

It is possible – as historian Jan Goldstein argues – that were it not for the controversy stirred by Esquirol's pupil Etienne-Jean Georget in 1825–6, monomania would have kept to the confines of the asylum. Instead, in the way of imperializing diagnoses – hysteria, multiple personality disorder and latterly OCD – it became something of a cultural phenomenon. To use the philosopher Ian Hacking's term, monomania made people up – shaped and stirred and suggested them into a configuration which for a while was contained by, then amplified, the diagnosis.

What Georget did was to give the profession of alienism a wider brief by taking this diagnosis of monomania into the courts. Like some talented contemporary reality-TV courtroom presenter, he graphically conveyed the case of what he called the homicidally monomaniac mad in order to distinguish them from the murderous bad. This is the moment at which alienists take on a key role as expert witnesses, usually for the defence: simultaneously the terrain, the popularity and the familiarity of the new diagnosis grow. Several criminal cases in which heinous, incomprehensible crimes are committed mark out the territory for the new alienism. Chief among these, for Georget, is the case of Henriette Cornier.

HENRIETTE CORNIER AND HOMICIDAL MONOMANIA

On 27 October 1825, Henriette Cornier, abandoned wife of a certain Berton, birth mother of two, took on a new post as servant to the Fourniers in Paris. She was twenty-seven years old. Over the last six months her normal ebullience had given way to a sad dreaminess, a sombre, taciturn manner which had resulted in her losing her previous job. The melancholy had gone so far as to lead her at the beginning of September to the parapet of the Pont au Change, where she was prevented from jumping only when passers-by threatened her with arrest. She reported this suicide attempt to her cousins, who eventually helped her find the new job.

In the house next door to her new posting, there was a grocery run by a Monsieur and Madame Belon. The couple had two small children, a nineteen-month-old called Fanny and a baby who was boarded out with a wet-nurse. Henriette seemed enamoured of the little girl: she liked to exclaim over her and caress her. On 4 November, a bare ten days after her arrival, Henriette was asked to buy some cheese for dinner while her mistress went for a stroll.

Henriette arrived at the grocers' at about 1.15. Madame Belon had little Fanny in her arms and Henriette took her, murmuring regret that she didn't have a child as sweet as this little girl. She already had a plan, she later said. The weather was fine and when Madame Belon said it would be lovely to go for a walk, Henriette urged her to run off and get ready while she looked after the child at her own place. Madame Belon protested, but her husband intervened. Covering little Fanny in kisses, Henriette quickly carried her off.

Back next door, Henriette went straight to the kitchen, found the big knife, and took the child to her room on the first floor just above the mezzanine. At the foot of the stairs she met Madame Drouot, the gate-keeper. Henriette cuddled the child fondly to her. When she reached her own room with its window overlooking the rue de la Pépinière, she stretched little Fanny out on the bed. With one hand she held up the small head and with the other, sliced it off. The child didn't have time to scream. Blood spurted everywhere – on Henriette, on the bed, and into a chamber pot placed at exactly the angle needed to catch the flow. Henriette put first head, then body, on the window ledge.

During all this, she later said, she felt no emotion, neither horror, nor pleasure, nor pain. Nor was she agitated. She performed the deed in a contained manner, not mechanically but with a certain careful preci-sion. The sheer quantity of blood did, however, startle her into a momentary trembling. They will kill me, she thought. The person who kills, deserves death. She had considered this before, but only now, after the act, did the idea hit home and frighten her. She ran to take refuge in her master's room. It was almost two o'clock.

From the bottom of the stairs, Madame Belon called for her child.

'She's dead,' Henriette shouted back from the landing. The woman rushed up, but Henriette blocked her entry. She pushed past into Henriette's room and let out a curdling scream.

'Get out, run. You'll be a witness,' Henriette shouted. It wasn't clear whether she wanted the witnessing or was ordering the woman out of the way. But simultaneously, she threw the little girl's head out of the window.

Roused by Madame Belon's screams, her husband rushed to Henriette's house. Any disbelief his wife's words had provoked was ban-ished when he found his daughter's head rolling towards the gutter. He just managed to take hold of it before a carriage clattered by.

Henriette Cornier didn't try to flee. She sat on a chair close to the body. The first person on the scene heard her moan, 'I'm a lost woman.'

By the time the police arrived, she was in the stupor that lasted the length of the interrogation period. Listlessly, she admitted to the crime, even confessed to premeditation. She gave no excuses, no extenuating circumstances, no motive. The idea simply took hold of her, she said. The action had to be carried out. It was her destiny. And why had she thrown the child's head out of the window? So that there would be no question of her guilt, she replied. She seemed to her first questioners, as well as to the judge who led the inquiry, completely in control of her reason – but for the fact that there was no reason, no motive of any kind, for this monstrous crime.[61]

Henriette Cornier's trial roused heated controversy. Was the woman insane? Or was she a murderer of the worst kind, cold and implacable in her malevolent determination? Commentators pondered her state of mind, her motives and the utter lack of them. They argued about the appropriate verdict, both before and after it was declared.

For the first time, there were commentaries feeding into the verdict from those new kinds of doctors, the alienists. The recently launched *Gazette des tribunaux*, a popular outlet which, not unlike a dedicated cable channel, brought court reports into the public arena, gave her case in full. According to French law and Article 64 of the Napoleonic Penal Code, those who committed crimes in a state of insanity were exempt from responsibility. But at the very core of Henriette Cornier's trial was the question of what exactly constituted a state of insanity, now that monomania had introduced a category of 'partial' madness.

Where Mary Lamb had been quietly spirited away into a madhouse with no more than a coroner's hasty verdict, Henriette Cornier's trial turned into a public debate and heralded a new moment in the relationship between the nascent psychiatry and the courts. Mary Lamb had needed no more than her actions and her brother's word to be deemed mad and therefore not responsible for her crime. Child-murdering Henriette Cornier needed a battery of experts, amongst them Esquirol, to attribute the category of 'insanity' to her brutal and seemingly motiveless act. The writing talents of Esquirol's pupil Georget made the case a defining one for the diagnosis of 'homicidal monomania'. It also set the new alienists up as border guards patrolling the line between reason and madness.

Georget's earlier pamphlet about a series of sensational murders had claimed that specialist doctors needed to examine the perpetrators of inexplicably hideous crimes to determine whether they were mad or not. It wasn't just for the courts to be sending 'unhappy imbeciles', who should be in asylums, or at least under lengthy observation, to the gallows. These forceful arguments advocating doctors in the court-room, and the ensuing public clamour, brought Esquirol and the specialists to the trial of Henriette Cornier. They examined her and asked for more time for observation. This was granted. When they claimed that yet more observation was needed, this, too, was granted. Arguably, medical evidence went some way to destabilizing a jury which finally skirted a verdict of madness, but determined that the abominable crime had been committed without premeditation. Instead of execution, Cornier was condemned to hard labour in perpetuity.

Georget's argument in Cornier's defence takes as its starting point that insanity isn't necessarily a set of visible actions and deluded associations – such as Hamlet had adopted in order to 'play' madness. The sufferer from monomania could well appear quite reasonable. Madness could be hidden, partial and for long stretches make its way in the world as sanity. Only expert interpreters could read signs that might lie to the uninitiated. *Monomanie homicide*, a subcategory of Esquirol's inclusive monomania, was a lesion of the *will* rather than the intellect, a perversion of the 'affections, passions and sentiments', and it could propel the person to sudden and brutal action.

Henriette's coldness, her lack of emotion, her stupor which was almost stupidity, all this together with her lack of motivation, her constant repetition to her interrogators that she simply wanted to do what she had done, that she was working out a desire, were all *symptoms*. They were signals to the experienced doctor of her monomaniacal state – or, to be more precise, of the 'homicidal mania' that Georget wants to see legitimated. So, too, was Henriette's *physiognomie* – her lowered and fixated gaze, her sadness of feature – and her preoccupation with a dominant idea. On the day of the crime a local doctor had already described these self-same symptoms, as well as a slow and depressed pulse, a difficulty in hearing her heartbeat, a great sluggishness of response.

In building his case, Georget pays little heed to the kinds of evidence a contemporary psychiatrist might have focused on to arrive at a diagnosis, probably of personality disorder. He mentions, but in no way stresses, Henriette's earlier depression and her suicide attempts. Her difficult childhood, where there seemed to have been violence, plays a negligible part in the picture. Her own prior children are simply not part of the case, nor is there any speculation – as there might be today – that the distress attendant on their loss might have been a contributory factor in her 'motiveless' killing. What Georget does note is that her failed suicide is linked to the brutal murder of the child which would in a roundabout way achieve the desired self-annihilation.

Cornier, herself, refused the designation of madness. During her observation at the Salpêtrière, she insisted that she shared nothing with the other inmates and refused to mix with them. The doctors argue that her very insistence on her sanity is the ultimate sign of her madness. This disagreement between doctors and patient indicates the new kind of medicine that is being constituted through the figure of Henriette Cornier. Georget is arguing that expert doctors can see beyond the patient's individual, subjective perception. They listen, they are alive to her words and her personal history, they take note of the physiognomy of her state, they observe carefully: their assessment is ultimately more neutral than hers, more 'clinical'.

Cornier's case is perhaps the first instance we have in the annals of psychological medicine in which the female patient resists the doctors' diagnosis: Henriette in that sense is akin to Freud's Dora, who refuses the interpretation he gives her and flees. Henriette cannot flee: she is a servant and a murderer. She can only resist. It is worth noting that Georget's argument in defence of her insanity is one that was later used in the 1950s by psychoanalysts giving evidence against the death penalty to Parliament and by psychiatrists against capital punishment in America: to execute the murderer is to give her exactly what she wants – to collude with her desire for death, to collaborate in that very murderousness through which she madly sought her own annihilation. People may murder in order to commit suicide.

In pleading, together with Cornier's defence attorney, for the establishment of a diagnosis of homicidal monomania, Georget is allying himself with the progressive forces of his time and making a passionate case for a 'just' society. Better to keep the homicidal monomaniac in hospital than to execute her, he is saying. Even better, to hospitalize her before the murderous act occurs.

The arguments of Cornier's prosecutor and defence and their supporters in the press persist into our day. Is preventive detention for the
dangerously insane – what we categorize as 'dangerous personality disorder' – a breach of civil liberties? Should individual rights prevail over
society's call for security?

> A battle is being waged between social interests which demand justice
> and new systems [of thought] which claim to be defenders of humanity.
> It is you [the jury] who will decide these important questions . . . Man is
> composed of two parts: unregulated appetites which ceaselessly agitate
> him; and that rich portion of divinity which is reason and which man
> must obey like the son the father and the soldier his captain.

Thus the Attorney General pleading that Cornier's supposed madness – testified to by doctors but unproven – was no defence.[62]

Countering this, Georget states that if we consider the mad to be
simply wild beasts or raging dogs, society might as well go all the way
and kill them off by the thousands. After all what difference is there
between a mad person who has already killed and the one who *may* kill?
But a mad person is not a wild beast. The mad need to be cared for and
can even be cured: humane attention in an asylum, not a prison, is
what is needed to keep both them and society safe.

Michel Foucault has signalled Cornier's case and 1826 as a turning
point in medico-legal discourse. Crime, here, became sickness, the inexplicable monster a matter for psychological investigation. He sees
Georget's argument as leading to a double incarceration: by naming
Henriette Cornier both mad and dangerous, she is being imprisoned
within a classification as well as within a prison/asylum. Georget, however, believes that in championing the new medical science he is striving
for a more caring and enlightened society.

The year 1826 is important in the history of psychiatry in a second way.
It marks a philosophical moment in which social and environmental
forces are clearly seen to produce madness, over and above biological
and hereditary ones. Society engenders alienation and shapes the symptoms of derangement. The proof of this lies partly in Cornier's much
publicized case, as Georget points out. In its wake, France is prey to a

series of copycat murders — a diffusion of the diagnosis of homicidal monomania. No sooner does a woman in Amiens who suffers from terrible head and stomach pains hear of the murder Cornier commits than she is seized by an irresistible desire to kill her own child, though she loves him. On the point of succumbing to this terrible temptation, she cries 'Fire!' When her neighbours arrive, she tells them of her plans and how she won't be able to resist killing unless she's hospitalized. Elsewhere a servant girl confesses to an urge to cut off her charge's head, a desire that has incapacitated her, thrown her into depression and made her stop eating. There are more.

Citing Esquirol as his model, Georget writes:

> the dominant ideas in a society, the grand conceptions and new opinions, important events, have generally influenced the character of madness. Amongst these we can count religious wars, the crusades, civil discord, magic and witchcraft, ideas about liberty and reform, the storms of our own revolution, the rise and fall of the Bonaparte family, the return of the Bourbons, and a host of other less general influences, amongst which one will soon have to place the importance of homicide trials by the mad.[63]

The best remedy for the latter is to forgo the publicized trial, which inflames the imagination of those susceptible to copycat acts. The mad person should immediately be examined by doctors and committed to an asylum — as English procedure has it.

MONOMANIA AND CHILDBIRTH

There was general agreement amongst Pinel, Esquirol and their school that, whatever the dominance of social and psychological factors in most monomanias, the dementia of the old, 'idiotism', and certain kinds of madness particular to women, had a bodily base. This has been a constant from the birth of psychiatry to our own time, whatever the period's understanding of 'biology', hardly yet a science.

When for a brief moment a suspicion arose that because of her low pulse rate Henriette Cornier might be pregnant, this seemed to provide a 'sufficient' motive for her crime and rendered it less inexplicable. Pregnant women were considered to be subject to wild and depraved whims, quite unlinked to their 'normal' state. Even more susceptible to madness, it was thought, were women who had just given birth, were nursing or had abruptly weaned their babies. 'Puerperal madness', as it came to be known, was responsible for a tenth of the intake of women at the Salpêtrière between 1811 and 1814, Esquirol notes – measuring as the new professionalism demands.

Subtracting the third of the intake who were over fifty, the proportion of women 'alienated' during this phase of their lives rises even higher. And richer women were apparently equally prone to this form of madness.[64] Given the difficulties of childbirth, the many stillbirths and dead children in all classes, this is hardly surprising. Queen Anne was pregnant eighteen times: no child survived beyond the second year. For some women, even when the birth was a healthy one, the chances were that it might bring back the horror of a prior death. However, all that said, Esquirol and other doctors' sense of the higher prevalence of madness in pregnancy and post partum has to be questioned. It is probable that in this historical period there were more pregnant women as a proportion of the total 16 to 40-year-olds in the population than 20 per cent, so the higher percentage in the ranks of the 'mad' is hardly disproportionate.

Nor does the actual character the post-partum madness takes vary greatly from that of other individuals. Of the 92 women Esquirol studied, he found 8 who suffered from dementia, 35 from lypemania, or depression, and monomania, and 49 from pure mania. Out of the fifty-eight he pronounced cured, two-thirds were returned to home and normality in the first six months after the birth. Interestingly, he notes that the recurrence rate is high if the root causes of the alienation *predate* childbirth. A way of avoiding the cycle of madness, Esquirol suggests in a statement which might look radical in some religious and pro-life quarters even today, is to prevent pregnancy itself.

In his cohort, Esquirol notes, there were six deaths. He wonders why the number of deaths from this puerperal madness is so much lower than that amongst women who have abdominal afflictions after childbirth. Post-mortem analysis of the six women who died after relatively long periods of alienation showed nothing unusual in any of their organs. There was no evidence of a material irregularity which might have caused their madness. Certainly – and Esquirol is emphatic in countering what were long-held medical dicta which he deemed pure superstition – there was no incidence of milk having travelled to the brain either because of lactation or lack of it, or because of abrupt weaning. There was no more milk to be found in the brains of these puerperally mad, he adds, countering another long-held superstition, than there was blood to be found on the brains of those women whose menstruation had ceased. Despite his preference for environmental over physical explanations for madness, Esquirol is quick to comment that analysis of the brains of those inmates who have suffered from long-term dementia of the kind most often associated with ageing shows that they do indeed differ substantially from normal brains. But this is very rarely the case with alienated post-partum women and can not be associated with the cause of their madness.

Throughout Esquirol's catalogue of case histories of post-partum alienated women, his tone is the humane, 'neutral' one of clinical observation. Woman, as the reproductive gender, may suffer a specific kind of alienation sparked by the difficulties of her condition, but there is no attempt to generalize this specific madness in a way that stigmatizes all women. Perhaps even more radically, Georget in 1821 insisted that his research at the Salpêtrière disproved the widely held assumption of a link between the uterus and hysteria: 'According to my observations, the action of the uterus is normal in more than three-quarters of the [hysteria] patients, even during the fit itself.'[65]

It is worth noting that in Britain, throughout the century, medical believers in the popular reflex theory, which found correspondences along the lines of the nerves between body parts, were rather less neutral in their observations and liked to trace mental symptoms back to women's reproductive system. They were quicker to stigmatize all women as 'more vulnerable to insanity than men because the instability of their reproductive systems interfered with their sexual, emotional, and rational control'.[66] George Man Burrows of the Chelsea Asylum noted in 1828: 'The functions of the brain are so intimately connected with the uterine system, that the interruption of any one process which the latter has to perform in the human economy may implicate the former.'[67]

Esquirol was more circumspect in his extrapolations. He was equally so in his treatments. He used purgatives, leeches, herbs and baths for calming or energizing, together, of course, with moral management. Kindness and time in the asylum away from the family — whether from a loving or a dictatorial husband, an abundance of children, or simply from duties and labour — seemed to be the best healers that the nascent medical science of alienism could offer.

What is innovative and far-reaching in his diagnosis of monomania is that it emphatically introduces into the new science the idea that, having come to the asylum, one may also leave it no longer mad. Madness can be both partial and, sometimes, curable.

3

ASYLUM

By 1826, the year that Georget composes his passionately argued plea for the criminally mad to be kept in special institutions, therapeutic asylums have begun to grow up across Western Europe. Managing the mad in a civilized and progressive way is a big idea. Management does not necessarily equal cure, but it is optimistic about the kinds of human rather than bestial lives the mad can lead. It is also optimistic about the possibility of treatment being found.

A year earlier, Esquirol had become chief physician at Charenton. He was turning it into a model institution much frequented by doctors from other countries. At Charenton there were separate sections for the paying and non-paying patients as well as for the women. A garden for recuperative walks and calming views, regularized activities such as sewing and military drills, and – for the paying patients – billiards and 'a salon where they may give themselves to various sociable games, to music and to dance, among each other and members of staff' were all part of the healing amenities. The pleasant aspect of the place as well as the kindness of the staff formed a direct part of the therapy. The general atmosphere, the abundance of staff and the zeal of the doctors all contributed to make mental illness treatable.[68]

Charenton may have served as a model institution, but there were few equivalents in France, despite Esquirol and his followers' efforts. Even the law of 1838 aimed at extending asylum services across the country did little to erect a Charenton in every department of France. In Germany, however, with its thirty-nine separate principalities, all competing with one another and many with their own universities, therapeutic asylums spread. Indeed, it was in Germany that the word psychiatrist was first used and that psychiatry and psychology became university sciences.

In Britain, after the early impetus given to moral management by the Tukes family and the York Retreat, therapeutic asylums burgeoned, their growth sanctioned by a series of parliamentary Acts which licensed and regulated madhouses, nudging them into a more professional and medical mould. The humanitarian impetus, a generalized wish to relieve the suffering of the poor, also expressed itself in local asylum initiatives: liberal papers like the *Northampton Mercury* championed the setting up of a facility which would better the condition of lunatic paupers, who suffered cruel treatment: 'It must be borne in mind that lunacy is a disease eminently dependent for its relief upon the moral no less than the purely medical discipline to which the patient is subjected.'[69] The General Lunatic Asylum in Northampton, which for many years housed the poet John Clare and later became the famous St Andrew's Hospital, was the result of public campaigning in tandem with government legislation.

Its first head, Dr Thomas Prichard, and his wife and co-worker took up the moral-management baton and went further, abolishing all mechanical restraints during their tenure from 1838. He reported that their success was echoed in the results of the 'largest and most celebrated hospitals in the kingdom; and that unanimity of opinion on this vital question is rapidly pervading not only our own country, but also the great continents of Europe and America'.[70] Prichard, unlike some of his fellows, did not believe that 'moral depravity is the essential cause of madness', nor 'guilt and sin', but physical malfunctions. Whatever the causes, help, however, was moral.

Kindness, a soothing relationship between doctor or carer and patient 'to calm the agony which reminiscence often generates'[71], and affectionate attention, were the watchwords of George Man Burrows in Chelsea and in the Clapham Retreat and William and Mrs Ellis first at Wakefield, then at Hanwell, as well as Prichard. So, too, was orderly occupation. In 1837 there were 612 patients at Hanwell, half of them 'paupers', of whom 75 per cent were engaged in some kind of regular daily work. So successful was the Ellises' combination of devoutly Methodist morning prayers, work and phrenology — which, administered by Ellis, involved a calming laying on of hands[72] — that in 1834, three years after the Ellises had taken over the management of Hanwell, the highly popular journalist Harriet Martineau sang the praises of the asylum as a model institution.

Like many of the reforming spirits of her day, Martineau was interested in bettering the condition of the pauper lunatic. But she was also interested in the fate of the 'lunatic rich': the absurd secrecy their families engaged in meant that they were kept in barbarous conditions, often strait-waistcoated and chained up in the attic and bereft of any 'occupation and the blessings which accompany it':

> Where is the right to conclude that because disorder is introduced into one department of the intellect, all the rest is to go to waste ? Why, because a man can no longer act as he ought to do, is he not to act at all ? Why, when energy becomes excessive, is it to be left to torment itself, instead of being more carefully directed than before? Why, because common society has become a scene of turmoil and irritation to a diseased mind, is that mind to be secluded from the tranquillizing influences of nature, and from such social engagements as do not bring turmoil and irritation ?

Considered a 'disgrace' when it is in all likelihood no more than an 'inflammation of the brain', the disease of insanity may be kept secret at home. But here it is not 'susceptible to cure'. However, if patients are placed in some public institution like Hanwell, 'where the inmates shall compose a cheerful, busy, orderly society; where there shall be gardening, fishing, walking, and riding, drawing, music, and every variety of study, with as many kinds of manual occupation as the previous habits of the patients will admit, they will in all probability be cured'.

Martineau was alive to another important aspect of Hanwell's management. This was Mrs Ellis's active role in it. Pinel had already noted the importance of his caretaker Pussin's wife. Martineau's stress, though, has a feminist ring – Mrs Ellis is an example to all, the harbinger of a new field in which women's dedication and moral intelligence can shine:

> The grandest philanthropic experiments which have hitherto proved undoubtedly successful, have been the work of men; and it has been thought enough for women to be permitted to follow and assist. Here is

an instance, unsurpassed in importance, where a woman has, at least, equally participated; an instance, too, where more was required than the spirit of love, patience, and fortitude, for which credit has always been granted to the high-minded of the sex. A strong and sound intellect was here no less necessary than a kind heart . . . Women who are dejectedly looking round for some opening through which they may push forth their powers of intellect as well as their moral energies, will set Mrs Ellis's example before them, and feel that the insane are their charge. They may wait till the end of the world, for a nobler office than that of building up the ruins of a mind into its original noble structure.[73]

Martineau's call has today been heeded.

It is clear that the asylum as a therapeutic tool had a certain success with those conditions we would now call depression or manic depression, perhaps also with what later became known as schizophrenia. Whether it was therapy, time away from family and from the pressures of life, or simply time itself which abetted cures is in some measure irrelevant. During its heyday, under doctors such as Ellis, John Connolly and Thomas Prichard, the morally managed or humane asylum helped a significant proportion of its patients – ninety out of a hundred, Harriet Martineau enthusiastically claimed in 1834.

But the rising medical professionalism of the alienists could also lead to certain abuses in which the doctors closed ranks against patients and refused to admit mistaken diagnoses. An understanding of madness as partial might engender therapeutic optimism. It might allow the professionals to see what the lay person was blind to. But it could also lead to diagnoses of madness where there might be none at all, or only of a passing kind; and with it a refusal to acknowledge that patients might be wiser about their state than a series of doctors, each of whom was afraid or unwilling to criticize a prior colleague's diagnosis. Patients could well find themselves the victims of a doctor's prejudice about what kind of behaviour constituted sanity: this could all too easily work against women who didn't conform to the time's norms of sexual behaviour or living habits.

Corruption – in the form of medical collusion with strict or cheating or abusive fathers and husbands – could also ensure confinement well beyond need, even if in the first instance this might have seemed necessary. Leaving the asylum in such cases became a near-impossibility, unless rescue came from family or friends on the outside. And even then, difficulties might persist. After all, insanity was so fluid a concept. When it wore the guise of lucidity, it was difficult enough for doctors to distinguish, let alone for lawyers setting out the limits of responsibility in a courtroom. Conversely, for the individual named insane, it was sanity that became all but impossible to prove. The law might want to protect the individual's liberty and civil rights – lost when he or she was declared insane and unable to manage estate and finances. Alternatively the law might want insanity named, attested to, and the person committed, since it had a duty to protect society from danger.

Charlotte Brontë was alive to this kind of danger. In *Jane Eyre* (1848), Mrs Rochester growls and grovels 'like some strange wild animal' in the attic where she is confined. She lunges and attacks and eventually sets fire to the house, blinding her husband in the process. Brontë – whatever other interpretations one might give to Bertha's animality – was worried by madness and alert enough, given her brother's condition, to delirium. But when she dedicated the second edition of *Jane Eyre* to William Thackeray, she had no idea that his wife Isabella had broken down after the birth of their daughter, attempted to drown her and then to commit suicide. Like Mrs Rochester, Mrs Thackeray was given to 'manic bursts of laughter' and was at times violent, even homicidal. Thackeray had her contained in a London madhouse, where two attendants looked after her.

Both the dangers of madness and the danger of asylums preoccupied Wilkie Collins. He and Dickens both visited asylums. Indeed, their jointly written mock travelogue of 1857, *The Lazy Tour of Two Idle Apprentices*, contains an asylum described as:

> An immense place . . . admirable offices, very good arrangements, very good attendants; altogether a remarkable place [in which there are] . . . long groves of blighted men-and-women-trees; interminable avenues of hopeless faces; numbers, without the slightest power of really combining for any earthly purpose; a society of human creatures who have nothing in common but that they have all lost the power of being humanly social with one another.

In his hugely popular novel of 1860, *The Woman in White*, Wilkie Collins put the many concerns Victorians had about insanity into dramatic perspective. Set in the decade after the law of 1845 was put in place – a law which *should* have eliminated the dangers of wrongful confinement by instituting stricter inspection of asylums and certification on admission – the book illustrates rampant social fears about mistaken incarceration and the ways madness can be induced. Collins graphically evokes the difficulty of an individual establishing a 'sane' identity once medical and social forces have combined to put the suspicion of insanity into play. He is alive to the way in which extreme circumstances – abusive relationships, the fatal power of suggestion by the strong over the weak, incarceration itself – can derail sanity. Through the fate of his two look-alike heroines, the ghostly Anne Catherick and the pure Laura Fairlie, Collins evokes the ways in which women are prey to corrupt men. Out to ensnare a wife's fortune or a girl's body, men in power can literally drive women mad, whether through marital sadism, drugs or sexual violation. Yet for all this, for Collins the sense persists that madness itself, however arrived at, can be dangerous – for the mad person as well as for those around her.

The novel opens with a declaratory preamble in which Collins's first narrator, the artist Walter Hartright, claims that the story will be told by witnesses to the events: the action is deliberately played out before the readers, who are in a sense invoked to become judge and jury. Who is to be judged mad, who bad, in the tumultuous stream of events that follows? The first of these is an encounter on a dark night on a lonely stretch of road just outside London with a woman in white. Lonely, helpless, gentle, beautiful, this intriguing creature asks nothing more of Hartright than that he let her leave him when and how she pleases – an apt request, given her history. When the smitten hero learns that the woman, Anne Catherick, is an escapee from an asylum, his musings sum up his time's perplexity about the constitutive features of madness, its mystery, and about the rights and wrongs of confinement.

> ... the idea of absolute insanity which we all associate with the very
> name of an Asylum, had, I can honestly declare, never occurred to me,
> in connexion with her. I had seen nothing, in her language or her

actions, to justify it at the time; and, even with the new light thrown on
her . . . I could see nothing to justify it now.

What had I done? Assisted the victim of the most horrible of all false
imprisonments to escape; or cast loose on the wide world of London an
unfortunate creature, whose actions it was my duty, and every man's
duty mercifully to control.[74]

Collins's novel highlights the ways in which asylum confinement can
be exploited by treacherous men against innocent women. Both men
and asylums drive women mad. Laura Fairlie, prompted into a disastrous marriage with Sir Percival Glyde, a man whose bullying hold over
her makes her grasp on reason slip. She finds her sanity slipping further
when he has her incarcerated – as he had Anne Catherick before her –
and the asylum doctors refuse to believe her protests that she is not
Anne. Her mad state is described as an extreme vulnerability, a child-
likeness which is an excess of her girlish femininity she inhabited before.
Anne Catherick's madness, in contrast, has a monomaniac feel: she is
reasonable until the villainous Sir Percival is mentioned, at which point
a rage beyond reason overcomes her.

The instant I risked that chance reference to the person who had put her
in the Asylum she sprang up on her knees. A most extraordinary and
startling change passed over her. Her face, at all ordinary times so touching to look at, in its nervous sensitiveness, weakness, and uncertainty,
became suddenly darkened by an expression of maniacally intense
hatred and fear, which communicated a wild, unnatural force to every
feature . . .

'Talk of something else,' she said, whispering.[75]

Is this the kind of madness that needs vengeance to calm it, or incarceration? Surely not the latter, Collins seems to be saying, since the
asylum proves therapeutic for neither of his victimized heroines. Even
though doctors and premises seem pleasant enough, the asylum's mer-
ciful control is simply a form of imprisonment: it mistakes sanity for
madness as easily as it takes one person for another. If the individual
cannot be recognized by medical authority, then what beneficial impact
can that authority have on the individual mind?

Collins's attitude to women is at once conventional and decidedly radical. His hero's preferred women – the beautiful, submissive, decorous, pious, elusive and good Laura Fairlie and her look-alike Anne Catherick – share that weakness of mind which is so susceptible to toppling into madness. The very childlike vulnerability which characterizes the period's ideal feminine and cries out for male protection thus shades into the distraught madwoman who needs the moral management the asylum offers. On the other hand, Collins gives us Laura's half-sister Marian Halcombe, a woman of great and outspoken intelligence, perfect grace and physical desirability, all marred by an ugliness of feature which is equated with the 'masculine'. The disjunction between masculine ugliness paired with such evident desirability tips the male narrator into another kind of madness state – the discomfort of dream:

> To see such a face as this set on shoulders that a sculptor would have longed to model – to be charmed by the modest graces of action through which the symmetrical limbs betrayed their beauty when they moved, and then to be almost repelled by the masculine form and masculine look of the features in which the perfectly-shaped figure ended – was to feel a sensation oddly akin to the helpless discomfort familiar to us all in sleep, when we recognise yet cannot reconcile the anomalies and contradictions of a dream.[76]

These unreconcilable anomalies, Marian's intelligence and evident sexuality, masculine in its directness, need to be conveyed as ugliness so as not to upset convention or seduce the narrator, thereby rendering Marian bad in the Victorian moral register. But to Collins's credit, he labels Marian neither a neurasthenic nor a hysteric as the alienists of the time might well have. Instead, while she remains utterly laudable, though never the object of his hero's desire, neurasthenia is attributed to the 'feminized' male, Uncle Fairlie, whose sensitivity is such that he can never leave his 'aesthetic' chamber to take part in life. As for 'absolute insanity', for Collins it exists not on that shadowy borderline where the sexes slip into each other and partake of each other's attributes, but at the extremes of the period's feminine where weakness is prey to the malevolence of men and the marital, hereditary and mental institutions they have put in place.[77]

The case of Hersilie Rouy

The memoirs of Hersilie Rouy share more than a melodramatic plot line with *The Woman in White*. Both books call on us to judge questions of sanity and the reigning system of confinement. Despite the inevitable one-sidedness of personal recollection and the heightening of experience that the writing of memoir often entails, Hersilie Rouy's *Mémoires d'une aliénée* remains a vivid document detailing the abuses inherent in the asylum system. It also shows how quickly the profession of alienism had grown, students attaching themselves to famous doctors, and medical loyalty displacing the needs of patients.

Born in Milan in 1814, Hersilie was the illegitimate daughter of the astronomer Henri Rouy with whom she lived until his death in Paris in 1848. Known as a proficient pianist by Paris society, she was mysteriously removed from her apartment, probably at the conniving of her half-brother, in 1854. Her belongings were seized and she was taken first to Charenton (where she may have been attended by Louis-Florentin Calmeil, who had served as inspector there), then to the Asile de Maréville and finally to the Salpêtrière. Here the well known alienist Charles Lasègue, a latter-day member of the Esquirol circle, though one who had fallen under the new wave of conservative clerical influence in the 1840s, examined her. In a way that foreshadows a modern entrapment within diagnosis, Rouy invokes the system of medical referrals which ensnare her. 'He saw me for only a minute or two. . . and he sentences me on the strength of Doctor Calmeil, who sentenced me on the strength of a doctor who had never seen me at all, who took me away as a favour to somebody else, on the strength of what they had told him.'[78]

From the 1850s to the 1870s Lasègue worked painstakingly on a clinical study of hysteria, not a fashionable diagnosis in those years. He proceeded by examining single symptoms such as the cough, anaesthesia or lack of sensation, loss of appetite, in order to try and recompose the whole malady, which according to anecdote he called 'the wastepaper basket of medicine where one throws otherwise unemployed symptoms'.[79] But despite her independence, her lucidity, her combativeness, her sense that writing kept her sane – all features that could have earned Rouy a diagnosis of hysteria – Lasègue, it seems from a letter she discovered, described her as suffering from something called *folie lucide*, or lucid madness. The diagnosis was based on the state she was in on her arrival in Paris. In her possession she had a 'delusional letter containing threats to the police station of the Seine [department]'.

Lasègue names Rouy 'Chevalier', the name given her by a doctor called Chevalier and one which, like a slave, she found herself bearing whatever her protests, as if the very fact of illegitimacy deprived her of an identity. Refused her birth name, Rouy signs her many letters to doctors and civil authorities with a variety of appellations not calculated to prove her sanity: the Antichrist, the devil, *sylphide*, Polchinelle – the latter the name the other inmates gave her because she understood them better than the doctors and, when called, took up their cause with the cudgel of her witty pen. Asked at one point if she still uses all these varying signatures, she tells the doctor, 'Of course! There is no law forbidding the use of pseudonyms, especially when one is officially anonymous.'[80]

When Rouy refuses to play the piano the doctor knows she can play, she is told she suffers from 'incurable pride'. When she protests against her incarceration and demands compensation for the wasted years, she is told, 'Your delusion is total, and all the more dangerous and incurable in that you speak just like a person who is fully in possession of her reason.'[81]

Sent to provincial Auxerre after she has proved too difficult at the Salpêtrière, and incarcerated there for five years, Rouy continually battles for her release with a passionate and justified sense of the wrongs she has suffered. There seems to be no way out of the trap: once one doctor has called her mad, all others follow suit. At last, Rouy meets the Inspector General of Asylums who is impressed enough with her to send two officials to see her: 'They came to test my thinking, my beliefs, to see if there were grounds for keeping me in perpetuity. ... How can you destroy the future of a woman and allow her liberty to be assaulted simply because she carries her head high and has the audacity to want to live from her own talent and her own writing? I have been buried alive.'[82]

Despite the fact that her half-brother, now the director of a newspaper, didn't want her released and conspired against her, the arrival of identification papers from Milan, fourteen years after her incarceration, linking her to a member of Napoleon III's household cavalry, changed everything. Suddenly release looked imminent. But because Rouy wanted to make her wrongs public, the medical profession closed ranks against her once more, all of them testifying to a madness that was belied by the reasonableness of her letters, which reached as high as the Minister of the Interior. He demanded an inquiry.

Calmeil, her early doctor at Charenton, defended his incarceration of her. The minister might well have seen 'Chevalier' when she appeared sane, but that was because she was in a 'latent state of alienation'. The source of her insanity, he wrote to the minister in a letter of 22 May 1869 was that 'she tired her nervous system by an excess of late nights and by her diligence in study and in her devotion to music . . . her life was filled with emotions'. This fatigue of the nervous system, the curse of books and music for impressionable women, are tropes that will appear again and again in a round of diagnoses from neurasthenia on. What seems unusual in Rouy's case is the length of time she is trapped in the claws of an intractable asylum system. She is early proof of the experiment set up by David Rosenhan in America in the 1970s, which showed how easy it was for a sane person to be admitted as insane into a psychiatric institution and, once admitted, how nigh-impossible it was to demonstrate sanity.[83] Rouy's difficulties are compounded by her demands for rights, for judicial hearings, for compensation and vindication. The doctors, the entire establishment that adjudicates on asylums, dig their heels in.

The Inspector General of Asylums puts the matter to the Minister of the Interior in what has become the classic way of professions:

> I cannot grant that ten, fifteen people with official titles, esteemed, honoured, of whom several are justly cited in the scholarly world as being masters, could have each of them become complicit in a bad action, in a crime . . . you are accusing not only these men, but also all the functionaries, judges, and others who had, during the long seclusion of your protégée, been forced to hear, listen to and judge her numerous and incessant protests.

Rouy, an early anti-psychiatrist, didn't give in: she had no intention of either hiding what she had undergone or excusing those responsible for her incarceration. In 1878, twenty-four years after her initial confinement, the Ministry of Justice at last saw the rights of her case and offered her 12,000 francs compensation, together with an annual pension. She was to benefit from it for only three years before she died, in 1881 at the age of sixty-seven, two years before her memoirs appeared.

THE DECLINE OF THE THERAPEUTIC ASYLUM

What Rouy's memoirs make clear is that the ideal of the therapeutic asylum of the early nineteenth century had foundered. As the pressure of numbers in the asylums built up over the coming decades, moral management with its advocacy of cure often gave way to simple, often brutal, containment. Despite their medical training, and faced by the intractability of many mental conditions, the alienists or psychiatrists in charge were no longer much better than the old Bedlam caretakers. A therapeutic pessimism set in, bringing with it matching theories of degeneration: biological inheritance, it was now thought, paved the way to madness as well as to criminality. Both were abetted by alcohol in an ever downward generational spiral which gathered physicality, morality and poverty in its swoop.

Dementia of the kind that was later discovered to be part of the progress of syphilis and led to what was called 'general paralysis of the insane' had never, even with Pinel's optimism, been a condition susceptible to cure. Nor had alcohol-related insanity, or the dementia linked to old age and 'imbecility', which might now be categorized under the large umbrellas of Alzheimer's and either 'learning difficulties' or 'autism'. As nineteenth-century family patterns changed in the crowded conditions of city and slum life, removing sufferers from the care of relatives, the asylums provided by the new state regulations were themselves gradually filled to bursting. Their very success became their failure. They grew into 'bins' – the 'snake pits' of horror movies, worse than any Bedlam. In 1827, the average asylum in Britain had housed 116 patients; by 1910, the number was 1072.[84] The vast Colney Hatch, which had opened in 1851 to house 1220 of the lunatic poor, was filled almost immediately. A census of the insane in 1854, including public and private asylums, noted a doubling of figures over ten years to a total of 30,538.[85] The English malady was on the rise. John Hawkes, the medical officer of the Wiltshire County Asylum, worried: 'I doubt if ever the history of the world, or the experience of past ages, could show a larger amount of insanity than that of the present day.'[86] Even the increasing presence of alienists – hardly in line with rising numbers – could make little therapeutic difference.

Contesting explanations for this rise in asylum numbers were rife. Few pointed to the existence of the asylums themselves and the changing family patterns urbanization brought as reasons, which is what historians today argue – unless, like Foucault, they postulated a disciplinary movement in a society which chose to incarcerate deviants of any kind, alongside the 'mad'. Was the apparent increase in madness 'a manifest fallacy', really due to new and more sophisticated diagnoses and statistics, as was claimed by the *Journal of Mental Science*, born in 1853 and first edited by the powerful quartet of medics and asylum heads, John Bucknill, C. Lockhart Robertson, Henry Maudsley and Hack Tuke? (The journal was later to become the *British Journal of Psychiatry*, but was already then the official voice of the budding profession.) Or was the rise in numbers due to the escalation of neurosyphilis, to chronic conditions and alcohol-related madness,[87] all of which could be linked to the growth of vice, which frightened Victorians and French moralists alike?

Emil Kraepelin (1856–1926), the leading fin-de-siècle asylum psychiatrist, gave the syphilis and alcoholism argument solid legitimacy. An exemplary Munich-based asylum diagnostician who eventually rejected Freud's dynamic psychoanalysis and put the periodicity of manic depression into the medical textbooks, he bemoaned, in his 1895 lectures, the fact that the asylum population in Germany had risen to two hundred thousand and become a much increased proportion of the population. Sufferers from syphilis and alcoholism accounted, he claimed, for one-quarter to one-third of the cohort. He feared for the increasing degeneration of his race. Kraepelin also underlined that the insane were dangerous to their neighbours and even more so to themselves: around a third committed suicide. The only therapeutic hope lay in attacking alcoholism and syphilis, together with the 'drug abuse' of morphia and cocaine. The 'prophylactic education of children' was called for.[88] None of these, needless to say, were therapies that could take place within the walls of the asylum. Rather, they required moral and social transformations.

The proportion of men to women in confinement has been much debated: while some have commented on the preponderance of women in asylums, particularly as the century progressed,[89] others have noted that the difference between the sexes was not statistically significant. What became known as general paralysis of the insane, for example, a condition later linked to tertiary syphilis, began to rise sharply during the Napoleonic Wars, and was far more common amongst men than women. Women, on the other hand, lived longer, and therefore made up larger numbers amongst the demented old. There were also more women in the poorhouses in Britain, and movement from these to asylums was common. Where there is a definite preponderance of women is in the diagnosis of 'neurotic' disorders, the milder hysterias and neurasthenias which are the property not so much of the large asylum doctors, particularly when the patients are middle- to upper-class, but of the growing number of 'nerve doctors' in private practice.

What is unarguable is that the rise and rise in numbers by the latter part of the nineteenth century led to a change in medical practice in the larger asylums. The clinical-pathological method, which moved back from post-mortem examination to attempt an understanding of the patient's symptoms in life, had been a strand of investigation into madness from the early 1800s when Antoine-Laurent Bayle had studied the inflamed meninges of Esquirol's patients and linked this to their mania and paralyses. Now this search for biological or physiological explanations moved to the forefront. In Germany Wilhelm Griesinger, known as the founder of biological psychiatry, definitively declared in 1867 that patients with mental illnesses were individuals with brain and nerve diseases. In Vienna Theodor Meynert, who taught Freud, was far more interested in his research into the frontal lobes of cadavers than in his living patients. In those overcrowded asylums where it existed, the march of science was increasingly separating itself off from therapy.

Henry Maudsley (1835–1913)

In Britain, one of the leading alienists of the high Victorian period and the fin-de-siècle was a sonorous proponent of the physical basis of all mental illness and a believer in degenerationist theories, which imagined the spread of insanity in the march of heredity. Through his many books and his editorship of journals, Henry Maudsley's influence travelled across Europe and to America as well as Australia. Endowed with prodigious energy and a sense of life as a 'stern duty', a believer in a Darwinian or, more accurately, a Spencerian struggle for which the mentally weak were not fit, Maudsley became head of the Cheadle Royal Hospital for the Insane in Manchester at the startling age of twenty-four. But he had none of the early nineteenth century's faith in the curative power of asylum life, and after a mere three years at Cheadle, in 1862 he moved to London where private practice and the *Journal of Mental Science* beckoned. Soon there was a professorship in medical jurisprudence at London University and a series of books, none more influential than his first, the widely translated *Physiology and Pathology of Mind*, published in 1867.

Maudsley's therapeutic pessimism, embedded in what seems to have been a native misanthropy, left no scope for any reformist hopes. Like the theoretician of criminal degeneracy, Cesare Lombroso, in Italy, heredity for Maudsley was destiny, physiology its sign. He had early taken up ideas of 'moral [90]'. The 'moral' in the term is a far-ranging concept — as it is in moral reason — embracing not only the ethical, but the psychological and social, and relates, according to the Oxford English Dictionary, to matter 'having influence on a person's character or conduct, as distinguished from his or her intellectual or physical nature'. The concept of moral insanity had been elaborated by the medical criminologist, James Bruce Thompson. It infects Maudsley's writing with a disciplinarian undertow devoid of compassion. Vice, for Maudsley, was everywhere, and everywhere visible in the 'stigmata of degeneration'. Here, physiology itself takes on an ethical dimension: individuals are born with madness and badness already in them. Crime and mental illness stalk the teeming pauperlands of the Victorian city like a disease, is the result of its inhabitants' parlous state. To talk of survival of the fittest, Maudsley underlines, hardly means to talk of survival of the best: 'it means only the survival of that which is best suited to the circumstances, good or bad, in which it is placed — the survival of a savage in a savage social medium, of a rogue among rogues, of a parasite where a parasite alone can live'.[91]

Natural selection is not the only idea Maudsley borrowed from

Darwin. He takes his cue from him where women are concerned, as well, though leaves out Darwin's more challenging propositions about the female choosing her sexual partner.

In his *Descent of Man and Selection in Relation to Sex* of 1871, Darwin emphasized the difference between the sexes emphatically to women's detriment, and with little sense that the source of what he described might have something to do with his own time's cultural conditions. Basing himself on the physical anthropologists and the cranial measurements they had taken, Darwin noted woman's smaller brain size and that she emerged with a skull 'intermediate between child and man'. Accordingly, her mental disposition showed 'greater tenderness' and 'less selfishness than man'. That male selfishness combined with ambition may be an 'unfortunate birthright', but these are qualities which nonetheless make man superior in the struggle for survival. In women, 'the powers of intuition, of rapid perception, and perhaps of imitation, are more strongly marked than in man'. But these are no advantage: indeed, they mark out women's inferiority since they are faculties 'characteristic of the lower races', and therefore of a past and lower state of civilization. Meanwhile, Darwinian men are endowed with greater 'intellectual powers' and attain to a higher 'pre-eminence' in any sphere 'requiring deep thought, reason, or imagination, or merely the use of the senses and hands'. But above all else, what mark man as superior in the ongoing struggle for existence are his 'higher energy, ongoing perseverance, and courage'. This stubborn perseverance is indeed what allows the male to win over the female.

As if struck by a sudden worry about his own progeny, Darwin remarks towards the end of this chapter: 'It is, indeed, fortunate that the law of the equal transmission of characters to both sexes prevails with mammals; otherwise it is probable that man would have become as superior in mental endowment to woman, as the peacock is in ornamental plumage to the peahen.'

Darwin's own genius, in perseverance as well as science, marks him out as his own superior male, while his woman is the frail, tender, maternal vessel of Victorian womanhood. The view was commonplace in Britain. Amidst alienists of the hereditarian school, like Maudsley, that frailty made women more prone to madness than men. Darwin and Maudsley were, of course, acquainted, each quoting the other.

Maudsley, however, was beset by a visceral misogyny, which is absent from Darwin. If, for both, women are so formed as to look after children, for Maudsley this is a lowly task, equal to what he thinks of as the excremental nature of parturition. Men's constitution makes them incapable of the necessary sympathy and attachment, let alone the 'base services' that the child requires. Maudsley urges men to examine potential wives carefully for any physical signs that might betray degeneracy: 'Outward defects and deformities are the visible signs of inward and invisible faults which will have their influence in breeding.'[92] As for those 'hysterics' who begin increasingly to populate the fin-de-siècle, Maudsley sees them as morally degenerate: 'believing or pretending that they cannot stand or walk', only to lie in bed all day asking for the sympathy of their anxious relatives. They are 'perfect examples of the subtlest deceit, the most ingenious lying, the most diabolic cunning, in the service of vicious impulses'.[93]

It was the very women Maudsley railed against, their nerves considered constitutionally frail, who would have a definitive impact on the course of his profession. As a therapeutic pessimism took over asylum doctors, private neurological practice rose and with it came a shift in diagnoses. Nerves and their attendant disorders gained in prominence as sites of illness and explanation. With the invention of neurasthenia and the reinvention of hysteria, a new kind of mind doctor came into being – one who had to listen to the patient as much as observe; one who would come to believe, as did Janet and Freud, Jung and Bleuler, that mental disorders had their roots in psychic problems whatever their expression in the body.

4

NERVES

By the 1870s, commentators everywhere in Europe and America were adamant that life had taken on a clang, clamour and speed that acted as an irritant on the nerves. Sensations forced themselves on any and everyone, whether in real or fictional streets. The times themselves, it seemed, were a shock to the nervous system, with their crowds and dirt, and the inevitable 'decadence' that followed. Trains chugged, hooted, smoked, crashed and produced the trauma of 'railway spine'[94] as well as a spate of railway murders. In Europe, driven by poverty or pogroms, people moved in ever greater numbers across borders and from countryside to town, or emigrated to the New World. Squalid housing, drink, that very crowding which gave birth to concepts of the mass and of degeneration, ensued.

In Britain, the 'undeserving poor' drank and reproduced in slums, as the vice and temperance squads would have it, or prostituted themselves on streets where no middle-class woman, protected though she was by metres of skirt, bustle and corset, could tread. Mayhew numbered unlisted prostitutes at some eighty thousand in London alone, a startling figure which underlines just how important it was somehow to keep 'the angel' who was the Victorian wife in the house, so that double standards along both sexual and class lines could be maintained.

In France, the Franco-Prussian War and the uprising of the Paris Communards left a legacy of death, displacement and class distrust: in *la semaine sanglante*, that single blood-soaked week of 21–28 May 1871, French troops, marching the length of Baron Haussmann's new grand and commodious boulevards, had fired on their own compatriots. The death toll had mounted some say as high as 30,000. The Third Republic, born out of civil war, saw an infernal increase in traffic on these very same streets – some 60,000 clattering vehicles a day powered by 70,000 horses. Between these and the trams, by the end of the century 12,000 people a year were being injured, and over a hundred killed; and new, speedier means of transport were coming into being as men burrowed underground to produce the metro in time for the Universal Exhibition of 1900.

America, recovering from the horrors of the Civil War with its five hundred thousand dead and countless wounded, moved into an expansionist phase in which the rapid accumulation of material wealth covered over any need for mourning – except by women, who became the guardians of that sensibility and culture the businessman might own, but have insufficient time for. Meanwhile, telegraphs ate up distance. Electricity invisibly produced instant light out of darkness. Vast new steamboats crossed the Atlantic in days, bringing the huddled poor one way and the travelling newly rich the other.

By the time the century had turned, it had definitely become, as the Viennese novelist Robert Musil noted in his *Man without Qualities*, 'a nerve-racked age' – one of 'restlessness and constant change, of speed and shifting perspectives, in which something was definitely amiss'.

Countless novels and stories dissected, described or emphasized what was amiss. As early as 1839, the American poet and great author of gothic tales, Edgar Allan Poe, had created characters whose nerves 'by long suffering had grown unstrung', particularly when their owners were scions of noble houses. The word 'nervous' had started off in the language as a synonym for strong, sinewy and energetic, and had grown, with the eighteenth century and Dr George Cheyne, to take on all the notions of an excitable, agitated, apprehensive and hypersensitive temperament. But by the mid-nineteenth century the word had become increasingly associated with mental features. In 1848, John Stewart Mill in his *Principles of Political Economy* notes, 'Labour is either bodily or mental; or, to express the distinction more comprehensively . . . either muscular or nervous.' This linkage of the mental and the nervous paralleled the neurologists' and alienists' focus on the brain as the centre of nerve and bodily activity. Evolutionary thinking collaborated in emphasizing the brain's primary place: it had became the location of the distinguishing features of the human.

As nerves and brain took on scientific and medical importance, they also became symptomatic sites of worry. Everything coalesced to produce a new kind of malady. Diagnoses focusing in on nerves coincided with symptoms which expressed a malaise with the stresses of the times as well as with gender restrictions. Any transgressing of the policed boundaries of what was appropriate to each gender took a toll on the nerves. In 1869, the condition was given its own name – neurasthenia – though the symptom picture had been more or less in place well before. *The Woman in White* (1860) had its Mr Fairlie, an 'effeminate', 'womanish' invalid who suffered from a disorder of the nerves. This entailed not only a hypersensitivity to light, sound, touch and motion and an attendant aesthetic over-refinement, but a weakened judgement.

Some twenty-five years later Mr Fairlie's French counterpart, Des Esseintes, the highly strung aesthete and hero of J.-K. Huysmann's *A Rebours* of 1884, last in a degenerating line of inbred aristocrats, has similar gender codings – ones we would now openly read as homosexual. But Des Esseintes, unlike Mr Fairlie, has his maker's sympathy. Indeed, Des Esseintes becomes the very icon of fin-de-siècle decadent sensibility, a man who is 'against nature' and, like a woman, is valued for his refinement. Depending on the critic's relations to those opposed poles of artistic modernity and moral Victorianism, Des Esseintes was hailed or reviled. His mother, meanwhile, was the very type of the neurasthenic: 'a tall, pale, silent woman, [who] died of nervous exhaustion'. The hero's chief memory of her is almost a stock memory – repeated in fiction from Poe, through Silas Weir Mitchell and in modernist, bluestocking garb in D.H. Lawrence – of a 'still, supine figure in a darkened room. . . for the Duchess had a nervous attack whenever she was subjected to light or noise'.[95]

The Duchess palpably suffers from neurasthenia, the diagnostic term generally attributed to the American physician George M. Beard, who coined it in 1869 in a leading medical weekly for 'the morbid condition of the exhaustion of the nervous system'. According to Beard, who went on to publish several widely translated books on the subject, the condition was one which grew out of the American way of life, with its race for money and power, its excessive pursuit of capital and technological progress. Beard blamed nervous exhaustion on the popular press, the telegraph and steam power, all of which had exacerbated the pressure of modern life. These had made striving, successful men prone to nervous prostration. As for women, who constituted a large proportion of the ranks of the neurasthenic, an incursion into the masculine sphere of intellectual labour together with the 'exhausting sentiment of love' were responsible for their nervous depletion.

It was soon to become clear that often enough a nervous woman was also a 'new woman'. The contradictions of a time which demanded compliance and quiescence of the idealized feminine while championing dynamism in the culture as a whole might drive a woman to action or to the couch. The escape into illness was the mirror image of rebellion. Emancipation, feminism and neurasthenia, or its sometime twin sister, hysteria, took shape in the same nervous soil.

Nerves, their relationship to the brain, temperament and mental life, were still mysterious areas for the scientists and doctors of the second half of the nineteenth century. As time moved on, however, they became increasingly confident about their ability to map the brain, understand the nervous system and diagnose its ill effects. Treatment, though bullishly applied, was often less certain. Particularly in America and Britain, it could look much the same as 'moral management', even if it came within the context of private practice for relatively affluent patients.

Silas Weir Mitchell, the Philadelphia-based nerve doctor whose *Lectures on Diseases of the Nervous System, Especially in Women* of 1881 made him famous, invented a much imitated 'rest cure', which allowed for no coddling of the 'couch-loving invalid' who was the patient, and no theatrical expatiating on her pains for an audience. Self-control, taking oneself in hand, was essential: 'I tell the patient her pains will be well when she gets well, and then cease to allow them to be further discussed.' What the rest cure entailed was 'the breaking up of old habits . . . the cutting off of many hurtful influences; but above all, it means the power of separating the invalid from some willing slave, a mother or a sister, whose serfdom, as usual, degrades and destroys the despot, while it ruins the slave'.[96]

Conceptualizing uncharted parts of the body, particularly in its relationship to mind, has always led to metaphors: these are particularly apt at revealing the preoccupations of their historical moment. Where the eighteenth century posited nervous energy as fluid, a kind of hydraulic or water power, the nineteenth understood it as an electric force. At first, this was in keeping with the galvanic physics of vital, animal electricity. Gradually, the conception shifted to take on Volta's chemistry, so that the brain emerged as a rechargeable voltaic battery generating electricity through the nerve fibres. It then played with thermodynamics and ideas about energy conservation, and finally moved on to Faraday's more complex model of electricity as a force that passes from particle to particle. Sometimes all these hypotheses functioned alongside each other.

The Handbook for the *Instruction of Attendants oo the Insane* of 1884 used the contemporary analogy of the telegraph to explain nerve and brain function:

> The grey skin of the brain may be compared to a great city, the headquarters of the telegraph system, and the grey clusters scattered through the white substance of the brain are the suburbs of the city, the grey clusters of the spinal cord are the towns, and the points of skin, muscle organs . . . where nerve fibres end, are the villages. The nerve fibres connect villages, towns, suburbs and the great city with one another . . . The internal nerves and the nerve cells of the mind connect with each other so as to form a network, which, while we are awake or dreaming, is in a state of busy activity, telegraphing ideas from cell to cell . . . In proportion as this network becomes broken or weakened does the mind fail in its functions; the snapping of a few fibres; the sickening of a few cells, makes a serious difference; and because of the delicacy of it, the structure requires constant repair and careful preservation.[97]

George Beard, who had some success with electrotherapy, postulated a chemical explanation of 'want of nervous force': 'My own view is that the central nervous system becomes dephosphorized, or perhaps loses somewhat of its solid constituents, probably also undergoes slight, undetectable, morbid changes in its chemical structure and as a consequence becomes more or less impoverished in the quantity and quality of its nervous force.'[98]

Whatever the metaphoric or speculative base borrowed from the sciences or the new technology, Victorians also turned the nervous system, as they did sexuality, into an economic model with an in/out ledger of income and expenditure. Each person had only a certain amount of nervous energy, an inherited capital fund that could more easily be depleted than replenished. 'Heedless overexertion, whether mental or physical, could drain an individual's supply, leaving an exhausted nervous system incapable of all endeavour. Failure of nervous power meant utter incapacitation.'[99] Just as bankruptcy was a form of sin in the public economic domain, so in the private sphere excessive expenditure which led to breakdown of the nervous system or to madness was tainted, and understood not only as physically depleting but as morally reprehensible. Sexual activity without a procreative aim was bad and incapacitating, doubly so masturbation. Excess was an abandonment of willpower – a faculty which, according to the public moralists and doctors, was already weaker in women. Duty was sacred, and for women it lay in marriage and the purity of motherhood.

With greater or lesser emphasis on such Protestant notions of willpower and duty, the language of the nerves was used throughout Europe and America. The resulting nervous illnesses – neuroses, breakdowns, neurasthenia – were conceived of as organic. Though the turn of the century swung the medical pendulum towards psychic explanations which had no proven physical base, this language of nerves and neuroses continued.

In 1895, the German psychiatrist Krafft-Ebing wrote in his *Psychopathia Sexualis*:

The mode of life of countless civilized people exhibits nowadays an abundance of anti-hygienic factors which make it easy to understand the fateful increase of nervous illness; for those injurious factors take effect first and foremost on the brain. In the course of the last decades changes have taken place in the political and social – and especially in the mercantile, industrial and agricultural – conditions of civilized nations which have brought about great changes in people's occupations, social position and property, and this at the cost of the nervous system, which is called upon to meet the increased social and economic demands by a greater expenditure of energy, often with quite inadequate opportunity for recuperation.

Since nerves fed the entire bodily system, overwork in one area, for example the brain, could result in a weakening elsewhere. Most usually for women, the link was with the vitality of the reproductive organs. Indeed, during the last part of the nineteenth century woman's reproductive system seemed to grow an intimate link with her frail, unstable nerves. Periodicity — the impact of menstruation on woman's body — childbirth and menopause had always played a part in the assessment of mental health, but not until the 1860s did these specifically sexual characteristics take on quite so prominent a public place in the interpretation of the 'nervous' symptoms that women might present.

The 'reflex theory' of the nerves had laid the ground for such thinking back in the 1830s. It proposed that nervous connections running via the spine regulated all organs, without any intervention from consciousness. If this 'message network' became weakened or was broken, the mind failed in its function. Breakdown could also lead to failures of internal and external sensation such as those anaesthesias suffered by hysterics, and of the motor system, such as spasms, jerks and palsies. Pioneered by the society doctor Marshall Hall in England, the reflex theory was extended to include the cerebral hemispheres by the prolific Edinburgh physician, Thomas Laycock, in a publication of 1845. Because of the continental fame of Laycock's earlier *Nervous Diseases of Women*, his speculations on the way in which reflex worked proved highly influential throughout Europe. Indeed, it was possibly Laycock's intervention that was the deciding one in making the reflex theory an early model for the links between the physiological and the psychological.[100] 'Woman, as compared with man,' Laycock proclaimed, 'is of the nervous temperament . . . Her nervous system is therefore more easily acted upon by all impressions, and more liable to all diseases of excitement.'[101]

Since the notion of reflex action could link organs far from the site of a symptom, the theory helped to provide a 'scientific' basis for implicating the uterus in a large variety of nervous afflictions. As Weir Mitchell emphasized, 'organic diseases of the ovaries and tubes in women react profoundly upon the nervous system'. Reflex action also had the disastrous effect of introducing a fashion for pelvic surgery and any number of other interventions in women's reproductive system as a cure for ailments as disparate as fatigue, headaches and vomiting. This impulse towards surgical intervention continued until the century turned.

Throughout this period, doctors and scientists seemed determined to raise the existing division of labour in the middle class to a universal given, and to transform women's place in the domestic sphere into a biological inevitably from which deviation of any kind would bring breakdown, not only of the mind but of the species. Women were understood as being fashioned by evolution for the home and maternity, nervously fragile, intellectually inferior. Moving away from that lesser birthright, allowing energies to be drained by intellectual or imaginative exertion would lead to nervous collapse or to that capacious list of symptoms which most often went under the catch-all diagnosis of neurasthenia or its near-neighbour hysteria. 'What a weak barrier is truth when it stands in the way of any hypothesis,' Mary Wollstonecraft had acutely observed in the 1790s, railing against Rousseau wanting to make woman a coquette by nature.[102]

By the 1870s, women's growing and concerted demands not only for the vote and for equality within marriage, but for education and greater freedom of activity, met with the newly mobilized strength of a scientific and medical establishment, specializing in nervous and mental illness. The medical warnings against any activity that might change women's domestic status, seen as a fact of God and nature, were deafening. They needed to block out not only women's voices, but advocates of the calibre of John Stewart Mill.

Mill stresses that women's subjection has everything to do with political will. Only in relations between the sexes, he points out, does it still seem just for the 'law of the stronger' to prevail. Where arguments for women's inferiority are concerned, the only thing that has changed since the last century is the move from social explanations to a call on innate, physical causes:

The reason given in those days was not women's unfitness, but the interest of society, by which was meant the interest of men: just as the raison d'etat, meaning the convenience of the government, and the support of existing authority, was deemed a sufficient explanation and excuse for the most flagitious crimes. In the present day, power holds a smoother language, and whomsoever it oppresses, always pretends to do so for their own good: accordingly, when anything is forbidden to women, it is thought necessary to say, and desirable to believe, that they are incapable of doing it, and that they depart from their real path of success and happiness when they aspire to it. But to make this reason plausible (I do not say valid), those by whom it is urged must be prepared to carry it to a much greater length than anyone ventures to do in the face of present experience. It is not sufficient to maintain that women on the average are less gifted than men on the average, with certain of the higher mental faculties, or that a smaller number of women than of men are fit for occupations and functions of the highest intellectual character. It is necessary to maintain that no women at all are fit for them, and that the most eminent women are inferior in mental faculties to the most mediocre of the men on whom those functions at present devolve.

Mill called for a proper psychological assessment which would show that the differences between men and women are only the differences of their education and indicate no inferiority given by nature. He wittily underscored that the size of the brain (is an elephant cleverer than a man?) might be less important in determining intelligence than its activity. He noted that men had cunningly and selfishly enslaved women 'by representing to them meekness, submissiveness and resignation of all individual will . . . as an essential part of sexual attractiveness'. He also pointed out that all arguments from 'nature' were undermined by cultural comparison: 'An oriental thinks that women are by nature peculiarly voluptuous; see the violent abuse of them on this ground in Hindoo writings. An Englishman usually thinks that they are by nature cold. The sayings about women's fickleness are mostly of French origin.' As far as medical practitioners were concerned, since almost none of them were psychologists, when they talked about women their comments were of no more use than any '"common" man's. It is a subject on which nothing final can be known, so long as those who alone can really know it, women themselves, have given but little testimony, and that little, mostly suborned.'

For Mill 'the principle which regulates the existing social relations between the two sexes – the legal subordination of one sex to the other – is wrong itself, and now one of the chief hindrances to human improvement . . . it ought to be replaced by a principle of perfect equality, admitting no power or privilege on the one side, nor disability on the other.' The greater nervous susceptibility of women, he contended, was in fact a feature of the 'higher classes' brought up as hothouse plants, physically inactive, yet unnaturally active where the emotions were concerned: 'It is no wonder if those of them who do not die of consumption, grow up with constitutions liable to derangement from slight causes both internal and external, and without stamina to support any task, physical or mental, requiring continuity of effort.'[103]

One of Mill's intellectual opponents most popular with the Victorian public was Herbert Spencer, whose writings on evolution, science and society incorporated Darwin's theories as well as those of the French naturalist Lamarck and his evolutionary model of acquired character- istics. It was Spencer, a prolific journalist and autodidact, who served, certainly in part, as the model for George Eliot's Casaubon in *Middlemarch* – a cold, sexless man whom Eliot had once wanted to marry and who was forever in search of a complete system of knowledge. It was Spencer, not Darwin, who coined the phrase 'survival of the fittest'. For Spencer, armed with a belief in the ever increasing 'specialization of functions', women were made for domesticity. From the beginning of time, they had perfected their intuition, submissiveness and skills in deception: hence their proper and natural place was in the home. Indeed, the patriarchal family was the model favoured by nature. Only within such an environment could healthy offspring be reared. Anything else would lead to the decline of the species.

As nature would have it, the theorists who most warned against women's straying from their natural sphere in reproduction, those who saw intellectual aspiration as a path towards a variety of nervous and physical disorders, were men who themselves suffered from any number of 'nervous' ills. Depression and a variety of physical symp- toms with no physical cause shadowed Darwin. Spencer's 'neurasthenia' plagued him throughout his life and he suffered from severe breakdowns. Indeed, that 'nature' which underpinned Victorian domestic arrangements did not extend to his own. He never married, nor fathered a child.

Such ironies hardly seemed to impinge on the pronouncements of the fin-de-siècle's alienists and neurologists.

Reacting against a nascent women's movement and John Stuart

Mill's call for women's education, Maudsley, the most influential of Victorian alienists, wrote an essay in 1874 on 'Sex in Mind and Education'. Here he made an emphatic case for the damaging effects on women's 'vital energy' of intellectual work combined with the bodily changes of adolescence. Women's physiology, unlike the male's, was simply not up to the nervous energy required. Menstruation was the bogey.

> This is a matter of physiology, not a matter of sentiment; it is not a mere question of larger or smaller muscles, but of the energy and power of endurance, of the nerve force which drives the intellectual and muscular machinery; not a question of two bodies and minds that are in equal physical condition, but of one body and mind capable of sustained and regular hard labour, and of another body and mind which for one quarter of each month, during the best years of life, is more or less sick and unfit for hard work.

Education, therefore, was an 'excessive mental drain' on the young woman's mind and, using the bank as a model of human resources, Maudsley argued 'What Nature spends in one direction, she must economise in another direction.' Woman's nerve centres, already unstable because of the energy needs of bodily change at puberty, would become deranged with the double effort of mental work and the kind of competition on which young men thrived. Menstruation would become irregular or cease altogether. The injuries to the menstrual cycle might lead, in some, merely to headache, fatigue or insomnia. In others the effects were graver: mental breakdown, epilepsy or chorea – which was the name the period gave to all kinds of fits. Worst of all, the young woman's reproductive system might fail.

Describing this failure, Maudsley fully exposes the prejudices and degenerationist sexual fears underlying his science. Mendacity is a key feature of the woman he evokes, a low creature determined to hoodwink the male: 'Those in whom the organs are wasted invoke the dressmaker's aid in order to gain the appearance of them; they are not satisfied unless they wear the show of perfect womanhood.' His description of the sagging breasts and loss of pelvic power of the unsexed, sterile woman, a freak who 'having ceased to be woman is yet not man', betrays a visceral disgust. Out of the girl grown nervously depleted through education, Maudsley brings forth the cataclysm of a sexless dystopia.[104] It seems that all of Victorian civilization, structured around the family unit, topples with a young women's education.

Maudsley's much quoted article was written in response to Harvard's Edward Clarke, whose *Sex in Education* argued that education would render women unfit for child-bearing. In Britain both had a ready following. The slightly younger alienist James Crichton-Browne (1840–1938), medical director of the large West Riding Wakefield Lunatic Asylum, where he established one of the few hospital-based neuro-anatomical laboratories, shared Maudsley's views. (It was Maudsley who introduced Darwin to him, when the latter wanted help with photographs of the mad, so that he could study their facial expressions for his work on the emotions in man and animals.)

Crichton-Browne's asylum provided him with ready and legally sanctioned access to the brains of dead patients unclaimed by their families. Measuring these and comparing his results with colleagues in two other asylums, he wrote a series of articles on the smallness of women's brains in comparison to men's and their comparative physiology. From this information he extrapolated a series of prejudices which gained influence because of their purported links with science. Women's smaller brains, the shallowness of the grey matter, the numbers of convolutions, all proved that women were intellectually inferior and childlike in their nature: they were over-emotional, had a deep sense of dependence, craved sympathy and were able mimics. Girls had 'sensitive and highly-strung nerve centres apt to be damaged by pressure', whereas boys were 'more obdurate and resistant'.[105]

Supposed expert facts breed more facts in the world. Just as contemporary 'expert' research linking women's infertility to the fact of work rather than to a thousand and one other potential causes helps to nurture panics about fertility, so the late nineteenth century stoked up a moral panic which envisaged that middle-class women's attempt to change their lives would result in madness and the decline of the species. The medical consensus about women's inferior intelligence and nervous frailty all linked to the vagaries of her reproductive functions did indeed, in turn, breed nervous illness and its over-diagnoses. Expert agreement led women to fear their periods and pregnancies, which apart from any impact on the 'nervous system' already had the dire side-effect of often enough resulting in death, either of mother or of child. Deprived of activity, warned off exercise and work, freedom of mind and movement, fin-de-siècle women with their 'mimic' capacity developed nervous troubles which the doctors then linked to their specifically female functions rather than to the overall conditions of their lives.

Elizabeth Garrett Anderson (1836–1917) struggled against great institutional odds, not to mention prejudice, to become the first woman doctor in Britain and the founder in 1871 of the New Hospital for Women in London, which had only women on its medical staff. She also married, had three children and engaged in numerous political activities. Her response to Maudsley and his cohort was not – though it might have been – that she was living proof of the fact that education did nothing to hinder women's reproductive abilities. Rather, she tactfully pointed out that working women were a fine example of the way women disregarded their 'special physiological functions'. The 'facts of their organization' did not stop them from working. Her patients had shown her that it was often the other way round. 'The break-down of nervous and physical health seems at any rate to be distinctly traceable to want of adequate mental interest and education in the years immediately succeeding school life. Thousands of young women, strong and blooming at eighteen, become gradually languid and feeble under the depressing influence of dulness.'[106]

The argument raged, women as often as not coming out on Maudsley's and the evolutionists' side. They found themselves between a rock and a hard place. Boredom would drive them mad; overexertion would not only drive them mad, but doom the species they were meant to serve. With a little variation and allowing for greater freedoms, not all that much has changed in our own day. 'Expert' voices reinvoke old prejudices, find statistics to fill the need, carry out studies in which the terms are already trapped in outworn hypotheses. They induce conflicts in working women by bemoaning the suffering child or the less than fertile womb, all the while warning of stress, emotional depletion or worse.

Alice James (1848–92) and the American nerve doctors

'[H]er tragic health was in a manner the only solution for her of the practical problem of life.' So wrote the novelist Henry James on 8 May 1894 to his brother William, the famous Boston psychologist, about their sister Alice, who had died two years previously.

Perhaps James, whose fictional heroines bestride the turn of the century, had a special flair for women's secrets and their need of them because he had so many of his own to protect. A mysterious ailment had prevented him from fighting in the Civil War, that historic testing ground of American masculinity. He seems to share women's and particularly the childless woman's lingering sense of ineffectuality. Better than the rest of his family, he understood the invalidism Alice had taken on from adolescence as a solution to the practical problem of life. In part through her, one imagines, he grew attuned to that fund of 'unused life' a woman like Alice contained and the frustrations of an independent nature housed in a woman's body. He imparted these in different portions to his heroines. James also understood the nature of Alice's talent, which had only latterly found expression.

For the last three years of her life, Alice had kept a diary. This had been sent to the brothers by the woman who had shared her life from 1879. Henry was acutely worried by the possibility of the diary's publication and the indiscretions it would reveal about himself and friends. Even so, he was astute and generous in his assessment of his sister's gifts: 'the life, the power, the temper, the humour and beauty and expressiveness of the Diary . . . It is heroic in its individuality, in its independence – its face-to-face with the universe for and by itself – and the beauty and eloquence with which she often expresses this, let alone the rich irony and humour, constitute . . . a new claim for the family renown.' The diary also provides us with an insight from the sufferer's point of view into what constitutes her 'nervous' condition.

Though distinctive in its particularities and in the soaring talents of its members, the James family shared with its social contemporaries that pattern of nervous illness which George Beard had attributed to the well educated American upper-class elite. The two elder brothers, Henry and William, as well as their father Henry Sr, a Swedenborgian philosopher, suffered from bouts of depression and a mysterious, unplaceable nervousness. But it was Alice, the single girl amongst four brothers, and the youngest, who took on the family's neurotic duty. It is the kind of division of energy and illness that Henry James portrayed in *The Sacred Fount*, where an emotional vampirism fuels the relations of his hero and heroine. The trajectory of Alice's condition, even if it is altogether her own, follows the general outlines that 'neurasthenia' and its sometime attendant category of 'hysteria' played out in many women of her time.

Henry Sr, who had no profession to take him out of the home, was an enthusiastic parent, intent, according to his philosophical under-standing, on being subordinate to his children's sacred 'natural instincts'. He turned their rearing, always loving but always vigilant, into an experiment in which they felt constrained to be happy. Alice was pampered by the doting Henry Sr, who happened also to believe that girls were born virtuous and capable of self-sacrifice. Faced with this vision of perfection, Alice tended to estimate any fault in herself as a fall into an abyss of badness. Much later, in her diary, she wrote, 'how sick one gets of being "good," how much I should respect myself if I could burst out and make every one wretched for 24 hours.'

Henry Sr's wife, Mary Welsh, shared little of her husband's sense of child-rearing, nor the philosophical leanings of the family's best-remembered members. She was the most conventional and practical of Victorian household angels. It seems she either neglected or disciplined the playful, energetic child little Alice was, though once Alice's illnesses begin, her letters — and the James family and their friends wrote count-less letters to each other — are replete with maternal care for her ailing daughter. Illness gives Alice a distinct place in the spectrum of mother love, spread as she sometimes thought rather thin over a brood in which she came last. Despite Alice's evident intellectual abilities, she was never educated to the level of her brothers, something she regretted throughout her life. During that restless European odyssey Henry Sr insisted was a necessary preparation for life for his American children, she often found herself left behind in shabby hotel rooms, while her brothers went to school or on cultural forays.

Back in America, Alice grew into a fraught adolescence. Love felt like a danger, something she would never be good enough to earn, even though it was women's only apparent destiny. She was plain, better at history classes than at the courting rituals of Boston. Men's eyes were not drawn. Mock social roles and rules as she does with all her acerbic wit, they nonetheless bear down on her and leave their mark on her sense of self. She can neither live up to feminine expectations, nor control her own unruly desires.

Illness provides a kind of solution to a life that accosts her sensibility, while all the while filling her with guilt about the unattainability of the ideal. That lifelong 'occupation of improving' she talks about in her diary can then take on a double significance: bettering herself and getting better. With illness, demands grow less, even if the weight of conscience and disappointment in herself continues. Illness means she needn't flagellate herself about her lacks, needn't compete intellectually with her brothers: she can be both interesting in her father's terms, and a failure, judged by outward measures.

The particular indeterminate condition from which Alice suffers also permits her the wild outburst of occasional delirium, a kind of hysterical rebellion against the imposed constraints of her situation. Interestingly, the very first entry in her diary, begun on 31 May 1889 when she is already forty, talks about those explosives within. Alice sees the diary as an 'outlet for that geyser of emotions, sensations, speculations, and reflections which ferment perpetually in my poor old carcass'. But before she enacted her ironic theatricals on the diary page, it was illness that gave Alice the permission to explode. Illness also allowed the opposite – a parody of a very proper feminine passivity in that enforced resting which is depression or neurasthenia. Indeed, nervous illness was an altogether useful way out.

By the age of fourteen Alice had already assumed what Henry James's biographer, Leon Edel, called a 'spiritual straightjacket'. She felt useless, imprisoned in a body 'struggling out of its swaddling clothes' but trapped by 'muscular circumstance', a lack of energy, into a renunciation: 'I had to peg away pretty hard between 12 and 24, "killing myself" as some one calls it, – absorbing into the bone that the better part is to clothe oneself in neutral tints, walk by still waters, and possess one's soul in silence.'

At fifteen, Alice began to suffer from the more serious breakdowns that marked the rest of her life. The family letters are full of her condition, its ups and downs, without ever precisely describing her symptoms. She lacks force. She is exhausted. She rallies, is riding or swimming, joins a sewing bee, which dwindles as the young women marry. She suffers mysterious pains and fainting spells. The pursued social life brings no necessary proposals of marriage. She wishes she were dead. She suffers from loneliness, while her brothers travel; a sense of desolation haunts her and occasionally overwhelms. She sets herself tasks of study, in keeping with her intelligence and the intellectual ethos of her father and the two elder Jameses, but her body, as she later says, rebels, and she is filled with thoughts of suicide or of wanting to murder her solicitous, sometimes seductive, father, who expects too much goodness from her.

A period of recuperation, a friendship formed with Katherine Loring, a capable woman who eventually becomes her partner in a 'Boston marriage' but who at first has to divide her time between Alice and her own invalid sister; a troubled engagement with Boston feminism – so well captured in her brother Henry's *The Bostonians* – and she is ill again, suffering from pains in her limbs, amongst much else. Her favourite brother William's marriage brings on a more severe collapse and a sojourn in an asylum – much as Charles Lamb's early passion helped bring on Mary's madness. After her mother's death, useful at last, she nurses her father. But he repudiates her usefulness by committing that slow 'gentle suicide' that he had once told Alice – parrying her desire to die – was the only fair way. Henry Sr's death brings another relapse. The pattern of nervous illness continues until her final cancer, which she suffers with a kind of relief that there is at last a nameable condition.

Neuralgia, spinal neurosis, nervous hyperaesthesia, rheumatic gout, all these were diagnosed for Alice, alongside headaches, stomach upsets, fatigue and nerves. Under neurasthenia, George Beard had listed over fifty symptoms, some of which shaded into the equally indeterminate nervous illness of hysteria: these included fainting, tooth decay, irascibility, paralysis, lack of appetite, vomiting, fits of laughing and crying, neuralgia, muscle spasms, morbid fears, constipation, insomnia and weariness. In 1866 at the age of eighteen, after the family had moved to their permanent home in Cambridge, Alice's condition so deteriorated that she was sent away for the first of her long cures. At the New York Orthopaedic Dispensary she underwent a regimen under the care of a

Dr Charles Fayette Taylor. It was not so very different from the one developed over the next decade by Weir Mitchell.

Indeed, like Weir Mitchell in his early days, Dr Taylor conceived of a link between orthopaedics and the nervous system. His treatment regimen included rest and a fattening regime, while the patient was distanced from her family. It seems slightly less autocratic than Weir Mitchell's in that enforced passivity was tempered with exercise. As Alice's biographer Jean Strouse points out, Dr Taylor, under the influence of a Swedish physiologist, had developed a movement cure which consisted of physical exercises, 'mechanical orthopaedics' and a goodly dose of therapeutic philosophy. He postulated, like so many of his fellows on both sides of the Atlantic, that girls who had been exposed too early to too much emotional and intellectual stimulation had their nervous systems 'perverted from tissue-making and absorbed, as it were, in the sensational life. The body is literally *starved*, while the nervous system is stimulated to the highest degree.' Emotions, for Taylor, were the most exhausting of all mental attributes. Too much education in a woman made her more emotional.

Taylor's therapeutic aim was therefore to 'accelerate the nutritive processes and cause muscular development, without taxing the nervous system'. He advised that the patient should be 'impressed with the idea that she must not regard her symptoms, be they temporarily pleasant or unpleasant, but should ignore them as much as possible, taking a course to secure ultimate immunity from them'. This latter advice has much in common with the tactics of 'moral management'. But as his paper on 'Emotional Prodigality' of 1879 reveals, Taylor had also taken on board evolutionary thinking and its attendant worries about the good reproductive vehicle:

> While men are calmed, women are excited by the education they receive . . . the woman of our modern civilisation becomes the bundle of nerves which she is – almost incapable of reasoning under the tyranny of paramount emotions; some are wholly incapable of becoming the mothers of rightly organized children . . .' 'For patience, for reliability, for real judgment in carrying out directions, for self-control, give me the little woman who has not been 'educated' too much . . . Such women are capable of being the mothers of men.

It was clear that Alice's mother was a far better exemplar of good womanhood than her daughter.

Alice spent longer than anyone had expected under Dr Taylor's care, six months from November 1866 to May 1867, during which the reports were that she bloomed. But no sooner is she home in Cambridge and engaged in the turmoil of social life, the loss of friends to marriage, the recognition of her own plainness, the pressures of that hothouse which is the James family, than early in 1868, at the age of nineteen, she suffers a far more serious collapse. James Sr comments on her state that year as being 'much of the time mostly insane'.

In 1890, after she had read her brother William's discussion of hysteria and the splitting of consciousness, Alice made sense of her own conflicts in his terms. She described to her diary the sheer terror of her youthful condition: she had felt morally constrained to keep herself in control, whereas some part of her, which she calls 'body' or 'muscle', had violently rebelled:

I have passed thro' an infinite succession of conscious abandonments and in looking back now I see how it began in my childhood, altho' I wasn't conscious of the necessity until '67 or '68 when I broke down first, acutely, and had violent turns of hysteria. As I lay prostrate after the storm with my mind luminous and active and susceptible of the clearest, strongest impressions, I saw so distinctly that it was a fight simply between my body and my will, a battle in which the former was to be triumphant to the end. Owing to some physical weakness, excess of nervous susceptibility, the moral power pauses, as it were, for a moment and refuses to maintain muscular sanity, worn out with the strain of its constabulary functions. As I tried to sit immovable reading in the library with waves of violent inclination suddenly invading my muscles taking on some of their myriad forms such as throwing myself out of the window, or knocking off the head of the benignant pater as he sat with his silver locks writing at his table, it used to seem to me that the only difference between me and the insane was that I had not only all the horrors and suffering of insanity but the duties of doctor, nurse, and strait-jacket imposed upon me, too. Conceive of never being without the sense that if you let yourself go for a moment your mechanism will fall into pie and that at some given moment you must abandon it all, let the dykes break and the flood weep in, acknowledging yourself abjectly impotent before the immutable laws. When all one's moral and neural stock in trade is a temperament forbidding the abandonment of an inch or the relaxation of a muscle, 'tis a never-ending fight.[107]

In this moving description of her inner struggle written in October 1890, over twenty years after her first major attacks, Alice folds her symptoms into the time's paradigms. She sees her sense that 'I had to abandon my "brain"' as being linked to her attempts at 'conscious and continuous cerebration'. Indeed, for all her rebellion, she accepts her own time's thinking on the limitations of women's capability and the effects of overreaching. She also understands herself as susceptible to nervous weakness through a hereditary strain. Her attacks are outgrowths of her body's weakness, its rebellion against the difficulties of study: her mind refuses to focus, even though she would like it to persist. There is no hint in her highly intelligent self-analysis of a description that takes her further than the American doctors around her diagnosed, even though she does note a part for the moral power of 'the constabulary' self in her breakdowns – that self-policing on which the Freudian mind doctors will elaborate in the next generation, when instinct and sexuality are opposed to the constraints of civilization. A quarter of a century later, a comparable women's analysing of her condition will use very different terms.

Meanwhile, it may not be going too far to speculate that William James's lifelong preoccupation with the 'principles of psychology' – the title of the two-volume work in which he explores the entire gamut of thinking in the field – owes not a little to the intricate play of consciousness in his own family and the very real problems posed by his 'delicate' sister's health. After years of treating his little sister flirtatiously, recounting his love affairs and writing to her at length from Europe about his escapades and tastes, his engagement and marriage in 1878 precipitated a major crisis in Alice, a suicidal despair through which Henry Sr nursed her.

The many treatments Alice underwent in her lifetime all bore the imprint of Silas Weir Mitchell (1828–1914), the pre-eminent American specialist in nervous diseases. Weir Mitchell, the son of a doctor, trained in Philadelphia before travelling to Europe where he worked with the eminent physiologist, Claude Bernard. He had a taste for both research and writing. His work on the impact of snake venom on the nerves is still considered first-rate; and his early writings on the split consciousness of an early figure in American psychological history, Mary Reynolds, were cited by many investigators in the field. But it was his 'rest cure' for neurasthenia and the accompanying books that brought him fame throughout America and Europe, where they were widely translated: *Wear and Tear; or, Hints for the Overworked* (1871), *Fat and Blood: An Essay on the Treatment of Certain Forms of Neurasthenia and Hysteria* (1877), and in 1881 his *Lectures on the Diseases of the Nervous System, Especially in Women.*

A prolific writer and astute observer of his patients, Weir Mitchell went on to give them fictional life in thirteen novels and countless short stories. Undoubtedly these portraits helped to fix the negative image of the neurasthenic woman in the popular imagination as a selfish, plaintive figure who manipulates those around her through her nervous disposition. Octapia Darnell, Ann Penhallow and Constance Trescott are all impatient, quasi-satirical portraits of invalids who shun the light and melodramatically enact their condition. In *Roland Blake*, Octapia Darnell spends her days in a darkened room, 'on a long reclining chair, and covered with a silken down-lined coverlet'. A 'long and attenuated figure', she has the pale-golden complexion of a woman 'originally dark-skinned and now lacking blood'. She complains about her weakness and chides her carer, the young Olivia, whose soothing caresses she seeks and whose life she sucks, vampire-like, to feed her own.

Cure, for these invalid heroines, often comes – as it does for Ann Penhallow – in a call to duty, a challenge to return to a life in which they are needed: 'Every physician of large experience must have seen cases of self-created, unresisted invalidism end with mysterious abruptness and the return of mental, moral and physical competence, under the influence of some call upon their sense of duty made by calamity, such as an acute illness in the household, financial ruin, or the death of a husband.'[108]

In his clinical writings, the spectrum of symptoms Weir Mitchell describes amongst his nervous women is broad. They suffer from tics and spasms, paralyses and aphonia, faints and sleeping, false pregnancies and 'fish-flaps', and veer between hysteria and neurasthenia, though distinguishing one from the other is rarely seen as necessary. He presents his cases with the vivid impatience of a practical misogynist:

> The patient was one of those stout, ruddy women, with good ovaries, and uterus where it should be, and yet hysterical to an exasperating degree. She weighed over two-hundred pounds, and was unhappily subject to what she called 'fish-flaps', which were really remarkable, because her body would be thrown up form the bed so high, and descend with such violence owing to her weight, that it was not rare to find the slats of the bed giving way. She grew better as her hysteria lessened, but is, I believe still subject at times to these unpleasant and undesired symptoms.[109]

While never altogether accusing his nervous women of inventing their symptoms or of being wholesale malingerers, Weir Mitchell is impatient at the intractability of illnesses which he nonetheless sees as caused by forces outside individual control. He attacks symptoms with the zeal of a terrier who doesn't like to let go. Of a woman whose leg had for months refused to move from its rigid right angle to her body, he writes: 'A multitude of therapeutic experiments ending always in failure, and the abandonment of the case, had been made by several physicians: nevertheless I undertook the treatment with a certain amount of hope, such in fact, as I always have, when an hysterical case is taken away from her own home and social surroundings, and subjected to new and revolutionary influences.'[110]

The primary features of the famous Weir Mitchell cure, his tenacity apart, were to take the patient away from familiar surroundings, to enforce rest and distance from any forms of stimulation other than those provided by doctor and nurse, to feed and to feed some more. In six weeks of isolation, the usual nervous patient was intended to gain some fifty pounds. On top of that there was massage; induction currents might be used to 'awaken unused muscles'; sometimes, too, as in the girl with the rigid leg, there were hypodermic injections. As Mitchell describes it, the treatment consists of 'an effort to lift the health of patients to a higher plane by the use of seclusion, which cuts off excitement and foolish sympathy; by rest [which sometimes meant immobility] . . . by massage . . . And by electrical muscular stimulation [which provided passive exercise].'[111]

All of this comes with goodly doses of the doctor's willpower and an avuncular firmness, just short of threat. Symptoms, like women, were there to do Weir Mitchell's bidding. The punishment of enforced bed rest and constant feeding, for a nervous patient who had already taken willingly to darkened rooms, could make movement and the stimulation health required at least momentarily attractive. If the patient proved obdurate, Weir Mitchell, it seems, was hardly above a little staged menacing. A story with all the force of legend has made its way into his biography. It has him telling a couch-loving patient, 'If you're not out of bed in five minutes, I'll get in with you', while slowly removing his coat, then his vest. Only when he started to take off his trousers did the angry patient leap out of bed.[112]

Mitchell had many women patients amongst the New England intellectual elite, including Jane Adams, Winfred Howells, Edith Wharton and Charlotte Perkins Gilman, who wrote a damning story, *The Yellow Wall-paper*, about the Mitchell cure. Her heroine is driven to insanity by enforced and infantilizing rest, during which she is prevented from writing.[113] Gilman sent the story to Mitchell who, she increasingly claimed, changed his treatment of neurasthenia after reading it, though there is no substantive evidence that he did so.

Alice James – though her *symptoms* were in line with his treatments – never went to Weir Mitchell. Both she and William had certainly read the man who, as a friend of theirs noted, cured 'all the dilapidated Bostonians'. William had also met him in Connecticut, and stated in a letter that his talk was very interesting, though his intellectual and artistic nature might 'be developed at the expense of his moral stability'.[114] Instead, in 1883, at the height of Weir Mitchell's fame, Alice checked into an asylum which treated 'nervous people who are not insane,' and stayed for three months. The Adams Nervine Asylum just outside Boston had been incorporated in 1877 by a bequest for the poor women of the state, though it also took in fee-paying patients. It had beautiful grounds overlooking an arboretum and a series of tastefully furnished Victorian Gothic buildings, all calculated to provide a fitting environment for its nervous patients and the Boston Brahmins who treated them. Places in the asylum, which prided itself, according to the *Boston Globe* of 18 April 1887, on 'aesthetic' surroundings, were in high demand.

In a report of 1883 to his managers, Dr Frank Page provided a survey of his patients conducted since the asylum's official opening in 1880. The results run counter to what some of his British fellow doctors might have predicted. In noting the causes of nervous illness he stated that in the 34 per cent who were housewives, their nervous condition was to do with 'overwork, care, anxiety and sleeplessness, incident to domestic afflictions'. But worry over the care of others was more important in causing breakdown than overwork itself. Amongst the 14 per cent of patients who were teachers overwork was rarely the cause of breakdown and was, in fact, 'productive of sound health'.[115]

For Alice and its other patients, the asylum offered what was a modified version of Weir Mitchell's rest cure: time in bed, food, vapour baths, massage and faradic and galvanic currents applied to nerves and muscles to relieve pain and provide the stimulation which stood in for exercise.

Temporarily better when she left the asylum, a few months later Alice was in search of treatment once more. As for so many nervous patients, cure was always sought and never found with any permanence. This time the instigating factor for Alice's collapse, or fear that she would, was her companion Katherine Loring's departure for Europe. The recommended doctor was an expensive New York specialist, a Russian who charged an exorbitant $100 a session for application of electrical currents, on the basis of a theory which had it that redirecting dormant impulses, or ones that had gone wrong, could cure fatigue and chronic nervousness. William Basil Neftel believed in exercise. It brought fresh blood and lymph to affected muscles. In 1875, he had written a book on galvano-therapeutics, which traced 'the action and therapeutics of the galvanic current on the acoustic, optic, sympathetic and pneumo-gastric nerves'.

Alice's letters about her two months with Dr Neftel provide a clue to the doctor–patient relationship undoubtedly key in the treatment of 'nervous' illness. There is a flirtatiousness in her tone, one she mocks, but can't or doesn't want to eradicate. The hope of cure produces a kind of love affair between patient and doctor which soon enough turns to disappointment and contempt for the doctor and, of course, for herself. On 5 May 1884, she writes to her old friend Sara Sedgwick, now married to Charles Darwin's son Darwin:

> I went to test the skill of a Russian electrician . . . of whom I had heard great things and who certainly either in spite or because of his quackish quality has done me a great deal of good in many ways. I was charmed at first with the Slavic flavour of our intercourse but I soon found myself sighing for unadulterated Jackson.[116] To associate with and to have to take seriously a creature with the moral substance of a monkey becomes degrading after a while, no matter how one may be seduced by his 'shines' at the first going off.

Alice's Bostonian moral sensibility may have been too refined for the mere foreign monkey, but the sexual metaphors underline that other kind of 'electricity' which was inevitably part of the therapeutic relationship. Doctors, in Alice's experience, were the only men who ever laid hands on her body. The touch could be restorative, but it was also humiliating, as she made clear in a letter of 1886 to William, when she once more needed help:

> It may seem supine to you that I don't descend into the medical arena, but I must confess my spirit quails before any more gladiatorial encounters. It requires the strength of a horse to survive the fatigue of waiting hour after hour for the great man and then the fierce struggle to recover one's self-respect . . . I think the difficulty is my inability to assume the receptive attitude, that cardinal virtue in woman, the absence of which has always made me so uncharming to and uncharmed by the male sex.[117]

Freud, who later spoke the unspoken for so much of the period, wrote about the cure through love and underlined the vagaries of the transference between patient and doctor. For Alice, as brother Henry was to write, her tragic health was the only solution for the '"nervousness" engendered by (or engendering) her intense horror of life and contempt for it'. It suppressed any need for 'equality or reciprocity', as impossible to find with a doctor as with any other man.

Her intense 'horror of life' was certainly entwined with its sexual element. But in puritanical America, diagnoses to do with that forbidden and unpalatable base matter of sex were not to arrive for some years. Before they did, that loose catch-all category of 'nervous illness' had to be contaminated by the dramatic proletarian atmosphere of Charcot's Salpêtrière in republican Paris and pass through the fire of that psychological crucible which was middle-class Vienna.

Alice was to die in London of cancer, the progress of which she met stoically and with a kind of relief that at last a *real* illness was the cause of her invalidism: nor did the doctors who dealt with this killing disease have any of the monkey-like quality of her prior healers. Henry James, whose books are filled with the mysterious ways in which illness, often either unnamed or unnameable, worms its way into and shapes the destiny of characters, was to survive his little sister by eighteen years.

5

HYSTERIA

In France, full-blown hysteria was a condition of the poor – not, in the first instance, of the neurasthenic rich. It began its new life as the choice diagnosis of a fiercely republican *belle époque*. Esquirol had hardly bothered to explore it, and had classified hysteria under mania with which it shared the characteristics of 'constant mobility, persistent agitation and inexhaustible loquacity'. The new hysteria took on prominence against the background of a society in rapid flux. Trains now sped between country and city, foreshortening geographical, if not cultural, distances. Scores of poor 'immigrants' and disoriented peasant travellers made their way to the capital, crowding its outskirts and slums. Their presence gave the city a sense of ungovernability. The influence of the Church was fiercely contested, as was the closeness between women and priests, which many thought only secular education and scientific medicine could rupture. In a speech in 1870, the republican politician Jules Ferry had urged: 'Women must belong to science, or else they will belong to the church.'[118]

Indeed, the French battle for secularism was now waged down among the women. If the Church had Bernadette, the peasant girl who had heard the Virgin and whose cult of faith-healing miracles at Lourdes it was eager to abet, the secularists had Augustine, Geneviève, Blanche Wittman and those women who made up Jean-Martin Charcot's remarkable panoply of hysterics at the Salpêtrière. Exhibited before a growing public not only of doctors, but of writers, artists and socialites – the chattering classes who made up *le tout Paris* – the extravagant St Theresa-like ecstasies and attitudes of demonic possession of

these madwomen could be proved to be aspects of a disease called
hysteria.

Whatever the proclaimed battle lines, the Church's sway over ordinary individuals went deep: the whispered orders of the confessional,
the influence of invisible powers, might no longer always be cloaked in
their traditional apparel, but the habit of listening to or being moved,
guided, taken over by the unseen was still in place. The mind doctors
would use it to bolster their new profession.

For women, whose roles and psychosexual potential were regulated
by Church and convention, the changes from a traditional to a modern
society brought a double burden of difficulties. They were no longer the
old version of their sex, at once cosseted and confined to the home, at
least if they belonged to the middle and upper echelons of society. Nor
were they yet the new: emancipation needed the First World War to take
a substantive step forward. Hysteria, the most fashionable diagnosis of
the latter part of the century, suited them. It described a sexualized
madness full of contradictions, one which could play all feminine parts
and take on a dizzying variety of symptoms, though none of them had
any real, detectable base in the body. It was a partial madness which
could in attacks mimic both epilepsy and ecstatic saintliness. The hysteric could be paralysed when awake, but perfectly mobile when
'asleep'.

Susceptible to 'invisible' forces such as hypnotism, easily and
unknowingly swayed, emotionally labile, often young and pretty,
Charcot's hysteric sums up the period's fears and aspirations. She is – in
her hypnotized, sleeping, paralysed or mute state – a parody, an excessive, caricatural version of that Victorian vision of the feminine which
would have woman passive, angelic, malleable, and utterly desirable
while undesiring, her skin anaesthetic. Yet the hysteric also embodies
the time's often secret desires for a certain sexual freedom from what
Freud later called '"civilized" sexual morality' – both for herself and for
the fascinated men who watch and help to invent her. Hysteria, with its
fluctuating symptoms, is *par excellence* the disorder that best expresses
women's distress at the clashing demands and no longer tenable restrictions placed on women in the fin-de-siècle.

Augustine and the doctors

The girl who became known as Augustine, though sometimes in the case notes she is called Louise or simply L. or X., came to the great Salpêtrière hospice, that women's city within a city near the Gare d'Austerlitz in Paris, at the age of fifteen and a half on 21 October 1875. Just thirteen years before, in 1862, when the formidable doctor who was to become known as the 'Napoleon of neurology', Jean-Martin Charcot, had first taken up his post, the hospital had been a veritable hell-hole, with one doctor for every five hundred of some five thousand women, many of whom suffered from chronic neurological conditions, were geriatric or, in the case of eight hundred or so, were 'alienated'. The vast majority were considered incurable.

By an accident of building layout, epileptics and hysterics, having been separated out from the mad, were housed together. With a zeal for establishing a science out of neurology, Charcot, a carriage-maker's son who had slowly risen through the medical ranks, set out to classify the contents of what he called the 'museum of living pathology'. Working with the hospital's resident population, he made detailed observations through time of the whole gamut of nervous and degenerative conditions – the choreas, ataxias and tabes dorsalis [a development of neuro-syphilis] – which manifested themselves in tics, shakes, loss of mobility or sensation, fits and paralyses of differing kinds. All of these could shade into mental conditions. Elevated in 1872 to the newly established chair of Pathological Anatomy, Professor Charcot soon set up a photographic atelier in order to put the new technology to use in the work of medical documentation.

Charcot was in the line of the great and theatrical French doctors. Like Pinel, a painting of whom he had hanging in his regular lecture theatre, and like Esquirol, he prided himself on his talent for observation, his eye for detail, his rigorous method. In the opening lecture of his *Diseases of the Nervous System*, he points out that unlike 'nosographers' who are interested in the abstract picture of a disease, 'the task of the clinical observer . . . lies more especially in individual cases which almost always present themselves with peculiarities that separate them more or less from the *common type*'.[119]

Sigmund Freud, who for five months in 1885–6 sat amongst Charcot's admiring pupils and achieved the desired honour of being invited to his famous soirées, stresses just this in his obituary of the great man.

> He was not a reflective man, not a thinker: he had the nature of an artist – he was, as he himself said, a 'visuel', a man who sees . . . He used to look again and again at the things he did not understand, to deepen his impression of them day by day, till suddenly an understanding of them dawned on him. In his mind's eye the apparent chaos presented by the continual repetition of the same symptoms then gave way to order: the new nosological pictures emerged, characterized by the constant combination of certain groups of symptoms... He might be heard to say that the greatest satisfaction a man could have was to see something new – that is, to recognize it as new; and he remarked again and again on the difficulty and value of this kind of 'seeing'.[120]

Focusing on the individual case, Charcot spoke what he *saw* and made a spectacle of diagnosis. Students as well as a growing influential and often international public flocked to his *leçons du mardi*, when the newly instituted 'outpatients', men amongst them, came for a quick and brilliant evaluation. When he was stumped, the *Maître* – for whom the post of Professor of Neuropathology in the Faculty of Medecine had been created in 1881 – would openly exclaim it. On Fridays, in his more formal lectures, the long-term residents of the Salpêtrière were presented for examination. Their cases had been under scrutiny for some time. They came before students and public to demonstrate, for example, the ease with which hysterics could be hypnotized. Asleep, they moved paralysed limbs or reproduced the traumatic scenes which had toppled them into their condition.

It is worth noting that for Charcot hysteria was equally a male illness, though, given the Salpêtrière's female population, most of his famous hysterics were women. Freud had emphasized in his obituary of the Master that 'Hysteria in males, and especially in men of the working class, was found far more often than had been expected; it was convincingly shown that certain conditions which had been put down to alcoholic intoxication or lead-poisoning were of a hysterical nature.'

Like his predecessors, including Georget, who believed in the power of physiognomy to reveal insanity, Charcot had his patients represented for medical purposes. He used not the old artisanal technologies of paint and plaster casts or wax, but the new 'objective' technology that couldn't lie: photography. The Salpêtrière photographs, it was thought, could provide a physiognomic map of the passions: traces, imprints on the body through time of maladies of the nerves and of the deranged emotions and mental processes they could produce. Trainee medics could learn diagnosis from such an amassed natural history of symptoms, as could doctors in hospitals and practices far and wide. If today the Salpêtrière photographs of hysterics can look melodramatically posed, and hardly useful as instruments for contemporary diagnosis, it is worth noting that their status in their own time was not unlike brain scans or magnetic resonance imaging today. Scans are no more an accurate rendition of a 'reality' than these older images once were; after all, they are computer-generated images processed, sometimes in glorious colour, in accordance with algorithms most doctors find incomprehensible, and then read using codes whose assured parsing requires great subtlety and experience.

Through the late nineteenth century's representational technology of photography, the Salpêtrière amassed a vast archive of the iconography of mental illness. Charcot's hysterics, like the early silent film stars who may well have imitated their expressions, went through the dramatic paces of their condition for the camera. Depending from where the judgement is made, either they provided the documentation, the evidence for the four stages of hysteria, or they enacted them as Charcot and his doctors had *suggested* them. From the careful and detailed observation of individual cases – a procedure which paid tribute to his admiration for the time's leading philosophy of positivism – Charcot arrived at what was the 'type' of the repeated mechanism of the hysterical attack.

All of these stages were captured on photographic plates redolent of the mystery which early photography, with its long, slow takes and erratic developing procedures, instils. They were also drawn and tabulated by the talented Paul Richer, Professor of Artistic Anatomy at the Ecole des Beaux Arts in Paris. So widely diffused were the dramatic images recording the four stages of the hysterical attack, so much talked about were Charcot's hysterics, it is hardly surprising that various forms of contemporary malaise found their way into an unconscious mimicking of the popularized symptoms.

The fact that Charcot proceeded by focusing on individual cases so as to arrive at general rules and a specimen type, a universal into which all hysterics fitted, allowed for what was almost certainly an over-recognition and over-diagnosis of the condition. It also allowed it to be *learned*, in the way that Charcot's first hysterical patients, housed as they were in the epileptics' ward, learned the enactment of fits. If a woman displayed any of the characteristics of the four stages – an anaesthesia, or a passional attitude – the other stages might be deduced and the categorization of 'hysteric' attributed. Just as with monomania, the culture of the times, the doctors and patients all collaborated in creating that pattern of illness and discontent which was hysteria.

Augustine came early. In 1876, just after her arrival at the hospital, the *Iconographie photographique de la Salpêtrière* series was established, and its splendid volumes recording patients through image and text began to be published by the wonderfully named Bureau de Progrès Médical. These books act as a testimonial to Charcot's Salpêtrière and the set of behaviours, postures and experimental procedures which make up what became its most famous diagnosis. They also serve as the fullest hospital guide yet available to the patients, containing not only the images Charcot was so intent on, but a record of their own words – that language of dream, delirium and memory which would form the focus of Charcot's most famous student, Freud's, practice.

The doctor who writes Augustine's case notes, and simultaneously reveals what, in a clinical picture, the doctors of the Salpêtrière found noteworthy, is D.M. Bourneville. It is he, together with the photographer P. Regnard, who gives Augustine to history and helps to make her one of the Salpêtrière's star hysterics. Introducing Augustine, Bourneville describes her as 'sweet, capricious, wilful, and far too saucy for her age'. Despite appearances, for she is tall and full of figure, she is pre-pubertal. Many had previously thought hysteria could only come with menstruation.

In the photograph taken of her fully dressed and depicting a 'normal state' – perhaps one of those intervals between attacks that Charcot noted as habitual in hysterics — Augustine gives the camera a fetching smile which reaches her light eyes. She leans back against a chair , a pretty, pneumatic figure, one hand raised to her carefully coiffed head, while her other arm, the tell-tale limb, lies in her lap — this is the arm which doesn't altogether feel sensations, and later doesn't move.

Bourneville tells us in his summary notes that Augustine is 'active, intelligent, affectionate, impressionable, temperamental and likes drawing attention to herself. She is coquettish, spends time on her appearance and in arranging her abundant hair in one style or another, taking particular delight in brightly coloured ribbons.[121] So far, were it not for the report of fainting fits and the arm, the portrait could be one of any ordinary teenager. A lack of mobility and sensation with no underlying physical cause is one of the determining features for a diagnosis of hysteria. Augustine is tested with all the existing indicators of neurological conditions, such as the Mathieu dynamometer, to see the difference in movement between left and right sides. She is pricked and scratched, her reflexes prodded, alongside her hearing, taste and sight. Charcot is first and foremost a neurologist, one who named and described a vast range of disorders while he taught the art of diagnosis.

Augustine's whole right-hand side is affected. The anaesthesia on one side is paralleled by an oversensitivity — a hyperaesthesia — in other parts. As for vision — and Charcot and his clinicians are highly alert to the links between perception and nervous disorders — acuity is diminished and Augustine's notion of colour itself is gone. All this marks only the beginning of the picture of hysteria that Charcot will flesh out with the help of photography and patients who, like most, are open to suggestion.

Bourneville's notes indicate that Augustine was brought to the Salpêtrière by her mother, a servant in good health, whose only possible neurological blemish lies in the migraines she suffered in youth. She is forty-one, to the father's forty-five, and he too is a servant, sober and rather stern of character. According to her mother, who supplies a part of this information, Augustine is the eldest of seven children, of which only she and her younger brother survived. She lived with her mother for her first nine months, was then sent off to relatives in the countryside, and from the age of six to thirteen and a half lived in a convent, where she learned to read and write, and sew lingerie. Her only illness before the bout that brought her to the Salpêtrière was bronchitis.

Without giving us the exact source of the information that follows, Bourneville then proceeds to fill in Augustine's story with dramatic flair. We later realize that a part of the material must come from her utterances during states of delirium, which is the last phase of a full hysterical attack as the Salpêtrière understood it. The story also emerges from her own reports of her dreams, or her 'hallucinations' under the influence of ether, amyl nitrate or hypnosis. Each of these 'drugs' is used as a means of gathering scientific data, as well as for soothing: Charcot's patients are always also experimental subjects, who will perhaps throw light on a disease entity. Hence the chemical 'tools', the careful recording of material, the attention paid to those traditional indicators – excretion, temperature (of various body parts), menstruation.

The machinations Bourneville depicts as background to Augustine's *hystero-épilepsie*, without in any way linking them absolutely or making them directly causative of her illness, might make us wonder whether Freud's hysterics were merely middle-class variations on the everyday narrative of *belle époque* life. Augustine's story is replete with violent sensation and melodramatic incident. In part because of this, certain aspects of her history feel more 'true' than others. But Charcot's doctors, even early on, were alert to the inventive side of hysterics, their ability to fabulate, on top of the protean nature of the condition. We can therefore only assume that the observational details Bourneville integrates in setting up Augustine's case are the ones he believed. From a Freudian perspective, of course, the evidential base is less important than the story itself.

In terms of a history of the Salpêtrière, however, it is worth noting that certain parts of Augustine's narrative, for example the evocation of scenes of religious ecstasy in the convent of her childhood, feel as if they have arisen from cues and suggestions within her present environment – as do the dramatic hysterical fits so akin to epileptic attacks which the women in the hospice perform and which occur as an aspect of hysteria almost nowhere else. In the convent, Bourneville tells us, the nuns often punish Augustine for what they see as her rebelliousness, her irreligious utterances, her fits of anger during which she purportedly turns black. Holy water is thrown in her face to calm her. The nuns think she is possessed and during a retreat she is sent off to be exorcised. On another occasion, because she and two other little girls touch themselves, the sisters punish them by tying up their hands at night. One of the other girls suffers ecstasies, which Augustine compares to those of a fellow hysteric at the Salpêtrière, Genevieve, another of Bourneville's documented cases. This is a patient Charcot uses to demonstrate that religious ecstasy, like demonic possession, is a component of hysteria.

While at the convent, Augustine sometimes goes to visit the wife of a painter/decorator. The woman drinks and rows with her husband, who grows violent. On one occasion he hits his wife, ties her up by the hair and turns on Augustine. He tries to kiss her and even rape her. She is terrified. Only that summer, when she is home on holidays, does her brother explain to her how babies are made. That same summer, her mother takes her to the house where she and her husband work as servants. Augustine is urged to call the man of the house, C., 'Daddy', and to kiss him.

When she leaves the convent at the age of thirteen and a half, she is brought to live in C.'s house. Her mother says that she will be raised alongside the other children here, and taught to sing and to sew. But C. makes use of his wife's absence to try and have sex with Augustine. The first time he fails because of her resistance. So, too, the second time. The third time he attempts seduction, promises beautiful dresses. He threatens her with a razor, and while she's in a state of terror, forces alcohol on her, throws her on the bed and rapes her. The next day she is in pain. She can't walk. When she finally comes to table the day after, she can't bring herself to give C. the customary kiss. His wife, also noticing her pallor, grows suspicious.

Meanwhile, C. throws her warning looks across the table. When she continues unwell, she is sent home. She vomits. Everyone thinks her malaise is tied to the onset of menstruation. But it doesn't come. What come are fits: when she is resting in her darkened room, she sees a green-eyed cat coming at her in the dark. She screams and suffers a convulsive attack which ends in laughter. For a month and a half there are daily attacks. One day, she meets C. in the street. He catches her by the hair. The convulsive attack which follows is particularly violent.

Later, at the Salpêtrière, the scene of the rape revisits her repeatedly. In a state of delirium she spits, makes small pelvic movements, calls out, 'Pig, pig! . . . I'll tell Papa . . . Pig! You're so heavy! You're hurting me!'[122] A year or so later, under the influence of ether, she rehearses the moment, adding a new element: 'Mr C. said he would kill me . . . I didn't know it was an animal that would bite.

Augustine is sent to work as a housemaid to an old woman. Her brother introduces her to his friends and she starts having sexual relations with one of them, Emile, for some six months. She also sleeps, perhaps only once, with his friend George: the tussle between the two youths is enacted during her attacks at the Salpêtrière, where she cajoles Emile not to be jealous of George, entices him to bed her, or rebukes him for trying it on at the Salpêtrière itself (where he has come to visit).

During the time before her arrival at the hospital, Augustine has frequent arguments with her parents, who also row with each other about her adventurous and irregular habits. She realizes that her mother has long had relations with C. to whom she delivered Augustine perhaps as a kind of proxy, or as a gift. She also learns that her brother might well be C.'s son, not her father's, with whom his relations have always been cold. In her delirium, she chastises her mother for delivering her to a man who put rats up her fanny.

Like Freud's Dora, Augustine gradually reveals to her doctors a highly sexualized fabric of daily life. It is one her parents, whatever their disapproval or strict behaviour on the surface, effectively deliver her to at a young age in order to cover up or facilitate their own sexual activity. Endemic to the family, it would seem, are certain forms of coercion and sexual exploitation, particularly of girls. Augustine shares this 'past' with others of the Salpêtrière's hysterics and with Freud's. The difference is that Freud sets out to focus on and understand the sexual genesis of the condition, and sees that understanding as part of the treatment. For him, the family and a hypocritical sexual morality are the instigating problem. A history of conflicts between what a child can see and feel and what she is told – the struggle, as he puts it, against accepting 'a difficult piece of reality' – often forms part of the clinical picture of hysteria.

Freud's appreciation of the arc of hysteria meets the case of Augustine in other respects, too. The disgust and attraction towards sex which she enacts so vividly and repeatedly during her hysterical attacks, the 'serpent' in the trousers she both fears and wants, foreshadow Freud's interpretation of Dora. Augustine's ability to perform passive and active sexual roles during these attacks, her double identification with male and female parts, the traumatic internalization of what is tantamount in her case to a rape (though it could be something far less, like a kiss, or a glance that cut across a face), also seem fundamental to Freud's picture of hysteria. Freud was certainly familiar with the specificities of her case. He possessed a copy of the Salpêtrière's *Iconographie photographique* as well as Charcot's archive.[123] When he attended Charcot's lectures in 1885, the resident hysterics must have proved just as vivid as Augustine.

What Freud also learned from the great teachers that were Charcot and his patients was something that Charcot never explicitly taught, though from an off-hand remark it was evident to him and became more and more so to Freud as his years of practice mounted. *La chose génitale*, conflicted sexuality, was often at the root of 'severe illness'. This fact seemed to be part of the unofficial knowledge of the medical profession, though it was never taught or actually stated.

In his history of the psychoanalytic movement, Freud reminisces about one of the moments of his research trip to France that marked him most profoundly.

at one of Charcot's evening receptions, I happened to be standing near the great teacher at a moment when he appeared to be telling Brouardel a very interesting story about something that had happened during his day's work . . . a young married couple from a distant country in the East – the woman a severe sufferer, the man either impotent or exceedingly awkward. 'Tâchez donc,' [keep trying] I heard Charcot repeating, 'je vous assure, vous y arriverez.'[I assure you, you will get there] Brouardel, who spoke less loudly, must have expressed his astonishment that symptoms like the wife's could have been produced by such circumstances. For Charcot suddenly broke out with great animation: 'Mais, dans des cas pareils c'est toujours la chose génitale, toujours . . . toujours . . . toujours' [But, in such cases it's always the genital thing, always . . . always . . . always]; and he crossed his arms over his stomach, hugging himself and jumping up and down on his toes several times in his own characteristically lively way. I know that for a moment I was almost paralysed with amazement and said to myself: 'Well, but if he knows that, why does he never say so?' But the impression was soon forgotten; brain anatomy and the experimental induction of hysterical paralyses absorbed all my interest.[124]

By the time Ida Bauer, the patient Freud calls 'Dora', came to him in 1899, Freud had left behind Charcot's experimental induction through hypnosis of hysterical paralyses and learned the unofficial lesson. Repressed sexual conflicts, perhaps produced by traumatic events – but equally occasioned by the difficulties of growing up a woman at a time when idealizations of the family were at odds with lived experience – were the seedbed of hysteria and a variety of neuroses.

Freud had learned other lessons too. For all his own high-handedness and patriarchal bullying that he himself draws attention to in his analysis of his teenage hysteric – offspring of a father who 'offers' her to the husband of his own mistress – Freud's talking treatment is humane when compared to that experienced by Augustine at the Salpêtrière. Candidly an experimental subject for her doctors, Augustine undergoes a series of interventions which are both exploratory and intended as teaching means. The hysterics at the Salpêtrière were routinely given a number of drugs to calm the fits they seemed to produce in growing numbers the longer they stayed in the epileptics ward and remained under Charcot's care. Inhalations of valerian or amyl nitrate or ether, ovarian compressors, baths, application of various metals, magnets, hypnosis in front of an audience, including pressing on the 'hysterogenic' zones so as to produce symptoms, electricity, the highly addictive chloral – all are used as research tools and to awaken sensation and mobility, or to suppress agitation, attacks, insomnia, and a host of other symptoms. Alongside these, and probably as effective as forms of treatment, were two particularly Charcotian specialities, subcategories of the curative powers of sheer medical attention: photography, and the public Charcotian lecture at which patients were encouraged to perform their condition, in and out of hypnosis.

Augustine became a model patient and, like all bright young women, learned from her peers and teachers in the hospital. In Regnard's photographs and according to Bourneville's notes, she produces all four stages of the hysterical attack as Charcot defined them, though most often separately. Bourneville records that in 1876 she suffered 1097 attacks; the following year there were more, and then fewer again the year after, though more complete attacks. Perhaps Augustine had consciously or unconsciously learned all the necessary stages. To begin with there is the 'aura', the lead up to the fit. This can consist of a seething pain in the right ovary, and is quickly followed by the sense of a ball rising from stomach to throat to form a knot, all accompanied by palpitations, agitation, speeding heart, difficulty in breathing, rapid eye movements. Sometimes, warned by these indicators, the hysteric, like an epileptic, will lie down. Then comes the loss of consciousness, the fixed stare.

In a photograph labelled 'Beginning of Attack' Augustine lies belted and tied to the bed by a straitjacket, her mouth wide in a scream. There follow all the stages of what became the 'typical' Salpêtrière attack. Charcot himself described Augustine as a 'classic' example, in part, perhaps, because she came to him before the height of his fame and seemed too young and innocent to be putting on what became the hysterical style.

First there was the epileptoid phase or 'tonic rigidity', which mirrored epileptic behaviour. Augustine's muscles contract, her neck twists, the heels turn out, her arms swing round wildly several times in a row, then her wrists reach towards each other while the fists gyrate outwards. She grows rigid, lies immobile, plank-like, eyes directed at space, unseeing.

Next came the circus-like acrobatics of the 'clonic spasms' or grands mouvements, also known as *le clownisme* – so very camera-worthy. This was followed by the representation of emotional states such as love, hate, fear, known as *attitudes passionnelles*. Here Augustine enacts seduction, supplication, erotic pleasure, ecstasy and mockery in a series worthy of silent film. Hallucinations often accompanied this stage. Augustine hears voices, is terrified, in pain, sees blood, rats; and when she slips into the delirium which marks the final stage of an attack these hallucinations often take on the shape of her rapist, lover or family. She pleads, says the scarf around her throat is choking her, refuses to drink, howls her pain. At the end, there are tears and laughter, both of which Charcot saw as a release before the patient comes back to herself.

Bourneville documents Augustine's narrative of her dreams, as well as those which come in her 'provoked sleep', including her wonderful aside when she doesn't want to talk about them: 'you think you've dreamed when you've only been hearing people speak'.[125] He notes the relationship between menstruation and fits, though also underlines, like a good scientific observer, that there is no regular pattern to discern. Prejudice would have come up with a link: the new science is more meticulous, though still hopes some causal relationship will occur. He notes her vaginal secretions after her voluptuous dreams on ether during which she enacts a sexual scene she writes down graphically for the doctor. There is a seductiveness in her postscript which suggests a kind of collusion between doctor and patient: he is allowed in on her secret life, may even have helped her with the imaging of it, but the crowd in front of whom she sometimes performs her hysteria is not: 'I've ended up saying everything you asked of me and even more. I would speak more openly if I could, but I fear doing it in front of everyone.'[126] Bourneville notes this, perhaps in a willing suspension of disbelief that the doctors haven't themselves provoked Augustine's dreams.

As she gets better towards the end of December '78, three years after her arrival, she begins to work as a nurse – a pattern Pinel had pioneered at the Salpêtrière years before and that we are to see again in the 'transmission' of psychoanalytic knowledge. In this later version, patients become practitioners, having learned the procedures through what might be called a training *illness* as much as a training analysis. In her new uniform, Augustine looks sedate and respectable. Some four months later, however, she suffers a relapse and is back in Dr Charcot's service. Her behaviour is violent and she has to be placed in a cell. Even Charcot, it seems, cannot now hypnotize her into sleep.[127]

In July, she takes the opportunity of a large public concert in the hospital to make her escape. She is caught on the Boulevard de l'Hôpital, just as she's getting into a carriage. During what seems to be a scuffle she trips and cuts herself. Back in the hospital, she climbs on a chair to see the crowd, falls off and breaks her kneecap. Only after a month can she walk again. Three weeks after the ability returns, Augustine flees once more, this time dressed as a man. The gender change is not insignificant. As a man, she can flee, can shake off her hysterical paralysis, which is a gendered, sexually linked inability to move unless the will of the hypnotist propels her. Since her escape, Bourneville tells us, Augustine has been living with her lover – a man she met at the Salpêtrière. He doesn't tell us whether this person is a doctor, some kind of assistant, or another patient. We are told only that when she suffers another relapse, she goes to another hospital, the Charité, before once more returning to her lover.

After that Augustine disappears from history. But she reappears as myth. She becomes the very 'type' of the young *belle époque* hysteric – beautiful, capricious, extravagant, sexually provocative, mysterious, attuned to the camera, capable of masquerading as a boy and, of course, masquerading sleep and paralysis in order to please her doctors. Léon Daudet, who attended Charcot's lectures, satirizes her and her kin as well as the whole Charcotian establishment in his novel *Les Morticoles*, where the hospital becomes the equivalent of a music-hall, the Folies Hystériques. In a more romantic vein Augustine returns, after the horrors of the First World War, as a muse for the Surrealists, who see her heightened sexuality, her disarray of the senses, her delirium and excess as the ideal of femininity, one which could, prophet-like, speak truths through madness.

HYSTERIA'S HISTORY

Immediately after Charcot's death in 1893, and despite his international reputation, the new generation at the Salpêtrière turned against the *Maître*'s diagnosis of hysteria. This may have in part been due to the now increasingly recognized professionalization of the patients, whom the younger doctors saw as making a mockery of their serious anatomical science. The rumour mills had it that the Salpêtrière was (inadvertently) courting the hirelings of 'magnetizers' or latter-day mesmerists, the kind of women who also made up the ranks of somnambulists, mediums and the popular hypnotists of theatrical spectacle. Here were jobs for aspiring working-class girls who had a talent for 'sleep' and who moved between music-hall and hospital stage with ease. These were women, some said, who could teach Charcot himself something about paralysis by suggestion; and if the medical, let alone the social, ranks had been more open, could have trained as hypnotizing doctors.[128]

Freud, a man of this next generation, did not agree with the rebels against Charcot. The theatricality of convulsive fits, at once erotic and religious, may have been a particular displacement of the gestures which were part of the Republic's love affair with boulevard spectacle. Hysteria would be enacted differently elsewhere. But the underlying logic of psychological distress finding itself converted into bodily symptoms, something Charcot came increasingly to see in the 1880s, was important. As Freud explained in his obituary of the Napoleon of nervous illness, what hysteria revealed was a whole new way of reading the human mind, which could express what it wasn't aware of through physical symptoms:

> if I find someone in a state which bears all the signs of a painful affect –
> weeping, screaming and raging – the conclusion seems probable that a
> mental process is going on in him of which those physical phenomena
> are the appropriate expression. A healthy person, if he were asked,
> would be in a position to say what impression it was that was torment-
> ing him; but the hysteric would answer that he did not know . . . If we
> enter into the history of the patient's life and find some occasion, some
> trauma, which would appropriately evoke precisely those expressions of
> feeling – then everything points to one solution: the patient is in a spe-
> cial state of mind in which all his impressions or his recollections of
> them are no longer held together by an associative chain, a state of
> mind in which it is possible for a recollection to express its affect by
> means of somatic phenomena without the group of the other mental
> processes, the ego, knowing about it or being able to intervene to pre-
> vent it.

Through Charcot and the hysterics, the unconscious begins to be theorized. With Freud, and the other researchers into the human psyche in which this turn of the century is increasingly rich, it takes on a key role in understanding both madness and ordinary everyday behaviour.

Hysteria, however, as a florid set of expressions in bodily form of mental problems – conversion hysteria, as Freud named it – ceased to be an illness prominent amongst Western women. As a diagnosis, it migrated with the First World War into the 'war neuroses' from which so many soldiers suffered, their blindness or muteness or paralysis an expression of the trauma of battle. Since then, conversion hysteria has all but disappeared. Certain psychoanalysts and therapists may still occasionally use the nomenclature for women who are dramatic, desperately seductive and alternately self-destructive, but the floridly dramatic symptoms its turn-of-the-last-century sufferers presented have largely gone. Increasingly, the complex set of bodily symptoms that had been hysteria was confused with the 'histrionic'.

The condition's component parts remain, however, alongside more contemporary patterns of symbolizing and diagnosing distress. Anorexia could easily be considered one of those component parts: Freud long saw it as one of the features of hysteria in adolescent girls, part of a number of disoriented appetites. So, too, did Charcot. For him, hysterics always functioned outside the norm: either they were in a state of lethargy and somnolent, or they suffered from insomnia; their organs functioned super-fast or slowed to the point of disappearance; their need to eat was exaggerated into what he calls bulimia, or reduced to abstinence. So-called dissociation or multiple personality disorder stresses one of the other aspects of the late-nineteenth-century.

The *Diagnostic and Statistical Manual of Mental Disorders* (*DSM*), the hymn-book of current psychiatry, no longer lists hysteria. Instead, it takes the fragmentation of the historic condition further and gives it nomenclature which fits more smoothly into the medical and behaviourist preferences of our own turn of the century: 'factitious illness disorder', 'dissociative disorder – conversion type', 'psychogenic pain disorder'.[129] It also lists a 'histrionic personality disorder' which medicalizes behaviour many would consider common, particularly in adolescents. This is characterized as a

pervasive pattern of excessive emotionality and attention seeking, beginning by early adulthood and present in a variety of contexts, as indicated by five (or more) of the following:

— [The individual] is uncomfortable in situations in which he or she is not the center of attention.

- Interaction with others is often characterized by inappropriate sexually seductive or provocative behavior.
- Displays rapidly shifting and shallow expression of emotions.
- Consistently uses physical appearance to draw attention to self.
- Has a style of speech that is excessively impressionistic and lacking in detail.
- Shows self-dramatization, theatricality, and exaggerated expression of emotion.
- Is suggestible, i.e., easily influenced by others or circumstances.
- Considers relationships to be more intimate than they actually are.

For once, the recommendation is that drugs are not indicated, unless this histrionic disorder is tied in with other conditions, such as depression. People who suffer from the disorder, mostly women, can be highly successful, we are told. They are more prone to come for treatment (being attention seekers) than those suffering from other kinds of personality disorder, and tend to do so when romantic attachments have gone awry.

Your and my favourite adolescent, be warned: your life is a psychiatric diagnosis.

Hysteria is one of those conditions that is reinvented for different times and has a cultural malleability almost as dramatic as Augustine herself. Elaine Showalter in her *Hystories*[130] has argued that in the 1990s the United States had become 'the hot zone of psychogenic diseases, new and mutating forms of hysteria amplified by modern communications and fin de siècle anxiety'. She lists amongst these new hysterical syndromes which often convert psychic problems into physical ills or use external sources as evidence for them: chronic fatigue syndrome, multiple personality, recovered memory and satanic ritual abuse.

The very malleability of hysteria might make us suspect the science-laden certainties with which the *DSM* names its component parts, let alone the possible cures. After all, hysteria's long and florid history stretches back to the Egyptians and the Greeks. Initially based on the idea that the womb, or uterus, was a free-floating entity which could leave its moorings, when a woman was dissatisfied, to travel around the body and disrupt everything in its passage, hysteria was thought to be able to produce any number of symptoms, both physical and mental. The wandering womb in search of gratification could make skin go numb (anaesthesia); engender fits, muteness, paralysis and, of course, that choking breathlessness of 'globus hystericus' when it lodged in the throat. In the *Timaeus*, where he explores origins and the relations between the sexes, Plato noted: 'The womb is an animal which longs to generate children. When it remains barren too long after puberty, it is distressed and sorely disturbed, and straying about in the body and cutting off the passages of the breath, it impedes respiration and brings the sufferer into the extremest anguish and provokes all manner of disease besides.'

With Christianity, some have contended, hysteria took on a supernatural configuration and became a sign of demonic possession: convulsions, muteness, fits – all became signals of concourse with the devil. Trial and punishment or exorcism were the only remedies. Only with the Renaissance did hysteria come back within the scope of medicine. In the late seventeenth century, when nerve-based theories began to be propounded, Thomas Willis proposed a medical model in which the condition was caused by an excess of animal spirits which travelled from brain through nerves to various body parts. George Cheyne gave it a dietary trajectory. Certain of the doctors of the eighteenth century linked it with hypochondriasis, the vapours, and a generalized 'neurosis'. William Cullen, the inventor of the term 'neurosis', placed its causes solidly, though not solely, back in the genitals, and saw it as a condition linked with an excess of sexuality which failed to find its completion in childbirth – hence its incidence among young widows:

> Observations of the dead bodies of patients labouring under hysterics, shew that in most of them the ovaria are affected. These are liable to a turgescence, which gives an irritability to the system; and hence a want of veneral pleasure is assigned as a very common cause of the disease. I will readily allow, that this turgescence, by producing such an irritability, may sometimes excite it; but I cannot consider it as a general cause, or hysterics would be a much more rare distemper. We may here observe, that though the seminal evacuation may in our sex prevent the attack of hysterics, it will not have that effect in females, for this reason: that by it the male purpose of the male economy is fulfilled: not so for

the females; they are also destined for the breeding and bearing of children; and hence evidently we are to account for our diseases attacking young widows.[131]

Cullen may conceive of women's sexuality as rampant, but – unlike many of the medical reporters on the condition – he also finds hysteria in men, if less often, and is unclear whether hysteria may not also be a version of dyspepsia. Following him, Pinel in his *Nosography* comments on the vagueness and over-generality of the category. This means that he is forced back to a primary observation of cases. He notes two: one is of a girl whose menstruation is not yet regular.

This seventeen-year-old is healthy and ruddy of colour: for no attributable reason she falls suddenly into a kind of 'mania' – or what he would rather describe as a sequence of extravagant behaviours which consist of talking to herself, jumping about, tearing off her clothes and throwing them in the fire. This lasts for some five months, then stops during the summer, perhaps because of many trips to the countryside which are followed by the oncoming of menstruation. Three months later the hysteria erupts again: the girl manifests a disgust for her ordinary activities, weeps for no reason, is sombre and taciturn. Soon enough there is loss of speech, spasmodic choking and a sense of strangulation accompanied by an engorgement of the salivary glands, then abundant salivation as in someone who has taken mercury. The girl's mouth, at this point, won't open and the rest of her body is rigid, the pulse almost inaudible, the breathing very slow. There is constipation, but the urine is clear. For three or four days the patient stops eating altogether, and then eats voraciously. Everything seems normal once more – before the whole cycle begins again. During this time the girl's periods stop for five months. Pinel sends the patient to the country for breathing in the open air, exercise and healthy food. And recommends marriage. Once this had taken place, he notes, and her *wishes* were satisfied, the patient recovered.

In his general description of the condition Pinel underlines, as predisposing factors for hysteria, a great physical and moral sensitivity, an abuse of sexual pleasure, lively emotions, voluptuous reading and conversation; deprivation of the pleasures of love after having experienced long satisfaction in that domain, and nursing. Flaubert's Madame

Bovary may well have gone to school in hysteria and helped to spread that version of the 'condition'. Pinel notes that symptoms can be minimal — over-paleness or ruddiness, loss of breath — or, when severe, fainting, fits and loss of sensation can take place. He also notes that the condition can be complicated by melancholy, hypochondria, even epilepsy. Indeed, throughout this time what we might call depression features as a symptom of hysteria. The best kind of treatment, Pinel suggests, is hearty exercise, various palliatives; and in the case of young, ardent women he recommends, like his precursor Hippocrates, marriage.[132]

By the time Charcot arrived on the scene of hysteria, this knowledge had something of the status of an old wives' tale to which the harder truths of neuropathology, drugs, the newly scientific hypnotism, and anatomy were preferred. It is to Charcot's credit that he did not treat the young women who came to him with a wide range of florid symptoms either as malingerers or as posturers. He understood hysteria as a genuine illness which had a neurological basis in a hereditary degeneration of the nervous system. Its status as a disease was provable by the very fact that it had a clinical pattern, the four stages, and could be *relieved* — by pressing on one of the hysterogenic zones, the *ovarie*, for instance — if not *cured*, which was the case for most neurological illnesses. It was the degeneration of the nervous system that made hysterics so susceptible to hypnotism, part and parcel of their illness. Environmental factors, traumas, sexual disturbances — all these for him were simply *agents provocateurs*.

If hysteria flourished under his aegis into a particular set of theatrical symptoms, it was perhaps not due only to malleable patients and the suggestive powers of hypnosis. In the naming of an illness, power relations between doctor and patient can be a delicate set of negotiations with mutual benefits. Hysteria burgeoned because it served as a useful tool in the armoury of fin-de-siècle republican anticlericalism, of which Charcot was such a champion. That anticlericalism went hand in hand with defining a new, more independent, status for women.

Nonetheless, we may not be surprised to find feminists in Charcot's very own time criticizing his condescension towards women, his 'sort of vivisection of women under the pretext of studying a disease for which he knows neither the cause nor the treatment'.[133] But neither should we be surprised that working-class women may have found some liberation in becoming his highly visible patients; and, indeed, to find middle-class women influenced by his patients into a greater openness of behaviour than their families might have approved. Freud's genius, perhaps, was to underline the wider cultural ramifications of hysteria, the collective features of conditions which so distinctly embodied the psychosexual conflicts of their time. One could say that Freud 'medicalized' the twentieth century by locating and naming sexuality as a problem; one could equally say the opposite. By underscoring the shallowness of sanity, our common thrall to the unconscious, Freud helped to destigmatize hysteria and the madnesses in which we all share.

6

SLEEP

Looking back at the last decades of the nineteenth century and the period up until the First World War, what strikes the eye is the peculiar and frequent emphasis on kinds of sleep. Sleep, indeed, is associated with a veritable boom in activity amongst mind doctors, whether they train as neurologists, alienists or psychologists, and whether their patients are poor and come to them in hospitals or more affluent and consult them in clinics or private practice.

There is the sleep which indicates illness – fatigue, exhaustion, hypnotizability. There is the sleep which is linked to therapy, whether as rest cure or the healing kinds of hypnosis. There is also sleep as mediumistic trance which is interpreted as either spiritualism, a communion with the dead, or hysteria. As illness, the medium's sleep, with its array of voices and characters, paves the way for a diagnosis of multiple personality, as explanations move inward, away from the metaphysical and the soul is 'scientized'.[134]

It is as if the period itself, with all its overt emphasis on work and achievement, on new speeds of travel and instant communication across distances – by telephone, telegram, telepathy – both deeply feared and passionately wished for nothing other than sleep. Nervous breakdown, collapse, exhaustion, fatigue, melancholia, punctuate the letters, diaries and case notes of the time, particularly for the growing number of nerve doctors in private practice in Britain[135] and the USA, but also in Germany. The ardour of industrialization and commerce gives way to the world of neurotic aestheticized torpor that Thomas Mann evokes so well, first in the family saga of the rise and fall of the German bourgeoisie which is *Buddenbrooks*, and then in *Death in Venice*.

To unpack the term 'decadence', so often associated with the period, is in fact to arrive at just this: heightened senses, tautly strung and attuned to the finest and subtlest – also need and long for rest, a dying sleep, the obverse of the call to rigid duty and discipline. The will, that backbone of character and action in the latter half of the nineteenth century, the very sign of Empire and industry, is weakening, even as it calls for power. It is worth noting that with Morton Prince and his famous 'multiple' Miss Beauchamp (see page 000), the will itself becomes the will to sleep, to enter the hypnotized state. *Aboulia*, that Greek term which became part of the diagnostic apparatus of the time and was attributed (mostly) to hysterics and neurasthenic women, means simply 'loss of will'. If this sleep of dissociation, for the woman, becomes the more radical will to open her eyes and become another – a spunky, smoking, rebellious gender-crossing Sally, in the case of the prim, timid Miss Beauchamp, say – then this is precisely because what women want is liberation from the indeterminate, hypnotized state into which the customs and morality of the times have penned them. Out of the end of the century's sleep, that waning of the disciplinary will, comes the Freudian dream with its double-edged wish at once for pleasure and for death. Indeed, one way of thinking about the shift is to note that with Freud, all the more rigid, determining and Victorian attributes of 'will' slip into the softer, murkier, and sexier, 'wish'.

Sleep, like wish, is, of course, most often culturally gendered feminine. And when the turn of the century researchers into the mind – whether psychiatrists, neurologists, psychologists, eventually the new century's psychoanalysts or simply philosophers and artists – begin to explore all the ramifications of sleep, their subjects more often than not are women. Sleep is a passive, feminine state, after all. But increasingly it is clear that activity takes place within it. That activity – whether it is dream, somnambulism, the emergence of different personalities or selves or aspects of the self, visitations, or just the nightly work of an unconscious mind – is distinctly other, altered, and seems to share not a little with the hallucinatory, non-rational spheres of madness. When sleep states intrude on waking, as in post-hypnotic suggestion, this is understood as 'pathological'; so too, the other way round, when the sleeper, rather than simply sleeping, walks or talks. The twentieth century is born with Freud's investigation into a sleep state: *The Interpretation of Dreams*, published in 1900. Just a few years later Marcel Proust, who hadn't read the Viennese, begins the novel that marks the modernist century with the words '*Longtemps je me suis couché de bonne heure*' (for a long time I went to bed early), and proceeds to move fitfully in and out of sleep for the next fifty pages.

If the hysterics of the Salpêtrière with their dramatic fits and star turns in lecture theatres hardly seem to be sleepers, this is to forget what Charcot thought of as their propensity for hypnosis, the ease of falling into sleep, into a state of somnambulism, which for him was intrinsic to their condition. In fact, part of the attraction of the Charcotian model of hysteria for the public may well have been that, like music-hall performance, it allows a dominant male to look into a woman's eyes and put her into a trance. In that sleep, like Trilby's Svengali, that great bestselling creation of George du Maurier's which had fin-de-siècle England enthralled, Charcot has the woman utterly in his control: even to the point where a mere touch supposedly brings on orgasm. Charcot is no exploitative Svengali, but he is part of the time's mounting fascination with sleep states, that other consciousness which escapes reason and duty.

Towards the end of the book Svengali's assistant, Gecko, evokes Trilby's double consciousness:

'I will tell you a secret. There were two Trilbys. There was the Trilby you knew . . . But all at once—pr-r-r-out! presto! augenblick! . . . with one wave of his hand over her – with one look of his eye – with a word – Svengali could turn her into the other Trilby, his Trilby, and make her do whatever he liked . . . you might have run a red-hot needle into her and she would not have felt it . . .

'He had but to say "Dors!" and she suddenly became an unconscious Trilby of marble, who could . . . think his thoughts and wish his wishes – and love him at his bidding with a strange unreal factitious love . . . When Svengali's Trilby was singing – or seemed to you as if she were singing – our Trilby was fast asleep . . . in fact, our Trilby was dead . . . and then, suddenly, our Trilby woke up and wondered what it was all about.'

Svengali's use of the French command '*Dors!*' for sleep is no accident, nor is the smattering of Italian and German. Hypnotism was a Europe-wide phenomenon. The papers and popular magazines were filled with stories about it and about trials concerning crimes committed under hypnosis. Performances of hypnotism were widely advertised. Nor was the gendered nature of the relationship between the male hypnotist and the female sleeper or patient something new. Ever since Franz Mesmer had travelled Europe at the end of the previous century and used animal magnetism and trance for various forms of healing, men had taken on the active role and deployed women as patient or subject. In the 1840s, the Scottish surgeon James Braid had medicalized the process he had first witnessed on the stage and had given it a new name, 'hypnosis', because he then assumed the trance state of the mesmerized was physiologically a kind of sleep. By the 1880s, when women had begun to clamour for greater freedoms and power over their own lives, controlling them by putting them to sleep might have felt even more apposite and expedient. Putting them to sleep *for their own good*, as the doctors did, adopting popular performers' means for experimental use, had a double advantage.

While there might have been some visible gains for working-class women in the 'performance' of sleep or trance on theatrical and hospital stage, or as mediums for the growing number of spiritualist séances, particularly in the Protestant countries, the immediate benefits of sleep for middle- and upper-class women are often less clear. The attractions of the invalid role with its sanctioned excuse from duty whether familial or sexual when no other possibilities are on offer, however, must not be underestimated. In a society such as the English, where fragility was a feminine attribute, the sickroom also wore associations with refinement and spirituality.[136] The various anaesthesias – the lack of sensation – that so many of those with hysteria suffered on various parts of their bodies also seem to hold up a mirror to the times: the body, the skin, is not that through which the late nineteenth-century woman, so well wrapped in her clothes, petticoats and corsets, is meant to feel.

Exploring the uses of hypnotism, trance and double consciousness as a key to an unknown province of the mind was high on the agenda for the leading clinicians of the 1890s, whether they called themselves

neurologists, alienists, psychologists or eventually, after 1896, psychoanalysts, as well as for philosophers and criminologists. In Paris, during
the Great Exhibition of 1889, while the Eiffel Tower displayed the feats
and conquest of the skies of which modern engineering was capable,
from 8 to 12 August adventurers in the mind sciences gathered at the
First International Congress for Experimental and Therapeutic
Hypnotism, which followed on from the International Congress on
Physiological Psychology.

The congress on hypnotism brought together famous names from
America as well as Europe. The philosopher and psychologist William
James came from Boston, seedbed of the new psychology. The most
famous medical user of hypnotism apart from Charcot, Hippolyte
Bernheim, spoke. An opponent of Charcot's and an expert in internal
medicine who had become head of what became known as the Nancy
School — where hypnotism, which he saw as a purely psychological
phenomenon, was used to treat 'organic' diseases of the nervous
system — Bernheim had influenced amongst many others the young
Freud, who came to Nancy for a month in 1889 just before attending the
Paris congress. Bernheim's hypnosis was intended 'therapeutically',
unlike Charcot's, which was simply understood as a test for a susceptibility to hysteria. August Forel, doyen of Swiss psychiatry, represented
the famous Burghölzli Hospital (see page 000), where the hypnotism he
had learned from Bernheim in Nancy was regularly practised on nurses
seeking quiet, as well as on the agitated patients they attempted to tend.

From England came Frederick Myers, founder of the Society for
Psychical Research, which had an impact not only on Bloomsbury and
English psychoanalysis, but on William James at Harvard and various
researchers around Europe. Cesare Lombroso, another pioneer in a new
field, came from Italy. A positivist and a progressive in terms of punishment, Lombroso's work in criminology had nonetheless attempted
to establish the hereditary nature of deviance, and posited an atavistic
'born criminal' whose degeneracy was identifiable through physical features such as fleshy lips, large jaw, pitcher-shaped ears and high
cheekbones. 1889 was the year in which Lombroso published his *Man of
Genius*, which argued a close link between genius and insanity.

The fame of the conference participants and the popularity of hypnotism as a subject meant that the conference attracted a host of

journalists from some thirty publications around the world. They would spread the word, along with the gestures and behaviours of the hypnotized. The altered minds and altered states that hypnotism could engender became not only clinical tools or psychological experiment for a growing cohort of specialists and researchers, but a subject that fascinated the masses just as monomania had before.

Amongst the conference participants that summer was Pierre Janet, then a doctoral student whose experiments with long-distance hypnosis and the sleep states of hysteria had captured the attention of professionals. A philosopher who was soon to be a doctor, Janet had been invited by Charcot to oversee the psychological laboratory of the Salpêtrière that very year. Janet's findings, his many books, his influence particularly on American practitioners, have been largely overshadowed by Freud. They have only come into prominent view again, after a century, with the rise of the multiple-personality movement in the United States, which needed a non-psychoanalytic precursor to give credibility to their ever more prevalent diagnosis.

DOUBLES, DISSOCIATION AND HYPNOSIS

Addressing the special centenary meeting of the Bloomingdale Asylum in New York in May 1921, Pierre Janet reminisced about his days with Charcot and underlined the strangeness of the divisions in the world of mind-doctoring.

> During the whole of the nineteenth century the radical division of neuroses and psychoses was accepted as a dogma; on the one side, one described epilepsies, hysterias, neurasthenias; on the other, one studied manias, melancholias, paranoias, dementias, without preoccupying oneself in the least with the connections those very ill-defined disorders might have. This division was accentuated by the organization of the studies and the treatment of the patients . . .
>
> This complete division did not fail to bring about singular and unfortunate consequences. In a hospital such as La Salpêtrière the tic sufferers, the impulsive, those beset with obsessions, the hysterical with fits and delirium were placed near the organic hemiplegics and the tabetics who

did not resemble them in the least, and completely separated from the melancholic, the confused, the systematically raving, notwithstanding evident analogies . . . This distinction between the neurotic sufferer and the mental sufferer was mostly arbitrary and depended more than was believed on the patient's social position and fortune. Important and rich families could not be resigned to see one of their members blemished by the name of lunatic, and the physician very often qualified him as neurasthenic to please the family.[137]

Janet's comments underscore the sense of the old adage that what is madness in the poor is mere eccentricity in the rich. They also look back with the wisdom of hindsight on what seem to be the aberrant classifications and odd mind/body divisions of the turn of the nineteenth century, a generational pattern which will repeat itself throughout the history of the mind sciences. As if trapped in the swing of a vast pendulum, the mind doctors focused their attention on physical or biological explanations only to be corrected by their followers, who emphasized the psychological and mental, and then back again.

Janet's criticism of his old master Charcot is, however, tempered. His work with hysterics pointed the way for those with a more psychological orientation, such as Janet himself. Born into a prosperous intellectual family, son of a Parisian legal editor, Janet began his academic career by studying philosophy at the elite Ecole Normale during 1879–82, where his contemporaries were Emile Durkheim, the founder of the new field of sociology, and Henri Bergson, the philosopher who was so to influence Proust with his work on memory – a major question for the epoch. Janet's interests were soon to move from a philosophical reflection on the self and memory to a more practical investigation of the problem.

It was in 1882 that Charcot publicized his use of hypnosis with the Salpêtrière hysterics. During the six years before, Eugène Azam (1822–99), son of an alienist, and a Bordeaux high-flier who was to become in turn chief surgeon at the asylum for women there, had published numerous papers on the strange doubling of personality he had witnessed and the scientific uses to which he had put hypnosis. These made an early patient of his, 'Félida X', famous. Félida, a seamstress, had from the age of thirteen suffered from a wide variety of hysterical

symptoms – terrible headaches, neuralgia, and eventually extreme pulmonary and gastric bleeding. There was no evident physiological basis
for her pain or the blood that poured from her mouth. On top of this,
she fell into daily trances, without the use of hypnosis. She awoke from
these after a few minutes into a better version of herself: pain-free, happier and, as Azam discovered when he did use hypnosis on her, far
cleverer. This second Félida knew everything about the first, had clear
memory of her 'ordinary' state in which she was most often morose and
depressed. But the first Félida, who returned after a few hours, knew
nothing of her more vivacious double. When she came to Azam to
complain of stomach pains and he determined she was pregnant, it was
only the second Félida who admitted to it and promptly went off to
marry her beau.

By the time he started writing about her, Azam was treating Félida X
once more. Now her secondary personality was longer in evidence than
her first one. But it was the first which was present through each of her
eleven childbirths. It was also the first Félida who worked hard in the
family grocery, and grew increasingly miserable with the growing severity of her pains and the dramatic bleeding from the mouth. Azam
found no cure for her condition. His hypnosis was largely a form of
experimental observation, part of the new science of psychology that
the Germans, principally, had pioneered.

Or so it came to seem from the writing of another major influence
on Pierre Janet – Théodule Ribot. Professor of the newly established
Chair of Psychology at the Sorbonne and then at the Collège de France,
Ribot had already discussed English experimental psychology when, in
1876, he wrote a history of the field in Germany, which at once traced a
lineage for the subject and set out what became the classic boundaries
of the discipline. In *La Psychologie allemande contemporaine* (translated ten
years later and widely disseminated as *German Psychology of Today*) Ribot
showed how psychology had been mapped out by Herbart, Fechner
and Wundt by refuting Kant's prediction that it could never be raised to
the rank of an exact natural science. These pioneering scientists had
shown that mathematics could indeed be applied to internal phenomena; and that these subjective phenomena were accessible to
experiment.

Ribot's ideas consolidated the new and radical positivist position, so closely allied with the secular thrust of the Third Republic. Like the English empiricists, the German scientists provided solid counter-arguments to any religious notion of a single and unitary transcendental consciousness, proposed by the French spiritualists and associated with the Second Empire. Taine, positivism's most powerful exponent, conceived of a Lockean self which was shaped out of 'sensations, memories, images, ideas, perceptions, conceptions, which are diverse and transient'.[138] For Ribot, hypnotism provided a powerful method of experimenting with this shifting self. Azam's Félida fell in perfectly with the notion. Her 'disease' was an 'experiment in nature', and he included Azam's description of her case in the series of monographs on diseases of memory, the will and personality which he wrote through the 1880s.

Paul Janet, Pierre Janet's uncle, an important philosopher of the spiritualist persuasion, was, despite his position, greatly influenced by these developments in psychology. He, too, wrote about Félida and other cases of doubling. Indeed *dédoublement*, or 'doublings of personality', had now been found not only in France, but in England, Switzerland and America.[139] Through the 1880s, such cases helped to shape the time's imagination and conception of itself. They became a popular feature in the literature of the day. Stevenson's *Dr Jekyll and Mr Hyde* of 1885,[140] Wilde's *Picture of Dorian Gray*, Dostoievksi's *The Double* can all be seen as part of the period's interrogation of the self. (Dostoievski, indeed, was dubbed by a contemporary 'the Shakespeare of the lunatic asylum'.) Poised on the edge of the Gothic in an idiom of good and evil that is already shaky, these are stories contemporaneous with the experiments in hypnosis and psychology. In the latter, the language of the moral, and certainly of the spiritual, gives way to the language of science and disease. Where demons reign, the 'positivist' neurologist or psychologist sees the slippages of conscious mind and identity. He attributes these to lesions and degeneration and/or to an un(sub)conscious which reigns in sleep and can produce doubles or alternative selves, aberrations of memory, alongside dreams and secret drives. French doublings, or *dédoublement*, were also translated as 'splitting', and were elided in the mid-twentieth century with American ideas about split personality.

Pierre Janet read Ribot while he was studying philosophy at the Ecole Normale and followed his monographs through the 1880s. Together with the case of Félida and Charcot's clear 1882 positioning of hypnosis as a scientific tool rather than a mere popular spectacle, set out in his paper to the Academy of Sciences,[141] Ribot's work helped to shape and feed Pierre Janet's interest in sleep pathologies. During Janet's second teaching job in Le Havre and while he was gathering material for his thesis – in part at the local hospital, where he was eventually given a small ward for hysterics that he nicknamed 'Salle Saint-Charcot' – he looked around for a suitable subject for psychological experimentation. He soon found her in 'Léonie', who could write while asleep, thus 'automatically'.

A forty-five-year-old peasant woman, Léonie was referred to Pierre Janet by a well known Le Havre doctor. She served as a subject for the first time with Janet for three weeks in September–October 1885. Highly susceptible to hypnosis, she even responded to it at a distance, and engaged in automatic writing during which a second 'sleeping' self emerged, an independent self, calling herself Léontine, who was also capable of commenting on Léonie's parlous state in a letter to Janet.

A paper presented in November about Léonie on Pierre's behalf by his Uncle Paul created a stir at the Société de Psychologie Physiologique in Paris, and in April 1886 a delegation arrived from Paris and from the Psychical Research Society in England to observe Janet's experiments. To Janet's chagrin, he was to find that Léonie's great suggestibility was in fact the residue of earlier 'experiments'. She was in that sense an unreliable subject, one already trained in the ways of hypnotism by earlier, 'unscientific' magnetizers, in particular one known as Dr Perrier. While Léontine, Léonie's second, hypnotized self, was in the throes of hallucination, she produced a third personality called Lénore. Lénore confessed to Janet that she had been created by the animal magnetizer. Astonishingly, this earlier self suffered from none of the anaesthesias that both Léonie and Léontine had. Perhaps produced as a cure for hysteria by Perrier, this Lénore was 'healthy' and had alternated with Léonie over more years than had Léontine.

Janet described Léonie's case in the papers which together made up his doctoral thesis, L'Automatisme psychologique (1889), where fourteen hysterical women, five men, and eight psychotics and epileptics are featured. Léonie had taught him several things. Namely, that it is essential to check patients' long histories to ascertain how they might have been influenced by past treatments; it is important to examine them alone, without observers, and to record everything that is said and done by them.

Janet concluded from his research that the human subject did not have a single consciousness: parts of the mind could live alongside each other in mutual ignorance. The waking or normal personality had no memory of the hypnotized state. The subject who arose in hypnosis, however, did remember and know about the waking state and sometimes about other successive or earlier states. Such states could come with their own mood or character and were called by other investigators, such as Morton Prince, 'alternating personalities', and more recently in America, 'multiples'.

Partial automatism, what we might call trance, could be induced in the subject: it was evident in feats of automatic writing or when instructions given under hypnosis were unknowingly carried out by the subject while 'awake'. Or the subject might suddenly burst into tears without being aware of the reason. Therapeutically, this existence of different areas of consciousness meant that symptoms could be worked on in one without the other being aware. What is perhaps most astonishing in Janet's experiments is that he found that, like Azam with Félida, he could replace the normal waking personality, with all its symptoms, with another personality that seemed altogether healthy. He gave this phenomenon the name of 'complete somnambulism'. Other patients were to repeat aspects of Léonie's case, even though they had not been subject to prior magnetizers.

Nineteen-year-old Lucie suffered from convulsions and delirium, brought on by terror, as well as from anaesthesias. These were labelled as 'hysterical' symptoms. They disappeared when Janet put her into 'hypnotic sleep', a state she forgot when she was woken. However, if Janet clapped his hands some time after she had woken, she would follow an instruction he had given her in her sleep state and do what he had asked, though without understanding what drove her to the action. Continuing his experiments into the existence of a 'subconscious' state that could propel actions without the subject's awareness, Janet would — while Lucie was distracted and talking to someone else — whisper questions to her. She answered these by 'automatic writing'. It was in this writing that she revealed the source of the fear that characterized her madness: when she was seven, two men hiding behind a curtain had frightened her, had done so as a joke.

Since Lucie roundly denied that she had written what was in front of her, Janet gave her writing second self, who could also feel sensation where Lucie could not, another name: Adrienne. Soon Adrienne began to speak and became the dominant consciousness. Unlike Lucie, she could remember everything, and like Félida's other self, she exhibited none of Lucie's hysterical symptoms. Janet called Lucie in her state as Adrienne another instance of 'complete somnambulism'. This second consciousness lasted only a short time before Lucie, with all her ailments, returned. Janet thought of a new 'therapeutic' experiment: he began to suggest anaesthesias to Adrienne, and as he did so, Lucie began to have sensation exactly where Adrienne lost it. Interestingly, when her ability to feel sensation had completely returned, she lost her suggestibility, her special pliant relationship to Janet the hypnotist, which had been part of her 'hysteria'. Now Adrienne could no longer be wooed back. Clearly, Janet deduced, anaesthesia was linked to amnesia. Lockean in this respect, Janet reasoned that memory was dependent on sensation. 'When a particular kind of sensation has been abolished, the images and as a result the memories of phenomena that have been created by that sensation are abolished as well.'[142]

Janet thought of Lucie as an hysteric, that catch-all diagnosis for the period. He understood the ability to dissociate, to have a *double conscience*, as a quintessential part of the pathology. Freud and Breuer in *Studies on Hysteria* (1895) acknowledge their debt to him:

> The longer we have been occupied with these phenomena the more we have become convinced that the splitting of consciousness which is so striking in the well-known classical cases under the form of 'double conscience' is present to a rudimentary degree in every hysteria, and that a tendency to such dissociation, and with it the emergence of abnormal states of consciousness (which we shall bring together under the term 'hypnoid'), is the basic phenomenon of this neurosis.

Freud in 1895 had 'nothing new to say on the question of the origin of these dispositional hypnoid states', except to note that women's work made them particularly susceptible to trance and its accompanying doubling. These hypnoid states, 'it would seem, grow out of the day-dreams which are so common even in healthy people and to which needlework and similar occupations render women especially prone'.[143] Shades of Mary Lamb.

As ever, with Freud, and this is certainly the origin of his pervasive influence over twentieth-century conceptions of the human, he normalizes pathological tendencies, situating what it is that might make us mad at the very heart of what we are. The tug in Freud's work is always and ever to bring into the open our kinship with the mental processes of patients who manifest the most extreme of symptoms, such as hysterics do in their dissociated condition: 'in their hypnoid states they are insane, as we all are in dreams. Whereas, however, our dream-psychoses have no effect upon our waking state, the products of hypnoid states intrude into waking life in the form of hysterical symptoms.'

These hysterical symptoms are translations into bodily ills, for both Freud and Janet in this early period of their work, of memories repressed because the horror the initial lived experience aroused was impossible for the patient to confront. This particular aberration of memory was one Freud dubbed 'conversion hysteria'. It played itself out in the case of Janet's Marie as it did in Freud and Breuer's Anna O, and in both cases led to similar forms of treatment.

Marie and Anna O

Nineteen-year-old Marie arrived at the Le Havre hospital suffering from extreme attacks of convulsive delirium. During these fits she saw blood and fire everywhere, and in horror would try to flee. Reverting to a childhood self, she would leap and jump on furniture and call for mother. Her attacks came on regularly and always just preceded menstruation. This was accompanied by intense pain, nervous spasms and shivering. Marie also suffered from blindness in one eye, and various anaesthesias with no physical basis – which Janet later linked to particular forgettings. During the months in which he merely observed her, Janet noted a pattern. Marie's period lasted for about twenty hours before it stopped suddenly and the girl went into her 'hysterical crisis'. This ended after two days, in a great vomiting of blood.

After eight months, Janet had the inspiration of hypnotizing Marie in order to find out how 'her periods had been inaugurated and had been interrupted'.[144] Under hypnosis, Marie told Janet that when she started her periods around the age of thirteen, she tried to stop the shaming flow by plunging herself secretly into a tub of cold water. Her period stopped, but violent shivering and several days of delirium came in its place. After that, her period didn't return for five years. During this time she was well. When the menstrual flow started again, it came with the symptoms she enacted in the hospital. The shivering was evidently related to her immersion in freezing water, as was the abrupt and now repeated stopping of the flow. Marie remembered none of this phase of her life when she was awake.

Janet set about removing the subconscious *idée fixe* which had stopped Marie's periods and brought on the accompanying attacks. To do so he had to bring her back to her thirteenth year and the initial circumstances of the delirium. Then, while she was under hypnosis, he convinced her that her menstruation had never been interrupted, and no subsequent illness had been suffered. In other words, he erased an unconscious memory. That done, Marie's next period proceeded without a hitch.

But there were more memories to remove: the fear of blood was also linked for Marie with the death she had witnessed of an old woman plunging down a flight of stairs. Janet replaced this with a scene which had the old woman merely stumbling, with no suicidal intention. Marie's 'attacks of terror' ceased. As for her blindness, under hypnosis Janet traced it to a scene in Marie's sixth year when she had been forced to share a bed with a child suffering from impetigo, one side of whose face was wholly covered in hideous pustules. Her fear of the child had been converted into an unconscious mimicking of the malady. Under hypnosis, Janet turned the feared child into a healthy, sweet and unfrightening creature, and after two sessions Marie's hysterical blindness disappeared.

This 'cathartic' method of removing symptoms while the patient is under hypnosis is one Joseph Breuer practised in what has been enshrined as the founding case of psychoanalysis. Anna O, or the real Bertha Pappenheim, is a prime exemplar of the ways in which symptoms are the expression of unconscious ideas – forgotten or repressed scenes of great emotional impact which return in disguise by imprinting themselves on the body.

Freud's early mentor, Breuer was a consultant in internal medicine, who like many internists of the time took on 'nervous' patients. He treated Anna O in 1881, though the case was only written up for *Studies on Hysteria* much later, in 1895. The young woman, daughter of a wealthy and respected but traditional and over-protective Jewish family, had fallen ill at the age of twenty-one while nursing her father, to whom she was greatly attached. Clever and imaginative, though schooled at home rather than permitted the formal education of her brother, Anna had early developed a habit of daydreaming, or entering her own 'private theatre'. With her father's illness, this imaginative escapism escalated into a *conscience seconde*, a dissociated trance state into which various hallucinations gradually entered, completely incapacitating her.

Alongside this doubling, Anna generated a series of severe symptoms — paralyses, anaesthesias, coughs and finally a deterioration in language which left her German a series of nouns without syntax and, in stretches, allowed her to speak coherently only in English. With her father's death, some eight months after his and Anna's illnesses had invaded their lives, her condition worsened. She could no longer recognize people. Often subject to states of manic anger, she couldn't sleep. She also refused food and water, though her doctor, whose love she craved rather more intensely than Breuer noticed, was able to distract her into eating far better than anyone else — and eventually into the 'chimney sweeping' which formed the basis of her treatment.

In her dissociated second state — the deep hypnotic trance she called her 'clouds', which took her over as evening approached — Anna would mutter and act out scenes. Breuer observed that if he or someone repeated her words back to her, she would incorporate these into tales, charming at first, though after her father's death they took on a horrifying aspect. Breuer encouraged her storytelling. After recounting the most ghastly scenes, Anna would feel better. This 'chimney-sweeping', the beginning of what she named the 'talking cure' was in place.

Not that any of this worked miracles. Anna grew worse, then better, then worse again. She was transported to a country house adjacent to a sanatorium and then back to Vienna for more regular sessions with Breuer. He had become aware that if Anna told a story that related to the first appearance of a symptom, it would disappear. Then, something bizarre happened. It became clear to Breuer that, in her night-time trance state, Anna was living out a period before her father's death and had forgotten everything that came after, whereas in the daytime, she inhabited the same time frame as everyone else. Freud and Breuer recount:

> The change-over from one state to another occurred spontaneously but could also be very easily brought about by any sense-impression which vividly recalled the previous year. One had only to hold up an orange before her eyes (oranges were what she had chiefly lived on during the first part of her illness) in order to carry her over from the year 1882 to the year 1881. But this transfer into the past did not take place in a general or indefinite manner; she lived through the previous winter day by day.[145]

Her mother's diary of the previous year confirmed Anna's revisiting of the past exactly. The realization brought on an intensive period of clinical work, during which each of Anna's symptoms was traced to its source in a scene or idea. 'In this way her paralytic contractures and anaesthesias, disorders of vision and hearing of every sort, neuralgias, coughing, tremors, etc., and finally her disturbances of speech were "talked away".'[146]

This was difficult work and it took its toll: Anna's symptoms intensified as she relived the past of each of them in turn. Her inability to drink, it transpired during this 'chimney sweeping', was linked to or 'converted' from a memory of asking her governess for a glass of water only to see the dog slobbering and drinking from it. Her hallucinated snakes, paralysis of the arm and disintegration of language came from a terrible night when, sitting by her sick father's bedside in a waking dream, she had seen a snake (there were snakes in the garden) slithering down the wall to bite him. She couldn't lift her arm to ward the creature off. It was paralysed, and the fingers had turned into little snakes with death heads. She tried to pray but language failed her, except for English and some childhood rhymes.

Anna's case proved, Freud later noted in one of his many formulations on the stepping-stones to psychoanalysis, that hysterical symptoms are residues [reminiscences] of profoundly moving experiences, which have been withdrawn from everyday consciousness, and that their form is determined (in a manner that excludes deliberate action) by details of the traumatic effects of the experiences. On this view, the therapeutic prospects lie in the possibility of getting rid of this 'repression', so as to allow part of the unconscious psychical material to become conscious and thus to deprive it of its pathogenic power.[147]

Freud and Breuer emphatically insisted that Anna, like all the other cases in the *Studies on Hysteria*, was a highly intelligent and accomplished young woman: 'Among hysterics may be found people of the clearest intellect, strongest will, greatest character and highest critical power.'

This insistence is important for a number of reasons. First of all, it obviates any slippage between inferior mental abilities and a proclivity for madness in women, who before the First World War form the majority of cases of what is diagnosed as hysteria. Such a slippage had long played into the hands of nineteenth-century nerve doctors. Then, too, Breuer and Freud want to distinguish their stance from Janet and indeed Charcot, both of whom were prone to find fundamental explanations for insanity in inherited degenerate tendencies, perhaps in part because their patients came from the poor in mental institutions rather than from the middle class. For Freud 'dissociation' or hysteria itself is not due to any constitutional incapacity in the patient for holding mental processes together. Rather, the disintegration of mental life, or dissociation, comes from the psychical process he calls 'repression' – a psychic procedure common in *all* human development. The exorbitant energy this splitting off of an unwanted part of a past self takes in certain people is what gives patients an air of mental incapacity. He suggests thinking of dissociation as akin to 'preoccupation', a mental activity which might make any ordinary person seem momentarily less than intelligent.

It is clear in all this that even as early as the *Studies on Hysteria,* Freud's project differs substantially from Janet's and the other psychologists who focused in on doubling or multiples, and the sleep states and hypnosis which produced them. None of Freud's hysterics are somehow navigated under hypnosis into a sphere where 'alters', or alternating personalities, with different characters take shape. Indeed, Freud is less interested in the startling phenomena splitting can give rise to, than in

what in life motivates it. These motive forces range as broadly as conflicts over the sexual morality of the day, which hypocritically enshrines
abstinence and ignorance as virtues, particularly for women, to childhood sexual seduction, to traumas occasioned by fears irreconcilable
with desires. More specifically, Freud talks of splitting as a psychic *defence*
against mutually incompatible ideas. Later in his work, he describes the
growing child as subject to conflicts which come from both within and
without and need defending against. Inner instinctual demands may be
coped with through repression: demands from the external world can
be so distressing that only disavowing any perception of them will leave
the child intact.

By the time the *Studies* is written, Freud is no longer practising hypnosis. He is as sceptical of it as he is of the cathartic method, even
though that may work well enough for the removal of hysterical symptoms and provide momentary relief for the patient. Hypnosis, however,
has often failed him therapeutically. Symptoms thus removed tend to
recur. Some patients cannot be easily hypnotized. Others are too malleable under hypnosis, produce symptoms or their relief simply to
please their doctor, or fall in love with him. Freud found he could get
to what occasioned the illness simply by insisting that the patient knew
what it was and by working through associations to his or her 'resistance' to knowing. But Freud's later work grows into another story,
which dominates the next century.

Meanwhile, Janet's ideas about therapeutic hypnosis and associated
sleep states such as automatic writing in order to remove 'subconscious
fixed ideas' continued to have a significant influence. In the United
States, his procedures, like his understanding of the doubling of personality were to be of particular importance both to William James and
to Morton Prince. In Switzerland, they helped to set the scene for a
ground-breaking study of a medium and the many personalities who
spoke through her.

SPIRITIST SLEEP

During the fin-de-siècle, the séance served as a popular site for those
interested in encounters with their dear departed dead or in reassurance

about the existence of a spiritual sphere. The rise of spiritualism — 'spiritism' for the French — alongside the theosophy of Madame Blavatsky and a general interest in the occult and reincarnation, gave equal and opposite rise to a rash of critics and sceptics. They judged the mediums' activities as hypnotic charlatanry performed for the ignorant and gullible. In the historical stakes, this latter perspective has won out. But at a time when wireless telegraphy made telepathy seem a scientific possibility worth exploring, when telephones brought disembodied voices into a room, when astronomers hailed the discovery of canals on Mars and the possibility of its habitation, science and spiritualism could occasionally be confused — or at least seen to have some common strands of reality and, through experimentation, a common goal.

Certainly, spiritualism's emphasis on proof, on giving evidence for the existence of an afterlife, took its impetus from science, its twin, rather than from traditional religion's emphasis on faith, belief, and the received wisdom of a hierarchy. Then, too, the high priests of this modern movement were largely in fact priestesses, thoroughly modern women who could transgress the boundaries of gender by taking on male roles in trance, who might even be paid for the wisdom that spoke through them.

Mediums, and the spirits they heard or embodied in trance, were also subjects of fascination for a wide variety of researchers into the new psychical sciences. Both philosophers and psychologists, amongst them William James, the Geneva-based Théodore Flournoy and Frederick Myers, considered automatic writing, crystal gazing, speaking in trance and — doing so in a number of languages unknown to the sleeper or perhaps entirely invented (glossolalia) — activities demanding scientific study for what they revealed about the human mind.

During the 1880s Myers, whom William James called the founder of 'Gothic' psychology, wrote a series of articles on the abnormal and the supranormal where he probed what he called the subliminal as it emerged in trance states and dreams. He was one of the founders, in 1882, of the Cambridge-based Society for Psychical Research, which attracted the attention of Freud and Jung and so impressed James that he founded an American equivalent some years later. The Society and its subcommittees set out to make an unbiased study of thought

transference (which Myers renamed telepathy), mesmerism, hypnotism and clairvoyance; of 'sensitives' and mediums; apparitions of all
types; levitations, materializations and other physical phenomena associated with séances.

Myers, like his friend the creator of Sherlock Holmes, Arthur Conan
Doyle, ended up believing in the mediums he studied and in the truth
of the spiritualist claims. Théodore Flournoy's research took him in a
more earth-bound direction, though the famous medium he studied,
Hélène Smith, travelled *From India to the Planet Mars* (1900), as he entitled
the bestselling and instantly translated book he wrote about her case.

Flournoy (1854–1921), two years older than Freud, had, like Janet,
both a philosophical and a medical formation. He had also studied
experimental psychology in Leipzig with its most famous protagonist
Wilhelm Wundt, and it was undoubtedly because of Wundt's influence
that when he was appointed Professor of Psychophysiology in 1891 in
Geneva he insisted on the post being in the Faculty of Sciences, where
he also founded a psychological laboratory. But, as he noted, where
human psychology is concerned, an hour spent in a nursery or in a
séance is worth several years in the laboratory.[148] Indeed, the medium
herself, with her many voices and many selves, provided a living laboratory for how the psyche worked.

In *Spiritism and Psychology* Flournoy described the medium as a person
'ordinarily of the feminine sex' who, having experienced nothing more
than a little sleepwalking, daydreams and presentiments, is thrust by
the death of a dear one into this new activity. She tries her hand at
table tapping or automatic writing, and finds she is receiving messages.
What makes the medium talented and distinguishes her from ordinary
people is simply the permeability of the usual barrier between sleep
and waking. In her, this borderline isn't stable: hallucinations, both
auditory and visual, submerged ideas and emotions easily make their
way across. Some doctors collided the medium with the hysteric and
bemoaned the popularity of mediumship. It encouraged dissociation
and increased the number of hysterics. Flournoy, however, made a distinction between the two and thought they should be studied
separately. Unlike hysterics, mediums were healthy when out of the
trance state which accompanied the séance. Through his medium
Hélène Smith he also noted that in the trance state a 'subliminal

imagination' was at work and at play. With its 'mythopoetic' potential, this was the source of all creativity as well as the source of the medium's revelations. Moreover, this subliminal sphere provided compensation for what life hadn't fulfilled, and offered psychic protection[149]. Flournoy thus gives us a conception of the unconscious as both the fount of creativity and play and the sphere that shores up the individual.

Given this understanding of the unconscious and of trance, it follows that Carl Gustav Jung, whose personal history incorporated a number of 'seers', should find inspiration, when still a young man working at the Burghölzli Hospital, in Flournoy's *From India to the Planet Mars* and in Flournoy himself, a teacher to set against Freud and his rationalism.[150] Jung's doctoral dissertation, 'On the Psychology and Pathology of So-Called Occult Phenomena', written in the first years of the new century, includes his own research into mediumistic states. The medium in question was his cousin Hélène Preiswerk, whose trances he had witnessed and probably influenced during the years leading up to 1900.[151] She has certain features in common with Flournoy's Hélène.

Helly, as the family called her, was interested in the Italian Renaissance and while still a schoolgirl had imagined herself in a previous life as betrothed to a nobleman named Sforza. In trance, she became a Renaissance princess who lived vivid romantic adventures. These florid accounts were interspersed with strange information about her family, which subsequently proved to be true, as if she had received the news telepathically. Helly developed a crush on Carl, who was six years older than her. When she heard that he claimed an ancestor in Goethe, she found her own ancestral worthies. She received visits from their mutual dead grandfather, a one-time head of the Swiss Reformed Church who now took her on far-flung spiritist journeys.

The 'family' séances which Jung attended began in 1895, when Helly was only fourteen. When he embarked on his psychiatric studies, he decided to observe Helly in controlled circumstances. The talented adolescent took on not only the elders voices, but could sing — something she couldn't do when awake. She also, he discovered as he explored her mediumship, incorporated present and long-ago reading into her 'visions'. These, as time passed, grew increasingly sexual: her trance persona became Carl's lover. It was clear to all that the séances were being enacted in order to attract Carl's attention. The family grew worried and when Helly, after one séance, could not be woken from delirium, her mother took action. By the autumn of '98, the girl had been sent off to France to apprentice as a dressmaker.

In his dissertation, Jung lightly masked Helly and the family's identity, though they were recognizable to themselves and upset at the terminology which linked their 'occult' propensities with medical problems and a weak inheritance. Not that Jung, himself subject to visionary experience, altogether disavowed the spiritualist content of what he nonetheless argued was mostly a psychological, rather than a mystical, state of trance in his cousin's case.

Flournoy left less room to occult possibility than Jung, even though the sources of his medium's spirit journeys were more difficult to locate in her own experience; and, unlike Helly, she had moved out of that adolescent impressionability and mimetic potential so close to the plasticity of hysteria. Hélène Smith, who, it seems, chose this name for herself – perhaps borrowing the Hélène from Flournoy's daughter – was in fact born Elise-Catherine Müller in Martigny, Switzerland, in 1861. At the time that Flournoy met her in December 1894 she was a highly placed employee in a department store, a woman of 'irreproachable character' who offered her mediumistic services 'unpaid' in séances, since she was a believer. Her father was Hungarian and had a capacity for languages, which Flournoy later linked to his medium's own skills in the invention of 'Martian'; while on her mother's side there was some experience of 'automatisms'. Tall, healthy, attractive, intelligent and with none of the tragic aspect of the sibyls of tradition, Hélène perfectly suited Flournoy's search for an experimental subject. After six months and some twenty séances, he wrote jubilantly to William James in Boston: 'this woman is a veritable museum of all possible phenomena and has a repertoire of illimitable variety: she makes the table talk, – she hears voices, – she has visions, hallucinations, tactile and olfactory, – automatic writing – sometimes complete somnambulism, catalepsy, trances . . . all the classical hysterical phenomena – present themselves in turn, in any order and in the most unexpected fashion'.

As Flournoy observed Hélène, he developed a theory to accompany the observations: 'the phenomena were evidently the automatic reproduction of forgotten memories – or memories registered unconsciously. There is actually in the nature of this medium a second personality who perceives and recalls instants which escape ordinary awareness.'[152] He calls this ability 'Cryptomnesia'. The medium, like all of us, knows more than she knows, and in that trance state which is a waking unconsciousness, exhibits the perceptions her unconscious has stored, transforming them along the way, adding a component of fantasy.

Flournoy understands buried memory and the unconscious as a storehouse for romantic fabulation. He is alert to the workings of suggestion. His medium effectively complies with his expectations. Her powers develop the more he observes, interviews, pinches, prods, asks her to repeat her strange linguistic structures:[153] 'Even if total somnambulism would have inevitably been eventually developed by virtue of an organic predisposition and of a tendency favourable to hypnosis states,' Flournoy writes, 'it is nevertheless probable that I aided in hastening its appearance by my presence as well as by a few experiments which I permitted myself to make upon Hélène.'[154] William James had already in 1890 made the point about the suggestibility of the medium or hysteric and the way in which visions or symptoms were joint creations. 'With the extraordinary perspicacity and subtlety of perception which subjects often display for all that concerns the operator with whom they are en rapport, it is hard to keep them ignorant of anything he expects. Thus it happens that one easily verifies on new subjects what one has already seen on old ones, or any desired symptoms of which one may have heard or read.'[155]

The wild 'subliminal romances' which Hélène produces in her new full trance state, her journeys to Mars and invention of Martian, are far more adventurous than anything she indulged in before Flournoy's observations. Then, too, the Hinduo Prince she meets in her persona as the daughter of an Arab sheik bears a marked resemblance to him. Revealing this to the reader, Flournoy offers a rare Freudian explanation and uses the German term *Abwehr Psychosen*[156] or defence psychosis. He is letting the sophisticated 'scientific' reader know that Hélène's move is a hysterical defence against a sexual attraction which is incompatible with her ideas and so expresses itself in this mediumistic fantasy. This is one of the few times in this potboiler of a journey *From India to the Planet Mars*, more Jules Verne than scientific investigation, when

Flournoy has recourse to a piece of psychological terminology in another language. He is, of course, tactfully protecting Hélène's honour, defending her from herself, since she will read the book. He is also, one suspects, protecting his own reputation.

Flournoy's book became a bestseller in both Europe and America, going into three editions in three months and far outstripping in sales Freud's contemporaneous *Interpretation of Dreams*. William James hailed the book as the decisive step in 'converting psychical research into a respectable science'. Spiritualists, however, were angry: Flournoy had exposed Hélène Smith's visions and trance journeys as fabrications; no theories of a creative subliminal consciousness at work could sugar the scientific pill which disproved their beliefs – not even Flournoy's allowance for the existence of telepathic transmission.

Hélène was equally distressed. Like many a biographee, she felt both exposed and traduced. She may have allowed Flournoy to write her story, may have collaborated with Flournoy's suggestions, but the fame it brought her radically changed her life. She insisted that she really was now Hélène Smith and could have no other identity, despite the mockery of her talents the book provoked. Flournoy had traced each of her great reincarnations back to her childhood or reading. Her visions, her spiritist travels, had been reduced to symptoms, a 'maladaptation of the organism, physical and mental, to the hard conditions of the environment' of her childhood. Hélène now stopped Flournoy from coming to her séances. She developed the Martian cycle, which had through Flournoy brought the attention of such famous linguists as Roman Jakobson to study her speaking in tongues, into new Iranian and lunar cycles or mediumistic journeys. She also demanded royalties from the book.

Flournoy eventually paid her half of the earnings and gave the rest to the *Archives de Psychologie*, the journal he established in 1901 with his cousin Edouard Claparède. Meanwhile, an American benefactress appeared, to look after Hélène. Psychological investigation apart, Flournoy's book had also presented a portrait of the artist as medium, a woman's version of growing up other and talented when there were so few vocations to choose from. Now the medium gave up mediumship to devote herself to painting. Even so, she long continued to feel that Flournoy was spying on her, that she somehow had to escape his grip and that of an entourage who 'tormented and agitated her'.[157] She remained unmarried, waiting for the 'fiancé of her soul' until her death in 1927. As for Flournoy, the scientist who had stepped in to become her trance lover, the Prince Sivrouka, he never again found as stimulating a subject. Hélène Smith had helped to create the idea of the 'subliminal imagination' for which he is remembered.

Boston's Miss Beauchamp and Morton Prince (1854–1929)

The very remarkable case of Miss Beauchamp, who in treatment developed three separate and competing alters, or others, unfurled itself between 1898 and 1904 for Morton Prince, Professor of Diseases of the Nervous System at Tufts College Medical School and Boston City Hospital. Prince came from a prominent family, numbered William James at Harvard amongst his friends and colleagues, as well as that other pioneer of American psychology, G. Stanley Hall, the man responsible for Freud and Jung's visit to America. After imbibing the influence of Charcot in Paris, Prince returned to Boston to become one of the new discipline's driving forces. A teacher as well as a physician, he was also editor from 1906 of the *Journal of Abnormal Psychology*. William James corresponded with him about the intriguing Miss Beauchamp and relished the mystery of the 'lovely' Sally, who helped to make multiple personality so popular a form of being woman that it eventually travelled to Broadway Theatre. Long after Prince would have preferred to forget her, Miss Beauchamp's potent influence also played its way through the psy professions, appearing, for example, in Cambridge psychology exams in the 1920s.

Prince recorded Miss Beauchamp's six-year-long treatment in over 560 pages complete with samples of writing in her personality as Sally, a feisty, outspoken, greedy and desiring character quite unlike the reticent and responsible student Miss Beauchamp, who had sought Prince's help for her troubles. In his opening pages Prince draws attention to Miss Beauchamp as 'an example in actual life of the imaginative creation of Stevenson', even though her split, unlike Jekyll and Hyde's, was along 'temperamental' and not 'ethical lines of cleavage'. The ensuing story makes exciting reading, a Gothic romance in which the Prince wakes the sleeping beauty who had gone into a trance of forgetfulness on a fatal and stormy evening in 1893.

Clara Norton Fowler, the real name of the patient Prince calls Miss Beauchamp, had a small but appreciative social circle in Boston. She came to see Prince at the age of twenty-three with 'headaches, insomnia, bodily pains, persistent fatigue and poor nutrition'. She was incapable of working, or indeed of exercise. Her 'bookish' nature, however, made her insist on pursuing her studies with what Prince saw as an excessive conscientiousness. He reports his case notes of the time as reading: 'Is a pronounced neurasthenic of extreme type; has never been able to pursue steadily an occupation in consequence. Tried three times to do professional nursing and broke down. Is now studying at ———— College; ambitious, good student; does good work, but always ill; always suffering. . . Is very nervous and different parts of body in constant motion.'[158]

Referred to as both a hysteric and a neurasthenic, Miss Beauchamp echoes the syncopation between the terms that was prevalent at the time.[159] She also suffered from aboulia – an inhibition of the will which prevented her from doing what she wanted to do, perhaps something as insignificant as picking an object up from the table or telling her doctor why she had come. Reticent, highly suggestible, often lost in 'abstraction', her family history was fertile 'psychopathic soil': on the paternal side there was 'violence of temper'. The mother, who died when her daughter was thirteen, 'exhibited a great dislike' for the nervous, impressionable, oversensitive child Miss Beauchamp was, one prone to headaches, nightmares and sleepwalking, as well as spontaneous trances and daydreams so intense she confused them with the real.

In the course of her long treatment, Miss Beauchamp splits into three separate entities, apart from her waking self. Prince is haunted by the fact that he has somehow called Miss Beauchamp's alters into being through hypnosis. The length of her cure may have been in part propelled by his desire to prove that her dissociation really is the result of emotional trauma and weak nerves.

Prince designates these dissociated personalities as Miss Beauchamp's earliest hypnotized self (BII); BIII, who comes into being in deep hypnosis, and is at first 'Chris' before she dubs herself in her obstreperous and rebellious way, Sally; and BIV, who appears after a year and is a rather limited self, whom Sally names 'the idiot'. Prince organizes his patient's personalities into types which reflect the prevailing vision of woman. In her waking state, Miss Beauchamp is the Saint — a woman who sees 'selfishness, impatience, rudeness, uncharitableness, a failure to tell the truth or a suppression of half the truth' as sins whose wickedness can be overcome by 'fasting, vigils and prayer'.

Sally is the Devil, a mischievous imp of the perverse whom Prince in fact finds irresistible without quite admitting it. He portrays himself and Sally flirting with each other. She suggests marriage, breaks all conventions to smoke like Prince, and constantly derides Miss Beauchamp, whom she plagues with her irresponsibility, making her miss appointments or turning up as an outspoken tomboy. Sally is a 'co-consciousness'. She knows everything about Miss Beauchamp; but this is not true the other way round, since Sally is in a sense her 'subconscious': she has been around from the beginning, as she reveals in the autobiography Prince has her write. She has all the wilful boyishness, outspoken desire to be an adventurous male, and the naughty flirtatiousness of girls before they are forced into the sexual mould and the long skirts of womanhood.

Prince designates Miss Beauchamp's third alter (BIV) as the Woman, a vividly misogynistic bit of naming, since this personality has all the 'frailties of temper, self-concentration, ambition and self-interest' of the ordinary 'realist'. In Prince's description, this 'Woman' is a walking parody of the New Woman who thinks she is 'capable of running the world'.

Given his social circle, Prince was well acquainted with the burgeoning women's movement. The American Woman Suffrage Association had, after all, had its home in Boston since 1868. Women's clubs — over 250 of them around the country by the turn of the century — were spreading, as was agitation for the vote, for property and divorce rights and university education. The first PhD awarded to an American woman came from Prince's own Boston University. In the dissociation of Miss Beauchamp, we can see some of the tugs and tensions women internalized during this period of historical transformation as they struggled with old dissatisfactions, new challenges and male hostility. And in Prince's description of the several personalities of Miss

Beauchamp, male fears about the strength and freedoms of the new woman are equally evident.

Yet Prince also strives for the 'objectivity' of the medical gaze. In summing up the 'health' of Miss Beauchamp's personalities, it is clear that the first Miss Beauchamp, the Saint, is the worst off. The Woman is far stronger and capable of greater exertion, while the pre-pubescent Sally, who has yet to confront the problems that sexuality and being gendered woman will bring, 'does not know what illness means'.[160]

Prince's reflections on the nature of gender and sexuality are part of the discussion of bisexuality then being held in progressive circles in both Europe and America. Weininger, Freud, Stanley Hall – all in different ways saw bisexuality as fundamental to the human. Prince was prepared to reject any notion of 'natural' and fixed sexual identities and imagined a spectrum of sexuality ranging from 'strong, vigorous masculine characters' through 'men with female personalities' and 'masculine females' to 'strongly marked feminine personalities'. Education and environment, he wrote, shaped the 'tastes and habits of thought and manners' of the child, and if the sexes were brought up differently, each could have the 'tastes and manners of the other sex'.[161] This culturalist view of gender and sexual behaviour is, however, underpinned by an understanding of homosexual orientation as being grounded in a nervous disposition: all *healthy* beings will turn to the opposite sex once puberty is scaled.

Prince wants to have it both ways: gender is a question both of biology and of social mores, but the latter will suppress homosexuality in the person of healthy mind and body. Adolescent Sally has permission to flirt with boyish behaviour and all kinds of love: she offers in a letter to marry Prince and also to run off with the mysterious William Jones, the dark hero of this romance. Miss Beauchamp's possibilities are far more constrained.

Like some psychic detective endowed with six years of stamina, Prince goes in search of the 'real' Miss Beauchamp. He tracks his patient back to the painful moment when the initial dissociation took place. Moving in trance between her alters, Miss B confuses Prince with the elusive William Jones who tries to embrace her and/or hypnotize her. He begins to see that the real Miss B is not the 'Saint' but the 'Woman', who split off in a frightening encounter with Jones on a stormy evening in June

1893 and has ever since been 'asleep'. Jones, an idealized older man who had taken care of Miss Beauchamp since her mother's death, unexpectedly came to visit her at the hospital where she was training as a nurse. Seeing a ladder, he climbed up to her room. Illuminated by lightning, his head terrified an unsuspecting Miss Beauchamp, who promptly forgot the event by dissociating her 'real' self from it and slipping into her saintly aspect. Retrograde amnesia, says Prince, had moved this traumatic encounter into oblivion. All Miss Beauchamp's ills, he gradually confirms by evoking the scene with each of her alters, can be traced back here.

It is difficult not to give this scene a Freudian, sexual reading: even the weather is accommodating with its stormy *Wuthering Heights* overtones, let alone the window nook at which the dramatic head appears. A similar storm attended Henry James's Isabel Archer when the aptly named Caspar Goodwood kissed her a little too forcefully, so that she, too, rushed into rather more saintly pursuits. The real Miss Beauchamp (BIV) has forgotten that the events of that fateful night didn't stop with her refusing to see Jones and going into the ward where a child was crying. In fact, as Prince induces her to remember, she went down to see Jones: they stood together outside with the lightning flashing across his face, and she was frightened because he was so nervous that he seemed perfectly mad. It is this shock which led to Miss Beauchamp/the Saint, taking over. BIV's memory then ceased for the next six years. What had brought everything back to her on that particular day was that in the university library a messenger had given her a letter from Jones which was couched in the same language as he had used during the encounter that *literally* blew her mind apart.

Prince's account of the scene is hardly explicit. Nor does Miss Beauchamp seem to recount enough of its terror for it to constitute the trauma, the external violence, Prince needs for his hypothesis of dissociation. Perhaps it is the very holes in the construction of the scene which, years later in the 1920s, made him reconsider the whole case in a Freudian perspective and ascribe a sexual conflict to Miss Beauchamp.[162]

In the second part of his book, Prince argues that a 'normal' personality is one which can adjust itself 'physiologically' to its environment as well as psychologically. So he begins the difficult business of reintegrating Miss Beauchamp into the 'Woman' that 'she was intended by nature to be'. This entails much hypnosis, automatic writing and play of alters, and at the end eradicating the rebellious Sally, making her 'subconscious'. It also means merging the saintly, 'emotional idealism' of the patient who had first approached Prince, with the strength of the 'Woman', who must give up her 'bad temper and wilful self-determination'. Only thus will the transformation into the real Miss Beauchamp be complete: the woman who remembers all her past, is physically and mentally strong, and resists hypnosis. This is the woman who can blithely say in 1904, following six years of the remarkable play of alters: 'After all, it is always myself.'

It was this 'myself', Clara Norton Fowler, who in 1912, after having completed three semesters at Radcliffe, ended up marrying the Boston psychotherapist Dr George A. Waterman, a well known colleague of Morton Prince.[163] In the history of the mind doctors, star patients in one way or another often end up staying in the profession.

Meanwhile, for several years following publication of her case, Morton Prince's Miss Beauchamp led to a wave of multiples. But Freud's rising importance in America following his trip there in 1909, together with the gradual disappearance of hypnosis from the treatment agenda, meant that multiple personality steadily vanished from the diagnostic spectrum. Ian Hacking in his important study of the memory politics that shaped the twentieth century, *Rewriting the Soul*, shows how by 1909 Prince himself sniffed at his own diagnosis. Janet, too, in his compendious 1919 *Psychological Healing* gives it only a single page and relegates it to the early days of pathological psychology. Diagnoses had changed. One might also say that women had woken up into a new world and a new range of symptoms. The stubborn, mischievous Sally with her masculine dreams had driven ambulances in the war and was no longer so easily to be put to sleep.

After this, if a young woman 'chose' mediumistic trance or hearing voices as a form of expression or of manifesting symptoms, psychologists would be far quicker to diagnose a sexual malaise. G. Stanley Hall, a student of William James and one of America's great founding psychologists, particularly in the area of child development, in 1918 in his article 'A Medium in the Bud' noted how a young woman in an 'incipient stage' of mediumship during which she had visited Mars, loved the abandon and the male masquerade that being a medium permitted her. Inhibitions were thrown to the wind. The 'most secret things in the soul . . . which ordinary social conventions would make impossible' could here be expressed: 'there is a sudden freedom from responsibility and sensitive, shrinking, repressed natures, who would above all things dread to shock or violate convention in phrase or manner, are freed from the necessity of even being agreeable or primly proper which must often become irksome, hedged about as they are by so many senseless taboos'.[164]

Once normal experience gave women the possibility of moving beyond senseless taboos, states of sleep receded. And as the mind doctors focused in on the sexuality of the patient, doublings, multiples and dissociation gave way to a new set of symptoms and diagnoses.

It is worth noting that neither Janet's *somnambules* nor Miss Beauchamp seem to have relayed a history of child abuse, which was underscored as a regular and necessary triggering event for patients who developed multiple personality disorder during the high point of the malady and its diagnosis in the 1980s and 1990s. What is common between the two historic moments of 'alternating' personalities is that these talking and walking other selves were most often consolidated, and sometimes only ever fully emerged at all, with induced deep hypnosis. It seems to be the very relationship between doctor and patient which produces the florid aspect of these alters: the patient pleases the doctor by producing 'symptoms' or 'states' which the doctor finds interesting, while the doctor alleviates the patient's symptoms (sometimes of his own making) and induces 'betterment' by the very force of his interest.

There is nothing necessarily suspect in any of this. It is intrinsic to an extended doctor–patient relationship and can often help engender 'cure', or at least an improvement of symptoms, whether the treatment comes by hypnosis, talk or pills. As for what both doctors are interested in and patients produce as symptoms, that does seem to bear the weight of a historical moment. Janet, Freud, William James, Flournoy, Morton Prince were all fascinated by and trying to find evidence for the existence of an unconscious or subconscious mind, however they then described its workings. Alternating personalities, or *la condition seconde*, were proof of this. During the decades of widespread multiple personality disorder in the USA, what the doctors were interested in was the link between childhood sexual abuse – the collective anxiety of the epoch – and dissociated selves in the adult: they found it everywhere, and symptoms grew to fit the diagnosis the greater the notoriety that attended them.

It was certainly the malleability of symptoms as he saw them in his patients, particularly those he called hysterics, that led Freud to pay less attention to their external manifestation than to the underlying nature of his patients' lives – the trigger that had determined or precipitated symptoms. And it was when Freud went in search of motivation, the inner emotional turmoil that engendered the splitting that took place in a state akin to sleep, that he came upon sex.

PART THREE

THE CENTURY TURNS

7

SEX

Late in 1914, just as the First World War was digging its trenches, a forty-five-year-old woman wrote to the Royal Edinburgh Hospital, then an asylum known for its outstanding and innovative psychiatric services, and asked to be admitted. Her letter is a riveting document from the inside of disorder: at once a gruelling depiction of the psychic pain she is in, a plea for help, and a searing attempt to make sense of her condition.

The sense she does make catapults us into a new epoch of psychological understanding. Somewhere along the line, and mysteriously, this woman has picked up a terminology to describe her disordered state and give it an explanatory narrative which is quite different from what has come before. With Celia Brandon[165] and far from Freud's Vienna, we somehow find ourselves in the midst of a Freudian case: one which emphasizes that the roots of a disorder lie in childhood and are linked to sexuality, to the tangled trajectory of desire, punishment and inhibition, much of it expressed through dream and fantasy. Celia is an indication that the Freudian paradigms, though of course still enmeshed with the language of the nerves and heredity, travelled quickly to Britain and informed not only local practice, but the patient's own narrative of psychic ills.

Throughout the nineteenth century, various prohibitions about sex and masturbation had increasingly combined with a medical and psychiatric discourse to make sex far more than an experience of the body. Sexuality as a 'possession of sexual powers, or capability of sexual feelings' – in other words as a complex of psychic features which carry with them abilities and lacks, a too-muchness or too-littleness – makes its first appearance in the *OED* in 1879. It is already manifestly a problem: the attendant quotation defining usage is from J.M. Duncan's *Diseases of Women* of the same year: 'In removing the ovaries, you do not necessarily destroy sexuality in a woman.'

Sexuality is other than anatomical. It is not simply a matter of physical parts, but something mysterious and perhaps threatening, constantly in need of investigation, attention, or control. It is fundamental to the make-up of the person, and in particular of the female person. 'Upon the nature of sexual sensibility, the mental individuality in greater part depends,' writes Dr Krafft-Ebing, the noted Viennese psychiatrist, in his *Text-book of Insanity*.[166] One of the period's growing number of sexologists, he readily constitutes humans by their perversions – whether masochist or sadist, fetishist or homosexual, nymphomaniac or frigid. In an article of 1894 on the sexual functioning of women, he clearly hypothesizes that the sexual centre in the brain is as important as any sexual organ. Like Freud, as the century moves towards its close, he sees illnesses such as hysteria arising from a psychological factor. Drawing not only on patients but on his many informants who over the years write letters to him on any number of sexual dysfunctions, he notes that coitus can be 'unsatisfactory' even if on a physical level it takes place altogether satisfactorily.[167] That ejaculation into the vagina constitutes only one part of a man's sexual pleasure is 'proven by so many husbands' confidential complaints to the doctor of the frigidity of their wives'.[168]

As the century turns, sexuality increasingly and openly becomes implicated in the way the Western world makes sense of health and happiness, identity and destiny. It becomes a key indicator of the kind of individual one is, normal or perverted, sane or mad. The focus on sexuality, as Foucault underlined, particularly problematized women and homosexuals, masturbation, and children.

The bathetic nadir of views on women is perhaps best represented by Otto Weininger in *Sex and Character*, the book that in 1903 took the German-speaking world by storm, was quickly translated and went into numerous editions. Weininger begins with a radical principle of human bisexuality. His feminine, however, is incapable of morality, voraciously desiring and 'organically deceitful'. Emancipated women were, for Weininger, sexual deviants, only one step above homosexuals and Jews (of which he was one) in the hierarchy of value.[169]

Other commentators, less interested in apocalyptic evocation, stressed the need for reform: in a world where marriage for men, the only breadwinners, came late, since they had first to establish themselves, prostitution was rife alongside debilitating venereal disease. In Munich one-third of all children were born to single mothers. (Another third, it was thought, though born in wedlock were not the children of their putative fathers.) The principle of monogamous marriage was both a hypocrisy and destructive, as that 'polygamist' and wild psychoanalyst Otto Gross, who for a while deeply marked the young Carl Gustav Jung, pointed out. In more academic circles, similar views took hold. The anthroposociologist, Ivan Bloch, in *The Sexual Life of Our Times* (1906), points out how modern society simultaneously ridicules the 'old maid' and 'condemns the unmarried mother to infamy'. 'This double-faced putrescent "morality" is profoundly "immoral"; it is radically evil. It is moral and good to contest it with all our energy, to enter the lists on behalf of the right to free love, to "unmarried" motherhood.'[170]

Thus, while problematizing sexuality, the new reforming discourse also had a liberatory force, especially for women who had been consigned to roles and rules, a double standard which severely restricted their human potential. The new attention paid to sexuality brought desire out of the depths that respectability, ignorance and oppression had forced it into.

Celia Brandon provides an example of the way a patient might have internalized the old punishing sexual order while acquiring some of the language of the new psychosexuality, a language which had become so commonplace by the end of the twentieth century that it is difficult to see it afresh and recognize it as a cornerstone in the making of a particular kind of human.

Celia Brandon

Celia Brandon had an extraordinary history, though in her own time its general trajectory was not untypical of women in families engaged in the colonial service. Her case underlines the difficulties the wives of those who worked in distant outposts faced as they negotiated the dangers of childbirth, the loneliness of a world where there was little mingling with natives, and the hothouse of damaging rumour produced in this closed society. Born in Shanghai in 1870 to a mother who died two weeks later, leaving the tiny infant and her older brothers in the care of a father in the British Chinese colonial service, baby Celia was sent home, first to relatives in Scotland, then to an aunt in England. Here she lived under the strict and self-righteous tutelage of a taciturn woman who could ill cope with the precocious child Celia was. The older Celia, already an adept of asylums, describes this aunt as 'cataleptic' and prone to periods of 'unconsciousness'.

In the letter to the Edinburgh Hospital in which she narrates her own 'case', Celia writes of terrifying punishments, too severe for the delicate child she was – one whom the doctor had thought might be stillborn. When she is three or four, she begins to have vivid dreams in which she is crouched on all fours and smacked from behind, 'which gave me a sexual pleasure in front . . . forgotten at the time, but remembered later'. Her formulation wonderfully parallels the Freudian understanding of child development from the early anal, oral and phallic stages, which are forgotten and then reinvoked during the sexual awakening of puberty – so that early sexuality is already always in part a created memory. Celia talks of remembering how her aunt told her to take a hairbrush to bed at night and punish herself behind – an injunction she names as the cause of her 'performing on her person in all manner of ways', including riding banisters. Discovered by her governess, little Celia learns to lie and carries on her activities, only to stop when she is returned 'home'.

At the age of twelve, Celia was shipped back to China to live with her father and brothers, one of whom worked as an engineer, the other as a teacher of navigation. Her mother, it was rumoured, had had a drinking problem; one of the brothers was unstable, and Celia's father described his own daughter as 'weak', referring to her nervous temperament as well as her physical delicacy. Celia's education may have been erratic but she was bright, as her own writing testifies, and her finishing school commented on her talents. She had a good singing voice and her liveliness made her popular in the fair-sized colonial community. So did her amateur theatrical performances, which were commented on in the local newspaper.

At the age of twenty, Celia met an ambitious functionary in the Chinese Office. Ten years older than her, Arthur James was a widower who had two children by a previous marriage. There is the sense of an exciting courtship filled with dance and music, so exciting that it over-stimulates Celia and her father takes her home, away from her fiancé, for something of an enforced rest. She talks in her letter of being in a nervous state during which excitement pulls her down again. The excitement is also evidently sexual and worrying.

Once married, the couple move to Peking where Arthur James rises through the service. The family live in the foreign compound, a small but active community housing a mix of European and American nationals, a lively society of diplomats, teachers, entrepreneurs and their staff. The compound has its own shops, library and entertain-ment, and is situated at the centre of Peking, just outside the walls of the Forbidden City. The James children live with Celia and her husband for a few years, before they are old enough to be shipped to boarding school in England. Meanwhile, Celia herself is pregnant, but the child is lost in a difficult miscarriage which takes its toll on both her health and her stability. Her accompanying illness just precedes the Boxer Rebellion. Sparked by growing resentment and nascent nationalism, fuelled by drought, this violent uprising against the foreign powers and their com-mercial interests, but also against the Empress who had sanctioned them, marks Celia profoundly, as it does the other inhabitants of the compound.

Barricades are built. A small military force faces some twenty thou-sand Boxers, as the members of the Society of Righteous Fists are nicknamed. They have marched from the countryside and want noth-ing less than to expel the 'foreign devils' by any means to hand. For nearly two months, the entire foreign compound is kept under siege and subject to daily incursions and bombardments. Captives are tor-tured. Houses are burned. Food grows scarce, along with medical supplies and ammunition. Over seventy foreigners die and many are wounded. Only when an international force is raised and finally marches on Peking are the inhabitants of the compound at last freed.

Soon after the Boxer Rebellion, Arthur James left Peking – partly, one imagines, on account of Celia. She was pregnant again and this time the birth of the child would be secured by a delivery in England. But even England couldn't guarantee the baby's safety, nor the mother's precarious mental and physical state. The child died just two weeks after birth. Eclampsia may have been the cause. Celia cites this frightening condition in her later letter to the Edinburgh Hospital. Eclampsia, literally 'a bolt from the blue', consists of a series of epileptic-like convulsions, jerky, repetitive, sometimes violent, involving muscles in the jaw, neck, limbs and eyes, leading to loss of consciousness and sometimes a stop in breathing. It is unclear when exactly the eclampsia occurred and whether Celia's baby died from asphyxia as a result of her convulsions, or had already been weakened by the lack of oxygen which is common to eclampsia. Whatever the actual medical cause of death, Celia's own puerperal fever and resulting condition were serious enough for her to be confined to an asylum, St Andrew's Hospital in Northampton. She stayed there for some six months.

St Andrew's Hospital was founded in 1838, as a belated result of the County Asylums Act of 1808 which empowered local justices of the peace to raise rates for asylums for paupers and criminal lunatics. Home for twenty-three years to the poet John Clare, St Andrew's had always, however, had a link to the middle classes. The great architect Gilbert Scott, who built St Pancras Station in London, designed its chapel. By the 1870s pauper lunatics had been moved to a separate asylum, and St Andrew's pushed ahead, becoming one of the most advanced of institutions in terms of patient comfort, offering gardens and grounds, a working farm, theatrical recreation and holidays in the Welsh hills. New technologies – first a telephone in 1881, then in 1898 an electrical generator – were installed.

This technological modernity hardly extended, it seems, to treatment and diagnosis. What the hospital provided was a rest home with all modern comforts. Its superintendent, Dr Joseph Bayley, had been there since 1865, and accounts of the hospital's history show him as far more interested in the management of the premises than in any new theories or treatments. It is unlikely that when Celia Brandon went home after six months, she had picked up from the hospital's two resident doctors either the terminology or the structural narrative of madness which permeates her letter of 1914. Something else, perhaps other patients, perhaps her own later reading and conversation in the cosmopolitan hub that was China's foreign community, must have influenced the narrative she makes of her life and 'peculiarity'.

Celia tells her story as if she knows that the beating fantasies which charged her sexual pleasure in childhood structured her adult sexuality. She seems to know that dreams – the human activity Freud described in 1900 in *The Interpretation of Dreams* as the royal road to the unconscious – are an expression of her wishes and fears. She also underlines the difference between fantasy and the real, and how masturbation is converted by shame into fantasy scenes foisting responsibility on to others, noting that on her marriage bed she struggled to tell her husband of the kind of masturbatory scenario she engaged in, but instead ended up telling him only that her aunt acted out the beatings which gave her pleasure. In fact, the *thought* of being beaten 'as in her dream' was enough to trigger pleasure for Celia. She names this beating fantasy her 'thought key', and she uses it during intercourse when her husband doesn't satisfy, the more especially so after her baby's death and the spell in the asylum. She also on occasion takes the 'whip' to herself, dutifully reporting this to her husband, who chides her and tells her never to do it again. Clearly she is ambivalent about her husband, who, she says, is worried about his own health, and doesn't give her all she wants. Her cravings, her need for self-punishment, shadow her marriage.

Celia's frankness to the doctors about her sexuality is astonishing: Freud's turn-of-the-century hysterics were hardly so well educated in their own conflicting desires, and manifested far more resistance to his sexual interpretations. What is even more startling is the way that in telling her story she openly links sexual needs and habits, formed in childhood, to her mental disarray – to the persecuting voices she now hears and wishes the doctors could rid her of – as if the masturbatory dream scenario and its eventual merging with the longed-for messages from a possible lover were *known* to be a sexual aberration that precipitated illness, and demanded both punishment and cure. There is far more in play here than a Victorian governess's punitive edict to a masturbating child, who is, unusually in this instance, a girl. What Celia gives us is the construction of a narrative of developing female sexuality and the conflicts on which it founders to produce illness.

Narratives such as hers are also the basis for Freud's understanding of the human and emphatically women's predicament. Freud listened, perhaps for the first time, to what women told him; made speech, rather than the clinical gaze of the Charcotian kind, a privileged part of treatment. It was out of what he heard in the consulting room, no matter how bizarre or against the grain of conventional beliefs, that he diagnosed the wrongs of his time's repressive sexual mores and built his theories of the formation of the human mind and its progress from infancy into adulthood.

When she leaves St Andrew's Celia, still delicate after the horror of the birth and death of her child, returns to her 'thought key' for sexual solace. She has sought help, or perhaps understanding, from her husband, wanting to 'change her thought key' since it isn't very 'nice'. But he won't or can't take any of this in, simply repeating, as he did on their wedding night, that she must put all this behind her. Celia's hold on the real grows tenuous once more. She talks of what she calls her 'black magic', her ability to predict and foresee the future, her refusal of it; but it is precisely this 'visionary' quality, this permeability of mind that she experiences, which comes back to persecute her later.

As she nears her forties, Celia is once more thought to be pregnant. The danger of this in her delicate state causes the physician to give her apiol, commonly known as parsley camphor, to bring on her period. But Celia isn't pregnant, is probably moving towards menopause, and the apiol in quantities has side-effects of vertigo and headaches. It is at this time that her husband is promoted and transferred to a regional posting. The move into a new community, which numbers few foreigners, is difficult for Celia, despite the comforts of the new home, the quantity of servants, the elevated social status. The new position also requires her husband to travel far more. Celia isn't well. A French doctor prescribes more apiol, which in her later letter she links to her precarious state, at once nervous and excited.

The local population was hostile enough in this new outpost for Arthur James to want protection for his wife when he was forced to leave her alone. An adjutant moves into their large house, to guard Celia against intruders. Instead, the young man himself becomes an intruder. He becomes her special friend, whether in bed or in fantasy isn't clear, though she denies the first. In any event, he invades Celia's dreams. When her husband returns, this young man begins to serve as the fantasy object who triggers her pleasure when she is with her husband. In her letter to the Edinburgh Hospital, Celia traces this change with a childish flourish: it occurred to her, she says, that it would be nicer to think of her friend than her usual 'thought key' when in bed. It worked: in her imagination intercourse with her husband is now accompanied by excursions with her friend.

Arthur James grew jealous and, after a row, publicly insulted both the young man and Celia. Celia's 'head trouble' followed. She protested that there had never been any impropriety, even though the man had entered her dreams. In her letter, which is both utterly cogent and has the associative tangents of a restless and troubled mind, she describes how one day at table, the young man rubbed his leg against hers. She withdrew, then reconsidered: it would be ungenerous, given how intimate they were, not to acknowledge his secret pressure. Her desire, like the affair itself, flourishes through signs both fantasized and intensely real, each of them bearing the conflict between secret desire and a doubly secret wish for exposure, which is also a fear. When the young man is sent away to another posting, Celia suffers a severe breakdown.

She spends almost a year in a missionary hospital. During this time, she begins to communicate with her young friend in a coded and quasi-hallucinatory fashion. It seems to her that he sends her messages through other people, as well as through animals, trees, flowers and wind. Her brain grows noisy with the process.

The missionary hospital did Celia no good. Arthur James decided she had to return to England. A nurse accompanied her on the arduous six-week journey during which her state grew worse. Celia becomes uncontrollable, running amok, throwing her suitcases into the ocean, attempting suicide, acting out with considerable violence. In England, she is committed to Bethlem,[171] where she spends some six months. Her fantasies have become hallucinatory, her sexual practices excessive. The persecution she describes in her letter has set in. There are warring voices in her brain, an inner 'telegraphy' which transforms the loving messages she receives from her friend into the old, self-punishing motifs of her thought key. Neighbours, 'others', do this to her. They convert a coded love signal from her friend, a message embedded in the smoke of his cigarette, into a vengeful and painful whipping. 'They take the faintest thought in my brain, even an unconscious idea sometimes – for a speech in the brain, which it isn't.' Her thoughts are dirty, rampant, her head like a telephone into which voices pour uncontrollably, and she cannot help listening and speaking to them aloud.

When she is calmer, Arthur James comes to fetch her and they return once more to China, only to come back to England with the outbreak of war. It is unclear whether Celia is ever altogether stable again, or indeed whether she has ever altogether been so since her first miscarriage, late in pregnancy. Indeed, there is an amalgam of precipitating causes for her mental condition: the repeated miscarriages, the traumas of war, the death of an infant, the love affair and the subsequent mourning for what is after all a double loss of child and lover – all this compounded with her own original motherlessness and constitutional delicacy.

Yet Celia somehow weaves all this into a narrative in which the sexual element is the one she chooses to emphasize as the salient cause and expression of her 'peculiarity'. By the time she writes her letter of 1914 to the Edinburgh Hospital, she is begging to be institutionalized because the persecuting voices have grown rampant: she has only 'unconsciously' to think of her husband or friend in the most innocent way, and the voices begin, rude, insulting, unbearable. The beating fantasies have grown into vengeful embodied punishments. Only the hospital doctors might be able to provide solace. The pain in her letter is a reminder of the great contemporary psychiatrist Emil Kraepelin's statement in his lectures to young doctors that 'Insanity, even in its mildest forms, involves the greatest suffering that physicians ever have to meet.'[172]

Celia Brandon, now a small stout woman with brown hair and clear, rather yellow skin, was admitted to the Royal Edinburgh Hospital in the spring of 1915. Under the supervision of George M. Robertson, soon to be Scotland's first Professor of Psychiatry, the Royal Edinburgh Asylum was a benign institution. Robertson had not only studied in Edinburgh and London, but in the early 1890s had visited Hippolyte Bernheim and J. M. Charcot in France to observe the use of hypnotism in the treatment of the insane. Although he was more interested in innovative practice, such as introducing the villa system with its separate small units and regular nursing into care, than in writing, two of his papers describe the findings of that early trip. By 1920 he is a convinced supporter of Freud's, and on 7 September 1923 he writes to the London *Times* to distinguish between spiritual healing and the mental therapies such as 'suggestion, auto-suggestion, or psycho-analysis, the curative effects of which are admitted by all'. It may be Robertson's knowledge of the scientific and secular medical practices of 'suggestion' and 'psycho-analysis' that accounts for the altogether 'modern' classification of Celia Brandon's problems as 'Freudian' in the hospital notes.

By the First World War, Freud was already well known in the medical literature in Britain and America. He had coined the word 'psychoanalysis' in 1896 to describe the new talking cure which displaced the cathartic method of treatment with its use of hypnosis, such as he and Breuer had described it in *Studies on Hysteria*. These years were productive for Freud, his activity spurred on by his father's death. Alongside a flood of papers, and his own self-analysis which gave him an insight into the Oedipal structure of family life, came ground-breaking books: *The Interpretation of Dreams* in 1900, followed in 1901 by *The Psychopathology of Everyday Life*, which Leonard Woolf, husband of Virginia and soon to be Freud's major publisher in English, applauded. Then in 1905, an annus mirabilis, came *Jokes and their Relation to the Unconscious*, and perhaps his most influential study, *The Three Essays on the Theory of Sexuality*.

With a radical coolness which had no truck with conventional morality, Freud separated out people's sexual aims from their choice of 'object', often enough of the same sex; postulated a psychic bisexuality, explored fetishism, perversion and sado-masochism in terms far more subtle than any previous writer had conceived of and without a trace of the voyeurism which turned those who exemplified these conditions into freaks. He attacked the sexual morality of his own time and showed how it made people ill: 'It is one of the obvious social injustices that the standard of civilization should demand from everyone the same conduct of sexual life – conduct which can be followed without any difficulty by some people, thanks to their organization, but which imposes the heaviest psychical sacrifices on others.'[173] Most dramatically, Freud transformed the supposedly innocent child of Victorian sensibility into a sexual being, and turned the idealized family into a zone of potentially tragic desires and conflicts. When it came to patients, those sufferers from neurosis and hysteria who made up his daily practice, he once more announced that their symptoms *were* their sexual activity: it was only through psychoanalysis that the libidinal component of these symptoms together with the defences which had helped to produce them, could be untangled and restored to more appropriate activity.

In 1909 Freud and Carl Gustav Jung, still his disciple, though not for much longer, were invited to lecture in America where psychoanalysis had already taken a foothold. In Britain, too, Freud's work was beginning to be known in medical circles, even before Ernest Jones set up the London Psychoanalytical Society in 1913. Lectures on 'Freud's Abnormal Psychology' appear in such provincial institutions as Liverpool's Medical Institute in 1912. By then his fame was also beginning to spread into the non-specialist, educated press. Four of his books had been translated, including *On Sexuality*. Even more importantly in terms of general reception, Bernard Hart's *The Psychology of Insanity* (1912) appeared. It included fine accounts of both Freud and Janet, had a wide readership and was rapidly and repeatedly reprinted into the 1960s, making it one of the most popular books ever in the field of madness.

As for the better journals, in January 1912 *The Strand Magazine* ran an article by William Brown entitled 'Is Love a Disease?', which talked of Freud's success and described Jung's early word-association experiments, noting that delayed response pointed to an unconscious emotional tendency at the root of the nervous disorder which could be cured by the psychoanalytic process of pulling this hidden matter into the light of day. By 1915 periodicals as diverse as *New Age, Blackwood's, The Cornhill* and *The Athenaeum* had run articles and reviews on Freud, while E.S. Grew in *Pall Mall* named him as 'the greatest of modern psychologists', and accepted the existence of the unconscious and its influence. When the *Psychopathology of Everyday Life* appeared in English in 1914, *The Saturday Review* likened Freud's investigations into the human mind to a 'high class detective story'. Soon he was being called the 'Sherlock Holmes of the Mind'.[174]

All this accounts, perhaps, for the ease with which Celia Brandon's case is labelled 'Freudian' by the admitting doctor in the Edinburgh

Hospital in 1915, and may go a little way towards explaining the way in which this intelligent woman understands and writes her own plight, easily linking sexuality and symptom.

Her admission report reveals the hospital regime as both enlightened and up-to-date. The word that is used most frequently to describe Celia's mental state and habits is 'peculiar' — a daily and non-medical term, but one that is free of Victorian moralizing. Under the description of her present mental state, the pre-printed categories note: Exaltation/Depression/Excitement/Enfeeblement/Memory/Coherence/ Delusions and Hallucinations. However, there is no ticking of boxes for Celia. The entry statement reads:

> Patient is . . . oriented and fully appreciates her pains and position. She is full of delusional ideas and gives a typical Freudian History. Her present trouble takes the form of old women tormenting her, putting all sorts of unpleasant thoughts in her head and saying vile things, often of a sexual character. She suffers from ideas of a masochistic type and has dreams and thoughts of whipping and of the genital region. The old women can cause what she calls 'sexual spasms in her vagina'.

Celia Brandon stayed at the Edinburgh Hospital until just after the war's end. Throughout the three years nothing much in her condition was altered. The persecutory voices in her head, the 'filthy old ladies' and 'dirty devils', retained their hallucinatory force, propelling her into outbursts, both day and night, of what the hospital considered appalling language. During such times she could also become destructive, smashing window-panes and crockery. The rest of the time she was sensitive to her environment and other people, played piano or tennis, and read. On occasion she was deeply depressed and despairing of her condition, but much of the time, when the voices didn't attack her, she was cheerful and her physical health was good. The hospital did not seem to provide any talking therapy. Certainly there is no specific reference to this in the case notes, though there is mention of the fact that the patient tells numerous stories about what her auditory hallucinations have done and how they affect her. One imagines these are told to a doctor, and if not, to one of the professional nurses Robertson had introduced to the hospital's management. Occasionally Veronal or sulphanol, which Celia asks for, is given to calm her.

By April 1918, Celia Brandon has complete outside 'parole' and when her voices aren't bothering her, she is permitted to leave the grounds. A year later, when her husband is back in the country, he comes to take her home. The final notes in her file state that she left 'relieved'. The diagnosis reads 'systematized delusional insanity' for which the prognosis is 'bad'. Partial relief, not cure, is what an enlightened asylum can offer.

Sigmund Freud (1856–1939)

Relief, not cure, is what Freud, too, most often offered. The most iconic mind doctor of the world that was to call itself modern, Sigmund Freud comes to us in many guises. Depending on the interpreter or historian, he is the heroic conquistador of the secrets of the unconscious, the great innovator whose talking cure definitively altered the treatment of madness, or the manipulative fraudster who launched a movement out of a mixture of fabrication and speculation. He is the good doctor or kind professor of some patients' memoirs, the Jewish swindler of others. His pervasive presence in popular culture is associated with slips or sex or Oedipal struggles in the battleground that is the family. It is also synonymous with that interesting condition which is neurosis – in itself a climate of being, proper to the imaginative outsider trapped in the stultifying net of suburban norms. Finally – though with Freud nothing is ever terminable – Freud is, all other things apart, one of the twentieth century's most fertile writers, at once the modernist who launches the discontinuities of self and dream emphatically on to the stage of literature and art, and the teller of gritty family romances replete with the narrative of childhood traumas and adult discontent.

Before he became a great many things even to people who had never read him or experienced a supposedly Freudian psychoanalysis, Freud was a neurologist, bent on 'understanding something of the nature of what were known as the "functional" nervous diseases, with a view to overcoming the impotence which had so far characterized their medical treatment'.[175]

Born in 1856 to a Jewish family in the small town of Freiberg in what was then Moravia, the Czech part of the sprawling Austro-Hungarian Empire, he was the first son in his father's second family, a status which gave him a nephew who was older than himself, amongst other extensions common enough in a time when second families were a norm because of death rather than divorce. The Freud family moved to Vienna when little Sigmund, always his mother's favourite of the eight children she eventually had, was four. He distinguished himself in school and gymnasium, before deciding on a medical career. These were times of growing liberalization in Austro-Hungary, and the professions were more open to Jews than they had ever previously been.

Vienna itself was rapidly growing into the great multicultural hothouse of the new. Immigrants speaking a variety of tongues poured into the capital from the far corners of the Empire. Shtetl Jews, Slavs from Poland and the Balkans, jostled with Hungarians and Ruthenians. Poverty was rife, as was prostitution; but the economy was buoyant and the city sprouted grand new streets and embraced outlying villages. As in all times of rapid transformation, old forms and ideas – in Vienna's case, of strict morality, religion and imperial hierarchy – coexisted with the new, that secular and scientific spirit which fed the arts, philosophy and politics. By the turn of the century, social-democratic reformers like the Adlers jostled with scientists like Boltzmann and Mach and modernist artists such as Klimt, Schiele and Mahler, their inventiveness feeding off each other through the very fact of proximity. The press for the first time felt as provocatively free as the 'associations' Freud drew from his patients, and fuelled reform. Writers like Schnitzler evoked the everyday life of the passions and sexuality with the same verve as Freud, while the radical satirist Karl Kraus simultaneously campaigned on behalf of much maligned prostitutes, attacked sexual hypocrisy and dubbed the nascent psychoanalysis 'the disease whose cure it purports to be'.

In 1881, Freud graduated as Doctor of Medicine from the University of Vienna. He had taken extra time over his studies, teetering as he did between interests in philosophy, a career in pure research and one in clinical medicine. He had worked under the famous Brücke at the Institute of Physiology and studied the sex life of eels in Trieste, applying the same ardour to their reproductive systems as Darwin had applied to the life of barnacles. Darwin remained his hero and first teacher in the painstaking observational skills necessary to a scientist.

Lack of finances and a wish to marry his sweetheart, Martha Bernays, meant that Freud opted for clinical medicine over research. He worked first at the Vienna General Hospital, focusing on cerebral anatomy and later, after a research trip to France where he was much influenced by the great Charcot, at the Kassowitz Institute in Vienna, with children who suffered from cerebral palsy and other neuropathological problems. His earliest physiological papers were followed by neurological work on aphasia, and only gradually as he moved into private practice, which would allow him a living, did he focus on psychopathology, hysteria and what he defined as the neuroses.

Like all ideas, Freud's ground-breaking observations and the theories which grew from them hardly came *ex nihilo*. The existence of an unconscious, a substratum or repository of feelings and ideas not always directly within the individual's grasp or control, the many problems of sexuality and the family, all of these had been talked and written about in various ways. What Freud gradually and magnificently added was a narrative and theories which provided pattern, motive forces and surprising explanations that did away with moralizing punishments and liberated sexuality.

Civilized sexual morality, the lack of libidinal satisfaction, its delay or distortion through the patterns of late-nineteenth- and early twentieth-century life and marriage, prohibitions against contraception and sheer ignorance about sex, produced, Freud underlined, anxiety and illness. He combined this early insight with a treatment which, by the century's turn, put not only the clinical gaze but both suggestion and hypnosis into the background, and substituted for them a talking cure which was also a careful listening to patients as they followed the rule of free association – of saying everything that came into their minds. In that twosome which was the listening analyst and the speaking patient, the fantasies and phobias that prevented the free flow of life outside the consulting room were re-enacted and re-imagined, resistances overcome, so that the blocks and fixations that had accrued from childhood could, both hoped, be released.

Freud's genius perhaps lay, above all, in the way he showed how the conflicts of sexuality in childhood not only shaped the person who might find her way into a clinic or to a mind doctor, but shaped us all. In one way or another, the adult human is a product of a family structure where the babe struggles to become a sexed human along the lines that differentiate the masculine from the feminine and can lead to that reproduction which Darwin had noted as the aim of life. Sex, for Freud, is not only pleasure and its attendant fantasies, or the fault-line along which illness or malaise can come, but the necessary animal goal. Our very humaneness, that extra which man and woman is, that plus which is civilization, may be what prevents us from fulfilling it.

Early in his career, Freud set himself apart from other neurologists and medical practitioners by declaring that neurasthenia – that condition which was contemporary to modernity – might have, but did not require, a direct basis in heredity. He pointed to a sexual aetiology not only for hysteria, but for the anxiety and obsessional neuroses as well. 'This, to tell the truth, is no new, unheard-of proposition,' he noted in 1896.

> Sexual disorders have always been admitted among the causes of nervous illness, but they have been subordinated to heredity . . . What gives its distinctive character to my line of approach is that I elevate these sexual influences to the rank of specific causes, that I recognize their action in every case of neurosis, and finally that I trace a regular parallelism, a proof of a special aetiological relation, between the nature of the sexual influence and the pathological species of the neurosis.[176]

The question of Freud's originality, the early rejection or acceptance of his insights, has been contested for almost a century now. Clearly, while some hailed his ideas, arbiters of psychiatric knowledge in his own time were often hostile, as Freud himself noted with a sensitivity all writers will recognize. In 1899 Emil Kraepelin mocked, 'If . . . our much-plagued soul can lose its equilibrium for all time as a result of long-forgotten unpleasant sexual experiences, that would be the beginning of the end for the human race; nature would have played a gruesome trick on us!'[177]

If Freud, while working with his early hysterics, first presumed, like Janet, that a disturbing childhood sexual encounter or 'trauma' had set in train the conflicts which resulted in mental disorder, as his case base grew he modified his thinking. The omnipresence of what he called childhood 'seduction', and we now call 'abuse', made him suspicious. Could it be that the instigating event did not *have* to have taken place in the external world but needed only to be imagined? – just as Celia Brandon had told her husband of a 'real' punishment, when she needed only an imagined simulated one as a thought key for pleasure? Freud determined that a fantasized sexual memory, re-evoked as real at a later date, could set neuroses in process as well as a real one. Intense childhood desires, one of the hazards of everyday life in a family understood as a hothouse of secret cravings and suppressions, could trigger illness by coming into covert conflict with an ideal or even acceptable image of the self and then going underground. These early battles between libidinal impulse and disgust, shame, censorship, these travails of 'civilized morality' as lived by the child, could form a base for later neurosis, just as could an actual seduction by a parent, uncle or sibling or, rather more rarely, a stranger. The movement between infancy and maturity is fraught, for Freud, with sexual compromises and conflicts, charged and changed by the process of reminiscence itself. Indeed, one of Freud's primary findings is that the child herself is already a sexual being who develops through desire and its forgetting or repression in a family were mothers, fathers and siblings all play their part in an Oedipal drama.

Looking back on the findings of his new science in his 'Short Account of Psychoanalysis', written when he was sixty-eight, Freud retrospectively once more underlined the importance of sexuality both in understanding neurosis and in ordinary human development. He summarized his major findings: a theory 'which gave a satisfactory account of the origin, meaning and purpose of neurotic symptoms', and which gave 'even the apparently most obscure and arbitrary mental phenoma . . . a meaning and a causation, the theory of psychical conflict and of the pathogenic nature of repression, the view that symptoms are substitutive satisfactions, the recognition of the aetiological importance of sexual life, and in particular of the beginnings of infantile sexuality'. To that he added the philosophical contention that the 'mental does not coincide with the conscious', the view that children have 'complicated emotional relations to their parents'. It became clear to him that in this Oedipal matter lay the nucleus of every case of neurosis; and in the 'patient's behaviour towards his analyst certain phenomena of his emotional transference emerged which came to be of great importance for theory and technique alike'.

As women analysts chipped away at and fed into his original theories, Freud came increasingly to see that for the girl the move from childhood to adulthood was even more fraught than for the boy. Becoming woman meant engaging in the complicated task of somehow learning to desire the male. Children of both sexes were first fixed on the mother or the maternal carer. For the girl, growing up entailed having to move her original Oedipal desires to the father, or the male who might give her a child. Along the way, the 'phallic' satisfactions of clitoral sexuality would need to be abandoned for the more 'mature' pleasures of vaginal sex and penetration. Freud locates the spur for this change in what he calls 'penis-envy' – the girl's discovery that she lacks the penis which is the organ of sexual pleasure. This discovery and its attendant disappointment can lead to sexual inhibition, neurosis, or to what Freud calls 'normal femininity'. It can lead the girl to deny her lack and mimic maleness in her various pursuits or sexual choices. Or it can resign her to what Freud calls 'femininity, that is, a settling into the "passive" role in which she expects to receive the penis in the form a child from her father or sometimes her mother'.

If Freud at first seems to make things easier for the penis-bearing boy, it shouldn't be forgotten that his path to maturity means measuring up to bigger Dad. The boy's attendant fears of castration, his murderous fantasies, are not exactly a sunny alternative to femininity. Indeed, Freud's view of the rocky path into adulthood makes Peter Pan a definite attraction, were it not that the whole trajectory is hardly the individual's consciously to choose. Like civilization, sexual maturity has its palpable discontents. For the ordinary neurotic, analysis is simply there to make these more bearable.

A proud paterfamilias himself, a firm believer that the birth of a child would sort out many women's hysterical or neurotic impulses, and that the 'masculine' pursuits of suffragette struggles or intellectual work might put a strain on a woman's psyche, Freud nonetheless – and despite the opposition of some of the early male psychoanalysts – welcomed women into the profession and numbered some of their leading lights amongst his closest confidantes. Always a pessimist, he was uncertain whether the difficult psychic trajectory he and analysts like Ruth Mack Brunswick and Hélène Deutsch had elaborated for women could ever be altogether satisfactorily accomplished. Nor did he lay any emphatic value on it. His daughter Anna, who in childhood had had beating fantasies not all that dissimilar to Celia Brandon's, never married nor bore a child. Freud called her his 'Antigone' and valued not only her work as a psychoanalyst and for the movement, but her indomitable courage. Confronted by the Gestapo, Anna had effectively saved the family. There was not a little help, too, from Princess Marie Bonaparte, another 'masculine' woman and one-time analysand. 'Women are the more capable,'[178] he wrote to Ernest Jones.

Indeed, for all his utterances about the 'normal' path of femininity, Freud seemed to prefer independent spirits who had a professional ardour rare for the times. H.D., the American poet Hilda Dolittle who memorialized her analysis with Freud ten years after the event, and who was not only an independent woman, but one whose sexual orientation wavered, returned the compliment, as had the writer and femme fatale Lou Andreas-Salomé and others before her, and evoked Freud as a 'blameless physician'.

Whether blameless or not, it is clear that Freud, in charting sexuality and putting it centre stage both as in need of reform and as a seedbed of problems, had no moralizing project at the core of his work. Perversion, fetishism, a disorder in sexual aim or object, seem to him an all too common matter. But the psychoanalytic profession, particularly in America, would take his findings and transform them into norms with which women must comply. In the process, new neurotic conditions would flourish, stigmatizing women with psychological diagnoses that had their basis as much in the needs of medical and social conformity as in sexual difficulties. The frigid woman and the nymphomaniac would become popular icons of psychic imbalance in post-Second World War America, where psychoanalysis flourished as a far more normative profession than Freud had ever imagined. The 'dark continent' which he had called woman and which he had set out to explore, without ever charting its outposts more than tentatively, had been given a grid-like map whose strip lighting led only to the suburban mall. Unlike Freud, who had never been able satisfactorily to answer the question, 'Was will das Weib?', these later analysts also seemed emphatically to know what women wanted – and it was home, hubby, and certainly no intellectual aspirations.

Meanwhile, elsewhere, the psychoanalytic profession would take hold with what became known as a more 'classically Freudian' configuration. The ever resisted notion of infantile sexuality – which most recently has found our cultural abhorrence of its existence writ large in the scapegoating of 'paedophiles' – has continued to be the manifold structure which analysts focus on within the analysis, precisely because it so often results in producing what is called the 'negative' transference. This elaborating within the relationship established with the analyst of the subject's nastiest hates, contempt, fears, is what the analysis will contend with. The Freudian profession would set to work to uncover what dark matter drove Celia Brandon's hallucinatory horror.

The easiest part of the Freudian project to describe is its radical educational aspect, together with the cultural importance of Freud's writings. The most difficult is to do with what a psychoanalytic therapy actually contends with shifts or treats within the individual in that long and sometimes interminable process which is an analysis. Moving around the ghostly furniture of the unconscious, finding the trace of wish beneath the heap of hate, may remain a novelist's or former analysand's business, even though some brain imagers and biochemical explorers have now found 'evidence' of hysterical desire and post-talking-therapy changes in the neural activity of the brain.

8

SCHIZOPHRENIA

Celia Brandon heard vile, persecutory voices who took her over and ran her life. Nowhere did the hospital even begin to consider she was suffering from schizophrenia. Others heard voices, too. They were diagnosed as hysterics, or dissociated personalities or mediums. Schizophrenia had not yet been named as a separate entity and when it was, hearing voices was hardly its primary symptom. Indeed, confusion over what schizophrenia might be persisted, and persists into our own time. This confusion stretches across the condition's – if it *is* a single condition – origins, causes and constituent parts, whatever the occasional casualness or certainty of a growing body of psychiatrists in attributing the diagnosis from the early years of the twentieth century on.

This has been due not only to a professional lack: the complexity of mental disorders, the wide range of their symptoms – a proportion of them overlapping with each other even for very different conditions – the changing spectrum of behaviours over time, make clarity a goal rather than a fact. *DSM-IV*, the most commonly used psychiatric diagnostic manual today, recommends that an individual be monitored over a six-month period before a diagnosis of schizophrenia is attributed. Of the characteristic symptoms that the *DSM* names – delusions, hallucinations, disorganized speech (frequent derailment or incoherence), grossly disorganized or catatonic behaviour, and negative symptoms such as 'affective flattening' – two are needed for a diagnosis. However, only one is needed if 'delusions are bizarre or hallucinations consist of a voice keeping up a running commentary on the person's behaviour or thoughts, or two or more voices conversing with each other'. Whether Celia Brandon, diagnosed by her medics in 1914 as 'peculiar', would at the same time in Vienna have been diagnosed as suffering from a paranoid hysteria, in Munich as suffering from dementia praecox, and in Switzerland then or in London today as a schizophrenic, is an open question.

Emil Kraepelin (1856–1926), Eugen Bleuler (1857–1939) and the Burghölzli

The history of the diagnosis of schizophrenia begins in psychiatric hospitals and with Freud's contemporary, Emil Kraepelin, arguably the greatest classifier in psychiatric medicine. A brilliant clinician and compiler of illness profiles, developed out of the programme he initiated for the systematic accumulation of hospital files, Kraepelin made Munich a centre for psychiatric research. He also utterly rejected Freud's psychodynamic technique. In his revised textbook of 1899, replete with those clinical observations which made him a model diagnostician and which are still pertinent today as descriptions of behaviour, Kraepelin elaborated and distinguished between the course and outcome of three separate diagnostic categories he had only mooted earlier: manic depression with its cyclical nature; paranoia; and a new entity, 'dementia praecox'. This last made a whole host of peculiarities into an elaborate disease process.

Drawing on a vast hospital base of case records, influenced too by the work of the pioneering Prussian Karl Kahlbaum, who ran the Gorlitz Sanatorium, Kraepelin described sample life histories for sufferers of dementia praecox which turned their existence into the narrative of an illness. Beginning with a working life in which the patients 'become negligent . . . pass no examinations, are turned away everywhere as useless, and easily fall into the condition of beggars and vagabonds', he underscored the pattern of a worsening of symptoms and general deterioration as time passed. Throughout, the patients showed a remarkable lack of concern for what befell them.

> Hopes and wishes, cares and anxieties are silent; the patient accepts without emotion dismissal from his post, being brought to the institution,

sinking to the life of a vagrant, the management of his own affairs being taken from him; he remains without ado where he is put 'till he is dismissed; begs that he may be taken care of in an institution, feels no humiliation, no satisfaction; he lives one day at a time in a state of apathy. The background of his disposition is either a meaningless hilarity or a morose and shy irritability. One of the most characteristic features of the disease is a frequent, causeless, sudden outburst of *laughter*.[179]

On top of the lack of affect, the flattened emotion which becomes a dominant part of the condition when it is recast as schizophrenia, Kraepelin also notes a lack of regard for surroundings, or what we might today call a lack of reality-testing; the loss of feelings of disgust and shame, so that 'sphincters' are loosened any and everywhere, bodies uncovered, sexual acts performed in public, obscene talk, improper advances and shameless masturbation indulged in. The patients may either grow monosyllabic and lose all wish to express themselves, even insofar as making complaints; or, in contrast, their talk can be a prodigious flow which has no link to need or situation and can simply be a torrent of abuse or cursing. Onset in males is with adolescence; with women a little later, often after the first child, and sexual activity in women is (inevitably) more marked.

Kraepelin understands all this as in some sense an early stage of senile dementia. It is a premature version of the same death-dealing syndrome and he maintains little hope, except through the vagaries of fate, of change or cure.

A hospital doctor who was more hospitable to Freud's findings and had written an early positive review of the *Studies on Hysteria* emphatically disagreed with Kraepelin's diagnosis. This was Eugen Bleuler, and his Burghölzli Hospital on the outskirts of Zurich became one of the premier hospitals of the early twentieth century. It was here that schizophrenia was diagnosed as a separate condition – not as Kraepelin would have had it, as an early manifestation of senile dementia, or dementia praecox. Unlike Kraepelin, Bleuler was convinced that schizophrenia was not irreversible, but was susceptible to improvement if patients were talked to and treated on a one-to-one basis, as well as given tasks in the real world.

Eugen Bleuler had been the first person in his peasant village of Zollikon, not far from Zurich, to go to medical school. Story would have it that as a former student at the Burghölzli, and then the chief of a secondary asylum in Rheinau, he was hardly in the front line for the senior post at the hospital, which was attached to a highly prestigious professorship at the University of Zurich. But Auguste Forel, the retiring head of the Burghölzli, wanted someone in place who would keep up his ban on alcohol – a potentially profitable trade for asylum chief and canton alike – and he knew Bleuler could be trusted in this. In 1898, a year before Kraepelin published his diagnosis of dementia praecox, Bleuler took over the Burghölzli.

Bleuler was a dedicated doctor who rose to new ideas, but was conscientiously cautious in their execution. At Rheinau, he had lived for ten years amidst the inmates; his personal rule, based on intimacy with the patients, meant that the mad had rallied in what many would have considered unthinkable circumstances. They had helped with the sick during a typhoid outbreak, for instance. Even the most dangerous had safely yielded axes when wood had to be fetched. These challenging tasks had helped alleviate and sometimes 'cure'. Unexpected discharges had ensued. At the Burghölzli, Bleuler ran a tight ship. Some, like the fiery young Jung, chafed under his stewardship. But Bleuler brought a fine team of doctors to the hospital and introduced a regime of new psychological medicine which would make the Burghölzli recognized as far afield as America as a model teaching institution.

As in most nineteenth-century hospitals and clinics, doctors and their wives at the Burghölzli lived amidst their patients. What was new with Bleuler was that patients had to be seen regularly and individually twice a day. This was not a matter of surveillance, since Bleuler was aware that surveillance itself 'awakes, increases and maintains the suicidal drive'[180] that schizophrenics so profoundly suffer. It was a question of talking therapy, of accommodation to the patient's way of seeing the world, of attentiveness. Doctors were instructed to write down *everything* a patient said, whether it sounded like nonsense or not. The entire medical staff did rounds together three times a week and discussed patient cases and care. All this reinvention of the Burghölzli took time, and although Bleuler knew that Kraepelin's diagnosis did not match his own experience of patients, he didn't publish his findings on schizophrenia until 1911, though his students were led into his thinking far sooner, as were those who came to his important 1908 lecture.

Disputing that there was such a thing as premature dementia, Bleuler suggested renaming the condition 'schizophrenia', from the Greek 'splitting' and 'soul' or 'mind'. It was intended as a dynamic concept. He didn't mean that the patient was inhabited by 'personalities' who lived side by side within her, but that she seemed prone to splitting affective states, was inwardly 'ambivalent' − a term he coined − as well as intellectually caught in the oppositional value of words and associations. Love and hate, wanting and not wanting, in the Bleulerian or indeed Freudian sense, coexist. They occupy the same moment. Bleuler's schizophrenia is difficult to diagnose since its most visible characteristics, when they are not at a peak of intensity, fall within the spectrum of health. Amongst these characteristics he cites 'indifference, lack of energy, unsociability, stubbornness, moodiness'. He combines this with symptoms like 'blocking, confusion of symbols with reality', creating neologisms.[181] Fundamental to the condition as a whole is not today's popular attribute of 'hearing voices' but a lack of affect and a loosening of associations, so that ideas don't cohere in a usual way, and facts which do not suit affects are split off and take on a symbolic life.

As Bleuler describes it in his long book on the condition, the schizophrenic can manifest a complete lack of interest in external events, yet register them in detail. It is the persistent indifference to vital interests that is indicative of the disease; this is not the negativity of depression but a profoundly flat affect, an absence − what Freud, partly in response to Bleuler's work with this general category of psychosis, described as a 'turning away of the libido from the external world'. At times, Bleuler points out, schizophrenia can look like hysteria or paranoia in its ravings, and only time will help the doctor arrive at a diagnosis. In his generalizations, which sometimes seem to grapple irresolutely with the ineffability of conditions − and which lack the clinical acuity of description that Kraepelin provides − there is an underlying sense that he is trying to contend with a person rather than a patient described in a hospital record. Bleuler's subject inhabits a changing reality both internal and external, not the fixity of a medical diagnosis which can only lead to deterioration.

Assiduous in his care of patients, generous to them and even to his renegade staff, Bleuler was perhaps a better doctor than theoretician. Yet he remained open to the new. Unlike his great student Jung, he also remained a lifelong friend of Freud's and the two kept up a lively correspondence. Bleuler corroborated Freud's insights about sexual disturbance in his own work with patients. Indeed, Bleuler applied the psychoanalytic method to the psychoses only to find that – despite Freud's caution in this area – it helped treatment. He and Freud shared a sense of the mind as a dynamic space, an area of conflict in which, as Freud noted, 'even the apparently most obscure and arbitrary mental phenomena invariably have a meaning and a causation'.[182] Much of this was, of course, also common to Carl Gustav Jung, who eventually fell out with both of the older men.

Jung joined the Burghölzli Hospital staff in the spring of 1901 just when Bleuler was primed to launch a 'laboratory' and a new set of experiments in psychology. These were modelled on tests that Emil Kraepelin, trained by the psychologist Wilhelm Wundt, had set up in Munich under the aegis of Gustav Ashaffenburg as a way of further studying the minds of the mad. The experiment consisted of a timed series of word associations: the doctor or experimenter would hold up a card bearing a word to which the patient would reply. Response was timed and everything carefully noted. In Munich, the tests were repeated with normal subjects, and then intoxicated normal subjects. These latter results were compared with sufferers from dementia praecox and found to have a kinship, in that both associated predominantly to the sound of the word, rather than to its sense.

Jung, well read in a wide array of psychiatric literature and familiar with Freud's early work, was an attribute for the Burghölzli. An ambitious young medic, he finished his dissertation under Bleuler. The older man also sent him to France, where he attended Janet's lectures. On his return Jung thought of applying the word-association tests to patients to investigate how internal distractions and competing ideas might affect the associative process. Intense emotional associations, it turned out, interfered with ordinary responses. This pointed to possible sites of repression, most of which were found to have a sexual basis, as Jung's paper, co-authored with another young researcher, Franz Ricklin, 'The

Associations of Normal Subjects', spelled out. This was indeed a find. A psychological test had been devised which gave evidence of the existence of unconscious, 'feeling-toned ideas' and also provided a tool for uncovering buried 'emotional complexes'. Jung barely bothered to acknowledge that all this corroborated Freud's theoretical findings. Nor did he reveal the identity of his subjects. In time-honoured scientific fashion, one of his first had been himself. The other was a young Russian woman he was later to label a 'schizophrenic hysteric', Sabina Spielrein. Her story is intricately enmeshed with the battle between the Titans of psychoanalysis, Freud and Jung.

Sabina Spielrein (1885–1942) and C.G. Jung (1875–1961)

Much has been written about Sabina Spielrein's relationship with the two men and particularly with Jung. Yet the importance of Sabina's own story as a *patient* early diagnosed with Bleuler's 'schizophrenia' and so permitted the possibility of getting better rather than languishing under what could well have been, given her extreme early symptoms, a Kraepelinian sentence of dementia praecox, has largely been neglected.

Spielrein began as Jung's patient, then latterly and secretly became his lover. Jung, in an attempt to rid himself of what he feared might be the scandal of her, 'gave' her up and handed her over to Freud, having used her interesting case to help establish his relationship with the founding father of psychoanalysis. In the partisan battles that afflict the history of psychoanalysis and what became Jung's 'analytic psychology', blame has been cast in different ways, depending in part on the source materials to hand. Jung has been targeted for allowing the 'transference' to go a tad too far, let alone for committing adultery with a patient and passing off – perhaps inadvertently – some of her ideas as his own. On the other side, Freud has been blamed for initially taking Jung's side and treating Sabina as a pawn in a relationship between two dominant, doctoring males, without ever taking her own contribution to psychoanalysis seriously enough. Finally Spielrein herself has been blamed as a seductive and plotting 'Jewess', who led the married hero Jung astray, indeed fantasized a passionate affinity and affair, then threatened to expose him after he had cured her of a serious illness.

Conventional morality aside, blame in this case may be rather more a matter of affiliation than of a cool view of the inevitably muddled progress of any psychological treatment or love affair, complex enough even when the key players at one time or another don't both rue and revel in their actions.

Sabina Spielrein was admitted to the Burghölzli on 17 August 1904, accompanied by policemen and an uncle. She had exhausted one private doctor, been refused by another and been violent at her hotel. Eighteen years old, she was the first of four surviving children of wealthy Russian Jews from Rostov on Dom, her mother already a university graduate, her father a merchant. Herself well educated, adept at a number of languages including Latin and Greek, and intensely intelligent, Sabina was in all ways a singular patient for the public facility that the Burghölzli was. A gymnasium graduate, despite her illness she had been admitted to the Zurich Medical School — which took only foreign women, and then only a small number. Withdrawn and difficult ever since puberty and the death of her younger sister, she had suffered a severe breakdown that summer. The private doctor her parents had taken her to could not manage the wildness of the young woman's deliria. The Burghölzli was a final resort.

Jung depicted Sabina anonymously in a lecture he delivered three years later, in 1907. He elaborated on her anal obsessions and her sadomasochistic relationship to her father, which it seemed lay at the root of her disorder.

> Puberty started when she was thirteen. From then on fantasies developed of a thoroughly perverse nature which pursued her obsessively. These fantasies had a compulsive character: she could never sit at a table without thinking of defecation while she was eating, nor could she watch anyone else eating without thinking of the same thing, and especially not her father. In particular, she could not see her father's hands without feeling sexual excitement; for the same reason she could no longer bear to touch his right hand . . . If she was reproached or even corrected in any way, she answered by sticking out her tongue, or even with convulsive laughter, cries of disgust, and gestures of horror,

because each time she had before her the vivid image of her father's chastising hand, coupled with sexual excitements, which immediately passed over into ill-concealed masturbation . . .

It was perhaps Sabina's involuntary fits of laughter alternating with deep depression, erotic activity and seemingly psychotic flights that earned her the occasional label 'schizophrenic'. There is a fluidity of attributions in cases such as this, which only underscores the difficulty of diagnosis. Sabina's condition on admission 'had got so bad that she really did nothing else than alternate between deep depressions and fits of laughing, crying, and screaming. She could no longer look anyone in the face, kept her head bowed, and when anybody touched her stuck her tongue out with every sign of loathing.'[183]

Jung described Sabina again as a case history of 'psychotic hysteria' in *The Psychology of Dementia Praecox* (1907). The masochistic aspects are reminiscent of Celia Brandon.

A certain young lady could not bear to see the dust beaten out of her cloak. This peculiar reaction could be traced back to her masochistic disposition. As a child her father frequently chastised her on the buttocks, thus causing sexual excitation. Consequently she reacted to anything remotely resembling chastisement with marked rage, which rapidly passed over into sexual excitement and masturbation. Once, when I said to her casually, 'Well, you have to obey,' she got into a state of marked sexual excitement.[184]

Despite the horror of Sabina's symptoms – which no one considered as a malingering hysterical performance – and her evident pain, the cure took less than a year. Whether this was due to time away from a manipulative and competing mother who insisted on keeping her daughter as sexually pure and ignorant as the 'clean play' of her name, from an authoritarian father and a loveless household, or to treatment by the new psychoanalytic method and 'word association', or to love for her handsome young doctor and the growing ability to play dirty, or a combination of all three, is not altogether an answerable question.

In Sabina Spielrein's hospital chart, recently made available, there is a letter describing her addressed to Freud from Jung. Access to these records has clarified the mountain of speculation about Sabina's case and her relations with Jung. Written some four months after her discharge on 1 June 1904, this 'referral' was never actually delivered – as evidently at one moment Jung feared it would be necessary – by Sabina's mother to Freud. The letter is at once a deft case history and a recognition by Jung that matters with this young patient had moved beyond his control: he needs Freud to cope with this very Freudian case.

25.9.1905
Report about Ms. Spielrein to Professor Freud in Vienna, delivered to Mrs. Spielrein for possible use.

Dear Professor Freud:

The daughter of Mrs. Spielrein, Miss Sabina Spielrein, a medical student, suffers from hysteria. The patient has a heavy hereditary taint, father and mother are hysterics, especially the mother. A brother of the patient is a severe hysteric since his earliest youth. The patient is now 20 years old, clearly clinically ill for about the last 3 years. However, the pathogenic events and experiences, of course, reach back to her early age. I have analysed the clinical condition almost completely with the help of your method and with a favourable result from early on.

Jung goes on to describe how after a childhood of being beaten by her father, threats or the sight of any aggression became enough to bring about sexual arousal, but after analysis there emerged 'a most intelligent and gifted person endowed with the highest degree of sensibility'. That summer, however, when her studies resumed, an inadvertent side-effect had manifested itself – one that Jung is a little too quick to blame on Sabina: 'In the course of her treatment the patient had the bad luck to fall in love with me. She continues to rave blatantly to her mother about this love and her secret spiteful glee in scaring her mother is not the least of her motives. Therefore the mother would like, if needed, to have her referred to another doctor, with which I naturally concur.'[185]

For whatever mixture of reasons, contact with Freud didn't take place for some time to come. Meanwhile the love, it emerged, was hardly only on Sabina's side.

Sabina was in many respects a model patient. She was the first patient that Jung – with Bleuler's constant support – treated with the new Freudian psychoanalytic method; and the one with whom he was so ably led to the emotional complexes behind word associations. Her treatment after the first three months, when her symptoms were at their most intense, became almost an exploratory collaboration in the ways of the new science.

The hospital notes speak of Jung's analytically dissolving Sabina's present symptoms, her tics and grimaces and defensive gestures, her masochistic dreams and daydreams, by tracing them back to her father's erotically charged beatings. The sexual basis is important, but, in line with Freud's own changing sense of the need for an original sexual trauma to provoke disorders, no single one is found here. Sabina suffers from fantasy. Jung 'educates' her in the reasons behind her symptoms and allows the aggression and rage embedded in them a discharge.

Towards the end of her hospital stay, when Jung deems her well enough to take up her medical studies and she registers at the university naming the Burghölzli as her address, Bleuler gives Sabina a medical statement certifying that she has undergone treatment for 'nervousness with hysterical symptoms', and recommends that she begin her studies at the medical school of Zurich University that autumn. Bleuler and Jung also write to Sabina's father asking him to release his daughter from any duties towards family members, whether it is writing letters or looking after one of her brothers who was to study in Zurich.

Sabina moved into an apartment in central Zurich and continued to see Jung as an outpatient at the Burghölzli. She saw him, it would appear, at irregular intervals and for a span probably ending in December of 1909. There is a correspondence about bills between her and Bleuler until then. It was probably during this period that the love affair – 'the poetry', as Sabina called it – between her and Jung rose to its romantic and passionate heights and tumbled into destructive disarray. In her diary in 1910, she looked back at that time: 'We came to know each other, we became fond of each other without noticing it was happening; it was too late for flight; several times we sat "in tender embrace". Yes, it was a great deal!'[186]

The great deal was not only sexual passion, which even without the naming of parts it is clear – given the tenor of letters and diary, the talk of contraception and birth – there was. Sabina also became the spur for

Jung's concept of the 'anima'[187] — that unconscious feminine component which is part of everyman and which, materialized in a loved
other, becomes a key to the self. He showed her a section of his diary in
which it became clear that he saw her, indeed had had a vision of her, as
a new edition of his mediumistic cousin, Hélène Preiswerk.[188] Then,
too, Sabina was Jung's stimulus to fresh ideas, a necessary party to his
work, not only as a patient but as an intellectual interlocutor. Certainly
she felt herself to have been Jung's collaborator. From early on, he had
given her psychiatric literature to read. They shared ideas and she
helped him with his thesis. Later, when everything had gone wrong, she
explained all this in a letter to Freud:

> We had numerous discussions about it, and he said, `Minds such as yours
> help advance science. You must become a psychiatrist.' I stress these
> things again and again so that you may see it was not just the usual
> doctor–patient relationship that brought us so close together. He was
> writing the paper while I was still in the mental hospital . . . I spoke of
> the equality or intellectual independence of woman, whereupon he
> replied that I was an exception, but his wife was an ordinary woman and
> accordingly only interested in what interested her husband.[189]

Only ten years older than his patient, Jung had allowed an eroticized transference to get the upper hand in his relations with Sabina and
had engaged in a full-scale affair, one which combined intellectual and
spiritual affinities with sex. On 20 June 1908, he writes to her to say,
'You have vigorously taken my unconscious into your hands with your
saucy letters.'[190] The letters move from being addressed to 'My dear
Miss' to 'My dear friend' to 'My dear'. He is happy at last to have hopes
of loving a person who isn't smothered in the 'banality of habit'. He feels
'calmer and freer' after their meetings.

That sex followed on from therapy was perhaps not altogether surprising in the heady atmosphere at the Burghölzli in those years. This is
evident not only from Sabina's highly charged and subtle diary, but
from Jung's adventurously 'wild analysis' of the rampant 'polygamist'
Otto Gross and his own descriptions of how women understand Freud
best of all. An erotic atmosphere pervaded the hospital wards as a
whole: 'It is amusing to see how the female outpatients go about

diagnosing each other's erotic complexes although they have no insight into their own.' With uneducated patients the chief obstacle seems to be the atrociously crude transference.[191]

Spielrein's affair with Jung climbed to dangerous peaks of intellectual romanticism. Half in love with each other's symbolic ethnicities, the 'other' they represented in myth and imagination, both prone to a heightened spiritualizing of experience, Jung and Spielrein, German and Jew, fantasized the birth of their own Wagnerian Siegfried, the hero of the new age – the symbol of a redemptive coming together of male heroism and feminine instinct, of destruction and creation. Each played out incestuous fantasies of the other in dreams and interpretation. Hope, doom, secrecy, a sexual charge doubled because of the intimacy forged in the doctor–patient dyad – all these are beautifully and intelligently evoked in the pages of Sabina's diary, where she emerges as a more generous spirit than the Jung she idealizes, who is naturally enough worried about his rich wife and his respectable career. But from that Spielrein–Jung coupling come the ideas which shape both their later work.

Both Freud and Jung later acknowledged, though never fully enough, their debt to Sabina. Freud seems uncomfortable with her formulations in the same way he would be with Lou Salomé's. High-sounding, philosophical and soulful, rooted in German philosophy and poetry, they always seem to sound meaningful but evanesce into vagueness. Freud seems at once to want to recognize the value of such grand pronouncements as the 'opposing forces of creation and destruction in the sex instinct' and to worry about the use of substantives which lack the grounded detail he tried to give even his pleasure principle and its opposing death instinct. Far closer to Sabina Spielrein is Jung's own work. The precognition she had lived during their affair, so close to his own experiences, made him reconsider the nature of the unconscious. Both thought in terms of polarized mythical and mystical forces. Jung's later work journeyed into the meanings of symbols and their transformative potential. In contrast to Freud, he hypothesized a collective, rather than individual, unconscious – a realm of shared archetypes and cultural narratives necessary to the journey towards an integrated self.

Jung's first communication to Freud was not the letter he had initially thought would go as a referral with Sabina. Instead, in April 1906, a year after that had been penned, he sent Freud his *Diagnostic Association Studies*, which of course included the association tests he had performed on Sabina. That summer, Freud wrote his study *Gradiva*, where the 'cure through love' was named. The cure, here, was enacted by a woman, and it is perhaps not coincidental that Sabina, the patient cured in the hothouse of association that was the Burghölzli, went on to become one of the first women analysts.

In that electric early part of their correspondence, where letters and ideas fly between Jung and Freud as if each has at last found a worthy interlocutor, Freud writes sometimes twice a day to the younger man; his hope – not all that distant in some sense from Sabina's – is of an extension of his all too Jewish science into the wider German world. On 6 December 1906, Freud writes – as if he might already in advance have sensed that Jung is in some erotic trouble – before the latter has recounted a dream where fears about his marriage are there for everyone except himself to see (29 December 1906). Jung defends himself from any Freudian imputation that there might be a sexual lack. Freud proceeds to give him a lesson in analysis, which rings uncannily, though in the kindest of terms, as if he somehow knows or empathetically imagines what Jung has been up to:

> You are probably aware that our cures are brought about through the fixation of the libido prevailing in the unconscious (transference), and that this transference is most readily obtained in hysteria. Transference provides the impulse necessary for understanding and translating the language of the ucs. [unconscious]; where it is lacking, the patient does not make the effort or does not listen when we submit our translation to him. Essentially, one might say, the cure is effected by love. And actually transference provides the most cogent, indeed, the only unassailable proof that neuroses are determined by the individual's love life.

Jung's rejection of Freud's interpretation, his unwillingness wholly to accept this succinct account of how transference works in psychoanalysis – its very existence generated by the patient's sexual difficulties – may have something to do with the whole Sabina muddle as much as with any growing intellectual unwillingness to accept Freud's sexual aetiology, already under attack elsewhere.

Nonetheless, Jung's stress that his patient base is usually so very different from Freud's, together with Bleuler's emphasis on the lack of affect in schizophrenia, may point to a wider problem in this understanding of transference as sexually charged, particularly with patients in whom the very nature of affect, its impossibility, is what has gone awry. It may be that transference with schizophrenic or 'psychotic' patients is precisely what can't exist. So while he was defending himself from acknowledging what was happening with Sabina, a matter perhaps not altogether unconnected with his later overt rejection of the whole sexual base of the Freudian project, Jung was also pointing to a real area of professional concern and theoretical difference. As ever, theoretical differences doubled up with personal ones: Jung, who found gratitude difficult and returned few favours unpunished broke with a Freud who too often wanted more loyalty than was either possible or reasonable from his growing psychoanalytic progeny.

Sabina Spielrein finally made her way to Freud – as herself, and not cloaked as case material – when her affair with Jung as well as their working relationship had broken down. An anonymous tell-tale letter had reached her mother – probably through Emma Jung, who might have sensed that her duplicitous husband had reached the end of his tether. In any case, with a new baby in tow, this time the much desired and symbolically feared male, Emma was seriously overstretched. Mrs Spielrein confronted her daughter, who wrote to Freud in great distress in June 1909 and asked for a 'brief audience'.

On the very day he received the letter, Freud wrote to Jung to inquire who this woman was. His tone is light, a note between professionals: is she 'a chatterbox, or a paranoiac'? Jung telegrammed, allowing Freud to write to Sabina to ask what she wanted of him more precisely: he cannot have her travel all the way to Vienna without knowing whether the journey will be expedient or not. Meanwhile, an explanatory and rather deceitful letter of 4 June 1909 arrives from Jung on Freud's desk. Jung explains that Freud already knows about Sabina as his 'test case, for which reason I remembered her with special gratitude and affection. Since I knew from experience that she would immediately relapse if I withdrew my support, I prolonged the relationship over the years and in the end found myself morally obliged, as it were, to devote a large measure of friendship to her, until I saw that an unintended wheel had started turning, whereupon I finally broke with her.'

All of which might just about be taken as a gentlemanly masquerade. But Jung goes on to add that all the while Sabina was 'systematically planning my seduction . . . and is now seeking revenge'. He accuses her of spreading rumours that he will soon get a divorce and marry her; and collides all this insidiously with the business of that arch seducer Otto Gross whose presence has legitimated amorous imaginings in everyone.

In his reply Freud pacifies, man to man, and explains again how treacherous the analytic business can be, particularly to one as young as Jung, when confronted with women who want to charm. He advises that Jung use the experience to thicken his skin so that he can dominate the '"countertransference" – which is after all a permanent problem for us'. The cure through love, Freud is saying, is not an actual love affair.

His next letter to Jung – who he has just learned has, like him, been invited to America – is to underline the point once more and advise that he must learn to handle such 'laboratory explosions'. Meanwhile, having found out independently from Sabina that she wants to talk to him about Jung, he uses diplomacy, and suggests to her that perhaps it is time to shed feelings that come out of the therapeutic situation: 'I would urge you to ask yourself whether the feelings that have outlived this close relationship are not best suppressed and eradicated, from your own psyche, I mean, and without external intervention and the involvement of third persons.'

Sabina's strength is visible in that what she took from Freud's advice was the sense that he loved Jung and was thus well placed to understand what they had been through. She wrote out their affair. That act itself helped her to regain some composure, and she was able to face Jung after a lecture and say she wanted peace. Eventually they found it: recently released documents reveal that after a cooling-off period they resumed an epistolary friendship, occasionally met at congresses and sent each other work. Sabina, now the peacemaker, even tried to bring some understanding between Freud and Jung. By 1913 they had thoroughly fallen out, ostensibly over the sexual question. Meanwhile,

Sabina had completed her medical degree, had married and had a child, and trained as an analyst to become one of the early women members of Freud's Vienna Psychoanalytic Society – the only woman member at the time. She later acted as the formidable developmental psychologist Jean Piaget's analyst, and became one of the leading figures in post-revolutionary Russian psychoanalysis, setting up an experimental school in Moscow with Vera Schmidt.

Her trajectory marks out what was to become a usual enough one in the field, perhaps already traced out at the birth of the profession with Pinel, who made warders of his patients. Sabina moves from patient to practitioner, having learned the lessons of the unconscious and, in her case, the particular dangers of the eroticized transference. Jung, of course, would repeat the process with Tony Wolff, another Jewish woman, one this time who would remain his lifelong mistress and intellectual partner.

Sabina Spielrein's medical dissertation, 'On the Psychological Content of a Case of Schizophrenia (Dementia Praecox)', was begun under Bleuler while she was working as a medical assistant at the Burghölzli. Bleuler was slow in reading the draft, and Sabina in the summer of 1910 decided to show it to Jung, who had by this time resigned from the Burghölzli and set up in his newly built estate as an independent practitioner. He was also now, in part thanks to Freud, President of the International Psychoanalytical Association and editor of its *Jahrbuch*. Bleuler, who independently of Sabina also referred her thesis to Jung, suggested it should be published in the *Jahrbuch*, where it eventually appeared in 1911.

The thesis, on which Jung congratulated her and which also marked 'a new era' in their relations, demonstrates the kinship in Spielrein's and Jung's thinking. It also shows just how adept Spielrein was – undoubtedly aided by her own recent experience and her literary bent, as well as her interest, like Jung, in mythological parallels – at chasing meanings in disconnected talk. No injunction to Freud's 'free association' is necessary with her 'schizophrenic' patient. The woman seems to have no inner controls at all, no resistance of that kind, at least, to overcome. The sense Spielrein is able to make of her fractured discourse, the patience she, and indeed Bleuler's entire team, brought to bear on their 'schizophrenic's' disquisitions, once more reminds one of R.D. Laing's later insistence that even his wildest patients were talking sense. Indeed, in Spielrein's well-educated, hostile and irritating woman whose compulsive flow of coded language circles around disease, dirt and dissolution, there is something of Laing's Mary Barnes, who painted with her faeces.

Spielrein's patient is a Protestant woman married to a Catholic, who is something of a womanizer and betrays her repeatedly. Spielrein uncovers a 'Catholicizing' complex in her. This includes images of the birth of mankind and a host of 'Sistine Experiments'. Underlying it is a fear of being overwhelmed by sexual ideas, a conflict between desire and resistance which brings with it hallucinated punishments. Shades, again, of Celia Brandon. 'Poetry' – a term Sabina's patient shares with her analyst for sexual congress overlaid with a religious patina, or what might be called a beneficent and transformative sexuality – seems to come from Auguste Forel's book, *The Sexual Question*, in which the psychiatrist who had preceded Bleuler as Director of the Burghölzli reflected on *abstinence*.[192]

Spielrein's patient had other things in common with her young doctor. She noted about Dr. J – that is, Jung – that this attractive doctor had everyone in love with him; that he wanted to get divorced once a year. He also lay at the root of her repeated comment about being 'flogged through Basel' – which Spielrein, in chasing associations, interpreted as her feeling humiliated by the Basel-raised Jung's initial tests on her which she experienced as a sexual assault.

Already looking forward to her later work on the linking of opposites – the doubling up of destruction and creation in sexuality – Spielrein noticed that her patient's preoccupation with images of death also had a sexual base. The fragile ego of the schizophrenic, already fragmented, feared the merging that sex is as a dissolution of the self, a death-dealing activity, whatever its opposing transformative powers:

I want to emphasize the enormous importance of 'description by the opposite', which was discovered by Freud, for the development of delusions. A particularly important instance of this is the description of sexual activity by death symbolism. The reason for this phenomenon is, as I see it, within the character of the sexual act itself, or to put it more clearly, in the two antagonistic components of sexuality.

If Spielrein's own experience informed her understanding of her patients, she was only following in Freud's and Jung's footsteps in this invention of the new science. The hallucinative force of her early break-down – her schizophrenia, or hysteria – was far more akin to Jung's experience of psychosis than to Freud's. Her comment about what she calls the schizophrenic's partiality for vague and abstract terms as a defence against a specificity which would put an always too porous, buffeted self on the line, marks yet another insight into the impetus behind symbol formation and the shoring-up benefits of religious thinking:

> In general, the schizophrenic likes to use vague and abstract terms and this for good reason . . . The less sharply circumscribed a term is, the less it means something distinct and concrete and the more it can contain. I have the impression that a symbol in general is generated through the striving of a complex for multiplication, for dissolution into the overall system of (collective) thought . . . By this means the complex loses its personal character for the schizophrenic.[193]

When Jung received a later paper of Spielrein's, 'On Destruction', and his one-time patient was already in Vienna and a practising member of the psychoanalytic society there, he wrote to her in terms which could as easily apply to her thesis, which he said Freud had also commended highly:

> The paper is unusually intelligent and contains excellent ideas whose priority I am willing to recognize . . . Nobody should think that you have borrowed from me. There is no basis for that . . . Perhaps I myself borrowed from you; I have surely unintentionally swallowed a piece of your soul as well as you mine. It depends what one does with it. You have made something good out of it. It pleases me that you are my represen-tative in Vienna.[194]

In those heady days before the First World War, ideas flew between the various psychoanalytical and psychiatric headquarters. Conversation buzzed between analysts and patients across frontiers and in consulting room and hospital. Karl Abraham, Freud's key follower in Berlin, had also worked with Bleuler at the Burghölzli during the Jung–Spielrein years, and he had corresponded with Freud about his observations. Combining all this input, Freud translated the findings on schizophrenia (dementia praecox) into his own language of the defences:

> Abraham has very convincingly shown that the turning away of the libido from the external world is a particularly clearly-marked feature in dementia praecox. From this feature we infer that the repression is effected by means of detachment of the libido. Here once more we may regard the phase of violent hallucinations as a struggle between repression and an attempt at recovery by bringing the libido back again on to its objects. Jung, with extraordinary analytic acumen, has perceived that the deliria and motor stereotypes occurring in this disorder are the residues of former object-cathexes, clung to with great persistence. This attempt at recovery, which observers mistake for the disease itself, does not, as in paranoia, make use of projection, but employs a hallucinatory (hysterical) mechanism. This is one of the two major respects in which dementia praecox differs from paranoia.[195]

Bleuler, Jung, Spielrein, the early doctors and patients at the Burghölzli, had between them invented a nascent disorder and inflected it with properties and understandings neither doctors nor perhaps patients had altogether seen before. The term 'schizophrenia' spread beyond the borders of Switzerland, though its use continued to be as erratic as the condition: sometimes it masked as hysteria, sometimes it fell within a more general rubric of the psychoses; at other times, it merged with the older and more genteel notion of breakdown. But in separating it out from dementia praecox, the Burghölzli, as Sabina Spielrein's case showed, had given patients with this serious disorder the possibility of a productive life.

Rooms of their own: Zelda Fitzgerald (1900–1998), Lucia Joyce (1907–1982), Virginia Woolf (1882–1941)

Switzerland had been the nineteenth century headquarters of sanatoria catering to tuberculosis patients. In the early twentieth, with a shift in illness patterns, it became the premier European site for mental clinics that more than rivalled their Austrian kin. When the famous American writer Scott Fitzgerald was looking for a sanatorium for his wife Zelda in June 1930, Prangins near Nyon was recommended. Run by Auguste Forel's son Dr Oskar Forel, Prangins had something of the aspect of a luxury resort. Located on the shores of Lake Geneva, amidst some hundred acres of beautifully landscaped grounds which included tennis courts and a winter garden, Prangins looked after its small number of 'guests' in four villas. Three others housed therapeutic staff. Forel diagnosed Zelda as schizophrenic.

Scott and Zelda Sayre Fitzgerald had been married for ten years. They were already a legendary couple, famous in the way that celebrity would only become again after rock and roll had invented pop stars. Precariously rich through the success of Scott's fiction — *This Side of Paradise, The Beautiful and the Damned, The Great Gatsby* and, most popular and lucrative of all, his many stories for the *Saturday Evening Post* — they spent and drank and spent some more that they didn't have in their peripatetic progression from the deep south of Zelda's childhood in Montgomery, Alabama, to the Midwest of Scott's, to New York, Paris, the Riviera, North Africa and back again, always and ever in search of the good, rich, leisured high life.

They were the very stuff of magazine copy, their life together a glittering and exuberant exhibition of what it meant to be young and daring in the Jazz Age. The twenties gaiety, the beauty and rebellious bravado they embodied — always already lost, a sweet memory before it had been fully lived — was the very stuff of Fitzgerald's art and sometimes hers. Of his novel *Tender Is the Night*, which turns Zelda's madness into fiction while steering, as so much of his writing does, perilously close to the autobiographical truth, Fitzgerald writes, 'The novel . . . should show a man who is a neural idealist, a spoiled priest, giving in for various causes to the ideas of the haute bourgeoisie, and in his rise to the top of the social world losing his idealism, his talent and turning to drink and dissipation.'[196] The man was a psychiatrist, Dick Driver, who saves and then is destroyed by the golden heiress, the little lost mad girl, Nicole Warren.

Somewhere along the way in the real life of excess and art, the Fitzgeralds had had a daughter, Scottie, born in October 1921, whom

Zelda, in the girl's early years, preferred not to notice. She was nine at the time of her mother's first breakdown. There had also been an abortion, and two love affairs – Zelda's, unlike Scott's, perhaps unconsummated, but both experienced as a betrayal by each. In the midst of all this, Zelda increasingly felt that she had nothing of her own, nothing that defined self and gave it boundaries: her writing, brilliant in its imagistic leaps, was not as successful as Scott's. Their child seemed to prefer him. Then, too, Zelda's idealized father, a strict and much respected judge, disapproved of her life.

Zelda had been a late child, a spoiled and much loved afterthought. Allowed to run wild by a mother who adored her, called 'baby' by the family into adulthood, she had grown in her teens into the wildly flirtatious and capricious belle of Montgomery, an expert in the performance of femininity if not of friendship. Handsome in his First World War captain's uniform, Scott had won her from a host of rival suitors. She recognized that jealousy both sparked and intensified his love, and that she needed him to feel it. She needed his desire, his attention, needed to be conquered to acquire definition. Somehow his jealousy limited what felt like her excessive depths of dependence.

When Scott's attention wandered, her acts grew increasingly reckless. In Los Angeles, legend has it, she burned all her clothes in the bath tub while Scott entertained next door. On another occasion, she collected dinner guests' jewellery and boiled it all in a great pot. When Scott knelt at the feet of Isadora Duncan at a restaurant in St Paul de Vence, Zelda plunged down a precipice of stairs.

As Fitzgerald drank more and more and lost himself in work or the inability to do it, since despite his alcoholism he could only write sober, desire dwindled. Zelda began to suspect him and accuse him of homosexuality, which rankled. They had always fought. Now they fought harder. In the late twenties, Zelda turned to dance both for escape and for a sense that here was something she could control, could succeed at. Ballet – practising, rehearsing, training, occasionally performing – became the compulsion that swallowed her days. In America, report has it, she would wordlessly abandon guests at the dinner table to practise ritualistically at the huge mirror and bar she had had installed. In Paris, ballet became as addictive as Scott's drinking, and more exhausting. It was her consuming ambition. It was also a ritual that allowed a certain sense of self-command. Zelda danced, rehearsed, danced and worried about her progress while Scott drank and sometimes wrote.

Then, in early 1930, came breakdown.[197] Eczema covered her. A recurrent asthma took hold. There were fainting spells. Terrifying voices, dreams, and phantoms of hallucinative force pursued her day and night. Dazed, incoherent, she attempted suicide to evade them. Morphine helped, but didn't stop the dreams' vivid pursuit. Scott took her to Malmont in Switzerland. The doctor's notes record that 'from an organic standpoint, there is nothing to report'. In calm moments, 'the patient understood quite well that she was at the end from a physical and nervous (psychological) standpoint and that she badly needed to take care of herself, but then an hour later she again wanted to know nothing about that and insisted on her return to Paris. Numerous discussions with her were fruitless because of all her real thoughts she expressed only a few incoherent ones.'[198] The call to Paris was the call of dance.

During one of her more reasonable moments, Zelda agreed to be transferred to Prangins for psychiatric treatment. With a friend, Scott came to collect her and delivered her to Dr Forel.

Fundamental to Zelda's treatment was separation from Scott. Both wanted to cooperate, yet three weeks in, Zelda wrote to him begging to be allowed home; urging him, also, to ask her beloved ballet teacher, Egorowa, where she thinks Zelda, who feels her legs are 'already flabby', stands with her ballet. Are her ambitions realistic? Scott asks for her. He is both relieved and surprised at Egorowa's judicious response. She tells him that Zelda started too late; but with that given, she has progressed well and could perform adequately in certain venues.

During the summer months and into the autumn, Zelda's treatment had little impact: lucidity alternated with descents into darkness. Her letters to Scott, regular enough, talk of panic, of things being 'barren and sterile and hopeless'. In this wavering condition, she is also able to describe something of what being inside her madness is like. She does it with all the panache of her extravagant, but utterly accurate, pen, conveying a sense of the limitlessness, the excitement, the intensity of colour and sensuous reality the experience brings.

> In Paris, before I realized that I was sick, there was a new significance to
> everything: stations and streets and façades of buildings – colours were

infinite, part of the air, and not restricted by the lines that encompassed them and lines were free of the masses they held. There was music that beat behind my forehead and other music that fell into my stomach from a high parabola and there was some of Schumann that was still and tender and the sadness of Chopin Mazurkas . . . And there was . . . a detachment as if I was on the other side of a black gauze – a fearless small feeling, and then the end at Easter – But even that was better than the childish, vacillating shell that I am now. I am so afraid that when you come and find there is nothing left but disorder and vacuum that you will be horror struck. I don't seem to know anything appropriate for a person of thirty. I suppose it's because of draining myself so thoroughly, straining so completely every fibre in that futile attempt to achieve with every factor against me.[199]

Other letters are more incoherent or violently hostile towards Scott, or simply plaintive. In the autumn, Forel, who had found Zelda uncommunicative and evasive, hit on the idea of having her write down her feelings about her family and herself. On paper, Zelda conveyed her family: her indulgent mother who came to her in striking images; the distant father for whom she had both respect and mistrust; her sudden sense of their unhappy marriage, though neither complained. She also wrote out her 'love affair with a French aviator'; the feeling that ballet provided an impersonal escape into a world in which she could express herself. And how one day 'the world between me and the others stopped'. No one, it seems, picked up on her accusing Scott of homosexuality at the same time as her ambitions focused on her ballet teacher as a signal that the boundaries between them had disintegrated. Her identification with Scott had taken on psychotic proportions which may well have played into their later mutual paranoia about whose life belonged to whose writing.

In September, Forel tried a new tack. He hypnotized Zelda, who succumbed like a perfect subject. In the thirteen-hour trance that followed, her terrible eczema oozed away. As she told Forel afterwards, she now realized the eczema was a warning device, signalling her deep conflicts with Scott. By November, it had returned, and Zelda was dull, unresponsive, lacking in affect. Under pressure from Scott, Forel called in Bleuler for a consultation. He wanted to be certain of his diagnosis, and discussing with the master this 'difficult patient . . . who was more intuitive than intelligent' would help. Scott reports all this in a letter to Zelda's parents, also noting that Forel had not been able to psycho-analyse Zelda for 'fear of disturbing and sacrificing what precious little equilibrium she possessed'.

Bleuler, according to Scott, was selected after some weighing up of the choices. Jung had been considered but, at the $500 Scott names as his consultation fee, at a time when a new Chevrolet coupé cost $600, thought too expensive. Scott was also under the impression that Jung handled primarily cases of neurosis, and Zelda's was more than that.

Bleuler travelled over from Zurich and spent an afternoon with Zelda, who treated him as 'a great imbecile', according to Forel. In the evening Bleuler, perhaps not so much an imbecile as all that, given the weight of his experience, reported to Forel and Scott. His diagnosis didn't differ from Forel's, but his prognosis was interesting – given the long-term pattern of Zelda's illness. Three out of four cases akin to Zelda's, Bleuler said – according to Scott's report to Zelda's parents – were discharged as cured, 'perhaps one of those three to resume perfect functioning in the world, and the other two to be delicate and slightly eccentric through life – and the fourth case to go right down hill into total insanity'.[200] Bleuler also indicated that Zelda's descent had begun some five years before and that though Scott might have retarded it, he couldn't have prevented it. He must stop blaming himself. Apparently, Scott asked the doctors if a change in his way of treating Zelda, who preferred men 'of a stable and strong character', might help. He was told that 'it was possible that a character of tempered steel would help, but that Mrs. Fitzgerald loved and married the artist in Mr. Fitzgerald'.

There is a possibility, of course, that Scott had finessed this last com-ment for the benefit of Zelda's strong and upright father. Sayre, an Alabama Supreme Court judge, was also – unlike Fitzgerald – utterly impervious to the mirror society turned on him and his ranking in the popularity stakes. The two men could hardly have been more different. Scott's residual grievance against Judge Sayre, the effect his emotional distance and unreachability had on Zelda, may have something to do with the way in which he transformed Nicole Warren's father in *Tender Is the Night* into a widowed seducer, whose sexual slips with his beautiful thirteen-year-old daughter had led to her breakdown a few years later.

It is as if Scott wanted to deflect responsibility on to the paternal figure. But there is no trace of any 'sexual abuse' in Zelda's actual history. In the novel, Fitzgerald introduces the matter almost blithely, thereby both giving sufficient reason for Nicole's breakdown and subsequent love–hatred of men, and chasing her father away from any further contact with his girl. She is saved by Dick Diver, only subsequently to destroy him.

Given that there are no grounds in Zelda's history for attributing sexual abuse, it is interesting, in terms of the 1980s 'discovery' of what has often been claimed in America as the patriarchal and psychiatric burial of women's real lived experience, that one of the country's most famous novels from an earlier era writes it large, but as a fictional invention. Zelda herself never mentioned an actual paternal seduction. She did, however, later trace or construct an Oedipal family narrative out of her childhood in her frankly autobiographical novel, *Save Me the Waltz*, where she pointed a finger of blame at her father, characterized as 'a living fortress', a stern, unloving judge as harshly correct as his wife was supple. The fictional father may give his daughter Alabama, security, but his inaccessibility is ruinous, and his unassailable integrity comes with a code of conduct the new generation can never hope to emulate. Safe when they are within his aegis, as soon as they enter the outside world the judge's children are crippled, unable to think for themselves, undone.

During his consultation, Bleuler had told Scott, it would be appropriate for him to see his wife occasionally. Fitzgerald moved to Lausanne and came for brief visits every two or three weeks. Meanwhile, there were letters on both sides trying to understand what might have gone wrong. Scott felt guilty; so did Zelda, by turns, though she veered between tenderness and vindictiveness: 'When you saw in Paris that I was sick, sinking – when you knew that I went for days without eating, incapable of supporting contact with even the servants, you sat in the bathroom and sang "Play in your own backyard".'[201]

Zelda's letters offer a finely honed insight into her schizophrenia, though they don't chart the violence that occasionally takes her over:

> My memories are mostly lost in sound and smell . . . Try to understand
> that people are not always reasonable when the world is as unstable

and vacillating as a sick head can render it – that for months I have been living in vaporous places peopled with one-dimensional figures and tremulous buildings until I can no longer tell an optical illusion from a reality – that head and ears incessantly throb and roads disappear, until finally I lost all control and power of judgement and was semi-imbecilic when I arrived here.[202]

Not so long after these letters she asked to see her daughter for Christmas, but when confronted by the child – a relationship which never ceased to cause her enormous difficulty – babbled incoherently and in a rush of violence destroyed the ornaments on the Christmas tree.

At the end of January, Scott's father died and he travelled back to America. In his absence, Zelda improved, eating regularly with the other patients for the first time and taking up skiing. Scott had always advised the doctors that regular exertion would help her, and it now seemed to. By spring, she had stopped recriminating him. On his return, they were able to go on brief outings together and contemplate a shared future. She also went out with other patients, revelling in the new freedom. In July 1931, after two weeks spent with both Scott and Scottie at Annecy, Zelda retrospectively conjured up the perfection of their holiday, the tennis, the warm nights dancing by the lake, 'white shoes gleaming like radium in the damp darkness. It was like good gone times when we still believed in summer hotels and the philosophies of popular songs.'[203]

She also wrote tenderly to Scott, offering herself and making light of her condition:

My dearest and most precious Monsieur,
We have here a kind of maniac who seems to have been inspired with erotic aberrations on your behalf. Apart from that she is a person of excellent character, willing to work, would accept a nominal salary while learning, fair complexion, green eyes, would like correspondence with refined young man of your description with intent to marry. Previous experience unnecessary. Very fond of family life and a wonderful pet to have in the home. Marked behind the left ear with a slight tendency to schitzophrenie [sic].[204]

Zelda's ability to mock herself was a sign of her improvement. After a trial of her ability to contend with life outside the clinic during a long visit to friends in Austria, Forel decided that she could leave Prangins. She had spent fifteen months in the clinic. The language in which Forel couches his prognosis shows a marked conservatism about woman's role, almost as if the whole feminist pre-war battle had to be fought again – which, of course, in most quarters, vote apart, it did. But his notions of inferiority are also the fashionable ones of Viktor Adler. Her case 'was a reaction to her feelings of inferiority (primarily towards her husband)'. Though Forel had also told Zelda that to keep writing was good for her, he estimated her ambitions in ballet as 'self-deceptions' which cause 'difficulties between the couple'. Prognosis was only favourable if conflict could be avoided.

In 1966, writing to Nancy Milford, Zelda's biographer, Forel 'put aside' his original diagnosis of schizophrenia, explaining that now, while 'certain symptoms and behaviours or activities, are called *schizoid*', this does not 'mean that the person is schizophrenic'.[205] Times had changed. By 1966 the wonder drug chlorpromazine had come along, eliciting differing definitions and diagnoses of schizophrenia – functioning, one might say, as a diagnostic agent in the same manner as Charcot's hypnotism: if it worked, then hysteria (or schizophrenia) was present.

Whether or not Zelda was schizophrenic in 1960s terms or not, she certainly couldn't follow Forel's injunction about conflict. It couldn't be avoided, and not only with Scott. Zelda turned out to be Bleuler's third kind of patient, delicate and eccentric throughout her life, with periods in institutions. These served a double purpose of providing an ordered existence, while removing her from an increasingly difficult life with an alcoholic Scott.

Another troubled young woman arrived at Prangins not long after Zelda had left. On 30 July 1933, twenty-six-year-old Lucia Joyce, a talented contemporary dancer, sometime member of Paris's racy Surrealist set, was confined to the asylum on doctors' advice and with her worried father, James Joyce's Consent. She stayed just long enough to get Forel's diagnosis of schizophrenia, reachable by 'persuasion and suggestion', before she was taken home again to Paris. Here her frenzied outbursts and violent acts – such as cutting the telephone wires – had her back in the asylum the following February.

As stormy and uninhibited in temperament as her romantic name-sake, Lucia di Lammermoor, Lucia didn't fare as well as Zelda had under the constant vigilance and order Forel and his staff imposed at Prangins. Far from the attention of her father, the one man in her life who – her biographer Carol Loeb Shloss[206] argues – had any impact on her, Lucia was amenable to neither care nor persuasion. She spent a fair part of her stay in closed, solitary quarters, less furious only when she could engage in sports. Like Zelda, physical exertion, preferably in dance, kept the inner demons or the chemical system in balance, if only partially. When her mother Nora and James Joyce came to collect her seven months or so later, she set fire to her room in some symbolically apt enactment of her need for her father. Joyce said of her that whatever 'spark' he pos-sessed had been transmitted to Lucia and 'kindled a fire in her brain'. Certainly Jung, whom Lucia next consulted, felt that 'fire' had much to do with her father. Jung hated Joyce's *Ulysses*. He judged it with undis-guised ferocity as the 'wreckage of a violently amputated boyhood', 'a delirious confusion of the subjective and psychic with objective reality', containing 'nothing pleasing', an analogy for 'schizophrenia'.[207]

For Jung, Lucia seemed to be not much more than her father's symp-tom. His first task was to separate the two psychically so that Lucia might be amenable to treatment. But despite the fact that he appointed a kindly minder, Cary Baynes, to act as something of a 'mother' thera-pist in the overseeing of Lucia, whose own mother seemed to have raised her with more resentment than love, Lucia did not improve. The bond with her father was unbreechable. Lucia remained closed to the transference Jung needed to establish for the talking cure to begin. He called her Joyce's anima, his *femme inspiratrice*. By January 1935, the treatment had stopped.

There was to be no real respite for Lucia: the bouts of unpredictable fury alternated with despairing lucidity for the rest of her days. The war separated her from her father, who died, blind and broken, in January 1941. Miraculously Lucia survived both the war years and the Nazis in a clinic outside Paris run by a Dr Delmas. Harriet Weaver, Joyce's bene-factress, looked after her far better than her mother or brother. With Delmas's death in 1951, Lucia was moved to St Andrew's Hospital in

Northampton, the asylum where Celia Brandon had earlier stayed. Lucia lived here until 1982, the straitjacket used to confine her eruptions of furious violence eventually replaced with phenothiazine.

After Zelda was released from Prangins, the Fitzgeralds moved back to America. The Depression was at its height. They settled near Zelda's family in Montgomery, both once more taking up their writing, Zelda with a new-found discipline and speed, which soon meant publication for her stories. Offered a contract in Hollywood, Scott left – both for financial reasons and because life in Montgomery, where the judge was dying, was stifling. He died in November, and Zelda coped with the funeral and her mother's grief. But after Christmas during a holiday with Scott in Florida, the eczema appeared again. Sleepless, Zelda found a flask of Scott's whiskey, drank it down and woke him at dawn in a tumult of irrational thoughts in which 'someone is causing the eczema and the eye –hurting with my connivance' – as Scott wrote to Dr Forel on 1 February 1932, asking for advice. He had earned enough money to buy him time to work on his big novel and he didn't want to have to spend it on a clinic for Zelda. But ten days later, Zelda's state once more scared them both, and she asked to be taken to hospital. The next day, having wired Dr Adolf Meyer, the director of the Henry Phipps Psychiatric Clinic of the Johns Hopkins University Hospital in Baltimore, Zelda moved in.

Swiss-born Adolf Meyer had not only studied medicine and psychiatry on his home terrain, but had visited key European centres before coming to America in 1892, where he was led to believe the scope for his ambitions might be greater. This proved to be the case: in rapid succession Meyer moved from staff pathologist at a mental hospital in Kamkakee, Illinois, to Worcester, Massachusetts, one of the many American asylums to have deteriorated into vast state 'bins'. It, too, wanted to shift into the new scientific age, with his help. From there in 1901, Meyer went to the Pathological Institute in New York City. Through these years, he shifted from a belief in pathology as the key to brain science towards a 'bedside' approach which involved extensive taking of histories, investigation of the patient's environment and record keeping. Kraepelin was his model, as he was for the nascent American psychiatric profession as a whole at that time: his textbook was the most widely used teaching instrument until Bleuler's arrived in translation in 1923.

American hospitals had traditionally kept science and the clinic separate: Meyer was one of the doctors who helped to build up a psychiatry which brought them together, and in 1910, when he took up an appointment as Professor of Psychiatry at Johns Hopkins in Baltimore, their union was precisely his goal. In 1913 the new four-storey Phipps Clinic, with its facilities for medical, psychological and laboratory investigation, proudly opened its doors to patients and to medical students. Given Meyer's wish to be all-embracing, it was perhaps inevitable that he would continue moving with the times towards a more psychosocial model of mental illness and potential cure. By the time Zelda arrived at the Phipps, it was the country's premier psychiatric institution, a training hospital which combined medicine with Meyer's own eclectic version of psychoanalytic practice and it also boasted that innovation, an outpatients' clinic.

By the 1930s Meyer had more or less put biological psychiatry behind him and was well on his way towards an understanding of schizophrenia as psychogenic.[208] In his influential doctoral thesis on paranoid psychosis, based on the case of Aimée, the famous French psychoanalyst Jacques Lacan cites Meyer approvingly as an example of a doctor who daringly took on psychoanalytic treatment of paranoid and hallucinatory patients.

Zelda was seen by Meyer, whose Germanic authority made her rebellious and uncooperative. Her resident physician, the young Dr Mildred T. Squires, fared better, and it was to her that Zelda eventually dedicated her one finished and published novel, *Save Me the Waltz*. But despite the presence of the young woman doctor, Zelda's history was almost entirely assessed from Scott's point of view: she was seen as irritable, over-ambitious, uncooperative in her marriage. The hospital was also worried about her plays on words and her sudden leaps of thought, suspecting there might be some kind of physical disorder present.

Another way of seeing this is that it is precisely in the sensuous or verbal leaps that Zelda makes – her surprising vantage point on experience – that her considerable literary talent resides. When Dr Squires read her work, she commented to Scott that, although it was vivid and had charm, it tended to break off and leave the reader in the lurch. Scott wisely corrected her apprehensions about the needs of modernist style – the fact that 'the form of so many modern novels is less a progression than a series of impressions, as you know – rather like the slowly-turned pages of an album'.[209]

Zelda was plagued by an involuntary smile and Dr Meyer's harping on her inability to make friends. She also feared she might spend the rest of her life in sanatoria. The talking therapy had a way of escalating neuroses, perhaps even the learning of a few new ones. She wrote to Scott early on in her stay:

> Life has become practically intolerable. Everyday I develop a new neurosis until I can think of nothing to do but place myself in the Confederate Museum at Richmond. Now it's money: we must have more money. Tomorrow it will [be] something else again: that I ran when mamma needed me to help her move, that my hips are fat and shaking with the vulgarities of middle-age, that you had to leave your novel . . . a horrible sickening fear that I shall never be able to free myself from the mediocrity of my conceptions. For many years, I have lived under the disastrous pressure of a conviction of power and necessity to accomplish without the slightest ray of illumination. The only message I ever thought I had was four pirouettes and a feueté [sic].[210]

Ballet was replaced at the Phipps by a strict writing routine. Zelda slept well. By March the first draft of her novel was finished and Dr Squires was pleased with her progress. Scott's reaction, however, was vituperative. Zelda had sent him the novel only after she had mailed it to their joint publisher, a certain sign that she had foreseen his rage. She had used some of the material he had read to her from a draft of *Tender Is the Night* – material, needless to say, which was about her. Reaching agreement on whose life belonged to which member of the writing couple wasn't to be easy, though eventually a very few, if telling, excisions ended up by satisfying Scott.

Luxuriant in its imagery, redolent in sensuousness, *Save Me the Waltz* contains particularly lucid insights into the mind of its heroine, Alabama, a barely masked version of Zelda. The description of Alabama's love for David/Scott looks forward, as her biographer Nancy

Milford so accurately points out, to the psychiatrist R.D. Laing's description of schizophrenia.

When she meets David, Alabama feels she is looking into a mirror at herself. As they kiss, she feels herself getting closer and closer until he becomes distorted in her vision and she senses 'the essence of herself pulled finer and smaller like those streams of spun glass that pull and stretch till there remains but a glimmering illusion'. Though she doesn't break, Alabama in love is a very small, suspended, ecstatic self who can through the kiss enter David's grey and ghostly brain, and run over 'a mystic maze of folds and ridges' until she loses herself in a worried frenzy wandering through the bleakness of his mind which is also the empty fragility of her own.

In *The Divided Self*, the sixties bible on what he sees as the family-induced madness that is schizophrenia, R.D. Laing conjures up the schizophrenic's tension between the desire to reveal himself and the desire to conceal himself. He feels both

> more exposed, more vulnerable to others than we do, and more isolated. Thus a schizophrenic may say that he is made of glass, of such transparency and fragility that a look directed at him splinters him to bits and penetrates straight through him. We may suppose that precisely as such he experiences himself.
>
> We shall suggest that it was on the basis of this exquisite vulnerability that the unreal man became so adept at self-concealment.[211]

Having read *Save Me the Waltz*, Dr Mildred Squires decided that, rather than only trying to talk to Zelda, having her write her version of what had happened to her would help in her cure. And so Zelda wrote her story for 'the eyes of the psychiatrist [which] moved back and forth under the heavy lashes, like the shuttle of a loom weaving a story from the dark heavy thread'. The injunction was to 'tell the story with no embellishments'.

'Very well,' began the sick one patiently, 'but it is the story of a fathomless solitude, of a black detachment of nothing. A vacuum can only exist, I imagine, by the things which enclose it.'

And so began what Zelda called her 'fairy tale' for the psychiatrists.

The aim of the therapy, now, on Scott's insistence, seemed to be to find Zelda's permissive mother at the root of her problems: her mother had been fixated on her, let her get away with everything, catered to the assertiveness Zelda's novel-writing gave voice to. By mid-April 1932, Scott was visiting daily, and a pattern emerged. The couple quarrelled; Scott reported the battles to the doctors; Zelda kept them to herself. His version of her problem was that she was reacting to him, competing, trying to use her 'values' to express herself, mistakenly imagining that self-expression had anything to do with the making of art. He adamantly didn't agree with this. Her writing had to be stopped. Zelda wouldn't give in to his view of things: he wasn't her doctor. His role should be 'to mother me and bear with a lot of unpleasantness which is not part of how I feel towards you at all but the result of my health'.

This talking and writing out for the doctors of what were the couple's deep-rooted problems and patterns went on for some years, even after Zelda left the clinic. The war between them about who owned the fictionalization of their lives, about Zelda's right to write given that Scott paid the bills, including the expensive private sanatoria, became a life-struggle in which Zelda's madness and Scott's drinking were the weapons of choice – to be used against each other before an audience of medics. The audience never made the battle less real, since the struggle existed even without the medical gaze: but nor is it clear that the doctors' presence ever made the battle less rather than more intense.

Squires left to be replaced by the young and handsome Dr Thomas Rennie, who was interested in literature. Zelda far preferred him to Meyer. The doctors sometimes backed an increasingly fragile Scott and asked Zelda to curtail her ambitions. At another point, Meyer actually defended Zelda, his patient, against Scott and wanted to take him in to tend to his drink problem. By this time, in the summer of 1932, the couple were living in a grand house not far from the hospital and Zelda was being treated as an outpatient. A strict routine was set down which allowed for no more than two hours' writing a day, followed by tennis and finally painting – all to be rigorously kept to in an atmosphere of calm reclusiveness.

Dr Rennie assessed their case as if he were a marriage therapist with a particularly difficult famous couple to contend with. With a nod to the Freudian matter of the sexual which might lie at the base of their 'problems', it was effectively their behavioural patterns that were at issue. He hoped that the reception of Zelda's novel might clear the air between them. It didn't. When *Save Me the Waltz* came out that October, the reviews were decidedly mixed and it sold only 1392 copies. America was still in the Depression. Reviewers talked of the novel's 'ludicrous lushness', of an inability to create character and of an 'undisciplined mind'; though one mentioned the 'dizzy delight' of her language and looked forward with interest to her next novel. Zelda, who was in fact trying to write a new novel, one which dealt with her own psychiatric history, in the face of Scott's adamant sense that the doctors mustn't allow her on to the terrain of *his* long-struggled-towards opus *Tender Is the Night*, began to sink into absences and incoherence once more, as well as attack and undermine her daughter.

By December Scott couldn't cope with her: he was drinking, taking Luminal and, as Dr Meyer wrote to Forel in Switzerland, had begun seeing a doctor at the Phipps. Their *folie* was, to a certain measure, always *à deux*. His own assessment of his marriage had early been sent to Dr Rennie:

> In the last analysis, she is a stronger person than I am. I have creative fire, but I am a weak individual. She knows this and really looks upon me as a woman. All our lives, since the days of our engagement, we have spent hunting for some man Zelda considers strong enough to lean upon. I am not. However, I am now so near the breaking point myself that she realizes she has me against the wall and that she can drive me no fur-ther. She is a little afraid of me at the present time.[212]

Scott couldn't stand the strain of tending Zelda unless he had the kind of authority over her which allowed him to order her to pack her bag and spend a week in an asylum. In May the couple met with Dr Rennie. A 114-page transcript documents what passed between them. It records Scott's worries about Zelda encroaching on the terrain of his writing: he hadn't published a novel for eight years, yet *he* was the professional. He needed her to stop writing. She wouldn't. She wanted independence.

When Dr Rennie finally asked her if being a creative artist would make up for a life without Scott, she refused the question. She couldn't contemplate living without Scott, yet she couldn't or wouldn't give in to his terms. Nine months later, she was back in residence at the Phipps. There is a possibility that the publication of *Tender Is the Night* in serial form, beginning in January 1934, had tipped her over the always beckoning edge. Her incarnation as the heroine, Nicole, was too close to bear: 'What made me mad was that he made the girl so awful and kept on reiterating how she had ruined his life and I couldn't help identifying myself with her because she had so many of my experiences.'[213]

Virginia Woolf

It is irresistible at this juncture to compare Scott and Zelda Fitzgerald to Leonard and Virginia Woolf, another literary couple who were unabashedly modern in their views, though of an older generation. Would Zelda have fared better, led a more productive life, under the assiduous and intelligent care of someone like Leonard Woolf, who tended to Virginia's talent and was so alert to her symptoms that he packed her off to bed and a necessary decrease of stimulus as soon as there was a signal of the return of her illness? Surely the criticism that some have made of Leonard as over-controlling and policeman-like in his vigilance vanishes when Virginia is placed alongside other sufferers from conditions akin to hers.

Though it is now broadly agreed that Virginia Woolf suffered from what Kraepelin had named around 1900 as cyclical manic depression, and Zelda from what Bleuler just a little later called schizophrenia, there is as much commonality in Woolf's and Zelda's experience of what they both jauntily designated as their 'madness', or in the way they resisted the controlling hand of the doctors, as there is difference in the kinds of characters their culture, accidents of geography and social place made them. They shared racing highs filled with vivid sensuous impressions, during which they might hallucinate and hear what were sometimes persecutory voices, followed by suicidal lows. In a diary entry of January 1924, Virginia evokes the curious visions she had in her room at Hogarth House, 'lying in bed, mad, and seeing the sunlight quivering like gold water, on the wall. I've heard the voices of the dead here.' On the occasion of her 1904 breakdown she talked of other 'horrible voices' – birds singing Greek choruses, King Edward using foul language in the garden.

Writing about the serious bout of illness when she was thirty-three which lasted for about nine months and was the second since their marriage, Leonard noted: 'She talked almost without stopping for 2 or 3 days, paying no attention to anyone in the room or anything said to her. For about a day what she said was coherent, the sentences meant something, though it was nearly all wildly insane. Then gradually it became completely incoherent, a mere jumble of dissociated words.' Virginia's incoherence, her total absorption in the world of her madness, parallels Zelda's – despite the different nomenclature for their condition. Both women also had 'nerves' and eccentricity in their closest family. Both at points blamed their husbands for their condition, complained about the doctors they had chosen for them, but largely felt guilty about the trouble their condition caused. Zelda often and Virginia before her suicide wrote tender letters to their partners thanking them for creating the only true happiness in their lives.

Virginia's breakdowns began in 1895 when she was thirteen, shortly after her mother's death, the grief over which her formidable, if histrionic, father manifestly took over, stealing it from the children. Irritable, increasingly engulfed in morbid self-flagellation, subject to her stepbrother's sexual molestation, Virginia entered a world from which suicide seemed the only escape. There were further attacks, of varying intensity: a difficult one after the death of her father, whom, like Anna O and so many other women in the period, she had nursed; one after Leonard proposed; a grave one, involving a suicide attempt, a year into their marriage and lasting really until 1915, perhaps in part occasioned by her less than happy sexual experience and then Leonard's decision, on the advice of their new and more modern doctor – a eugenicist in the spirit of the times – that children should be avoided. Later breakdowns were milder, one imagines partly because of Leonard's watchfulness. If her early breakdowns had been sparked by deaths – her mother's, her favourite brother Toby's, her father's – the later ones tended to come after she had sent off the manuscript of a novel. The last 'breakdown' came in 1941 after she had completed *Between the Acts*. This time it was so bad, so much a replay of the most difficult crack, that she took her life.

In the midst of all this, Virginia wrote a brilliant array of fiction and criticism, not to mention the most riveting journals, diaries and letters of her era. Two principal doctors, each of a status equal to the doctors who treated Zelda Fitzgerald, in turn oversaw Virginia's illness. The treatment she received was, however, very different, at least in the way it was theorized. Early on there was certainly no question of talk therapy — not that Virginia's attitude to it, despite Bloomsbury's adamant modernism, was ever less than ambivalent. She and her husband may have become the English publisher of Freud's *Collected Papers*, but Virginia remained sceptical of the whole psychoanalytic enterprise, perhaps coming closer to Freud only once she had read him and realized that the inner life he had set out to chart was rather more darkly textured and marked by the irrational than that which the philosopher G.E. Moore, so important to the pre-war Bloomsbury Group, had evoked.

The doctor who oversaw Virginia Stephen's serious illness following her father's death when she was twenty-two, was George Savage (1842–1921), President of the Medico-Psychological Association and of the Neurological Society, and the editor of the *Journal of Mental Science*. He was an alienist of the old school, who wrote his major work, *Insanity and Allied Neurosis*, in 1884. Though he had resigned as head of Bethlem in 1888 — because under his aegis deaths there had occurred at twice the rate of other asylums — he remained a bastion of the British medical profession. The Stephens family doctor, he was first consulted directly about Virginia in 1904. He promptly diagnosed a general 'neurasthenia' and sent her off to a Twickenham nursing home where treatments were largely benign: rest, quiet and not too much sedation, though in the course of her life Virginia was given everything from chloral to the veronal on which she overdosed in 1913.

Savage, like all the members of the family, knew that George Duckworth, Virginia's stepbrother, her mother's son by a former marriage and fourteen years older than her, had sexually molested Virginia, beginning at the time of her mother's death and continuing until her breakdown of 1904, when she had flung herself out of the window. George, who 'prowled by night', had also abused her sister Vanessa and poor, mad Laura, abnormal from birth and long incarcerated, their father's daughter from his first marriage to Thackeray's child, Minnie, the very child whose birth had precipitated the older writer's wife into puerperal madness. Savage apparently lectured George over his sexual misconduct, but any direct sympathy for Virginia is more likely to have come from the kindly Violet Dickenson, who nursed her back to health after her suicide attempt.

It is clear that the early incestuous activity had a disturbing effect on Virginia's sexuality: from all reports, sex was to prove perennially problematic for her, though not, it seems, for her artist sister, Vanessa. After Leonard Woolf proposed to Virginia on 11 January 1912 she went through a period of turmoil, and over the next two months Dr. Savage had her in and out of nursing homes. Then, as recent historical digging has revealed, Virginia herself went to see a doctor who only a year later was to become a founding member of the London Psychoanalytical Society.[214] On 9 March 1912, independently of Leonard, who was waiting for her response, she consulted Dr Maurice Wright, whom she called a 'psychologist'. What they talked of is not known, but it would not be implausible to imagine her sexuality might have been on the agenda. In any event, something turned, for on 29 May she accepted Leonard's proposal. She returned to Wright probably only once more. Virginia and Leonard's honeymoon proved, sexually at least, less than satisfactory, though their sexual relations persisted and there was talk, at least at first, of having children. The marriage was one that buoyed them both up.

Whether it was the sexual disturbance that made Virginia wary of Freud, as some have claimed, is unclear. Like all the members of bohemian Bloomsbury, Virginia was altogether forthright in her use of sexual language, alert to and experienced in homosexuality, and seemed to relish the shock of 'dirty' words. It is more likely that what kept her from a talking cure was what became the twentieth-century artist's perennial fear that the insights garnered during 'madness' were somehow related to literary talent and might be disturbed by psychoanalysis – a therapy as potentially penetrative as sex itself. To the composer Ethyl Smith, Virginia noted in 1930: 'As an experience, madness is terrific I can assure you, and not to be sniffed at; and in its lava I still find most of the things I write about. It shoots out of one everything shaped, final, not in mere driblets as sanity does. And the six months – not three – that I lay in bed taught me a good deal about what is called oneself.'

In a 1920 review entitled 'Freudian Fiction', Virginia scoffed at the reductionist simplicities of the new science: 'A patient who has never heard a canary sing without falling down in a fit can now walk through an avenue of cages without a twinge of emotion since he has faced the fact that his mother kissed him in the cradle. The triumphs of science are beautifully positive.' The patient, here, is more than likely Woolf herself, and her irony points to the fact that no 'psychologist's' revelation has lessened the intensity of the singing birds for her. She will not be turned into a 'case' – any more than Nabokov, ever scathing about the 'Viennese witch-doctor', would later be. Her own experience aside, she is adamant that the turf of the inner life and the imagination rightly belongs to novelists and artists and needs protecting from the reductionist inanities of these psychological interlopers. Yet Virginia's husband thought of himself as an out-and-out Freudian. He reviewed Freud early, had read *The Interpretation of Dreams* by 1914, and he and Virginia certainly discussed dreams.[215] Her brother, Adrian Stephen, became one of Britain's first psychoanalysts.

Later, her own views towards Freud, if not the efficacy of his practice, changed with reading. In her notes on the writing of *To the Lighthouse* she tellingly states: 'I wrote my book very quickly; and when it was written, I ceased to be obsessed with my mother. I no longer heard her voice; I do not see her. I suppose I did for myself what psycho-analysts do for their patients. I expressed some very long felt and deeply felt emotion. And in expressing it I explained it and then laid it to rest.'[216]

Woolf's diary note, after meeting Freud on 28 January 1939, is amenable enough for a woman who was known for her tart verdicts on the people she met: 'Dr. Freud gave me a narcissus . . . A screwed up shrunken very old man: with a monkey's light eyes, paralysed spasmodic movements, inarticulate: but alert . . . Difficult talk. An interview . . . Immense potential, I mean an old fire now flickering . . .' The following day, she added. 'Freud said, It would have been worse if you had not won the war. I said we often felt guilty – if we had failed, perhaps Hitler would not have been. No, he said, with great emphasis; he would have been infinitely worse.'[217]

As Robert Hinshelwood has argued, it is likely that for Virginia and many of her circle Freud was acceptable culturally, but not therapeutically. In the first half of the twentieth century Freud equalled the modern, the emphatically new, the sexually open and unrepressed. The package included a toppling of the securities of the Victorian era. The very hypothesizing of an unconscious meant that the individual's grip on reason, on a controlled self, was undermined, by slips, by laughter, by desires. For writers, the erratic stream of the inner life, rather than the character in action, became the subject of fiction.

The cultural Freud, as Virginia gradually read him, might be fine, but that hardly equalled Freud as a mind *doctor*. Alix Strachey, a close friend, analyst and James Strachey's wife, noted in her reminiscences about Virginia that she didn't agree with James that analysis would be of help to Virginia: 'Leonard, I think, might well have considered the proposition and decided not to let her be psychoanalysed . . . Virginia's imagination, apart from her artistic creativity, was so interwoven with fantasies – and indeed with her madness – that if you stopped the madness you might have stopped the creativeness, too.'[218]

Alix Strachey was probably right. Virginia recognized that psychoanalysis had as its object the individual's unconscious processes and not just clinical symptoms: hers had uses apart from illness.

Freud aside, Virginia had little time for mind doctors in general. It is unlikely that she would have felt any more friendly to the posthumous uses of her supposed manic-depressive cycle and its relationship to her artistic productivity than she did to contemporary experts'. The fact that after the span of serious illness at the start of her marriage all that the detailed charts of her illness can show is that there was no significant decrease in literary output, whatever the ups and downs of mood, might have induced one of her usual hoots of laughter.[219]

Woolf's second principal doctor, whom Leonard, always well informed and progressive in his views, decided to consult rather than the ageing Victorian Savage during Virginia's prolonged bout of illness of 1913–15, was Dr Maurice Craig. A Cambridge graduate like so many of the Bloomsburys, and in his later career thoroughly integrated into the elite circle of Cambridge medical psychologists, Craig had worked as an assistant at Bethlem. He had written a textbook on *Psychological Medicine* (1905) and had succeeded Savage at Guy's Hospital. He also ran a nursing home, played a crucial role, when part of the War Office's group on shell shock, in securing pensions for many thousands of 'nervous' soldiers, and was the doctor Leonard Woolf himself consulted about the tremor in his hand. Craig certified in 1914 that Leonard was unfit for 'military service'. He eventually became the President of the Psychiatric Section of the Royal Society. For all his modern dislike of Savage's older designations of 'moral insanity', and his move into a more Kraepelinian nomenclature, Craig's handbook on *Nerve Exhaustion* of 1922 offers little that is new. Cautious about Freudian therapy, since the 'distressing ideas' it revealed might threaten the 'mental stability' of patients who couldn't stand the strain, Craig thought of breakdowns as 'nervous' and therefore requiring primarily physical treatment rather than the Freudians' 'clearing up of amnesias'.[220]

Virginia's early biographer, Quentin Bell, describes the breakdown which brought her to Craig thus:

> She thought people were laughing at her; she was the cause of everyone's troubles; she felt overwhelmed with a sense of guilt for which she should be punished. She became convinced that her body was in some way monstrous, the sordid mouth and sordid belly demanding food — repulsive matter which must then be excreted in a disgusting fashion; the only course was to refuse to eat. Material things assumed sinister and unpredictable aspects, beastly and terrifying or – sometimes – of fearful beauty.

During this prolonged bout of madness, which also brought with it violence, hallucinations and a refusal of food, Craig had little more to offer than a dose of foul-smelling and sedating paraldehyde and the Weir Mitchell regime of bed rest, quiet inactivity and regular intensive feeding. Writing – when it once more became possible – was to be kept to a minimum, a maximum of one hour daily. Craig was a conservative when it came to women's abilities. Under his care, Virginia put on over three stone in a year, sixty pounds over the two years of her illness. She was not averse to the treatment. Ever after, as she wrote to a friend in 1922, she associated plumpness with health: 'I'm glad you are fat; for then you are warm and mellow and generous and creative. I find that unless I weigh 9 stones I hear voices and see visions and can neither write nor sleep.'

That said, Virginia was hardly complimentary about Craig. He was the doctor who had advised, unlike the buoyant Savage, against her and Leonard's having children.

In *Mrs Dalloway*, a novel which is in part about the competing languages of mental illness, the sufferer's and the doctor's, Woolf's principal male character, the suicidal war veteran Septimus, feels 'exasperation' in his encounters with the various branches of the medical profession. His general practitioner can only offer 'no nonsense common sense and recommend porridge, golf and three grains of Veronal' for his 'nerve symptoms'. As for Sir William Bradshaw, the smug Harley Street psychiatrist who is an amalgamated portrait in which both Craig and Savage figure, Woolf describes him in the most scathing terms. Indeed, her contempt for the disciplinary regime doctors impose on patients rivals that of Michel Foucault. Her portrait of Bradshaw suggests a conspiracy between social engineering, the restraint of the mentally ill and the patriarchal self-protection of the Establishment. Bradshaw shuts up his lunatics in 'nice' homes in the interests of the 'goddess of Proportion' and of his ever-growing bank balance.

To his patients he gave three-quarters of an hour; and if in this exacting science which has to do with what, after all, we know nothing about — the nervous system, the human brain — a doctor loses his sense of proportion, as a doctor he fails. Health we must have; and health is proportion, so that when a man comes into your room and says he is Christ (a common delusion), and has a message, as they mostly have, and threatens, as they often do, to kill himself, you invoke proportion; order rest in bed, rest in solitude, silence and rest, rest without friends, without books, without messages, six months' rest until a man who went in weighing seven stone six comes out weighing twelve . . . Worshipping proportion, Sir William not only prospered himself, but made England prosper, secluded her lunatics, forbade childbirth, penalised despair, made it impossible for the unfit to propagate their views until they, too, shared his sense of proportion.[221]

Zelda's last years

Like Virginia, Zelda Fitzgerald rebelled against her doctors' discipline. Talk may have been part of her treatment, but it was talk of a kind which was intended to make her comply with the doctor's or husband's view of the world – though even had it been otherwise, there is no guarantee that it would have been more palatable, or served her. Unlike Virginia, however, Zelda's control over her own talents was never great enough to result in more than one book.

At the Phipps, through the winter of 1934, Zelda grew worse. She wanted to leave the hospital, go to Europe. Instead, Scott found her a place at the sumptuous Craig House, located on 350 acres adjacent to the Hudson River some two hours from New York. Here patients were free to roam: there were swimming pools, tennis courts and a golf course – all for a handsome fee. The hospital's assessment of Zelda was that she was madly confused, emotionally unstable and, oddly, mentally retarded. She continued to write from her plush new quarters to Dr Rennie. Scott, ever guilty and assiduous in bursts, arranged for an exhibition of her paintings at a gallery in New York. The reception of the work was not what either of them might have hoped. Zelda's letters to Dr Rennie begin to show more confusion. To Scott she says she wants to start on a new novel, if he will allow it. But things quickly became too serious for her to begin. On 19 May 1934, Zelda was transferred to the Sheppard and Enoch Pratt Hospital just outside Baltimore in what was described as a 'catatonic' state, a term which probably refers to her listless apathy, a lack of expression and affect, which signalled a serious relapse.

Auditory hallucinations of the persecutory kind she had experienced at Prangins had returned. This time the voice was Scott's and it terrified her in its repetition of her name, or of her own words. 'I have killed her,' the voice also said. 'I have lost the woman I put into my book.' She told the doctors that despite the tricks her eyes were playing on her, the doublings of things, the distortions, she wasn't thinking of killing herself, but death was the only way out.[222]

The Sheppard and Enoch Pratt Hospital was a leading site for the use of psychoanalysis. Harry Stack Sullivan, the pre-eminent American psychiatrist to apply psychoanalytic treatment to the psychoses, came to the hospital in December 1922. Though he left in 1930 for private practice in New York and Washington, the hospital was already imbued with his methods. Hardly an orthodox Freudian, Sullivan had trained with the feminist Clara Thompson, close colleague and analysand of Sandor Ferenczi, and a follower of Karen Horney's. Horney had challenged Freud on his concept of penis-envy, regrounding it as a biologically ordained attraction between the sexes and positing an equal and opposite womb-envy, an envy of women's natural creativity, as a structural principle in the male.[223] This was an idea Zelda might not have been unfamiliar with.

What is clear from both Scott's and Zelda's writings, as well as their letters, is that whatever Zelda's prognosis and current state, the understanding of herself in relation to Scott and her parents shifted through the course of her various treatments. Both learned from the doctors, in that continual redescription of illness which seems to be part not only of the history of mental medicine but of the patient's own experience and interpretation of symptoms. In certain respects Scott and Zelda's changing perspective keeps pace with the changes in psychoanalytic and psychiatric theory themselves. At first, in France and Switzerland, Zelda is concerned primarily with sexuality; by the time she is through with the Phipps and in the Pratt, she and Scott are talking about relations with each other and with parents, about strengths and fears, competition and security. The developing American psychodynamic psychiatry privileged 'interpersonal relations' and that 'anxiety' which mounted to a veritable panic in the dreams and delusions of schizophrenics. It was 'anxiety' that was said to characterize the sick patient's early relation to a family which, though Oedipal in its power relations, was not understood as sexual. This same anxiety was replayed in the social world and again in the doctor–patient couple.

Frieda Fromm-Reichmann, a leading German-trained American analyst who worked with extreme or psychotic patients just after the Second World War, explained this shift in an attempt to bring different kinds of practitioners together, while all the time heeding Freud:

Among the reasons for this shift in therapeutic emphasis among analysts, the historical fact should be mentioned that Freud's original concepts of analytic therapy and theory were gained from his experience with the psychoneuroses, mainly hysteria, whereas the majority of the patients with whom we work now, are character disorders [sic], obsessionals, and also many borderline cases and outright psychotics. The repressed and dissociated material of these patients is somewhat more easily available to consciousness than that of the hysteric. Their anxieties are greater than those of the hysteric and in the borderline cases and the psychotics not infrequently nearer to the surface. These facts, I believe, explain in part the psychoanalytic shift in therapeutic emphasis from unearthing repressed material and investigating its meaning, to the investigation of its dynamics. This includes, above all, therapeutic concern with the manifestations of the anxiety which is aroused by the resolution of repressed material, and in the patients' operations with the therapist. At this point, then, the theoretical and therapeutic conceptions of classical psychoanalysts and other dynamic psychiatrists run in close dynamic confluence . . .

Sullivan . . . shares with Freud the concept of the anxiety-arousing power of unacceptable thoughts, feelings, wishes and drives. But in the framework of his interpersonal conception, he sees the expected punishment for these forbidden inner experiences as entailed in the anticipated disapproval of the significant people of an anxious person's early life and of their emotional successors in his present life . . . it seems that the feeling of powerlessness, of helplessness in the presence of inner dangers, which the individual cannot control, constitutes in the last analysis the common background of all further elaborations on the theory of anxiety.[224]

For Sullivan, repressive religious educators and overbearing, moralizing mothers featured prominently as anxiety producers. Their penalizing prohibitions against masturbation were part of the picture that produced schizophrenia. 'A hand on the penis is a hand against God'[225] was an all too prevalent sentiment that needed to be fought by sexual education. Sullivan's patients were taught that sexual experience was a good. Sullivan himself was known for his marked personal success with patients he diagnosed as schizophrenic, in particular the men amongst them. One of the reasons he took on an analysis with Clara Thompson was that he failed with women. He thought of schizophrenics as singularly gifted and socially significant people, and understood their condition as an unsuccessful reaction to anxiety. Everyone needed safety, security, let alone that attribute of 'self-esteem'[226] that was later to dominate so much American psychological thinking. Sullivan's patients were given hours of close attention. Drugs, often ethyl alcohol, were also widely used in the period to put patients into a curative state of sleep, or to make them amenable to talk therapy by dismantling their defences.[227] Though, given Scott's objections to Zelda having anything with an alcoholic content, since it tipped her over the edge, it is unlikely that it would have been used in her case.

By July 1935, in any event, the doctors had concluded that talk about her illness in her present serious state was futile. Zelda swung between violence and an uncooperative, inaccessible apathy in which she would have nothing to do with the other patients or the doctors. Scott, who visited regularly, had suggested that he help her pull together a collection of her stories, but the timing wasn't right. Zelda was incapable. She talked of suicide to her doctors and tried to harm herself in whatever way she could, once racing towards the railway tracks so that Scott caught her only moments before the onrush of a train. She wrote only to Scott, who was also unwell, sometimes calling up the good times they had had together. But even if he was her 'dream', the only 'pleasant thing in her life', her tone, for herself, was now without hope:

> My dearest Sweetheart:
>   There is no way to ask you to forgive me for the misery and pain which I have caused you. I can only ask you to believe that I have done the best I could and that since we first met I have loved you with whatever I had to love you with . . . Please get well and love Scottie and find something to fill up your life . . .[228]

By April 1936, though she wanted to leave the hospital, Zelda was no better. As Scott noted in a letter to mutual friends, she was claiming to be in direct contact with 'Christ, William the conqueror, Mary Stuart, Apollo and all the stock paraphernalia of insane-asylum jokes . . . I was her great reality, often the only liaison agent who could make the world tangible to her.' But in his own precarious state, he was seeing her less and less.

He had her moved to Highland Hospital in North Carolina, since he was temporarily in the state for his health. Zelda was to be in and out of the institution for the rest of her days. The Dr Carroll who had founded the hospital was an eccentric in contemporary psychiatric circles: a throwback, a believer in the therapeutic value of diet and exercise. But something in the treatment helped. In July, Scott was reporting to Scottie that Zelda 'looked five years younger' and had stopped her 'silly praying in public'. They met for lunch and walks. Dr Carroll, in 1937, was saying that Zelda was 'quite charming'; while a fellow staff member underlined:

We were careful with Zelda; we never stirred her up. She could be helped, but we never gave her deep psychotherapy. One doesn't do that with patients if they are too schizophrenic. We tried to get Zelda to see reality; tried to get her to distinguish between her fantasies, illusion and reality . . . We let her talk about things which bothered her. Discussed her reading and what things meant to her. Explained the 'why' of her orders and routine. She often rebelled against the authority, the discipline . . . She didn't like discipline, but she would fall into it.[229]

There was no simple or single treatment method or cure, and Scott was having difficulty paying hospital and school bills. He took up an offer in Hollywood where he met the the English-born Hollywood columnist, Sheila Graham, who would be with him till the end a mere year later. Scott wanted to continue to care for Zelda. For Easter 1939 he arranged a Cuban family holiday for the two of them and Scottie, but it proved a disaster, partly because of his drinking and brawling. It was the last time Scott and Zelda were to meet.

Back at the hospital Zelda had town privileges and helped with gym classes. She was particularly good with patients who were far worse off than herself. In return for her help, her expenses were reduced. At Christmas that year she was permitted to go home to her mother in Montgomery, as long as she kept to the advised routine. She did so well that Carroll, in March 1940, wrote to Fitzgerald signalling that she was ready for release. Her mental health would always be precarious and she was incapable of mature judgement, he said, and though she might again become irresponsible and suicidal, for the time being she was 'gentle and reasonable'.

Four years and one week had passed since her admission. Approaching her fortieth birthday, Zelda was now to live with her mother in the straitened circumstances which were all that Scott could afford. She would spend her last years between her mother's home and the Highland Hospital.

On 20 December 1940 Scott Fitzgerald's heart, already weakened by a first attack, gave up. Zelda wasn't well enough to attend the funeral. When his unfinished novel *The Last Tycoon* was published in 1942, it triggered the repetition of a pattern. She started to write her own once more: *Caesar's Things*, which occupied her through her six last years. The book reworks the terrain of her childhood and youth, her sense of rejection by her father, her lost great love. But its incoherence is a testimonial to the debilitating effect of her illness. Delusions and religious fantasies have overtaken her, as has a sense of utter solitude. Her hold on the real slipped unpredictably.

At the beginning of 1948, she was given insulin treatment – a course of injections to reduce blood-sugar level, which eventually induced hypoglycaemic shock and attendant convulsions or coma. The treatment had been pioneered in Berlin by Vienna University-trained Manfred Sakel. Before long, it travelled through Europe and America. At the Maudsley in London, it was a favourite of that stern advocate of the physical therapies, including ECT and leucotomy, William Sargent. Insulin-induced coma was administered when schizophrenic or depressed patients were restless and agitated, grew violent or suicidal. When they emerged from their deathlike sleep, the patients were transformed, reborn into a new calmer self, or so the treatment story went. In fact, this chemical version of ECT – based on a notion that epileptic convulsions were the biological antagonists of schizophrenia – often came with memory loss, physical and mental disorientation and a substantial weight gain of twenty to sixty pounds. With its sugar and starch diet it also infantilized patients, and in this respect resembled the nineteenth-century rest cures for women. Adolf Meyer, ever eclectic, had given the therapy his blessing in 1937 and from then on it became common in American custodial hospitals, particularly with intractable patients.[230]

After her treatment, Zelda was recovering on the top floor of the hospital with the other insulin-coma patients. She had just written to her daughter, who had given birth to her second child, to say that maternity clothes would probably do very well for her, Zelda, so much weight had she put on. But she was buoyant, indeed reborn. She noted the promise of spring in the air and how she longed to see the new baby. It was not to be. During the night of 10 March 1948 a fire leapt from the kitchen of the building in which she was housed. Zelda Fitzgerald died along with nine other women. She was just under forty-eight years old.

Virginia Woolf had committed herself to a watery grave seven years before, on 28 March 1941. Between them, the two women had been through the span of treatments the twentieth century thus far offered. None of them worked, if permanent cure acts as the main criterion.

The schizophrenia that Zelda had on occasion been diagnosed with would, in the fifties and sixties, become America's most common diagnosis. Shortened to 'schizzy', it grew into an everyday synonym for crazy, or odd, or weird, or peculiar. Marilyn Monroe, amongst many others, was called 'schizzy'. Committed into the asylums, however, those labelled schizophrenic could easily enough develop a career path of craziness. Learning the illness behaviours that got attention from doctors and formed a bond with other patients was, as Erving Goffman convincingly argued in his *Asylums* (1961), an inevitable part of life in a 'total institution'. While the governing principle of the asylum is that treatment should lead to 'cure', the compliance it generates in patients, even when treated by well-meaning doctors, can lead to entrapment in a schizophrenic role and a pattern of recurrent institutionalization.

Being schizzy could all too easily become a way of life.

9

DISTURBANCES OF LOVE

In France after the First World War, a new kind of woman was born. She wore some of the clothes of the liberated flapper and was a sister in spirit if not in arms to bluestocking and suffragette. But her closest kin was the convulsive hysteric, marked in body and mind by the conflicts of her condition, her social place and her rampant desires. Unafraid, unabashed, utterly reasonable in the excesses of her erotic logic, she was nonetheless mad, often criminally so. The Surrealists, those postwar artists who grouped themselves under the banner of a rebellion against a reason that had ended in the madness of the trenches, where war was fought in the name of what kings called peace, sang the praises of this new woman and helped to invent her and spread her fame.

Hysteria, for the Surrealists, as their *révolution surréaliste* of 1927 proclaimed, was a 'supreme vehicle of expression'. Young Augustine, who had entered Charcot's service back in the 1880s, was delectable in her excess, a subject for poetry and emulation rather than for pathological dissection and psychiatric classification. In his novel *Nadja*, structured as a case history, Nadja, the case, becomes Surrealist supremo, André Breton's seductive model of the artist as a charter of new frontiers of the mind and of metaphorical possibility. For the first time, madness, a Rimbaldian derangement of the senses, became a glamorous cultural property, a barometer of the new, particularly where female desire itself was concerned.

The Surrealists were inspired by mind doctors like Freud and Janet. They also took not a little from Gaëtan Gatian de Clérambault (1872–1934), medical head of the Sainte-Anne Hospital's Special

Infirmary for the Insane attached to the Paris Préfecture de Police, who reinvented the condition of erotomania and entered the annals of psychiatric diagnosis with a syndrome named after him. In turn, they inspired readers and a new generation of mind doctors – Jacques Lacan, their friend and contemporary, principal amongst them. In the sixties Lacan, the French Freud, would become one of France's most celebrated intellectuals, a kind of philosopher of excess, the excesses of meaning and desire. Early anti-psychiatrists, the Surrealists both learned from the profession and the patients and attacked its more disciplinary side, as well as the underpinnings of its laws on insanity.

Elisabeth Roudinesco, the historian of French psychoanalysis, reports how in November 1929, when *Nadja* was the subject of a meeting of the Medico-Psychological Society, Breton was accused of inciting inmates to murder their psychiatrists: a dangerous maniac had underlined in blue the poet's insults against psychiatry and caused a commotion in the asylum.[231] Heavyweights of the older generation, Janet and Clérambault, attacked the upstart Surrealists, and the proceedings found their way into the press. Breton counterattacked, accusing the mind doctors of being jailers and executioners who abused their power, rather than true physicians. The following year, those who had targeted the Surrealists figured prominently in the Second Surrealist Manifesto as prime agents in society's 'system of degradation and cretinization', part of the sterile crowd at whom the surrealist revolver was aimed. Virginia Woolf had put it more decorously and with English irony, but the criticism was the same. Though culturally they were inextricably linked, artists and the mind doctors now stood ranked against each other across the terrain of the human soul. And that terrain was often symbolically, as well as actually, signposted feminine.

Little enough had changed for French women despite the greater need for their labour during wartime. If the right to spend their own earnings had recently been won, many of their civil and property rights were still in question. Values might now be more openly disputed; customs were challenged; but for every question the left put, the Catholic and moralizing right had an answer. The Surrealists' invocation to a free sexuality, a rebellion that could be deemed criminal, a seeing afresh of the world, coexisted, for women, with this standard school textbook call to tradition:

What is a woman's greatest duty? To have children, then to have more children, always to have children! A woman who refuses, who seeks to control or to suppress her maternal destiny, no longer deserves any rights. That woman becomes nothing.[232]

Way back in the revolutionary year of 1791, the radical Olympe de Gouges in her *Declaration of the Rights of Women* had stated that if women had the right to mount the scaffold, they should also have the right to mount the hustings. In the interwar years the scaffold was still in place, although out of chivalry it was rarely used for the weaker sex. The hustings had to wait until 1944. In terms of crime, not all that much had altered since the days of Henriette Cornier. Clemency, in the form of a lifetime of penal servitude, might be granted murdering women, but the war of the lawyers and psychiatrists over baldness or madness was to be waged all over again in the cases of 'criminal' women that galvanized the early thirties.

It is hardly surprising if the conflict between new liberties and old laws played itself out in both symptoms and diagnoses. Erotomania had already been noted as a condition by Esquirol. In its newly amplified guise, compounded with persecutory delusions, it reflected some of the disorder of the times, the contradictory liberties, demands and prohibitions which tugged at women's minds and emotions, as well as a fraying class system and its attendant resentments. With a Kraepelinian zeal, Clérambault detailed erotomania in his police infirmary as a madness, a 'mental automatism' of the ambitious, often sexually wayward and most usually female imagination. With an admixture of paranoid delusions, erotomania frequently carried its own punishment for any excessive overreaching. It also often came with a glossolalia, a fervid verbal outpouring and flagrant mixing of metaphors, syntax and literary registers. The Surrealists found this as inspiring as the more conservative literary critics found their 'modernist' outpourings mad.

Amongst a rush of cases of women imagining that priests or high-ranking men have singled them out for love, Clérambault describes the case of Léa-Anna, a fifty-three-year-old delirious erotomaniac suffering from persecution. She was brought to the Sainte-Anne special infirmary in 1920 after an arrest for the usual banal causes: she had approached a policeman, accused him of laughing at her and slapped him.[233]

From a broken peasant family with an alcoholic father, Léa-Anna had made her way to Paris, become a milliner, and taken on a rich, well placed lover, who supported her in high fashion for eighteen years. After his death, a second relationship with a younger man having come to an end, Léa-Anna began to believe that the King of England was in love with her and had sent emissaries. She went to England, stood in front of Buckingham Palace and began to interpret everything that happened to her as signs of the King's love.

Emotion fuelled the hopes which the aristocrat Clérambault understood as one of the stages of a disease of which an over-reaching pride is the underlying feature. Doubt marks the next stage. If the King can love, he can also hate. The one thing the delusion won't permit is indifference. With doubt comes the paranoiac phase of the condition: the King is persecuting her, playing tricks on her, preventing her from finding a room in London's better hotels, making her lose her luggage and money. He is, she now believes, also responsible for the poverty and humiliation she has generally been forced into as well as for her present incarceration.

Clérambault calls the tale Anna-Léa reveals, the 'novel' of the *érotomane*'s passion. Like Freud, his nomenclature is literary. The twentieth-century self, as understood by the mind doctors, tells stories, whether they're family romances, self-aggrandizing passions, or the kinds of case histories Freud worried might be too close to novelettes, the chick lit of its time.

A social conservative who believed the insane were a danger to public order, Clérambault was interested above all in classifying his 'criminal' patients, whose condition he saw as constitutional and therefore untreatable. Yet he had stumbled on a 'mental automatism' – an unstoppable charge of ideas in madness – of which the erotic content was undeniably modern, and proximate to the Viennese he despised.

Clérambault's 'stalkers' suffer from a disturbance of love which parallels and parodies true 'forbidden' romance at every juncture: first comes the sense of being desired and desirable through countless secret signs and glances, then come the hurdles and misunderstandings, then the disillusion, the *chagrin* or sadness; finally the rupture, with its anger and texture of paranoia. His women are the heirs of Madame Bovary, taking her sentimental aspirations into a world of delusional excess. Indeed Madame Bovary, penalized for her dreams and ambitions, gave her name early in the century to a condition, *bovarysme*, which signified illusions about the self, dissatisfactions, the desire to be another. In the courts, the condition Flaubert had given birth to in the heroine of whom he had said, '*C'est moi*', was used to insist on the irresponsibility of the accused. Bovarysme was the sign of madness which would place a woman in an asylum rather than in a prison.

Clérambault is said to have possessed a terrifyingly acute clinical gaze, an eye for detail and difference which was honed by his artistic pursuits and which abetted his zeal for classification. A descendant of an old aristocratic family, alert to social rank, he was hardly himself lacking in the pride he so regularly found in his erotomaniacs. Like them, he was also adept at secret passions: one for photography, the other for the arrangement of women's drapery, its folds and fall, an art he had studied and photographed with a fetishist's obsessiveness during his war years in Morocco when he served in the French army. Clandestinely, he now attired wax figurines, alert to the feel of fabric, the erotic charge of silks and velvets he had so graphically described in his account of the fetishism of textures and female kleptomania in an early review for a criminology journal.[234]

Whatever his dislike of artists, Clérambault's own clinical notes are filled with an artist's attention to the look and dress and movement of patients, all communicated in a resonant, telegraphic style. When his sight failed him and a cataract operation removed his ability to see depth, he arranged an elaborate suicide. Like a detective, sight was crucial to his being: he couldn't face the loss of it. He staged his own murder, pistol in mouth, watching himself in the mirror before falling back on to the divan he had carefully placed behind his chair. When police entered his house in Montrouge on the morning of 17 November 1934, they found not only the dead body of the reputedly misogynistic doctor, who had never allowed women into his lectures, but hundreds of wax mannequins, intricately draped dolls and photographs of Morocco (now in the collection of the Musée de l'Homme). The man who had popularized a medical category describing erotic obsession was thus no stranger to it himself. He left his name to a stalking syndrome organized around a false but persistent belief that one is loved by a famous or prominent person and entailing the obsessive pursuit of a disinterested object of love.

It is perhaps no wonder that under the problematic tutelage of Clérambault, with whom he shared a high Catholic aestheticism, his charismatic pupil Jacques Lacan grew alert to the vacillations of desire, not to mention the significance of mirrors. From Freud, whose primacy of influence he was later to claim, Lacan learned the importance of the unconscious and of sexuality in the structure of the paranoid psychosis. But his psychiatric training in the Sainte-Anne Hospital, where delirium and the clinical gaze were the norm, always informed his later psychoanalytic work.

Whether it was because of his link with the Surrealists, or his participation at the first reading of Joyce's *Ulysses* at the Shakespeare and Co. Bookshop in Paris, Lacan also showed an early interest in the way language functioned amongst the patients at the Sainte-Anne. The theorist who would later declare that the unconscious was structured like a language was already alert to the slipperiness of syntax, sound and meaning, the inherent ambiguity and overflow of language – all evident in the speech as well as to writing of his deluded and particularly his paranoid patients. How easy it is for meaning to slide away from authorial and indeed authoritative intent is evident in such ambiguous signs as 'Refuse to be put in this basket!' or 'Dogs must be carried on the escalator!'[235] Cultural and gender codings are assumed; a slight shift on speakers' or hearers' part can indicate 'madness': it seems to be perfectly all right for a major South African politician, for example, to say that a woman's short skirt sent him the message that she wanted sex – he is deemed neither mad, nor a rapist.[236] But if in a similar instance a woman had said, 'His short trousers sent a message to me', she might well be regarded as eccentric; said often enough in the early part of the last century and accompanied by irritable behaviour, the eccentricity might catapult into madness. Later on, Lacan was also to show how words could take on the force of acts and seep into the unconscious of hearers to shape their symptoms.

One of Lacan's first case presentations, made in 1931 with two of his colleagues, featured the 'inspired writings' of a thirty-four-year-old teacher, Marcelle, classified the year before as an erotomaniac by Clérambault because of her fixation on her superior, who had recently

died. Clérambault had the woman committed because she was claiming twenty million francs' worth of damages from the state (her
employers) on the grounds of privations and dissatisfactions, both
sexual and intellectual – an early, contested instance of sexual harassment, one might say.

Marcelle saw herself as Joan of Arc. Through her revolutionary writings she wanted to regenerate a decadent France, caught in an economic
crisis and with a rising far right. 'All those old forms need shaking up,'
she said. 'I shall make the language evolve.'[237] The declaration has one
wonder whether Marcelle had read the Surrealist manifestos. Certainly
Lacan saw in her prose something which resembled their attempts at
automatic writing, at allowing the unconscious free rein on the page,
exploding grammar and syntax and, in the poets' case, perhaps willing
those wild puns of sound and sense, metaphors and leaps of significance that Joyce nurtured and which seemed to come so readily to
Zelda Fitzgerald and Virginia Woolf. In this early stage of a long career,
Lacan was prepared to classify Marcelle in a traditional psychiatric way,
while at the same time analysing her *schizographie*, her untranslatable
and surreal mode of writing. The young teacher's letter to the French
President began: 'Monsieur le Président de la République P. Doumer
holidaying amidst spiced bread and sweet poets. Monsieur le Président
of a Republic overcome with zeal. I would like to know everything in
order to make you the corn mouse of coward and canon, but I'm much
too long to guess.'

'Aimée' and Jacques Lacan (1901–1981)

On 3 June 1931, some three weeks after Marcelle had written her letter,
a woman whose core condition was labelled as erotomanic was sent to
the Sainte-Anne from the Saint-Lazare women's prison infirmary. She
had languished in a delirium for twenty days after having attempted to
assassinate a well known *comédienne*, Huguette Duflos, the lead in a popular boulevard comedy, *All Is Well*. All wasn't well with Marguerite
Pantaine. At the Sainte-Anne, she was put in the care of Jacques Lacan.
Under the name of Aimée, or 'Beloved', the heroine of one of her own
ambitious unpublished fictions, Marguerite was to become a famous

case: the subject of Lacan's medical dissertation and the first of his theoretical disquisitions: *Of Paranoid Psychosis in its relations with Personality*. The thesis had all the panache of a contemporary *Madame Bovary*, a story of love, ambition and tragic delusion narrated with a novelist's care. It also came with a modernist twist, a tale within a tale. Lacan included lengthy sections of Marguerite's own fictions, side by side with interpretations of her delusional interpretations of the world.

The thesis bears a parallel to Freud's *Studies in Hysteria*: it is a founding text in the history of French psychoanalysis. But forty years on, hysteria has given way to psychosis.[238] The dissertation is also Lacan's *Interpretation of Dreams*. If Lacan's subject is woman, language and psychosis rather than Freud's autobiographical self, dreams and neurosis, it is perhaps because in Aimée, Lacan can think through his own family structure, the ties to siblings, the play of unconscious identifications within the family so that children re-enact parental lacks or buried wishes, and the grand dreams which will catapult him from provincialism to the very centre of Parisian intellectual and artistic life. The debt to Freud lies in the way Lacan makes use of his insights about the links between the structure of paranoia and a repressed homosexual identification. Lacan had that very year been translating Freud's 1922 essay on 'Some Neurotic Mechanisms in Jealousy, Paranoia and Homosexuality'.

At 8.30 p.m. on 18 April 1931, thirty-eight-year-old Marguerite Pantaine, well dressed, gloved, polite, had approached Huguette Duflos just as the celebrated actress of stage and screen reached the actors' entrance to the theatre. Having confirmed the woman's name by her response, Marguerite opened her handbag, took out a large knife and struck out at the woman's heart. Duflos kept her cool and stopped the blade with her hand, suffering a serious cut through 'two flexor tendons'. Two assistants rushed to constrain Marguerite and hustled her off to the nearest police station.

Here, she refused to explain her act, though she answered questions about her identity normally enough. She claimed that for some years Duflos had been conspiring against her, stirring 'scandal', threatening. She had teamed up with the famous academician and writer, Pierre Benoit, the film of whose book she starred in as a duchess. Benoit had portrayed Marguerite maliciously in numerous passages in his books and had stolen the plots of Marguerite's own fictions. This very Benoit was also the man, Lacan later learned, who 'loved' her and who had persuaded her to leave her husband. Together, *comedienne* and writer had prevented Marguerite's books from being published. Though Benoit had met her once when she had accosted him at his publisher's, whom she haunted, there was in reality no relation between them except in her troubled imagination.

At the prison infirmary, Marguerite was diagnosed by the forensic doctor, Benjamin Truelle, who concluded that she suffered from a 'systematized persecutory delirium based on interpretation and with megalomaniac tendencies and an erotomanic substrate'. No civil suit was brought by Duflos, but the story made the papers with all the hyperbolic stereotypes that female criminality even today still receives. *Le Journal* contended that Marguerite was a *masculine* woman, with few friends except for two women teachers with whom she was preparing exams. She had been deranged by too much reading of fiction and attempting to write her own. She was an 'declassed' peasant, who had risen to the rank of clerk at the post office, where she earned a good living.[239] (In fact, on the very day that she was arrested, notice had come of her promotion.)

Jacques Lacan, then a hospital-based psychiatrist, observed Marguerite/Aimée for some eighteen months.

In his substantial case history, he changed her name, provenance and some details, turning her into a railway clerk. No sooner had the twenty-day delirium following the assassination attempt subsided and Aimée arrived at the Sainte-Anne than she became a reasonable and compliant patient. The attempted homicide had 'apparently resolved the preoccupations of her delirium'. There might still be some holes in her memory and she was convinced her act had been undertaken in order to protect her child from those who wanted his death. But Aimée spoke her story, and wrote. Before an audience, her generally reserved manner grew deeply expressive, her very posture that of a heroic mother. Lacan not only interviewed his patient but gathered all available evidence about her. This included reading her copious writings and calling in her family. Her estranged husband was now living with her sister: together they looked after Aimée's son, apparently with her acquiescence since she had asked to be transferred to a post in Paris, while her husband, a postal worker like her, remained in the outlying region. She visited regularly enough, though her frightened sister would have preferred her not to.

The bright daughter of a peasant family, Aimée had made her way up the educational route to a good post. Though she had still not attained her baccalaureate, she was ambitious, and, as Lacan notes, 'themes of persecution are intimately linked with delusions of grandeur'.[240] Aimée had dreams of rising to a new and better life, of accomplishing some great social mission. Her aspirations extended to achieving idealistic reforms. These were linked with an erotomanic fixation on the Prince of Wales.

Having had a secret affair at the age of eighteen, Aimée had married seven years later, in 1917. Apparently frigid, her first pregnancy had not come until 1921. During the pregnancy, then twenty-eight, she had begun to suffer from an overwhelming sadness and a sense that her colleagues at the office — at that time the same as her husband's — were laughing contemptuously behind her back and wishing her baby dead. She felt her husband resented her earlier relationship. They quarrelled frequently. Coded messages began to appear for her in the newspapers and she had terrible dreams. Her vehemence during this period frightened her family. She slashed a friend's bicycle tyres, threw first a pail of water, then an iron, at her husband.

A girl child was born dead on 20 March 1922. Aimée blamed the death on her enemies, in particular a woman of higher class who had for three years been her best friend, but had now moved office. She had telephoned Aimée during the pregnancy to ask after the child.

Aimée's second pregnancy brought back her fears and depression. Once the boy was born, she gave herself up to him with a passionate ardour, nursing him until he was fourteen months old. Everyone else irritated her and she interpreted all actions as hostile to her child. She was overwhelmed by a sense that both familiars and strangers were insulting her, that the whole town saw her as depraved. She wanted to run away. Secretly, she applied for leave from her post and for a passport to America, using a false name for the request, since otherwise it would have needed her husband's consent. She would have abandoned her child, she claimed, for his own good. Her grand schemes were beginning to take shape.

The family had her confined in a private asylum. She started writing letters to a famous author, asking him to rescue her. Asylum staff reported her saying: 'There are those who have built stables in order to trap me as a milk cow'; 'I'm too often judged other than I am.' After six months, her family took her home. She was better, if not cured. She moved to Paris. The delusionary structures which would lead to the assassination attempt took a firm grip. Huguette Duflos, much in the news because of a court case, became a fixation when office staff spoke of her in flattering terms: Aimée interrupted, saying the woman was nothing but a whore. It was this comment, Aimée believed, that had set Duflos against her and implanted the wish to kill Aimée's son.

What Lacan calls her 'interpretative madness' then moved into full swing. Newspapers, posters, ads, everything Aimée came into contact with added up to the single fact that Huguette Duflos was about to target Aimée's son in revenge for his mother's slander and bad character. Soon any celebrated or successful woman became part of the plot against Aimée and her son. Lacan notes that her hatred had a core of ambivalence. The women she loathes and fears are the very women she wants to be. As for the author she has fixed on, Benoit, too, is present in his minions, the many writers and journalists who steal her ideas and use them wrongly. Aimée would save the world, do good, while they only harm. They propagate war, Bolshevism, murder and corruption, exploit our misery for their selfish ends.

Aimée's aspiration to do good emerges as part of her erotic fantasy about the Prince of Wales, to whom she writes poetry and who acts as her protector. This 'relationship' has long been in place. The Prince seems to be part of the good world Aimée wants to create, one where women and children will dominate and be safe. Yet the Prince is also linked to a dissolute aspect of her life: she stops strangers in the street, apparently in order to tell them of her mission to convert them to better ways, but the encounters often lead her to hotel rooms from which she has to flee.

At the height of her madness, Aimée is leading a double life. Still a successful post office clerk, she goes to work daily and carries out her duties. Afterwards, she moves into the wilder life of her fantasies. She studies. She goes to a newspaper office and insists they carry an article of hers against the 'decadent' novelist Colette. She writes two novels, one a pastoral idyll dedicated to the Prince of Wales, called *The Detractor*, in which the hero David is in love with a young woman called Aimée, a perfect country maiden and older sister. A painted harlot arrives in this innocent village with her consort and sows discord, hatches plots which have Aimée and her family as their victims. Her brothers and sisters die, her mother grows ill. She takes refuge in her dreams and follows them to their grave, leaving her mother in despair.

In a second novel, also dedicated to the Prince of Wales, the heroine instead of succumbing to the evil woman goes off to Paris, like some Balzacian hero, to battle her way to the top. The book is a jumble of medieval, revolutionary and contemporary elements in which the heroine confronts a puritanical Robespierre figure, as well as communists and the writers and actors who want to kill her in effigy, before returning home to the safety of her family and the peaceful countryside.

When this book was rejected by the publishers Aimée demanded an interview. She leapt violently at the throat of an editor. 'Band of assassins!' she shouted, 'band of academicians!' Stopped in time, this attempt to strangle was the first in an escalating series of acts which culminated in the assassination attempt. Meanwhile, she sent her manuscripts off to the Prince of Wales, hoping for his favour and help. With deadly irony, the manuscripts came back with the traditional note saying His Highness could not accept presents, on the day after Aimée was committed.

During the time leading up to her violence, Aimée visited her son daily, waiting for him at the school gates. She worried with an ever-growing anxiety that matched her increasing ferocity that he might be killed at any moment. She accused her husband of brutality, told her sister that she wanted a divorce, wanted the child; was ready, if her husband didn't grant it, to kill him. At night, she was haunted by dreams of the war that would take her son away. That would be her fault. She was a criminal mother.

A month before the assassination attempt, Aimée bought a large hunting knife. The night of the crime, she later told Lacan, her state was such that she could have targeted any of her persecutors. The 'justice' her act represented followed her into the early part of her incarceration. She wrote to the prison director complaining that the newspapers had slandered her in calling her 'neurasthenic', something which could damage her future career as a woman of letters. She told fellow inmates of the terrible persecutions she had suffered. And then, suddenly, her delirium disappeared, 'the good as well as the bad.' 'All the vanity of her megalomaniacal illusions became clear to her,' Lacan writes, 'as well as the silliness of her fears.'

According to Lacan, the delusional delirium goes because the act has carried with it Aimée's self-punishment. In striking out at her externalized ideal, she was also hitting out at herself. This was a fulfilment of her subterranean wish, a punishment for her own repressed desires.

Much of Lacan's handling of Marguerite's case has a Clérambault-like descriptive ring. Yet he emphatically shuns any of the organic underpinnings his psychiatric masters would have called up. He also holds out the possibility of cure. Though he did no formal psychoanalysis with Aimée – his training as a psychoanalyst had to wait for his own analysis with Rudolf Loewenstein which began sometime in 1932 – his interpretation of her case already has a distinct Freudian emphasis.

Bleuler apart, there were no models for conducting analysis with psychotic patients, and Freud, ever pessimistic, had misgivings that success in this area. Lacan rehearses these, but from his long conversations with Aimée and her family and friends, he constructs a detailed and distinctly Freudian analysis of the way in which her delusions have been built up. In a brilliant passage, he also uses Janet to show exactly the opposite of what later American recovered-memory theorists will go to Janet for: that is, Lacan demonstrates how memories are created through a mixture of fantasy images coinciding with associations, events, and *feelings* about the past. These come together to give weight not only to the memory but to the individual's perception of that memory, its familiarity and hence its reality – so that Aimée's fantasized memories take on the full density of lived experience. She 'knows' that persecutory messages have been sent, when plots began and what brought them about.

Lacan tracks back to his patient's family history, not to find inherited madness, but to unearth a 'special' relationship with her mother, who always singled Aimée out for her intelligence, made her special.[241] Her mother, like her daughter after her, it transpires, had a tendency to feel persecuted and to read signs in her neighbours' actions – a reading of the two women's inevitably hostile unconscious, as Freud points out in his essay on jealousy, rather than the mask that consciousness puts on it. Her elder sister became Aimée's principal carer, a maternal stand-in, until she left home for work at the age of fourteen and then married her employer. It was his death that brought her home again, herself childless, to look after Aimée's child: Aimée, the clever dreamer, was ever incompetent around the house, the family story runs.

Lacan determines that Aimée's persecutory delusions have in fact all along been her attempt to punish herself not only for past and present acts and lacks, but for a deeply buried homosexual identification with her sister — besides herself, the underlying target of all her violence. He locates Aimée's psychic homosexuality and her conflicted rejection of it in a number of areas. He cites her confessed inability to enjoy sex — according to her husband, too, she was sexually cold — her attachments to women, the vivacity of her intellectual attraction to men, her sense of affinity with them and the unconscious slippages into the male voice in her fiction, her Bovaresque ambitions, her Don Juanism — that is, her casual liaisons with men which are in fact an anxious search for herself, propelled by sexual dissatisfaction.

Aimée's unconscious homosexual desires, he concludes, explain the structure of her paranoia, her erotomania, and her wish for self-punishment. Everything, Lacan notes, points to this. After her first breakdown, when her childless sister returned to supplant her, desire and guilt were compounded. The resentment and anger that couldn't be felt or directed at an ambivalently loved member of the family had to be displaced. The close upper-class friend Aimée made at work served that purpose. She turned the loved woman into an enemy, a new edition of the sister she couldn't permit herself to hate. And so that woman became linked to her dead child, Aimée's own failed destiny as a woman.

Charting the structure of her unconscious drives and desires, Lacan describes how, from that moment on, Aimée projected her hatred and aggression on to objects further and further away from her real target. 'Their very distance makes them difficult to access and so prevents immediate violence. A mixture of happy coincidence and deep emotional analogies will guide her to her objects.' While her insanity appears to be a reaction against aggressive acts she thinks are perpetrated on her, it is actually a flight from the aggressive acts she wants to perpetrate.

Not surprisingly, her sister senses this. She tells Lacan that she is terrified of Aimée and doesn't want her home.[242]

To show the genesis of paranoia in psychic homosexuality, Lacan quotes Freud's structure of denial in homosexual love:

'I love, him' (the homosexual object) can become 'I don't love him, I hate him', which is projected as 'he hates me', which becomes the theme of persecution.[243]

The second possible form of denial gives birth to erotomania: 'I don't love him, I love her' (the object of the opposite sex). Secondarily projected, this becomes 'she/he loves me', which is the erotomanic theme. This gives birth to a pure delirious fantasy, according to Lacan, which Freud leaves out.

The third possible form of denial goes: 'I don't love him. I love her.' This results, with or without projected inversion, in jealousy, another paranoia.

Finally, there is the form of denial which underlies all of these: 'I don't love him, I love no one. I only love myself.' This explains the theme of self-aggrandizement which, with regression, circles back to a primitive narcissism.

Once again acknowledging his debt to Freud, Lacan notes the difficulties analysis can confront in such cases:

> It is of primary importance to correct the narcissistic tendencies of the subject by a transference which is as long as possible. However, the transference to the analyst, by awakening the homosexual instinct, tends to produce a repression, which . . . is the major mechanism for unleashing the psychosis. This puts the analyst in a delicate position. The very least that can happen is the patient puts a rapid stop to the treatment. But in our cases, the aggressive reaction is most often aimed at the analyst himself. This can last for a long time, even after the reduction of major symptoms, and often to the surprise of the subject herself. Which is why many analysts propose as a primary condition that the therapy has to take place in a closed clinic.[244]

Another problem is that the patient's necessary resistance to the analytic procedure can become part of her own delusional armoury. Which is why, he concludes, with psychosis a psychoanalysis of the ego may function better than one that focuses on the unconscious. Reflecting on Aimée's family situation, Lacan concludes what R.D. Laing will later: the role of the family in the patient's history as the producer of psychosis needs to be taken on board. Despite her 'cure' Aimée refuses to confront the very sister who has set in motion the entire displacement process which is her psychosis. She decides instead to settle on a resignation that doesn't implicate her family, in particular her beloved mother (whom her sister has replaced), who is herself now in the midst of a breakdown because of Aimée. (Later researchers have pointed out that Aimée's illness may indeed have been occasioned by her mother's own illness following the death of a child, a pattern her daughter unconsciously repeated.)

The reflection on families brings Lacan on to a social and political register. Aimée's kind of self-punishing paranoia with its self-aggrandizement and homosexual undertow affects many individuals with superior idealized selves. They are people who want to do good in the world – teachers of both sexes, governesses, women in lowly intellectual jobs, the self-taught. Modern society can leave these individuals in cruel isolation. For them, stably structured hierarchical religious communities, militant political groups or armies, in which they can sublimate their homosexual impulses and work for a higher good, are a real boon. In the subjection to rules, their self-punishing needs are met. This solution to one of the difficulties life presents is an excellent one.

It is worth noting that Lacan's own younger brother had chosen the monastic life, much to his sibling's disquiet.

Aimée's family was to come back and haunt Lacan, as if it were his own. Not her childhood family, but her own son. In one of those returns of the repressed which mark psychoanalytic history Lacan was – unknowingly, it seems – to find himself the training analyst of Marguerite/Aimée's son, Didier Anzieu, who himself became a well known analyst. Lacan claimed never to have seen or certainly not to have remembered his foundational patient's married name, nor did Anzieu know his own maternal history very precisely. Stumbling upon the link with his estranged mother, he found her case in the library and read it in a frenzy. When he questioned his mother, Marguerite had little good to say of her doctor at the Sainte-Anne. She would not have let him analyse *her*. He was too seductive to be trusted. Nor had he ever returned her books and papers. By another twist of fate too implausible to figure in a fiction, Marguerite at around this time became the house-keeper to Lacan's father. He would see her on his irregular visits to his ageing parent, an affable and successful grocery wholesaler who had been married to a conventionally religious woman who was Lacan's mother, until her death in 1948.

If the case of Aimée does not lead directly to what Malcolm Bowie has wittily called the 'surging glossolalia' and 'loosely moored concep-tual mobiles' of Lacan's often impenetrable but hugely influential later seminars, which schooled successive generations of warring French analysts, it does present the germ of some of his major ideas. We begin to see in his analysis of Aimée and her fictions his understanding of the unconscious as being structured like a language, slippery, punning, dis-placing objects and meanings; and the manner in which a symbolic world impacts on the individual. Indeed, Lacan's early work with delu-sionary patients, his familiarity with paranoia, is fundamental to his later conception of the way in which the other is constituted so as to contain the subject's own lacks, hates and fears; while the other's very existence allows the self to see its subjectivity as superior. Hegel's insight into the master–slave relationship, so important to Simone de Beauvoir's conception of woman as the second sex and to later con-structions of the identity politics of race and colonialism, played into Lacan's thinking, here, as well.

Lacan's intervention in a second famous case at this time underscores this. His intervention also points to a growing feeling amongst psychi-atrists and a contingent of the new French psychoanalysts that not only can their insights bring an understanding of criminal behaviour, but that changes need to be made to the legal system to accommodate the existence of the unconscious. Princess Marie Bonaparte, one of Freud's earliest disciples in France, whom Lacan and the younger analysts were to mock as 'Freud-a-dit' because her statements so often began with a reference to the man she claimed not only as her analyst but her per-sonal friend – the man she would do a great deal to rescue from Nazi Vienna in 1938 – had bravely championed the case of one Madame Lefebvre against popular will. In 1925 Madame Lefebvre, a seemingly ordinary middle-class woman, had suddenly taken out a pistol and shot her daughter-in-law who was pregnant with her son's child. Abhorred by press and populace as a monster of motherhood, Madame Lefebvre faced the death sentence. Perhaps reminded of the rumours of murder which surrounded her own father in her childhood, Marie Bonaparte stepped in. She interviewed the woman, became the first expert psychoanalytic witness in France, and in a fine, impassioned paper tracing the way in which Madame Lefebvre in a state of delirium was in fact enacting a long-buried wish to murder her own pregnant and hated mother, argued the case for her irresponsibility.

The Papin sisters

The case of the Papin sisters, the subject of a later play by Jean Genet, brought with it a renewed battle of the mind doctors over the terrain of what constituted madness. In a particularly brutal double murder with an aura of class war, two hardworking maids, Christine and Léa Papin, on the night of 2 February 1933 in Le Mans murdered and sexually maimed their mistress and her daughter, pulling out the eyes of the first. The only provocation seemed to have been the mistress's cold distance, and the hint of an accusation that the ironing had not been done because of an electricity failure. The case kept newspapers and public enthralled for the six months of an extended judicial process in which expert witness was called for from psychiatrists. Dr Truelle, a traditional hereditarian, having examined the sisters poor peasants, brought up in turn in Catholic institutions and by a mercenary mother – contended that there was no hereditary or constitutional condition and thus no grounds for diminished responsibility. The elder Papin sister was simulating delirium, he concluded.

The psychiatrist called in by the defence was Benjamin Logre, a 'progressive'. Not permitted to visit the girls, he assessed them from the magistrate's records and put forward a very different perspective. He rebutted the official psychiatrists' statement that the girls were liars and described a disturbed passion between the older, commanding Christine Papin and her passive sister Léa, which had led them in a *folie à deux*, a double madness, to commit a sadistic, erotic crime.

Despite the vigorous case of the defence, the investigating magistrate's evident qualms about the sanity of the sisters and Dr Logre's testimony, the jury brought in a predictable verdict of guilty: Christine Papin was condemned to death, a sentence commuted to life imprisonment. A year into her imprisonment, the severity of her delirium had her transferred from prison to the Le Mans Psychiatric Hospital. There she never ceased calling for her sister. She refused to eat and died in 1937. Léa served eight years and returned to live with her mother. She worked as a maid for many years, dying only at eighty-two or, some say, eighty-nine.[245]

The full proceedings of the trial were published as soon as it was over. Jacques Lacan entered the fray with an article in the surrealist journal Le Minotaure of 3 December 1933. Fresh from his work on Aimée, he emphasized the structural underpinnings of the sisters' paranoid psychoses and its homosexual nature. He stressed the way in which their employers' odd lack of human sympathy must have been echoed in the servants' proud indifference: one group 'didn't speak to another'. This silence, however, could hardly have been empty, even if the key players couldn't see what was at play. An interpretative paranoia must have been long at work, certainly in Christine, for her to have exploded into aggression.

Lacan describes how the utterly banal electricity failure triggered a passage à l'acte – the moment in which the 'obscure', the hidden depths, suddenly take on material form and are transmuted into violent action. While paying homage to Dr Logre's interpretation, Lacan disagreed. His own diagnosis was delusional paranoia: the sisters, particularly Christine, suffered from a mental delirium around the themes of grandeur and persecution which can breed aggressive, often murderous reactions. Underlying this are social tensions: a conflict between what the self, which incorporates an ideal, wants and what society demands. For Lacan, delirium itself is a camouflage – rather than any straightforward expression – of aggressive instincts which can find no compromise with the individual's understanding of social demands and ideals. Murder serves as a punishment for inner, unconscious desires.

The crime of the Papin sisters, he shows, contains a symbolic meaning in the very atrocity of its details. 'Pull out her eyes,' shouts Christine, as if this were merely the everyday expression of hatred it is – and then literally does so, making the symbolic actual, taking language to its logical conclusion, castrating her employers, tearing away their power — the power of the gaze — and taking it into herself. This power is sexed male, as is Christine's relationship to her sister whose 'husband' she has once been. It is clear to Lacan that the sisters' delirious ideas, their *délire à deux*, pre-dated the murder. There was a slow build-up of delusionary ideas. Their tenuous hold on the reality of their crime is part of its continuation.

Aimée, with her ambivalent hatred of her sister, had struck out at a displaced version of her ego ideal which she both loved and hated. The Papin sisters, with their Siamese twinning, didn't turn against each other but acted as one in two parts. By turning against their mother/daughter mistresses, castrating them, pulling out their eyes, they enacted their own murderous punishment for the sins of their homosexual desires. They were also engaged in a symbolic language of rebellion against, and hence castration of, the masters. In this last we all share.

Such cases, Lacan wants to say, are susceptible to analysis. The unconscious motivation of the Papin sisters, their delirium with its underlying disturbance of love and social rage, is readable. He doesn't, however, call for the sisters' pardon or release. They are guilty of a crime — whether or not we are all *potentially* guilty of it as well.

10

MOTHER AND CHILD

Freud's psychoanalysis had its origins in the idea that psychic disorders were prompted by conflicts related to sexuality. A simple description might have it that civilized sexual morality, with all its strains and hypocrisies, its punishment of childhood masturbation, its enforced ignorance, acted through parents, nannies and schools upon the curious, growing child with her instinctual desires and polymorphous perversity. Gradually internalized through a process fraught with inevitable Oedipal difficulties and, for the boy, the fear of castration, repression ensued. Psychic troubles of varying degrees alongside a panoply of symptoms emerged. The very same process also produced all the goods of civilization. Psychoanalysis could treat underlying problems by giving the adult a space in which to remember, re-enact, and work through blockages that the drama of family life had created. Symptoms – always the markers of deeper psychic problems in this narrative of the self – would then be relieved, transformed, reworked. The individual would be released into the ability to work and to love, with only an ordinary everyday unhappiness to bear.

In the consulting room, Freud's child was always a creature of memory, evoked through free association, hidden in the interstices of dreams or behind screens, misremembered, pushed and pulled, teased and seduced by adult desires and her own forgettings, all the while re-enacting a family romance in relation to the analyst. This child was both buried within and instrumental to the adult's analytic agenda. It stood at doorways peering into the parental bedchamber, was struck by a glance from a shopkeeper, experienced sexual stirrings and fantasies, loved and hated its parents of the same and opposite sex, raged at the infidelities of its parents and the resulting competing intruders, was punished for masturbation, feared castration, developed fantasies, anxieties and phobias. Above all, this child was ever-curious and conducted sexual research into the origins of life. The Freudian child is an energetic, sensual being, an adventurer and a seeker after truth. No innocent in terms of sensuous pleasures, he nonetheless has everything to learn about the world.

Though for much of the 1890s as a specialist in children's nervous diseases, Freud, rather like Winnicott later, saw thousands of children, he never treated any but one analytically, his own children apart. That was Little Hans whose predicament, complete with his phobia of horses, was brought to Freud by parental report. Hans's father was a member of Freud's early psychoanalytic Wednesday group and Freud only once saw the little boy, whose sexual researches fuelled parts of two papers as well as a case history. Daughter Anna provided an occasional case: Anna's greed for 'stwawbewwies' features in her father's dream book and her own rescue fantasies in his paper 'A Child is Being Beaten'. Freud's grandson, Ernst, son of his favourite daughter Sophie, appears as the child in *Beyond the Pleasure Principle*, where he manages his mother's coming and going, absence and presence, by making a game of it: repeating it and controlling the emotions through play.

Women were the first psychoanalytic practitioners to deal directly with the living child. Psychoanalysis had opened its doors to them, if not without a little dissension amidst the original members of Freud's circle. But Freud prevailed and women came into the new profession in proportionately significant numbers.[246] In Germany by the early thirties, women analysts made up about 40 per cent of the profession, whereas they constituted only 6.5 per cent of doctors.[247] The British Psychoanalytic Society in the thirties was also 40 per cent female, and women were numerous in the ranks of the Tavistock Centre.

Even if the early women analysts, such as Helene Deutsch, were all too eager to get away from the 'tyranny of the mother' or, as in Anna Freud's case, treated the maternal home-maker with an edge of contempt tinged with discomfort, they showed a marked interest in re-creating women as mothers. They focused on women in relation to their biological destiny – menstruation, pregnancy, menopause. Or they zeroed in on the child as if, despite their professionalism, they were playing out their own mothers' concerns. Given the constrictions on women's work, this was in part a social imperative: children were their permitted domain. But the exceptions – like the flamboyantly independent Princess Marie Bonaparte who wrote about adult female sexuality, or the feminist Karen Horney who worried about the pathologization of the feminine, about marriage and the monogamous ideal – only highlight the regularity with which most of the early women analysts, feminist in their social concerns or not, concentrated in writing as well as in practice on children or motherhood. Many, like Helene Deutsch, saw in the mother the consummation of the feminine trajectory, or, like Melanie Klein, theorized her as an adjunct to the child. Many were or became mothers and their own experience fed into their work.

The earliest impetus of the child analysts was to enlighten children about the sexual secrets which damaged them by the very fact of secrecy. Hermine Hug-Hellmuth, one of the first female members of the Vienna Society, was lauded by Freud for her researches into the sexual life of the growing child, and for her intelligent application of psychoanalysis to the 'prophylactic upbringing of healthy children'.[248] The *Young Girl's Diary*, which she claimed to have edited rather than written, caused a scandal on its appearance in 1919 because of its honesty about a middle-class girl's fantasies and sexual curiosity.

In her first article in the International Journal of Psycho-Analysis Melanie Klein writes:

We can spare the child unnecessary repression by freeing – and first and foremost in ourselves – the whole wide sphere of sexuality from the dense veils of secrecy, falsehood and danger spun by a hypocritical civilisation upon an affective and uninformed foundation. We shall let the child acquire as much sexual information as the growth of its desire for knowledge requires, thus depriving sexuality at once of its mystery and of a great part of its danger. This ensures that wishes, thoughts and feelings shall not – as happened to us – be partly repressed and partly, in so far as repression fails, endured under a burden of false shame and nervous suffering. In averting this repression, this burden of superfluous suffering, moreover, we are laying the foundations for health, mental balance and the favourable development of character.[249]

This thrust was echoed in any number of social campaigns in Europe and America. Marie Stopes's *Married Love* and *Wise Parenthood*, as well as her subsequent clinics, and Margaret Sanger's work in America, are both part of a sexual education project that comes hand in hand with advice on birth control, so that the new child will be a wanted child and grow into the best possible environment. At its most politically idealistic, such educative campaigning formed part of a larger socialist enterprise: the creation of the new man and woman, who would leave behind the murderous aggression that world war had so tragically highlighted.

Schools influenced by psychoanalytic thinking were founded in Vienna and Berlin, England, Russia and America. Delinquency moved from being a 'moral' problem to becoming a psychological one with roots in disturbed or broken families, or disciplinarian orphanages. New professions such as social work grew, and older ones — nursing, teaching, medicine, psychiatry itself — often took on a psychoanalytic gloss. This coexisted with changes in psychoanalytic practice and a proliferation of related and sometimes warring theories. While Freud in the post-war period moved beyond the pleasure principle to posit a death drive, explore the psychology of the group, or move back in historical time to find the roots of monotheism, others moved back to explore infancy before language, which had thus far been the only tool of analysis.

This shift towards child and mother gradually dislodged sex as instinct from its central place in psychoanalytic thinking. Thwarted desire, sexuality and its attendant anxieties and fantasies moved aside as the key set of explanations for illness. Mothers displaced castrating fathers as the crucial authority dominating both childhood and the inner life: it was on the base of that earliest and fundamental relationship, not the paternal one, that all future relations, of love and power, of attachment and dependence, would be replayed.

Undoubtedly a world war, followed within a single generation by another, fed into the process that made a healthy mother and child — the so-called nursing couple — a prime preoccupation for the mind doctors. They were part of a larger cultural impetus. The twenties brought a need to repopulate after the devastation both of war and of the 1918 flu pandemic, which had taken a terrifying fifty million lives worldwide. Women were urged back into the home from wartime work and often went willingly. A backlash occurred against what many saw as rapacious feminist demands for an equality which included sexual equality. While all forms of sexuality and sexual orientation were on permanent display in its night-life, the Weimar Constitution forbade the public display of contraceptives and description of their use. The French rewarded mothers of five children with motherhood medals. In 1930 the Pope issued an encyclical that permitted marital sex *only* when the intention was to reproduce. Pro-natalism was widespread. Fascists monumentalized woman as mother. Although they didn't share in their politics, women mind doctors hardly demurred from urging women to motherhood. Increasingly they emphasized the importance and complexities of his majesty, the child.

Becoming a mother now took on an added 'psychological' interest, at once troubling and intelligible[250], a subject for professionals and social authorities, as well as for those older moral arbiters, the religions. All were now engaged, alongside mother and child, in determining conduct, measuring health and development, and attributing meanings to a function and relationship which was, after all, as old as humanity itself.

Anna Freud (1895–1982) and Melanie Klein (1882–1960)

Anna Freud and Melanie Klein were the two most influential early child analysts, not only through their writings, but through that form of diffusion which is the training analysis itself. In a sense, each took up different aspects of Freud's capacious legacy and moved it in new directions. Rivals, they battled for the supremacy of their views and for the paternal mantle.

Having trained as a teacher, undergone a partial analysis with her father and another with that most alluring of Freud's early women followers, Lou Andreas Salomé, the work of Freud's youngest daughter always had a pedagogical and normative cast. She stressed the importance of working with parents and schools in order to shape the developing child into a well integrated adult. In 1927, with Dorothy Burlingham, she set up the experimental Hietzing School, and as early as 1936 pioneered nurseries for children under two. At the Jackson Nursery toddlers were observed and information gathered about their eating habits (she herself had suffered from an eating disorder), play, and general development. Anna shared the socialist hopes of Vienna's therapeutically inclined radicals, such as Siegfried Bernfeld and August Aichhorn. The latter's *Wayward Youth* set out to show a repressive, militaristic society that delinquents were not criminals but children whose inner development had gone awry. Psychoanalysis, for Anna, could help that development: its role was not only to focus on the unconscious psychic life, the repressed instinctual impulses and fantasies, but to strengthen the ego, so that the child could become a responsible adult.

Counter to Melanie Klein, whose focus lay on the infant's earliest inner life and its rampant instinctual desires and aggression, Anna Freud emphasized that 'From the beginning analysis, as a therapeutic method, was concerned with the ego and its aberrations: the investigation of the id and of its mode of operation was always only a means to an end. And the end was invariably the same: the correction of these abnormalities and the restoration of the ego to its integrity.'[251] Ego psychology, as well as the understanding of the ego's defences – which she detailed in her 1936 book *The Ego and the Mechanisms of Defence* as repression, regression, reaction formation, isolation, undoing, introjection, identification, projection, turning against the self, reversal and sublimation – owe much to Anna Freud's thinking, and although she, like Melanie Klein before her, settled in Britain, it was in the United States that her influence would be greatest.

In 1933, the new Nazi government in Germany had effected a purification of the 'Jewish' science of psychoanalysis. On 10 May, some four months after it had taken power, Freud's books were burned in Berlin. By the end of the month, sex counselling and birth control clinics were shut down. Eighty per cent of German psychoanalysts were Jewish, and emigration to the United States, Britain, France and Palestine began. Freud had felt he was too old to leave Vienna, but with the Nazi takeover of Austria in 1938 and ensuing threats to the family which Anna, his Antigone, fended off with great personal bravery, they moved to

London. Freud died there on 23 September 1939, just as war was taking Europe over.

As part of the war effort Anna, with her long-term partner Dorothy Burlingham, set up the Hampstead Nurseries for evacuated babies and children. Caring for displaced children also provided a rich field for gathering insights into the nature of the child's life and family relations. Experience began increasingly to show that children were often less affected by the blitz, the war from the skies, than by their mothers' anxiety, or by the separation itself. What emerges above all in the books based on the nurseries, *Infants without Families* (1944) and *Young Children in War-Time* (1942), is the crucial importance of the mother in the child's emotional life: 'A child in the infant stage of 1, 2, 3, 4 years of age will shake and tremble with the anxiety of his mother, and this anxiety will impart itself the more thoroughly to the child the younger he is. The primitive emotional tie between mother and baby, which in some respects still makes one being out of the two, is the basis for the development of this type of air raid anxiety in children.'[252]

Separation from the mother has a formative impact on the child. Taken away from its mother, the youngest child will, out of need, adapt to a new carer. But for the three- to five-year-olds, separation can do severe damage to everything from toilet training to the acquisition of language. Killing a parent in fantasy, which, of course, is part of the ordinary Freudian child's Oedipal desire, is tolerable when the parent is present and maintains the bond with the child. If the parents are absent, 'the child is frightened. . ..and suspects that their desertion may be another punishment or even the consequence of his own bad wishes. To overcome this guilt he overstresses all the love which he has ever felt for his parents. This turns the central pain of separation into an intense longing which is hard to bear.'[253]

The Hampstead Nurseries served the immediate needs of war work. But the observations garnered there also helped to shape postwar fostering, institutional and welfare policies. They crucially determined Anna Freud's focus on the developing child, on learning disturbances, delinquency, eating disorders, and eventually family law. Her later work was instrumental in forging the concept of 'the best interests of the child' and in laying the foundations of children's rights. Judgements in custody cases came to be shaped by a psychological view of the child as a highly sensitive and malleable creature. For the 'sound development' of the child, Anna Freud argued, stable bonds had to be formed. A child's need was for 'unbroken continuity of affectionate and stimulating relationships' which could, of course, be provided by a caring, and not only by a biological, parent. From this it followed that protracted custody decisions, shuffling between foster parents or institutions, and joint custody, might not be in the child's best interests. On the other hand, a social worker's 'rescue fantasies' might be more detrimental to the child than continuity with parents the social worker didn't altogether approve.

Anna Freud's work emphasizes the importance of the environment in relationship to the child's development, an environment which in the first instance is the mother, whom the analyst must not displace but rather work alongside. The child is understood as a being in search of instinctual gratification: this is what will drive it in its first attachments and on its all-important path to the outside world to which a series of difficult adaptations will have to be made as its ego matures.

A wider-ranging hypothesis about the workings of the unconscious inner life of the baby was not what primarily interested Anna Freud. That pre-Oedipal, pre-linguistic world was the dramatic terrain of Melanie Klein. Her insights gave birth to an increasingly complex infantile psyche, an inner landscape which brought with it a host of new psychological tropes – such as projection, introjection, and manic defence – to describe the dynamic psychic life of the child and its object relations. A new very British emphasis within psychoanalysis was one of the results.

Melanie Klein was born in Vienna, the youngest of four children, a late arrival to an ageing, father, Dr Moriz Reizes, and his considerably younger ambitious wife, Libusa Deutsch. Her favourite sister died when Melanie was four; the brother who coached her in Greek and Latin died while still at university. These losses shadowed her. Abandoning her own aspirations to study medicine, Melanie married at nineteen, leaving university early to follow her husband, an engineer, in the various moves which eventually took them to Budapest in 1910. The couple had three children by the time Melanie decided, having read Freud and in the wake of her mother's death, that she wanted to study psychoanalysis.

After an analysis with the brilliant and innovative Sandor Ferenczi, she began to analyse children, worked in his Budapest clinic during the war years and participated in the early life of the profession, lecturing at meetings and congresses. In 1921, on the cusp of divorce, she moved with her children to Berlin and worked with Karl Abraham, her great supporter, who sadly died in 1925. Bloomsbury's own acerbic Alix Strachey, wife of James, who was having an analysis with Abraham while her husband was pining in London, described Klein in a letter at this time as a vulgar Cleopatra, an 'ultra heterosexual Semiramis in slap up fancy dress'. But she valued Klein and translated her from rather woolly German into a precise Bloomsbury English – a fact which certainly helped Klein's eventual British reception.

Invited to London to lecture by Ernest Jones at the Stracheys' behest, Klein gave six lectures at the home of Virginia Woolf's brother, the psychoanalyst Dr Adrian Stephen. The following year Klein emigrated to Britain, where she had a galvanizing impact on British psychoanalysis, sowing love and hatred, passionate affiliation and radical dissent, in a mirror image of her own dramatic view of the inner life, with its splittings, projective identifications and persecutory forces. Bloomsbury, itself constituted out of relationships and valuing their importance, continued to be kind to her. Virginia Woolf, who dined with Klein on 15 March 1939, left a telling portrait of her exact contemporary in her diary: 'a woman of character & force some submerged – how shall I say? – not craft, but subtlety; something working underground. A pull, a twist, like an undertow: menacing. A bluff grey haired lady with large bright imaginative eyes.'[254]

One of Klein's innovations was to posit that the child experienced the Oedipal situation with weaning or earlier, its world by then already riven between love of one parent, hatred of the other, an attendant guilt and fear of castration. For Klein the deprivations that weaning brings topple into those suffered by the child's inability to stand in for the parent of the opposite sex. Such deprivations can affect a child's toilet training, seemingly inadvertent self-injury, and ability to learn.

At a very early age children become acquainted with reality through the deprivations which it imposes on them. They try to defend themselves against it by repudiating it. The fundamental thing, however, and the criterion of all later capacity for adaptation to reality, is the degree in which they are able to tolerate the deprivations that result from the Oedipus-situation. Hence, even in little children, an exaggerated repudiation of reality (often disguised under an apparent 'adaptability' and 'docility') is an indication of neurosis and differs from the flight from reality of adult neurotics only in the forms in which it manifests itself. Even in the analysis of young children, therefore, one of the final results to be attained is successful adaptation to reality. One way in which this shows itself in children is in the disappearance of the difficulties encountered in their education. In other words, such children have become capable of tolerating real deprivations.[255]

Even if the psychoanalytic world itself was small, particularly so at the time in Britain, Klein's focus gradually spread into a wider social arena through her prominent analysands. England provided fertile ground for Kleinian ideas, helped by the abiding English interest in the child, a legacy of Romanticism made vivid in a thriving and altogether uncontinental children's literature. By the mid-1920s, Christopher Robin and what would become the classical 'transitional object', Winnie the Pooh, were already alive and well. And their little Freudian friend, James, James, Robertson, Robertson, Weatherby George Dupree, was taking 'good care of his mother, though he was only three', and knew very well that she must never go down to the end of the town without 'consulting me'.

The Kleinian baby is a dramatic creature, a site of internal warfare between aggressive and libidinal demands. Attached or distant from the breast – its focus of attention, or object – this babe inhabits a world of dark and extravagant passions, full of sucking and biting and kicking. The mother, meanwhile, is mostly breast, at best compliant and ever available, unhampered by her own moods and needs which are inevitably instantly communicated. This breast stands in for the whole of the babe's world, site of satisfaction, or lack, and when lacking, taken in as attacking and therefore demanding retribution. The baby internalizes, or 'introjects', this good and bad breast as separate forces. The split between the two cannot be reconciled as ambiguity or into a single whole person until later, if ever. The good is idealized, loved, mostly unattainable. The bad is persecutory. Primitive warfare between the two is fundamental and can be re-enacted at any difficult point in an individual's life. Indeed, a Kleinian analysis usually takes the patient back to this early pre-sexual world of fears, guilt, anxiety and retribution, so fundamental they are tantamount to original sin.

Klein recounts the case of a five-year-old boy who used to pretend he had all sorts of wild animals, such as elephants, leopards, hyenas and wolves, to help him against his enemies. They represented dangerous objects – persecutors – which he had tamed and could use as protection against those enemies. But it appeared in the analysis that they also stood for his own sadism, each animal representing a specific source of sadism and the organs used in this connection. The elephants symbolized his muscular sadism, his impulses to trample and stamp. The tearing leopards represented his teeth and nails and their functions in his attacks. The wolves symbolized his excrements, invested with destructive properties. He sometimes became very frightened that the wild animals he had tamed would turn against him and exterminate him. This fear expressed his sense of being threatened by his own destructiveness (as well as by internal persecutors).[256]

Kleinian anxiety is a fear of annihilation, which exists in the unconscious together with a life force: the mother's breast, the first bit of reality the child meets, represents both:

first the mother's breast (and the mother) becomes in the infant's mind a devouring object and these fears soon extend to the father's penis and to the father. At the same time, since devouring implies from the beginning the internalisation of the devoured object, the ego is felt to contain devoured and devouring objects. Thus the super-ego is built up from the devouring breast (mother) to which is added the devouring penis (father). These cruel and dangerous internal figures become the representatives of the death instinct. Simultaneously the other aspect of the early super-ego is formed first by the internalised good breast (to which is added the good penis of the father) which is felt as a feeding and helpful internal object, and as the representative of the life instinct. The fear of being annihilated includes the danger lest the internal good breast be destroyed, for this object is felt to be indispensable for the preservation of life. The threat to the self from the death instinct working within is bound up with the dangers apprehended from the internalised devouring mother and father and amounts to fear of death.[257]

The Kleinian child has a punishing, sadistic super-ego which comes into being through that deprivation which is weaning, or even earlier — certainly far sooner than Freud or Anna had postulated. Ordinary pleasure, for Klein, seems most often to be a way of avoiding psychic pain. In the child's inner world, which is already a version of the others it has come up against, the super-ego attacks it for having murderous thoughts about the people who gradually come into three-dimensional focus as first mother, then parents. In this process, the omnipotent (and utterly helpless) babe moves out of the initial struggle for survival and begins to recognize what were 'part objects' in its own world as people on the outside, or 'whole objects'. This relational element is the foundation of the Kleinian world — hence the world of 'object relations' as this kind of analysis came to be called.

Simultaneously the child also begins to recognize its dependence on mother and see that what it both loves and hates is one and the same person. The mother it hates and attacks is the loved object and, conversely, loving her means loving what is hated and feared. The child feels guilty about the hatred, though this guilt is not as ferocious as that persecution the earlier super-ego inflicted. It also fears that the mother will abandon it as a result of its aggression. Depression, or the 'depressive position', comes with this sense of loss. During this phase, the child may either defend against the sense of loss or mourning by being 'manically' busy or cheerful; or it may try to repair the damage its own aggression has caused, thereby paving the way for good future relationships or indeed for the various creative tasks which it may later undertake.

Inescapable as a force, essential, the Kleinian mother has little of an individual person about her apart from her task of mothering. But the mothering is what serves as a spur to the child's eventual recognition of a world separate from itself, a world of objects or others, to which the child will relate in the manner which these first of relations set down. In the helpless infant's grappling to form links with the real, those eventual 'object relations', its inner life becomes filled with dark phantasies. These phantasies form the basis of later 'projections' on to others. With the same infantile literalness that makes the breast the world, they also resemble and form the root of later psychoses.

In Klein's savage scenario of developing infant and appended mother, the latter can be as helpless as the child in bearing the brunt of murderous attacks and emotions which, because of their very unspeakability, feel far more violent than Freud's postulated Oedipal attacks on the father. Within the world of psychic illness, Kleinian ideas had a distinct impact on the treatment of psychotic conditions and on the care of patients, child or adult, immured in their own imaginations, with little link to the outside real. In the culture at large into which Klein's complex hypotheses gradually fed in a simpler form, her sense of the mother as both utterly passive and infinitely responsible helped to induce in women a feeling of lingering culpability with regard to their children. Everywhere in the postwar magazines, paediatric services and childcare manuals, the business of raising children became something so difficult as to drive both mothers and children if not altogether mad, then certainly to seek out help.

D.W. Winnicott (1896–1971)

Donald Woods Winnicott, a paediatrician by initial training, forged a crucial link between the medical and the psychoanalytic care of children in Britain and, through his many books and articles, much further afield. Winnicott made babies interesting.[258] There is more to a baby than blood and bones, he reiterated in any number of ways. His status as a male and a doctor gave the contention a great deal of weight.

Born into a prosperous Plymouth family, Winnicott studied medicine at Cambridge, then interrupted this to serve as a probationer surgeon on a destroyer in the First World War. Having completed his medical studies, he began to work at the London Queen's Hospital for Children in Hackney and at Paddington Green Hospital in 1923, the very year in which he started a ten-year analysis with Freud's translator James Strachey. His interest in psychoanalysis had been spurred by his reading of Freud's *Interpretation of Dreams* in 1919, which opened him up to a new way of thinking – one he wanted instantly to redescribe in English. In 1927, the year that Melanie Klein arrived at the British Psychoanalytical Society, Winnicott began his psychoanalytic training. Melanie Klein became his supervisor. In 1936, fully trained, he nonetheless began a second analysis, this time with Joan Riviere, Klein's foremost champion and her talented translator: Klein's insights permeate Winnicott's thinking. That said, he was ever a rebellious sceptic about theoretical formulations, whether (Sigmund or Anna) Freudian or Kleinian. He preferred to pioneer his own course, and steered a very British one through the 'continental wars' between the two women , insisting on that plain speech which the BBC listening public, not to mention doctors, could readily understand. During the so-called Controversial Discussions of 1943, in which Klein and later arrival to Britain, Anna Freud, and their respective followers battled over Freud' s legacy – a controversy which almost tore apart the British Psychoanalytical Society – it was Winnicott who pointed out that while the verbal salvoes were being fired, there were actual bombs falling overhead.

Needless to say, Winnicott became the leader of what emerged as the so-called Middle Group, the Independents within the very British compromise that postwar training within the British Psychoanalytical Society offered, with its A (Klein), B (Anna Freud) and Middle Groups. He served for two terms after the war as the Society's president, and for twenty-five years as the head of its training institute's Child Department.

Winnicott's preoccupations reinforced the emphasis on the nursing couple of mother and child, and further removed from the terrain of analytic concerns consideration of any indecorous sexuality that might involve actual coupling rather than childhood fantasies. For Winnicott, as the much cited phrase has it, there was no such thing as a baby, since wherever you found a baby, you would always find someone else, most notably, a mother. The phrase astonished him when it first slipped from his lips, but he realized what he meant by it was that the two must always be considered as a couple.[259] One might almost conclude, to take his daring thought to its logical end, that for Winnicott there was rarely enough such a thing as a woman, since she existed entirely as part of the mother–child dyad.

During his forty years at the two hospitals where he worked, his 'psychiatric snack-bar', Winnicott saw some sixty thousand children and their mothers, fathers and grandparents. Unlike many of his psychoanalytic contemporaries, he was prepared to engage in brief psychotherapies with his patients. This not only had the potential of disseminating psychoanalysis more widely, but helped to bring a new way of thinking into the medical arena. Winnicott believed that since illness and cure were rarely altogether to do with physical factors, doctors should have some knowledge of the unconscious and its mechanisms. He would have liked this knowledge to be largely intuitive and spontaneous. He had an optimistic sense of human possibility, an idea of an authentic self and creative potential instilled by the relationship with a 'good-enough mother'. This romantic sense coexisted, perhaps paradoxically, with a predilection for Klein's tormented agonist of an infant, born to the terrors of an inner world split into warring good and bad.

His work as psychiatric consultant to the government's wartime Evacuation Scheme in Oxford, where he managed several hostels, had underscored the importance of the mother's role for him. The child who had not had good-enough mothering couldn't adapt to his placement. A failure in early mothering could lead to later delinquency. The 'curable' kind was often instigated by a failure in mothering or a separation from mother which occurred *after* the child's ego was already integrated. Antisocial activity for Winnicott is an expression of the delinquent child's sense of loss, a rupture of an earlier integration the child carried within him, as he carried his entire early environment. The fact that there was 'activity' was itself an expression of hope: what had been lost would be found again by freeing a development that had been stopped too soon. Winnicott also recognized that a continually dependable environment helped the problem children as much as therapy.

This underscored his postwar sense of therapy as only partly to do with Kleinian deep interpretations which insisted on the underlying, Oedipal meanings of the child's play and utterances. Therapy, equally and increasingly, became for Winnicott a question of providing a 'holding environment', of allowing a constant and reliable space in which the troubled child could express the worst without fear of punishment. Therapy, particularly with the seriously damaged, was a question of 'managing' the transition from the terrible fantasies and omnipotence of the babe's inner world – so akin to a psychotic's – to an acceptance of a reality beyond the child's magical/diabolic control and all the guilt and anxiety that attended this control.

The therapist became 'real' for the child when she could hate him

without destroying him, move from 'illusion' to 'disillusion' and perhaps 'reillusionment'. The therapist, in other words, was a later version
of a 'good-enough mother' ferrying the child into the real. Freud had
once said he was uncomfortable when asked to take on the mother's
role in transference. Not so Winnicott. Even if Freud had not written
much about the maternal function, 'it turned up in his provision of a
setting for his work, almost without his being aware'.[260] The analyst, like
a mother, would always be reliably there, alive and breathing. The
shift – in terms of the mind doctors' practice – is from Freud's form of
analysis which deals largely with neurosis, to a therapy which can also
deal with psychosis, since it probes back to the earliest pre-verbal relationships.

After the Second World War, Winnicott lectured not only to analysts
and professionals, but with increasing prominence and frequency to
social workers, childcare organizations, teachers and priests. A member
of UNESCO and WHO study groups, his thinking fed into public policy
and, through his BBC broadcasts, helped shape public opinion. Not
only his focus on, but his understanding of, the mother–child couple
slipped into common knowledge. It seemed both 'natural' and
'common-sensical', its theoretical status veiled by Winnicott's felici-
tous common English.

So what was this mother–infant relationship that made the good-
enough mother so decisive in the infant's development? If Winnicott
took from Klein her description of the infant's inner world, he corrected it by grounding it in the ordinariness of mother-love, that
unconditional acceptance by the mother of the child's early 'ruthless'
needs. The child's attempts to hurt the mother in nursing or play – to
bite, stab, kick, yell and generally to wear her out – are his primitive
form of love. Only a mother can tolerate such needs; her acceptance,
indeed her continuing presence and survival, are essential to the child's
development.

If the mother does not have the capacity to accept this ruthless love,
to be a good-enough holding environment for it, and to emerge
unscathed by the infant's attacks, later problems or delinquency can
emerge. Indeed, from his psychotic patients, Winnicott learned that it is
the mother who takes the infant through from a primary stage of

'unintegration', in which the self is not yet anchored to the body and its various parts. By handling, bathing, rocking, naming, she gathers the baby's bits together, integrates him. Gradually through that continuum of sight, sound and smell, which she provides, she also becomes a whole being in the world outside the baby's fantasy. The breast gives the infant the capacity to conjure up – to hallucinate – what is available, while its conditioning reappearance provides the relief of the real, which limits fantasy. The sense of unreality, the disintegration which is part of psychoses, are caused by a rupture or failure in early mothering[261] or by the mother's depression – as Winnicott had learned from his wartime evacuees and patients.

Winnicott posited a 'primary maternal preoccupation' as a necessary state for infant health. This was in part a response to Anna Freud's insistence that to blame 'neurosis on the mother's shortcomings in the oral phase is no more than a facile and misleading generalization', since 'disappointments and frustrations are inseparable from the mother–child relationship.' For Winnicott the tiny, utterly dependent infant is not susceptible yet to disappointments and frustrations, which are later emotions. Needs can only be met or not met, but their meeting is crucial. And when she is in that state of 'primary maternal preoccupation' – a kind of heightened sensitivity or fugue, a 'normal illness' which lasts through the last period of pregnancy and through the babe's early weeks – the mother meets them. Her lulling attention, her feeling herself into the child's place and letting the ruthless child have his way with her, is all-important.

> A good enough environmental provision in the earliest phase enables the infant to begin to exist, to have experience, to build a personal ego, to ride instincts, and to meet with all the difficulties inherent in life. All this feels real to the infant who becomes able to have a self that can eventually even afford to sacrifice spontaneity, even to die.
>
> On the other hand, without the initial good-enough environmental provision, this self that can afford to die never develops. The feeling of real is absent and if there is not too much chaos the ultimate feeling is of futility. The inherent difficulties of life cannot be reached, let alone the satisfactions. If there is not chaos, there appears a false self that hides the true self, that complies with demands, that reacts to stimuli, that rids

itself of instinctual experience by having them, but that is only playing for time.'[262]

An awful lot hangs on a few weeks in a mother's life in which the all-important breast needs to be presented in the right intuitive way so that 'it is of a piece with the child's desire' and enables him to build up 'the basic stuff of the inner world that is personal and indeed the self'. If the rapport between herself and the child is not in place, if she is depressed or inattentive, or has a 'strong male identification', the babe may experience a 'threat of annihilation', or begin to develop a false, compliant self which eventually feels futile and breaks down. Later development will in any case be impaired: may result in thieving or delinquency, that psychosis which Winnicott characterized as a 'deficiency disease' – the risks attending mere 'good-enoughness' are huge. A believer in spontaneity, Winnicott's hypotheses hardly leave the mother much room for either artful or artless meeting of the babe's needs. Luckily the analyst, by replicating the good-enough environment, could sometimes make good the mothering lacks the child had undergone.

Anna Freud remained unconvinced about the direction the new object-relations school of psychoanalysis was taking. The 'false generation' missed the essence of psychoanalysis, she noted, looking back in 1974 – the 'conflict within the individual person, the aims, ideas, and ideals battling with the drives to keep the individual within a civilized community. It has become modern to water this down to every individual's longing for perfect unity with his mother, i.e., to be loved only as an infant can be loved. There is an enormous amount that gets lost this way.'[263]

The Piggle

Few of Winnicott's published case histories are longer than examples within a text. One of these is the moving case of Gabrielle, or the Piggle, as her endearing nickname has it, a highly intelligent and talkative little girl who came to Winnicott at the age of two years and four months. Her parents were known to him and the mother in a sense co-authors her daughter's case: her letters describing Piggle's state and progress are exemplary descriptions by a woman who is both psychoanalytically informed and optimistic about therapeutic success. She is in some ways the best existing mother in Winnicott's work: alive to her daughter's state, interested in her fantasies and childhood weirdness and alert to her progress. Though it is never stated, one can only imagine that her early mothering was 'good-enough', and that the happy resolution of Piggle's problems, partly the result of that common enough occurrence, the birth of a sibling, is an indication of this. We can only speculate that this may be one of the reasons Winnicott decided in the last year of his life to prepare the case for publication.

Extracts from the mother's two initial letters to Winnicott, which precede the first consultation on 3 February 1964, reveal her sensitivity to her child and to what is amiss in her. They also reveal an astute sense of what this particular analyst needs to know. This analysis is, in some ways at least, a double act. In the first letter Winnicott is given a sense of the normal progress of nursing, Piggle's great poise and inner resources, her passion for her father and her 'high-handed' attitude to her mum; then the change sudden in her at the arrival of a sibling when she was twenty-one months, when she became 'bored and depressed' and very conscious of her relations and her identity. Piggle also developed an intense and troubling fantasy life, which had her scratching her face and waking her with nightmares:

> She has a black mummy and daddy. The black mummy comes in after her at night and says: 'Where are my yams?' (To yam = to eat. She pointed out her breasts, calling them yams, and pulling them to make them larger.) 'Sometimes she is put into the toilet by the black mummy. The black mummy, who lives in her tummy, and who can be talked to there on the telephone, is often ill, and difficult to make better.
>
> The second strand of fantasy, which started earlier, is about the 'babacar'. Every night she calls, again and again: 'Tell me about the babacar, all about the babacar.' The black mummy and daddy are often in the babacar together, or some man alone. There is very occasionally a black Piggle in evidence (we call Gabrielle 'the Piggle').[264]

The astute mother is worried about the present. She also has the very Winnicottian worry about the person Piggle may become if she 'hardens' herself against her distress, erects defences against pain. In the second letter, the mother points out that the Piggle is worse: she no longer plays with any concentration or admits to being herself at all. 'The Piga', who is now black and bad, has gone away to the babacar. When told that her mother has written to Dr Winnicott who understands about black mummies and babacars, the little girl asks twice to be taken to him.

Much is astonishing in Winnicott's account of the Piggle. Although in its progress it is clearly a psychoanalytic case, one which extensively probes the child's unconscious fantasy life, Winnicott doesn't see the Piggle daily. In fact, between the start of the treatment and the final session when the Piggle is five, he sees her only fourteen times and does so 'on demand'. The family live far from London. Like Anna Freud and unlike Melanie Klein, Winnicott also engages the parents in the treatment process. He does more. He emphasizes that the 'on demand' model has contributed to the unfolding of the case: too often the frequency of analysis means that the parents give the child over to the doctor and assume that everything in the 'rich symptomatology' she presents is part of her illness. 'It is possible for the treatment of a child actually to interfere with a very valuable thing which is the ability of the child's home to tolerate and to cope with the child's clinical states that indicate emotional strain and temporary hold-ups in emotional development, or even the fact of development itself.'[265]

In that sense Winnicott's treatment is an aid to good-enough parenting, and the written exchanges between himself and the Piggle's mother are exemplary of a mutual process. The case itself is a fascinating narrative as much for the door that it opens into the consulting room as for the magic of the child's relations with Winnicott, as she plays her way out of her fears and worries and into an understanding that Winnicott, who had become part of her once black and rapacious inner world, can be left and still continue to exist independently of her, liking her, even if she hates. Along the way, the Piggle clarifies her confusions and imaginings about babies, comes to terms with her little sister and her Oedipal jealousy of her father, and puts together her primitive split-apart good mother and black mother. 'Black mummy as a split-off version of mother, one that doesn't understand babies, or one who understands them so well that her absence or loss makes everything black,'[266] Winnicott's observes, in a text which is filled with an array of brilliant observations.

Perhaps the most riveting aspect of the case is the way it illuminates what Winnicott means both by play and by treatment. The first is no half-hearted pretence, but integral to the relationship the child and doctor form. The many anecdotal accounts of Winnicott's clinical skills become visible in *The Piggle*. Winnicott really is down there on the floor with the child, the toys and the roles the child attributes to him. He provides a consistent environment in which she can feel safe and 'held'. He is hard at play, that process which amongst much else is an unconscious enactment of the bits and pieces within the child's inner life, their taking apart and putting back together again. Importantly, mutual play is entrenched well before any interpretations are offered.

The Piggle's father, who brings her, sometimes participates in the play. (Indeed, Winnicott writes to express his admiration for the way he allows himself to be used without quite knowing what is going on.) If needs be, Winnicott continues to play even after the toys have been tidied up (though sometimes, when the Piggle is almost better, she can afford to leave a mess behind her): 'I stayed where I was, being the black angry mummy who wanted to be daddy's little girl and was jealous of Gabrielle. At the same time I was Gabrielle being jealous of the new baby with mother. She ran to the door, they went off and she waved. Her last words were: "Mother wants to be daddy's little girl."'

As for the treatment, Winnicott suggests its success is in large part really up to the child and the parents. The doctor is there to facilitate, to be available, not to interpret too quickly according to theoretical rote. Winnicott is careful to stress his 'not understanding what she has not yet been able to give me clues for'. Only the Piggle knows the answers, and they cannot be provided for her. 'When she could encompass the meaning of the fears she would make it possible for me to understand too.' She does.

After the fifth session, Winnicott writes to the Piggle's mother: 'The Piggle is a very interesting child, as you know.' He adds wryly, 'You might prefer that she were not so interesting, but there she is, and I expect that she will settle down into being quite ordinary soon. I think a great number of children have these thoughts and worries, but they are usually not so well verbalized, and this in Piggle's case has a lot to do with your both being rather particularly conscious of childhood matters and tolerant of childhood questions.[267]

The Piggle is an interesting child and she shares her interesting thoughts and worries with a great number of children. Her exemplary nature lies in her ability to articulate these thoughts which, here, if not always elsewhere, Winnicott attributes to her good-enough mother and to that father who is so often absent from his writings.

John Bowlby (1907–90)

Another analysand of Joan Riviere's and a supervisee of Melanie Klein's was to become instrumental in the focus on the mother–child couple and to give it a wider bearing in that psychology which came to govern everyday life outside the consulting room. The son of Sir Anthony Bowlby, head of the Royal College of Surgeons, who had organized the treatment of the wounded in the First World War, and the patrician Maria Mostyn, John Bowlby had easier access than any immigrant psychoanalyst to the centres of British institutional power. His ideas about 'maternal deprivation' as the cause of a child's problems and his emphasis on 'attachment' between mother and child took root quickly. Alongside Winnicott, and with more institutional connections, Bowlby played a major role in shaping the postwar establishment consensus on parenting. Bowlby was also one of the few clinicians to play an influential part both within British psychoanalysis and in the setting up of the National Health Service after the war — something Winnicott, fearing regimented standardization, opposed.

A graduate of Dartmouth Naval College, a dab hand with a yacht, a devoted ornithologist, Bowlby studied natural science and psychology — a newly inaugurated discipline — at Cambridge in the twenties, then medicine, though he didn't complete his degree until after he had taught disturbed children in a Norfolk school. It was this experience which led him to a psychoanalytic training, first with adults, at the same time as he completed his medical degree and specialized in psychiatry. He worked first at the Maudsley Hospital as a clinical assistant, then at the London Child Guidance Training Centre, and after the war became head of the Department of Children and Families at the Tavistock Clinic.

In 1937, partly influenced by Klein's *The Psycho-analysis of Children*, he decided to train as a child analyst with her. The supervision was not what he had hoped.

> His first child patient was a 3-year-old boy, who was very hyperactive and allegedly out of control. Bowlby thought that his mother was very anxious and disturbed, and that this was one of the key factors in the little boy's wild behaviour. At the Tavistock Clinic he would have been able to take the deteriorating state of the mother into account, but Melanie Klein seemed to him only interested in the boy's play and the reports of the sessions. His relationship to his real mother did not seem to interest her. After a few months the mother had a psychiatric breakdown and was moved to a mental hospital. The treatment had 'inconveniently' broken down. What upset Bowlby was that Melanie Klein seemed to refuse even to discuss the effect that the mother's illness and behaviour might have had on his child patient.[268]

All of Bowlby's experience had made it clear to him that the child's environment, in particular the kind of mothering he or she received, caused and shaped any later psychopathology. Already in his paper of 1940 for the *International Journal of Psychoanalysis*, he was alert to the effect of intergenerational repetition:

> For mothers with parenting difficulties, a weekly interview in which their problems are approached analytically and traced back to childhood has sometimes been remarkably effective. Having once been helped to recognize and recapture the feelings which she herself had as a child and to find that they are accepted tolerantly and understandingly, a mother will become increasingly sympathetic and tolerant towards the same things in her child.[269]

This kind of insight, though familiar to Anna Freud in whose wartime nurseries one of Bowlby's key postwar researchers, James Robertson, trained, was hardly calculated to please or interest the Kleinians, with their intense focus on the child's inner world.

During the war, Bowlby served as an army psychiatrist and a member of the medical corps. As part of the War Office selection boards, he worked with psychological and social researchers. This collaboration would have a marked effect on the postwar therapeutic communities and civil resettlement units; and indeed on the Tavistock Clinic's social agenda, and on his own research. Statistical work, unlike that which the psychoanalytically trained usually conducted, fed into Bowlby's postwar book on delinquent children, *Forty-Four Juvenile Thieves: Their Characters and Home-Life*. Various articles, one in the magazine *The New Era* in a special issue on the emotional problems of evacuation, had already broached his thesis about the effect separation from the mother had on a child. He would argue the thesis throughout his life, focusing in on maternal deprivation, or the later attachment. Here he argued that prolonged separation of small children from their homes and their mothers led in many cases to the development of a criminal character.

On the strength of these findings, Bowlby was asked by the World Health Organization, concerned about homelessness, to prepare a report on the mental health aspects of postwar displacement.[270] For six months in 1950, he travelled to Switzerland, France, the Netherlands, Sweden, the USA and around Britain and gathered evidence from care professionals working with disturbed children. The resulting report, *Maternal Care and Mental Health*, appeared in 1951 and went into numerous printings in many languages, making of Bowlby a world authority. The report called passionate attention to the grave medical and social significance of the long-term institutionalization or maternal deprivation of the child. It was essential for mental health that an infant and young child experience a warm, intimate and continuous relationship with his mother or her permanent substitute. The child who didn't would be likely to show signs of partial deprivation – excessive need for love or revenge, or depression. Complete deprivation could lead to utter listlessness and retardation.

Maternal deprivation was akin to a vitamin D deficiency, Bowlby argued with the zeal of a campaigner. If the second caused rickets, the first seriously damaged the 'psychic tissue' of the child, who could be scarred by separation for life. 'This is a discovery comparable in magnitude to that of the role of vitamins in physical health, and of far-reaching significance for programmes of preventive mental hygiene.'[271]

Bowlby called for more interdisciplinary research on the disrupted emotional relationships of early childhood so that the 'embryology of the personality' could be established with authority. He also argued for changes that would ameliorate or prevent ill-effects, notably as he himself remembered in a 1986 article, 'by supporting a child's family to enable it to care for him or her, and if this was not possible, by arrangements such as adoption and fostering. For children in hospital, unrestricted visiting by parents was recommended.'[272]

The impact of the report on health and care institutions internationally was considerable. An abridged Penguin version appeared in 1953 as *Child Care and the Growth of Love*, running into many editions. Denise Riley notes that this is the 'book above all responsible for defining the "Bowlbyism" of 'keeping mothers in the home'. Followed as it was in 1958 by a pamphlet for the National Association for Mental Health (now MIND) called *Can I Leave My Baby?*, it consolidated the need for mothers to stay as close to their infants as possible, while fathers were removed to a quasi-symbolic realm where they provided money and morale. The reward for mothers who cared for the mental welfare of their child, Bowlby writes, is the feeling 'that they really matter, that no-one else will do'.[273]

Bowlby's work seems utterly commonsensical until one remembers that all his findings moved backwards from a child who had a problem or pathology. Looking for separation or maternal deprivation, it was often enough found in the histories of problem children: the correlations with poverty and other kinds of deprivation were not carried out, though Bowlby was well aware of the economic factor and parents' dependence on a 'greater society for economic provision'.[274]

But economics and welfare were not the principal factors in what became known as 'Bowlbyism'. Bowlby's own gloss that any continuity of care would do didn't stop the emphasis on the role of the mother, which became increasingly amplified in the handbooks and parenting guides of the postwar world. If the analyst's work in the nascent welfare state was to be a second mother and make good what the natural mother had left undone, then in the public imagination, women's place, whether she was working or not, was with her babe at home. Only later would Bowlby himself and other theorists find psychological problems in children whose mothers were overattached and didn't allow for sufficient separation.

Despite his institutional links with psychoanalysis, in the 1950s

Bowlby moved further and further away from any interest in the inner life of the child. Instead he turned to Konrad Lorenz's ethology and the animal world, where he found a scientifically credible model for infant–mother attachment, as well as for observing 'animals' in their natural habitat, which echoed his own team's observation of children. A psychobiology group began to meet at the Tavistock through the fifties. It included key figures from anthropology (Margaret Mead), ethology (Konrad Lorenz, Julian Huxley), and Erik Erikson, one of the doyens of American psychoanalysis. In Bowlby's thinking, attachment now emerges as an instinct necessary for survival: its component behaviours such as sucking, crying, clinging, following, bind the child to the mother in the first twelve months of her life. Presented to the British Psycho-analytical Society, Bowlby's work on this new 'instinct' of attachment caused a stir of opposition, but, ever-practical, Anna Freud pointed out to her colleagues that Bowlby was too valuable a person for psychoanalysis to lose.

If attachment was animal-based, so now was separation. Bowlby had earlier postulated three stages of separation – protest, despair (related to mourning) and denial of grief and of the object/mother from which separation took place. Now he talked of separation anxiety being provoked when a situation activated both escape and attachment behaviour but no attachment figure was present. If the mother continued to be unavailable, grief and mourning would ensue. Children who had too many mother substitutes and suffered this mourning too often would not be capable of profound attachments in later life.

Bowlby's theories fed into psychological research studies and into mainstream American thinking in part through his collaborator Mary Ainsworth, who worked with him at the Tavistock. She questioned his use of animal observation as a model for children and went on to carry out infant observation studies in Uganda. These observations, published first in 1958, shored up Bowlby's work: Ainsworth concluded that securely attached children were those with mothers who were sensitive to their cues and enjoyed breast-feeding. As a result the children cried little and were adventurous in their play, happy to explore while in the presence of their mothers. Children of mothers who were less sensitive to their child's 'signals' – that is, those who were insecurely attached – were prone to cry more and explore less.

When Mary Ainsworth moved in 1955 to Baltimore to teach at Johns Hopkins and do clinical work and psychological diagnoses at the Sheppard and Enoch Pratt Hospital, the link with Bowlby was not only maintained but intensified. The architecture of attachment theory now took shape on both sides of the Atlantic. It quickly became part of the accepted lore of child-rearing: the bridge from the child with a *problem* whose difficulties were 'psychoanalytically' traced backwards to conflicts between desire and a reality which was first of all parental, to 'psychological' guidance on how to be a good parent and raise a healthy/normally attached child, now had firm structural underpinnings. This link to psychology grew ever more important in the United States, where batteries of tests for disorders, personality determinants and development were put into constant use in clinics, schools and prisons. In Britain and elsewhere, Bowlby's ideas became received truth, shaping adoption regulation and troops of unquestioning teachers of social work.

Bowlby's famous trilogy on attachment and loss, beginning with *Attachment* (1969), then *Separation* (1973), and finally *Loss, Grief and Mourning* (1980), gave his concepts such currency that the patterns of intimate attachment he traced even re-emerged in the analytic setting as patterns re-enacted in the transference.[275] Their positioning as contemporary science – rather than old-fashioned Freudianism – abetted Bowlby's 'expert value'. To the 'signals' of animal behaviour Bowlby then added the language of cybernetics and information systems, of cognitive working models and evolution: attachment behaviour was seen as an 'evolutionary' function which protects the infant from danger. If the mother or 'attachment figure' acknowledged the infant's needs for comfort and protection, while also respecting his needs for independent exploration of the environment, he or she would develop an internal working model of the self as valued and reliable. The alternative was an unworthy and incompetent self.

Winnicott had positioned the mother-child relationship within an artistic/creative nexus, with the good-enough mother acting as a 'holding' environment, putting all the infant's component parts together, enabling imaginative play and a 'potential space' which is a transition towards building authentic relationships with the world and enjoying its cultural goods. Bowlby positioned the mother–child within a world of empirical observation – of animal behaviour married to cybernetics. Whatever the theory, whether the child analysts found it deep in the inner life or in animal models, for the mother in her relation to the child it all meant an examined relationship with new internal as well as external tests to confront, which sometimes came in the form of welfare services. Mothering had not only become visibly important. It was also problematic and potentially now a double burden for the woman – something that the experts seemed to think they knew how to do better.

Winnicott, perhaps revealing his own ambivalence about 'mother', wrote a telling postscript to the popular set of talks he did for the BBC, published under the title *The Child and the Family*, in 1957. Because of their importance for the child, he noted, women are feared. Men, especially, are terrified of them, hate Woman because she represents their utter dependence, their absolute helplessness as babes. They owe her an infinite debt. Not that they remember it, or even necessarily know it. It is for this reason, Winnicott urges, that we ought all to recognize the 'mother's contribution to society':

> The result will be a lessening in ourselves of a fear. If our society delays making full acknowledgement of this dependence, which is a historical fact in the initial stage of development of every individual, there must remain a block both to progress and to regression, a block that is based on fear. If there is no true recognition of the mother's part, then there must remain a vague fear of dependence. This fear will sometimes take the form of a fear of WOMAN, or fear of a woman, and at other times will take less easily recognized forms, always including the fear of domination.[276]

In every dictator there is a man who is trying to control the woman whose domination he unconsciously fears, all the while demanding total subjection and love. We can make a plausible guess that Winnicott also feared there might be a dictator in many men, or his shadow, in many a mind doctor.

Perhaps the very immensity of society's debt to women, combined with male fear, played into the ways in which postwar American psyprofessionals enshrined the mother as all-responsible and therefore, soon enough, a prime object for hate. The attachment–separation nexus manifested itself in a more intense register in the United States, where there was no cushioning provided by a welfare state. It helped to create the monster that was Mom. Childhood had been made interesting by the psychoanalysts, motherhood imbued with a new and exacting responsibility: together this fixed women into a single identity. Mom became both less and more than human.

11

SHRINK FOR LIFE

Hitchcock's film *Spellbound* of 1946 captures something of the triumphant cultural position psychoanalysis, and the psychiatry it became increasingly identified with in postwar America, came to occupy. Set within a psychiatric clinic, the film has novice shrink Ingrid Bergman restoring the new head of the clinic, Gregory Peck, to health through love and therapy. Peck is a walking exposition of the power of the unconscious: he isn't who he purports to be, though he's not sure he knows it. The merest glimpse of parallel lines terrorizes him and induces blackouts.

Bergman guides him back to the traumatic origin of his amnesia and out again into cure with a little help from an all-wise, European-accented psychiatrist, who is Bergman's training analyst. Meanwhile, through the forensic method of detection, evil is unmasked. Analysis emerges as a near-magical therapy, working through dream analysis and insight, to restore memory by its re-enactment: this cathartic cure, the kind so many soldiers had undergone in the war, brings back to life and full consciousness an individual of heroic dimensions. As a side-effect of the treatment, Bergman's woman doctor is unfrozen from ambitious professionalism and herself cured by love and marriage.

Spellbound was the first film to have a paid psychiatric consultant standing in the wings, Hollywood's own May Romm, a feisty Jewish Momma, who serviced the film industry. She helped with the opening card, which talks of psychoanalysis's ability to overcome 'the evils of unreason'. Since the unreason included some murderous shrinks, the film ended up unleashing not a little unreason in an envious and ever-critical analytic profession,[277] which in America was solidly married to that bastion of traditional professionalism: medicine.

Fleeing the Nazis and war, a substantial number of analysts had arrived in America.[278] Amongst them were Heinz Hartmann, Frieda Fromm-Reichmann, Franz Alexander and Karen Horney: though all different in their orientations, they helped cement the American trend towards an ego psychology focused on the personality and its reorganization towards a new and happily normal maturity. This entailed an adjustment to reality and the leading of a responsible life. It was a form of psychoanalysis which lent itself to psychotherapy, with its less frequent sessions, and to that eventual 'scientific' demand for statistical results that could prove the therapy efficacious, even, in the event, for insurance companies.

Through the fifties, American psychiatry grew increasingly conservative, shoring up a vision of 'therapy as a tough, painful exercise that resulted as a rule in marital happiness, personal equilibrium and vocational success'.[279] Freud, who had shown, if nothing else, how the individual mind was always peopled by others and how humans had a propensity to unhappiness, might have marvelled at the ease with which his work was adapted for the church of the self and its happiness. But then, whatever Freud's popularity, many analysts considered his writings old hat. Unlike him, they pathologized homosexuality as a mental disorder and severely narrowed the range of sexual and human possibility that the profession's pioneering founder had opened up. Some have said that it was the move away from 'lay analysis' and into paramedical standardization, with its bogey of science, which helped to foster this conservatism. The mind now had 'cures' as effective as those for the body.

In Britain and France psychoanalysts did not need medical training to practise. In America, they needed both a medical degree and an internship in psychiatry. Psychoanalysis was thus integrated into the specialization of psychiatry which swung, roughly between 1940 and 1975, towards mental rather than biological modes of explanation. The link with medicine gave psychoanalysis in America both a more conservative cast and more social power. Although it did its best to keep out some of the most talented of the European analytic refugees, who lacked medical degrees, the field burgeoned and became an inescapable cultural force.

Psychoanalysis had played an important role in the Second World War effort. So had the new, growing field of clinical psychology, propelled by Carl Rogers's influential *Counselling and Psychotherapy* (1942). Psychoanalytically informed doctors, given basic principles by William Menninger, head of the US Army's neuropsychiatry division, had diagnosed soldiers fit or unfit for duty, rejecting one million from the ranks. Their success with war neuroses, from which some 860,000 soldiers had suffered, had heightened the reputation of the talking and particularly the cathartic cure, while glorifying the men's fate.

True-life stories, in which soldiers broke down under the strain of battle, were puffed in the press. Their therapy was popularized in any number of films in which the soldier's ability to remember or relive the moments which had resulted in his blindness or paralysis precipitated a cure. *Time Magazine* informed its readers in its issue of 29 May 1944 that these soldiers were heroic 'high strung, nervous people . . . who cannot face certain difficulties without developing bothersome symptoms such as headaches, tiredness, weakness, tremors, fears, insomnia, depression, obsessions, feelings of guilt'.[280] The doctors who brought them round with a cathartic talking treatment were equally heroic in their flashes of insight, their understanding and their charismatic ability to enable cure.

Freud, inventor of analysis both terminable and interminable, and ever a sceptic about cures for the human condition, might have chuckled at what America had now made of him – and would make of him again, when the backlash came.

War had also heightened a sense of the value of psychosomatic medicine: it became clear from soldiers' experience that stress, fear, anxiety and the emotions in general could produce any number of physical ailments. In the USA a new postwar cohort of medics took up psychiatry. Their numbers swelled more than sixfold between 1948 and 1976 to 27,000, thanks in part to the new National Institute of Mental Health, which encouraged and subsidized research into such areas as suicide and delinquency.[281] Increasingly taught by those who had a psychoanalytic training, themselves analysed, the new recruits worked in clinics, as consultants and in private practice, but also took on key university posts in psychiatry and spread the psychodynamic word. Only a small number of these analytically oriented psychiatrists serviced the large state mental hospitals – some 16 per cent in 1958 – which had grown

into the unwieldy 'snake-pits' where the poor and incurables were pre-
dominant. This state asylum population of some 750,000 was treated by
the older biological psychiatrists, whose function was largely custodial.
In Anatole Litvak's 1948 film *The Snake Pit*, a new-style analytic psychiatrist stands up to the older doctor and effectively works with a patient's
anger, rather than punishing with confinement.

In the years around his 1956 centenary, Freud became an American
cultural hero. There may have been only 942 practitioners who were
members of psychoanalytic societies in America (or as *Time Magazine*
stated, 619 hardcore Freudians), but their impact and Freud's were
swelled by the rise in the number of psychologists, psychiatrists, therapists and social workers who practised versions of the talking cure.[282] In
its Freud centenary issue (23 April 1956) *Time Magazine* claimed that millions had not only been taught a new way of thinking about themselves
by Freud, but were affected by the penetration of Freudian theory into
social work, the probation service and the courts. President Eisenhower
sent Freud birthday congratulations. Ernest Jones's monumental three-
volume biography, which began to appear in 1953, abetted the process.
It turned Freud into an icon: a daring, perspicacious, if all-too-human
scientist, who had launched a great revolutionary adventure. Though
the work is now seen as idealizing, *Time* then noted that Jones belonged
to the warts-and-all school of biography, given his intimate charting of
Freud's own neuroses and foibles.

A version of Freudianism-lite permeated American society. As
Nathan Hale states, Freud was 'sanitized and made the author of most
of the gifts of liberal culture – progressive education, psychiatric social
work, permissive child-raising, modern psychiatry and criminology'.[283]
Benjamin Spock's *Common Sense Book of Baby and Child Care* of 1946 had sold
some twenty million copies by 1965. It put a narrative of Freudian child
development and anti-disciplinary practice into every home, introducing in plain commonsensical language Oedipus, the family romance
and sibling rivalry, alongside the need for hugs.

Meanwhile, on Broadway and in the movies, the psychoanalytic
story was reiterated in any number of variations, most of them optimistic. Badness was largely a matter of bad parenting and
misadaptation, which therapy could somehow put right. In the musical *West Side Story*, the 'delinquents' standing up to arresting officer

Krupke replay a mid-twentieth century American version of that old dilemma of mad versus bad. Mocking themselves, and the whole apparatus of state control – the police, the doctors, the courts, the social workers – they both parody and play up to those who would tell them they are either 'psychologically disturbed' or 'socially sick'. With mothers who are junkies and fathers who are drunks, they never had the love that every child needs, after all. So it's no wonder they're misunderstood punks, shunted around from one professional's office to the next.

Deriding this world where awareness will magically initiate improvement, *West Side Story* nevertheless asks us to understand rather than condemn. When the ensuing decades of American history fought back against the Freudian psychoanalytic myth – first because its overemphasis on the individual buried the McCarthyite politics of the Cold War, then for its complicity in condemning women to 'penis-envy' and second-class lives, and finally for its disregard of the supposed neurological, genetic or biological underpinnings of mental illness – they forgot that the Freudian moment in America had come with a hope that understanding rather than punishing the 'bad', or demonizing it into 'evil', might engender a better society. If the psychological society carried its own constraints and categories – some of which emptied themselves out in the democracy of popularization – the impetus to reform hardly deserves the wholesale flagellation it received from subsequent generations. Medicalizing or psychologizing ethical dilemmas may not have provided the best answers, but to treat a soldier for war neurosis was, after all, better than to shoot him.

FREUD MEETS MOM

This widespread belief in the psychological nature of illness, encouraged by the popular media, had a particular effect on women, whose role as pioneering mothers and keepers of culture had always been important. Exalted as the all-American mothers of our boys at the front, as the makers of apple pie and the backbone of the nation, they were to suffer a backlash of scapegoating proportions from the mind doctors who blamed them for the weakness of their 'boys'. The castrating Mom, the pop-culture version of Freud's purported penis-envier, was born.

In 1946 Dr Edward Strecker, Surgeon General of the Army and Navy, published *Their Mothers' Sons*. The book indicted the American Mom for the majority of men who were either rejected for military service or discharged on neuropsychiatric grounds, often after only a few days. These men lacked 'the ability to face life, live with others, think for themselves and stand on their own two feet'. And the fault, of course, was Mom's — whether she was an empty-headed 'addlepate' following a cult of beauty, or a 'pseudo-intellectual' forever taking courses:

> A mom is a woman whose maternal behavior is motivated by the seeking of emotional recompense for the buffets which life has dealt her own ego. In her relationship with her children, every deed and almost every breath are designed unconsciously but exclusively to absorb her children emotionally and to bind them to her securely. In order to achieve this purpose, she must slam a pattern of immature behavior on her children . . .
>
> . . . the emotional satisfaction, almost repletion, she derives from keeping her children paddling about in a kind of psychological amniotic fluid rather than letting them swim away with the bold and decisive strokes of maturity from the emotional maternal womb . . . Being immature herself, she breeds immaturity in her children and, by and large, they are doomed to lives of personal and social insufficiency and unhappiness . . .[284]

This tirade against the mother, now for being overattached, came hand in hand with the injunction for women to be mothers and nothing else. To be a housewife and mother had become both all-consuming obligation and an internalized ideal, difficult to escape.

As Betty Friedan pointed out in her ground-breaking study *The Feminine Mystique*, paving the way for feminism in the late sixties, Strecker's book was used in any number of articles and speeches to persuade women that they must once more nurture their femininity and 'rush back home again and devote their lives to the children', even if, in fact, he had been saying exactly the opposite.

The blinding mystique of postwar femininity had taken over. The American woman was enjoined into the suburban home, characterized as the only possible site of fulfilment and of marital happiness. Here the woman could be a perfect (rather than good-enough) maternal giver, with a child appropriately attached to each apron string, though with the rising birthrate, she would have needed four or five of these.

Uneasy in the shadow of the Cold War, America tried to turn back the clock to a mythic period of domesticity. The rule of McCarthyism coincided with the widespread desire of new immigrants to adapt to their new country, to produce an era of abject conformity. In a parallel with Victorian England, the sign of success and middle-class decency was the stay-at-home wife devoted to her children. The proportion of women at universities, let alone in medical schools, declined significantly in these years.

The baby boom, however, was on its way and would last into the sixties. This was not only a matter of our boys coming home to rut and of a widespread tendency to counter death with reproduction. There was an ideological impetus shaping consciousness here. The combined force of media and experts signalled that home and motherhood were where satisfaction lay. Teenage pregnancies rose by 165 per cent between 1940 and 1957; the number of women with three or more children doubled. Most surprising of all, educated women led the family stakes, often producing an above-average three or more children. Women were dropping out of university to marry; if they went to work, it was to support their husbands through their degrees. Half of all American women had tied the knot by the age of twenty. So strong was the collective need to stigmatize working and particularly educated women that, unconsciously or not, trends were misinterpreted. When early figures of Kinsey's reports on American sexuality were released and showed a correlation between frustration and level of education in women, these were misinterpreted as indicating that nearly 50 per cent of university-educated women had never experienced orgasm. Ten years later, Kinsey's full statistics were published and corrected these early reports: women of 'upper educational backgrounds' had far higher rates of orgasm in every period of marriage, it was now announced.

Idealized in her perfect kitchen with her four or five scrubbed children and hardworking hubby who would come home to a fulfilling kiss, prey to her own much publicized myth, Mom was also to find herself split apart into a desexed virago of horrific proportions – as if Melanie Klein herself had orchestrated the split.

Written at the very same time as Dr Strecker was gathering his notes on neurotic soldiers, Philip Wylie's *Generation of Vipers* (1942) showed how that all-American creation, Mom, was a social disaster. By 1955, the book had gone into twenty editions. Once the shining-haired, starry-eyed, ruby-lipped *Virgo aeternis* or Cinderella, by menopause Mom was all-powerful and all-demanding, even if brainless and destructive. No one, not even women, liked her. Accused of misogyny, Wylie, in later editions, defended himself with sardonic verve:

> I showed her as she is — ridiculous, vain, vicious, a little mad. She is her own fault first of all and she is dangerous. But she is also everybody's fault. When we and our culture and our religions agreed to hold woman the inferior sex, cursed, unclean and sinful — we made her mom. And when we agreed upon the American ideal of Woman, the Dream Girl of National Adolescence . . . we insulted women and disenfranchised millions from love. We thus made mom . . . Freud has made a fierce and wondrous catalogue of examples of mother-love-in-action-which traces its origin to an incestuous perversion of a normal instinct. That description is, of course, sound. Unfortunately, Americans, who are the most prissy people on earth, have been unable to benefit from Freud's wisdom because they can *prove* that they do not, by and large, sleep with their mothers. That is their interpretation of Freud.

The period's interpretation of Freud played an important part in furnishing the ideology that kept women chained to maternity and home, simultaneously enshrining them and attacking them in that biological identity which is motherhood. The psychologists and their popularizers had made the whole business of sexual satisfaction and child-rearing so exacting that it precluded the desire, let alone the ability, to be human.

Enjoined to a watchful, nurturing love for her children, to be attentive to nursing and weaning, to toilet-training, sexual arousal, masturbation, to the meanings of food — not to mention its careful, loving preparation — to sibling rivalry, and to the too much and too little of everything — all this even before hardworking hubby, who worked just for her and the kids, came home — the American mother both complied with and felt frustrated in her confinement to a role that might be wrapped in mythical banners, but locked her out of full participation in the world. Helene Deutsch and her followers' insistence on a fundamental female passivity, even when glossed as activity directed inward, together with a masochism which underpinned all the functions that made women female, began to chafe and irritate educated women, even if they might at first accept the premises.[285] When the feminism of the late sixties and seventies took wing, Freud and the psychologists would be in the front line of attack.

The exactions of idealized psychological motherhood apart, the doctors played an even crueller trick on mothers. In a replay of the attachment–separation axis, American mothers, responsible or not for any of the number of crimes that parenthood inevitably brings in its trail, found themselves targeted as disease agents. The psychosomatic understanding of the body, in which emotional conflicts were seen as attacking specific organs, meant that someone had to be responsible for those emotional conflicts. Enter all-powerful Mom, maker of asthma, as well as autism, schizophrenia and a host of other mysterious ills.

The argument, where asthma was concerned, went like this. No somatic base or cure for asthma had been found. Children's asthma was observed to lessen when they left home and worsen when they returned – even, in one sample of children, when dust from their homes was sprayed into their hospital rooms. Franz Alexander speculated that asthmatics suffered from 'excessive, unresolved dependence' on the mother, a deep-seated conflict between independent and dependent impulses. Asthma attacks were a substitute for feelings of intense anxiety. The 'asthmatogenic' mother was pathologically overprotective or, as the case may be, unconsciously hostile and rejecting, so that the child became increasingly clinging.[286] Though these generalizations were soon challenged as simple-minded and the 'bacillicus asthmaticus psychosomaticus' ridiculed, Mom's relationship to her child remained the seedbed of other ailments.

AUTISM

Autism was a category Eugen Bleuler had used in 1908 to identify a type of abnormally introverted behaviour he associated with the group of schizophrenias. His adult sufferers were withdrawn and didn't respond to social cues. Infantile autism was first described by the Austrian-born Leo Kanner, one of the first American child psychiatrists. In 1943 he published his paper, 'Autistic Disturbances of Affective Contact', in which he described what for him was the altogether unusual case of Donald, a child who would never make eye contact or recognize faces, and who spoke, but not in order to communicate. 'Donald wandered about smiling, making stereotyped movements with his fingers . . . He shook his head from side to side, whispering or humming the same three-note tune constantly . . . he completely disregarded the people and instantly went into objects, preferably those that could spin. He angrily shoved away the hand which was in the way.'

At the age of two and a half, Donald had been able to name all the presidents of the United States in order both backwards and forwards; as well as the twenty-five points of the Presbyterian catechism. He was upset by changes in routine and was hypersensitive to loud noises.

Kanner decided that Donald's condition stemmed, at least in part, from his mother and her lack of warmth and responsiveness. He designated her as a 'refrigerator mother' – a bit of nomenclature that caught on both in the literature and in the popular imagination. Mothers now had a new potential stigma: if they weren't attached enough to their children, they could produce autism.

Bruno Bettelheim then entered the field. A talented writer, with the authority of a survivor of Dachau and Buchenwald, Bettelheim ran the Orthogenic School for the rehabilitation of emotionally disturbed children at the University of Chicago. Many of the children there were diagnosed as autistic or schizophrenic. Bettelheim linked both to bad parenting. Indeed in his *The Empty Fortress: Infantile Autism and the Birth of the Self* (1964), prefaced by Leo Kanner, the refrigerator mother is akin to a guard in a concentration camp, the child, her prisoner. 'The difference between the plight of prisoners in a concentration camp and the conditions which lead to autism and schizophrenia in children is, of course, that the child has never had a previous chance to develop much of a personality.' Which could be taken to indicate that prisoners were rather better off than Bettelheim's autistic children with their improperly attached moms, and had more hope . . . The condition itself, as

Bettelheim understood it, was a kind of defence mechanism against bad parenting – a process of reasoning that anti-psychiatrist R.D. Laing was simultaneously initiating on the other side of the Atlantic in implicating the family as the crucible of schizophrenia.

The refrigerator-mother explanation of the aetiology of autism was soon disputed, notably by the father of an autistic child: the psychologist Bernard Rimlaud argued that his own son had had the condition from birth. Bettelheim drew on opposing proof from the psychologist Harry Harlow. The refrigerator mother and autism thesis now found backing in monkey experiments, just as attachment had found reinforcement in ethology.

Harry Harlow had begun to work with rhesus monkeys in 1957. He devised a set of experiments which studied child–mother bonding or attachment. Taking baby monkeys – born more independent than humans but still needing to be nursed – away from their biological mothers, he put them in cages with a hard wire 'mother' fitted with a milk-producing nipple and an electric light for warmth; as well as with a second softer cloth-and-cardboard 'mother', who had no bottle. The monkeys spent far more time clinging to the cloth mother, whom they markedly preferred, playing with her, manipulating her odd face, cuddling, while they used the wire mother only for quick nourishment. When 'monsters' were introduced and the monkeys frightened, they invariably ran to the cuddly mother. Frequent and intimate contact with the mother's body, Harlow's experiment seemed to prove, was far more important than food. Nursing was more about the first than the second. He also noted that the experimental monkey's love for the cuddly mother was no less than the ordinary monkey's love for his real mother.

A year on, however, the monkeys raised by these surrogates displayed odd and troubled behaviours. They clutched themselves, rocked back and forth, bit themselves, self-harmed – indeed, displayed 'autistic' features.[287] Their sexual lives were equally disturbed. They didn't know the correct mating postures; females attacked males. Harlow had to retract some of his pronouncements. As for mothering when their time came, the 'motherless mothers' were either negligent and failed to comfort or protect their young, or abusive, biting and injuring their babies and eventually killing them.

In Bowlbyesque style Harlow concluded that early deprivation resulted in the failure to create secure attachments later in life, and with their own offspring. It also drove the monkeys mad. They were akin to Bettelheim's autistic children. In 1971 in the *Journal of Autism and Childhood Schizophrenia*, Harlow compared his tortured monkey infants to human infants. Both exhibited 'marked social withdrawal'. They retreated to a corner to 'avoid social contact' and to shut out all outside stimulation. Deprived of maternal affection, the isolated monkey was a mirror image of the autistic child.

There is little doubt that children who are cruelly treated and severely deprived can develop later emotional or mental disturbance. However, that 'refrigerator mothers' produce autistic children is now generally discredited. Mothering can not be held responsible for everything.

Navigating the good ship Mom between the Scylla of early warmth and the kind of attachment that would serve their children appropriately and the Charybdis of suffocation if separation was inappropriately timed, women also had to confront the frustrations of everyday psychosexual life. Cold, unavailable, detached, they could find themselves labelled frigid or castrating by the mind doctors; or, most hideously of all, schizophregenic – producers of poor, blighted schizophrenic children. If they erred on the side of warmth or too much actively expressed desire, they were not merely sluts but nymphomaniacal. With a kind of iatrogenic effect, the growth in mind-doctoring and its diagnostic formulae resulted in the growth of the need for therapy, and not only of the retail variety rampant enough in this time of Stepford Wives. As the gulf between prescribed ideals of behaviour and satisfaction widened, the perception spread that therapists could step in to assuage the misery. Male or female, they often enough became America's good-enough mothers, the ones who could help where the family had failed.

THE GOOD-ENOUGH SHRINK

According to some statistics in the 1950s and 1960s twice as many women in America suffered from depression and anxiety disorders as men. Whether increasing psychologization of the nation augmented the numbers of sufferers, or demand for psychological medicine increased the supply of mind doctors, is unclear. Undoubtedly a conjuncture of forces came into play and popular culture both reflected and propagandized the symmetries of illness and cure. Leading women's magazines, like *Mademoiselle* in October 1953, ran attractively illustrated spreads with the headline question 'Should you be psychoanalyzed?', while the confessional answer below ran 'Illness, worry, deep depression brought me to the analyst . . . I stayed to work the puzzle to the end.' Moss Hart's *Lady in the Dark* had moved from enormous success on Broadway to Hollywood. Ginger Rogers, the star who played more psychiatric patients than any other, enacted a career woman on the edge of a nervous breakdown whose sessions on the couch bring deep Oedipal knowledge and a release into love and marriage.

While popular culture educated America in the ways of analysis and the slips of the unconscious, New York; and California's intellectual and artistic elite used analysts in the way that the rich in the past had used personal spiritual advisers and father confessors. The church of the self, after all, had its painful stations of the cross, and a personal analytic adviser could help on the journey through life. Daily sessions on the couch, advice from the analyst on how to lead your life and cope with its intimate problems, as well as your children, while all the while achieving some insight, some inner truth and maturity, were part of a covetable and glamorous lifestyle.

Chris Mankiewicz remembers that his director father Joseph Mankiewicz made sure that his children, as well as his wife, were seen by psychiatrists:

> My father used to say to me, 'You obviously have a lot of problems and a lot of hostility. You and I could never relate, so you need to talk to someone impartial.' Just as English families consigned their kids to private school so they didn't have to deal with them until they knew Greek and Latin, people like my father used psychiatry for one-on-one dealings . . . Most of us progressed from nannies to nurses to housekeepers to psychiatrists. There was always a surrogate parent around . . . the shrinks were always there.[288]

Brenda Webster in her memoir *The Last Good Freudian* depicts her artist mother's reliance on her analysts through mourning, breakdowns and suicide attempts. The support such well known analysts as Muriel Gardiner and Marianne Kris gave her extended to help with the children. The advice the young Brenda Webster received on sex, on contraception, on men and on life paths came from them too. There was an implicit double bind here: if mothers couldn't cope with their children and had to send them to shrinks, they had obviously failed in their primary calling and could only be resented by the children.

Increasingly conservative as they became part of the medical establishment, America's supposedly Freudian analysts were by the mid-sixties to find themselves attacked either because they had betrayed Freud's legacy or because the whole psychoanalytical package was retrograde and ineffectual. Happiness was neither a penis, nor the child it helped to produce. Nor was the envy of it — so often interpreted as everything that a woman might want that didn't include the attached man — a sufficient explanation or a good-enough put down for women's growing desire for a wider sphere of activity.

But if the generation of women who came to young adulthood in the late sixties and early seventies and made up 'women's liberation' attacked Freudian patriarchy, they also and inevitably criticized the Moms who had been suborned by it. In fact, often enough they endowed them with the same all-influencing power that the culture as a whole popularly attributed to Moms. With intimate resentment, when it came to their own psychological ills, daughters blamed mothers for loving them not enough or suffocating them with too much love. Cold or fawning, always and inevitably sensed as controlling since they were the all-important centre of love or attachment in the family, its keepers and makers — these mothers also inevitably emerged as responsible for their daughters' breakdowns. They had failed to safeguard the rites of passage into womanhood. In the spate of fictions describing women's mental illness — from Sylvia Plath's *The Bell Jar*, to Susanna Kaysen's *Girl, Interrupted*, to Hannah Green's *I Never Promised You a Rose Garden*, to Marie Cardinale's *The Words to Say It* — it is the mother who in an uncannily Oedipal scenario becomes the focus of the daughter's illness, the bearer of her inability to come to terms with self, men or world.

Mother-analysts, transferential doubles – reliable and, it is hoped, not ultimately controlling – stand in for mothers and allow the girls to separate from their childhood Moms. They can also stand in the way of getting to or at the fathers. Meanwhile, they oversee the girl's growth into woman.

I never promised you a rose garden

Hannah Green is the pseudonym of Joanne Greenberg, the author of some twelve fictions. Her bestselling novel, *I Never Promised You a Rose Garden* (1964), which became a Hollywood film, is a fictionalized account of her three-year experience as a patient in the famous Chestnut Lodge, one of the United States' finest private mental hospitals. Greenberg, or Deborah Blau, as she is in the book, is sixteen, and has made a suicide attempt. This has led to a diagnosis of schizophrenia and the parents' difficult decision to have her institutionalized.

The girl, the book gradually reveals, has increasingly lived in isolated torment in a symbolic world, the Kingdom of Yr, which has its own language and demanding, persecutory gods. The real of her parents, a precise, emotionally controlling mother and a lonely father, confused by her illness, is available only with effort. Arriving at the asylum, 'Deborah Blau smashed headlong into the collision of the two worlds . . . where she was most alive, the sun split in the sky, the earth erupted, her body was torn to pieces, her teeth and bones crazed and broken to fragments. In the other place where the ghosts and shadows lived . . . an old red-brick building stood . . . There were bars on all the windows.'

During a time when electro-shock, insulin and early forms of drug treatment were common, Chestnut Lodge was one of the elite asylums to specialize in psychoanalytic therapy with severely disturbed patients. Run primarily by highly trained psychoanalysts, it took between forty-five and fifty-eight patients at a time, who were looked after by a staff of some 165. Treatment revolved around intensive therapy, not only the four-times-weekly hour with the psychiatrist, but life within an ethos in which each staff member saw mental illness as a condition potentially common to all, and listened carefully to what patients said since it might give a symbolic lead to the inner world they inhabited. Frankness was a watchword. Parents, particularly mothers, were to be kept away since their presence affected patients badly.

That said, the picture Greenberg gives of asylum life is hardly rosy: warders can be frightening and insensitive; other patients violent as well as suffering. What is acutely portrayed is the solidarity and understanding that exist between patients, their nervous gossip about those who leave and may return, their knowledge that acts of violence are unintended or find mistaken objects. For all its travails, this asylum emerges as a place of refuge from a world which fears and fails to understand the motors of insanity and the overwhelming pain it brings.

The Dr Fried (or Furii), who treats Deborah, is based on Frieda Fromm-Reichmann, a pioneer of analytic treatment with schizophrenics. One of the first women doctors in Germany, she had worked with neurologically damaged soldiers during the First World War and had run an asylum along Orthodox Jewish lines with her then husband, Erich Fromm. Both had trained as psychoanalysts at the Berlin Institute in the twenties. He went on to become one of the cultural theorists of the influential Frankfurt School and moved to the United States in the mid-thirties. Frieda, a medic, became a leading practitioner. Four foot ten, apparently straight-talking and charismatic, she was an advocate of Harry Stack Sullivan's interpersonal psychiatry and by all accounts a formidable clinician. She is one of the 'mothers' Greenberg's book is dedicated to. Persistent and sensitive, her long experience with the most intractable of mental patients leads to Deborah/Joanne's cure after three gruelling years as an inpatient between 1948 and 1951, and then, until 1955, as an outpatient while she completes her education.

Greenberg evokes a psychoanalyst whose treatment methods are far more interventionist than the norm, who prods her patient into response until she uncovers the secrets that won't be divulged, in Deborah's case a humiliating and disturbing uterine operation when she was five, which the child feels poisoned her: 'They had gone in with their probes and needles as if the entire reality of her body were concentrated in the secret evil inside that forbidden place.' The analyst communicates her anger. Her voice is 'full of indignation' for the five-year-old who stood before them both:

'Those damn fools. When will they learn not to lie to children! . . .'

'Then you're not going to be indifferent . . .'

'You're damn right I'm not!'[289]

Fromm-Reichmann, like the various doctors who worked with schizophrenics and the severely disturbed, doesn't rely on what had become the standard technique of detachment, silence and rare interpretation of the patient's free associations – the norm of the profession in America. Instead, she is talkative, asks questions and answers them, intervenes actively and builds up trust. She offers support and is wise. As her last paper makes clear, she understood the profound, incommunicable loneliness – like the 'helpless loneliness of a child whose cry is never answered' – which underlay her patients' condition and against which their madness was a defence. The trust built up in the novel between Dr Fried and Deborah is one of the cords that tugs her back into the world as they do battle together against Yr, its persecutory authorities and its buried meanings. The doctor is a responsible guide through and out of the depths.

Deborah's 'poisoning' operation, one of the points of origin of Yr, leads her to believe that she poisons everyone she meets, including the ugly new baby sister she is certain she has tried to fling from the window. The attendant guilt is given symbolic shape in Yr. So, too, is her Jewishness, and the fate of the European Jews in the war that her grandfather evokes. Then there is her father, who constantly warns her against the filthy world of men's desires, so much so that she palpably feels his and her own. As the therapy digs backwards, she sees a place without colour where a child is utterly alone, cold, far from love, her mother gone. She gradually recognizes that her sense of abandonment was triggered by her mother's miscarriage. Locating the real and reasonable event is not enough to dispel the madness. We are made to see that this underlying aloneness has been reinforced time and again by each subsequent abandonment in the child's life, has accrued in terror so that escape to her secret world becomes a habit and then a parallel universe which takes over.

Yr is both the expression of Deborah's illness and the illness itself: the once compassionate idealized world she could flee to has turned on her and now threatens to destroy her altogether. Let into the secret, Dr Fried's task is in part to interpret this world and then to wean her away from it by allowing her patient to experience her ability to live without its ambiguous protection. Deborah's first active step away from her symbolic world is the assumption of responsibility for a fellow inmate who has been beaten. She acts on her roommate's behalf by coming out of the lethargy which her struggles in Yr impose and complaining to one of the doctors. She comes to Dr Fried, too, who talks tough and pragmatically underlines that neither justice nor happiness is necessarily part of the 'real' world they are working together to usher her back into. There is no rose garden, only the ability to fight for it.

> 'Look here . . . I never promised you a rose garden. I never promised you perfect justice. And I never promised you peace or happiness. My help is so that you can be free to fight for all of these things. The only reality I offer is a challenge and being well is being free to accept it or not at whatever level you are capable.'[290]

The fight takes time. Deborah gets worse, recedes, self-harms, burning herself time and again. Coming into the real is not easy, as all patients' narratives testify. The doctor's belief that there is a core of strength in her, however, is one of the forces that can pull the patient through.

In her own writing, Fromm-Reichmann talked of the stormy therapeutic interviews, the severe persecutory ideas of her patient, as well as her hostility towards her and the dependence that had been built up. Not unlike Winnicott, though her language is different, she understood schizophrenia to come from a failure of early mothering at a time when it was essential to the child's survival. In terms resonant with the force of splitting into good and bad, Fromm-Reichmann elaborated the conflict between dependence and hostility in the child, a split which produced intense anxiety. The fear of her destructive impulses, her fury and violence, made the child resort to hiding in her own self-enclosed world.[291] The analyst's task was to clarify the causes of these impulses as they were reinvoked through the defences – in Deborah's case, through the symbolic world of Yr. Gradually the patient could recognize the irrationality of those defences, relinquish them and be tugged back into reality.

Chestnut Lodge had more success than most in dealing with

schizophrenia. From a group of seventy-seven paranoid schizophrenics treated by psychotherapy, 17 per cent were much improved, while 49 per cent were improved. Thirteen per cent remained unchanged, got worse, or died. For patients often considered incurable these are good figures; though the attendant costs in staff and time were such that only the wealthiest could afford them.[292] Another elite institution known for its famous patients and for its mix of treatments from ECT to psychotherapy was McLean's in Belmont, Massachusetts. It was here that another talented young woman was sent on 14 August 1953, after she had taken an overdose of sleeping pills and almost died.

Sylvia Plath (1932–63)

Sylvia Plath's case is well known. Part of its iconic status comes from her 'fiction' *The Bell Jar*, where she evokes the downward spiral of a young woman, hungry for both creative work and experience, but vaulted by the limiting choices of her time into depression and the suicide attempt that take her to McLean's. Plath's own ultimate suicide at the age of thirty propelled the poet into an iconic stardom. For the women's movement, particularly in America, she grew into a saint of female victimization, her madness and suicide themselves signals of what patriarchy did to talented women who dared to aspire, and dared doubly by also loving passionately. Sylvia Plath's graduating class at Smith in 1955 were exhorted by the presidential candidate, Adlai Stevenson, to write 'laundry lists' rather than poems.[293]

Almost ten years passed between Plath's first suicide attempt, her hospitalization, and the writing of *The Bell Jar*, which appeared pseudonymously in Britain in 1963 – the year *The Feminine Mystique* came out – and just months before her death. Plath had been worried about her mother's reaction and the book, though circulated in its British edition, didn't come to America until eight years after her death. In the years between her first breakdown and the writing of *The Bell Jar*, Plath had moved to Britain on a Fulbright fellowship, met and married and was arguably on the point of divorcing the British poet Ted Hughes, had had two children, published *The Colossus*, and composed amongst others the great poems of *Ariel*.

The Bell Jar is Plath's only novel. It was written with the hope of making much-needed money. Provoked by 'mental health articles' in *Cosmopolitan*, she notes in her *Journals* on 13 June 1959 that she wants to write 'a college girl suicide' story, 'THE DAY I DIED' . . . a novel even, since there is an increasing market for 'mental health stuff'. She has, she says, Mary Jane Ward's *The Snake Pit* in mind, the gripping asylum exposé made into a film with Olivia de Havilland. Plath produced something quite different. In the tough unsentimental idiom of an urban thriller, she explored the question of what being a productive woman might entail, – one who can write, love and have children, not to mention relate to the world. The question harries her heroine, Esther Greenwood, into a suicide attempt. Becoming a woman in the fifties, when the choices are restricted to suburban motherhood or a spin-sterish professional life, entails a descent into madness, a symbolic death by ECT , followed by a reawakening, a birth into rebellious woman-hood. This last is signalled by the ritual bloodletting, which is her heroine's triumphal stage-managed sacrifice of her virginity. Greenwood's is not the 'schizophrenic' symbolization and splitting into parallel worlds that Deborah Blau suffered from, but a far more common adolescent picture of depression, or of what Plath later called the 'disintegration' of her mind.

Like her heroine, Plath had, in a writing competition, won a highly coveted month guest-editing the annual college edition of *Mademoiselle* in that capital of life and glamour, New York. That very month, on 19 June 1953, Ethel and Julian Rosenberg, allegedly Soviet spies, were elec-trocuted – and 'goggle-eyed headlines' blared – a chilling event that Sylvia both recorded in her journal and used in the opening of her novel, where the heroine talks of feeling 'very still and very empty, the way the eye of a tornado must feel, moving dully along in the middle of the surrounding hullabaloo'.

The month passed in an agitated whirl of activity, unfulfilled sexual exploration and self-doubt. At the end of it Sylvia was torn between taking a summer writing course at Harvard, the expense of it, and spending the next months before her senior year at Smith at home, learning shorthand, meeting the challenge of writing alone, and making her mother's vacation 'happy and good'. In July her *Journals* record the self-laceration of an ambitious and highly achieving young woman who drives herself with a frenzy, drives herself to love and work so hard that a paralysis of indecision and inertia takes her over. Plath's vivid notes capture a spiral of self-hatred and confusion, a hothouse emotional excess made up of ardent desire, fear, lack of confidence and injections to bolster it. Her inner life is reminiscent of many a troubled young woman's. On 6 July, she chastises herself: 'why blind yourself by taking course after course' when you should be able to think and not 'retreat into a masochistic mental hell where jealousy and fear make you stop eating'? She orders herself to stop thinking selfishly 'of razors & self-wounds & ending it all' and at the same time of 'noise, names, dances'. She should be getting a job, or learning shorthand. 'Nothing ever remains the same,' she tells herself.

On the 14th, she's in a panic about failing academically and not living up to past prizes, while at the same time she has a 'perverse desire to retreat into not caring'. She has visions of herself in a straitjacket, murdering her mother and killing the 'edifice of love and respect'. All her relations with both men and women are at an impasse. She feels incapable of feeling.

Less than a month later, having gone home to the 'motherly breath of the suburbs' which 'smelt of lawn sprinklers and station-wagons and tennis rackets and dogs and babies', Sylvia took an overdose. Deep depression had followed the tensions of New York: disappointed at failing to get into the Harvard writing course, unable to write or sleep or eat, hating the babies and suburban women who plague her, terrified by the unravelling of her mind, the constant thoughts of death, and on top of it all an unsympathetic psychiatrist and a first, deadening course of ECT, she had swallowed the pills, crawled into a dug-out space beneath the house and waited for death. She was found by her brother two days later in a semiconscious state. Her moans had alerted him. Sometime in those two days, the pills had been vomited up. For the rest of her life, there was a scar on her face where the skin had been scraped by the rubble beneath the house.

Plath was taken to the local hospital, then to a psychiatric unit where things went from bad to worse. (She would work at this same clinic at the Massachusetts General Hospital in 1958 as a secretary while she and Hughes were in Boston. Part of her work included recording patients' dreams.) Finally, thanks to her patron, Olive Prouty, a place was found for her at McLean's, with its psychotherapeutic care facilities, its lawns, golf course and badminton court. Here for five months her doctor was Ruth Beuscher – Doctor Nolan in the novel – a young attending psychiatrist in 1953. Beuscher had apparently recently taken courses in psychoanalysis at the Boston Institute, but had not been accepted as a member because of a prior application by her husband. Her relations with Sylvia seemed to provide what this depressed and suicidal young woman needed and Plath kept up a relationship with her until the end.

If Doctor Nolan's therapeutic function in the novel is hardly elaborated, she nonetheless emerges as the good, holding mother, in stark contrast to Esther's own. When Mrs Greenwood comes to visit Esther, she wears the 'sorrowful face' of sacrificial motherhood which begs her daughter to tell her what she has done wrong. 'She said she was sure the doctors thought she had done something wrong because they asked her a lot of questions about my toilet training, and I had been perfectly trained at a very early age and given her no trouble whatsoever.' Her mother's refusal to see that she is implicated in Esther's state makes Esther throw out the birthday roses she has brought her. Passionate at last, she tells Doctor Nolan what she really thinks about this all too strong and self-sacrificial figure. '"I hate her," I said and waited for the blow to fall. But Doctor Nolan only smiled at me as if something had pleased her very, very much and said, "I suppose you do."'

The permission to hate her mother is a crucial step in Esther's treatment.

Equally important is ECT. At their first meeting, Nolan has Esther talk about her earlier psychiatrist. He had given her ECT and under his charge it had terrified her and done nothing to avert her suicidal wishes. Doctor Nolan reassures her that they won't use ECT here. If they do, she'll be told beforehand and it won't be anything like what she previously experienced. 'Why, some people even like it,' Doctor Nolan tells her. When insulin treatment does little except fatten Esther, leaving her imagining that she looks pregnant, Doctor Nolan breaks her word. Despite this, under her tender guidance, ECT does indeed prove as beneficial as she has promised and after five sessions, Esther's depression lifts.

Electroconvulsive therapy had first been developed in Rome in 1938 by Ugo Cerletti. He had seen pigs in a slaughterhouse becoming more manageable and less agitated when an electric prod was administered. Since the idea, later disproved, was around that epileptics didn't develop 'schizophrenia', it was thought that if epileptic-like convulsions could be administered in patients, this would stop or ameliorate other forms of mental illness. The thinking behind shock treatment of any kind has always been and is still disputed, but some, amongst them the established figures in psychiatry, claim that producing a fit and then unconsciousness in the patient has a beneficial effect in some cases.[294]

ECT was welcomed by asylum psychiatrists in Britain as an advance on Cardiozol, an unreliable camphor-based convulsive, and on insulin therapy, which took an unpredictable period to build up the desired reaction of a convulsion or coma/sleep. In America, ECT first met with a certain resistance. Important asylum doctors like Harry Stack Sullivan refused to use it. The general favouring of psychodynamic rather than physical treatments in the postwar period meant it had far less popularity than in Britain, where it quickly became a staple therapy for major depression and schizophrenia.[295] Many patients loathed and feared the passivity, the scrambling of memory, the zombie-like condition of those who came back from treatment. Others found it beneficial, calming agitation and lessening anxiety, particularly after it began to be administered with a general anaesthetic — the way McLean's used it, an innovation at the time.

The final step in Doctor Nolan's treatment is that she allows Esther to go to a doctor to be fitted for a diaphragm. Sanctioned both to distance herself from her mother and to make the long-awaited entry to full womanhood, Esther returns to university, her spiralling depression left behind. Instead, her friend and double at the hospital commits the suicide that Sylvia would only implement after *The Bell Jar* was published.

The Bell Jar is emphatically a woman's book. The men in it, though desired in fantasy, are in fact distant — either dead, like the father whose grave Esther visits just before her suicide attempt, or like Esther's boyfriend tucked away in a TB sanatorium while she nurtures her wish to rid herself of him. The mathematician who deflowers her at the end is a prop to a shedding of her virginity. She never wants to see him again. Their final transaction is a financial one in which she asks him to pay the hospital bill she incurred after sex brought on haemorrhaging.

Nor is Esther friendly or kind to the women in the book who represent the dead ends of possibility. But a few of the women penetrate the bell jar of depression, and when she is at last 'patched, retread, and approved for the road', in a ritual which is more like being born again than married, it is Doctor Nolan – the woman who told her that what other women see in each other is tenderness – who carries her across the threshold into her new life.

The Doctor Nolan who sees Esther into her new woman's life will, as Ruth Beuscher, stay with Sylvia as either therapist or adviser for the rest of her days. The often irreconcilable demands of writing and being wife and eventually mother with the perfectionist zeal and passion Plath demanded of herself, together with the underlying tug of depression, led her to rely on the help of psychiatrists throughout her life.

At Cambridge in the spring of 1956, some two weeks after she had first met Ted Hughes and bitten him on the cheek with lustful, drunken frenzy as they danced, Sylvia went to see the university psychiatrist Dr. Davy whom she liked – 'calm and considered, with that pleasant feeling of age in a reservoir; felt Father: why not.'[296] But it is Beuscher she calls on dramatically in her journal. Running through names, it is hers she focuses on. She asks Ruth to take her into her heart, to let her cry and cry and to help her be strong. Beuscher increasingly takes on the mothering of the Sylvia who needs help. She is the 'psychologist-priestess', her voice internalised as the 'permissive mother figure'. Meanwhile, to her real mother, Sylvia writes regular letters of astonishing calm and enthusiasm, always presenting the successful façade Mrs. Plath wanted of her.

Sylvia Plath and Ted Hughes were married on June 11, 1956. In the autumn of 1958, during the couple's second year in Boston, while Ted Hughes's poetry met with increasing success, Sylvia struggled with writing, sexual jealousy, and writer's envy. Depression, a sense of her own worthlessness and the impossibility of the battle with language and form, gripped. She turned at first secretly and then openly to Ruth Beuscher for psychotherapy. On December 12th 1958, a fresh section of her journal records her 'interview notes'. They show Sylvia in combative mood, pledging herself to use her sessions with Beuscher to the full. If she is going to pay hard-earned money for her therapist's time and brain, then she will treat therapy as she would a tutorial about the emotional life. She will work 'like hell', interrogate and probe the 'sludge and crap' of her inner life, and get the most out of it.[297]

Her 'sludge and crap' is not mainly to do with her tendency to turn her men into all-powerful fathers, the boot-wearing Fascist of her Daddy poem. It is to do with her mother. Beuscher has given her permission to hate her self-sacrificing vampire mother, and that, in a process more efficacious than shock treatment, makes a 'new person' of her.

Sylvia fills in the detail here of that therapeutically sanctioned hatred. Aurelia Plath married an old man, sick as soon as she got him and 'heiling Hitler' in the privacy of his home. The children came as her salvation: she worked and aspired for them, gave them the best. After she had killed off the father, she sacrificed herself some more, being man, mother and woman in 'one sweet ulcerous ball', making everything perfect for her perfect children. Sylvia disgraced her by going mad. 'I hate her because he wasn't loved by her,' Sylvia notes, and the consequence of that is she hates men because they don't stay around to love her like a father, because they don't suffer like women do. The vision of love this hateful mother gave her is also hateful – security, house, money, babies, and a loved vision of Sylvia, which isn't her. She wanted to kill her mother's idea of her, to kill her mother, but she was too nice for murder, so she decided to kill herself instead. Do unto yourself as you would do to others.

But that's in the past. Sylvia is now – with the help of Beuscher – herself, and she won't allow her mother to 'kill' Ted the way she 'killed' her own husband.

So this quintessential vampire of an American Mom can be neutralized with the help of a better mother, one with whom Sylvia can cry and think; one through whom she reads Freud's *Mourning and Melancholia* and recognizes her depression as his 'draining of the ego', a transferred murderous impulse from her mother to herself, a self-abasement which is a transferred hate and which keeps her from writing. With Beuscher she also sees that what stops her from writing or having babies is spite, since she will have to give her mother the writing and the babies and her mother will appropriate them. She hates this witch-mother because Sylvia's not writing proves Mrs P. correct about the need for Sylvia to do something that brings security – like teaching, which in turn makes her like her mother.

Plath's notes sound the clarion call for the coming generation of rebelling women – but the answer she provides is not the political one. `What to do with your hate for your mother and all mother figures?' she asks. What is the woman to do when she feels guilty for not behaving in the manner prescribed by the mother who has after all gone out of her way to help her? Where is one to look for an alternative figure who has the wisdom to tell you what you need to know about babies and the facts of life. The only person Sylvia trusts to fulfill this function is Beuscher, who won't *tell* her what to do, but will help her find out what is in herself and what she 'can best do with it.'[298]

Beuscher did help Plath through this cycle of depression. She began to go to Robert Lowell's writing class, make new friends, amongst them the poet Anne Sexton, whose own trajectory involved a mentoring analyst. She wrote, despite the rejections. None of it was easy, but the poems of *The Colossus* emerged – a creative surge Plath linked with 'the buried male muse and godcreator'. And Frieda Hughes, despite Plath's worries about being barren, was conceived. To be deprived of having a baby, Plath writes, is death indeed: 'to consummate love by bearing the child of the loved one is far profounder than any orgasm or intellectual rapport'.[299]

Plath's notes from her sessions with Beuscher also include pointed queries from her analyst about the suitability of Ted Hughes as a husband for her. 'Would you have the guts to admit you'd made a wrong choice?' Sylvia says she would, but she is sanguine about the question since her husband supports her in soul and body and she loves his 'being-there'. Does Ted want her to get better, Beuscher asks again in a later note, and again Sylvia offers an emphatic yes. The queries don't upset her or make her link Beuscher up with the 'bad' mother, who had equal criticisms of Ted. Yet, in the light of Beuscher's last intervention in Plath's life, in that final terrible year before her suicide, what may be signs of an early mistrust of Hughes take on a slightly ominous note. Beuscher was one of the women who later urged Plath to divorce Hughes and seek a legal settlement.

We have no way of definitively knowing whether Beuscher's advice was one more element in the gathering storm of circumstances that led Sylvia in her last depression to take her life. On top of her jealousy and the prolonged split with Ted, which finally seemed to have come to a head in October 1962, there was that winter's unusual and persistent cold, the children's flu, her finances, and what she took to be the cool reception for her pseudonymous *The Bell Jar*. As her biographer Diane Middlebrook notes, that book itself might have held up too terrible a mirror to her current depressed state. To Beuscher Plath wrote, 'I can feel my mind disintegrating again.'[300]

In anguish, she asked her therapist whether she could come to London. Beuscher couldn't, and in her last weeks Plath went to the enlightened general practitioner John Horder, who provided a live-in nurse while the children's flu took its course, then wanted to arrange hospitalization for Sylvia, so severe did he judge her condition. Space wasn't instantly available, and on 4 February he prescribed the antidepressant, Parnate. This was meant to work more quickly than others then on the market. He saw her daily. But six days later, on the evening of Sunday 10 February, 1963, Plath carefully prepared her children's breakfast, set the trays beside their beds, opened their windows and sealed their door. Then she went downstairs to place her head deep within the gas oven. She was thirty years old; her son Nicholas had had his first birthday a month before, and Frieda was not quite three.

Hughes and her mother both thought that the act had been provoked at the last by the antidepressant medication: the tranylcypromine was used as an alternative to ECT and it seemed that Plath's American doctors had established that she was 'allergic' to it. Hughes believed it induced the very suicidal thoughts it was intended to prevent. He had held out hope, after their meeting just a week before her death, that they might come together again, but time had run out on them.

Aurelia Plath was ill and didn't come to the funeral: she learned only later that Sylvia had taken her own life and determined that she must have been in a state of 'chemical' confusion. Ever anxious to put the best face on things, she prevented publication of *The Bell Jar* in the USA for eight years. When it came out in 1971 at the height of the women's movement, she countered its portrait of her mothering by having Sylvia's upbeat and loving letters to her published as well. Together with the intensity of Plath's poetry, fiction and journals, they provide a record of a life which made up for its tragic brevity by its depth.

In an interview she gave to the *New York Times* on 9 October 1979, when the letters were being staged, Aurelia Plath intimated that it was the psychiatrists who had turned her daughter against her:

'My mother was always my best friend and I'd hoped that my daughter would be too,' Mrs. Plath said. 'She became ashamed of our friendship during her breakdown. I don't want to accuse anybody. I don't want to blame anybody, but . . . I came one Saturday, and then Sylvia held me off with her two arms straight out and she said, "I don't hate you." You see, somebody had to be the scapegoat. She couldn't understand why she had had the breakdown. I think psychiatry has moved a long way since the 50's. They don't shut out the family. The doctors and the family work together. When Sylvia was sick, only one visit a week was allowed.'

Had Ruth Beuscher, the other mother in Sylvia's life, allowed her one-time patient to become too dependent on her? Apparently in the 1960s, when she was Clinical Assistant Professor of Psychiatry at Harvard, Beuscher had blamed the rash of suicides at McLean's on psychoanalytic treatment. There is no way of knowing whether this assessment was linked to the tragic culmination of her own therapeutic interventions with Sylvia Plath. Whatever the case, Beuscher began to move in a new direction, which was also an old one. She took a Master's degree in theology, focusing on spiritual aims, and received it in 1974. Her father had been a well known Presbyterian clergyman. Six years later she was ordained, and towards the end of her career taught at a theological seminary in Texas. Psychiatrists, she thought, were often insufficiently aware of when they needed to call in a member of the clergy.[301]

By then traditional American psychoanalytic psychiatry was being re-examined from all directions. Ruth Beuscher was hardly alone in moving towards religion. In 1973 Hollywood, the weathervane of American culture, had already evoked one extremity of that particular route. In the landmark film *The Exorcist*, the hero is both psychologist and priest: only when he gives up his secular role can he save the possessed twelve-year-old heroine from demonic clutches. Marilyn Monroe's Hollywood analyst, Ralph Greenson, stepped into the critical frame to attack the film as dangerous and for the way it degraded the

medical profession and psychiatry. His intervention was already beginning to look like a retrograde action. A decade earlier and while she was
under his care, Monroe had committed suicide just six months before
Sylvia Plath. It was becoming clear to America that psychoanalysts were
neither foolproof surrogate parents, seers, nor spiritual guides.

Marilyn (1926–62)

In October 1959, towards the end of her time in America, Sylvia Plath
dreamt of Marilyn Monroe. She appeared to her as a kind of 'fairy god-
mother'. Sylvia tells her how much she and Arthur Miller meant to her
and Ted. Marilyn, the woman who understands the body and the ways
of desire, gives her an expert manicure. Sylvia asks her about hair-
dressers. The good fairy Marilyn invites her to visit during the
Christmas holidays and promises her a new, flowering life.[302]

Marilyn Monroe was appearing in many dreams at that time, perhaps because her own life at the end of the fifties had the structure of a
tinseltown wish-fulfilment. She was everyone's figure of fantasy – from
Moji, Japan, where her famous nude image had been hung in the
municipal assembly building in an effort 'to rejuvenate the assembly-
men', to the radiation control lab of the world's first atomic submarine,
where she featured amongst the table of elements. So *Time* had asserted
in a cover story of 14 May 1956, hailing her 'frolicsomely sensual figure'
and the path she had taken from 'slithering vamp' to 'good-natured
tramp' – a journey that had, over five pictures, grossed more than $50
million. And now, everyone's favourite 'dumb blonde' had been to Lee
Strasberg's famous Actors' Studio in New York, and had become the
darling of the intellectuals. She was also, on 29 June that year, to be married to America's premier dramatist, Arthur Miller – the man who
announced their wedding at the same press conference in which he
refused to cooperate with the House Un-American Activities
Committee, pleading the First Amendment, and thereby standing up to
Senator Joe McCarthy's witch trials. The union of Monroe with Miller,
whose name was synonymous with the death of the American dream –
hollowed out by the fate of the world's most famous salesman, Willy
Lomax – seemed in popular mythology to indicate the dream might

have one more chance. On top of this, Miller had testified to Marilyn's talent, her 'terrific instinct for the basic reality of a character or a situation. She gets to the core.'

It was no wonder that the iconic duo had invaded Plath's dreams. Like Marilyn, Sylvia had transformed herself into a blonde, though only for a summer. The scholarship girl and the blue-collar 'orphan' whose mother was regularly institutionalized, may have come from backgrounds miles apart, but both were trying, within the strictures of the times, to invent themselves, forge some kind of working alliance between the feminine, the sexual and the thinking parts of their identity. Like Sylvia, Marilyn had also worked hard to get where she was. She had worked at her body, her carriage, her way with the cameras, yes, her unschooled intellect – despite the jeers at her pretentiousness – and above all, her acting.

According to Miller's rendition of her in *After the Fall*, she was a perfectionist, like Plath. She was also touchy, and resentfully insecure about her place in the world and her husband's love. If her skin was thin, her temper volatile, her ambition was great. The 'dumb blonde' was no one's fool, as Truman Capote makes clear in his memoir and others echo.[303] Given the gossip mills, Sylvia may also have known that Marilyn, like her, had recourse to an analyst: in the media it was recurrently signalled that she had been deeply affected by the absence of her father. Not only did she do a heartfelt, if comic, rendition of 'My Heart Belongs to Daddy', but that was what she called all three of her husbands. When she died, apparently from an overdose of Nembutal, a common barbiturate used to counter insomnia and relieve anxiety—though as with much in the Marilyn story, including her Cinderella-like childhood, this too is disputed – the story of celebrity, female sexuality and its price took on its full mythical arc.

Born Norma Jeane Mortenson, but known as Baker, her mother's maiden name, Marilyn was 'illegitimate'. Her father, who worked as her mother did in the blue-collar side of the film industry, had abandoned his wife during the pregnancy, taking his two other children with him. Twelve days after Marilyn's birth, her mother broke down and was institutionalized. Marilyn was boarded out to a family of religious zealots somewhere on the dirt-poor borderlands of LA. They talked of little but sin and hellfire and had her working in the house by the age of five. She took to hiding in the woodshed, the site of fantasies and escape from pervasive guilt. When she was six, a friend of the family raped her. Side by side with the sermons and the praying, this unsettled her enough to produce hallucinations. The family sent her away, worried that she would repeat her mother's madness. She was shunted off to another foster home.

When Norma Jeane was eight, her mother broke down a second time. She couldn't meet the costs of fostering and Norma Jeane was sent to an orphanage, which had all the qualities of a Victorian workhouse. She loathed it and developed a stutter. From the age of eleven, when a friend of her mother's took her in, until the age of sixteen when she first got married, there was a series of twelve families, each one poorer than the next. Norma Jeane's education suffered. At school she was an unhappy stringbean of a child, much maligned. But as her 'own' narrative would have it, a sweater transformed her from being the despised orphan girl to the budding sex goddess. She had borrowed the blue garment from a friend. It metamorphosed her. The boys who had teased were now rapt, attentive, her slaves. 'For the first time in my life people paid attention to me . . . I prayed that they wouldn't go away.'[304]

The early marriage, on the advice of her guardian, to Jim Dougherty, then an aircraft worker, soon failed. But while she was working at a defence plant, some publicity stills were taken by a photographer who recognized her possibilities and marched her off to the Blue Book School of Charm and Modelling. The Hollywood make-over included the bleach-blonde hair, a deeper voice and a new smile. By the spring of 1947, Norma Jeane was a covergirl, smiling from the front of five magazines. The film studios beckoned. When she went to Fox, the casting director took her straight on and gave her a new name, taking the Monroe from her mother's maiden name.

The rest is Hollywood history, inevitably mingled with myth, gossip and press releases. There was fame and drugs and too much (or too little) sex, alongside a series of glorious performances in films that still matter. There was the damaged, insecure waif within the beautiful woman, the angel of sex — all warmth, goodness, vulnerability and innocent responsiveness — who was by all accounts so terrified of filming, so eager for perfection, that she was perennially late, or absent or heavily sedated, or vomiting on the studio stairs before coming in. There was the rapacious 'nymphomaniac', the 'castrator' — terms that inevitably embody the male's fear of his own hated and rapacious sexuality projected on to the woman — who seduced and seduced and abandoned. There was the unsatisfiable and dissatisfied 'frigid' woman, the woman's own response to the male's rapacity, compounded by her loathing of her own sexuality. There was also the addict, the heavy drinker and the suicidally depressive madwoman. There were a disputed dozen abortions, 'hysterical pregnancies' and miscarriages, perhaps one after the fraught filming of her final movie, *The Misfits*. Arthur Miller was apparently not the father, though he had fathered the script of the film. They had already more or less separated. But it was on the set of the doomed film — in which, according to Clark Gable's wife, Marilyn's tantrums killed Clark, who died a week after the end of filming — that Arthur Miller met his next wife, the film's photographer.

Part of this story belongs to the annals of psychoanalysis. Indeed, for all the stumbling, childlike innocence with which her own 'intellectual' statements seem to be made, Marilyn had by the late fifties learned a sophisticated version of the patter of psychoanalysis quite as well as Woody Allen enacted it later on. 'I'm always running into people's unconscious,' she once told a reporter in an interview,[305] underscoring in a Freudian way the whole history of what it means to be a celebrity, an object of desire to millions, each of whom has a pre-emptive persona for you.

Marilyn's stories of her life seem to move easily from analyst's couch to casting couch: sometimes the sexuality is troubled, (de)formative; at others, triumphal. Her own structuring, with a little help from the studio, of the key moments of her history — from abandonment, rape, guilt, to burgeoning pubescent sexuality — all play into a couch narrative, a case history of Freudian screen memories, though this time enabling a screen image. Even the childhood dream she remembers, from some unspecified date, has the feel of a rehearsed and interpreted couch dream, which is also a Hollywood extravaganza: 'I dreamed that I was standing up in church without any clothes on, and all the people there were lying at my feet on the floor of the church, and I walked naked, with a sense of freedom, over their prostrate forms, being careful not to step on anyone.'

Marilyn's training in psychoanalytic meanings and her attempt to deal both with her baggage and with the demands of her celebrity status formally began in 1955 after she had ended her nine-month marriage to the baseball legend Joe DiMaggio, had left Hollywood and Fox for New York and started training at the Actors' Studio. This famous 'method' called on actors to look into themselves to find the truth of a character. Lee Strasberg, the studio's director, more or less demanded psycho-analysis of his actors. It was perhaps on his recommendation that Marilyn started analysis with Dr Margaret Hohenberg, at 155 East 83rd Street. Hohenberg had arrived as a refugee in America in 1940. Her medical degree from the University of Vienna had been obtained in 1925, the same year as Marilyn's second analyst, Marianne Kris. Hohenberg had become a full member of the New York Psychoanalytic Society in 1950. She was part of New York's European cultural elite, an appropriate figure for a star in search of self-improvement.

Monroe's biographer Donald Spoto, whose narrative posits a waif of a Marilyn of little brain, done down by the analysts, would have it that 'Excessive introspection exacerbated her lack of self-confidence. Intuition suffered at the expense of a forced, conscious intellectualism that paralysed her and pushed her further back into herself.'[306] Suicide has retrospectively made Marilyn into a victim. But the world-famous star Marilyn was neither stupid nor stable before she went to the ana-lysts, whose aura at the time – and aura in the therapeutic and medical professions has always been part of the placebo effect so essential to feeling better – was rather more potent than it is now. She seemed both to need and to want the bolstering and confidence the cultural sphere could bring. Arthur Miller was part of the same picture. So, too, were Lee and his wife Paula Strasberg, who served not only as teachers but as surrogate parents. Paula accompanied her on all her films from 1955 on, as her acting coach. Marilyn also stayed with them in New York on Central Park West.

In the summer of 1956, when she and Arthur Miller were in London and she was filming *The Prince and the Showgirl* with Laurence Olivier, Marilyn had a crisis. Whether one believes the dramatic versions of her biographers or Miller's own earlier dramatization in *The Misfits*, it is clear that Marilyn had found something that Miller had written just two months into their marriage that showed he didn't love her in the way she had thought and wanted. In the play, Maggie, the Marilyn character, says, 'You know when I wanted to die? When I read what you wrote, judgey. Two months after we were married, judgey.' What the Miller character, Quentin, had written was: 'The only one I will ever love is my daughter.' Miller explains he had written it when confronted by his own sexual jealousy, her enraged response that it made her feel she didn't exist, and his fear, in turn, that he didn't know how to love.[307]

In the version of the daughter of Paula Strasberg who was with Marilyn in London and on the set, Miller's diary passage that sent Marilyn into a spin expressed his disappointment in her, 'how he thought I was some kind of angel but now he guessed he was wrong'. Paula's reassurance that diaries were for talking to oneself about everything you think, good and bad (not unlike free association, perhaps), met with Marilyn's: 'Yeah, but I wouldn't leave my head wide open for the person I was thinking about to see. That's a little too Freudian.'[308]

The event tumbled Marilyn into depression. Olivier, who was directing, demanded an end to her show of temperament. Dr Hohenberg was flown over to see her patient through. When she could no longer stay, Marilyn was apparently sent to see her fellow Viennese, Anna Freud. The maid Paula Fichtl, who had been with the Freuds since the Vienna days, notes triumphantly – though her account is not always to be trusted – that Marilyn arrived in a black Rolls at the Freud house in Maresfield Gardens in Hampstead. Whether it was due to the exemplary care of the joint analysts or not, the film was duly finished in November. During her stay, Marilyn had been presented to the Queen, and had been asked to perform the title role in *Lysistrata* for the BBC. Apparently on Anna Freud's recommendation, Marilyn on her return to New York took up analysis with Anna's old childhood friend, Marianne Kris.

Dr Kris had the advantage of living in the same building as the Strasbergs. She was the daughter of Oskar Rie, who had been a close friend of the Freuds in Vienna and the family paediatrician. Marianne, something of a favourite, had been briefly analysed by Freud. Her husband, the famous art historian and psychoanalyst Ernst Kris, had trained alongside Anna, and was one of her collaborators on the journal *The Psychoanalytic Study of the Child*. On Marianne Kris's couch, Marilyn

Monroe was in regular contact with the Viennese 'aristocracy' of the profession and its high culture.

Eric R. Kandel, who trained and practised as a psychoanalyst before moving on to neurology and the study of the storage of memory in the Californian sea slug, aplysia, for which he won the Nobel Prize for Physiology and Medicine in 2000, knew the Krises in the fifties through their daughter Anna, named after Anna Freud. The family was influential in shaping his early interest in psychoanalysis. In his Nobel Prize speech, he writes:

> It is difficult to recapture now the extraordinary fascination that psychoanalysis held for young people in 1950. During the first half of the 20th century psychoanalysis provided a remarkable set of insights into the mind – insights about unconscious mental processes, psychic determinism, and perhaps most interesting, the irrationality of human motivation. As a result, in 1950, psychoanalysis outlined by far the most coherent, interesting, and nuanced view of the human mind than did any other school of psychology. In addition, Anna's parents, who rep resented academic psychoanalysis in its most intellectual and interesting form, were extraordinary people – intelligent, cultured, and filled with enthusiasm . . . By frequent interactions with them and their colleagues, I was converted to their view that psychoanalysis offered a fascinating new approach, perhaps the only approach, to understanding the mind, including the irrational nature of motivation and unconscious and conscious memory.[309]

Marilyn's analysis with Marianne Kris, it can be assumed, was an education as well as a therapy, private tuition after the correspondence course in literature she had taken from UCLA. In practice, the analysis was far more like one of Freud's early and irregular ones than what America had come to expect in terms of standardized technique. Over the four years she saw Marianne Kris, Marilyn was often away filming. Her perennial lateness swallowed up the hour, though it was in part that persistent lateness that had brought her to analysis. From Brenda Webster's account of her mother, the painter Ethel Schwabacher's, analysis with Kris, which began after Webster's father had died, Kris was warm and casual. She used her patient's first name in a companionate way, was maternal and caring rather than distant and neutral. Indeed, Schwabacher's 'happy' analytic relationship, in which the analyst urged her patient to paint her 'grief and rage', lasted for thirty years until Kris's death.[310]

There is no record of what was discussed in Marilyn's analysis or what effects it had. Her acting improved, but her marriage to Arthur Miller didn't: it was effectively over in 1959. Celebrity was stressful. The insomnia medication – Demerol, sodium pentothal, amytal – had the side-effect of impairing judgement. The strains of filming had got worse over the years with the demands of her own perfectionism. The unhappy termination of her brief affair with her co-star in *Let's Make Love*, Yves Montand, in the midst of the shoot in 1960 may well have precipitated Marilyn's collapse. He told reporters he had only taken up with her to make the screen love affair more plausible. Marilyn was so severely affected she stopped coming in to work altogether. From New York, Marianne Kris arranged help. She called Los Angeles analyst Dr Ralph Greenson, a well established Californian doctor, to Marilyn's side. Greenson had experience in the hothouse world of stardom. He was the analyst to celebrity which, given its pattern of extremes under media spotlight, created its very own psychic ills. Frank Sinatra, Peter Lorre and Vivien Leigh, amongst many others, had had recourse to Greenson. Since he was also a friend of Anna Freud's, Marianne Kris trusted him.

The referral has been read by some as a conspiracy of shrinks intent on profiting from Monroe, particularly since Greenson's brother-in-law was Marilyn's lawyer and her will left a bequest to Marianne Kris. She in turn bequeathed it to the Anna Freud Centre in London, which also received funding from the West Coast research foundation Greenson had set up. Kris died in London in 1980 in Anna Freud's house in Maresfield Gardens, now the Freud Museum. But there is little real evidence that Kris was particularly mercenary. It is probably more accurate to see in her contacting of Greenson the usual medical system of referral at play.

Then, too, if Marilyn was to have recourse to psychoanalysis, Greenson was eminently qualified. When he arrived at her bungalow at the Beverly Hills Hotel, he was quick to note her slurred speech and sedated manner. Asking for a list of the stimulants and sedatives

Marilyn was on, he told her she had taken enough medication to put five people to sleep.' I promised she would sleep with less medication if she realized she is fighting sleep as well as searching for some obvious oblivion which is not sleep.'[311] It was the beginning of a therapy which would last until Marilyn's suicide: the wish for oblivion won out. Greenson never altogether got over it.

Ralph Greenson (1911–79)

Ralph Greenson was born Romeo Greenspoon, alongside his twin sister Juliet, on 20 September 1911, to Russian Jewish immigrants in Brooklyn. By dint of hard work and imagination, his pharmacist father became a doctor while his wife, who had worked alongside him while he went to medical school, transformed herself into a successful artists' manager. The children's names give away the family's love of theatre, opera, music and the arts; before he became Ralph – or Romi to his friends – Greenson had already had an education in the cultural classics and the high drama that its interpreters could engage in both on stage and off. The great Russian ballerina Pavlova was one of his mother's clients. In 1931, after university, Greenson went to medical school in Berne (a quota for Jews still applied in America). Here he met his wife Hildi, and learned to read Freud in German. Drawn to Vienna, he had an analysis with the indefatigable Wilhelm Stekel, one of Freud's earliest followers who had been abandoned by Freud to go his own way.

By all accounts a charming, loquacious enthusiast of a man, with a great gift for lecturing and none for modesty, Greenson came to Los Angeles in 1936 to find himself rejected by the existing psychoanalytic society because of his links with Stekel. He did a second analysis with the highly respected Viennese analyst Otto Fenichel who had recently arrived in America, and effectively completed his analytic 'training' during the war, when he headed the combat-fatigue unit at the Army Air Force Convalescent Hospital in Fort Logan, Colorado. His experience in dealing with war neuroses found its way into *Captain Newman MD*, in which Gregory Peck plays the heroic army psychiatrist who brings three distressed soldiers back to normal life after their traumatizing war experience. Greenson had dramatically recounted his war stories for the film's writer, Leo Rosten, and when the film appeared in 1963, the same year as John Huston's *Freud*, it played to packed houses – unlike the Huston film, in which Marilyn Monroe, possibly on Greenson's advice, had refused the part of Freud's young hysterical patient.

In 1960 Greenson had helped Marilyn enough to see her through the filming of *Let's Make Love*. Then she returned to New York and to Marianne Kris. In July and August of that year, the fateful shoot of *The Misfits* took place in Reno, Nevada. The heat was as intense as the passions that swirled around the set, not least between Miller and Monroe. The film was based on a short story he had written about her early in their relationship. It portrays a vulnerable, sensual, supremely feminine young woman whose sensitivity is such that she manages, mostly through her trembling passivity, to bind together a group of male 'misfits' and stop them preying on the wild horses they hunt.

Marilyn felt she was being called upon to play what was effectively a 'misconstrued concept of herself'.[312] This idealized Marilyn – for which Marilyn Monroe Productions had paid Miller $250,000 – eradicated the shameful and shaming past that had made her. Miller had never been able to acknowledge that past; nor, it seems, the Marilyn she was. She is quoted as saying about the scene in which her character, Roslyn, persuades the cowboys not to kill the wild horses: 'I convince them by throwing a fit, not by explaining anything. So I have a fit. A screaming crazy fit . . . And to think, *Arthur* did this to me . . . If that's what he thinks of me, well, then I'm not for him and he's not for me.'[313] Meanwhile, the film's director John Huston lauded Marilyn, by saying that she had not been acting. 'The role was Marilyn, but Marilyn plus. She found things, found things about womankind in herself.'[314]

Portraying this naked, wounded creature, Marilyn felt isolated and abandoned, 'worthless', merely the sexualized female of the male unconscious she was always bumping into. She was drinking heavily. In the first week of August, she collapsed and had to be flown back to LA, where Greenson tried once more to wean her from alcohol and pills. He put her back together enough so that she could return to finish the shoot. But when the film wrapped in January and she returned to New York, Marianne Kris judged her state and threats of suicide so frightening that she had her hospitalized at the Payne Whitney Clinic in Manhattan. Monroe voluntarily signed in as Faye Miller, but then realized that this was no rest and rehabilitation centre. 'There was no empathy . . . The inhumanity was archaic . . . There were screaming women in their cells,' she later wrote to Ralph Greenson.

Marilyn herself was amongst them. She was put in a locked, padded room and threatened with a straitjacket when she screamed her demands to be released. This was too close to the demented maternal reality. She spent three days at the hospital and finally managed to reach her ex-husband Joe DiMaggio, who flew in and demanded her release. The torrent of rage Marilyn subsequently released on Marianne Kris had the older woman trembling: 'I did a terrible thing, a terrible thing. Oh God, I didn't mean to, but I did.'[315]

A place was found for Marilyn at the Columbia Presbyterian Hospital. From here she wrote to Greenson to ask him to become her primary analyst. She was moving back to LA. By June she was hailing him as her saviour. Perhaps this second cultivated Jew was in some ways a stand-in for the Miller who had never, she felt, properly understood her. Greenson evolved a radical form of treatment for Marilyn. In the early days of psychoanalysis it would have been called 'wild'. It was certainly unconventional in the world of neutral American analysts. Some said he had simply fallen under Marilyn's spell. Greenson not only had erratically long sessions with his star patient, sometimes allowing these – when she was in serious trouble at the studio, for example – to extend to five hours. He also took to seeing her at the end of the day and in the informal environment of his own home, where she might then stay on for dinner, and later help with the washing up or attend one of the chamber concerts the Greensons held. She became friends with his wife and children – unusually for Marilyn, coming early for sessions so that she could chat to them. She attended Greenson's art school daughter's birthday party, taught her dance steps, gave her advice on boyfriends. She went to lectures – indeed, one by Greenson – with his student son, or, disguised in a black wig, helped him flat-hunt. She phoned Greenson at home at any hour of the day or night, to the point where he himself began to feel trapped by her. He delayed a long-planned trip to Switzerland with his wife in order to be on hand for Marilyn who was once more in trouble over filming, this time the Cukor comedy *Something's Got to Give*.

Greenson had a rationale. Marilyn, he determined, was a borderline personality: addictive, needy, impulsive, prone to bouts of rage and feelings of self-abasement compounded by sexual and emotional excess, unstable in her relationships as well as in her own identity. An amorphous term often redefined (for example, by feminist therapists) as embodying one of the personality disorders or a post-traumatic stress disorder arising from childhood abuse, borderlines, though not psychotic, can also sometimes somatize like old-style hysterics. Analytic hearsay has it that the mark of borderlines is that they can talk about themselves for five hours at a stretch without the analyst getting a realistic picture of who they are. Indeed, borderlines were most often considered unreachable by psychoanalysis, certainly in its American fifties configuration. However, analysts like Frieda Fromm-Reichmann, let alone the British Kleinians and French Lacanians – as Greenson was well aware judging from his many reflections on technique, particularly post-Marilyn – had devised methods of using talking therapies with more extreme cases. As Greenson writes in 1974:

> Most Freudian analysts believe that the borderline and psychotic patients . . . suffer predominantly from a deficiency in the ego's capacity to form and retain mental object representations and are therefore not suitable for psychoanalytic therapy . . . Analysable patients have a relatively well developed and intact ego, with the capacity to distinguish inside from outside and self from others. In addition they have the ability to develop and sustain both a transference neurosis and a working alliance in order to work effectively and endure the demands of the analytic situation. Patients lacking the resilient ego functions necessary for these developments will not be able to comprehend, feel, integrate and utilize interpretations of their unconscious reactions . . . Conflict disorders with an intact ego usually respond well to interpretive interventions. The ego deficiency disorders require primarily structure building techniques.[316]

Marilyn had an ego deficiency and there was work to be done before analysis could bite, before she could use interpretations. There was no hope here for a conventional analysis. What was clear to Greenson was that her childhood had given Marilyn no indication of how to live. The mad mother, the lack of a father, the changing foster homes and the abuse, though invoked in her erratic, earlier analyses, had done no more than educate her in a language. She would speak easily enough of 'Oedipus' – in fact, on several occasions, she talked of finding her father and sleeping with him. She elaborated a fantasy, reported as real, of donning a wig and seducing the ageing Lothario, so that she could then confront him with his own history of seduction and abandonment. For Greenson, to create a therapeutic alliance with this wild Marilyn would mean first of all laying down the foundation of what a life with attachments might mean. Attachments here, as they were for Bowlby, are real – not only, or also, unconscious fantasies. So Greenson set out to provide a version of the good foster home, a model surrogate family for orphan Marilyn to internalize. He had her buy her first house and furnish it. He found her a kind of nurse/housekeeper who displaced her cadre of fawning helpers. He tried to keep her working. She tried, too. It needed time. But time ran out.

Undoubtedly an ever flamboyant Greenson also revelled – at least to begin with – in his seductive celebrity patient, who dazzled and was helpless by turn. He became her surrogate father, battling for her with the studios, always available on the phone. The vagaries of the transference were hardly in control, and Marilyn seems to have ended up repeating with him some of the patterns of her other love affairs. She became deeply dependent on him. One of the case histories cited in his *Explorations in Psychoanalysis*, 'On Transitional Objects and Transference', bears a marked resemblance to Marilyn. In this case of 'an emotionally immature young woman', Greenson can only absent himself from the patient who has developed a 'very dependent transference to me' when she finds a 'transitional object' to stand in for his presence. This is a 'white knight' from a chess set she has been given which she thinks looks – through a champagne glass – just like him. She wraps this talisman in a handkerchief and keeps it with her to protect her from 'nervousness, anxiety or bad luck'.[317] The case history makes one wonder what Winnicott might have made of Marilyn.

Before judging Greenson too harshly – as many, particularly fellow analysts, did and as his own later attempts at self-justification imply he did too, gutted as he was by Marilyn's suicide – it's worth noting that his unconventional 'therapy' with Marilyn bears many comparisons with recent reports on best practice for the National Health Service in

Britain. This recommends that borderline patients are given what is effectively education and support for 'life' — a resident treatment scheme which combines detox with regular therapy, teaching and work-monitoring.

In May 1962 Greenson, who had been in thrall to Marilyn, her break-downs and absenteeism from the shoot of *Something's Got to Give*, at last took his delayed trip to Switzerland. He left Marilyn in the care of a col-league and, one can only assume, the protection of some talismanic 'white knight'. But things took on a treacherous momentum. *Something's Got to Give* was going badly. On 19 May, a terrified Marilyn flew to New York to perform in the much publicized fund-raising gala at Madison Square Gardens for John F. Kennedy's forty-fifth birthday. Her breath-less rendition of 'Happy Birthday Mr President' has become history. It was perhaps only made possible by long phone calls to Greenson in Switzerland, with his son and daughter stepping in to comfort and reassure — an attentive, supportive family for the waif who had never had one. John F. Kennedy and some fifteen thousand members of the public watched her give a dazzling performance in a dress which left little room for secreted talismans. The President, whose purported fling with Marilyn later acquired notoriety, commented, 'I can now retire from politics having had Happy Birthday sung to me in such a sweet, wholesome way.'[318] Kennedy's comments have an eerie ring, given that he had only another eighteen months before his retirement was forced upon him by a gunman. The woman who said to feminist Gloria Steinem, 'That's the trouble, a sex symbol becomes a thing. I just hate to be a thing', had even less time than that.

On her return to LA, the studio executives were hardly pleased with Marilyn's New York performance. In something very like executive pique, they fired her from *Something's Got to Give* and mounted a publicity campaign against her. It was the first time Marilyn had been fired. Greenson cut short his trip. Marilyn's state on his return was such that he considered having her hospitalized, but feared that might make things even worse. The concatenation of being fired, the bad press, combined with the news of Arthur Miller's new wife's pregnancy, exac-erbated what was already a precarious state.

On Saturday 4 August, Greenson saw her, noted that she was depressed, but no worse than she had often been before. She rang him at home later and they chatted before he went out to dinner. Then, at three in the morning, the fateful call came from her carer-companion. Marilyn Monroe, at the age of thirty-six, was dead. According to the coroner's report her blood contained a dose of the barbiturate Nembutal amounting to forty or fifty capsules. This was no accident. And there had been no intercourse that night.

But in this final act of Marilyn's life, it is harder than ever to unravel all other facts from fiction. The rash of biographies implicate a range of culprits from furtive presidential brothers to the mafia and the FBI, to slandering studio bosses who hounded what was already a wreck of a dope-ridden actress in a daze, to a lone, possibly murderous, Svengali or Comintern agent of a shrink who tried to counter the effect of an overdose of pills by prescribing a killing enema of chloral hydrate. The truth is probably rather more prosaic: like Plath, it is likely that Marilyn found life intolerable and, in a confusion of drugs, took her own life. Whether any form of drugs prescribed by her GP, or a therapy that was more radical, more responsible or more conventional, could have saved her at this stage is impossible to answer. She would not then, in any event, have been Marilyn.

Ralph Greenson never got over her death. He wondered what grandiosity had provoked him to think he could succeed where other analysts had failed, but he had always been something of a gambler. For the ten last years of his life, he replayed his handling of Marilyn by worrying over transference and counter-transference in his articles, and pondering what was the most effective technique. Even though he had often counted himself a traditional Freudian in the American sense – which implied a technique of studied neutrality and an analyst who was as objective as the later computer programs some said they preferred[319] – Greenson's wide reading of Ferenczi and the British school has him coming down, if a little restlessly, on the side of the unconventional therapist who can allow empathy or some kind of holding environment into the analytic twosome.

> one cannot work effectively unless one is willing and able to become emotionally involved. It is not possible to empathize with a patient unless one feels a goodly amount of liking . . . The only time indifference may be a therapeutic response is in regard to intense and prolonged

emotional outbursts in borderline and psychotic patients. They may need your indifference to reassure themselves that their hostile or sexual assaults are not deadly or overwhelming to you.

Whether Greenson had withdrawn into temporary indifference at the wrong moment remains an open question. This argumentative, some said charismatic, man who held top posts both at the LA Psychoanalytic Institute in the fifties and throughout his career at the UCLA School of Medicine, and published widely, remained a controversial figure amongst both analysts and patients until his death at the age of sixty-eight in 1979. As Anna Freud wrote for a memorial meeting in 1980, 'we have not yet discovered the secret of how to raise the real followers of people like Romi Greenson, namely, men and women who make use of psychoanalysis to its very limits; for the understanding of themselves, of their fellow-beings; for communicating with the world at large; in short, for a way of living'.[320]

As for Marilyn, *Time*'s obituary stated: 'her life kept hopeless plans alive, her death was the trigger of suicides in half a dozen cities'. Indeed, Marilyn's death made suicide attractive – a dramatic conclusion to a life of glamour, emotional extremes and pills taken to counter psychic anguish.

For young women growing up in the sixties, her plight as a beautiful woman tossed on the stormy seas of her gender and sexuality and trapped by the unconscious of others also reinforced their sense of a need for radical change. That need for change encompassed the psychiatric and psychoanalytic professions, which as guides for 'a way of living' seemed to have failed both Marilyn and Sylvia Plath, let alone countless unsung others.

In her 1987 biography of Marilyn, the feminist Gloria Steinem charges Freudian assumptions of female passivity and penis-envy – applied to Marilyn by her analysts – in Marilyn's indoctrination to dependent status. Steinem also raises Marilyn's childhood rape to the level of fact, using as evidence the commonness of abuse in women's childhoods and the widespread nature of men's disbelief. Her Marilyn emerges as a double victim: both male society and the world of the mind doctors have conspired against her. Steinem's feminist reading of Marilyn's life and her attack on the psychoanalytic way of seeing that allegedly helped to give it a tragic turn are informed not only by the seventies and eighties history of the women's movement, but by a more generalized attack on the mind doctors and their institutions which began with the sixties.

PART FOUR

INTO THE PRESENT

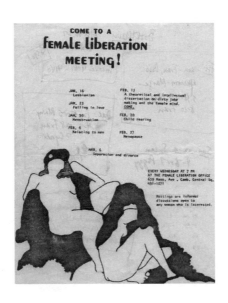

12

REBELS

I think I'm so absolutely centred on the one thing – it's, well, to get her well . . . since she's ill, she's never accepted anything any more. She's had to reason it out for herself, and if she couldn't reason it out for herself, then she didn't seem to take my word for it.

Mrs Abbott, mother of the 'schizophrenic' patient, Maya[321]

By the end of the fifties it was becoming increasingly evident to some that the triumphalist mind doctors, whatever their status in the media and as paid personal helpmates, couldn't tell a troubled and rebellious growing girl, let alone a non-conforming all-American male, from a raving madperson. Defiance, unruliness, disobedience were character-istics they translated all too readily into the language of illness. Meanwhile, many asylums were little better than prisons where drugs, experiment and punishment were legitimated as treatment. Their clas-sifications, though increasingly dressed in the powerful jargon of solid science and physical medicine, were as vaporous as smoke rings – and more dangerous. Even the most cultivated of analysts couldn't avert a patient's suicide.

A part of the more general sixties political attack on the bastions of power and science, the anti-psychiatry movement was launched from a variety of sites. Primary amongst these were not the patients' groups that were to evolve later, but the ranks of the psychiatric profession itself.

Thomas Szasz's ground-breaking *The Myth of Mental Illness* of 1960 launched the first conceptual missile at the burgeoning ranks of American psychiatry and exposed the hollowness of the category itself.

The notion of mental illness derives its main support from such phenomena as syphilis of the brain or delirious conditions –intoxications,
for instance – in which persons are known to manifest various peculiarities or disorders of thinking and behavior. Correctly speaking,
however, these are diseases of the brain, not of the mind. According to
one school of thought, *all* so-called mental illness is of this type. The
assumption is made that some neurological defect, perhaps a very subtle
one, will ultimately be found for all the disorders of thinking and behavior. Many contemporary psychiatrists, physicians, and other scientists
hold this view. This position implies that people *cannot* have troubles –
expressed in what are *now called* 'mental illnesses' – because of differences in personal needs, opinions, social aspirations, values, and so on.
All problems in living are attributed to physicochemical processes which in
due time will be discovered by medical research.[322]

Mental illness as a category was being questioned and criticized as the
self-serving creation of an ambitious profession which sought to med-
icalize the very troubles being human brought in its train. Also under
attack were the diagnostic ineptitude and the dangerous coerciveness of
treatments within asylums. Ken Kesey's *One Flew Over the Cuckoo's Nest*
(1962) vividly satirized the asylum's straitjacketing of the scope of human
experience, its disciplinary use of ECT and lobotomy. The novel was
based on Kesey's LSD trials and employment in a veterans' hospital in Los
Angeles: its point of view is that of the giant native American 'paranoid-
schizophrenic' Chief Bromden who pretends to be a deaf mute and sees
the action as a contest between good, as embodied in anarchic R.P
McMurphy, and the evil psychiatric order of Nurse Ratched. The 1975
film of the book took the action to a state hospital in Oregon and had
actual patients playing secondary parts to wisecracking Jack Nicholson –
the seductive individualist at war with frigid Nurse Ratched.

Erving Goffman's *Asylums* (1960) arose out of the time he spent in
1955–6 at St Elizabeth's Hospital in Washington DC, where he observed
at first hand the daily life of mental patients and staff. He concluded that
in the 'total institution' the asylum was, doctors and patients were
bound in a masquerade in which the first had to behave in an authoritarian fashion while the second enacted variations on the theme of
manic craziness: even if power lay with the doctors, both colluded in a

social order which perpetuated madness rather than the vaunted and hoped-for cure.

Meanwhile in France and in a different critical register, but prompted by the same liberatory impetus, Michel Foucault's *Madness and Civilization* (1961) explored the ways in which the very discourse and 'scientific' discipline of psychiatry – a form of knowledge – had defined madness, and instituted its own power over its forms. Simultaneously its ways of seeing had become naturalized. Unreason had been bound into cases and diagnoses and lost its oppositional force to ever-narrowing understandings of 'reason'.

Even without having recourse to Foucault's overarching critique, it is clear the asylum system had reached a nadir in its chequered history. Scientific hypotheses about cure, a desire to experiment with surgery or drugs, coincided in many hospitals with 'snake pit' conditions and growing numbers of patients. Andrew Scull's *Madhouse* (2005) charts a compelling and emblematic microhistory which begins in the first part of the twentieth century: the story of Henry Cotton, superintendent of the Trenton State Hospital, New Jersey. In the name of a scientific theory postulating that the source of psychosis was 'focal sepsis' or chronic pus infections which poisoned the brain, Cotton carried out an obscene campaign of surgery on the tonsils, stomach, colon and uterus of patients alongside removal of teeth. In the process he maimed and killed thousands.

One of Trenton's patients was a certain Martha Hurwitz. Her case, culled from hospital records, charts the tragic trajectory of a woman subjected over the course of half a century to every change of treatment asylum fashion dictated. Born in Russia in 1902, poor but intelligent and adept in three languages, she had been abandoned by a drinking, gambling husband and had fallen into a depression which brought with it occasional bouts of violence. This violence seems to have been simply troubling acts, inappropriate female behaviour in the eyes of old-world Jewish parents. After a short stint in a private hospital, and temporary improvement, Martha Hurwitz had broken her ankle and became so 'talkative and restless' that her parents had her admitted to Trenton. Here she was diagnosed as a case of 'Septic Psychosis Schizophrenia', for which she was treated with typhoid vaccine, tonsillectomy and had several teeth extracted.

Released within a few months, Hurwitz was back in the asylum in
the late summer of 1929, 'nervous and excitable' and depressed after she
had broken a leg. In a state of panic about readmission, she was also 'violent'. This time the same diagnosis resulted in the extraction of her
remaining teeth. Hospital notes talk of her being 'rational' but 'restive
and uncooperative' – a resistance, as Scull notes, which was defined as
pathology. Twenty colonic irrigations were followed by a course of 'surgical bacteriology' – puncturing of the sinuses in search of sepsis, and
Lane's bowel operation in which a section of the colon was removed.
This assault on the body defeated Hurwitz's resistance; becalmed, she
was sent home six months later. 'Cure' lasted for almost two years,
then on 4 April 1931 she was readmitted for five years, discharged, but
after a short remission came back to Trenton, this time to stay, in March
1938. During the coming years she was given fifty insulin treatments.
Hospital transcripts record her feeling that these are punishments for
her good health, which is resented by others: 'the people here resent the
fact that she is so healthy so they give her needles to make her sick'. Her
'flattened emotional tone' and near-muteness now led to fever treatment – inoculation with malaria – and then, in 1949, to a series of
electro-shocks.

Martha's condition had now become chronic, and no treatment
made any discernible difference. In September 1951, notes showed her
'greatly deteriorated', but not selected for the course of lobotomies the
hospital was then undertaking. Instead, in 1955, her mental faculties in
decline so that she now claimed to have been born in the Trenton State
Hospital, but still quarrelsome, she was given the new treatment for
psychosis, Reserpine, but on double the recommended level and escalating. By November, she was receiving seventy times the 'therapeutic'
dose. Still psychotic after forty-two doses, Martha was selected in 1956
for a trial of the new drug Thorazine, and six months later a further
escalating course of Reserpine. Early in the 1980s, she was, as Scull
vividly notes, 'a burnt-out case, a demented old woman who had somehow survived repeated surgeries, the extraction of all her teeth and
tonsils, fever therapy, insulin comas, electric shocks and massive over-
doses of drugs, during a confinement that had stretched over five
decades'. It was now that the powers that be decided Martha Hurwitz
should be de-institutionalized and released into a community she had

left in 1938. Luckily, she fell and broke her hip, contracted pneumonia and died on 7 May 1982, fifty-four years after her first admission.[323]

This distressing example of a patient whose chronic craziness was more than partly induced, and certainly exacerbated, by the tortures of asylum life shores up both the broad and narrow claims of the anti-psychiatrists by highlighting the power of the asylum as a total institution, the dangers of unchecked medical experimentation on vulnerable people and of the treatment fads the profession is prone to. By the fifties and sixties the catch-all diagnosis of schizophrenia had become so widespread – and most decidedly so in America – that any 'normal' person could find herself incarcerated and unable to leave the institution once its threshold had been crossed. This was what David Rosenhan's famous experiment showed.[324]

In the early seventies, Rosenhan and eight friends, including one psychiatrist, presented themselves at the psychiatric emergency rooms of a range of state and poshly private hospitals and asylums. They had prepared themselves minimally. They were hairy, unshaven and unwashed, their teeth unbrushed. They probably emitted a pong. Apart from their appearance, their only spoken symptom was that they had heard a voice say 'thud'.

All eight were admitted and all, save the one who with the same symptoms was labelled manic depressive, were diagnosed as paranoid schizophrenic. They were given drugs, which they had learned not to swallow. Despite their subsequent pleas of normality and truth-telling, they were kept in for varying lengths of time. Their 'therapy' records showed that, although each had merely recounted his or her life, their histories were given meanings conforming to the diagnosis of schizophrenia. Only other inmates seemed to suss that they were not 'mad'. They saw them writing notes, after all.

Rosenhan published the results of his experiment, 'On Being Sane in Insane Places', in the influential *Science*. His charge that the profession misdiagnosed and held 'patients' against their will plunged the American discipline of psychiatry and asylum practice into a nosedive. Psychiatric diagnosis was clearly a dangerously inexact and unreliable science, capable of making 'massive errors'. Shock therapy, the treatment of choice in institutions, was used far too indiscriminately, as were a whole range of stupefying drugs. Despite the profession's good intentions, it was clear that labelling a patient insane and bracketing him with a diagnosis resulted not only in the stripping of the usual rights of a citizen, but in a depersonalization which was difficult to correct.

In Britain, well before Rosenhan's experiment, a series of case histories had been published which set out to show how families, not biology, produced the pathology of schizophrenia. On the way they made it brazenly, if inadvertently, clear that women in particular were trapped by the neat fit of family and doctor's expectations of female behaviour. Psychiatric illness emerged as the diagnosis of choice for a great deal that might now look like defiance or adolescent unruliness. These women are the pseudonymous contemporaries of Marilyn Monroe and Sylvia Plath. They painfully reveal how the difficulties of becoming and being woman during these years, combined with a rebellion against broadly held, constricting expectations, both induced and shaped what doctors, families and society were all too ready to label as 'schizzy'.

R.D. Laing and Aaron Esterson's ground-breaking *Sanity, Madness and the Family* (1964), without drawing attention to any specificities of gender, focused on the cases of eleven women in two pseudonymous institutions, East Hospital and West Hospital. Laing and Esterson's starting point is that schizophrenia is not a biochemical, neurophysiological or even psychological fact. Seen within the 'phenomenology' of family life, it emerges as an 'intelligible' response to the interaction of its members. The experience and behaviour of women labelled as 'schizophrenic' – the wildness, the content of the voices, the non sequiturs – make complete sense when apprehended within the family system.

In Britain, unlike America, the assault on psychiatry was often enough launched from a psychoanalytic stance. Since the talking therapies and their underlying hypotheses had rarely been combined with medical psychiatry in institutional treatment here, Laing's initial position was that the first could act as a corrective to the second, which had far too long relied on medication and shock treatment, as well as damaging power relations between doctor and patient. The drug-giving, lobotomizing, ECT-using, diagnostic psychiatrists with whom Laing and his colleagues had trained and worked throughout their lives needed correction from various psychoanalytic and existential stand-points. Only thus could sense be made of what looked like madness, which was in fact a condition produced by family and society and exac-erbated by the evils of confinement and psychiatric treatment.

MADNESS, SANITY AND THE FAMILY

Laing and Esterson's eleven cases were aged between fifteen and forty and had been diagnosed as 'schizophrenic' by at least two senior psy-chiatrists. The women had no organic condition that might have affected their actions, nor were they of 'subnormal' intelligence. They had had no brain surgery and had received no more than fifty electro-shocks in the last year (which effectively means one a week) and no more than 150 in all. After that, the suggestion is, there would be visi-ble deterioration. The coolness with which the selection criteria are noted points to the radical physical treatments that patients were sub-mitted to as a matter of course in the mid-fifties, the era from which these cases come.

Maya, twenty-eight, had spent nine of her last ten years in West Hospital. An only child, initially very close to her father, the manager of a general store, she had lived with her parents until the age of eight, had then been evacuated and returned home at the age of fourteen. A month before her hospital admission, she had suddenly told her parents that her headmistress wanted her to leave school. She had also begun to imagine her father was trying to poison her, certainly get rid of her. Unravelling the clinical description of Maya's 'affective impoverish-ment', her 'autistic withdrawal', lack of ego boundaries, depersonalization, auditory hallucinations and impulsiveness, Laing and Esterson describe a young woman who experiences herself as a machine rather than a person. She has no sense of her 'motives, agency and intentions belonging together'. She speaks with 'scrupulous cor-rectness': her thoughts are controlled by others; her voices often do her thinking for her.

Almost fifty hours of interviews were held with the patient and her family in different configurations, the majority of them with mother and daughter together. What emerges is a riveting portrait of how a girl's need for autonomy once she returns to the family home at the age of fourteen fills her parents with alarm. Maya's desire to read alone, her refusal to swim or walk with her father, her efforts to separate herself from them, are interpreted as her being difficult, or selfish, or greedy, or as part of her frowned-on 'forwardness', and in retrospect as 'illness'. She in turn experiences her parents as intrusive, complicit, disapproving, at once patronizing and anxious about her so that she has to assuage their concern. They are ambivalent about her cleverness, both want it and see it as 'too clever perhaps'. She feels they laugh at her when she wants to read, though they deny this, only to ask, 'Why do you want to read the Bible, anyway?'

In interview, they enact the double bind. They continuously disavow Maya's lived reality, both past and present, contradicting her perceptions and experience, so that she grows confused. They exchange glances, winks and gestures which they deny exist, so that Maya 'mistrusts her own mistrust' of them. When she has tried in the past to tell them her sexual thoughts, they asserted that she didn't and couldn't have any and even during interview when she acknowledges it, they deny that she masturbates. They insist so regularly she has powers of mind-reading and telepathic exchange with her father, that she no longer trusts her own thoughts as her own.

It emerges that all the 'signs' and 'symptoms' that the psychiatric world would regard as 'caused' by Maya's pathology are induced by her parents, who undermine her at each possible occasion and refuse to acknowledge her separateness:

> Not only did both her parents contradict Maya's memory, feelings, perceptions, motives, intentions, but they made attributions that were themselves curiously self-contradictory, and, while they spoke and acted as though they knew better than Maya what she remembered, what she did, what she imagined, what she wanted, what she felt, whether she was enjoying herself or whether she was tired, this control was often maintained in a way which was further mystifying . . . The close investigation of this family reveals that her parents' statements to her about her, about themselves, about what they felt she felt they felt, and even about what could directly be seen and heard, could not be trusted.[325]

It is hardly surprising that Maya withdraws to repudiate a world in which she can't read the signs. Her schizophrenic behaviour is a response to the social reality she has experienced.

Laing and Esterson structure their reports of these cases so as to underscore that what in an ordinary family might be seen as normal development or reaction on a child's part is here understood and reinforced as aberrant and gradually becomes the 'illness'. Lack of recognition or acknowledgement of the growing child's experience and need for independence can indeed induce that 'illness', which the doctors, in unwitting collusion with families, then label schizophrenic and proceed to reinforce.

Sarah's parents, the Danzigs, Orthodox Jews, listen in to their daughter's phone calls, secretly investigate the boys she goes out with. Her reading the Bible at night is translated as laziness, whereas the very fact of her thinking seriously worries them: 'Sitting up all night thinking and not telling anyone what she thought. Not that we particularly want to know what Sarah's thinking or doing, although it's only natural that a mother should be curious . . . She's thinking and thinking . . . It's enough to twist anybody's mind.'[326] Sarah's mind was duly twisted.

Not so very much had changed in cultural attitudes towards women's intellectual work, it seems, from 1887 to the 1950s. Then, Charlotte Perkins Gilman, the now famous author of that document of women's madness, *The Yellow Wall-paper*, and suffering from a postnatal depression, was finally released from Weir Mitchell's rest cure only to be instructed to 'Live as domestic a life as possible . . . Have but two hours' intellectual life a day. And never touch pen, brush or pencil as long as you live.'[327]

Claire's mother insists that she knows her daughter's feelings better than she does. She mystifies Claire by constantly shifting her position on things, negates and muddles her meanings in conversation, so that nothing can be criticized or attacked. Her own omissions and hypocrisies destroy Claire's inner world and render her speechless.

Ruby has bangings inside her head and voices outside calling her 'slut', 'dirty'. One moment she says her mother loves her, the next that she is trying to poison her. People lie on top of her at night to have intercourse with her, and she has given birth to a rat. Her sense of reality is in shreds. It turns out that two months before admission she has had a miscarriage. The family lives a texture of lies, hiding the fact of Ruby's own illegitimacy from her, though everyone else knows: in this extended family ménage her biological father (who doesn't live with them) is known to Ruby as Uncle; her mother as Mummy, her aunt as Mother, her Uncle as Daddy, her cousin as Brother. The family unite in trying to make her feel both 'mad and bad' when she perceives what is going on beneath the chatter about this 'lovely family' who are 'really good' to her.

Ruth, twenty-eight, who has been hospitalized six times, was, according to her parents the Golds' account, a happy, considerate, respectful, normal child, who had never posed any problems until her sudden and unaccountable breakdown at the age of twenty. She then became inexplicably uncontrollable, abusive, resentful, dressed 'strangely' and tried to 'ape' her brother who was a writer. The sum of these descriptions makes up what her parents and the doctors name as Ruth's 'illness'. It emerges that Ruth's mother has secretly, and without admitting it to herself, stepped in to cut off Ruth's first love affair in parallel with what her own mother had done to her sister, also named Ruth, many years earlier. The act resulted in the sister's suicide. After her mother's breaking up of her relationship, Ruth attempts to live a less limited, 'bohemian' life, not unlike her brother's, but these attempts are labelled 'illness' by her family. While her account is being written, Ruth has returned home to live with her parents. When the interviewer asks her if she feels she has to 'agree with what most of the people round you believe', she answers, ' Well, if I don't, I usually land up in hospital.'

The hospital or asylum was where many young women 'landed up' in these difficult decades of the fifties and sixties when doctors read normality off a code book that had strict and repressive rules for women. Both Sylvia Plath and Anne Sexton,[328] who like Plath had a trajectory of psychiatric 'illness' and suicide, expose the way in which the existing limits of sanity disavow their own experience as women. In several of her early novels, where she charts histories of breakdown, Doris Lessing evokes madness as an appropriate response to an impossible situation. Breakdown is an honest reaction when life as it is lived at every turn contradicts both what people say is the case and the accepted rules of behaviour.

But what was it about Laing's own trajectory that made him so astute and radical a listener to the voices of these women, even if he never understood their experience as being particularly tied in with their gender?

R.D. Laing (1927–89)

R. D. Laing, whose widely read books – in particular, *The Divided Self* (1960), *The Politics of Experience and the Bird of Paradise* (1967) – catapulted him into being a hero of the counterculture, was born into the rough Glasgow neighbourhood of the Gorbals to lower-middle-class Presbyterian parents who seemed so astonished at his conception that his mother hid her pregnancy until just before Ronald David was due and went into a decline after his birth. His father was an electrical engineer and the principal baritone of the Glasgow University Chapel Choir. Paternal beatings, a cruel maternal discipline, sexual repression, together with a fastidious Puritanism in relation to food, characterized a childhood so difficult that perhaps without the recourse to music, avid reading and the attention of good teachers, Laing would have suffered the 'schizophrenia' of his later patients. For many years he shared a room with his mother, who insisted that she could read her child's mind to fathom any lies – a claim he tested by lying. The 'fear and trembling' of this experience, the punishments meted out, are key to the existential fragmentation Laing evokes in *The Divided Self*. Parental denial of the child's reality, 'knots', double binds and a kind of double-think which claimed love where there was hate – what he later called a deep-programming against living – were part of the coercive and unloving atmosphere his mother created.

But an adolescent Laing shored up childhood vulnerability with the rigours of philosophy, literature and the classics. He found heroes in the *Dictionary of National Biography*. This wide reading is evident in all his later books. Arguably not unlike Freud, his considerable literary gifts as a writer of harrowing scenes from family life and the inner adventures of the modern soul are key to the contagious spread of his ideas in the late sixties.

After studying medicine at Glasgow University, Laing in 1951 began

National Service and served as a lieutenant at the British Army Psychiatric Unit at Netley until 1953. There was a particular horror to the neurosurgical ward there. Patients had been placed into deep insulin comas, which narrowly avoided the epileptic fit the treatment could so easily induce. Since 'light is extremely epileptogenic under a lot of insulin', the ward was entirely blacked out and the stomach tubes through which the waking glucose would be poured had to be administered with only a torch strapped to the head. With patients whose veins were completely collapsed, finding the right target was hardly easy. The roots of Laing's anti-psychiatry were firmly laid down during these years: the patients he treated here, the padded cell in which he spent the night in trying to understand a patient, Peter, whom he took home with him, despite the diagnosis of schizophrenia, so as to save him from ECT, made their way into his first book.

From 1953, Laing completed his psychiatric training in the women's wards of the Gartnaval Royal Mental Hospital. Here he experimented with a special 'Rumpus Room' – an early version of Kingsley Hall (see page 000) – in which refractory patients could both be quiet and receive more attention as well as participate in activities – knitting, drawing, music. Both his early postings underlined for Laing the radically dictatorial powers psychiatrists had over their patients' lives as well as the paradox, from the patients' side, of treatments that could be both feared and sought.

In his final book *Wisdom, Madness and Folly*, part memoir, part reflection on psychiatry, Laing returned from his wilder views of madness as psychedelic prophecy to reflect on the problems of his profession. Psychiatry is unique, he noted, in that it treats people physically in the absence of any known physical pathology, often treats them against their will, and imprisons them if it judges necessary. Yet who is to fulfil a function that society wants fulfilled, if not the psychiatrist?

It is not easy. What do we do when we don't know what to do? I want that guy out of sight, out of sound, out of mind . . . The situation keeps cropping up in our society, when, no matter how liked, esteemed or loved, some people become insufferable to others. No one they know wants to live with them. They are not breaking the law, but they arouse in those around them such urgent feelings of pity, worry, fear, disgust,

anger, exasperation, concern, that something has to be done. A social
worker or psychiatrist is 'brought in'.[329]

There is a 'consumer demand' for the service psychiatry provides, Laing
notes in the language of the eighties. If psychiatrists don't perform it,
the police or some other body will. But if the psychiatrists take on the
task of changing 'undesirable states of mind and forms of conduct into
less undesirable or even desirable ones', the point has to be to do so
humanely.

Laing decided he would not do to patients what he wouldn't want
done to himself. The politics of humane relationship needed to enter
the psychiatric hospital, where violence, in the name of cure, and an
authoritarian medical structure inflicted the very condition it intended
to treat. Diagnosis itself, as Laing describes so powerfully in his first
book *The Divided Self*, prevented apt treatment: 'in his eagerness to find
signs and symptoms, the psychiatrist has not time to simply try and
understand the patient'.[330]

For Laing, the schizophrenic patient is someone who has never been
born into full existence: she is 'ontologically insecure', terrified that
the world will implode or that she will turn to stone, and so hides her
frightened, chaotic true self, instead offering to the world a compliant,
ambassadorial, false self.

The Divided Self ends with Laing leaving his post as Senior Registrar at
the Southern General Hospital to take up a job at the Tavistock Clinic
and to train at the Institute of Psychoanalysis. Here his analyst was
Charles Rycroft, who later chortled that, for all Laing's anti-psychiatry,
he himself had resigned from the British Psychoanalytical Society long
before his famous analysand. Laing's training supervisors were Marion
Milner and Donald Winnicott. The influence of Winnicott's writings on
Laing is everywhere evident in *The Divided Self*, which Laing sent to
Winnicott before its eventual publication with a letter noting that in
describing the transition from 'a sane to a mad way of being in the
world' he had drawn his 'inspiration largely from your writings'.[331]

Despite this and for all his evident brilliance, Laing was never wholly
accepted by an increasingly conservative British Psychoanalytical
Society: there was malaise over his more radical pronouncements, even
though Laing's initial anti-psychiatry was fed from within their own

ranks. Indeed, the training committee itself was split over Laing's qual-
ification: for all his knowledge, they felt 'Dr Laing is apparently a very
disturbed and ill person and wondered what the effect of this obvious
disturbance would be on patients he would have to interview'.[332] Laing's
later experiments with the hallucinogenic LSD with patients, as well as
his problems with drink in the last decade of his life, may well have fulfilled the worst fears of the conservatives on the committee. But during
the sixties and early seventies, while the Vietnam War raged and the
counterculture grew, the potency of Laing's analysis made of madness
a radical politics. The 'psychedelic psychiatrist' who thought of schizophrenia as a kind of epiphany, far superior to normal experience,
became a prophet of that counterculture.

In 1962, while on a research visit to the United States, Laing met the
Cambridge anthropologist Gregory Bateson, whose ideas on the double
bind fed directly into his thinking on the genesis of schizophrenia. Since
1956, Bateson had been publishing papers on a specific pattern of disturbed communication in which one member of the family is subjected
to a pair of conflicting injunctions, or 'binds', in a situation from which
there is no escape. For example, the mother persistently repeats that
sweets are bad for the child, but offers them as rewards. The child loses
out in both instances. Choices in double binds are always part of a
lose–lose game. The child begins to avoid interaction and to lose confidence in the validity of her own perceptions. The groundwork for
schizophrenia is laid down.

On Laing's return from America, an anti-psychiatry group coalesced.
It included the South African psychiatrist David Cooper, with whom
Laing was to write *Reason and Violence*, an introduction to Sartre's philosophical thinking; the American, Joseph Berke, and Aaron Esterson, a
fellow Glaswegian. All were hospital doctors who found work in the
existing mental health system demoralizing. They formed themselves
into the Philadelphia Association and established, in 1965, an alternative:
an anti-psychiatry unit in Kingsley Hall in London's East End. Here,
instead of the shock and drug treatment the hospitals provided, patients
could in theory travel back to childhood and reforge the early experience which had left them psychically maimed, in order to become
creative adults.

From a speech delivered at London's Institute of Contemporary Arts in January 1964, it becomes clear that Laing's thinking had evolved. The illness of the times was normality, not schizophrenia. He was now the guru of an age in which madness was the signal of a revolutionary strategy.

> From the moment of birth, when stone-age baby confronts the twentieth-century mother, the baby is subjected to forces of outrageous violence, called love, as its mother and father have been and their parents and their parents etc, mainly concerned with destroying most of its potentialities. This enterprise on the whole is successful. By the time the human being is 15 or so, we are left with a being like ourselves. A half-crazed creature, more or less adjusted to a mad world. This is the normality of our age.[333]

In this new understanding, schizophrenia was no longer a psychiatric condition, an illness produced by a disabling family life, but an indictment of the 'one-dimensional' imperialist world's violence and limitations which repressed both sexuality and transcendence. Schizophrenia was a stage in a psychic healing process. It contained the hope of an entry into a mystical 'hyper-sanity'.

Kingsley Hall was the sympathetic space in which the cyclical voyage which led to an existential rebirth could take place. The Hall's star patient, Mary Barnes, was a veteran of psychiatric hospitals, something of a career patient who had been subject to ECT and drug treatment time and again. She had applied for and been refused analysis with Anna Freud. Under Dr Joseph Berke she regressed to nappy-wearing infancy, created her famous 'shit paintings', smearing her faeces over the walls of the increasingly chaotic but internationally infamous Kingsley Hall, only to re-emerge from the ardour of the anti-psychiatry cocoon as the artist she had always wanted to be. The story of her case, written in two versions within one book by Berke and herself, is an instance of the new democracy of anti-psychiatry.

Laing and his colleagues destigmatized madness for the sixties and gave it the cachet of a rite of passage for troubled souls. Schizophrenia became an intelligible response to harrowing existential conditions, nurtured in the family and in a troubled society. In two of Doris Lessing's novels of the period, *The Golden Notebook* and *The Four-Gated City*, breakdown and madness function as radical stimulants to new insight. Madness provides an alternative way of seeing to be set against the cold, repressive world of Establishment normality. The doctors' antipsychotics – aimed at inducing a zomboid, controllable normalcy – are to be rejected at all costs.

But Laing 's therapeutic practice was more problematic than literary versions of journeys into madness could suggest. Kingsley Hall might be a site where the disturbed could 'safely get in touch' with their earliest selves and supposedly come out the other end, after a not illiberal quantity of hallucinogenics were imbibed by both doctor and patient. But the wild tripping was rarely as safe as all that. In fact, it was often downright dangerous. It could provoke ugly behaviour and encourage breakdown – as the original of Anna Wulf's American lover in *The Golden Notebook*, Clancy Sigal, learned and later evoked in his satirical novel *Zone of the Interior*. Sigal had initially gone to Laing for a conventional analysis to overcome his writer's block. He had followed Laing to Kingsley Hall and fled in the midst of a drug-exacerbated breakdown. *Zone*, deemed libellous by publishers, remained unpublished in Britain for years. Sigal's Meditation Manor is an unruly and dangerous place: its charismatic head is a tripping, irresponsible, egomaniacal Dr Willie Last. Its schizophrenic 'existential guerrillas ' are fought over while doctors, oblivious to yet-to-be-invented sexual politics, vie for the most attractive patients; and while Mary Barnes, the real-life schizophrenic star, lives in a corrugated tin tank in the cellar of Kingsley Hall where her nursing includes regular hosing down.

Laing himself moved off the premises before the end of the Hall's five-year lease, which was not renewed. The experiment was not one to be replicated. But the experience led to the creation of a series of halfway houses, alternatives to asylums, safe points on the way out of institutionalized life for schizophrenic patients still needing attention. Indeed, such halfway houses held out the promise of more humane treatment and a partial integration into society. Once the asylums began to shut down in the seventies, these halfway houses could have benefited from an expansion which sadly never took place, though Laing's colleague Aaron Esterson created the model Arbours Association, which still runs three houses.

*

The shutting down of asylums in Europe and in the USA had as much to do with government cutbacks and a general attack on outmoded institutions as with a specific anti-psychiatric impetus. Most important to their demise, however, was the contemporaneous rise of new drugs such as the antipsychotic chlorpromazine (Thorazine) and the mood stabilizer lithium used in manic depressive illness, or bipolar disorder. These could keep the most visible signs of madness – psychotic mania – under control. Treating madness through outpatient centres was now a real possibility.

After an initial use by Henri Laborit at the Val de Grâce Military Hospital, the first to pioneer chlorpromazine was the Sainte-Anne in Paris, where Jacques Lacan and Clérambault had worked. Henry Ey, its head and founder in 1950 of the World Psychiatric Association, together with Jean Delay, inventor of the term 'psychopharmacology', and Pierre Deniker introduced it to patients here in 1952 and found that it calmed mania and returned reason.[334] Testing its efficacy on nine patients, they discovered chlorpromazine to be far superior to ECT and insulin and less dangerous. By 1953, a psychiatric revolution was under way. In a moment as radical as the one in which Pinel had relieved patients of chains, the howls and the straitjackets of the mental ward became things of the past.[335]

An experimenter on various fronts, Delay in the fifties also gave Jacques Lacan space at the Sainte-Anne to hold his increasingly influential and popular seminars. Here, until 1963 when Lacan moved to the College de France, the 'return to Freud' was teased out. But by 1968 things had changed, and Delay was seen as a reactionary. It was his office at the University of Paris that the May 1968 students attacked, seeing in his brand of newly successful psychiatry a bastion of the imprisoning social order that demanded toppling. Psychiatry, for them, was the sadistic twin of CIA mind-control and brainwashing experiments, the kind Ewan Cameron had notoriously carried out in Montreal, and which they understood as synonymous with Delay's culture of psychopharmacology.

In Germany the greatly respected psychoanalyst Alexander Mitscherlich's books, The Inability to Mourn and The Fatherless Society, became key in the nation's attempts to deal with its unpalatable Nazi past. These functioned during the sixties as ' banners and slogans for a newly coalesced psychoanalytically informed social vision' which affected mass society and the whole West German educational system.[336]

In Italy, Franco Battaglia, who had been director of vast asylums in Gorizia and Trieste, led a distinctly political 'Democratic Psychiatry Movement'. This resulted in the passing of the famous Law 180 in 1978, which saw the closing of the large asylums. The United States under its seemingly progressive Community Mental Health Center Act of 1963 had opened some 640 local centres in which de-institutionalized patients could be treated and low-cost outpatient care made readily available. Sadly, there were insufficient funds and insufficient centres to meet demand. Poor, lonely, disoriented people with few social or work skills were left to roam the streets, often a danger to themselves and sometimes to others. Similarly in Britain, the movement to provide 'care in the community', from the 1970s on and under various governments, all too often led to the discharging of patients into no care anywhere.

For all the interest of its writings and its cultural status, the new anti-psychiatry could promise no more stability for its treatments and cures than the less humane physical/chemical therapies or more traditional talking therapies had done. Mary Barnes herself, when in 1977 she came to the opening of David Edgar's stage adaptation of her and Joseph Berke's book about her 'case', admitted to recurring acute attacks of depression and withdrawal.[337]

After the sixties peak of the Dialectics of Liberation conference which brought together black leaders, psychiatrists and political thinkers, Laing left Britain and – like his contemporary cultural heroes, the Beatles – the blighted materialism of the West to travel East in search of spiritual enlightenment. As it did for so many of the period's celebrities, the tripping, drugs and alcohol took their toll. In the seventies Laing produced little that had the audacious mark of his earlier work. He became a casualty of the very culture he had helped to create. When he returned to the ICA at my invitation in the eighties, it was to talk to the American poet Allen Ginsberg and meditate with him to the beat of an Indian drum: the event was a pastiche of a ritual which no longer carried its radical origins. On another occasion, in 1985, when he discussed his memoir, it was clear that he had more or less returned to the initial moment of his anti-psychiatric project, leaving behind the romantic terms of the spiritual journey of the schizophrenic and the political impetus to cull universal insights from the schizophrenic mind. In his last books, Laing once more emphasized his attempt to make the speech of the schizophrenic intelligible and to provide compassionate treatment for the disturbed. No longer the guru, he became once more the reforming doctor – one who couldn't quite heal himself.

In conversations recorded before his death at the age of sixty-one on a Saint-Tropez tennis court in August 1989, Laing described his own therapy thus: 'You could call some of it psychoanalytic, some of it existential, some of it gestalt, some of it psychosynthesis, some of it primal – all these little bits and pieces were all fragments of an integrated whole array of possibilities.'[338] At the end Laing had returned to the starting point of his critique of psychiatry – the talking therapies rather than the physical ones were the most humane of possible treatments.

If the spiritual adventure of Laing's latter-day schizophrenic trips lost its glow in the sobering light of the later seventies, this didn't diminish his and the anti-psychiatrists' impact. Whatever their therapeutic successes or failures, their influence is still there to be read. Setting out to make schizophrenia intelligible, Laing ended up not only destigmatizing madness, but making its 'language' available and in some measure glorifying it. Paradoxically this not only helped to make the mad feel more kin and made crises or breakdowns more acceptable, but fed into the ageing century's increased willingness to read unhappiness and malaise in terms of symptoms. Never mind Freud's neuroses – psychotic symptoms, too, were now to become part of the growing democratic repertoire of illness. Schizophrenia, anorexia, PTSD, manic depression, multiple personality disorder, obsessive-compulsive disorder – even these terrible diagnoses, by making the unbearable seem intelligible in a name and an ordered set of symptoms, gradually took on the glow of fashion

The scorpion's sting in the tale of anti-psychiatry was that paradoxically, it helped turn everyone into a patient. This was not the cowed patient of old but a patient who could be on increasingly equal terms with a doctor, even if both were women.

WOMEN REBEL

Laing and his colleagues had paid little attention to the gender-speci-
ficity of their patients' problems. But their descriptions of the lives of
women unwittingly brought women's very specific plight into dramatic view. Through the eyes of hindsight, their patients, from the
hospitalized schizophrenics to Mary Barnes, seemed to cry out both
for explicitly gendered consideration and for liberation. Nor were the
sexual politics of the doctors themselves any more enlightened than
those of the sixties radicals in general. The sexual revolution, for all its
emphasis on freeing desire, more often than not meant freeing male
desire. Women paid for this in many indeterminate ways, some large,
some small, whether they were patients or not. The anti-psychiatrists'
radical attack on social control and the structures of power both in
and out of the asylum hardly extended to their unexamined control
over women. Laing himself had ten children and three wives, and along
with David Cooper, who advocated 'bed therapy', exemplifies what
Elaine Showalter described as the fundamental anti-psychiatric constellation: a 'combination of charisma in the male therapist and
infantilism in the female patient'.[339]

For the women's movement, which championed before all else
taking control of one's own life, including its sexuality, it now grew
evident that what men, doctors, and the world they had created had
always done was to drive women mad by limiting their possibilities – by
insisting on their sexual identity and their secondary status, by turning
them into the 'seen' of the clinical, voyeuristic gaze, which was
inevitably interiorized, so that a persecutor inhabited every woman.

The feminists of the late sixties and seventies set out to wake women
from the long sleep during which they had acquiesced to their secondary status. They did so not only in terms of economic and social power,
though these were primary. Psychological characteristics, attributed to
them by the patriarchy, had been naturalized and internalized as truth.
Where men were active producers, women were passive reproducers
and care-givers. Where they utilized rational intelligence, women's lot
was the emotions. The only dream permissible in this long night of
inferior status was the enslaving fantasy of romance, which would bring

woman to her acquiescent knees before the godlike glory that was phallic maleness.

Simone de Beauvoir had set down her encyclopaedic tablets in 1948–9: translation into English came in 1953. *The Second Sex* punctured the myths of femininity and deftly showed how woman had always been defined in relation to man – a secondary term, the other to his absolute, the object to his subject. Her agenda for women underscored independence and freedom, that ultimate existentialist goal. Happiness, an American pursuit, was not a stated part of the picture. De Beauvoir attacked, if not psychiatry, then the one related form of it which had philosophical status: psychoanalysis and its inventor Sigmund Freud, who stands in for a way of seeing, despite an elusive fluidity which irritates the rigorous French philosopher she is. She begins, however, by applauding Freud's exemplary recognition that the body does not exist simply as the biologist's object. It is the body as lived in and experienced by the human subject that is significant, the cultural body. It follows that a woman is female only to the extent that she feels herself such. Change that experience, and woman could be free, her destiny unshackled from biology and anatomy.

But having understood this, de Beauvoir argues, Freud then falls into the patriarchal trap and makes the phallus both signifier and actual subject of power. He bases his world on a masculine model which inevitably results in woman emerging as castrated, a mutilated man, envious of the penis and of an authority she doesn't possess. Elevating his views to the position of a universal truth, Freud gives them the legitimacy and inevitability of fact, thus positing a determining force which removes choice from the world. He fails to see that the primacy attributed to the phallus is a historical construct: 'if woman should succeed in establishing herself as subject, she would invent equivalents of the phallus'.[340]

Betty Friedan and Kate Millett in America, Germaine Greer and Juliet Mitchell in Britain, amongst many others, took up the feminist baton. The first pointed out the part Freud's psychoanalysis, in particular, had played in women's oppression in America.

Freud was accepted so quickly and completely at the end of the forties that for over a decade no one even questioned the race of the educated

American woman back to the home . . . After the depression, after the
war, Freudian psychology became much more than a science of human
behavior, a therapy for the suffering. It became an all-embracing
American ideology, a new religion . . . Freudian and pseudo-Freudian
theories settled everywhere, like fine volcanic ash.[341]

Relegated to depression-inducing routines of housewifery, to the
masochism and passivity which the influential psychoanalyst Helene
Deutsch had laid down as basic to female sexual make-up, women
developed the 'problem with no name' which was variously treated by
drugs, alcohol, ECT and psychotherapy. Now women needed to expose
the forces that had created their condition. Principal amongst these,
Kate Millett noted, even before the publication of her important *Sexual
Politics* (1970), was the category ploy of the 'individual case' begat by
Freud and his 'very private science'. This undercut an engagement in
sexual politics, the very possibility of women acting as the collectivity
they in fact were. It condemned sexual relations to an endless series of
unique instances and converted resistance to sterile stereotypes of
motherhood and wifeliness into neurosis. Any woman who dared not
to conform was 'clearly off her nut'.[342]

For Millett, Freud was the 'strongest individual counter-revolutionary force in the ideology of sexual politics', the man who 'clothed the
old doctrine of separate spheres in the fashionable language of science'.
Betraying his initial radical insights into sexuality and the need for liberation, he had effectively been responsible for the demise of the first
wave of feminism by turning protest into illness.

Feminism, particularly in America, which valued empirical research,
could also draw fuel from Masters and Johnson's physiological proof
that Freud and the psychoanalysts had been altogether mistaken in
their views on what constituted mature female sexuality. The developmental model which stated that clitoral satisfaction was replaced in
the well adjusted adult woman by vaginal orgasm was hokum.
Feminists officially declared the vaginal orgasm a myth and with it that
psychoanalytic diagnosis of 'frigidity'. The contraceptive pill was the
technology of liberation. It freed women's sexuality from the age-old
hold of reproduction. Women were now free to listen to their own
bodies, and freed to a measure of control over childbirth. They no

longer had to strive for what the shrinks laid down in terms either of
sexual pleasure or of female roles.

Phyllis Chesler, a psychologist, brought the feminist critique more
closely into line with the anti-psychiatry project. In *Women and Madness*
(1972) she questioned the very construct that was mental illness and
argued, using historical examples, that it was an expression both of
female powerlessness and of the attempt to overcome it. Symptoms of
mental illness, Chesler argued, were directly linked to conventional
understandings of masculinity and femininity. They were 'norm viola-
tions'. Any transgression of the core attributes of male and female
identity were understood as madness. But women were more likely
than men to be categorized as insane or ill for the simple reason that the
standards of health – independence, autonomy, objectivity, self-suffi-
ciency – ran counter to any description of a well adjusted woman, who
was meant to be submissive, emotional, dependent.

In a double bind of health and femininity, women could be labelled
crazy whether they rebelled against, or accepted, the feminine role.
Men, on the other hand, exceeding the demands of masculinity and
deviating from the norm, were more likely to be branded 'sociopathic'
or criminal. Stereotypical assumptions about the sexes therefore made
it inevitable that women would exhibit more symptoms of mental illness and be more often hospitalized. Institutions exacerbated women's
plight by subjecting them to the same degradation and disempower-
ment they suffered within the family. Chesler's interviews with
institutionalized women of all ages gave graphic examples of the ways
in which 'unfeminine' behaviour – 'troublesome, needy'- or indications of a 'fighting spirit' could land women in hospitals when families
couldn't or wouldn't keep them. Her interviews were backed up with
graphs of hospital and private clinic admissions, which clearly indicated
that even with corrections for population size and age, the number of
institutionalized women of all races exceeded that of men, often by as
much as 10 per cent or more; only in outpatient services for the under-
eighteens did men exceed women.[343]

The first wave of feminism had been closely entangled with Freud's
invention of psychoanalysis. The founding study in hysteria, Anna O,
the woman who had given the talking cure its name, had metamorphosed into Bertha Pappenheim, the altruistic women's leader who

had campaigned against the sexual exploitation of women and children throughout Europe and the Middle East. The philosopher Martin Buber had lauded her as that rarest being of all, a passionate spirit. Hysteria, rebellion and feminism, as women's liberation was quick to underline, were intricately linked: their sources lay in the same discontent. To express their anger at the circumscription of their lives, women got ill or got organized. Sometimes they did both in turn.

If the marriage of psychoanalysis and feminism sometimes looked like a Strindbergian dance of death, it was also often fruitful. Rethinking sexuality and gender in both personal and political terms, women from a variety of intellectual formations found themselves coming back to the crucible of psychoanalytic ideas.

Freud, in any number of manifestations, together with Lacan but also and increasingly Klein, Winnicott and the object-relations school, shadowed and informed the entire feminist project. In examining the construction of femininity, sometimes phallus and its reinterpretations were prioritized, sometimes breast. A startling number of key feminist thinkers – from France's Julia Kristeva to Juliet Mitchell in Britain – also became practitioners. Meanwhile, Freud's Dora and later Ladwig Binswanger's Ellen West, a troubled woman who died while refusing food, took on the aura of patron saints: women who through body and psyche had rebelled against the patriarchal doctors. As women's studies began to take shape, feminists recovered a history which needed to be voiced or reinterpreted. Virginia Woolf provided an early lead. In *Three Guineas* she had written, 'the public and private worlds are inseparably connected . . . the tyrannies and servilities of one are the tyrannies and servilities of the other'. 'The personal is political', as one of the key slogans of the early seventies had it, was already enmeshed in her work, as it was in women's experience.

In her early book, *Women's Estate* (1971), Juliet Mitchell noted that the first step on the path from an individual complaining woman towards the creation of a women's political movement was the consciousness-raising group. It was through women meeting together to share the 'unspecified frustration of their own private lives' that the personal problem – abortion, a miserable sex life, the look of a body – became political. 'The process of transforming the hidden, individual fears of women into a shared awareness of the meaning of them as social problems, the release of anger, anxiety, the struggle of proclaiming the painful and transforming it into the political – this process is *consciousness-raising*'.[344]

Mitchell likens the process of consciousness-raising both to group therapy, a tag its critics needlessly deride it with, and to the Chinese practice of self-criticism, speaking 'bitter thoughts' in a group. 'Speaking the unspoken,' she notes, is, of course, also the 'purpose of serious psychoanalytic work.' Given that their condition has been made to seem 'natural', women's oppression is hidden from them, unconscious. Thus this task of consciousness-raising, which bears a distinct relationship to psychoanalytic practice, is both necessary and a political step.

Three years later Juliet Mitchell's influential *Psychoanalysis and Feminism* (1974) appeared and began the task of salvaging psychoanalysis and marking out Freud's crucial importance for the feminist project. Mitchell underlined the feminist fallacy of assuming a direct translation between the social order and the individual subject. There was no mirror that reflected one in the other. Women were not simple victims on which the social order inscribed itself: if that were the case there could be no escape from the patriarchal condition, no breaking of the mould of oppression. To give way to an essentialism, a fixed entity that was woman, forced woman into the position of being 'nature' to man's 'culture'. But both sexes, Mitchell argued, functioned in the cultural sphere. Freud had offered a theory of what it means to become woman. He had not trapped her in fixed, unchanging characteristics. Reinterpreted by Lacan, whom Mitchell followed in this respect, the 'penis' which Freud had understood women as 'envying' was the phallus of symbolic function, the signifier of sexual difference. Both sexes are marked out by their desire for its power. Both suffer from its lack. Lack (not unlike Freud's discontent) underpins both sexes' relation to 'civilization'. Psychoanalytic thinking, which posited a dynamic psychic reality and no gendered essentials, was women's best hope of escaping a reduction to essentialist terms.

Mitchell's stance, which refused a reading of women as passive victims and redeemed Freud as an important thinker, was more influential in Europe than in America until, through the eighties and nineties, academic feminism there took on and talked back to the masters of

French theory. Mitchell herself, after a degree in literature, trained at the British Psychoanalytical Society and became a practising psychoanalyst. But even in the United States, where Freud often acquired demonic proportions, a fair number of the early feminists took up one of the psy professions or returned to the field for theoretical formulations. In America, on the whole, they didn't train within the conventional institutes which, until 1989, required a medical degree. Instead they joined the looser, more multidisciplinary, university-based post-doctoral programmes, such as the one at NYU where Jessica Benjamin worked.

With their diverse backgrounds in the social sciences, literature or anthropology, these feminists brought new optics into psychoanalysis. From within the existing institutes women, emboldened by the wider social movement, challenged old models of therapy and began to insist on more 'relational' practices, an empathy with the patient's needs.[345] They helped to transform American psychoanalysis. Freud, who had been quite clear that he didn't like being the mother in transference and that women analysts worked better with pre-Oedipal matter, would have been pleased. He would also have applauded the rupture between psychoanalysis and medical psychiatry.

Chesler became a psychotherapist, and often appeared as an expert witness in cases where mad and bad needed distinguishing. The prominent feminist theorist Nancy Chodorow became an analyst. She found her mentors not in Freud, but in Karen Horney and Melanie Klein. Her highly influential *The Reproduction of Mothering* (1978) traced her contention that the gendered specificity of the mother–child relation made it harder for girls to separate from their mothers and made women more alert to relations so that they reproduced the mothering bond. The boy's core identity was constructed out of a repudiation of the mother and lay at the origin of the fear and hatred of women in Western culture. The only solution to this vicious circle was mothering by both sexes.

In Italy, the educational psychologist Elena Belotti in the bestselling *Little Girls* analysed the ways in which girls are prompted into secondary status and into little-womanhood by their mothers and teachers, their time at the breast briefer than boys', their hugs less ardent, their toys a preparation for mothering, which will entail the greater orderliness already demanded of them. Back in America, the psychologist Carol

Gilligan conducted research which underlined how gender-specific mothering created the different modes of being in the worlds of boys and girls. She showed how girls' morality is based on a sense of responsibility to others, whereas boys have a more mechanical ethics of rights and abstract notions of justice. Dorothy Dinnerstein's *The Mermaid and the Minotaur* argued that the power of the mother in infancy resulted in adults of both sexes in fear of women, and an internalized misogyny which made men repudiate closeness while women hated their own bodies and distrusted female power. In 1981 Alexandra Symonds founded the American Association of Women Psychiatrists, which looked at sexism within the profession.

Everywhere in Europe and America there was a refocusing on the female body and sexuality, so that old and all-but discarded diagnoses, such as Esquirol's puerperal madness and the links between erratic behaviour and menstruation, came back in a newly emphasized manner. To look at woman as woman, after all, meant to re-examine her difference from man, which lay first of all in the body and the way that body was lived   as the ground-breaking *Our Bodies, Ourselves* by the Boston Women's Health Book Collective did in 1971. In an opposing motion, by the late seventies and into the eighties other feminists — particularly those influenced by Lacan, such as Juliet Mitchel and Jacqueline Rose — refused gendered categories and set out to expose the arbitrary and constructed character of the binary opposition between male and female. As it was in language, gender here became an assigned and then internalized identity, not an essential or biological given.

With the spur of an increasing number of women in the profession, female madness from the seventies also took on a new variety of symptoms and diagnoses, as well as treatments. If these didn't always turn out to be very much kinder than the ones poor Mary Lamb had received two hundred years before, then at least symptom and diagnosis often came with a support group — modelled in part on the women's consciousness-raising groups of the seventies — rather than a solitary brother. What that astute critic of late-twentieth-century society, Philip Rieff, had called the 'emergent democracy of the sick' was taking hold. If the Freudian revolution had ushered in a stoical psychological model of the self, the 'therapeutic' model was now in ascendancy, with its newly trained hordes of professionals poised to answer and explain all needs.

Meanwhile, in a shadowy inversion of the trajectory in which mid-wives had historically been displaced by doctors, as women moved increasingly into the talking therapies in America the profile of the profession itself fell. The psychiatric wing emphasized its scientific and medicalized aspect and gradually shifted away from therapy into a 'harder' drug- rather than talk-oriented definition of mental illness and cure. Here the body of illness reverted to its centre in neuro-wiring and chemistry, and away from the 'softer' model of relational triggers or the search for meaning.

And although the number of women doctors increased many-fold in this period, and in the USA by 2002 women made up half of the medical student population (up from 9 per cent in the 1960s, when quotas for women were still in operation), the overall number of doctors special-izing in psychiatry fell. In 1979, *Time* had already noted: 'The U.S. has 27,000 psychiatrists in active practice, up from 5,800 in 1950. But now the bloom is off the therapeutic rose. Today only 4% to 5% of medical school graduates go into psychiatry, vs. 12% in 1970. Says one doctor: "Psychiatry is not where the action is."'[346]

Applications to the prestigious Columbia Psychoanalytic Clinic for Training and Research fell by 90 per cent from 1960 to 1980. In 1989, a resisting New York Psychoanalytic Society, propelled by the trend, had to open its doors to training lay analysts.

But if the American marriage between psychiatry, psychoanalysis and the psychotherapies was temporarily over, separation hardly dissi-pated the importance of the mind doctors overall. On the one hand, with the rise and rise of the new drug cures, there was a rush towards psychopharmacology. On the other, the psychotherapies proliferated. In December 1985, over seven thousand practitioners from around the world gathered in Phoenix, Arizona, for a meeting dedicated to the 'Evolution of the Psychotherapies'. They represented some twenty-seven different schools, from behavioural therapy to Freudian psychoanalysis. Heavyweights like R.D. Laing, Bruno Bettelheim and Thomas Szasz were there, along with Carl Rogers, the 'guru of Human Potential', and Virginia Satir, a Palo Alto family therapist who regularly drew audiences of two thousand.[347]

The anti-psychiatric rebels may have attacked the face of the profession. The result was that it had grown a few more. Group therapy received a new boost from the women's movement and was increasingly used in hospital as well as in outpatient and private settings for any number of psychological ills. Family therapy burgeoned, spurred by pre-war work with troubled children, but also by the anti-psychiatrists' findings about schizophregenic families. Each of these had a variety of orientations.

Meanwhile, patients or clients seemed increasingly in need or in pain. The very speed of cultural change in women's roles and expectations, the impact on men and assumptions about masculinity, the continuing contradictions of demands, desires and needs, the increase in images that bombarded the sex that had always been the object of the gaze – all this made the helping hand therapy of any kind offered seem essential. New freedoms made life more interesting, but not always any easier.

At the end of her history of women's mental illness in Britain, *The Female Malady*, Elaine Showalter had raised the hope that a new feminist psychology of woman together with a feminist therapy movement would liberate women from the chains of madness which 'obtuse and misogynistic' medical practice had kept them in, whatever their leading doctors', from Pinel's to Laing's, claims to freeing them. Whether that hope can still be kept in place is an open question. What is clear is that the increasing number of women involved in mind-doctoring both responded to, and helped create, new clusters of illness.

13

BODY MADNESS

I was just struggling to find my place, like anyone experiencing change, and nothing seemed certain anymore, except what I did or did not eat.[348]

Grace Bowman

The dizzy rapture of starving. The power of needing nothing. By force of will I make myself the impossible sprite who lives on air, on water, on purity.

Kathryn Harrison, The Kiss

Over a century has passed since Charcot had the Salpêtrière hysterics photographed. Posed for and captured by the new technology of the camera, their passionate attitudes, simultaneously erotic and saintly, played a part in initiating a local fashion in hysteria. These expressions and gestures also affected the actors of the silent screen, where they were in a sense normalized into histrionics and disseminated once more. Hysteria became every woman's expression of intense passion. Though now occasionally re-enacted as spectacle, the hysteria that has been transmuted into the disorder the *DSM* classifies as 'illness behaviour' has taken on other bodily manifestations. Simultaneously, the interaction of disorder, image and unconscious mimicry has taken on a new intensity.

Images now suffuse daily life in the West. From the high street to the shopping mall, from public to private space, from big to small to tiny mobile screen and all the paper surfaces in between, images surround us and invade our imaginations. Increasingly, the very same images circle the world, implanting themselves in minds and within cultures distant from their source of production. Whole new professions, technologies and burgeoning industries – from fashion to film, advertising to the World Wide Web, diet to food processing – depend on their unstoppable flow. Women's bodies, blown up to be larger than life or reduced to the smaller-than-lifeness of everyday TV screens, but always incarnating an idea of beauty, are a key part of that flow. They are also used to confer magic, that ineffable charm which is glamour, as elusive as a will o' the wisp to those who might be seduced into thinking that the bought commodity contains its extra-special happiness within itself. These immaterial bodies constantly seen, present from cradle to grave, inevitably impact on material ones. They can engender body madness.

Over the last thirty years, as the West's plenty increasingly separates it from famine and war zones, glamorous images of women have shed weight. In the victim-chic of post-colonial guilt, they echo the gaunt faces and shapes of famine-struck children – the ones who might somehow have survived into pubescence. Curves have disappeared, to be replaced by countable vertebrae and pin-thin arms and wrists. A once voluptuous turn of a shoulder is now a sharp-angled jab. The rounded, procreative body of a living woman has been displaced by that of a hunger-artist. By twenty-first century standards, the Marilyn Monroe of *Some Like It Hot* or the Brigitte Bardot of *And God Created Woman* are fat. They weigh in a good thirty pounds heavier than the clothes-hanger models of catwalk and soap screen.

These stars, from Calista Flockhart to Victoria Beckham, whose eating disorders are ever mooted and ever negated, or given that fashionable label of 'recovery', are the envied celebrities of teen magazines. Anorexia is the pet disorder of the fashionistas, invading the minds of girls as young as seven who, doctors report, are already affected by eating problems. On the Internet chat rooms of 'pro-ana' sites, 'thinspiration' is available for anorexics who would prefer to categorize their condition as saintly protest against the consumer culture rather than a mental disorder. Dieting for a hungry planet is confused with dieting for a smaller jeans size. Lost weight is celebrated, descriptions of fasting states and their attendant highs and lows exchanged, together with notes on how to hide unwanted food. Friendship is provided where it might otherwise not exist and, dangerously, that ultimate stage in the campaign, which is death, is cheered on.

Anorexics become the suicide bombers inside the bourgeois family. Their refusal of appetite and consumption marks them out as the perfect anti-capitalists.

In more conventional Net support groups for anorexia, fasting girls or their parents can obtain information on doctors and clinics, exchange notes on how to get help and how to survive an illness which kills in the region of 20 per cent of its subjects. For bulimics, that other even faster-rising category of food disorders amongst women, there are 'pro-mia' sites which specialize in tips on how to vomit more effectively and keep the condition secret from family and friends.

Meanwhile obesity, from young to old, is on the rise in America and Europe.[349] In 2004, reversing a prior policy, the US health department named it a 'disease', making health insurance and medical research monies available for its treatment. Using the Body Mass Index, defined as the ratio of the weight of a person in kilograms divided by the square of their height in metres, the World Health Organization in 1998 came up with a definition of overweight as a BMI of over 25 and obesity as a BMI of over 30. Marilyn Monroe's BMI moved between 21 and 24, so she was verging towards the overweight by today's standards. According to this scale to be underweight is to have a BMI below 18.5. In the past twenty years, the BMIs of *Playboy*'s centrefold have gone down from 19 to 16.5, while the average weight of an American female is un unprecedented 163 pounds (75 kilos); and 3.8 million people weigh in at over 300 pounds (136 kilos).[350]

This imposition of measured norms, backed by experts and by a pharmaceutical industry searching for the magic capsule of certain weight loss is one more way of 'making people up' as a classification, in this case 'obese', on the pretence that this is some kind of total identity.[351] In the UK the Royal College of Physicians, participating in the Western moral panic around obesity, has warned that 'if current trends continue, conservative estimates are that at least one-third of adults, one-fifth of boys and one-third of girls will be obese by 2020'. Being overweight, they underline, harms 'health, self-esteem and social life.[352] In Germany, obesity was declared an epidemic by the Consumer Affairs Minister in 2004: 'Every third child and every fourth teenager is massively overweight', as a result of inactivity and the fast food industry.[353] In the West, it seems that obesity is a property of the working class, or of ethnic groups who don't suffer from the compulsion to disavow the fleshy fruits of imperial gain.

Clearly, discrepancies between the idealized image of glamorous womanhood and the realities of fat and everyday life are huge and growing. Constant warnings from health authorities, prepared foods that carry contents lists more detailed than a lab report and flash their low-carb or low-fat banners, the fashion and diet industries – both worth billions – have all combined to create a situation in which fat is, for many girls, a nearer and greater terror than war; while thin is perfection, a dream sphere to be constantly sought in which all problems will magically vanish. With 'thin' come men, wealth and happiness. Fairy godmothers for the contemporary Cinderella carry slimming tablets rather than a wand.

Bodies may be made of hard matter but we perceive, understand and shape them in coded ways. A thin pop star with shorn hair on a billboard carries different meanings from a concentration camp survivor, no matter what the intended references. So, too, does the illness she may have. Our zealous concentration on food, on feasting or fasting, and the attendant body image, has given rise to a series of culture-bound psychopathologies, which, like hysteria, fold in crucial contradictions and core anxieties of time and place.[354] Most categories of mental illness, by their very basis in classifications which separate off sick from well, sane from insane, healthy from ill, are culturally linked. But particular illnesses, from their spiralling proportions in given historical periods together with the spiralling literature which surrounds them, are more clearly visible as expressions of the malaise of their times.

Since the 1980s this has been the case with anorexia nervosa, bulimia and the various conditions which rotate round their borders. They now have their own specialists, clinics and scientific apparatus, including (since 1981), an *International Journal of Eating Disorders* to investigate and communicate a field that has grown globally, shadowing the rise of McDonald's They have a popular culture of diet and self-help books, magazine columns and pop songs that lyricize the condition alongside that other teenage disorder of self-harm – again, more prevalent amongst women – to which eating problems are often linked: both are expressions of a woman's attack on her own body. Meanwhile, an academic culture has grown up alongside: histories – such as Catherine Bynum's *Holy Feast and Holy Fast* or Joan Brumberg's *Fasting Girls*, which uncovers the meanings of past fasts; and literary criticism which looks back, as Maud Ellmann writes in *The Hunger Artists*, to Kafka, Byron and Richardson (who, incidentally, was told to slim by that first great dietitian-doctor, George Cheyne). The eating disorders are illnesses of the McLuhan age, as Ellmann aptly notes, 'disseminated by telecommunications rather than contact'.[355]

Food fuels life and answers to that primary appetite of hunger. Like all appetites, humans sporadically attempt to control it. Food has always, also, carried a diversity of uses and meanings. It separates out insiders from outsiders, believers from non-believers. It can designate wealth and status or, served to a stranger, friendship and hospitality. It can signal love from mother to child, or communion between humans and God in a rite where it stands in, cannibalistically, for body and blood. Some of its transformations as it moves from raw to cooked, or penetrates the body to metamorphose from tantalizing titbit to excrement, retain their mystery even for sophisticated, information-weary adults. Food can succour and it can poison. It can make the female body mimic pregnancy or return to pre-pubescence. By an invisible process food alters the eater. That invisibility, itself, has always been a crucible for religion or science, let alone the imaginings of an adolescent girl.

Indeed, in the permissive West, eating has arguably now outstripped sex as the key psychic experience of the body. It underlies the sense we make of health and happiness, identity and destiny. The way we eat separates rich from poor, good from bad, moral from deviant, reward from punishment, thin from fat. Eating now has its attendant medical, scientific and psychiatric discourses, a code of moral prohibitions and injunctions. It has its perversions and its normality: its decadent, over-refined or over-processed and its natural or organic. It has its secret delights, sinful excess and social rituals, just as sex has masturbation, brothels and marriage. Nutritionists and dietitians invoke standards of health, investigate chemistry, invent a new expert language of contents and effects, always insisting on and changing what constitutes appropriate eating activity. Photographers, television cookery programmes, books and supermarkets fetishize, create food porn, while doctors warn and prohibit, invoking fresh terrains of science — from the effects of good and bad cholesterol to the hypothesis of a set-point mechanism, a kind of inner thermometer made up of genetic and metabolic factors, which regulates body weight and may account for the notorious failures of diet.

Food is no longer matter for simple home economics taught to high school girls. It is the very stuff of science and genetics, replete with scares and protests. A sure sign of its status is that male celebrity chefs have taken over the kitchens of the world, while aspirants to the now noblest profession write serious literary evocations of their stations of the cross on their own path to the altar of cuisine.[356] Needless to add that eating also has its own politics and power relations: from sanctions on food coming from ostracized countries to altruistic vegetarian purity and animal rights, to an enmeshment with a beauty industry which some have said sells 'thin' in order to enslave women, once more constricting their lives to their bodies. Hardly surprising, then, that psychic disorders related to eating have escalated radically from the 1980s on. And it is women, who as mothers have traditionally been the providers of food, from breast to table, despite the recent gender-bending of celebrity chefs, who are also most directly implicated in these disorders; though the number of men to be affected is rising.

ANOREXIA NERVOSA

Most prominent amongst these disorders and most intractable is the fasting disease anorexia nervosa, which commands such attention that it yields an astonishing fourteen million hits a year on the Internet. There are three times more sites for anorexia than for schizophrenia — the disorder which had such a metaphoric quality for the sixties. Anorexia is only topped in the Google lists by depression. The ubiquitous prominence of the disorder in the media, its many prize-winning memoirs of 'survivors', gives the condition the feel of an epidemic, even though the actual number of sufferers hardly constitutes epidemic size.

The figures, however, are bad enough. According to the American National Institute for Mental Health anorexia takes hold of from 0.5 to

3.5 per cent of the American female population. In the UK, the most cited figure is 0.1 per cent of women, or sixty thousand individuals. The worrying statistic is that the number of anorectics in America rose threefold through the nineties, while the most recent indicator in Britain shows a rise of 130 per cent in incapacity benefit claimed on the basis of eating disorders.[357] Whether this rise is linked to the guidebook effects of media and memoirs as well as more general cultural factors isn't clear, but it has resulted in the fashion industry responding to criticism and in certain countries banning skeletally thin models from the catwalk.

Anorexia and its slightly less intractable twin, bulimia, ravage girls' schools and campuses with fierce copycat mimicry and take a disproportionate toll on young lives; while its sister act, 'self-harm', follows suit — sometimes an indicator of suicidal wishes, at others, like an addiction, bringing release when confusion, a roller-coaster of incoherent emotions and pain, needs gouging out. 'I cut myself to get the pain out,' Kurt Cobain, lead singer of the grunge band Nirvana, famously said before committing suicide. Britain's self-harm figures are now the highest in Europe, and in 2004–5 some twenty-five thousand were severe enough to result in hospital admissions. Young women outnumber men by seven to one in these statistics, and Asian women are high in the figures.

The 'illness-patterns' that anorexia and bulimia now take are popularly known, but these have not always been fixed in diagnostic stone.

Anorexia nervosa was designated as a disease entity in the 1870s at the height of Victorian restrictions on women's possibilities. Fasting was hardly new. Deliberate self-denial and starving had long been part of the arsenal of sanctity: the holiness of women in the High Middle Ages was evidenced by their control of appetite and dedication to the Eucharist, wafer and wine miraculously providing the necessaries of existence. With secularization, fasting took on new meanings. No longer a saint, the girl engaged in starving as a means of self-definition and protest. Permitted, as Florence Nightingale so aptly noted in her book *Cassandra*, 'no food for our heads, no food for our hearts, no food for our activity', and with 'Our bodies . . . the only things of consequence', woman became a patient — or perhaps a hunger-striking suffragette.

Anorexia has its origins firmly in the particular conditions of the bourgeois family: relative affluence, a sexual division of labour making the domestic woman's realm, a template of parental love in which daughters are long infantilized, dependent and sexually ignorant, while being groomed for the competitive rites of courtship and marriage. Here a slim figure and the spirituality which a restrained appetite evokes are useful assets. Asceticism and purity are valued.

The term 'anorexia' sprang up all but simultaneously in France, Britain and the USA, to designate a condition of adolescent girls who refused to eat. Sir Willliam Gull (1816–90) a society doctor in London attached to Guy's Hospital, used the term to designate a 'morbid medical state' differing from tuberculosis – that other wasting disease accompanied by a lack of appetite. Anorectic patients were girls between sixteen and twenty-four who demonstrated, to begin with, an excessive energy. This eventually led to amenorrhoea and starvation. Rest, regular – if necessary, forced – feeding, and removal from the family were recommended treatments. William Smoult Playfair (1835–1908), a reputed obstetrician and gynaecologist, recognized the disease's prevalence but refused it a separate category status, subsuming it instead under neurasthenia.

In France, in 1873, the leading alienist Charles Lasègue classified anorexia as a 'hysteria of the gastric centre'. Interested in the psychological aspects of the condition, he wrote an influential paper which charted a progress from the anorectic girl's general uneasiness after eating and vague sensations of fullness, to a reduction in food intake on a variety of pretexts including headache, distaste or fear of pain, to the point when eating was reduced to almost nothing and the disease was declared. Hyperactive in the initial stages of the condition and able to pursue a 'fatiguing life in the world', the patient was obstinate about eating meals at home. Meanwhile, parents swung between spoiling the child with titbits, entreating and punishing. Lasègue aptly characterizes the discourse of love and rejection that food in the family takes on: the patient is 'besought, as a favour, and as a sovereign proof of affection, to consent to add even an additional mouthful to what she has taken; but this excess of insistence begets the excess of resistance'.[358] The daughter, dutiful in all ways but this, chose food as her form of rebellion against family love and as a troubled call for attention.

Though he never focused on anorexia at length, Freud stressed its prevalence: 'It is well known that there is a neurosis in girls . . . at the time of puberty or soon afterwards, and which expresses aversion to sexuality by means of anorexia.' He linked anorexia to other conditions, sometimes to melancholia or depression; or saw it as one of the manifestations of hysteria — as did most early analysts, given its greater incidence in girls on the cusp of womanhood. When the young woman refuses to eat, finding food disgusting and dangerous, she is also refusing that adult sexuality which will engage her in taking the other, the male, in, and in making babies, like her mother.

For Freud, as for Klein, eating and sexuality had a complicated relationship. The Freudian child, satiated by mother's breast, radiates a bliss which is the prototype of all sexual satisfaction.[359] Breast and milk, however, separate out, and the child has to lose the breast, this first object of desire, to form an idea of the whole person to whom this object that brings it satisfaction belongs and to form a sense of its own separateness. All future pleasures will be an attempt to find again this lost object, which always exceeds in scale and sense the food it produces. Eating maps out the zones of gratification that continue to bear the memory traces of maternal care. The child will retrace these within itself during a phase of auto-eroticism.

Klein's infant is a cannibal: it devours all the objects of the outer world to install them inside itself in fantasy, constructing its inner world by a process of incorporation. This inside can become a nightmarish tomb, the child's greed or need having made it devour too much so that these inner objects, these internalized parents, threaten in turn to devour the child, and rob it of all mastery.

Freud's gloss on femininity in his late essay on Female Sexuality (1931) offers a further clue to eating disorders. He argues, as he had before, that girls reproach their mothers for depriving them of a penis, but also — and here he seems to draw an equivalence between penis and breast — because 'the mother did not give them enough milk'.[360] He doubts that any quantity of food could satisfy the infantile libido. The passage has led later theorists to question whether femininity itself is structured on an insatiable need.[361]

For Klein, the mother is the storehouse of all hidden treasures — penis, food, babies — all of which the infant wants to devour. Split off and taken in so that it becomes part of the girl's identity, the mother's dangerous body is also a persecuting and far too powerful devouring object, which may demand excision by self-harm or elimination by puking, or starvation.

This linkage between sexuality, the mother's body, food, need and feminine identity plays through most of the contemporary accounts of anorexia. Interestingly, the therapy Freud notes for advanced anorexia is not in the first instance talk. Twice he warns that 'Psycho-analysis should not be attempted when the speedy removal of dangerous symptoms is required, as, for example, in a case of hysterical anorexia.'[362] The starving girl, whatever the origin of her symptoms, needs more radical help than psychotherapy can at first provide.

Sometimes, it seems, what she also needs, needs most of all, is social change – or so one could interpret the suffragette's use of self-starvation as a form of political protest. Needless to say, the hunger-striking suffragettes were not anorectic, but the fact that they turned to self-starvation, the most passive and conventionally feminine form of dissent and the one which needs no external tools, is emblematic of the closeness of food to women's armoury of protests as well as symptoms. If authority quelled that protest by the use of force-feeding, it only underlined what women already felt: reduced to body, even that body wasn't ultimately their own.

After the First World War, anorexia as a psychiatric disorder was less often noted. It re-emerged again in the sixties. Hilda Bruch (1904–84), a German Jewish doctor from one of the early generations of women to struggle their way into higher education and a medical degree, pioneered contemporary psychological explanations for 'eating disorders', the title of her 1973 book. Bruch had fled Nazi Germany to come first to Britain and then to the USA, where she worked with Theodore Lidz, theorist of the 'schizophrenegenic mother', in Baltimore during 1941–3. At the same time she trained as an analyst with Frieda Fromm-Reichmann. Taking her cue from them, she looked to the shaping influence of the family and argued that anorexia, like obesity, had to be seen within that developmental context: it was most often a child's neurotic response to an unnatural rejecting or over-nurturing mother. Sander Gilman contends that Bruch rebelled against the racially and biologically defined textbook arguments about obesity that she had imbibed during her medical training in Germany with a view to providing a new 'treatable' model. The Nazi discourse had linked obesity to Jews and stereotyped it as non-productive: the fat Jew, sluggish, lazy and stupid, was opposed to the thin, healthy German who found joy in work. Haunted by deterministic racial explanations, Bruch transformed the eating disorders into curable conditions.[363]

Bruch argued that both anorexia and obesity revolved around the girl's problem with body image and needs distorted during early development. In the case of the anorectic there was a delusional misperception of the body as fat. This was combined with the girl's inability to distinguish hunger from a range of other needs and desires; and an overriding sense that neither emotions, nor thoughts, nor actions come from within, but passively mirror external and maternal expectations. She distinguished a form of primary anorexia, in which the girl was compulsive in her pursuit of thinness, and felt a deep sense of self-estrangement. In a secondary form, self-starvation had a symbolic function, though the underlying problems were not necessarily linked to a distorted body image. Bruch popularized her ideas in the women's magazines and became an adviser on weight matters for the agony aunt, Ann Landers.

The women's movement within the psy professions took on body-image and eating disorders from the first. In her *Fat Is a Feminist Issue*, psychotherapist Susie Orbach records that in March 1970 she went to the Alternate University in New York City and registered for a course on compulsive eating and self-image. The structure of the course had grown out of consciousness-raising groups, where problems were shared and discussed. Here the problem was compulsive eating – 'a very painful and on the surface self-destructive activity. But . . . feminism had taught us that activities that appear to be self-destructive are invariably adaptations, attempts to cope with the world.'[364] The compulsive eaters ate when they weren't hungry, thought about food, diets, and thinness much of the time, felt out of control around food and submerged by the activities of dieting or gorging.

They also felt terrible about being out of control, and about their bodies. As the group talked and thought over their individual and common difficulties, it emerged that beneath the desire to be thin lay an equal and opposite desire to be fat, to fill a larger social space unhampered by men's eyes, advances, and the rat race of attraction. When the brackets of fat and thin, what they represented, and what each individual perceived were the characteristic personalities of both were gradually filled out, the focus on diet and food fell away. In the place of a woman who felt out of control about food, there emerged a woman unafraid of the categories and their relation to sex and maternity.

The particularities of the female body, its sexual and reproductive aspects as well as its image, continued to preoccupy the women's movement. The highly mediatized rejection of bras and the display of female flesh at the Miss World Competition played its part, alongside the more mediated search for an understanding of the ways in which women had taken in the feeling of being the object of the male gaze and incorporated it into the structure of their inner lives. In *The Female Eunuch*, Germaine Greer charts all parts of the body that make woman, woman. She also sounds the clarion call for thinness as a rebellion against traditional, oppressed femininity with its 'hallucinating sequence of parabolae and bulges . . . The characteristics that are praised and rewarded are those of the castrate: timidity, plumpness, languor, delicacy . . . All repressed, indolent people have been fat.'[365] Free women are thin, free and active, is the message.

Since women treat their bodies as the object of the male gaze that they have interiorized, inevitable distortions between how the body is imagined from within and how it appears to others are common enough. But the gulf between inner and outer perceptions can be so deep as to produce wild distortions, which is when anorexia or dysmorphia can occur This latter has now become known as BDD, the body-dysmorphic disorder listed in *DSM IV*. The condition is common not only amongst anorectics (there is apparently a 32 per cent co-morbidity between dysmorphia sufferers and eating disorders)[366] who have little sense of their real size, but amongst adolescents and seekers after plastic surgery obsessed by the shape of a purportedly ugly nose or breasts around which all anxiety and hopes of happiness are concentrated.

According to some figures, one in fifty adolescents suffer from BDD: whether, like the accompanying 'social phobia' that it can produce, this should qualify as a psychiatric disorder is another question. What is clear is that the prevalence of images, many of them other than life size and constantly morphing from the hugeness of a billboard or movie screen to the smallness of a home screen, cannot but impact on our inner sense of our bodies and their size and shape in the world. Nor is it difficult to imagine that living in the presence of screen beings may make their embodied and real versions frightening: they look different, perspire and smell, they can't be zapped or moved by a mouse; nor can they be stopped, rewound, repeated; they require response – speech, movement and facial gestures.

The coincidence of the rise in the eating disorders and dysmorphia with the women's movement also suggests that in the very process of elaborating and focusing in on the difficulties of being woman at the end of the twentieth century, the movement unwittingly combined with the attendant beauty, fashion and diet industries to forge and consequently swell the numbers of individuals who expressed their conflicts and unhappiness, their identity, in ills related to body size and shape. Was it this very focus on the body, the venom of the backlash, the conflicting values of thinness in the twin mirrors of freedom from femininity and designer-chic that turned women so violently against their own bodies? Marya Hornbacher in her memoir *Wasted* wonders if she might not have channelled her 'drive, perfectionism, ambition and excess of general intensity' into quite so self-destructive an illness as anorexia, if she had lived in a culture where 'thinness was not regarded as a strange state of grace'. The damage to her body, the radical distortion of her sense of who she was, might have been less if the eating disorder hadn't taken hold with its bulimic beginnings at the age of nine.[367]

Devastating in its detail of the growing insanity of a condition that can begin simply enough, Hornbacher notes how the early prevalence of talk of food, fatness and thinness in her parents' communication with each other and with her played an important part in the progress of her condition. These were the sites over which her parents stated their pronounced difference from each other, and their discord. Each wooed her, the pawn in their battles, with their preferred foods, which also stood in for their modes of being – her father's excessive, her mother's restrained. 'Watching the two of them eat played out like this: My father voracious, tried to gobble up my mother. My mother, haughty and stiff-backed, left my father untouched on the plate. They might as well have screamed aloud: I need you/I do not need you.' The child distracts them from their tension and becomes their common ground, their symptom bearer. They both urge her to eat. By the time she is five, as her mother tells her to behave herself, restrain herself, stop acting like a child, she feels that if only she can stop herself from spilling out into space, she can contain herself.[368]

As the progress of the eating disorders was mapped, psychologists and doctors largely agreed that the characteristic profile of an anorectic was of a highly achieving, hardworking, often attractive and amiable teenager, good at sports, with top grades and a competitive desire to do as well as possible and to please those around her. Internally, like so many adolescents – except that the gap here is wider – this budding academic or sports star feels worthless, insecure and unable somehow to fulfil what she perceives as both her parents' and her school's expectations. Perhaps she doesn't feel ready to grow up and away, doesn't want to grow into her mother or cease being her father's favourite. A university entrance exam, a falling out with a friend, a grandparent's death, a new stepparent – any distressing situation can shatter the brittle carapace of confidence she wears. She tumbles into a confused low, feels empty, not herself, out of control. The sense of being out of control demands controlling. The culture tells her she will feel better if only she sheds a few pounds, that lingering puppy fat. Diet and exercise are the answer. She begins to lose weight. She feels good. Energetic. Has a sense of achievement. And the reinforcement from her mother and her friends gives her a sense of power. So does the ordered control of her food intake, the counting of calories, the subtracting of those used up in vigorous exercise, the saying no to herself and no again and again, the near-obsessional ordering of the day and what comes into her body. Meanwhile, she works even harder. The near-fast produces a high. The thinness now attracts the fuel of attention: though this may be of a morbid kind, it doesn't matter. The body that she has created is after all not really hers.

Once a certain point in the weight loss is reached, the family usually wakes to the dissonance of compulsion and wilful fasting. The mother begins to try and persuade the girl to eat. This has its own rewards – the rewards of attention and wilful refusal. The helplessness of the parent met by the child's hostility and rejection is painful for the first, but may well produce a sense of triumph in the girl, who is daring at last to overstep the boundaries of what contemporary families accept as tolerable rebellion. The girl's symptoms, after all, are her solution to her problem. She hasn't so much lost her appetite as overcome it. She is in fact hungry all the time. But the greater the anorectic's control, the more she may also feel out of control. The inner battle is reflected in her relations with any authority figure who attempts to make her eat.

If the girl comes from a more traditional or an ethnic background, where food and familial meals carry more joint importance, such as in France, the point at which parents notice thinness and what from the family's point of view is a terrible problem may come earlier. If it comes too late, the struggle with the eating problem may well take on the proportions of a war.

Therapists, today, often implicate in the anorectic process the girl's need to separate herself out from a powerful mother who may behave like a friend and has put few generational boundaries in place. Alternatively, the mother may be strict, herself self-restraining, or experienced by the child as devouring. She may in some way need the child to make up for what she herself lacks, say a fulfilling marriage or a career, perhaps entangling the child in what has gone wrong with her life. Like a double bind, this maternal lack can induce guilt either if the girl constrains herself to the mutually despised maternal image, or if she rejects it.

Separating from mother is a conscious process, but it brings unconscious matter in its train. The girl may need to be alone to distinguish which bits are her, and simultaneously fear the fragility and guilt that brings. Her expressions of hostility to mother and family may indicate both the strength of her attachment and her terror at its presence and at letting go. The inner confusion, the war of conflicting desires and demands, can find its ordering anchor in the double rejection of food and of the menstruation which would thrust her down there amongst the women where her mother is. Her cruelty to others is bound up with her cruelty to herself, which she asks others painfully to witness.

The anorectic is a liar and also deludes herself. Once the starvation pattern is in place, she finds secret, deceiving ways of not eating the food she may have agreed to eat; or of storing laxatives and purgatives in secret places. This is the case even when it is the therapist, the parental stand-in, who has prepared the eating pact in collaboration with her. She may both need, and need to reject, any care the mother (belatedly) offers. In any event, it always feels belated to her. Internally, the girl still sees herself as fat and needs to defend her weight loss. The mirror, in which she examines every inch of herself for hours, reflects the bulges and blemishes no one else sees. Not even her boyfriend or any of the men she may sleep with – perhaps surprisingly in a Freudian register, but less so at a time when sex can see as important as a supermarket commodity – for these days, the anorectic is often enough sexually active. She will cannily hide herself and her thinness from others with loose clothes; and deny it to herself. By now, all her thoughts are of food and, like an addict obsessed with her habit and the need, in this case, not to feed it, she can do nothing else. Friends and work fall away. She can no longer concentrate. She is utterly alone with her obsession – suffering from weakness, muscle fatigue and cold. She must wrap herself up all the more, lie in bed under blankets, depressed enough to die.

Medically, the anorectic now shows all the signs of malnutrition. Her potassium and chloride levels will be down and her cardiovascular system affected. Her heartbeat may be irregular. She sometimes passes out. Her life is in danger, unless her system can be renourished. Later in life, if she survives, the effects of this early starvation will play themselves out in loss of bone density and early osteoporosis.

In gruelling detail Marya Hornbacher describes a process in which the common and recognizable adolescent excess of emotion and confusion catapults into craziness, as compulsive self-starvation takes its toll. The round of hospitalizations doesn't breach it: the anorectic, she notes, likes hospitalization, the constant attention, the returning to an infancy in which all needs are taken care of. Once out and fed just enough to walk and pretend, the girl will starve herself once more, playing with death, fearing to sleep in case she won't wake up, yet unable to eat unless it's to make herself puke again or exercise through the night. Even though she loves her 'stoned boy', that doesn't stop her from leaving him to wander through the city streets all night, shivering, always cold, 'murmuring to no one, nothing, tumbling through the strange unreal dimensions in the head'.[369] Her hands are birdlike, papery blue and numb, and don't grip so well any more. They just about manage the cigarettes she steals, the crusts of eaten sandwiches she doesn't know why she picks up from dirty streets and stuffs in her pockets. She's afraid to sleep.

Back in hospital once more, the psychiatric notes read: anorexia nervosa, malnutrition secondary to severe starvation, 'bulimia nervosa, major depression, recurrent'. The attendant medical notes add: bradycardia, hypotension, orthostasis (taken together, this simply means that the heart isn't up to allowing the person to stand up without rushes of dizziness or fainting), cyanosis (skin discoloration due to impoverished blood supply), heart murmur, severe digestive ulceration. The diet that will make the young woman beautiful grips the mind and kills the body.

Psychotherapist Susie Orbach's *Hunger Strike*, based on her experience of women with eating disorders who have come to her in private care or to the London and New York Women's Therapy Centres she co-founded, gives a feminist inflection to anorexia and its treatment. She interprets the disorder as the woman's battle against her own emotional needs, her attempt to control them in a world which, with its contradictory demands of women, refuses her the possibility of satisfaction. Anorexia is indeed a hunger strike, a protest against times which hold out the promise of independence and a life lived beyond the home while simultaneously demanding that women, as lovers, wives, mothers or carers, service the needs of others. Within the individual woman, anorexia plays itself out as a metaphor of what society wants of her: that she not take up too much space, that she be vigilant about her own needs and restrain them. The transition between the psychic and the social is hardly, however, a straightforward mirroring.

Writing about the mother–daughter relationship, Orbach notes the way in which women are taught by maternal actions not to be emotionally dependent, but rather to be midwives to the aspirations of others. 'Girls . . . suppress many needs and initiatives that arise internally. The result is that they grow up with a sense of never having received quite enough, and often feel insatiable and unfulfilled. As an attempted solution to this psychic state of affairs, they seek connection with others and learn that this connection, especially with men, depends on the acceptability of their bodies.'[370]

The echo of Freud in this positing of the girl's insatiability, the more emphatic recourse to object-relations theories, take on in Orbach and in many of the feminist psychotherapists a positive hope. If the world could be changed and the relations between the sexes altered, then the psyche would attain an equilibrium and women would attain satisfaction. This underlying hope of individual happiness is one that Freud never held out for civilization, which doomed the individual to discontent — even if he criticized the double standards of his time and wanted change.

Orbach draws attention to the fact that the times condemn the mother to giving her infant daughter an unsatisfactory sense of her own body, restraining and containing it, so that it becomes appropriately gendered female. Restraining and curtailing her daughter's needs, she creates a girl who feels ashamed that she has any, who defends herself against them, fails to recognize and express them and won't let anything — not love or food — in. This would make her needs public, even to herself.

Extending Winnicott's idea of the false self, Orbach argues that when the infant has not had a chance to experience its physicality as 'good, wholesome and essentially all right, it has little chance to live in an authentically experienced body'. The result can be a 'false body' which conceals the insecurity of the undeveloped inner body. Girls who develop an eating disorder are trying to shape their false body along acceptable lines. This plastic body, which can represent the negative, hated aspect of the unfulfilling mother, the bad object, can be shrunk into nonexistence. But at the same time, it is her body and it is all that she has: her real self is just a tiny, confused infant. Giving up on the hunger strike, says one patient after two years of therapy, is like giving up on one's 'whole identity'. It may not be the loss of anything good, 'like a bad mother you don't need anymore',[371] but it's still a difficult loss. Anorexia is often intractable to treatment.

Theories about its causal base and development abound. Some analysts interpret the food the young woman rejects as the mother she is distancing herself from. Seeing mother as food, rather than care, is a failure in symbolization, another lack linked to the infant's early relations with the mother. Biological psychiatrists talk of anorexia being linked to depression. Parental depression may indeed have played a part in shaping the girl's illness if a carer suffered from it during the girl's early infancy and failed to give her an appropriate sense of her bodily reality. But the sense here is a questionable one: the girl is said to suffer from depression because she responds to antidepressants, a line of reasoning that drug-based therapies too readily employ, offering a diagnosis tailored to a response to a drug. Still other therapists see starving, with its loss of feminine shape and menstruation, as an attempt to replace the female body with a masculine one.[372] In the 1990s, with the rise of interest in obsessive-compulsive disorder and its rituals, equations were made between OCD and anorexia, which certainly in its minute structuring of eating activity has a deeply compulsive side. It remains unclear, however, whether obsessionality can indicate a predisposition to the eating disorder and whether the serotonergic medications such as Prozac have any impact at all on patients at the lowest points of starvation.[373]

Anorexia is not only a middle-class disease. Today the eating disorders are seen in women from all social groups. As forensic clinicians Estela Welldon and Anna Motz have both noted, based on their experience of working with psychiatric patients in prisons, eating disorders are often coupled with self-harm and what psychiatrists designate as borderline personality disorders, which in turn regularly enough bear a history of early abuse. For these women, refusing food is often linked to an unconscious wish to stop their periods and in this way violently to reject their sexuality and the hated, sometimes complicit, mother they have incorporated. When they cut themselves, these women are not only trying to stop the pain or to come out of a state of numbness, but to cut a neglecting or abusive mother out of themselves and, with her, cut out their abused sexuality.[374]

Whatever theorization of anorexia clinicians prefer, one note persists in all accounts. The anorectic's fear and rejection of food are also a rejection of any form of intrusion – which is precisely what therapy is. This makes any treatment difficult. Anorectics perennially sabotage therapy. They are as aggressive to those who attempt to help them as they are cruel to themselves. Doctors and therapists often find themselves enmeshed in a power struggle: the fading girl insists that she is just fine and must be left to her own devices. Persuasive attempts at feeding can easily grow coercive. Doctors attempt to follow procedures that the Hippocratic oath and duty tie them to. The patient's victory over forced feeding is too often also her death.

Margaret Lawrence describes a patient who looks like a 'dying child', insisting everything is under control and she is just fine. The patient's intransigeant insistence that there is no 'need' at all in her, coupled with the presence of the dying body, is characteristic of the illness.[375] Help is food in the anorectic's lexicon. This translates into therapists' and parents' frustration and often enough the violence of force-feeding. Since, as Orbach notes, force-feeding reinforces gender stereotypes of the powerful male doctor applying invasive tubes to the female body, the procedure threatens the anorectic, whose refusal to eat is about control and overcoming appetite. Although hospitalization may be necessary and re-feeding may initially save the girl, without more comprehensive psychological treatment there will inevitably be a new cycle of illness. Few anorectics will continue the hospital diet without other kinds of help. Group work inside the hospital or on an outpatient basis can be useful. It can overcome the patient's loneliness. She may also be better able to see the illness outside than inside herself. As for individual treatment, Orbach recommends structuring a therapeutic alliance in which eating is left in the patient's control until she herself asks for help with it.

There is a great need for genuine sympathy from the therapist — especially since the anorectic may have been to many professionals in the past. On the open terrain the therapy can provide, the girl-woman's feelings of disgust and despair, her inner maps, her body image, can gradually be placed alongside the rejected food which has given them symbolic life. Eventually the geography of a new self can be charted.

Hilda Bruch noted the usefulness of family therapy with anorectics. Many have followed her lead. The anorectic can be the bearer of psychological problems between parents, or enacting a struggle with her mother, all of which makes itself evident when the family is together. Mara Selvini Palazzoli (1916–1999), the Italian therapist who understood the familly as a transactional system which attempts to perpetrate itself, pointed out that anorectics' families often cover over deep resentments with a show of excessive solicitousness towards their children, inappropriate by the time they reach adolescence. She pioneered the 'prescription' of rituals and shock injunctions or paradoxical interventions, much imitated and redeployed by family therapists in Britain and the USA. Palazzoli's rituals provide precise counter-games which can budge the family out of its habitual patterns. The paradoxical intervention has the same purpose, though it functions through a few deft sentences which illuminate the family drama and redirect it. A starving girl, for example, might be told not to gain weight, since if she puts on curves her father will feel estranged in a family which is uniformly made up of women. Running counter to the expectations of the patient, such prescriptions lay bare the family power system and rupture the deadlock which has kept it in place.

CBT, or cognitive behavioural therapy – the subsidized health services' therapy of choice because of its limited length and apparent high success rate – is also said to have some initial success with anorexia and other eating disorders. CBT takes its model from the behaviourists' experiments with animals and conditioning in the first part of the twentieth century. It is based on the simple principle that if behaviour has been learned, it can be unlearned. Brainwashing is the popularized political version of the science, visible in a thousand films in which spies or soldiers are frazzled, punished or drugged into adopting the ideology of their enemies. CBT practitioners think of the unconscious as a woolly and unscientific idea. For them, thoughts determine emotions. Sort out the correct thoughts and beliefs about phobias or anorexia, encourage them, and health will follow.

The brainchild of a dissatisfied psychoanalyst, Aaron Beck, and a clinical psychologist, Albert Ellis, CBT has thrived under managed care in the USA and is on the rise and rise in Europe. Health services want treatment plans with visible goals, boxes with symptoms that can be ticked off as soon as eradicated – as if the troubled human mind and psyche were easier to treat than chronic diabetes, more like a leg with a fracture that resetting will fix in a matter of months with only the slightest trace of a scar left behind.

Focusing on the present and the future rather than the past, and on symptoms to be eliminated, CBT sharpened its tools on depression and anxiety. Patients were shown the fallacy of negative thoughts and low self-esteem, how to cope with irrational thinking and misperceptions, dysfunctional thoughts and faulty learning. Therapists often give patients a series of inner exercises and homework to do so that their mental processes through callisthenics can be rejigged into a more positive form. Claims are that depression, often with a side treatment of SSRI's (selective serotonin re-uptake inhibitors), is lifted, anxiety and phobias disappear. Beck has now gone on to treat schizophrenia and personality disorders. With anorexia, CBT therapists highlight the significance of the disorder as a means of gaining a sense of self-control. They focus in on the girl's eating patterns and weight, attempting change here, but leave aside the unconscious components that bind into the condition and give it its individual shape. Anorexia, like so many disorders, is not simply a behaviour, but a response to inner knots and tangles invisible and individual to the young woman.

In America, the NIMH (National Institute of Mental Health), in its advice to anorectics, has become a little cautious about CBT, specifying that it is best used in conjunction with other therapies. With anorexia, which results in twelve times more deaths in the eighteen- to twenty-five-year-old female population than any other single cause, they recommend a procedure which includes hospitalization in conjunction with ongoing CBT or other interpersonal therapies, individually or in groups, to combat perennial low self-esteem, social difficulties and dysmorphia.

BULIMIA

In 1987, the revised *DSM-III* for the first time included the diagnostic category of 'bulimia nervosa'. More fully fleshed out in *DSM-IV*, bulimia entailed 'an awareness of loss of control' in recurrent episodes of binge eating; compensatory ways of preventing weight gain, in particular vomiting and misuse of laxatives, and a 'self-evaluation unduly influenced by body shape and weight'.

Bulimia, the binge–purge cycle, comes in several forms, which can slip into one another. One is its noisy adolescent manifestation involving group bingeing and group vomiting. This can have a fashionable air of adolescent defiance, parallel to binge drinking and other stormy weekend excesses. Another form is the *secret*, ritualized vomiting after meals that often begins in the later teens. More troubling, this bulimia can persist as a lifelong extension of dieting. The most serious form,which prodded the change in the *DSM* entry, has a compulsive aspect: binges are built up to over weeks, thoughts of them increasingly insistent, the urge and the final experience felt as a possession. Once the secret binge begins, the woman can consume gallons of ice-cream and pounds of food. With the giving in to the food comes both a release of tension, almost sexual in nature, and an accompanying shame, compounded by the guilt of inevitable weight gain. The vomiting that follows brings momentary peace.

Bulimics are not the saints of eating disorders, but the impulsive sinners. They're garrulous, often as incontinent in their relationship to words as they are to food. Bruch notes their 'exhibitionistic display . . . their lack of control or discipline . . . a deficit in the lack of responsibility'.[376] They blame their symptoms on others, and often claim to have 'learned' the behaviour. They characterize themselves as victims. Sometimes they steal the food they binge on and explain this as 'kleptomania', similar to bulimia in the compulsive force which guides it. Interestingly, kleptomania is a disorder at the end of another women's spectrum of behaviour, this time related to shopping and its attendant need to acquire, loosely interpreted as a need for love. Despite the compulsion involved in the act of a kleptomaniac's theft, courts in Britain and America will not accept it as a plea to reduce sentences. With the eating disorders, and particularly obesity and bulimia, it shares, as Bruch's own tone underlines, a low status, as if the disorder also entailed self-indulgence, or a disreputable moral falling-away from civilized standards.

Robert Lindner, that brilliant teller of tales from the consulting room, describes his unstoppable patient Laura and his overwhelming feelings of disgust when she arrived in his consulting room following a binge. Her face was 'hideous'. 'Swollen like a balloon at the point of bursting, it was a caricature of a face, the eyes lost in pockets of sallow flesh and shining feverishly with a sick glow, the nose buried between bulging cheeks splattered with blemishes, the chin an oily shadow mocking human contour, and somewhere in the mass of fat a crazy-angled carmined hole was her mouth.' Out of that foul-smelling mouth come curses, a spout of grievances and accusations, and finally a call for help.[377]

Laura's case was first told in the fifties in the United States, before eating disorders had gained in prominence and notoriety. Lindner's description captures his patient's own sense of disgust, which is one Hornbacher echoes, emphasizing how disgust and need in the bulimic are part of her excessive emotion and inner violence. But she sees the bulimic's impulse as more realistic than the anorectic's because the former knows the body is inescapable.[378] Lindner eventually tracks his own patient's pathological craving for food back to a startling Oedipal desire for her father's child: a father whose abandoning of an already impoverished family when she was a mere girl she blamed on her chair-ridden mother. The bingeing is an enactment of pregnancy, correcting a childhood lack — her overwhelming need for her absent father — coupled with a disgust for her crippled mother.

Such interpretations and indeed enactments can seem florid amidst the current understandings of bulimia, which some say is endemic amongst teenagers in the West, though numbers are hard to come by since treatment is not regularly sought. But Lindner's case provides a glimpse of the unconscious elements which can activate a binge–purge cycle. This old 'tale' also underscores the compulsive nature of the condition and the displaced meanings which food can hold for the individual — the way in which food, particularly for women, can stand in for love.

Bulimia has had some high-powered women in its thrall. The condition allows for a controlled, successful, pleasingly thin façade beneath which a secret world can swing wildly into messy rage. Often the bulimic feels this is her true self. Unlike the killing anorexia, and like alcoholism, bulimia doesn't necessarily visibly impede work patterns or even family relations. The quotient of inner malaise, however, is high. Princess Diana was a bulimic and sought treatment. Indeed, psychotherapists see bulimia in a wide range of women: some suffer from a false self; others have passing adolescent problems; still others are borderline personalities who engage in savage fluctuations of behaviour from self-harm to sexual promiscuity to alcoholism, and who have often had childhoods in which abuse features.[379]

In her autobiography *My Life So Far*, actor and political activist Jane Fonda describes how with her thirteenth birthday a sense of her own imperfection attacked her, and centred itself on her body. Her father estimated it 'fat'. It was 'the outward proof of my badness'. Her mother, who had a history of breakdowns, had recently committed suicide. Around the time of her divorce from Henry Fonda, she had shown Jane the ugly scar left by a kidney operation and the botched effect of a breast implant. Eleven-year-old Jane associated these with her parents' divorce and vowed that she would be flawless.

In retrospect, her overwhelming desire to make her body thin and thus perfect also emerges as a way of postponing a womanliness that was associated with being a victim like her mother. The perfection of thinness was her aim. At school she responded to a newspaper advertisement for a 'tapeworm', which never arrived. With a friend who had similar problems with her body image, Fonda binged and purged. The school secret grew into an adult ritual enacted alone. She would go into a grocery store and buy 'comfort' foods, ice-cream and pastries, all the time telling herself this would be the last time, her breathing quickening, fear and excitement mounting together. No sooner was the secret feast finished than 'the toxic bulk which had seemed so like a mother's nurture' had to be got rid of. Eliminated before it took up residence inside her. Otherwise it would kill her. Only years later did she overcome her denial of the addictive nature of the illness. Like alcoholism, bulimia is an addiction, which the addict lies about to herself, saying she is in control, that the addiction can be stopped at any time by an act of will; couching it in moral terms, equating it with a sense of weakness and worthlessness.

Fonda's secret food addiction sometimes expressed itself as bulimia, sometimes as anorexia. It persisted into her forties and through two marriages and two children. No one knew about it. She became expert at dining in the best Beverly Hills restaurants and retiring to the toilets to puke, before returning, smiling, her make-up perfectly in place. The condition would grow worse when she was sustaining 'inauthentic' relationships. Increased anxiety about food and numbness would then take her over, cocooning her from life, so that the toilet became the only place where she felt she was herself – not the false self which acts as a defence against the chaotic, undeveloped, needy infant within.

Fonda's case exhibits the characteristic persistence of the eating disorders, their deep hold on their sufferer's psychic structures. In a study carried out by the Massachusetts General Hospital in Boston, women were seen again after three years of various treatments: out of thirty only 69 per cent were diagnosed as fully recovered. In another study at the University of Minnesota, after a ten-year period, 30 per cent of the women continued to engage in bingeing and purging.[380]

During all those years when she herself was part of the flagellating body industry and encouraged women through books, audio and seventeen million video tapes to work out and 'let it burn', Jane Fonda was a 'recovering food addict'. The paradox here is of women's complicity – even a feminist's, which Fonda is – with the social coercion of her time. Fonda's ringing voice, together with her super-svelte form, did indeed burn itself into the minds and eyes of eighties women who worked out to find a semblance of her outward perfection.

Always emblematic of her times, it is interesting that Fonda, a consummately successful woman in every sphere she has engaged in – as an actor, political activist, exercise guru, film producer, mother, high-profile wife, writer – couches her life in the victim narrative so crucial to American feminism and popular culture since the 1980s. In her sixties, at last 'recovered' from a lifetime of feasting, vomiting and fasting, still slender and beautiful, she has entered 'the infancy of her new adulthood', a new beginning where she at last feels 'embodied' and can acknowledge her mother's part in her life. A life story is also a therapeutic tale in which the woman is a patient who at last recovers. There is evidently hope for us all.

Fonda's story underlines the way in which the lives, particularly of women, have now become therapeutic tales. Their confessional tone and the stepping-stones they choose to chart are not, however, the Freudian narratives of mid-century in which struggle, part of which is linked to rampant desire, leads to insight and stoical resignation to a civilization in which discontent is inevitable, but achievement possible. Now the therapeutic women's narrative has a religious thrust. Born into a doomed world in which mothers, like Eve after the Fall, are never, and can't be, good enough, daughters are wounded in their bodies and emotions, suffer the slings and arrows of fortune, and are eventually redeemed, often with the help of a replacement good-enough mother-therapist. Under her aegis, they are healed and born again into a wholeness which also means peace. Interestingly, the inflection here is on the life of the body and the emotions.

Therapeutic feminism rightly added the missing cultural dimension to women's psychic ills and put eating disorders, as well as others prominent amongst women such as self-harm, into an appropriate social perspective. It nudged medical psychiatry and traditional psychoanalysis into an awareness of the way in which the cultural emphasis on thinness and on women's bodies played into illness; how treatment had to take into account a woman's wish to control her body. In the process, feminism seems to have given back to women what they always had: the body, emotions, and a penchant for the softer sides of religion as the prime means of self-definition.

14

ABUSE

Trawling through the sizeable psychiatric and psychoanalytic literature of the twentieth century, it is surprising to find that the mind doctors rarely put their minds to matters that today are prominent above all others. Rape, incest – that whole package compounded within child abuse, trauma and its ensuing disorders – hardly surface in their writings until the mid-1980s. Abuse, neglect, the mistreatment of children are a social matter: the fact that love, compassion and understanding, let alone warmth and food, are necessary to development is a question of common sense, not material for the investigation of mind doctors. When rape and incest do appear in the literature, they're most often linked to anthropological matter, to investigations of myth; or to theoretical discussions of unconscious fantasy. In considering hysteria, Freud notes that rape is a 'severe trauma' which reveals 'to the immature girl at a blow all the brutality of sexual desire'. But in the consulting room it emerges that such trivial matters as the tender stroking of a hand or the rubbing of a knee under a table can prove as traumatizing an event in one young girl's psychic life as the far more serious rape in another's.[381] Some individuals, it seems, can digest the assault of triple Macs and milkshakes, while others have trouble with thinly pared celery.

Transmuted in memory, screened by a bundle of emotions, the real of the individual's history, the external and documentable events of a life, most often become for the analyst what the patient has 'experienced'. Except in dealing with child analysis or full-blown episodes of mania when psychiatrists take histories from family or witnesses, what is remembered, re-presented and re-enacted in the consulting room is the principal stuff of therapy. What is crucial within analysis is the way in which the mind manages the relationship between inner and outer reality. Damage, the manner in which the individual has responded to or been stopped in her tracks by the blows of life, the meaning she makes of them, is what is on the table for treatment. As the American Psychoanalytic Association's plenary meeting heard in 1992, data gathered by the researcher William D. Mosher had shown that there were only nineteen articles mentioning either sexual abuse or incest in English-language psychoanalytic journals from 1920 to 1986.[382] Since rape, abuse and incest have hardly been absent from human history until the 1980s – were indeed well documented throughout the late nineteenth century – clearly, the mind doctors considered these as social problems to be dealt with by social workers, the police and politicians, all those professions that contend with the order of the social world and real events, rather than the meanings the mind can generate from these events and the disorders of the inner life.

Then, in the last decades of the twentieth century, several forces came together to alter the concerns of the mind doctors radically and to put precisely these matters centre stage. The West became more inclined to find individual solutions to what were often social and political matters. Poverty and deprivation were repressed as categories in favour of identity and fitness. There was a shift, too, of demarcations and focus in the professions. The old talking-cure dividing lines between social work, psychiatric social work, clinical psychology, any number of therapies, psychoanalysis and psychiatry began to blur. Particularly in America, the high status of analysis in its link with psychiatry was disappearing, and analysis had to catch up with the other talk therapies if it was to find patients. The psychiatric world began to organize itself around the diagnostic schema of the *DSM* which fell in with the bureaucratic needs of 'managed care' insurance or welfare services.

If slightly more than half of patients had always been women, then women, too, had changed. Liberation and the focus of feminism had transformed sexuality itself and reproblematized it. The women's movement had pinpointed wrongs: these were to do not only with the culturally ordained look and feel and experience of the body, but with what physically penetrated it – men. Rape and other sexual violence came early and importantly on to the women's liberation agenda as key crimes against women. Rape was first characterized as stranger rape, a violent assault by an unknown. It was quickly extended into boy-next-door or date rape, and rape in that part of the world women have always known best, the family, which had its very own embodied patriarchs.

Battered wives, pornography, sexually abused women and child abuse began to preoccupy the women's movement. In the English-speaking world, these gradually through the eighties became more prominent than the original calls for social and sexual equality – the right to contraception, abortion, liberated sex, alongside the very free-dom to desire. These latter – the very matter implicated in the birth of psychoanalysis – remained well after '68 the calling-cards of French feminism. With its close links to Lacanian and post-structural theory, the women of Psy et Po (Psychanalyse et Politique), for example, pos-tulated a new feminine language grounded in the passions of hysteria. French feminists' points of attack, alongside social ills, were the organ-ized systems of knowledge which had always excluded women. They were concerned to show how meaning itself was entangled in a hierar-chy of power-relations which placed masculine reason at its pinnacle.

If French ideas circulated in academic spheres worldwide, they didn't percolate on to the streets with quite the immediacy of rape and incest. Through the seventies and eighties, a vocal part of the women's move-ment in Britain and America took on the aura of a Victorian vice squad, the original purity movement from which one branch of early femi-nism had sprung, a moral brigade for whom the sexual slid with hardly an intervening moment into rape. Men, those agents of patriarchy, emerged less as lovers, let alone husbands and fathers, than as perpe-trators of sex crimes and exploitative pornographers. Whereas at first these crimes were against women, by the late 1980s and 1990s they had become crimes against children, or against the girls the women had been. Consciousness-raising had initially involved speaking out and breaking the silence so as to change present and future. Remembering soon displaced it as a collective injunction. The very identity politics that feminism had given birth to robbed it of its agenda of change. Constituting identity meant not only having the flexibility of the masquerade, the trying-on of parts and the gender-bending that the postmodern theorists explored. It also meant looking into the past where the causes of what had made life go wrong could be found. The bonding narrative of women's identity moved from liberation to abuse.

Borrowing the prevalent tropes and mood of Holocaust history and slavery narratives, women found their identity in past wounds and wrongs. All of these caused illness and made that very illness a badge of courage. 'Hysteria', as the influential psychiatrist Judith Herman proclaimed, 'is the combat neurosis of the sex war.' In a replay of late-nineteenth-century politics, women became the walking wounded, trauma and its effects their clarion call. The talking cures, now heavily populated by women therapists, both played into and helped to shape this newly vulnerable woman trapped in bad (remembered) sex and a fragile body; a woman newly infantilized, extending, perhaps projecting, her 'abused', tortured state on to children, so like the child she had once been. To be a woman who had been molested as a child and entered the path to recovery was to be a 'survivor'. Life had become all too quickly an afterlife filled with shady memories all but impossible to shed. Already in 1971, the New York Radical Feminists had held a Rape Speak Out, in which women shared their rape experiences. Their manifesto read:

> It is no accident that the New York Radical Feminists, through the technique of consciousness raising, discovered that rape is not a personal misfortune but an experience shared by all women in one form or another. When more than two people have suffered the same oppression, the problem is no longer personal but political – and rape is a political matter . . . The act of rape is the logical expression of the essential relationship now existing between men and women.[383]

In 1975 with the publication of Susan Brownmiller's mass bestseller *Against Our Will*, the battle against rape became a primary rallying call of the women's movement. Positing rape as the fundamental relationship between the sexes, Brownmiller argued that 'man's structural capacity to rape' corresponds to woman's 'structural fragility', and is as basic to sex as the primal act itself. 'Man's discovery that his genitalia could serve as a weapon' has meant that from prehistoric times to the present 'rape has played a critical function', which is to intimidate women and keep them in a state of fear.

That fear and fragility were at first to be fought. In 1976, the International Tribunal of Crimes against Women met in Belgium and held the first Take Back the Night march – a candle-lit demonstration protesting violence against women. Marches followed in quick succession in Italy, Germany and in various centres in Britain through 1977. In November of that year, in San Francisco Andrea Dworkin addressed some three thousand women, who walked through the city's red-light district to demonstrate not only against rape but against pornography and the sexual exploitation of women. By December, the twenty-five-point action plan that grew out of the vast National Women's Conference in Houston, and which included a large proportion of pro-life, pro-family Republican activists, called for education in rape prevention, shelters for wives who were physically abused by their husbands and state- funded programmes for victims of child abuse.

Mobilizing against rape had many benefits. Rape crisis centres and hotlines sprang up in every city and on every campus. Speaking out about rape lessened the terrible shame women had long borne in secret. Judges, men, fathers and even mothers, who had indulged in blaming the victim for the crime in such recurrent asides as 'She was asking for it', were contested and brought up short; it is clear that many still need to be. Battles to increase sentencing and change the procedures related to rape legislation were engaged in, and continue.

But the ideological battle-cry which made all men (potential) rapists had a debilitating side-effect. The very fear and vulnerability Brownmiller had evoked as fundamental to femininity reinforced women's self-image as powerless. Woman as victim became a core identity for American feminism. If men were all rapists, then women were always in danger. No amount of self-defence training could counter the anxiety of constant alertness. With potential predators everywhere, who didn't ever and always attack, violence against women began to slip from its initial designation of forced, non-consensual sex to encompass a wide set of behaviours: molestation, harassment, aggressively flirtatious speech. A Canadian government-financed survey by two sociologists revealed that an astonishing 81 per cent of university women had suffered what they called 'sexual abuse': it transpired that the ambit of abuse included taunts and insults during quarrels.[384] By the eighties, sexual violence had tumbled into a generalized category of 'abuse' which increasingly also embraced children.

The idea of 'child abuse' both transfixed and indelibly marked the moral climate of the turn of the century. Here, too, the initial focus had a radical intent: if child abuse could be eradicated, the generational recycling of violence could be stopped in its tracks and society emerge as a humane place. The many books of Alice Miller – the Polish-born, Swiss-based psychoanalyst who turned against her profession for what she saw as its wilful blindness to and perpetuation of abuse – focused attention on the way in which children were deformed by parents who had themselves been neglected, unloved, unprotected, uncared for, not to mention beaten, battered and humiliated. Miller, who as a ten-year-old had experienced Hitler's rise to power in Berlin, was, as she stated in a 1992 interview, scarred and transfixed by the experience: 'I watched dumbfounded as millions of supposedly "civilised" people were transformed into a blind, hate-filled mass who enthusiastically allowed a primitive, arrogant monster to lead them to murder their fellow human beings . . . I have tried to understand how it is that people can be so easily manipulated and where are the invisible sources of their latent hatred.'[385]

Miller found her answer to the riddle of Hitler's monstrosity in his brutalization by a father who was partly Jewish; she also found evidence of abuse in all the greats from Dostoievski to Joyce, Proust and Kafka. In the next round of psychological fashion, manic depression would be attributed to a similar list. Miller came to believe the old adage that we grow into our parents was true. Although she was a renegade to the psychoanalytic fold, she believed it in a particularly analytic way: adults were destined unconsciously to repeat what they themselves had suffered but forgotten. 'It is well known that fathers who bully their children through sexual abuse are usually unaware that they had themselves suffered the same abuse.' Only in therapy, even when it is ordered by the courts, do they discover that they have been re-enacting 'their own scenario just to get rid of it'.[386] The cycle of abuse could only be broken with the help of an 'enlightened witness', to whom the child or the child within could recount and replay her history of suffering.

A similar strategy would make its way into the care professions together with its underlying paradigm that children were more likely than not to be abused, and the adults they became were unlikely to remember. Only by eradicating abuse could society be saved.

In Miller's understanding, the abuse was not only sexual or disproportionately aimed at women: it extended broadly to include both sexes and almost all behaviours – 'a poisonous pedagogy' that the inevitably powerful parent might enact before a helpless babe. It became a version of original sin. But Miller's ideas, including their Holocaust colouring, played into the women's movement and the care professions, helping to legitimate the notion of 'recovered memory' that fired America through the nineties.

The philosopher Ian Hacking has brilliantly teased out the ways in which child abuse became a defining category for our times, enmeshing science, popular culture and institutions of state, to make up a new kind of person.[387] What began in 1962 with a medical notion of 'battered child syndrome', designed to draw attention, with the use of X-rays, to children who had been beaten and were physically damaged, escalated into a growing nationwide problem. In January 1965, *Time* noted that if all cases of parents who 'beat, burned, drowned, stabbed and suffocated their children with weapons ranging from baseball bats to plastic bags' were reported, the number killed would be far more than ten thousand and would top deaths by 'auto accidents, leukaemia or muscular dystrophy'. Newspaper headlines and media programmes merged with added social-science definitions, to extend the abused- or battered-child category into one which accommodated both physical abuse and neglect – a category which psychiatrists at that point thought was far more damaging to the child, nullifying emotional life and development.

In the USA statistics for abused children rose and rose, together with official bodies to count and care for them and experts to advise. Forced to attention, politicians could not allow the obvious equation between battery, poverty and neglect to be made, for fear of a rising demand for costly welfare programmes: instead, a generalized cross-class and national abuse problem had to be emphasized. By 1969, all fifty states had new 'child abuse' statutes on their books, and in twenty states some form of law asking doctors to report cases to a central register was in place. In 1976 the scale of reported abuse was still growing. The

American Humane Association found that 413,000 cases had been reported to state and local authorities that year. By 1981 the count had doubled to 851,000 and was still climbing.[388]

Into this thicket the women's movement tossed the flame of incest and *sexual* abuse, which had until then been kept quite distinct from the child abuse classification. In April 1977, *Ms Magazine* carried an article headed 'Incest: Sexual Abuse Begins at Home'. Just as women had joined children where battery and physical abuse were concerned, children now joined women as victims of sexual violence. The lived horror was real enough, as Maya Angelou's 1969 autobiography had so movingly evoked. But the noisy proclamations of vice and virtue, evil and innocence, which attended the brutality of the experience fanned abuse into insurmountable atrocity.

As the forest fires of moral panic leapt and spread, they touched everything within their reach. Child abuse grew to encompass everything from touch (which could be good or bad – though how could your neighbours tell?) to fondling, to molestation to intercourse to purported satanic rituals. Analysed in articles in a growing number of journals dedicated to child welfare and documented in any number of real-life programmes, emotive fictions and memoirs, discovered prevalence of abuse escalated. Ellen Bass, who was later to write what became a popular manual for discovering multiple personality disorder, in 1983 put together a collection of writings by survivors of child sexual abuse, *I Never Told Anyone*. In her preface she states:

> Like rape of women, the rape and molestation of children are most basically acts of violation, power, and domination. Parents United . . . estimates that one out of four girls and one out of seven boys will be sexually abused. Other studies find the ratio of girls to be higher, closer to ten girls for each boy. The sex of the molester, however, is consistent from study to study. At least 97 percent of child molesters and rapists are men; 75 percent are family members . . . The true numbers may be greater.[389]

The anguish of the contents of this volume is real enough. So, too, in the retelling of sexual violence, is the unintended whiff of pornography. By 1991 researchers were estimating that between 200,000 and 360,000 cases of child abuse occurred each year in the United States. The help-lines were up. There were reports of satanic rings, horrifying accounts of abuse so vile, their iconography seemed often enough to have leapt out of the wilder reaches of the porn industry. The family, nuclear or extended, had become an increasingly dangerous place.

Throughout Britain, too, in the eighties and nineties, cases of child abuse and the satanic child abuse which soon joined it were, it seemed from arrests in Cleveland, Newcastle and elsewhere, on the rise. The NSPCC sponsored a series of adverts that chilled with its figures and its portrayal of victimized waifs. Everywhere slips of girls with bruised faces looked plaintively out of billboards expressing their plight. Primed by their American kin, British social workers in a dawn raid in February 1991 took – with all the force and attendant terror of kidnappers – five boys and four girls aged between eight and fifteen from their homes on South Ronaldsay in Orkney and subjected them to a month's interrogation in order to discover the shameful satanic secrets the social workers 'knew' existed on the island. If the judge, in this instance, ultimately threw the case out and deemed there were no secrets to be discovered, the social workers remain convinced to this day that sexual abuse had taken place. As a 2006 BBC documentary made clear in enacting interview tapes of the time, what can only be termed an ideology which insisted that secrets existed and were always held back fuelled the questioning. There was a passionate moral crusade on the march here, one aimed at righting the great injustice that was the sexual abuse of children.

The most articulate exemplar of that moral conviction is the American psychiatrist Judith Herman, who presents a cogent analysis of the ways in which an abused child adapts to her condition by various defences and so can present the appearance of normality so important to her family:

> The child's distress symptoms are generally well hidden. Altered states of consciousness, memory lapses, and other dissociative symptoms are not generally recognized. The formation of a malignant negative identity is generally disguised by the socially conforming 'false self'. Psychosomatic symptoms are rarely traced to their source. And self-destructive behavior carried out in secret generally goes

unnoticed . . . Most abused children reach adulthood with their secrets intact.[390]

If the underlying notion of care workers is that children can keep abuse so well hidden, then extracting the assumed secret from them can take excessive forms. In the Orkney case, the experience for the children – with its surprise dawn raid, forced separation from parents, clothes, toys and everything they knew, hours and days of repeated interrogation by overbearing adults, the horrors of borstal or fostered life – took on an aura of torture which was not unlike abuse itself. The vice squads in the modern garb of care professionals had become the keepers of a punishment park which paraded as a space of safety, an asylum.

The rounding-up of the abused, let alone those who would be accused once testimony was obtained, made everyone aware that a new kind of being had gradually taken shape: one who could not speak her or his sexual secrets without the help of professionals to guide her through the horror, fear, inner stigma, helplessness – in a word, 'the trauma' – of the experience. The trauma, it was gradually accepted, involved a vast range of behaviours, from rape itself to being photographed. The truth, it also seemed to be agreed, must come out, since early abuse would destroy adult lives.

A dynamic abuse narrative had been moulded: it took for granted that the entirety of a life was misshaped by the experience of early sexuality; without help, the once chronically abused would remain eternally damaged, would fail in life and repeat the abuse on their own nearest and dearest, as well as unconsciously eliciting it from encounters with others. The developmental story line was at once potentially true and a self-fulfilling prophecy, particularly in the disciplinary hands of an interventionist state and its often police-like social services, which too readily tore already vulnerable children away from the world they knew, however vile some of its dimensions.

This understanding of child abuse demanded the acquiescence of all right-thinking people – in the way that earlier vice of self-abuse had of the Victorians. Sexual cruelty to powerless children came to seem, as Hacking notes, 'the most heinous of crimes' because it bundled together four distinct kinds of harm: 'We used to have quite different types of moral revulsion against a parent wilfully neglecting a baby, against a person savagely beating an innocent, against a stranger molesting a child, and against incest.' But when these are run together into child abuse, 'a compelling new constellation of absolute moral evil' is born. Though loath to state that evil is in part 'merely relative to our culture', Hacking suggests that 'there is so much morality, so much righteousness here that one can begin to suspect that some sort of pseudomorality is creeping in'.[391]

From knowing that abuse is an intensely kept but widespread secret to conceiving of it as *forgotten* if one 'experiences' all the signs and symptoms the experts say it produces, is a mere slip of a step. Recovering memories of sexual abuse became a way of explaining the malaise of the present. Speaking the horror in front of sympathetic witnesses, perhaps in a women's group or in therapy or most controversially in the courts, took on, particularly in the USA, the force of a moral injunction. From recovering memories to recovery itself – a usage familiar from Alcoholics Anonymous – was a mere matter of a few therapeutic steps away. Being part of a wide network of 'incest survivors' held out the promise of salvation.

In 1988 the bible of what quickly became a recovered-memory movement appeared, laying out the steps by which the ills of the present could be found in past abuse. Written by Ellen Bass and her student Laura Davis, the emotive *The Courage to Heal* sold over eight hundred thousand copies. It was directly aimed at 'you' – everywoman. And 'you' could tick a checklist of seventy-eight effects of incest, to see whether you qualified as a survivor. Given the questions, it wasn't difficult to qualify. Here's a random sample. 'Do you have trouble feeling motivated? Do you feel alienated or lonely? Can you accomplish things you set out to do? Do you feel you have to be perfect? Do you feel yourself clinging to the people you care about? Are you satisfied with your family relationships? Do you have trouble expressing your feelings? Do you ever use alcohol, drugs, or food in a way that concerns you? Do you feel powerless, like a victim?'[392]

Bass and Davis also described 'coping mechanisms' – eating disorders, super-achieving, denial, leaving the body and, of course, forgetting. Healing takes courage. It means recovering all of the painful past, stored in the fibres of the body, and letting it out. The pain of therapy, feeling the pain burn again, is part of the process. So too is confronting those responsible for the abuse. At the end of the process, every woman is welcomed into the sisterhood of incest survivors. The 1992 edition of *The Courage to Heal* contains a resource guide of not only some six hundred books, but support groups, organizations and newsletters, even a board game.

Being alive as a woman at the end of the twentieth century meant to be an incest survivor. In 1991 Oprah Winfrey, as well as former Miss America Marilyn Van Derbur and the famous television comedienne Roseanne Barr Arnold, shared their abused pasts with the world. *Time Magazine* reported: "'It's the secret that's been killing me my whole life,' Arnold, 38, says. "I feel like screaming; I feel like running; I struggle hard not to forget again." . . . And for every celebrity who has gone public, thousands of ordinary people have found the courage to confront their own pain, tell others about it and seek help.'393

Help, of course, means help from the therapeutic professions which had no little hand in constructing the illogicality of a killing secret so terrible one struggles *not* to forget it. Everywhere vulnerable people woke up to the possibility that their ailments, discomforts and failures, their sense that something was wrong, had a cause in a secret they had forgotten. A sizeable industry of therapists, psychologists, counsellors and social workers was at hand to diagnose, root out, suggest or simply cue repressed memories of abuse in their clients. They did so through any combination of hypnosis, journal-keeping, 'guided imagery' (A programme of 'guided' thoughts and suggestions), dreamwork and sodium amytal. The movement had its ambulance-chasing lawyers primed to sue accused parents at the first rush of memory. And as the abused took the accused family members to court for 'reparations', in high-profile cases which by 1994 had topped the three hundred mark and included murder and satanic abuse charges, a backlash set in.

The turning point may have come around 1988 when in Olympia, Washington, Paul Ingram, a sheriff's deputy who belonged to a religious group, the Church of the Living Water, which actively believed in Satan, confessed to child abuse and to murdering twenty-five children in satanic rituals. The case was brought by his daughters Erica and Julia, who recalled the abuse by their father and his poker friends, from when Erica was five until she left home. Ingram's recollections of his wildly abusive past came during intensive interrogation. He was persuaded that he suffered from multiple personality disorder and so couldn't at first remember the events. He confessed to a series of horrendous charges and was jailed, only later to withdraw his confession. This wasn't accepted, despite the reports of memory experts such as Elizabeth Loftus, which showed that his original testimony had nothing to do with remembering. Ingram served fourteen years in prison. Investigated by Lawrence Wright, the Olympia story was published in The *New Yorker* in 1994 and fed the backlash, which by then included cases against therapists.

Melody Gavigan, thirty-nine, a computer expert from California, checked into a local psychiatric hospital. She was severely depressed and needed help. During her five weeks of treatment, a family and marriage counsellor suggested that her depression stemmed from childhood incest. Desperate for any answers, Gavigan took the cue and started writing her journal of emerging memories. As *Time Magazine* reported on 29 November 1993: 'She told about running into the yard after being raped in the bathroom. She incorporated into another lurid rape scene an actual girlhood incident, in which she had dislocated a shoulder. She went on to recall being molested by her father when she was only a year old – as her diapers were being changed – and sodomized by him at five.'[394] On her therapist's advice, Gavigan confronted her father with her accusations. She broke off relations with her family, moved away and formed an incest survivors' group. More memories came. Something in the college psychology course she had signed up for, however, made her sceptical of what she had 'recovered' and she concluded her memories were false. She filed a suit against the psychiatric hospital for the pain she and her family had suffered.

The 'memory wars' were well under way. Where therapy was hailed as salvation, it was also now under attack, sometimes by patients, sometimes by theoreticians, sometimes by accused parents who banded together in America in the False Memory Syndrome Foundation early in 1992, and in the British False Memory Society. The new memory scientists – a grouping which included cognitive psychologists like Elizabeth Loftus, biochemists, neuroscientists and the new brain imagers – came together to dispute therapists' recovered-memory findings. They argued that memories decayed, could easily be changed by suggestion or wish, and made to feel real by repetition. Freud's name was bandied about by both sides: either he was responsible for having abandoned his original hypothesis that really occurring and later forgotten childhood seduction was a trigger to hysteria or, as the philosopher of repression and the unconscious, he was responsible for the entire package of recovered memory, with its real or therapy-induced rememberings.

Memory had become the fin-de-siècle's favourite conceptual cluster. It gathered under its aegis Holocaust museums, memorials and survivors' reminiscences, which had never been *forgotten* but had rarely been spoken as fully. Alzheimer's, the disease of forgetting, was the time's shadow side, the great memory fear of the older generation. Abuse could be recovered or invented to create an identity. Sufferers from Alzheimer's had nothing at all — no memory and no remembered subject to experience it. But as the most feared neurological condition of an ageing Western population at the end of a dying century and in the 'decade of the brain', it did have a great many investment dollars to nourish it.

Phyllis Greenacre (1894–1989)

In America, as elsewhere, it took traditional psychiatrists and psychoanalysts, even the women amongst them, a while to wake to the new, emphatically proclaimed evils contained in the package called sexual abuse and its prevalence as a central medical and morally defining category.

The redoubtable Phyllis Greenacre, doyenne of American psychiatry, had experience of all sides of the profession. Beginning in 1916, she had served as an intern at Johns Hopkins and worked in the psychological laboratory of the Henry Phipps Clinic under the pioneering, if erratic, Adolf Meyer. One of the first women in the profession, she was then engaged to assess the experimental research of the notorious and delusional Henry Cotton at Trenton State, with his theory of chronic infection causing madness. To her credit, she bravely damned his research.[395] She became director of the outpatient unit at New York's

Payne-Whitney and from 1932 began a psychoanalytic training, rising to become President of the American Psychoanalytic Association, as well as a professor of psychiatry at Cornell. She was also one of the founding editors, with Anna Freud, of the *Psychoanalytic Study of the Child*. Though Greenacre had written specifically on trauma and early childhood, the trauma here is not understood as necessarily sexual: it could be the effect on the child of an external act such as hospitalization or a mother's depression.

J. Laplanche and J.-B. Pontalis in their deservedly famous dictionary of psychoanalysis give a succinct, classic definition of trauma:

> An event in the subject's life defined by its intensity, by the subject's inca-pacity to respond adequately to it, and by the upheaval and long-lasting effects that it brings about in the psychical organisation.
>
> In economic terms, the trauma is characterised by an influx of exci-tations that is excessive by the standard of the subject's tolerance and capacity to master such excitations and work them out psychically.[396]

In a 1950 paper on trauma in girls before puberty, Greenacre explores the case of Daphne, a thirty-year-old woman incapable of sustaining relationships with either men or women. Daphne is exceptionally tense, suffers from a fear of what she calls a 'black presence', as well as a dread of 'growing up and wearing white stockings'. She goes to pieces when-ever any public pressure is put on her: taking exams, speaking in front of people, or indeed watching sadomasochistic events such as fights. Such events cause her to 'flood' — experience a spontaneous discharge (orgasm, blood, urine, excrement) — or faint. Like other patients in the more classical literature who have experienced a 'trauma' after the age of about four or five, Daphne has little trouble in remembering in analysis the event from which her troubles dated. The accuracy of the memory is not the question. She relates the episode, the details of which will be analysed, on her second visit. Greenacre recounts :

> At the age of about ten the girl was roller-skating in the cellar of her own home when a man entered to read the gas meter. She spoke to him and he offered to show her the meter, thereupon lifting her so that she could see the movement of the little hands upon the dials of the meter.

In lifting her he put his hand under her dress and stimulated her genitals. She recalls having become extremely excited, ashamed and frightened; she squirmed free and the man quickly left. She could not recall exactly how the experience ended; she had the feeling that she lost consciousness or 'went blank'.[397]

The 'traumatic' event happened during a period when Daphne and a girlfriend had been chatting excitedly and at length about matters sexual. Soon after this, thanks to her friend, she discovered a 'peculiarly pleasant' form of masturbation in the bathtub which continued up until the time of her analysis. After the event with the meter-reader, Daphne's family moved, she suffered a humiliating rejection by her favourite male cousin; then they moved again, for no related reason. Daphne's puberty coincided with the pregnancy of an aunt whose namesake she was and the birth of a boy whom Daphne thought of as her brother and who soon developed epilepsy, much to her fascinated distress.

After a series of associations amplifying on the case, Greenacre draws what would, after feminism and the establishment of the classification of child abuse, be an almost impossible conclusion. She argues that in all of the patients she has seen of which Daphne is an exemplar, the 'prepuberty trauma was induced by the child generally . . . under the stimulus of an adolescent or an older woman'. The traumatic situation was also 'precipitated' by the child who was curious and preparing for puberty. It represented the condensation of pre-Oedipal, far earlier experiences which had disturbed the girl, and it was in that sense a repetition.

In Daphne's case, there were a number of earlier events which had stirred her pleasure and mixed it with fear – including the exhilaration of her father lifting her and hurling her around wildly, watching her mother perform what she interpreted as fellatio while her father was confined to bed and encased in a white cast (interpreted as the white stockings she fears as part of growing up). These earlier incidents, together with the event at the gas meter, were then mobilized by the patient as evidence of the (exciting) danger of sexuality and used as a defence against it. In Daphne's case this also carried the masochistic gratification of 'flooding'. When the traumatic event takes place with an adult, Greenacre also notes, 'the guilt can be the more readily shifted'.

The child's own part in the trauma, together with the earlier events which have produced the pressure of provocation, can be more readily concealed.

According to Greenacre's paper, Daphne seems to have done well enough through her treatment, whether Greenacre was right or wrong in her interpretations and the points she draws. What is interesting from the vantage point of the present is the way in which she implicates the patient, ascribes an active part to her in her own life story. Daphne is not – though Greenacre herself followed Hélène Deutsch in understanding femininity as passive and charged with masochism – treated as a victim. A latter-day therapist might say that the analyst here is repeating the trauma which victimizes the patient by wrongly attributing a partly willed participation in a traumatic sexual act, by not taking Daphne's story at face value; by enacting the patriarchal view of implicating the victim in the act of perpetration. All this may also be true. But what underlies Greenacre's analysis is the understanding that children can and do experience sexual pleasure, that all sex is not an irreparable violation, a rape, an insurmountable evil. Daphne's trauma is something that can be got over, and a life with sex (no matter what the orientation) lived. Our turn-of-the-century idea of 'sexual abuse' hardly permits this possibility through the door. To be molested by a stranger becomes an event as deeply shocking to the woman as an act of war: it indelibly colours life thereafter, marking all life as an afterlife, transforming it into a survivor's tale.

Greenacre's cases in her 1950 paper are middle-class. Hospital and outpatient child psychiatrists and psychotherapists were, if anything, even more accustomed to seeing children who had been beaten, sexually violated by elders or siblings, or who had witnessed the kinds of scenes that Freud called 'primal'. After all, separate bedrooms were relatively new in history and then only the property of the better off. The class aspect of the abuse and incest dilemma is now rarely noted.

THE FRONT LINE

In a talk at the December 1989 meeting of the American Academy of Psychoanalysis, Margaret Tsaltas, MD, looked back at her records over thirty-three years of psychiatric practice with 'abused' children to sift the changes that had taken place in theory and treatment.[398] She noted that the children referred for outpatient treatment because of reaction to sexual abuse made up the *smallest* number in her case load: a total of forty-seven over a lifetime's practice from 1953 on. But her account suggests that not only had numbers grown (which might have to do with the readiness of reporting), but so too had the brutality of the violence the children suffered.

In the first five years of her practice in a teaching hospital she saw nine 'sexually molested' girls under twelve. The term in this context meant any kind of sexual behaviour other than penetration. All the abusers were fathers, who in this period were dealt with by being put on probation. This involved psychotherapy, though not being taken away from the family, which was understood as needing the father's financial support. The child was placed in a foster home until such time as the acting social worker was confident the father would not repeat his acts. The treatment goal with the child was to relieve the conflict 'between their guilt (over having to lose their family and their pleasure in what they regarded as their father's special love for them) and their fear (of what their abuser might have done next and their fear of losing their mother's love)'.

It is worth remarking that Tsaltas, who is of a pre-feminist generation, records and stresses the child's *pleasure* in the sexual activity, the conflict between love and fear. This is something which disappears altogether in later understandings of abuse, where any sexual activity is equivalent to violence (which it may indeed by the turn of the century have become). Tsaltas notes that the girls saw their being taken away from the family as 'punishment for the pleasure they had in their father's manipulations of their bodies and they fantasised that their mothers would never forgive them for talking to outsiders about their guilt'. Invariably, the girls' attempts to talk to their mother had met with the mother's denial of their experience.

Between 1958 and 1963, Tsaltas moved to another hospital outpatient department. Here, out of her case load, she saw twenty-three children who had been molested and six raped, four of whom were already teenagers. The state now prosecuted both molesters and rapists, and since the guilt of the latter was easier to establish, they were usually imprisoned for long terms. Mothers, left destitute with families, blamed daughters for 'lying and fantasizing' and bringing accusations against fathers, thereby precipitating poverty. All the girls needed to do to get the families off welfare was to retract what they had said. Tsaltas states as her primary treatment goals the resolution of conflicts 'about personal integrity versus family interest as well as concerns about paternal betrayal and fear of bodily harm'. Rather than the usual play therapy, she feels she needs here to be both more intrusive and more educational in her approach.

Twenty-two years later, between 1985 and 1990, the social fabric of everyday life of the families whose raped/and or abused children Tsaltas sees has so deteriorated that she has altogether shifted her goals 'from direct efforts at unconscious conflict resolution to the more indirect but more effective method of re-establishing maturational tracks'. In other words, her psychiatric work has become directly remedial: families are involved, dialogue with the children in trying to establish a narrative of their lives may accompany play, and certainly take more of the treatment time; education and future planning about how they can return to school and cope forms part of the psychiatric plan. The children are designated as 'traumatized'. They come to the psychiatrist on a referral from a rape crisis centre and their assailant has usually already been dealt with by the criminal courts and is locked up.

In the world in which they live, single-parent families, absent jailed fathers, step-boyfriends are the norm. Poverty is endemic. Aids makes sex even more dangerous. And between 1988 and '89, crack cocaine use has doubled the murder rate. Even at the start of this period, so prevalent are fears of abuse that mothers tell her that they must be present when she interviews their children – just in case. The doctor is now also a potential abuser – a fear that had become so widespread in the USA at this time that polled university students said they would prefer to have therapy with a computer program than with an analyst. Tsaltas in fact finds that the parent's presence diminishes the child's anxiety and, in turn, the child is shored up by the shrink's presence. She can divulge the family 'secret' in front of a parent who has *promised* not to react. Five of the girls she saw during this time had been not only raped, but sodomized, and one of them had been gang-raped by her father and his druggy friends. Another had been prostituted for drug money.

The level of violence, associated with sex or not, has risen incremen-
tally. In this urban world, brutalized by poverty, mind-doctoring feels
like a plaster applied to an arterial haemorrhage. The psy worker can
provide a little remedial help, can educate in emotions and social
values – as, for instance, lessening the child's continuing fear by reducing the rapist 'to the emotionally disturbed, sexually immature figure
he really is' and showing her appropriate adult behaviour, so that she
understands how 'her formerly beloved assailant deviated from that
role and those behaviors'.

What is at issue here is not psychic disorder so much as social deterioration of a radical kind. One of the problems of our time is that mind
doctors are called upon to deal with ills that have to do with endemic
poverty and social breakdown. The theorization of trauma that grows
out of this period – with its origins in war neurosis – may have not a
little to do with the psy professionals' own terror at what is being asked
of them during a peacetime in which the brutalization and distress of
poverty, displacement and drugs take the emotional toll of war.

NEW DIAGNOSTIC CATEGORIES

In 1976, the *Comprehensive Textbook of Psychiatry* by A.M. Friedman, H.I.
Kaplan and B.J. Saddock still claimed that the rate of father–daughter
incest was one in a million. Anyone who recognized this text as authoritative would, of course, doubt the reality of a patient's claims of sexual
abuse. Little wonder that women trainees in the therapeutic professions during these years rebelled against the received wisdom. The new
generation were not afraid to voice issues their teachers and supervisors
would have found too shameful to speak. Following Jeffrey Masson's
lead in *The Assault on Truth*, many attacked Freud's shift from an early
understanding of sexual seduction as real and traumatic to a focus on
fantasy and the psychic life. They mutinied against analysts who refused
to give enough weight to the 'real' of their lives and turned to his disciple Ferenczi, who in a late paper, 'The Confusion of Tongues,' upheld
the importance of distinguishing the real from the fantasized both in
childhood and in the consulting room.[399]

Amongst this new generation was Judith Herman, who had a

background as a civil rights and women's movement activist. Moulded by consciousness-raising, which she said taught her to trust the personal testimony of women, and her experience as a Harvard-trained psychiatrist working within a 'victims of violence' unit, Herman had the authority to contest the ways in which the psychiatric establishment tended to misdiagnose abused women by seeing their ills as a function of their character: a fundamental masochism coupled with promiscuity, for instance, would be said to elicit violence from the male. The perpetrator's crimes and behaviour were thus repeatedly laid at the feet of the victim.

Herman recounts how in the eighties when the *DSM* was coming up for revision, a group of male psychoanalysts proposed a diagnosis of 'masochistic personality disorder' to be applied to a person 'who remains in relationships in which others exploit, abuse, or take advantage of him or her, despite opportunities to alter the situation'. Women's organizations protested, as did Herman, who participated in the *DSM* revision process. Many of the male psychiatrists failed to see what the women, who during this period worked with the battered and abused in crisis centres and the courts both in America and Europe, learned: that chronic abuse renders a victim passive and dependent on the perpetrator who often has also isolated her from the rest of society.

Like captive to kidnapper, or prisoner to warder, the relationship between battered wife or child and her abuser generates helpless passivity, robs initiative, and induces that numbness which is also a means of enduring repeated violence. Since for the woman and child what is at issue here is a dismantling of the nature of love, the ability to trust is fundamentally damaged. In front of medics or courts, a perverse loyalty may make her unwilling or too ashamed to reveal the full scale of abuse. As the campaigning barrister Helena Kennedy has also argued, male judges, alongside doctors, trapped in an old double standard about sexuality, were used to blaming the victim for the crime, whether it was rape or repeated abuse, and slow to see the nature of the psychological damage inflicted.[400]

Herman and her women colleagues won a victory over the 'masochistic personality disorder' diagnosis and its stigmatization of the victim. The compromise diagnosis, now relegated to the appendix of the *DSM*, became 'self-defeating personality disorder', and the criteria stopped it being applied to anyone who had been physically, sexually or psychologically abused.[401]

In line with one school of feminists, Herman's major book of 1992, *Trauma and Recovery*, attacked Freud for reducing psychoanalysis to psychic and unconscious determinants, and so ensuring that the dominant psychological theory of the twentieth century was founded in the 'denial of women's reality'.[402] Drawing on clinical work with the victims of sexual and domestic violence, combat veterans and the victims of war and terror, Herman's book has the zeal of a political campaign. The elision of battered women and political prisoners, rape survivors and combat veterans, of 'the survivors of vast concentration camps created by tyrants who rule nations and the survivors of small, hidden concentration camps created by tyrants who rule their own homes',[403] is rhetorically powerful. There is no doubt that the book 'validates' women's experience of sexual violence and raises it to a top-grade category of suffering where the worst and most heroic forms of degradation certainly belong. But the very notion of 'validation', like that of empowerment of victims, may sit more readily in a human rights court or a political campaign than within a psychiatric environment.

However, since diagnoses do make their way into court in the form of expert witnesses, since they do affect divorce, custody or the rarer murder trials and also serve to release insurance expenditure for treatment, the battle to find a diagnosis for the abused of the private sphere had a sense of justice about it. The diagnosis which Herman and her colleagues battled to attach to abused women was PTSD – post-traumatic stress disorder. PTSD has a dramatic history of its own, which brings together hysteria, the disputed war neuroses, the search for reparations from the Germans after Nazi atrocities, and the protracted campaigning by Vietnam veterans for compensation for the debilitating psychic after-effects of war.[404] PTSD found its way into the *DSM* in 1980.

Classified as an anxiety disorder, its criteria were expanded in the revised *DSM III-R* of 1987:

a. The individual has experienced a *traumatic* event that (1) is 'outside the range of usual human experience' and (2) would be 'markedly distressing to almost anyone'.
b. The traumatic event is persistently reexperienced in at least

one of the following ways: (1) recurring and intrusive distressing recollections of the event; (2) recurring distressing dreams of the event; (3) sudden acting or feeling as if the traumatic event were recurring; (4) intense psychological distress when exposed to events that symbolize or resemble an aspect of the traumatic event.

c. The individual persistently *avoids* stimuli associated with the trauma or experiences a *numbing* of general responsiveness. To meet this criterion, a person has to evidence at least three of the following: (1) efforts to avoid thoughts or feelings associated with the trauma; (2) efforts to avoid activities or situations that arouse recollection of the trauma; (3) an inability to recall an important aspect of the trauma; (4) a markedly diminished interest in significant activities; (5) feelings of detachment or estrangement from others; (6) a restricted range of affect; (7) a sense of foreshortened future.

d. The individual experiences persistent symptoms of increased *Autonomic arousal* not present before the trauma. The person must exhibit at least two of the following: (1) difficulty falling or staying asleep; (2) irritability or outbursts of anger; (3) difficulty concentrating; (4) hypervigilance; (5) exaggerated startle response; (6) physiological reactivity when the individual is exposed to events that symbolize or resemble an aspect of the traumatic event.

On the committee to help write the definition of PTSD for *DSM IV*, Herman succeeded in having the phrase 'outside the range of usual human experience' removed, as well as 'would be markedly distressing to almost anyone'. This left the way open for the sexually abused and battered wives to be diagnosed as sufferers of PTSD, an affliction that had already gone to court on numerous occasions, particularly with war veterans in America, and won compensation. It is said that the diagnosis has risen by some 50 per cent since the definition was enlarged. Breslau and Davis, who have also carried out gender-based research on PTSD, say that women are at greater risk than men as a result of 'assaultive violence' and that because of their helplessness, suffer far longer from its effects.[405]

There is now a movement afoot for the new edition of *DSM-IV* and
the ICD (*International Classification of Diseases*) to contain a 'complex' version of the diagnosis, which would make further reference to the effects
of chronic or persistent abuse. Herman argues that victims of prolonged
and repeated trauma such as Holocaust survivors, or those who have
been subject to totalitarian control – which can include totalitarian
systems in sexual and domestic life – hostages, survivors of some religious cults, 'develop characteristic personality changes, including
deformations of relatedness and identity'. They may withdraw from
others, disrupt their intimate relationships, suffer from persistent distrust, despair of life, be preoccupied by suicide, fail to protect
themselves, be jumpy, and see threatening situations or recurrence of
the traumatic events as possible everywhere. They suffer from numbing, insomnia, nightmares and hyperarousal, part of the disorder of
the fear/flight mechanism.

Victims of prolonged abuse in childhood develop similar problems
and in addition are 'vulnerable to repeated harm, both self-inflicted
and at the hands of others'. Most dramatically, perhaps, they suffer
from 'alternation in consciousness', not only in the form of the intrusive recall of traumatizing event(s), but in the form of transient
dissociative episodes during which amnesia sets in. The standard explanation of this is to do with the abused child coping with repeated
brutalization by blocking out existing experience and entering a trance
state. This defence is learned; what is called a vertical splitting becomes
habitual (rather than the horizontal notion of a Freudian repression
into the metaphorically buried unconscious). During this splitting,
alternative personalities or alters can emerge – or so they have been
interpreted in the literature ever since Janet described his hysterics and
Morton Prince his Miss Beauchamp.

Herman's battle to include abused women alongside survivors of
war, disaster and terror under the diagnosis of PTSD did indeed elevate
women from the much maligned implication of hysteria or, often,
from that classification so loathed by psychiatrists and analysts,
Borderline Personality Disorder. But a concept of dissociation, linked
with a presumption of incest which could be remembered, had side-
effects: it rendered suffering symptomatic and a signal of a psychiatric
disorder. 'Suffering from intimacy, an inability to create safe and

appropriate boundaries between the self and others, having a tendency to idealize or denigrate'[406], could, after all, more or less describe any woman at the end of an affair.

Herman's therapy for recovery, inspired by the cases that human rights lawyers build with torture victims, involved providing a safe environment in which the patient could trust the therapist. In that safe haven, remembering and reliving horror could occur. The cathartic effect was enabled by the scripting of a trauma narrative which filled in the patient's missing moments. In putting together the details over many sessions, the therapist acted as prompt and ghost writer. What the patient didn't remember, the therapist filled in to provide coherence. At all points, the therapist's role was actively to believe the patient's story and encourage it.

Since traumatic events re-invade the patient's mind as images, are incoherent and inarticulate flashes, putting words to these images, providing them with context, sense, history would offer relief. Where there were amnesiac gaps, hypnotherapy, the truth drug sodium amytal or drama therapy were used. Throughout, the therapist acted as a trusting and 'compassionate witness'. There was one further stage to the therapy: the trauma document validated the patient's experience and suffering fully only once it was made public as testimony — and perpetrators confronted. Abusers, like war criminals, need to be taken to court.

Herman's technique is part psychological, part political. The mixture of the two, the use of recovered memory to indict sexual abusers, went against the grain of the more psychoanalytically based part of the profession. Freud had long ago said that the logic of the unconscious, with its uncertain differentiation between the imaginary and the real, and its lack of punctuated time, had no place in the courtroom. The truths of the psyche were not the same as legal evidence. Recovered-memory therapy was based on the assumption that they were.

MULTIPLES

Dissociated memory with its roots in trauma was linked to that other great illness epidemic of the last part of the century, Multiple

Personality Disorder, or MPD, which came into the *DSM* in 1982 and was later revised as Dissociative Identity Disorder, or DID, in 1992. Based again on the prolonged horrors of child abuse from which the victims dissociate, the florid sufferers of MPD, like Charcot's earlier hysterics, performed an acrobatics of alteration, moving between good and bad, male and female personae. At least two distinct alters were necessary for the *DSM* classification, but in the lore of what Ian Hacking has described as a 'down home', 'egalitarian' movement, as many as thirty-two alters have been documented in the same person. An illness of both identity and memory which made the vulnerable all too susceptible to the suggestions of therapists, MPD travelled America remembering satanic abuse and a whole vivid string of horrors which far outranked anything Miss Beauchamp had managed to remember in Prince's consulting room.

The popularizing of illness descriptions, particularly where the drama of multiples was concerned, was ripe for unconscious mimicking by the vulnerable, often depressed, possibly self-harming and suicidal, certainly suggestible: the behaviour could then become all too real. Human beings are complicated creatures, subject to being 'made up' by medical and psychological inquiry, authoritative group or institutional descriptions, so that they can be changed or bettered or simply emulated.[407] Since people are not static, they interact with their own classifications, through support groups or lobbies, and in a 'looping effect' create new kinds of people. The 1990s multiple with her support groups and websites was a different being from the mediums or hysterics investigated by the psychologists of the turn of the nineteenth century. What remained the same was that the behaviour needed a little learning, just as had the various acrobatic postures of Charcot's arc of hysteria.

As Hacking observes in *Rewriting the Soul* (1995), fewer than fifty cases of multiples had been noted in the medical literature between 1922 and 1972. In 1973 *Sybil* appeared, Dr Cornelia Wilbur's case of a *grande hystérie*, and captured the public imagination, eventually becoming a popular movie. Sybil, as told by her psychiatrist to the journalist Flora Rheta Schreiber who came to live with Sybil, Wilbur and her other multiple patients, is a multiple with sixteen alters whom Wilbur treated first in Nebraska, then took along to New York as a graduate student when she moved there to do a psychoanalytic training, and who finally followed Wilbur to Kentucky.

An intelligent young woman, Sybil suffered from fugue episodes in which she woke up in strange places without knowing how she had arrived there. Amongst Sybil's warring personalities, some were children; two were men. Some remembered childhood: they had emerged to cope with the terror of a perverse mother, who punished the little Sybil with cold water enemas tied so as to prevent expulsion, sharp objects in her vagina and a sordid list of other tortures. Wilbur went on to confirm that the implements existed in Sybil's childhood home. Whether – as Hacking underlines – they had been used in the manner Sybil's alters remembered did not really matter by the time the story had percolated and then been dramatically recreated in the public arena. The links between dissociation, multiple personality and childhood abuse had been made.[408] The swell of abuse findings and narratives over the coming years would mostly change the sex of the abusing parent.

Wilbur chaired the first panel on MPD at the 1977 meeting of the American Psychiatric Association. Thanks to workshops, meetings, and what was effectively lobbying for the inclusion of an ever more ample diagnostic description in the *DSM*, multiple personality arrived. It had its own international association, and by 1988 its own journal, owned by therapist Richard Kluft, an advocate of multiples and one of the association's prime movers. Loosely educated therapists now discovered multiple personalities in growing numbers of patients. Using hypnosis and sodium amytal to unearth the abuse trauma they were convinced lay at the base of the patient's problems, dissociations appeared and personalities developed. Multiples grew to some twenty thousand and Dr Colin Ross, a leading party in the MPD movement, speculated that over two million Americans 'fit the criteria for being a multiple personality'.[409]

The therapeutic procedure for diagnosing a patient with MPD is revealing. Frank Putnam, whose 1989 textbook on the subject is the most influential in the field, points out that he begins by taking a full chronology of the patient's life, and if there are significant gaps or confusions, that is an indication of a possible multiple. Recall is an uncertain function and most people would find this task daunting. Then there are questions about flashbacks, nightmares and intrusive images. Since 'patients are masters at appearing to say one thing while actually saying another', it may take some time before memories rise and alters appear. So the clinician can prod, ask questions: for instance, do you ever feel that there is 'some part of yourself that comes out and does or says things that you would not do or say'?[410]

Being a multiple is a frightening condition. Though its presence in court has most often been in conjunction with cases in which the multiple is accused of committing a crime 'while in a dissociated state', in a 1990 trial a diagnosed multiple, Sarah, sued one Mark Peterson, an Oshkosh grocery worker, who she alleged had raped her while she was moving between personalities. Peterson had invited the twenty-six-year-old, who called herself Franny, to go dancing with him, despite the fact that he saw her personality undergo profound shifts even as they sat by a Wisconsin fishing hole, and the group she was with told him she suffered from MPD – or so the prosecution witnesses stated, since Wisconsin law makes it a crime to engage in intercourse with a person you believe to be mentally ill and who cannot assess your conduct.

Peterson rang Franny, took her to a coffee shop where she told him about a personality, Jennifer, who likes to dance and have fun. When, later in the car, he asked 'Can I love you', and this Jennifer said OK, he drove her to a park and they had sex, at which point six-year-old Emily intruded, whom he asked to tell Jennifer to keep their tryst a secret. But Franny and Emily told Sarah, and she phoned the police to report an assault.

During the pre-trial hearing, three of Sarah's twenty-one personalities were sworn in separately. 'In each instance, she closed her eyes, paused, then opened them to speak and act as different people. At one point, Sarah was given a glass of water by the judge. Later another personality did not remember having taken the drink.'[411]

The increasingly high profile of multiples encouraged the disorder to come out, as anorexia and bulimia had, as a badge of courage. A website called Angel World sets the tone:

Perhaps you are also a Multiple. I hope to be able to show you that there is no need to be frightened. Inner families can learn to work together.

Research has shown that multiples are blessed with enormous creativity. Indeed, multiples had to be very creative in the first place to develop such unique solutions to escape the horrors of childhood . . . The thought I hope you will hold close is that you can lead an extraordinarily productive, creative, and fulfilling life, and that you can do it with abilities which are totally unavailable to singletons.[412]

But the increasing wildness of the disorder made even its original proponents, such as Putnam, issue cautionary warnings. Compliant patients were evidently attempting to satisfy what therapists wanted of them by producing fascinating alters, which were then increasingly difficult to reintegrate into the dominant personality – the ultimate goal of treatment. The psychiatric establishment had always been sceptical about the proliferation of alters. The chair of the dissociative disorders committee for the 1994 *DSM-IV* noted: 'there is a widespread misunderstanding of the essential psychopathology in this dissociative disorder which is failure of integration of various aspects of identity, memory and consciousness. The problem is not having more than one personality; it is having less than one personality.'[413] By 1994 MPD had been reclassified as Dissociative Identity Disorder with an emphasis not on the existence of separate personalities – which suggests distinct people more or less functioning in the world – but rather on the experience by the patient of their presence. The distinction between external and inner, the objective and the psychic realities, indeed between the measurable or evidential and the experienced, has always haunted any classifications the psy professions attempt to make.

Dissociated identity, for the mind doctors' profession if not necessarily for the multiples of the world, increasingly became a delusional sense of inner disintegration, an uncertainty about who one is, accompanied by varying degrees of amnesia and a sense of severe depersonalization – an experience of feeling out of one's body. MIND, the leading British mental health charity, often sensible and judicious in its characterizations of illness, notes that the spectrum of dissociative disorders, amongst which it includes PTSD, is most often linked to a history of trauma, usually childhood abuse, since children 'generally have a greater ability to dissociate' than adults, unless repeated trauma in childhood has turned it into a habit.[414]

Traditional psychoanalysts found themselves under attack from all sides during this period, as the British analyst Mary Target attests:

> On one side, which sees all or most recovered memories of abuse as false (i.e. historically untrue), the accusation is that these 'memories' are planted in the minds of suggestible patients by irresponsible therapists. On the other side, there is anger at the thought that survivors can be re-traumatised, by therapists who label painfully revived memories as fantasies, and who turn a blind eye, repeating the denial of reality that may at times be the most bitter betrayal in child sexual abuse.[415]

The question of what analytic stance to take in such cases is tricky. There is the danger of the patient's compliance and suggestibility, which may create the very memories the therapist, let alone the culture as a whole, implies are present. On the other side there is the fear that if the analyst doesn't ally herself with that part of the patient that is trying to overcome denial and repression, then the patient may experience the whole therapy as a repetition of an earlier failure to perceive and protect.[416] The image of Freud pursuing Dora's seduction, perhaps a little too relentlessly, haunts the profession.

Another matter underlies the wary psychoanalyst's hesitation over recovered memory. Why all these years on, and sexual revolutions later, is it only memories of abuse that recovered memory therapists, not to mention patients, insist need 'validation'? After all, if it were a fundamental question of the status of the 'real' and the 'fantasized' throughout a patient's therapy, or indeed of 'trust', then many other aspects of life would have to be put in the 'reality' scales:

> the analyst is not seen as having to say whether a patient's mother was really depressed, whether the patient was really left alone too much in hospital, whether she was really very close to her grandmother who died when she was small; these things are worked on as the patient's reality, which is not to dismiss them as fantasy. It is the expression of her current internal world, or present unconscious.'[417]

Whatever the more wary of the European psychoanalysts' responses to the status of trauma and recovered memories of abuse, child abuse itself remained a central social preoccupation and a continuing problem in the therapeutic and care sectors. Sometimes it also expressed itself, with the help of a goading popular press, in a mass hysteria about paedophiles and child sex rings, which from time to time throughout this period rocked Britain, France and Belgium. At other times, it found its focus in frantic attempts to repress or criminalize Web porn sites. In New York, where a licensed registration system has been put in place for psychoanalysts and therapists, they are now asked, in addition to the 'professional education requirement', to 'complete coursework or training in the identification and reporting of child abuse'.

THE SCIENCE OF TRAUMA

Throughout the 1980s and '90s, research in adjacent fields brought a boost to theories which postulated that childhood trauma, even of the neglectful rather than abusive kind, affected later behaviour, as well as stress levels and neurochemical activity. Mother—child relations, it now seemed clear, were imprinted on the physiology, the very chemistry of body and brain, and not only on the psyche. Earlier theorists might not have presumed that there could be a clear-cut difference, but now in any case it was eroded. Neurochemistry could chart the evidence.

Harry Harlow's student, the psychologist Stephen J. Suomi, conducted a subtle experiment with infant monkeys. The monkeys were reared by humans in the presence of inanimate surrogate 'mothers' for the first thirty days of their lives, then put in a group of peers and then into a larger mixed troop. Apart from thumb-sucking, these 'peer-reared' monkeys behaved normally, unlike Harlow's own sad, mad, monkeys raised in isolation. Their only irregularity was that they clung longer to other monkeys, and were rather more timid and slow to explore. In yearly periods of social separation from their group, the peer-reared monkeys showed significant signs of distress and withdrawal — signs which are linked to depression — such as huddling, rocking, passivity, and anxiety evidenced in increased grooming and picking. Monitored over time, these same monkeys showed a marked abnormality in their biochemical distress indicators. Their cortisol levels were high and their norepinephrine activity abnormal, compared with

monkeys raised by their mums. Cortisol and epinephrine, or adrena-
line, the fight-or-flight substance, are the two hormones responsible for
regulating stress in the body. They have also been found to be related to
mood regulation.

The conclusion drawn from these experiments was that disruption of
social bonds affects the physiology and neurochemistry of stress, leaving
the monkeys more neurochemically sensitive to stress even much later
in life. Their condition deteriorates with time, each separation from
the group bringing greater signs of depression and anxiety, with its
attendant change in hormone and neurotransmitter systems.[418]

Monkeys may not be humans, but a 1991 NIMH-funded study found
similar physiological abnormalities in stress hormones following what
this time was abuse, rather than what might be termed neglect. Here
160 girls from the ages of six to fifteen were followed from six months
after they had experienced documented sexual assault by a family
member for a period of four to five years. Compared to a control group,
the girls were found to have consistently above normal cortisol levels
and disruptions in the rise and fall of their stress hormone system. This
was later correlated to high levels of depression in the girls some years
after the abuse.[419]

PTSD as a diagnosis in America received a new boost and new
research monies with each 'traumatic' social event — from scares of
child abuse in schools to shootings to the attack on New York's Twin
Towers, when the trauma therapists came out in full force. Increasingly,
American trauma therapists travelled the world of crises and offered
psychiatric services to hurricane and war survivors. With the rise of
brain imaging and the neurosciences, a whole new set of 'scientific'
descriptions came into place to bolster diagnosis and further research.
Trauma, it now seemed to be clear, altered the chemistry of the brain
for life – though it was possible that talk, and more certainly – or so it
seemed – drugs, could have a therapeutic effect. Even the psychoanalysts and therapists who had been trained to think in terms of
unconscious conflicts were drawn into the new trauma science.

It has been found, for instance, that when patients suffering from
PTSD are confronted with a number of sensations that match the initial
traumatizing experience – such as being touched in a particular way, or
finding themselves exposed to smells or visual reminders – their

biological systems make them react with fight-or-flight responses, as if they were being traumatized all over again. Studies have shown that this is to do with abnormalities in the neurotransmitters that regulate arousal and attention. Sufferers from PTSD or indeed from depression have low levels of the stress hormone cortisol and secrete too much norepinephrine. Their continuously high physiological arousal engenders a tendency to call up emotional memories that were laid down during past states of arousal, resulting in the flashbacks and nightmares which are part of the condition's description.

Brain imaging has shown that when people are frightened or aroused, the frontal areas of the brain which control analysis and language are cut off in favour of the more primitive parts, the limbic system and the brain stem, not under conscious control. The amygdala, responsible for creating emotional memories, interprets the threat level of incoming information: once it has been imprinted with the memory that particular sensations are dangers, it triggers fight-flight reactions, and indeed behaviour that might look irrational.

According to Bessel van der Kolk, Director of the Boston Trauma Clinic and, along with Judith Herman, a leading medic and researcher in the field, the difficulty of traditional talk therapies with patients who suffer from PTSD is that not only does their traumatizing experience happen upon them, but it overcomes them with sensation. They cannot talk about it to a therapist. Nor do they want to confront the experience. How, then, to help patients process traumatic memories? Van der Kolk recommends the use of SSRIs (selective serotonin re-uptake inhibitors, amongst which are antidepressants such as Prozac, Paxil, etc.), which have been shown to allow patients some emotional distance from the traumatizing stimuli. Eye movement, desensitization and reprocessing (EMDR), has a similar effect, though no one seems to understand quite why following the therapist's hand while remembering trauma should have any calming impact, unless one hazards the notion that it might have something in common with mild hypnosis.

Only in their newly found calm can patients begin to make sense of the intrusive memories. With the therapist they find a language in which to communicate the worst in all its detail, encoding it in time, overcoming their helplessness. In that way it can become the past, while the patient emerges into a potential future. Achieving perspective, realizing that remembering is not reliving, can result in symptom reduction. However, van der Kolk warns, the fall-out rate with PTSD sufferers is high.[420]

The fall out rate of those *wanting* trauma therapy seems to be high outside the USA as well, despite predictions after the Bosnian War that everyone there was traumatized. The more recent advice of the World Health Organization to NGOs was that the one billion victims of war, torture and terrorism needed less therapy and more compassion and assurance that their basic physical needs would be met. After the tsunami disaster in Sri Lanka, the chief of their psychosocial services dealing with the aftermath told the New York Times, 'We believe the most important thing is to strengthen local coping mechanisms rather than imposing counselling.' Therapists were criticized for rushing in to impose Western-style group therapy and 'debriefing' techniques in which victims are meant to express their feelings and relive the traumatizing event as vividly as possible. Little attention was paid to local healing systems and conceptions of what mental illness might be, let alone to current needs. From Beirut to Bosnia, what refugees want far more than trauma therapy is help in rebuilding their lives through training or education.[421]

PERSONALITY DISORDERS

Josetta Marino is an attractive thirty-five-year-old Hispanic woman, separated from her husband, mother of a twelve-year-old girl and nine-year-old boy. After a suicide threat in the midst of depression, she was admitted to the psychiatric unit of a New York hospital. There had been two previous attempts at suicide, the first having taken place just after her daughter's birth, the second three years before her current admission to hospital.

Mrs Marino lives in an area where drugs and violence are an everyday part of the life of the streets. She herself has a history of on-and-off drug use and heavy drinking, though until six months ago she was fairly regularly employed as a nurse. The drug-taking varies in seriousness, depending on how 'worthless' and 'helpless' she feels. The two drug treatment programmes she has been on seem to have had little permanent effect. Most recently, the patient said she had been taking drugs to 'numb the pain'. Mrs Marino is highly sensitive to pain and to slights. In her time, she has left various jobs where she felt she wasn't treated with sufficient respect. She has also found herself fired from them.

For the last six months Mrs Marino has been unemployed. Seven months ago she kicked out her boyfriend, who the daughter had told child protection services was molesting her. Though her mother didn't believe her and the boyfriend denied the charge Mrs Marino threw him out after one of their repeated violent rows. The children's biological father disappeared for good when the children were small and Mrs Marino thinks he might be in prison. Since then she has engaged in any number of stormy sexual liaisons. These inevitably prove harmful to her, often physically as well as emotionally, but she is incapable of being alone for any length of time.

Since her first suicide attempt, Mrs Marino has had a history of diverse symptoms ranging from depression, to insomnia, to weight loss; in addition to hospitalization, there has been a long pattern of outpatient treatment with various therapists. She does not follow up treatment recommendations, and has abruptly terminated two therapies. With her therapists she is alternately suicidal and seductive, hostile and dependent. Various medications have been prescribed over time: antidepressants, anxiolytics and neuroleptics. None have had any long-term benefit.

Mrs Marino tells doctors that since the 'trouble' between her daughter and her last live-in boyfriend, she has been suffering from intense 'flashbacks' of being abused by her uncle. This was not in her files because she didn't think it worth mentioning before, and in any case assumed no one would believe her. Her mother certainly hadn't when she had complained of him at the time. But then, when her mother wasn't 'silent as the grave', she was usually blinded by a haze of alcohol.

A diagnosis of borderline personality disorder was made.

Roxy Grant, a slim, pixie-like twenty-three-year-old was admitted to a psychiatric unit after a serious suicide attempt. Her parents and ten-year-old stepbrother were away on holiday and she was home alone, depressed and desperately lonely. She mixed herself a killing cocktail, downed it, then rang the therapist she had been seeing erratically over the past months.

Roxy had been the family darling until her thirteenth birthday when she took up the clubbing life and fell in with a slightly older crowd who did an assortment of drugs and drank to excess. At sixteen, she ran off with an older boy, lived with him in a squat for several months, and dropped out of school despite her parents' pleading. The 'couple' returned to live with her parents when their other accommodation fell through. After a few weeks here, their relationship ended in tempestuous recrimination, accompanied by the destruction of much of Roxy's attic rooms. She made her first suicide attempt.

At her parents' and the hospital's insistence, Roxy started to see a therapist three times a week. She also saw any number of men and played out scenarios of great passion and excitement, some of them violent. The serial polygamy left her feeling increasingly vulnerable. She hid the helplessness in drink, binge eating and drugs, had flings with women partners, but here too, her therapist noted, the relationships ended in dramatic confrontation. Her narratives displayed a manipulativeness which she also replayed with her therapist. She showed little capacity for the insight the therapy demanded of her. She spent sessions complaining about family and friends, and the insults she suffered. She railed at the therapist for not listening to her well enough or sympathizing appropriately. She rang him often between sessions, her moods fluctuating wildly. When he went on holiday, she felt utterly abandoned, and punished for her worthlessness.

Roxy had started to work in her stepfather's office and was by turn competent and absent, depending on her night life. Her parents complied with all her erratic demands, fearful that she would once more try to kill herself. But one day, when she complained of the boredom of her job, her stepfather grew angry and exploded, firing her on the spot. She locked herself in her room. After a while, when her mother didn't hear her and feared the worst, the door was broken down. Roxy was mixing herself a cocktail, which hadn't yet been drunk. The family debated as to whether she should be institutionalized for her own safety. Roxy refused, promised she would get her life in order and enrol in a sixth-form college.

After some weeks of low-level depression, she started to see a new therapist. An antidepressant was prescribed. The pattern of drink and drugs and clubbing started again. A particularly violent and exciting bout of sexual activity with a new acquaintance resulted in her refusing to accompany her family on holidays. Just after Christmas, she found herself dumped with a black eye on the pavement. She went home and tried to kill herself.

The hospital diagnosed borderline personality disorder

Dawn, twenty-eight, was admitted to a secure unit after her conviction for the infanticide of her eleven-month-old son, Gabriel, who had been living with foster parents from birth. Quiet, with a polite, girlish and whispering quality to her speech which drew people near, Dawn had a long history of severe depression, suicide attempts and hospital admissions. In and out of children's homes through her childhood, she had been abused by residents as well as, in one, a staff member. Her mother had a history of psychotic depression. Dawn's husband, baby Gabriel's father, had abandoned her when she was four months pregnant.

On the night of the murder, Dawn had paid a visit to her son's foster family. Pitying her predicament, Gabriel's foster mother had broken the rules and allowed her to go up and spend time with the babe alone. She wasn't aware that Gabriel's father had recently asked Dawn for a divorce, thereby setting the seal on her sense of rejection and abandonment. In Dawn's eyes, Gabriel was intimately linked to his Dad, in some sense stood in for him. So she suffocated, then strangled, the boy. During the police interview, she betrayed no emotion about her act. Even six months later, with the therapist in the secure unit, that emotion was still absent.

Before coming to see Gabriel, Dawn had rung the police and announced her intent to kill unless she was stopped. But she had given no address and her warning went unheeded. The lack of help enabled her to feel like the passive victim of her own violent act.

In psychotherapy, she had vivid recall of waiting for her mother to come and take her away from her children's home. Yet she still showed no remorse whatsoever or, indeed, any understanding of the murder she had committed. When she talked of her son, there was no sense of his having an identity separate from her own.

Anna Motz, the forensic therapist who saw her, observes that Dawn was incapable of 'mentalization', that fundamental process which permits a person to imagine what another feels or thinks. Psychoanalysts relate this ability to a stage in self-development where the child looks for a reflection of her own inner states in her mother or primary caregiver. Dawn had never found this mirroring in her mother; thus her inner despair couldn't be converted into understanding. Instead it manifested itself in violence. During the act, she was herself the abandoned infant rejected by a mother she had never been able to separate herself from. In the infanticide, she compounded her own child, her husband, her mother and the child she herself had once been. The act was also a tragic request for containment by psychiatric services.[422]

According to Anna Motz, Dawn, though psychotic while committing the murder, had features of borderline personality disorder.

Josetta and Roxy are my own inventions based on a cross-section of cases given the designation 'borderline'. They have in common with Dawn a certain wildness or impulsiveness of action and what used to be called 'deviance'. Together these women demonstrate what has been a historical category problem: are people like them mad, or simply bad? I could have written Mrs Marino as a mother trapped in a dysfunctional and impoverished estate — a woman who needed not a psychological diagnosis, but help with a life she was leading in a way that harmed her own life and her children's. Roxy could have been characterized as a relatively ordinary selfish adolescent who would — if suicide wasn't pathologized in our society and the many lyrics which extol it didn't intervene — eventually grow into a new and calmer phase of life. Whatever else she may be, Dawn is clearly also 'bad' and society has imprisoned her for her crime. But is she also sick, in the way that the champions of the new psychiatric diagnoses in the mid-nineteenth century argued Henriette Cornier, another infant murderer, was?

What are now called the 'personality disorders' have long taxed both mind doctors and the legal profession. They have also called ethical categories and notions of 'normality' into question. What is society to do with a whole spectrum of people who may be dangerous to themselves and to others; people who don't and perhaps can't, without help, follow the rules of everyday behaviour that society sets down?

Distinguishing mental illness from what some have called sin, vice or crime, the mind doctors have come up with various categories. In his *Treatise on Insanity* (1835) J.C. Prichard coined the term 'moral insanity' to describe individuals of 'a singular wayward, and eccentric character' who display 'an unusual prevalence of angry and malicious feelings, which arise without provocation or any of the ordinary incitements'. At the more extreme end, such people migrated into Cesare Lombroso's category of 'degenerates' (see page 000), then became psychopaths or sociopaths. Now we have the 'antisocial personality' of the *DSM*, with its characteristics of deviance, deceitfulness, aggression, impulsiveness, reckless disregard for others and failure to feel remorse.

Though, as a whole, modern Western society has tended to pathologize crime, this has hardly meant an accompanying ability to treat disorders. Nor has it meant of late an increase in the number of hospitals where treatment is provided for criminals. Quite the other way round: statistics tell us that one in six prison inmates in the USA suffer from mental illness, often accompanied by illiteracy, a rate three times higher than in the general population. American Human Rights Watch reports that 'prisons have become the nation's primary mental health facilities', though without providing the kind of care that might eventually make reintegration into society possible. In women's prisons, borderline personality disorders are rampant. An August 2006 report on women in British prisons showed that out of the 4494 prisoners, three-quarters suffered from mental health problems, half had histories of domestic violence, and a third had been sexually abused, while two-thirds were drug- or alcohol-dependent. Drug charges and theft, often enough of clothes or food for their young children, were the main reasons for their imprisonments.[423]

In 2000, the Labour government introduced a Dangerous People with Severe Personality Disorder Bill in an attempt to establish legislation which would enable people who 'might' commit serious violent crimes to be preventatively arrested. The idea behind the legislation was to take 'psychopaths', violent sex offenders or potential murderers off the streets before they committed a crime, rather than having them turned away by mental health services as 'untreatable'.

Many psychiatrists relegate the personality disorders to a diagnostic dump bin. 'Psychopathic disorder', for example, is a legal term used in the current mental health legislation to refer to people who have 'a persistent disorder or disability of mind . . . which results in abnormally aggressive or seriously irresponsible conduct'. It is not a psychiatrically agreed condition. There was an outcry from much of the psychiatric profession when the bill, which had sizeable costs attached to it, was brought forward. The Royal College of Psychiatrists contended that there was no 'entirely satisfactory' diagnosis of antisocial traits that threaten public safety. The *Lancet* warned that dangerous severe personality disorder (DSPD) was so vaguely defined that six people would have to be detained to prevent one from acting violently.[424] The concern for civil liberties meant the bill was severely amended so that patients' rights were respected alongside the concern for public safety. Historically, the mad or bad conundrum has swung between the two poles as much as a result of social demand and governmental attitude as of psychiatric fashion. It has proved ever intractable and in need of correction. Alienists who, in the early days of the profession, might have wanted to extend their domain now feel wary of taking responsibility for what seem non-medical imperatives or social rehabilitation, for which they may have few skills.

The category of *borderline* personality disorder – neither quite mad, nor altogether bad – is another diagnostic dump. Until the precisions of recent *DSMs*, it designated an individual whom traditional therapies had found it all but impossible to treat, though they often asked for treatment or were assigned to it by social agencies. According to the NIMH, 2 per cent of American adults, most of them women, are borderlines: emotionally unstable, they may attempt to seduce, manipulate, attack the therapist or simply leave the treatment. They have a pattern of rapid emotional fluctuation, as well as of shifting aspirations, jobs and relationships. They account in America for some 20 per cent of psychiatric hospitalizations, often because of suicide attempts or threats.

In the early days of the women's movement, the analytic characterization of borderlines was derided. It was understood, in parallel with hysteria, as a controlling classification – a label to be applied to any woman who wouldn't conform – from Dora to Marilyn Monroe.

Wildnesss, desire, extreme language, excessive, impulsive, indeed rebellious behaviour were simply not allowed into the feminine repertoire;
and so its expressions were categorized as mad, morally insane, hysterical, borderline.

More recently, as classifications in our therapeutic society become
something of a desirable attribute, a sanctioned identity which can
confer meaning and a lifestyle to misery, 'borderline' has become an
acceptable, certainly accepted, classification. It describes an illness and
holds out the hope of recovery, even if often it is a condition linked to
certain social determinants: poverty, drugs, violence.

Patients designated as 'borderlines' have now also been recognized as
suffering in many instances from PTSD. This link to childhood trauma
or neglect has rescued the diagnosis from the untouchables pile. Judith
Herman offers a description that has fed into the diagnostic manuals.
'Borderline patients find it very hard to tolerate being alone, but are also
exceedingly wary of others. Terrified of abandonment, on the one hand,
and of domination on the other, they oscillate between extremes of
clinging and withdrawal, between abject submissiveness and furious
rebellion.'[425] Often understood as suffering from a failure of development in their early years because of parental neglect or abuse,
borderlines – the professionals now agree – have never managed to
form an inner representation of trusted people. They feel empty, need
others to fill that emptiness, and so may frantically seduce or please.
This need, however, can all too soon transform itself into a feeling of
being invaded, combined with the contradictory terror of being abandoned. Unstable, with no sense of boundaries or inner security, their
intimate, sexual or parenting relations often fail. Their precarious inner
state is one in which good and bad, ideal and demonic, are split off from
one another, so that no links between the two exist.

Forensic psychiatrists and analysts in Britain, while accepting that the
symptoms of the borderline patient can lie in early abuse, often find its
perpetrator not in the father but in the mother – the point where the
cycle of neglect or violence starts. Estela Welldon, Juliet Mitchell and
others after them have postulated that violence of the kind enacted by
women can best be understood as a form of female perversion, a perversion of motherhood: its site is the whole body and its extension, the
child. When women attack their own bodies by self-mutilation,

starvation or bingeing, by repeated placing of their body in relation to an abusing male, they are avenging themselves on a perverse or cruel mother whose extension they are, just as the child is theirs. Child abuse, or chronic infant neglect, is the reproduction of perverse mothering.

Recent treatment methods for borderline patients recommend a mixed package of therapies. No longer considered unreachable, patients are now understood to need SSRIs for their depression or anxiety, particularly if they are threatening suicide; a talk therapy, and thirdly, a measure of re-education and support over the years while they learn to deal with their volatility, which is often exacerbated by drug or alcohol use. England's National Institute for Mental Health (NIMHE) has recently put forward a plan which attempts to rescue borderlines from exclusion. This plan for a 'personality disorder capabilities framework' combines psychological treatment with a programme of education for employment alongside vocational or professional training, and continuing therapeutic support services. What is effectively a life-support system is seen as useful because the alternative is a sequence of failed drug rehabilitation programmes, erratic hospitalizations, and damage or danger to the woman and her children.[426]

The favoured psychotherapeutic approach to personality disorders is Washington Professor of Psychology Marsha Linehan's dialectical behaviour therapy, or DBT. This sets out to teach patients how better to control their lives, their emotions and themselves through self-knowledge, emotional regulation and that cognitive restructuring which is a feature of all the behavioural therapies. New ways of coping with the world, with social and intimate relations, and in particular how to handle stressful situations without recourse to drugs or violent upheaval, form a key part of the therapy, which also imports 'mindfulness' training from eastern religions. The use of the word 'dialectical' in the name of the therapy signals that this treatment both takes the patient as she is and 'validates' and supports her while confronting the imperative of change – which is the therapeutic aim.

The therapy assumes that on top of an 'invalidating environment', the patient's condition has a biological underpinning in the failure of her 'emotion regulation system', which may be due to genetics, intrauterine factors, and/or traumatic events in early development that permanently affected the brain.

It is clear that recent neurological studies of trauma have had an impact on the treatment of borderline patients, who, it is reported, share the predisposition to aggression because of impaired regulation of the neural circuits that modulate emotion. 'Impulsivity, mood instability, aggression, anger, and negative emotion' are characteristics supposedly implicated in the malfunctioning of the amygdala, and dependent on those key chemical messengers serotonin, norepinephrine and acetylcholines. Happily, we're told, 'such brain-based vulnerabilities can be managed with help from behavioural interventions and medication, much like people manage susceptibility to diabetes or high blood pressure'.[427]

Over the last twenty years, the work of the mind doctors has increasingly fallen into line with the more medical and neurochemical side of the profession. Physical, even genetic, explanations of illness have predominated. These made a sideshow of more diffuse dynamic arguments that placed less emphasis on classifiable symptoms and diagnoses and more on the patient's history, relations, and her unconscious. But in order to attract patients or research monies, theoretical leg-work needed to be done by the talking therapies. Diagnoses changed, proliferated and acquired a precision, hand in hand with the new drugs. Some would even say that symptomatology and diagnosis tailored themselves to the pharmaceutical industry. But this was in part what increasingly savvy patients, who could self-diagnose from Web, book, memoir or magazine, wanted.

Ian Hacking tells the story of a doctor in Ontario who, when a patient arrives and announces that she has multiple personality disorder, promptly asks to be shown her health insurance card, which contains a photograph and a name, and then says, 'This is the person I am treating, no one else.' There are many meanings that can be drawn from this story, but one, surely, is that diagnoses have the hypnotic power of master words. In a rampantly medicalized age, the classification of depression or borderline carries not stigma but the hope of cure.

15

DRUGS

I start to get the feeling that something is really wrong. Like all the drugs
put together – the lithium, the Prozac, the desipramine and Desyrel
that I take to sleep at night – can no longer combat whatever it is that
was wrong with me in the first place. I feel like a defective model . . . I
start to think that there really is no cure for depression, that happiness
is an ongoing battle, and I wonder if it isn't one I'll have to fight for as
long as I live.

Elizabeth Wurtzel, Prozac Nation

In 1963 Karl Menninger, one of the most important figures in American
post-war psychiatry, wrote: 'We tend today to think of all mental illness
as being essentially the same in quality, although differing quantita-
tively and in external appearance.'[428] For Menninger, with his
psychoanalytic orientation, symptoms were expressions or conversions
of an underlying inner conflict. This conflict produced anxiety which
could manifest itself in everyday or exaggerated neuroses at one end of
the spectrum, or at its other extreme in the severe disintegrations of
schizophrenia. Psychotherapy, the dominant mode of treatment and
explanation, could work with all of these. In its principal understanding and treatment of mental illness, America was then arguably the
least biologically oriented of the Western nations. Nowhere else, neither in Britain nor in France, where they played their important
cultural, though less medical, part, did the psychodynamic and talk
therapies have such prominence, even with disorders that might need

hospitalization. European psychiatry had remained what it had been from its origins, primarily hospital-based, while in America the private or office model of psychiatry, which lent itself to the talking cure, had grown to have great importance.

Then, while in Europe through the seventies the talk therapies rose up the popularity scale both in treatment and theoretical value, in America there was a radical turn towards a biochemical model of mental disorder. Apart from attacks by homosexual, feminist and anti-psychiatry critics and the detrimental presiding sense that the talking therapies, from the wildest encounter groups to the most conservative 'Freudian', were somehow one, several key factors played into each other to determine this shift.

One was the rise and rise of the pharmaceutical industry and its bopping, hip-hopping shadow, the street drugs trade. Arm in arm came the making of a transformed *Diagnostic and Statistical Manual* under the aegis of Robert Spitzer, who wanted above all to give the psychiatric profession a reliable medical look. From its earlier psychoanalytical imprecision, in its 150 spiral-bound pages, the *DSM* grew into that internationally used 900-page bible, which listed and described more varieties of mental disorder than even that arch-classifier Kraepelin had been able to dream of as he piled up his patient records and coded them into illness descriptions. A substantial proportion of these disorders, often characterized by behaviour, mention an associated 'recommended' drug treatment. In about 50–70 per cent of mood or anxiety disorders, there is also mention of a co-occurring 'substance abuse', though not the alcohol which plagued the populations of turn-of-the-nineteenth-century asylums, but more often a street drug or another prescription drug.[429]

Announcing the new scientific trend, *Time* in April 1979 put old-fashioned psychiatry on the couch and diagnosed depression and an identity crisis:

Patient's name: Psychiatry.

Age: In middle years.

History: European born. After sickly youth in the U.S., travelled to Vienna and returned as Dr. Freud's Wunderkind. Amazing social success for one so young. Strong influence on such older associates as Education,

Government, Child Rearing and the Arts, and a few raffish friends like
Advertising and Criminology.
Complaint: Speaks of overwork, loss of confidence and inability to get
provable results. Hears conflicting inner voices and insists that former
friends are laughing behind his back. Patient agrees with Norman Mailer:
'It's hard to get to the top in America, but it's even harder to stay there.'
Diagnosis: Standard conflictual anxiety and maturational variations,
complicated by acute depression. Identity crisis accompanied by compensatory delusions of grandeur and a declining ability to cope. Patient
averse to the therapeutic alliance and shows incipient overreliance on
drugs.[430]

Unlike their psychoanalytic kin, medical researchers working on
brain biochemistry were already optimistically predicting wonder
drugs.

People with titles like biochemist, psychobiologist, neurophysiologist
and psychopharmacologist are attracting scarce federal funds and
replacing traditional psychiatrists as chairmen of hospital psychiatry
departments. The field offers what psychiatry seems to have been yearn-
ing for all through the 1970s: scientific expertise, medical underpinnings
and an escape from the troublesome subjectivity of the human mind.

At about the same time as *Time* ran this article, a Dr Rafael Osheroff
was admitted to the famous Chestnut Lodge, where he spent seven
months being treated for the symptoms of 'psychotic depression' by
intensive psychotherapy. He requested medication but apparently it
was denied him, in favour of a 'regression' to childhood, so that he
could build himself up anew from there. Osheroff obtained a transfer to
another clinic where he was treated with phenothiazines and antidepressants. Within three months, he had returned to his old life. Sadly,
in the interim, that life had changed: his wife had left him and he had
been ousted from his medical practice. Osheroff sued Chestnut Lodge
for malpractice and was awarded $250,000. Ways of curing him had
been available and had not been used.
The case had major repercussions for psychoanalysis in the context
of American psychiatry: it now seemed that *not* to use drugs on patients

could constitute malpractice.[431] Young doctors, already hesitating between psychiatry and better-paying specializations, chose to go into less contested areas. Soon, to make up for the growing lack of medics, psychoanalysis in America would open its doors wider and wider to the ranks of lay analysts – from psychologists to social workers. In tandem, psychiatry became a more firmly biochemical practice.[432]

That 'troublesome subjectivity' that was the human mind and its messy emotions had hardly been drug-free throughout the twentieth century, nor even the nineteenth. Chloral hydrate, the first of the popular sedatives, and 'the first rehearsal of the "Prozac" scenario', was synthesized in 1832 and by the 1870s had a great public following as a drug that could relieve common symptoms from insomnia to anxiety and the vapours – or 'melancholia'. Virginia Woolf amongst many others was prescribed it for home use.

Various other drugs – such as apomorphine, a derivative of the opium that held sway in the seamy 'dens' of nineteenth-century cities – were enlisted to still mania. Potassium bromide, with its bitter taste, was used in 'hysterical epilepsy': in 1891 the Paris asylums were employing a thousand kilos of potassium bromide a year as a sedative.[433] Barbiturates, synthesized in 1864, modified into Barbital by Emil Fischer and Joseph von Mehring in 1903 for hypnotic and sedative use, then named and marketed in 1904 by Bayer as Veronal and by the Schering firm as Medinal, soon became the drug of choice in private asylums and nervous clinics. It had few side-effects and the working dose was far lower than the toxic dose, always a concern for doctors with patients who might be suicidally inclined. Its offshoot, phenobarbital, marketed as Luminal by Bayer in 1912, became for a time the pink elixir of asylum psychiatry and the housewife's calming friend, though it had a longer life as an anticonvulsant successful in epilepsy treatments.

The post-Second World War psychiatric pharmaceuticals story has two main avenues. One leads through the work with antihistamines – anti-allergy drugs – to the discovery of their sedative side-effects, and thence to chlorpromazine, used as an anaesthetic, then as an antipsychotic in France, Eastern Europe, Britain, Canada and finally America. Technically a neuroleptic, chlorpromazine could both quieten delirium, such as in the manic phase of bipolar disorder, and reduce confused states. It also had a startling impact on long-term psychotics and schizophrenics, waking them from the deep sleep of madness and emptying the mid-century asylums. It quickly outdistanced insulin and electro-shock treatment for such patients, and all but put an end to lobotomies and leucotomies. Smith-Kline & French (now GlaxoSmithKline), who bought the drug from its developers Rhone-Poulenc and licensed it in America in 1954, made some $75 million from it in the first year of its sale.[434] Now displaced by what are called the atypical antipsychotics such as risperidone, which have far fewer side-effects, chlorpromazine was one of the great psychiatric drug successes, despite the 'tardive dyskinesia' it eventually produced in patients – that is, those Parkinsonian-like involuntary and repetitive movements from the sticking out of tongue to blinking, to piano-playing finger exercises and leg or arm thrusts. Though there have been many splendid speculations, no one has altogether agreed on exactly what it is that makes these newer drugs work.

The second wing of the pharmaceutical story perhaps begins with Frank Berger, a Jewish Czech refugee from Hitler's Europe, who landed in America in 1947. At once a doctor and a bacteriologist interested in the physiological basis of nervousness, overexcitability and irritability, Berger went to work for Wallace Laboratories. Soon, Meprobamate was proven to calm anxious monkeys and went on the market as Miltown and Equanil. At the American Psychiatric Association meeting of 1955, there was a buzz that doubled as a whispering campaign. The axiolytic (anti-anxiety drug) Miltown was said to be terrific. A few months later, pharmacists were routinely running out of supplies. 'Happy pills' were up and away, the first of America's long list of mood enhancers, in this case lesser in side-effects than alcohol.

Following in Miltown's footsteps came Benzodiazepine and its derivatives, first the powerful Librium, then the Diazepams, the best known of which is Valium, child of another refugee chemist, Leo Sternbach, who worked for Hoffmann-La Roche. Stronger than Miltown, in the sixties Valium became the world's favourite and seemingly least toxic tranquillizer, making it on to the World Health Organization's essential drug list. Between 1969 and 1982, Valium was America's bestselling pharmaceutical. In a good year for the drug, immortalized by the Rolling Stones in 1966 as 'Mother's Little Helper', some 2.3 billion little yellow pills were sold. Famously, the Stones linked the pill to the constitutional right to the pursuit of happiness. But too many 'little helpers' made that pursuit seem 'a bore', and soon the 'shelter' they provided 'was no more'.

Not technically addictive — though the difference between what is called addiction and dependence may have more to do with social control than chemistry in this druggy world — Valium users could nonetheless develop a 'dependency' which was hard to break. In 1975 the Food and Drug Administration imposed special reporting requirements to control refills of both Valium and Miltown. In *Prozac Nation*, Elizabeth Wurtzel describes how her father slept through her childhood and their 'quality time together', a prisoner 'of nerves and Valium, Librium, and Miltown and whatever else too'.

Usually, in the stories and in the statistics, it is women who are the pill-swallowers, tranquillized into the stupor of Stepford Wives and depressed to the point of suicide, without — and sometimes even with — the magic of the nineties' Generation X prescription drug of choice, Prozac.

Women are, indeed, deeply enmeshed in this saga of everyday drug use, depression and anxiety. The question needs to be addressed: why do women figure in so much greater numbers and percentages on all the statistical indicators, particularly in the category now called 'mixed depression and anxiety'? The *Psychiatric Morbidity Survey* published in 2000, listing the main conditions suffered by gender, shows that whereas women suffer only marginally more than men from the main categories of mental disorder, they suffer in significantly greater numbers from that everyday mixture of depression and anxiety.

The question of why more women suffer from depression than men has received a variety of answers, none of them singly suitable for all circumstances. It's a fact, as the old adage has it, that women go to doctors where men go to the pub — or to deviance and crime. When they feel low or disturbed or perturbed, women do pharmaceuticals where men in far greater numbers do booze and street drugs. Even though, with greater equality and changing cultural habits the figures are creeping up, in Britain only 19 per cent of known street drug offences are committed by women.[435] Women, however, consult physicians more regularly and frequently than men, outstripping them by some 5–6

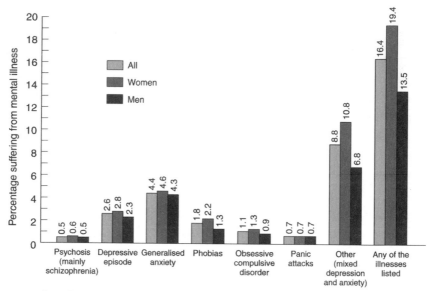

Source: Psychiatric Morbidity Survey, 2000, adults aged 16–75. More than one condition is possible.

FIGURE 1 Percentage suffering from mental illness

Source: Psychiatric Morbity Survey, 2000, as cited in *The Layard Report on Depression*, 2004. Adults aged 16–75; more than on condition [in the same patient] is possible.

per cent – a figure more or less equal to the greater statistically-recorded proportion of anxiety and depression amongst women.

In part, women are drawn into the medical habit by the very nature of reproductive physiology. In the West and in all countries where a welfare system of medicine presides, women go to doctors from the age of menstruation, when conception or contraception becomes a question, onwards. Pregnancy and birth are medical issues where state surveillance and self-care coincide. Once the child is born, it is most often women who will take it to doctor or nurse. Talking to doctors, taking advice, seeing professionals who may make you feel better – indeed, swallowing pills – is part of being a woman in the modern world. Women's larger showing in the statistics of mental disorders may therefore be as much a matter of self-reporting and a tendency to consult, as of any particularly greater incidence of depression and anxiety than men.

Even should a susceptibility be posited, then it may well be related to the starts and stops of women's hormones in relation to the reproductive

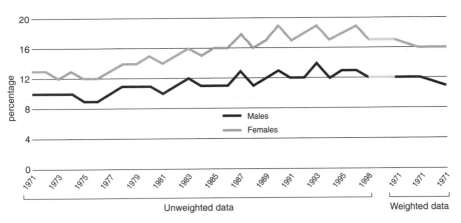

FIGURE 2 Percentage of males and females consulting an NHS GP in the 14 days before interview: Great Britain 1971 to 2001

Source: http://www.statistics.gov.uk/lib2001/Section3533.html

process. As long ago as Pinel, women's menstrual, pregnancy and birth cycles were linked to various mental, emotional, and what we now call 'mood' or 'affective' disorders. Social and cultural factors which produce malaise inevitably play into this, but it isn't as clear as we once thought that equality, however unequal, would erase the misery that topples women either towards anorexia or what our times understand as 'depression'.

If this risks sounding like a reactionary stance towards older feminist readings of women's condition or towards the very many social gains that Western women have achieved over the last forty years, it isn't. What needs to be emphasized in this continuing debate is that – despite the many volumes of depression or breakdown or anorexia memoirs that line the shelves – the greatest percentage of both men and women who consult doctors, old age apart, are those who have no regular work or those engaged in manual labour. Although in Britain the 2004 Layard report – which looked into the scale of mental illness in relation to overall disability and its costs – found depression and anxiety disorders were higher predictors of unhappiness than poverty, it is nonetheless the case that an impoverishment of potential, together with life on the most deprived estates or streets, does much to enmesh people in the mental health or its neighbouring prison system.

DEPRESSION

Elizabeth Wurtzel's streetwise and lippy *Prozac Nation* powerfully captures the frenzied spirit of nineties youth, the so-called Generation X, whose drug-charged highs too often descended into the terrifying and recurring lows of depression, which themselves became the target of more drugs – this time, prescribed. The confessional presents a portrait of an intelligent, sensitive New York child trapped and pulled apart by vocal divorcing parents whose differences are acted out over the expense, management and love of her, though it's sometimes hard in the midst of this to catch their attention.

By the age of twelve, Elizabeth is cutting herself at school. Talk therapy with a doctor who postures about his fame never quite seems to make enough difference. The psychiatrist feels more like the referee in her parents' battles than someone who is there for a sensitive child. She spends much of her time in a state of distress encased in earmuff size headphones listening to Bruce Springsteen, a friend in the desolate emptiness of despair, in which life has no meaning despite sex, more drugs and the kind of high-octane education that gets you to Harvard. Then, after still more drugs – cocaine, Ecstasy – troubled loves and a manically fuelled summer of writing for a Texas newspaper, comes a major down and a suicide attempt. In what increasingly emerges as a portrait of the artist as a young, depressive, often self-destructive woman, aka Sylvia Plath, Wurtzel begins to see a woman psychiatrist, Dr Sterling, who tries to help. Despite this, she finds herself hospitalized first at Stillmans Hospital, then like Plath at McLean's in Belmont, Massachusetts, and eventually, with the appearance of Prozac, diagnosed as suffering from 'atypical depression'.

The 'atypically depressed' are the 'walking wounded, people like me who are quite functional, whose lives proceed almost as usual, except that they're depressed *all* the time, almost constantly embroiled in thoughts of suicide even as they go through their paces'. The condition, though severe, allows an 'appearance of normalcy'.[436] Wurtzel is simultaneously productive and living in constant despair, pursued by the 'cognitive dissonance' of the two side by side. If untreated, her condition gets worse. Wurtzel is treated. She is given Prozac. It helps. She is also, over the years, given much else.

In 1999, ten years after the appearance of Prozac in Britain, she describes her drug regime as consisting of two Prozac capsules in the morning, followed by lithium. Lithium is the salt that, because it was found in the nineteenth century to dissolve urate stones, was used to treat gout and was drunk as waters in spas and at first in the soft drink 7-UP. It produced a sense of well-being and by the 1880s it had been found to have a beneficial effect on manic patients in asylums. Then forgotten, it found its way back in the 1950s in one of the first randomized controlled trials in psychiatry.[437] However, the American Food and Drug Administration didn't license it for use in mania until 1970. It is now regularly prescribed to keep the mood swings of manic depression on an even keel, so that the mania in the cycle doesn't result in the dangerous activity that can have sufferers from bipolar disorder sectioned in psychiatric wards.

Alongside lithium, Wurtzel recounts that she also takes a pink caplet called Depakote, the trade name for valproic acid, an anticonvulsive drug once prescribed for epilepsy, but now used to control mood. Then comes the blood pressure medication atenolol, which alleviates the shakiness in her hands that the other drugs produce. With dinner, she takes one of the older tricyclic antidepressants that act on the dopamine and norepinephrine systems of the brain, alongside the evening doses of the other drugs. Lethargic all day, she can't sleep at night, so she also takes a sleeping tablet that has a blackout effect.[438]

In the memoir *Prozac Diary*, psychologist Lauren Slater describes her own troubled trajectory. Daughter to a mother whose intensity had manic dimensions, Slater, as a child, starts hearing voices – a blue baby who cries, a girl in a glass case. She has a history of self-harm and has undergone five hospitalizations for depression twinned with anxiety which, when the book opens, manifests itself in an obsessive and compulsive need to 'touch, count, check and tap over and over again'. The man she describes as the Prozac Doctor gives her what is in 1988 the recently licensed wonder drug. He tells her how 'Prozac marked a revolution in psychopharmacology because of its selectivity on the serotonin system; it was a drug with the precision of a Scud missile, launched miles away from its target only to land, with a proud flare, right on the enemy's roof.'[439]

Slater is one of Prozac's earliest recipients. She wonders whether the

Prozac Doctor has displaced her subjectivity, her history, with a series of biochemical equations. Since illness, as she says, is part of the self and something one gets attached to, there is a struggle before she begins to take the prescribed pills.

This resistance to taking the drug the psychiatrist offers is telling. It is oddly reminiscent of Freud's own, sometimes disputed, contention that a patient resists interpretations and is unwilling to give up the accumulated habits and conflicts of the self, for which illness has provided some kind of solution. Kay Redfield Jamison echoes this in her memoir *An Unquiet Mind*, charting the course of her own manic depression. After years of just about containable mania, she finally goes, in the midst of a psychotic flight, to see a psychiatrist. She is ambivalent about his diagnosis, both relieved and resistant. Nor does she want the prescribed lithium which will remove her symptoms and which she knows she will have to take indefinitely.

Recognizing oneself in the straitjacket of a diagnosis, accepting an interpretation or a prescription, means giving up the self one knows. There is a double fear here, common in bipolar disorder, that the brilliance, the speeded-up activity, the elation, which accompany the milder forms of mania, will go with the drug.

In Slater's case, through Prozac she is effectively born into the youth she never experienced. Better than well, she walks around arcades, is alive to sound, people and colour; goes to rock concerts unafraid, gets a job; a place at Harvard; completes a PhD in record time and eventually goes on to become a therapist and edit a book on women's mental health. Along the way, there are the side-effects: a certain intensity which is also creative goes from the world. She misses her 'illness identity' — a factor that Wurtzel also explores, noting that suicide attempts most often come when the pills have eased the worst of depression and the young woman no longer knows who she is. After a while Slater's sexual pleasure wanes, the bleakness of depression re-emerges; the drugs have to be adjusted. But the *Diary*, written ten years after her first contact with the drug, is undoubtedly a Prozac success story.

Jamison is clear in retrospect that she needs both her lithium and her psychotherapy: lithium prevents her 'seductive but disastrous flights', diminishes depression, 'clears out the wool and webbing from my disordered thinking', keeps her out of hospital and makes psychotherapy possible. The latter heals, 'makes some sense of the confusion, reins in the terrifying thoughts and feelings, returns some control and hope and possibility of learning from it all'.[440]

It is interesting that these depression narratives still broach childhood and history in old quasi-psychoanalytic terms. Freud provided the twentieth century with the best story of the self available and the one which carries the most meanings – though sex, desire and becoming woman have become less important now than the quality of parenting and the upbringing that grow the child's identifications and illness. This is the case even when the depression or other condition has a possible inherited factor. But this psychoanalytic shaping of the family is now overlain with a version of 'cure' which is biochemical and neural, the dominant psy language of our turn of the century.

Today Big Science is called upon to lend authority to descriptions which may be as old as the hills in their actual content. For example, to say, as is the pattern now, that brain chemistry is implicated in mood or depression may be little more than to say that humans have bodies. To say, as Slater does in an article, that 'touching, talking, feeding, rocking, smiling, giggling' with one's baby are expressions of love or neural messages which have an impact on the limbic system, or the emotional brain, and imprint themselves on the child[441] is to repeat Winnicottian injunctions in what today counts as a scientific register. All this is fine and well. But what the pharmaceutical industry does with such neural and biochemical language is to feed it back to us as a medicalization of feeling and behaviour for which, when things go 'wrong', it can provide the drugs that cure. The fact that we may need or want the cure does not necessarily make the supposed scientific legitimacy or power of the drug prescribed any greater than sipping the (lithium) waters at the nineteenth-century spa or than a session with the hypnotist.

In its *Global Burden of Disease, 2000*, the WHO ranked depression as the fourth 'leading cause of burden' amongst all diseases; and the one most affecting productive life, resulting in 11.9 per cent of years lost from life's span due to disability. Predictions are that worldwide, depression will soon be second only to heart disease in its seriousness, while in the developed world it will rise to be the highest cause of the burden of disease. These are astonishing figures. They can be read to say that either the contemporary world (war, poverty, politics, terror, inequality) or biology (genetic inheritance, population rise) increasingly inflicts on people what are now called 'mood disorders'. They could also be read to say that we are measuring something we never measured before. Sadness, even disabling sadness, has only recently become a classified illness that swallowing a pill can cure.

Once, sadness and its accompanying inactivity might have been linked to sloth, the sin of accidie, the torpor of ennui, that mental prostration which was a lingering suicide and that some attributed to the spiritual aridity attendant on God's grace departing from the individual. Discipline might be recommended as a cure. Melancholy, the early term most usually linked to today's medicalized depression, described a profound sadness, due, according to humoral theory, to an excess of black bile in the body. The *OED* gives 'ill-temper, sullenness, brooding anger' as definitions, and also points out that in the Elizabethan period and for a long time afterwards 'sadness, dejection, esp. of a pensive nature; gloominess . . . introspection . . . perturbation' formed a 'fashionable mark of intellectual or aesthetic refinement'. Hamlet suffered from it; George Cheyne recognized it. In Charles Lamb's time, the sadness was subsumed under 'hypochondriasis' (which became the illness of suffering from imagined illness).

Jean-Paul, the early German Romantic, whose *Hesperus* (1795) was the most popular novel there since Goethe's *The Sorrows of Young Werther* had led to a wave of suicide amongst the young, gave melancholy the inflection of 'world weariness' or *Weltschmerz* — a term the post-punk Goth sub-culture picked up as emblematic of the eighties, when 'death rock' also emerged. Harking back to humoral resonances, Baudelaire called his utter lassitude, that dejected weariness of 'limping days', *spleen*, the very site of black bile's production. Spleen transformed him into 'the bored prince of a rainy country, rich, but impotent, young and yet very old', his memories straining over some thousand years. For him as for Coleridge, it now seems clear that the condition was linked to repeated use of opium, then a legal substance and often used as a sedative, though whether the condition or the drug use came first remains, even today, an open question. In the second half of the nineteenth century, depression was often subsumed under neurasthenia, or an attack of nerves. As such, it was both plague and affectation, a fashionable attribute which might also savagely debilitate.

Esquirol and the developing French psychiatry — seeing a disease of the emotions where melancholy with its popularly understood attributes of sadness had been — described a condition named *lypémanie*, (from the Greek *lype*, or sadness), a partial madness which was attended by chronic delusions and an overwhelming tristesse. Esquirol, whose asylum population came largely from the poorer classes, found rates of the condition increased from May to August; that it was most prevalent in twenty-five- to forty-five-year-olds; and that while heredity played a role, domestic crises, disturbed relations and grief precipitated the condition. In Germany and Britain, the term 'melancholia' was maintained by the nascent alienists. Sir William Gull used it in 1868 as part of his description of 'hypochondriasis': 'its principal feature is mental depression, occurring without adequate cause'.

The word 'depression' itself, to describe a condition rather than a sharp drop in the landscape or of vigour in trade, only gradually came into the English language. Always a good indicator of the mood of the times, George Eliot was one of the first to use the term as a noun to refer to an emotional condition: Daniel Deronda finds the beautiful Gwendolyn after she has been betrayed and widowed 'in a state of deep depression, overmastered by those distasteful miserable memories'. G.E. Berrios notes that by the end of the nineteenth century, depression came to be defined as 'a condition characterized by a sinking of the spirits, lack of courage or initiative and a tendency to gloomy thoughts'.[442] The term migrated into Kraepelin's nomenclature. Importantly, Kraepelin broke down the large, generalized category of psychosis to classify a pattern of symptoms as manic depression, now more commonly known as bipolar disorder. Kraepelin's genius lay in stressing the cyclical nature of an illness which most often presented itself to doctors in its depressed state: when sufferers were high, they rarely thought anything was wrong with them — though, of course, their relatives might.

For Freud, common depression is of no substantive interest in itself: he mentions it several times in passing, either as an accepted and usual part of everyday life or as part of a larger condition such as hysteria, where it can be linked with anxious excitation. In the *Psychopathology of Everyday Life*, he talks of a man 'overburdened with worries and subject to occasional depressions'. Only when he compares mourning to

melancholia do the kind of obsessional states of depression which characterize melancholia take on a dynamic interest for him: a pattern links
these to a loss about which the subject is ambivalent and so sadistically
attacks herself.

> The self-tormenting in melancholia, which is without doubt enjoyable,
> signifies, just like the corresponding phenomenon in obsessional neu-
> rosis, a satisfaction of trends of sadism and hate which relate to an object,
> and which have been turned round upon the subject's own self . . . It is
> this sadism alone that solves the riddle of the tendency to suicide which
> makes melancholia so interesting – and so dangerous.[443]

This sadistic attack on the self is in full play in many of today's depression memoirs, though they are rarely Freudian. Freud also links this
severe kind of melancholia to a manic high, a cyclical rhythm which
makes him consider the possibility that certain unknown 'toxins' are in
play here, linking the physiological to the psychogenic.

By the time we arrive in 1962 when pills are on the market in a handy
form, the Oxford English Dictionary suggests that the physiological or
chemical has altogether taken over from the psychogenic. Depression
has become so medicalized that it usurps the place of experience: the
Lancet of 2 June notes: 'events at the onset of depression . . . must be
interpreted with caution for failure at work . . . or in a love affair may be
early symptoms, rather than causes'. Failure has slipped from being a
cause of misery or even a precipitating factor of a psychological condition into becoming a symptom underlying a disorder called depression.

Since then, depression has often enough become 'tantamount to
dysphoria, meaning unhappiness, in combination with loss of appetite
and difficulty sleeping'.[444] The shift in emphasis from depressed mood to
visible symptoms marks the objectivizing psychiatrist's victory: there is
hardly a need for subjective states of mind at all in the diagnosis. In 1991,
just three years after the launch of Prozac by Eli Lilley, Edward Shorter
notes in his History of Psychiatry, the NIMH began a 'National Depression
Screening Day' as part of its mental health awareness programme.
Athough the intentions were worthy – to inform family doctors how to
diagnose depression in their patients in order to refer them to psychiatrists, since a missed major depression might result in suicide – the

ultimate effect was 'psychiatric empire-building' against other kinds of care. As a consequence of this emphasis on depression, it became the 'single commonest disorder seen in psychiatric practice, accounting for 28 percent of all patient visits'. The existence of Prozac has moved hand in hand with the process of spreading depression: 'Physicians prefer to diagnose conditions they can treat rather than those they can't.'

On its official website, the British Royal College of Physicians notes that there are some thirty different kinds of antidepressant available today. Their use began in the fifties and they are divided into four main types: the older tricyclics, which are dangerous in overdose, the MAOIs (monoamine oxidase inhibitors), now hardly used because of their serious side-effect of high blood pressure; the preferred SSRIs (selective serotonin re-uptake inhibitors), amongst which is the famous Prozac, better known since its patent ended in 2001 as Fluoxetine; and the trickier SNRIs (serotonin and noradrenaline reuptake inhibitors), prescribed only when the others don't work. The Royal College admits quite openly that there is no complete certainty about how these medications function, 'but we think that antidepressants work by increasing the activity of certain chemicals in our brains called neurotransmitters. They pass signals from one brain cell to another. The chemicals most involved in depression are thought to be Serotonin and Noradrenaline.' There is more certainty about what these antidepressants are used for as well as what the disorders they work on might be:

Moderate to severe depressive illness (not mild depression).
Severe anxiety and panic attacks
Obsessive-compulsive disorders
Chronic pain
Eating disorders
Post-traumatic stress disorder.[445]

If women seem to get depressed more than men do, the website states pragmatically, 'this is possibly because men are less likely to admit their feelings [; they] bottle them up or express them in aggression or through drinking heavily'. It adds, perhaps less helpfully, 'Women may be more likely to have the double stress of having to work and, at the same time, look after children.' True enough, though the underlying suggestion that there is a free choice in the offing here, that women could either have the men look after the children or look after them alone rather than go out to work in a mere snap of the fingers, is insidious. There is also an implication that working and mothering together – something surely that most women have done through most of Western history – marks the downward path to depression. One might say with as much 'truth', that when men both work and father, there is a downward path to war.

GENERALIZING DIAGNOSES

The admirable certainty that all websites and handbooks now display about the nature of the above 'disorders' reminds us that we are once more in an age of Kraepelinian classifications. Illness descriptions and categories produced by the American *DSM* and its international kin, the *International Classification of Diseases*, govern the medical and psychiatric worlds. Such manuals, which bear the accolade of science, are useful for unifying practice vis-a-vis insurance providers, bureaucrats and statistics gatherers. They may also help sufferers who want the 'liberation' that a diagnosis can give together with the attendant and sometimes helpful medication. But the way in which such illnesses come into being and the function of description should not be forgotten.

A psychoanalytically trained psychiatric graduate and member of the Columbia University Psychiatry Department in the 1960s, Robert Spitzer in 1966 took over the task of chairing the *DSM-III* task force. Psychiatrists at the time in America seemed to agree on little: one might name a patient a textbook hysteric, while the same patient might be labelled a 'hypochondriac depressive' by another.[446] Psychiatric diagnoses did not have what the period's scientists understood as 'reliability' – that is, they failed to produce results that were both consistent and replicable. And if psychiatrists disagreed about diagnosis, they would inevitably also disagree about treatment and cure. Underlying this emphasis on reliability are the needs of Big Pharma, as the massive combined weight of the international pharmaceutical industry is known: 'How can you test the effectiveness of a new drug to treat depression if you can't be sure that the person you're testing is suffering from that disorder?'[447] The answer of course might well be – and sometimes became – that if the patient responds to the drug, then there is a disorder and it's called depression; but that's to get ahead of oneself and the period in which the new, more authoritative, DSMs came into being.

Spitzer established twenty-five committees charged with arriving at detailed descriptions of mental disorders. He chose scientifically inclined, and therefore anti-psychoanalytic, psychiatrists to sit on these committees. They were to be guided by data. The data, however, didn't yet exist. Spitzer sat in on committee meetings and from the mass of psychiatric talk sifted argument and anecdote into the disorders to be included in the *DSM-III*. New disorders emerged to match the times: attention-deficit disorder which eventually became – together with the rise and rise of Ritalin, the drug which 'treats' the disorder in children – attention-deficit hyperactivity disorder (ADHD). The illnesses that characterize our fin-de-siècle took on their full amplitude: autism, anorexia nervosa, bulimia, panic disorders, post-traumatic stress disorder, anxiety disorder, obsessive-compulsive personality disorder – to name the ones, apart from depression, that have grown empires of sufferers.

Each of the *DSM-III*'s disorders came with a handy checklist of symptoms, and the warning that in order for patients to 'qualify' for the disorder (and the attendant insurance monies to pay for the treatment), doctors must make sure that at least a certain number of the listed items were present. For example, for a diagnosis of major depression in *DSM-IV R*, the patient must exhibit depressed mood over a two-week period, plus five of the following:

Feelings of overwhelming sadness or fear or the seeming
    inability to feel emotion (emptiness)
A decrease in the amount of interest or pleasure in all, or almost
    all, activities of the day, nearly every day
Changing appetite and marked weight gain or loss
Disturbed sleep patterns, such as loss of REM sleep, or excessive
    sleep (Hypersomnia)
Psychomotor agitation or retardation nearly every day
Fatigue, mental or physical, also loss of energy
Feelings of guilt, helplessness, hopelessness, anxiety, or fear
Trouble concentrating or making decisions or a generalized

slowing and obtunding [medicalese for deadening] of
cognition, including memory

Recurrent thoughts of death (not just fear of dying), recurrent
suicidal ideation without a specific plan, or a suicide attempt
or a specific plan for committing suicide

Other symptoms sometimes reported include:

A decrease in self-esteem

Inattention to personal hygiene

Sensitivity to noise

Physical aches and pains, and the belief these may be signs of
serious illness.

Fear of 'going mad'

Change in perception of time.

The checklist aspect of the *DSM* meant that the American Psychiatric
Association now had a manual with a biomedical 'viability'. The 'reliability problem' was solved. Or so they thought. When they spoke of a
psychiatric illness, diagnosticians would now all be speaking about more
or less the same thing. Patients, too, could recognize themselves, and
indeed band together according to a classification, to form support
groups – and, if it came to court cases, legally recognized 'classes'. In its
various editions – from the first Spitzer edition, *DSM III* in 1980, its
revision in 1986 (*DSM III-R*), the new *DSM IV* in 1994 (by which time
Spitzer's aegis had passed to Allen Frances) and its next revision in 2000 –
the *DSM* has had a marked influence on psychiatry worldwide. Indeed,
its global intentions are visible in its accompanying case books, which
present cases complete with diagnoses from Africa to Latin America to
Europe and back home again. The boon of the *DSM* is that psychiatry
now has order in its disorders.

There are side-effects as well. The long, structured diagnostic history-
taking interview the *DSM* puts into place for standard psychiatric
practice has given the drug companies the capacity to assemble research
populations sharing similar properties for clinical trials. These double
blind randomized clinical trials are the standard for drug-testing across
medicine. As a result, it is now easier to test psychiatric drugs, and

arguably the procedure is more reliable, though statistical results can often fudge matters for all those less than expert in statistics, and this includes doctors. The controversy over Prozac and whether, as the *British Medical Journal* asserted, its manufacturer had concealed facts about suicide in the trials of the drug, is an example of the way in which results can be either fudged or massaged or overlooked – certainly, they may often not be unambiguous. The kind of advertising to doctors, let alone the public, that the pharmaceutical companies undertake[448] may also confuse independent judgement, even where there is no particular corruption.

Then, too, the very existence of 'reliable' double blind trials demands competition from the talking treatments, who need to prove equal 'reliability'. The diffuseness of psychoanalysis (which sets out to treat not symptoms but the underlying life) and many other psychotherapies has made the kind of hard evidence that governments and insurers want difficult to extract – though some studies have been done to prove that expense and working hours saved, for example, are not so different in medicalized and talking therapies. For these purposes cognitive behavioural therapy (CBT) is most often the talking treatment of insurers' and welfare-providers' choice.

DIAGNOSES AND TREATMENTS: A DOUBLE ACT

CBT in part grew out of the psychological side of the psy professions in America – those which traditionally dealt with standardized testing of children and adults along the 'normal/abnormal' divide, or personality tests to serve army and industry, most prevalently along lines developed by Eysenck from an originally Jungian provenance – extroversion or introversion. Fun as parlour games, less so for job applicants, these tests are also serious and supposedly 'scientific' business, gathering data on which to build statistics and then reapply them as norms. In *Cult of Personality* Annie Murphy Paul tells the story of some 2500 kinds of personality tests, which in the USA form a $400-million-a-year industry. One of the most popular tests worldwide is the Myers-Briggs Type Indicator (MBTI), which categorizes psychological types along axes of extroversion/introversion, intuition/sensing, thinking/feeling, judging/

perceiving. Twenty minutes will give you a summary of your personality type in some combination of the above. Eighty-nine firms out of the Fortune 100 make use of the Myers-Briggs for hiring and promotion.

Aaron T. Beck, one of the founders of CBT and a longtime critic of the unreliability of psychiatric diagnosis in America during its psychoanalytic imperium, has a test named after him: the Beck's Depression Inventory, or BDI. First published in 1961, the BDI was revised in 1996 as BDI-II. An objective multiple-choice questionnaire, it is intended to be filled out by the 'patient' in the presence of a clinician, who then scores it – in the manner of newspaper quizzes. Above a certain score, the indications are that you need professional help, most likely a course of CBT, plus an SSRI. The questions ask the test-taker to indicate among the four states in each grouping which best describes how she has been feeling during the past few days. The first group runs:

0   I do not feel sad.
1   I feel sad.
2   I am sad all the time and I can't snap out of it.
3   I am so sad or unhappy that I can't stand it.

Other questions query the subject's view of herself as a failure, her guilt, her suicidal thoughts, her irritation, her interest in others, her decision-making, her sleep patterns, appetite, tiredness, weight, interest in sex, and so on. A score of 1 to 10 indicates normal ups and downs; 11–16, a mild mood disturbance; 17–20, borderline clinical depression; 21–30 moderate depression, which goes to severe and extreme at over 40.

There is a kind of challenge, indeed inevitability, for a score of depression to result. We all want to do well, after all. And if a person is taking a test for depression, then there is already the suspicion of a problem. But what young person doesn't feel depressed? – particularly perhaps after a week of student exams, or a split with a boyfriend, even after a little use of recreational drugs and forgetting to eat; let alone the constant flow of pop songs chanting the emptiness of life, the nowhere we inhabit, the soul assassins, the cavalcade of clowns, the yawning abyss, the sanity whose upkeep is a full-time job – all to hypnotic rhythms booming in on the inner ear. A sense of hopelessness, a teenage irritability, may be a phase, even if one that lasts several years.

One of the effects of such tools as the Beck's Depression Inventory and the *DSM*'s chartable diagnoses is that they can produce the very results they are looking for. Easily replicable not only as tests but as illness behaviours, they bubble on to the web and into general circulation, spreading the very disorders they were intended to cure. The world of the emotions and the imagination is always open to suggestion and it's a simple business to tick off a list of ailments for oneself and a group to which one belongs. As a way of assessing personality and its supposed aberrations, the recipe approach, which reduces the complexities of mind and experience, can have an insidious aspect.

Take the recent 'Teen Screen program' emanating from highly respectable Columbia University. This has been unfurled in some four hundred communities across the USA. It sets out to screen youths between the ages of eleven and eighteen for the 'likelihood' that they may be *prone* to depression or constitute a suicide risk. In some ten minutes or so the youths fill out a fourteen-item self-completion questionnaire, which asks them about 'depression, suicidal ideation and attempts, anxiety, alcohol and drug use, and general health problems'. Teen Screen also provides a general-purpose fifty-two-item computerized interview that can be administered and scored by trained non-professionals. This indicates the likelihood of a youth having a significant mental health problem.

The young are offered Big Macs and various incentives to fill out the forms. Although Columbia has emphatically denied any link with finances from Big Pharma in the running of the project, there is an inevitable down-the-line feeding of the mental health industry in such predictive work. The good intention may be to 'catch them early'. The result may well be that 'in making mental health a priority' and 'offering all youth an opportunity for voluntary screening', more learn the brackets and language into which they can wedge their often inchoate feelings. These are then arranged into today's fashionable diagnoses: panic disorder, social phobia, generalized anxiety, social anxiety disorder, for which Paxil has been widely sold. The programme may indeed also have helped edge the common teenage 'social anxiety' into the category of illness. Other oft-diagnosed conditions, now that medication exists to better them, include OCD with its ritualization of common anxieties (Do I have bad breath? Did I brush my teeth? Did I turn off the iron, lights, cooker?) and, of course, depression – which, it is hardly astonishing to hear, can be treated with antidepressants and quick courses of CBT.

Outside the mental health world, it comes as no surprise that most young people at some time or another are anxious, harbour suicidal thoughts or behave, feel, or fantasize in ways which form-ticking professionals may find aberrant; though when out of their own bureaucratic straitjackets, they may have listened to the same songs, gone to the same websites, taken the same 'recreational' drugs and felt the same tug of anomie after the fall from rapture. Teen Screen sounds like yet another formula for medicalizing and then somehow getting rid of adolescence itself by naming it 'disordered'. Indeed, one study has shown that three brisk thirty-minute walks each week have greater effects on reducing depression than drugs from the Prozac family. Out of 156 subjects monitored by Duke University, only eight following this regime saw their depression return.[449] Perhaps Teen Screen might ease more depression and suicidal thoughts if it were transmuted into a 'build up Teen Steam'.

Clearly, locating a mental illness or a disorder in people will create a demand for an ever-expanding range of treatments and drugs that can contain or ameliorate the illness. Simultaneously the very existence of a Big Pharma drug can help to name a condition. Elizabeth Wurtzel writes that from the start her psychiatrist, although she had never specifically said so in the course of a therapy which began with pronounced suicidal conduct, had suspected Wurtzel's cache of feelings and behaviours fell into the category of 'atypical depression'. But there had been no reason to 'name' her condition unless a medication were to be prescribed. When Fluoxetine appeared on the market and was said by many doctors, including famously Peter Kramer in his *Listening to Prozac*, to make patients with just such life symptoms 'better than well', it made sense for her psychiatrist to offer a diagnosis.

> It seems oddly illogical. Rather than defining my disease as a way to lead us to Fluoxetine [Prozac], the invention of this drug has brought us to my disease. Which seems backward, but is a typical course of events in psychiatry – that the discovery of a drug to treat, say, schizophrenia, will tend to result in many more patients being diagnosed as schizophrenics.

Writing in 1999 some six years after the first appearance of her book, Wurtzel noted how much had changed in the mental health world since her initial diagnosis. The psychiatrist who had first put her on Prozac now ran a mental-health clinic in California where no long-term therapy or counselling of the kind Wurtzel herself had had was on offer. Instead, a great deal of prescription-writing was taking place. The psychiatrist felt that this way, instead of a very few people getting a lot of help, many got some. Then, too, the exhaustion of talk therapy with suicidal patients was averted and she at long last had the 'emotional wherewithal' to deal with her family. Wurtzel concludes: 'It is not just patients who are desperate for whatever relief Prozac can provide — doctors too are overwhelmed; the needs that their deracinated, unstable and alienated clients bring to therapy in an age of divorce are almost too much to be handled without non-human intervention.'[450]

It's said that between its introduction in 1988 and Eli Lilley's loss of the patent, Prozac was prescribed to over thirty-five million people worldwide. In 1999 one million children in the USA were reported to be taking antidepressants, including mint-flavoured Prozac. In 2000 alone, Prozac earned its parent company $2.6 billion. Eli Lilley are hardly alone in the antidepressant bonanza. Promotional budgets for the large pharmaceutical companies continue huge, larger than the amount spent on research and development.[451]

Now that the risk of suicide for those under nineteen on antidepressants has been found to be twice as likely as for those who are unmedicated (and those on antidepressants are fifteen times as likely to complete the act), wholesale prescribing of antidepressants to the young has slightly fallen off.[452] The size of the depression problem has not, and for most, antidepressants continue to be both prescribed and desired. As for therapy, CBT remains the recommended insurable and efficacious accompanying treatment. In Britain, the Layard report noted that there weren't enough trained therapists to meet demand. Luckily, in case none of the preferred CBT therapists are available, there is now a computerized CBT package available for depression: you can engage in 'Beating the Blues' on your very own computer screen . . . which may have given you the depression in the first place.

One of the difficulties of the cognitive therapies is an underlying assumption that people are rational beings always and ever capable of self-assessment, without any self-deception, and that a good dose of problem-solving pep talks and strategies for getting rid of 'negative thoughts' will sort things. It may and it's always good to learn a little more about the self, but the promise of happiness and a short-term fix may be far more than can always be delivered. Patients usually re-engage with CBT after a first round; and after a second. Many also find a need to stay on their antidepressant, the habit of which is difficult to beat. Coming off can be a slow process, not always achievable.

Even if help is what one wants when vulnerable or depressed, in evaluating the way in which the marketing of diagnoses and therapies can spread the disorder itself, it is well worth remembering that many of the most common depressions will disappear after some eight months on their own and without treatment. The Royal College of Psychiatrists affirms this on its website. Nor, in the usual British and understated fashion, do they recommend seeing a psychiatrist for depression, when a GP for prescriptions and a course of talk therapy will do. One would be hard put to find similar recommendations in a fee-paying mental health economy.

As for antidepressants, the Royal College spells out the odds. All trials have shown that 24–35 per cent of people will get better with a placebo after three months; whereas of the 50–65 per cent who improve with drug treatment in that time, some of that benefit, too, is due to the placebo effect. Care helps, it seems, as long as it is well intentioned. And placebos produce fewer side-effects, such as that radical decrease in sexual desire associated with SSRIs . Since the World Health Organization reckons that 33 per cent of diseases today are caused by medical treatment – that is, are iatrogenic, or doctor-induced – it may be safest to have less drug-related care, particularly after the exposure of some of the hidden aspects of the Big Pharma drug trials and the fiddling that creates our 'safe drugs'.

THE CHEMICAL SOCIETY

One of the difficulties of our chemical society is that the leap from illicit recreational drugs to what Peter D. Kramer aptly dubbed 'cosmetic psychopharmacology' is just a hop across the street. Not only are the patterns of taking drugs to alter moods well established on both sides of the road, but it's sometimes hard to tell whether having taken one kind may in fact help to bring on the mood swings and the underlying depression which lead to taking the other; or whether an underlying neural proclivity to depression of the atypical or cyclical variety makes individuals more likely to seek out and be sensitive to the effects of street drugs, so that in taking them they are effectively self-prescribing, as doctors may do for them later on. The traffic between street and prescription drugs is rarely one-way. The SSRIs are, after all, mood enhancers, just as many of the street drugs are. Though hypotheses of how they work and why they work on some and not others are rife, no scientists have produced conclusions that have lasted more than a few years. Meanwhile, Big Pharma is now researching one of Britain's favourite club drugs, ketamine, initially used to dope horses, for its medical potential.

If the pharmaceutical companies took over street drug manufacture and marketing, would we find ourselves listening in a different manner to the 'better than well' way people occasionally feel on them, as we did with Prozac? Is feeling 'better than well', in any case, something of an aspiration to 'mania' – that 'up' in which mind, imagination and emotions race and inhibitions fall away that those with bipolar disorder say they are loath to relinquish, particularly before it spirals too high. Unsurprisingly, urban anthropologists have indicated that big American financial firms see a certain degree of manic behaviour as an asset in their employees, who most often effect it by recourse to the more expensive illicit drugs.

Our times have produced a terrible confusion about drugs, mood, illness and behaviour. The licit and the illicit, big medical science and street traders, have combined to create a chemical view of the human which traps the full range of human possibility into categories of mental disorder or criminality, with little in between. While both classes of drugs have attractive aspects and simultaneously carry a stigma, both inevitably reduce the fullness of human life and put a stress on mood, on upness or downness and whatever produces it, above all else. The neuro view of life with its accompanying psychological tick-list is simply not enough to see most people through its many phases. Even Spitzer, creator of the contemporary *DSM*, has acknowledged as much in the 2007 television documentary, *The Trap*.

If our chemical society, with its erratic flare-ups of faith in magic-bullet cures, at times gives the illusion to patients, doctors and researchers that conditions can be got rid of or be easily controlled, reality usually insists on another picture. Nowhere is this clearer than in the stories of those self- and medically categorized as depressed or bipolar. Here pain is palpable, together with confusion and a sense of life gone awry, ever teetering on the brink of suicide. Even when these narratives are structured around the poles of illness and recovery, life seeps through with its inevitable messiness to produce a far larger picture. Depression stories like Wurtzel's *Prozac Nation* or Lauren Slater's *Prozac Diary*, or even the remarkable Kay Redfield Jamison's various books on manic depression, or bipolar disorder, which link the condition – perhaps just a little aspirationally – to the many 'geniuses' Western culture has produced, reveal nothing so much as that life escapes the current medical categories and what is labelled as cure. Of course Sylvia Plath – whose trajectory is much emulated – can be thought of as depressive or even manic-depressive, but that hardly sums up the entirety of either her life's achievement or the many moods, emotions, aspirations, responsibilities taken and work produced in between. There is a temptation to ask whether a chronic condition, to its causes understood as genetic, constitutional, chemical or environmental, might not be better considered simply as part of the human condition.

The late and famous French analyst Pierre Fedida, sometimes known as an existentialist, wrote his last book on depression. Worrying about the rise of a condition which affected only 3 per cent of the population in the seventies but which had risen by the turn of the century to 15 per cent, he noted that depression could not but be inherent to a rapidly changing society which demanded performance and enterprise at all cost despite the fact that technology and codes of love were both metamorphosing at an exceptional rate. In such a world, being depressed is a way of going underground, holding oneself quiescent, refusing performance, while desires are rekindled. If drugs are now less toxic and can have an effect, the real work, Fedida suggests, is still that of understanding, through the talk and listening of therapy, where you can get to know yourself better so as to be able to confront the frontal shocks of our times. Happily there are still some within the psychiatric professions whose worlds are not summed up by diagnostic manuals.

It's useful to be reminded, as history is prone to do, that today's 'conditions' have been both seen and lived otherwise. Freud might well have thought of some of the contemporary sufferers from depression – with their energy, vivacity, intelligence and suicide attempts – as hysterics; and one or two transported to mid-century America might well have found themselves classified as schizophrenics. In the pre-psychiatric world that Mary Lamb inhabited, with all the horrors of its asylum life, they might have had little choice but to rely on time and the love of a responsible 'carer' to help them through.

This book is not a condemnation of our psychiatrically medicalized times. Much of the care, medication, therapeutic talk available does make life better for people in distress. But the trip through history provides a cautionary note: mental illness is also the *name* given to a set of ills by various sets of mind doctors. The illness may provide meaning and definition for a time for the sufferer; or it may inflict a stigma. There is certainly no basis for the last: in most people's lives at some point they will live through aspects of some of the states we now call mental illness or chronic mental conditions. But nor are there, for most mental conditions, however they are named, absolute cures or chemical cures that produce lasting equanimity or happiness. Recovery, salvation, healing, are neither absolutes nor a simulacrum of heaven.

Lives span across time. They contain moments that are better and worse, and sometimes so bad, it looks as if you won't get through. People have. Women have. They have got through the danger points: adolescence with its dramatic ups and downs, its crises about identity and image, its inner chaos and uncertainties. They have got through childbirth with its hormonal spurts and depletions and motherhood upon which so much is blamed. They have even got through mourning. They have got through with the kindness of relations, friends, doctors, therapists, and strangers.

If in recent years the proportion of the doctors and therapists who are women has grown, this can only be to the good: they bring to their task a greater understanding of what growing up woman means. But it is perhaps too early to tell whether their place in the profession will ease the lot of women, or substantially shift the mind doctors' historic recruitment of women to 'illness'.

EPILOGUE

Ten days after the birth of her second child, Fiona Shaw, a young, vibrant, well educated and literary young woman in the north of England in the 1990s, found herself in a 'mood of unease' she couldn't shake off. The tears came and engulfed her. So did screams, self-loathing, a fear of the outside world, stretches of numbness, and an inability to understand why she was in a state of despair when she had nothing to be depressed about. She could barely bring herself to feed and bathe her baby. People talked of 'baby blues'. Her general practitioner told her to 'grin and bear it', unless she wanted antidepressants, which might mean giving up breastfeeding. It would pass, he said. It didn't. A second doctor came to the house, kinder, and recommended the Mother and Baby Unit of a psychiatric hospital.

She spent the next months there, suicidal, surreptitiously burning and cutting herself, refusing food. The psychiatrist gave her an explanation of her condition which was hardly different — in its mix of environmental, biographical and physiological causes — from what Esquirol might have offered two hundred years earlier in considering that oldest of those madnesses specific to women. Dr A, an intelligent, matter-of-fact woman, talked of a combination of factors: a traumatic event (the birth) 'triggering a reaction to past history, perhaps compounded by drastic hormonal shifts'.[453] Her treatment, however, was more radical than what Esquirol had on offer, though his cases did not seem to go on any longer than contemporary ones. Hers was no regimen of purges and hot baths. When Shaw didn't respond to antidepressants and chlorpromazine, and was still not eating (Esquirol's post-partum patients mostly didn't, either), she was sectioned and given ECT, twice a week for four weeks. She suffered from the inflicted brutality of the treatment and a severe accompanying memory loss.

When she returned home after two and a half months, she was still in need of help. Psychotherapy, which she wanted, wasn't available. Only the shocks were, now as an outpatient. For a total of six amnesiac months, the substance of life was eviscerated for her. After that came another six on antidepressants. When she came off these, the depression returned, debilitating and difficult to bear.

Shaw decided not to go back on pills. 'They would simply have delayed the dilemma. They enabled me to survive an impossible crisis and helped me compose myself sufficiently to begin life again. But they had no answers for me and they hadn't erased the questions.'[454] She stopped eating again and eventually found the money to go to a therapist.[455] She wanted some understanding – of herself, the breakdown, what had led her there. She wanted meaning. Alongside looking after her children well, she also wanted to write, which is another form of exploration and understanding.

Human beings are odd animals. Whereas they're sometimes pleased to give over responsibility for an illness to a 'physical' explanation or remedy, with illnesses that involve mind, emotions, behaviour, the physical is rarely enough. After all, we may be our bodies, but our bodies are hardly all that we are: for some this even extends beyond the corporeal limit of death. And though our bodies largely inhabit a present, the mind roams through time. The past affects it: so does the (im)possibility of a future. Even when pills or hot baths (and, as some swear, even the barbarism of ECT) help, there's a residue of questions and needs.

Shaw met some of these by psychotherapy and some others by writing. Both fleshed out a story in which her own early childhood abandonment by her father at the moment that a sibling was born produced a flurry of conflicting emotions, which replayed themselves in the self-hatred, defensive aridity, even mourning over an old loss, when her own second child was born. We are not simple creatures.

Recently, though the figures on depression continue to rise, there has been something of a patients' backlash against the easy and sometimes loose prescription of antidepressants for all forms of ills. A report from the Healthcare Commission in Britain stated that of the eighty-four thousand people who had used mental health community services in 2005 a third had not been able to get access to the talking therapy they wanted.[456] An expansion in the availability of clinical psychologists and primary care therapists is a government priority. This can only be a good: on the whole, talk therapies of most kinds are a huge advance on the physical therapies such as insulin coma or psychosurgery, with their sadistic component. But here, as in the USA and to a certain extent in France, there is a sense that cognitive behaviour therapy, with its forward thrust, its vocabulary of aims and self-esteem, is the only therapy that provides a so-called evidence base of success. With its supposedly limited term, its spoken therapeutic goals, its 'proven' cost-benefits in relation to patients' lowered use of other parts of the health services, CBT seems to share a language of government targets and savings.

If nothing else, the history of these past two hundred years of the growing psychiatric and psychological imperium should make us sceptical of any single 'therapy' suiting all situations for more than a brief period. Therapies, after all, can create their own best patients, though once created they have the human creativity to change and need other therapies. If government were cagey, or rather, intelligent, it would hardly be putting all its therapeutic eggs in one basket, no matter what the supposed evidence base or financial saving. Evaluations of various kinds of therapy from CBT, to interpersonal, to attachment-based family therapy (ABFT) – which works on 'relational reframe, alliance-building, parent education, re-attachment, and promoting competency '– to simple educational interventions, show that all have had their degrees of success with depressed adolescents and also their families. The only substantial differences in success are seen in those people who experience some kind of intervention as against a control group who are on a 'waiting list' and fare worse.[457]

Since often, after a first 'acute' intervention, further therapy is called for, it is probably not far-fetched (as other studies have shown) to imagine that the more traditional psychotherapies which attempt an understanding of the self that marries past with present might also serve a purpose, and provide some form of cost-benefit. After all, anecdotal evidence has it that while people are in psychotherapy, they rarely fall ill or go to their GP.

There has been a recent move by some practitioners in even the most traditional psychoanalytical wing of the therapies to provide an 'evidence base' for their work — partly in order, perhaps, to police the boundaries of a profession that too often spills over into quackery, partly to keep pace with the needs of government health programmes.

Though psychoanalysis – with its individual, long-term and confidential nature and its aim of dealing with inner conflicts that may have the accidental benefit of getting rid of symptoms – hardly lends itself to the kind of replication that evidence-based studies need, the Stockholm Outcome of Psychoanalyis and Psychotherapy Project (STOPPP) set out to provide just such a study.[458]

Designed for a Swedish national health programme which wanted to test the viability of providing insurance for such therapies, STOPP set out to measure the effectiveness of therapy. Seven hundred and fifty-two patients – 202 in subsidized analysis or psychodynamic therapy with known clinicians, the rest on a waiting list – all of them diagnosed and rated on *DSM-IV* criteria, were followed over a period of three years. Comparisons were made between the two kinds of clinical work and the group on the waiting list. 'Outcome was assessed in terms of symptoms, social relations, morale or existential attitudes, general health, health care utilisation, working capacity etc., by qualitative interviews, self-report inventories, questionnaires and official records.'[459]

For 'norming' purposes, a well-being questionnaire was given to the participants and to a non-clinical group of 650 people in Stockholm. The results indicated that both therapy and analysis saw a substantial improvement in terms of morale and relief from symptoms. The surprise was that analysis effected the greatest improvement – though not in social relations. This was despite the therapists', a proportion of them cognitive behaviourists, far greater emphasis on curative factors: stated aims, concrete goals, adjustment to prevailing conditions; helping the patient avoid anxiety-provoking situations. Surprisingly, given prevailing assumptions, it seems that the therapists' stress on kindness, supporting and encouraging the patients, and their own self-disclosure, had little beneficial effect on the therapy, whereas the supposed neutrality of the traditional (and often older) psychoanalysts did.

Of particular moment in this context is that STOPPP patients with female therapists had significantly better outcomes than patients with male therapists, irrespective of the patient's own gender and the kind of treatment involved, though the difference was not so substantial amongst the psychoanalytic patients. Indeed, the manner of the psychoanalyst mattered far less to the outcome of the analysis than the manner of the therapist did to the therapy. It may be that insight –

which the study designated as 'helping the patient to understand that old reactions and relations are repeated in relation to the therapist; helping the patient see the connection between his/her problems and his/her childhood; encouraging the patient to reflect, in the therapy, on earlier painful experiences' — may after all have more to do with Freud's invention of the analytic technique than with the immediate personality of the analyst.

Later 'evidence-based' studies of therapeutic outcomes — such as those conducted by Peter Fonagy and Mary Target of the Anna Freud Centre and the University of London's Psychoanalysis Unit in collaboration with the Yale Child Study Center — have investigated the impact of therapy on diabetic children who need to resolve conflicts in order to control their insulin levels better. Substantial and lasting improvement has been found here.[460] A study of 352 children in therapy for depressive and anxiety disorders showed marked improvement in 72 per cent of those treated for at least six months, with the best results in serious cases for those treated intensively and daily. Another, of adolescents, not yet complete, showed amongst a plethora of results that girls responded far better than boys to both analysis and therapy.

Such results can only give way to speculation: is it possible that women, who made up so talented a portion of Freud's early patients, have a gift for the talking therapies and/or for pleasing their therapists? One needs to beware of generalizing too much on the basis of a confined study, but the thought is tempting, particularly given that in Britain in 2004 there were an estimated nineteen thousand suicide attempts by depressed adolescents, one every thirty minutes, and the majority of the 'attempts', though not of their successful and tragic conclusions, were made by girls, who outnumber boys in suicide attempts here by nine to one.

The mind doctors may indeed be helping women. Then, too, the simple presence of an interested 'other', whether an interlocutor, an attentive friend or spouse, has been shown to have far reaching effects on our immune and nervous systems as well as on our emotions and minds.[461] So why not, after all, an attentive therapist. But perhaps we can not rely on a single profession to cover all bases on its own. If the mind doctors over these last two hundred years have shown us anything, it is that our model of the human mind needs to be capacious.

Narrowing or medicalizing definitions too much limits the boundaries not only of so-called normality, but of human possibility. Lacan observed that some of his 'mad' would have functioned quite well in a religious community, in closed networks or in social organizations or political parties. Such possible lives might have kept them from stumbling into prison or madhouse.

Thinking back over the lives that have punctuated this history – from Mary Lamb, Théroigne de Méricourt, Henriette Cornier, through Alice James, Zelda Fitzgerald, Virginia Woolf to our contemporary sufferers from anorexia or depression – and putting them side by side with their times' understanding of the mad, bad and sad, certain features come into relief. It is clear that symptoms and diagnoses play into each other and cluster to create cultural fashions in illness and cure. Whatever the sophistication of the diagnosis, however, and its attendant treatment, this may not alter the *recurrent* or chronic nature of an individual's suffering. Pinel, in that sense, was as effective or ineffective a medic as the most 'scientific' of psychopharmacologists.

What is clear is that as we have moved through the twentieth century and into the twenty-first, an ever wider set of behaviours and emotions have become 'symptomatic' and fallen under the aegis of the mind doctors. A vast range of eccentricities or discomforts that seem too hard to bear shape suitable cases for treatment. But if what is understood as illness grows, symptoms have been attributed to an ever narrowing set of 'chemical' factors. It is as if the greater the terrain of possible malaise, the more 'scientifically' and organically precise we would want the cause and cure to be. There is a contradiction here, which may serve a drug industry rather better than it serves those who have become designated as patients or indeed the social sphere as a whole. Our times may need 'cures' that are broader and other than those that can be found in therapy alone, whether of the talking or the pharmaceutical kind.

Meanwhile, the mind doctors – whether they're GPs on the front line, therapists of an increasing number of varieties, psychoanalysts, psychiatrists or psychopharmacologists – trudge along, doing what they can, which is sometimes all that can be done. The danger, perhaps, comes when we ask them to do too much.

NOTES

Abbreviations

CW *The Collected Works of C.G. Jung*, ed. Sir Herbert Read, Michael Fordham and Gerhard Adler, trans. R.F.C. Hull (London: Routledge & Kegan Paul, 1944–78)

FJ *The Complete Correspondence of Sigmund Freud and Ernest Jones, 1908–1939*, ed. by R. Andrew Paskauskas (Harvard: Harvard University Press, 1995)

FJung *The Freud–Jung Letters*, ed. Wiliam McGuire, trans. R. Manheim and R.F.C. Hull (Princeton: Princeton University Press, 1974)

IJP *International Journal of Psychoanalysis*

SE *The Standard Edition of the Complete Psychological Works of Sigmund Freud*, 24 vols, ed. James Strachey in collaboration with Anna Freud, assisted by Alix Strachey and Alan Tyson (London: The Hogarth Press and Institute of Psycho-analysis, 1953–74)

Introduction pp. 1–10

p. 3 1. *up by 234 per cent* Rufus May, 'Britain on the Couch', *Independent*, 8 Oct. 2006, p. 12, available at http://news.independent.co.uk/uk/health_medical/article1819643.ece

p. 3 2. *mental health problems* Nigel Mossis, 'Suicidal, Sexually Abused, Scarred', *Independent*, 2 Aug. 2006, p. 12, available at http://news.independent.co.uk/ uk/crime/article1209749.ece

p. 4 3. *high blood pressure* *Our World*, BBC World, 14 Nov. 2006

p. 5 4. *specific hormones* Ray Moynihan, 'The Marketing of a Disease: Female Sexual Dysfunction', *British Medical Journal* 326 (2003), pp. 45–7, available at: http://www.bmj.com/cgi/ content/full/326/7379/45

p. 6 5. *anxiety and depression* See website for the ADD Health Centre: http://www.add-adhd-help-center.com/Depression/statistics.htm. See also the website for the National Institute of Mental Health, National Statistics Online (UK), the WHO document *The Global Burden of Disease, 2000*

p. 6   6. *majority are women*   'Mental Illness Benefit Claims Up', *BBC News*, 1 Feb. 2007, available at <http://news.bbc.co.uk/1/hi/uk/6319593.stm>

p. 6   7. *Service are women*   *Cambridge University Newsletter*, Apr./May 2007, p. 4

PART 1

1 Mad and Bad pp. 11–49

p. 14   8. *frilly bonnet*   Mary and Charles's portrait was painted by Francis Stephen Cary and is in the London National Portrait Gallery Collection

p. 15   9. *too much business*   *Morning Chronicle*, 26 Sept. 1796, in Sarah Burton, *A Double Life* (London: Penguin Books, 2004), p. ix

p. 16   10. *holy infant's head*   'To a Friend', in Samuel Taylor Coleridge, *Poems*, ed. John Beer (London: Dent, 1974), p. 43

p. 18   11. *she is mad*   Richard Hunter and Ida Macalpine, *Three Hundred Years of Psychiatry 1535–1860* (Oxford: OUP, 1963), pp. 310–11

p. 18   12. *until 1948*   Edward Shorter, *A History of Psychiatry* (New York: John Wiley & Sons, 1997), p. 5

p. 19   13. *they administered*   William Battie, *A Treatise on Madness*, and *Remarks on Dr Battie's Treatise on Madness* by John Monro, reprinted from the 1758 edition with an introduction by Richard Hunter and Ida Macalpine (London: Dawsons of Pall Mall, 1962)

p. 19   14. *Earth and Heaven defies*   Anonymous, in Roy Porter, *Mind-Forg'd Manacles* (London: Penguin Books, 1990), p. 123

p. 19   15. *as a lunatic*   Burton, *A Double Life*, p. 91

p. 20   16. *paroxysms of insanity*   *State Trials*, 1800, vol. 27, columns 1307–30, quoted in Valerie Argent, 'Counter-Revolutionary Panic and the Treatment of the Insane', available at Andrew Roberts's website: http://www.mdx.ac.uk/www/study/index.htm

p. 21   17. *under five thousand*   Shorter, *A History of Psychiatry*, p. 5

p. 21   18. *was 74,000*   See Roberts's website http://www.mdx.ac.uk/www/study/mhhtim.htm#1800

p. 22   19. *use of violence*   Porter, *Mind-Forged Manacles*, pp. 131, 137

p. 27   20. *wrong principles*   John Locke, *An Essay Concerning Human Understanding* (London: Everyman, 1961), book 2, ch. 11, p. 127

p. 30   21. *melancholy to hypochondria*   George Cheyne, *The English Malady: Or, a Treatise of Nervous Diseases of All Kinds* (London: Stratham & Leake, 1733). ed. and with an introduction by Roy Porter (London: Routledge/Tavistock, 1991), p. 262, passim 260–74 for following material

p. 30   22. *nervous minds*   Letter to Moxon's, Sept. 1833; letters to Thomas Manning, 24 Feb. 1805, 10 May 1806

p. 31   23. *Resource of Ignorance*   Cheyne, *The English Malady*

p. 32   24. *associations and judgement*   Dr William Cullen, *First Lines of the Practice of Physik* (Edinburgh, 1778–84), vol. 2, pp. 121–2, quoted by Porter in *Mind-Forg'd Manacles*; see also *Clinical lectures, delivered in the years 1765 and 1766, by William Cullen, M.D. . . . Taken in short-hand by a gentleman who attended* (London, 1797), available at 'Eighteenth Century Collections Online', Gale Group, http://galenet.galegroup.com/servlet/ECCO

p. 32   25. *society is afflicted*   Thomas Trotter, *A View of the Nervous Temperament* (London: Longman, 1807), p. xvii, quoted by W.F. Bynum, 'The Nervous Patient in Eighteenth- and Nineteenth-Century Britain', in W.F. Bynum, Roy Porter and Michael Shepherd (eds), *Anatomy of Madness*, Vol. 1 (London: Tavistock, 1985), pp. 89–102

p. 33   26. *Roy Porter*   Porter, *Mind-Forg'd Manacles*, esp. pp. 89–110

p. 33   27. *newly invented types*   Michel Foucault, *Interviews and Other Writings, 1977–1984* (London: Routledge, 1988), pp. 125–51. Foucault argues in his essay on 'The Dangerous Individual' that in consolidating itself as a specialized branch of medicine, psychiatry invented a new human type, the homicidal maniac, and turned murderers into mad people, the madness calling out for expert witness from specialists in court, since it was often visible only to them, the specialized readers of its signs, and the increasingly trained custodians of their treatment. The period in which this new human type emerges runs alongside the consolidation of the specialization of psychiatry in the first half of the nineteenth century. Mary Lamb's life coincides with its development, though her homicide just pre-dates it. Whereas the arguments put in pleading Hadfield's assassination attempt on George III could have been spoken by later psychiatrists, in 1800 there were no expert witnesses for Erskine to call. His arguments, however, were familiar to Pinel and Esquirol, the founding fathers of French psychiatry

p. 36   28. *his last years*   Porter, *Mind-Forg'd Manacles*, pp. 88–9

p. 37   29. *to escape*   It is telling that Charles writes an essay entitled 'The Sanity of True Genius' in which he emphatically states that genius, the greatest wit, is always to be found in the 'sanest writers'. 'It is impossible for the mind to conceive of a mad Shakespeare.' Poetic talent, for Charles, who was always unsure of his own and worried over Coleridge's excesses, manifests itself in the 'admirable balance of all the faculties'

p. 39   30. *report of 1825*   Burton, *A Double Life*, pp. 294ff. See also Anon. [John Mitford], *A description of the Crimes and Horrors in the Interiors of Warburton's Private Mad-House*, (London: Benbow, 1822); and J.W. Rogers, *A statement of the Cruelties, Abuses and Frauds, which are practised in Mad-Houses* (London: printed by E. Justins, 1815)

p. 40   31. *asylums in Britain*   See Andrew Roberts's biographical resource on Mary and Charles Lamb, available at http://www.mdx.ac.uk/www/study/yLamb.htm

p. 41   32. *that was necessary*   W.W. Webb, rev. Patrick Wallis, 'Tuthill, Sir George Leman (1772–1835)', *Oxford Dictionary of National Biography* (Oxford: OUP, 2004), available at http://www.oxforddnb.com/view/article/27900

p. 42   33. *most valuable asylum*   W.L. Parry-Jones, *The Trade in Lunacy: A Study of Private Madhouses in England in the Eighteenth and Nineteenth Centuries* (London: Routledge & Kegan Paul, 1972), pp. 183–4.

p. 43   34. *good citizenship*   See Samuel Tuke, *A Description of the Retreat*, 1813 (reprinted London: Dawson's, 1964); Michel Foucault, *Madness and Civilization*, trans. Richard Howard (London: Random House, 1965), pp. 241–7, provides what has become the classic critique of moral management

p. 43   35. *female insanity*   Elaine Showalter, *The Female Malady* (London: Virago, 1985), p. 10

p. 45   36. *of a kaleidoscope*   Thomas Noon Talfourd, *Final Memorials of Charles Lamb* (London: Moxon, 1850), pp. 351–2, quoted in Burton, *A Double Life*, pp. 241–2

p. 45   37. *bear this out*   See, for example, Andrew Scull, *Social Order, Mental Disorder* (Berkeley: University of California Press, 1989), p. 270; and Nancy Tomes, various articles including 'Feminist Histories of Psychiatry', in S. Micale and Roy Porter (eds), *Discovering the History of Psychiatry* (Oxford: OUP, 1994), pp. 348–83, 364–6

p. 45   38. *ever met with*   See Burton, *A Double Life*, pp. 164–5

p. 46   39. *those of women*   Porter, *Mind-Forg'd Manacles*, p. 163

p. 46   40. *30 per cent*   Parry-Jones, *The Trade in Lunacy*, pp. 49–50

p. 46   41. *1056 to 1000*   Figures quoted by Showalter, *The Female Malady*, pp. 52, 259

p. 46   42. *nineteenth-century asylum* Jonathan Andrews and Anne Digby (eds), *Sex and Seduction, Class and Custody: Perspectives on Gender and Class in the History of British and Irish Psychiatry* (Amsterdam: Rodopi, 2004); see, esp. the editor's introduction

p. 46   43. *in either jaw*   John Haslam, *Observations on Madness and Melancholy*, first published 1798, 2nd revised edn (London: Callow, 1809), p. 317, quoted in Shorter, *A History of Psychiatry*, p. 5

p. 47   44. *Scabs dried up*   William Black, 'Dissertation on Insanity', in Hunter and Macalpine, *Three Hundred Years of Psychiatry*, p. 646

p. 49   45. *category of masturbation* Arthur Foss and Kerith Trick, *St Andrew's Hospital, Northampton: The First 150 Years* (Cambridge: Granta Editions, 1989), pp. 193–4

PART 2

2   Passions pp. 53–81

p. 53   46. *the medical gaze*   Michel Foucault, *The Birth of the Clinic*, trans. A.M.
Sheridan Smith (New York: Vintage, 1994); see, for example, preface,
pp. ix–xix and 71–2. Foucault's definition of the gaze is far-reaching: it
includes an ocular probing which, translated into speech, renders the
patient's disease visible in a series of signs which become a subject both
for natural history and for the education of students in the new medical technology of *la clinique*

p. 54   47. *of his volition*   J.E.D. Esquirol, '*Délire*', in *Dictionnaire des Sciences
Médicales, par une Société de Médecins et de Chirugiens, Paris*, p. 251, quoted in
German Berrios and Roy Porter (eds), *A History of Clinical Psychiatry*
(London: Athlone Press, 1995), p. 31

p. 54   48. *or faith cures*   Jan Goldstein, *Console and Classify* (Cambridge: CUP,
1987), pp. 72–7

p. 55   49. *the Paris police*   Ibid., pp. 47–8

p. 55   50. *machine à guérir* Jacques Tenon, in *Mémoires sur les hôpitaux de Paris* (1788),
quoted by Goldstein, *Console and Classify*

p. 56   51. *of the passions*   G.-F. Etock-Demazy, 'Statistique medicale de l'asile
de la Sarthe', *Bulletin de la Societé d'agriculture, sciences et arts du Mans* 2 (1837),
quoted in Goldstein, *Console and Classify*, p. 160

p. 59   52. *from their chains*   Sigmund Freud, 'Charcot', *SE*, vol. 3, p. 18

p. 61   53. *brain disease*   Ibid., p. xx

p. 61   54. *reassuring words*   Quoted in Goldstein, *Console and Classify*, p. 79

p. 64   55. *in their capitals*   Quoted in DoraWeiner, 'Le geste de Pinel:
Psychiatric Myth', in Mark S. Micale and Roy Porter (eds), *Discovering the
History of Psychiatry* (Oxford: OUP, 1994), pp. 232–47. The description
comes from a report Esquirol undertook for the Minister of the
Interior in 1817, when he travelled across France investigating the con-
ditions in which the mad were kept

p. 65   56. *virtually vanished*   Goldstein, *Console and Classify*, p. 155

p. 65   57. *buoyant [gaies] passions* J.E.D. Esquirol, *monomanie*, in *Dictionnaire des Sciences
Medicales*, M.M. Adeslon, Alibert, Barbier, et al. (eds), vol. 34 (Paris:
1819), p. 115; and below, passim to p. 122

p. 65   58. *despair and suicide*   J.E.D. Esquirol, *Des Maladies Mentales* (Paris:
Balliere, 1838), vol. 1, pp. 399–401, for an introduction to the condition

p. 68   59. *roller-coaster-like excesses*   See, for example, Elisabeth Roudinesco,
Théroigne de Méricourt, trans. Martin Thom (London: Verso, 1991)

p. 69   60. *to the soldiers*   Esquirol, *Des Maladies Mentales*, vol. 1, p. 447

p. 74   61. *this monstrous crime*   Etienne-Jean Georget, *Discussions médico-légales sur la folie ou l'aliénation mentale* (Paris: 1826), pp. 71–9

p. 77   62. *was no defence*   Quoted in ibid., p. 94. Georget's contemporary text is the main source of material for the trials which laid the foundations of French law in this sphere

p. 78   63. *trials by the mad*   Ibid., p. 116

p. 79   64. *form of madness*   Esquirol, *Des Maladies Mentales*, pp. 252–3. Later figures cited by Elaine Showalter in *The Female Malady*, p. 54, show that the balance for post-partum madness was greater amongst the poor – though none of these comparisons are altogether reliable. Poverty could breed what was called 'lactational insanity', a condition caused by anaemia and malnutrition in mothers who nursed their babies for long periods for lack of other food and as a means of contraception

p. 80   65. *the fit itself*   Etienne-Jean Georget, *De la physiologie du système nerveux* (Paris: 1821), vol. 2, p. 279, quoted in Edward Shorter, *From Paralysis to Fatigue* (New York: Free Press, 1992), p. 202

p. 80   66. *rational control*   Showalter, *The Female Malady*, p. 55

p. 80   67. *implicate the former*   Ibid., p. 56

3   Asylum pp. 82–98

p. 82   68. *mental illness treatable*   Esquirol, *Des Maladies Mentales*, vol. 2; see pp. 695, 701–2

p. 83   69. *patient is subjected*   *Northampton Mercury*, Oct. 1834, quoted in Foss and Trick, *St Andrew's Hospital, Northampton*, p. 17

p. 83   70. *Europe and America* Report by Dr Thomas O. Prichard in 1838, cited in ibic. pp. 30–1

p. 83   71. *often generates*   George Man Burrows, *Commentaries on the Causes, Forms, Symptoms and Treatment, Moral and Medical, of Insanity* (London: Underwood, 1828), p. 667

p. 83   72. *laying on of hands*   Shorter, *A History of Psychiatry*, p. 43

p. 85   73. *original noble structure*   Harriet Martineau, 'The Hanwell Lunatic Asylum', *Tait's Edinburgh Magazine*, June 1834, quoted in Roberts and Andrew, *The Lunacy Commission* (1981) available at http:// www.mdx. ac.uk/www/study/01.htm

p. 88   74. *mercifully to control*   Wilkie Collins, *The Woman in White* (Oxford: OUP, 1991), p. 22

p. 88   75. *she said, whispering*   Ibid., p. 91

p. 89   76. *contradictions of a dream*   Ibid., p. 25

p. 89   77. *put in place* English novelists of 'sensation' continued to be preoccupied by madness and confinement. The bestselling *Lady Audley's Secret* ends with the heroine's confession that she murdered her husband because she was mad, a gloss of sorts on its author Mary Braddon's relationship with the man she couldn't marry because his wife was insane and confined in an asylum. Charles Reade's *Hard Cash* provides a thin disguise for John Connolly, head of Hanwell, and accuses him of confining a man after receiving payment from his father: in fact, Connolly admitted taking money from a wife in order to inter her husband

p. 90   78. *had told him*   Hersilie Rouy, *Mémoires d'une aliénée* (Paris: Paul Ollendorff, 1883), pp. 92–3, trans. by and quoted in Jeffrey Masson, *Against Therapy* (London: Collins, 1989)

p. 90   79. *unemployed symptoms*   Goldstein, *Console and Classify*, pp. 324, 328

p. 91   80. *officially anonymous*   Rouy, *Mémoires d'une aliénée*, p. 216, quoted by Masson, *Against Therapy*, p. 56

p. 91   81. *of her reason*   Rouy, *Mémoires d'une aliénée*, p. 133, quoted in ibid., p. 54

p. 91   82. *buried alive*   Ibid., p. 257, quoted in ibid., p. 57

p. 92   83. *demonstrate sanity*   David Rosenhan, 'On Being Sane in Insane Places', *Science* 179 (1973), pp. 250–8

p. 93   84. *number was 1072*   Shorter, *A History of Psychiatry*, p. 47

p. 93   85. *total of 30,538*   E. Fuller Torrey, MD, and Judith Miller, *The Invisible Plague* (New Jersey: Rutgers University Press, 2001), p. 74

p. 94   86. *the present day*   Ibid., p. 75, quoted from the *Journal of Psychological Medicine and Mental Pathology* 10 (1857), pp. 508–21

p. 94   87. *alcohol-related madness*   Shorter, *A History of Psychiatry*, gives astonishing statistics on the rise of alcohol consumption throughout Europe: for example, in France the production of alcohol rose fourteen-fold between the end of the eighteenth and the beginning of the twentieth centuries. The result was a huge rise in alcohol-related conditions which fell under the category of madness – hallucination, memory loss, confusion – and resulted in confinement. Cf. pp. 00–00

p. 94   88. *was called for*   Emil Kraepelin, *Lectures on Clinical Psychiatry*, facsimile of the 1904 edn, revised and ed. by Thomas Johnstone with a new introduction by Oskar Diethelm, (New York: Hafner Publishing Co., 1968)

p. 95   89. *the century progressed*   See Showalter, *The Female Malady*, passim, esp. ch. 3.

p. 96   90. *moral insanity*   'Moral insanity' was in fact first introduced in 1835 by the physician J. C. Prichard. He – and the courts after him – applied it to 'insanity without delusions', a Scots, then English, equivalent of Pinel and Esquirol's 'partial insanity'. See G.E. Berrios, 'Délire', *History of Psychiatry*, vol. 10, part 1, no. 37 (Mar. 1999)

p. 96   91. *alone can live*   Henry Maudsley, *Body and Will* (London: Kegan Paul, Trench, 1883), p. 237, quoted in Showalter, *The Female Malady*, p. 119

p. 98   92. *influence in breeding*   Henry Maudsley, *The Pathology of Mind* (1895), p. 536

p. 98   93. *vicious impulses*   Ibid., pp. 397–8

                                  4   Nerves pp. 99–124

p. 99   94. *railway spine*   See Allan Young, *The Harmony of Illusions* (Princeton, Princeton University Press, 1997), for a full discussion of nervous shock originating in railway accidents

p. 101   95. *to light or noise*   Joris-Karl Huysmans, *A Rebours*, trans. Robert Baldick (London: Penguin Books, 1966), p. 18

p. 102   96. *ruins the slave*   S. Weir Mitchell, *Lectures on the Diseases of the Nervous System, Especially in Women*, 2nd edn, (Philadelphia: Henry C. Lea's Son & Co., 1885), pp. 263–4, 270–1

p. 103   97. *careful preservation*   *Handbook for the Instruction of Attendants on the Insane, Prepared by a Sub-Committee of the Medico-Psychological Association* (London: Baillière & Co., 1884), p. 13

p. 103   98. *nervous force*   George Beard, 'Neurasthenia or Nervous Exhaustion', *Boston Medical and Surgical Journal* 80 (29 Apr. 1869), pp. 217–21, quoted in Shorter, *From Paralysis to Fatigue*, p. 221

p. 104   99. *utter incapacitation*   Janet Oppenheim, *Shattered Nerves* (New York: Oxford University Press, 1991), p. 81

p. 105   100. *physiological and the psychological* Michael Barfoot, 'Thomas Laycock', in *Oxford Dictionary of National Biography*, available at http://www.oxford dnb.com/

p. 105   101. *diseases of excitement*   Thomas Laycock, *Mind and Brain*, 2 vols (London, Marshall Simpkin, 1860), vol. 2, p. 317, cited in Oppenheim, *Shattered Nerves*, p. 187

p. 106   102. *coquette by nature*   Mary Wollstonecraft, *A Vindication of the Rights of Woman* (Boston: Peter Edes, 1792), ch. 3, available at http://www. bartleby.com/ 144/3.html

p. 108   103. *continuity of effort*   J. S. Mill, *The Subjection of Women* (London: Long-mans, 1869), ch. 3, available at http://etext.library.adelaide.edu.au/m/ mill/ john_stuart/m645s/, facsimile of 4th edn available at http://oll.lib-ertyfund.org/Home3/Book.php?recordID=0130

p. 110   104. *sexless dystopia*   Henry Maudsley, 'Sex in Mind and Education', *Fortnightly Review* 15 (1874), pp. 466–83

p. 110   105. *obdurate and resistant*   James Crichton-Browne published many articles on the brain in his journal. See Oppenheim, *Shattered Nerves*, pp. 188–93. See also Trevor Turner, 'James Crichton-Browne and the anti-psychoanalysts', in Hugh Freeman and German Berrios (eds), *150 Years of British Psychiatry*, vol. II: *The Aftermath* (London: Athlone Press, 1996), pp. 144–55

p. 111 106. *influence of dulness* Elizabeth Garrett Anderson, 'Sex in Mind and Education: A Reply', *Fortnightly Review* 17 (1874), p. 590

p. 118 107. *never-ending fight* Alice James, *The Diary of Alice James*, ed. Leon Edel (New York: Dodd, Mead & Co., 1964), pp. 149–50

p. 119 108. *death of a husband* Silas Weir Mitchell, *Westways* (New York: Century Co., 1913), p. 387

p. 120 109. *undesired symptoms* Silas Weir Mitchell, *Lectures on the Diseases of the Nervous System* (Philadelphia: Henry C. Lea's Son & Co., 1885), p. 181

p. 120 110. *revolutionary influences* Ibid., p. 125

p. 121 111. *provided passive exercise* Ibid., p. 270

p. 121 112. *out of bed* This story is told by Jean Strouse in her biography *Alice James* (Boston: Houghton Mifflin Co., 1984)

p. 121 113. *prevented from writing* For a fine analysis of *The Yellow Wallpaper*, see Elaine Showalter, *The Female Malady*, pp. 140–2

p. 121 114. *moral stability* Strouse, *Alice James*, p. 223

p. 122 115. *sound health* Ibid., pp. 221–5

p. 123 116. *unadulterated Jackson* Probably the great Boston pioneer of neurology, James Jackson Putnam, who taught at Harvard and worked at the Massachusetts General Hospital and who was known to all the James's

p. 123 117. *the male sex* Quoted in Jean Strouse, *Alice James*, p. 236

5 Hysteria pp. 125–146

p. 125 118. *to the church* Quoted in Goldstein, *Console and Classify*, p. 374

p. 127 119. *common type* J.M. Charcot, *Lectures on the Diseases of the Nervous System* (London: New Sydenham Society, 1881), trans. and ed. George Sigerson (New York: Hafner Publishing Co., 1962), pp. 2–3

p. 128 120. *this kind of seeing* *SE* III, p. 12

p. 131 121. *brightly coloured ribbons* D.M. Bourneville and P. Regnard, *Iconographie photographique de la Salpêtrière* (Paris: Progrès Médical, 1876–80), vol. II, p. 125

p. 134 122. *hurting me* Ibid., p. 131

p. 135 123. *Charcot's archive* Ernest Jones, in his three-volume work *Sigmund Freud, Life and Work* (New York: Basic Books, 1953–7), talks about Freud's one extravagance in Paris being the purchase of a complete set of Charcot's archives (see vol. 1, p. 202). His library also contained a copy of the *Iconographie photographique de la Salpêtrière*, though he didn't take it to London with him

p. 136 124. *all my interest* On the History of the Psychoanalytic Movement, *SE* XIV, pp. 13–14

p. 138 125. *people speak* Bourneville and Regnard, *Iconographie photographique de la Salpêtrière*, vol. III, p. 199

p. 138   126. *front of everyone*   Ibid., p. 188

p. 138   127. *her into sleep*   Ibid., p.198

p. 140   128. *hypnotizing doctors*   Jacqueline Carroy, *Hypnose, Suggestion et Psychologie* (Paris: Presse Universitaire de France, 1991), pp. 72–5

p. 141   129. *pain disorder*   See Mark Micale, *Approaching Hysteria* (New Jersey: Princeton University Press, 1995), p. 4; Steven E. Hyler and Robert Spitzer, 'Hysteria Split Asunder', *American Journal of Psychiatry* 135, no. 12, pp. 1500–4. For *DSM*, see http://www.psychnet-uk.com/dsm_iv/_misc/_complete_tables.htm

p. 142   130. *her Hystories*   Elaine Showalter, *Hystories: Hysterical Epidemics and Modern Media* (New York: Columbia University Press, 1997)

p. 144   131. *young widows* William Cullen, *Clinical lectures, delivered in the years 1765 and 1766, by William Cullen, M.D. ... Taken in short-hand by a gentleman who attended* (London, 1797), pp. 265–7. See 'Eighteenth Century Collections Online', Gale Group, available at http://www.gale.com/ EighteenthCentury/

p. 145   132. *Hyppocrates, marriage*   Philippe Pinel, *Nosographie philosophique*, vol. 3, Bibliothèque Nationale de France, electronic version based on Paris, J.A.B. Rosson, 1810, pp. 279–85

p. 145   133. *the treatment*   Quoted in Goblstein, *Console and Classify*, pp. 37f. from 'Charcot dévoilé', *Revue scientifique des femmes* 1 (1888), esp. p. 245

6   Sleep pp. 147–178

p. 147   134. *scientized*   Cf. Ian Hacking, *Rewriting the Soul* (New Jersey: Princeton University Press, 1995); Sonu Shamdasani's introduction to Théodore Flournoy, *From India to the Planet Mars* (New Jersey: Princeton University Press, 1994)

p. 147   135. *practice in Britain*   See Janet Oppenheim's excellent *Shattered Nerves* for a thorough analysis of 'depression' in the Victorian age

p. 150   136. *refinement and spirituality* Alison Winter, *Mesmerized* (Chicago: University of Chicago Press, 1998), pp. 213–17

p. 153   137. *please the family*   From Pierre Janet, 'The Relation of the Neuroses to the Psychoses', in Howard Townsend, Bronson Winthrop and R. Horace Gallatin (eds), *A Psychiatric Milestone: Bloomingdale Hospital Centenary, 1821–1921* (New York: Society of the New York Hospital, 1921), available at http://www.gutenberg.org/etext/15365

p. 155   138. *diverse and transient*   H.A. Taine, *De l'Intelligence* (1870), quoted by Hacking, *Rewriting the Soul*, p. 164

p. 155   139. *Switzerland and America*   Hacking, *Rewriting the Soul*, pp. 169–70

p. 155   140. *of 1885*   Stevenson corresponded with Pierre Janet while writing *Dr Jekyll and Mr Hyde*. Cf. Hacking, *Rewriting the Soul*, p. 278

p. 156   141. *Academy of Sciences*   Charcot, 'On the Various Nervous States Determined by Hypnotization in Hysterics' (1882)

p. 158   142. *abolished as well*   Pierre Janet, *L'automatisme psychologique* (Paris: Alcan, 1889), pp. 136–7

p. 159   143. *especially prone*   Freud, *SE* XI, pp. 12–13

p. 160   144. *been interrupted*   Janet, *L'Automatisme psychologique*, pp. 436–49 quoted by H.F. Ellenberger, *The Discovery of the Unconscious* (London: Allen Lane, 1970), pp. 361–4

p. 162   145. *day by day*   *SE* II, p. 33

p. 162   146. *talked away*   *SE* II, p. 35

p. 163   147. *pathogenic power*   *SE* XII, 'On Psycho-analysis', p. 207

p. 166   148. *the laboratory*   Flournoy, *From India to the Planet Mars*, ed. and introduced by Sonu Shamdasani, cited in the introduction, p. xiii

p. 167   149. *psychic protection* Ellenberger, *The Discovery of the Unconscious*, pp. 317–18

p. 167   150. *and his rationalism*   C.G. Jung, 'Flournoy', in *Memories, Dreams and Recollections* (New York: Pantheon), 1963

p. 167   151. *up to 1900*   Deirdre Bair, *Jung: A Biography* (New York/London: Little Brown, 2004), pp. 47–52, 62–4. See also H.F. Ellenberger's seminal 'The Story of Hélène Preiswerk', in *History of Psychiatry*, vol. 2, part 1, no. 5 (Mar. 1991

p. 169   152. *ordinary awareness*   William James and Théodore Flournoy, *The Letters of William James and Théodore Flournoy*, ed. R. Le Clair (Madison: University of Wisconsin Press, 1966), pp. 47–8

p. 169   153. *strange linguistic structures*   Mireille Cifali, Appendix in Flournoy, *From India to the Planet Mars*, p. 274

p. 169   154. *upon Hélène*   Ibid., p. 11

p. 169   155. *heard or read*   William James, *Principles of Psychology*, 1890 ed. (London: Macmillan, 1918), p. 601

p. 169   156. *Abwehr Psychosen*   *From India to the Planet Mars*, p. 207

p. 171   157. *agitated her*   Ibid., quoted and trans. by Sonu Shamdasani, from Waldemar Deonna and C.E. Muller, *De la Planète Mars en Terre Sainte* (Paris: 1932), which explores Hélène Smith's life after Flournoy and as a painter-medium

p. 172   158. *in constant motion*   Morton Prince, *The Dissociation of a Personality* (Cambridge: CUP, 1905), pp. 14–15

p. 172   159. *at the time*   In *Studies on Hysteria*, Freud is at pains to distinguish between hysteria and anxiety neuroses, since patients with either diagnosis sometimes somatize in the same way – using their bodies to express inner conflicts. Dissociation, however, and certainly the more extreme somnambulistic multiples are categorized as hysteric. Multiples seem to disappear from the diagnostic repertoire for women around the same time as hysterics

p. 174   160. *what illness means*   Prince, *The Dissociation of a Personality*, pp. 15–17

p. 174   161. *the other sex*   Morton Prince, 'Sexual Perversion or Vice? A Pathological and Therapeutic Inquiry' (1898), quoted in Ruth Leys, *Trauma* (Chicago: University of Chicago Press, 2000), pp. 64–5

p. 175   162. *Miss Beauchamp*   Leys, *Trauma*, p. 79fn

p. 176   163. *of Morton Prince*   Ibid., p. 42

p. 177   164. *senseless taboos*   G. Stanley Hall, *American Journal of Psychology* 29 (1918), pp. 144–58; see p. 154

PART 3

7   Sex pp. 181–201

p. 181   165. *Celia Brandon*   For reasons of confidentiality, the patient's name and family details have been changed. I am grateful to Lothian Health Services Archive, Edinburgh University Library, for their help here

p. 182   166. *Text-book of Insanity*   Richard von Krafft-Ebing, *Text-book of Insanity Based on Clinical Observations*, trans. Charles Gilbert Chaddock (Philadelphia: 1904), p. 81. See also Arnold I. Goldman, 'Sex and the Emergence of Sexuality', *Critical Inquiry* vol. 14, no. 1 (Fall 1987)

p. 182   167. *altogether satisfactorily*   Richard von Krafft-Ebing, 'Neuropathis sexualis feminarum', in W. Zulzer, *Klinisches Handbuch der Harn- und Sexualorgane* (Leipzig: F.C.W. Vogel, 1894), pp. 88–91

p. 182   168. *of their wives*   Ibid., p. 93

p. 183   169. *hierarchy of value*   Otto Weininger, *Sex and Character* (New York: Putnam, 1907)

p. 183   170. *unmarried motherhood*   Ivan Bloch, *The Sexual Life of Our Times in Its Relation to Modern Civilization* (London: Rebman, 1910), p. 276 and passim

p. 189   171. *committed to Bethlem*   I am indebted for this information to Dr Cyril Cannon who has done extraordinary research on the British in China

p. 190   172. *have to meet*   See Emil Kraepelin, *Lectures on Clinical Psychiatry*, ed. Thomas Johnstone (New York: Hofner Publishing Co., 1968)

p. 191   173. *on others*   'Civilized Sexual Morality and Modern Nervous Illness', *SE* IX, p. 192

p. 192   174. *Holmes of the Mind*   For the early reception of Freud in Britain, see Dean Rapp, 'The Early Discovery of Freud by the British General Educated Public, 1912–1919', *Society for the Social History of Medicine* 1990, pp. 217–43. See also W. Brown, 'Dreams: The Latest Views of Science', *Strand Magazine*, Jan. 1913, pp. 83–8; E.S. Grew, 'The Factory of Dreams: How and Why We Have Them', *Pall Mall Magazine*, Sept. 1913, pp. 358–65; *Saturday Review*, 11 July 1914, p. 51

p. 194   175. *their medical treatment*   *SE* XIX, 'A Short Account of Psychoanalysis' (1924)

p. 197   176. *of the neurosis*   *SE* III, p. 149

p. 197   177. *gruesome trick on us*   Cited in Hannah Decker, *Freud in Germany* (New York: International Universities Press, 1977), p. 102

p. 200   178. *the more capable*   *FJ*, Freud to Jones, 28 Apr. 1938

8   Schizophrenia pp. 202–251

p. 204   179. *outburst of laughter*   Emil Kraepelin, *Dementia Praecox and Paraphrenia*, trans. R.M. Barclay (Edinburgh: E. & S. Livingstone, 1919)

p. 205   180. *suicidal drive*   Eugen Bleuler, *Dementia Praecox or The Group of Schizophrenias*, trans. Joseph Zinkin (New York: International Universities Press, 1955), p. 489

p. 206   181. *creating neologisms*   Ibid., pp. 294, 295

p. 207   182. *a meaning and a causation*   'A Short Account of Psychoanalysis', *SE* XIX, pp. 191–212

p. 210   183. *sign of loathing*   Jung, 'The Freudian Theory of Hysteria' (1908), *CW* IV, pp. 20–1

p. 210   184. *marked sexual excitement*   John Kerr, *A Most Dangerous Method* (London: Sinclair-Stevenson, 1994), pp. 112–13, citing Jung, 'The Psychology of Dementia Praecox', *CW* III 46

p. 211   185. *I naturally concur*   Zvi Lothane, 'In Defense of Sabina Spielrein', *International Forum of Psycho-Analysis* 5 (1996), pp. 203–17. I am indebted to Zvi Lothane's excellent article for the Burghölzli admission records

p. 212   186. *a great deal*   Sabina Spielrein 'Secret symmetry', diary, 11 Sept. 1910, in Aldo Cartenuto (ed.), *A Secret Symmetry* (London: RKP, 1984), p. 11

p. 213   187. *of the anima*   See Kerr, *A Most Dangerous Method*, pp. 506–7, and Lothane, 'In Defense of Sabina Spielrein'

p. 213   188. *Hélène Preiswerk*   H.F. Ellenberger, 'The Story of Hélène Preiswerk', *History of Psychiatry*, vol. 2, part 1, no. 5 (Mar. 1991), p. 52

p. 213   189. *interested her husband*   Cartenuto, *A Secret Symmetry* SS to Freud, 13 June 1909, pp. 101–2

p. 213   190. *your saucy letters*   Quoted in Kerr, *A Most Dangerous Method*, p. 196 ff.

p. 214   191. *crude transference*   *FJ*, Jung to Freud, 12 June 1907, p. 63

p. 219   192. *reflected on abstinence*   Kerr, *A Most Dangerous Method*, p. 297

p. 220   193. *for the schizophrenic*   Sabina Spielrein, *A Case of Schizophrenia*, quoted in ibid., p. 298

p. 220   194. *representative in Vienna*   Quoted and trans. in Lothane, 'In Defense of Sabina Spielrein'

p. 221 195. *differs from paranoia* *SE* XII, pp. 76–7, 'On an autobiographical account of a case of paranoia' (Schreber case), 1911

p. 222 196. *drink and dissipation* Quoted in F. Scott Fitzgerald, *Tender Is the Night*, preface by Malcolm Cowley (London: Penguin Books, 1988), p. 13

p. 224 197. *1930 came breakdown* Zelda's life is fully portrayed in Nancy Milford's dazzling biography, *Zelda* (New York: Avon, 1970)

p. 224 198. *few incoherent ones* Ibid., p. 197

p. 225 199. *factor against me* Jackson R. Bryer and Cathy W. Barks (eds), *Dear Scott, Dearest Zelda* (London: Bloomsbury, 2002), pp. 81–2 (Letter number 53, Summer 1930)

p. 226 200. *into total insanity* Matthew J. Bruccoli and Margaret M. Duggan (eds), *Correspondence of F. Scott Fitzgerald* (New York: Random House, 1980), p. 254 (Paris, 1 December 1930)

p. 227 201. *play into you own backyard* Bryer and Barks (eds)_, p. 87 (Letter number 57, June 1930)

p. 228 202. *arrived here* Ibid.l, p. 83 (Letter number 54, Summer 1930)

p. 228 203. *popular songs* Matthew J. Bruccoli (ed), *Zelda Fitzgerald: The Collected Writings* (London: Abacus, 1991), p. 429 (From '1931' in 'Show Mr. and Mrs. F to Number —')

p. 228 204. *slight tendency to schitzophrenie* Byer and Barks (eds), p. 104 (Letter number 72, Spring/Summer 1931)

p. 229 205. *person is schizophrenic* Ibid., Milfords letter of 9 March 1966, p. 473

p. 230 206. *Carol Loeb Shloss* Carol Loeb Shloss, *Lucia Joyce: To Dance in the Wake* (London: Bloomsbury, 2004)

p. 230 207. *analogy for schizophrenia* C.G. Jung, 'Ulysses: A Monologue', *The Spirit in Man, Art and Literature* (London: Routledge & Kegan Paul, 1971), pp. 112–17

p. 232 208. *schizophrenia as psychogenic* Shorter, *A History of Psychiatry*, pp. 91–3, 109–12 and passim

p. 233 209. *pages of an album* Scott Fitzgerald to Mildred Squires, 8 Mar. 1932, quoted in Milford, *Zelda*, p. 261

p. 233 210. *and a feueté* Bruccoli and Duggan (eds), pp. 283–4 (after February 1932). This appears in Zelda's phonic spelling and is evidently fouetté, though the eds. have strangely changed it to finité which has no link to any ballet step

p. 234 211. *adept at self-concealment* R.D. Laing, *The Divided Self* (London: Penguin Books, 1965), p. 37

p. 236 212. *the present time* Milford, *Zelda*, p. 315; see also 315ff. for reviews

p. 237 213. *many of my experiences* Ibid., p. 342

p. 240 214. *London Psychoanalytical Society* I am grateful to John Forrester for the information on Wright, some of which is also noted on I.M. Ingram's highly useful website on Virginia Woolf's psychiatric history, available at http://www.malcolmingram.com/vwframe.htm

p. 241 215. *certainly discussed dreams* Hermione Lee, *Virginia Woolf* (London: Chatto & Windus, 1996), pp. 197–8

p. 241 216. *laid it to rest* Quoted in Jeanne Schulkind (ed.), *Virginia Woolf, Moments of Being* (New York: Harcourt Brace Jovanovich, 1976), pp. 80–1. See a similar account that includes both parents and written just a year after *To the Lighthouse* (1927) in Virginia Woolf, *A Writer's Diary*, p. 135 (entry dated 28 Nov. 1928)

p. 241 217. *been infinitely worse* Virginia Woolf, *The Diaries*, vol. V, *1936–41* (London: Hogarth Press, 1977–84), p. 202

p. 242 218. *stopped the creativeness too* Alex Strachey, 'Recollections of Virginia Woolf' (1972) in Joan Russell Noble (ed.), *Recollections of Virginia Woolf* (London: Cardinal, 1989), pp. 172–3; quoted in Robert Hinshelwood, 'Virginia Woolf and Psychoanalysis', *International Revue of Psycho-Analysis* 17 (1990), p. 367 (Letter)

p. 242 219. *hoots of laughter* http://www.malcolmingram.com/vwframe.htm

p. 243 220. *clearing up of amnesias* Maurice Craig, *Nerve Exhaustion* (London: J. & A. Churchill, 1922), pp. 122–6

p. 244 221. *sense of proportion* Virginia Woolf, *Mrs Dalloway* (London: Penguin Books, 1964), pp 109–10

p. 245 222. *the only way out* Craig, *Nerve Exhaustion*, p. 356

p. 246 223. *structural principle in the male* See also Lisa Appignanesi and John Forrester, *Freud's Women* (London: Weidenfeld & Nicolson, 1992), pp. 434–5

p. 247 224. *theory of anxiety* F. Fromm-Reichmann, 'Psychoanalytic and General Dynamic Conceptions of Theory and of Therapy – Differences and Similarities', *Journal of the American Psychoanalytic Association* 2 (1954), pp. 711–21; see pp. 716–17

p. 247 225. *hand against God* Nathan G. Hale Jr, *The Rise and Crisis of Psychoanalysis in the United States* (New York/Oxford: OUP, 1995), pp. 175–6

p. 248 226. *attribute of self-esteem* Freud had defined a more complex version of this 'self-regard' which he deals with in his paper 'On Narcissism', *SE* XIV

p. 248 227. *dismantling their defences* See Harry Stack Sullivan, 'The Modified Psychoanalytic Treatment of Schizophrenia', *American Journal of Psychiatry* 11 (1930), pp. 519–49, esp. p. 533. Also Shorter, *History of Psychiatry*, pp. 204–5

p. 248 228. *fill up your life* Bryer and Barks (eds), p. 87 (Letter number 57, June 1930)

p. 249 229. *she would fall into it* Quoted from an interview with Mary Porter by

Milford, *Zelda*, p. 373

p. 250   230. *with intractable patients*   Shorter, *A History of Psychiatry*, pp. 210–12; Showalter, *The Female Malady*, pp. 205–6

9   Disturbances of Love pp. 252–271

p. 253   231. *commotion in the asylum*   Elisabeth Roudinesco, *Jacques Lacan and Co., A History of Psychoanalysis in France*, trans. Jeffrey Mehlman (London: Free Association Books, 1990), pp. 27–8

p. 254   232. *woman becomes nothing*   Jean Doléris, *Néo-malthusianisme. Maternité et féminisme. Education sexuelle* (Paris, 1918), p. 14

p. 254   233. *and slapped him*   Gaetan Gatian de Clérambault, *L'Erotomanie* (Paris: Le Seuil, 2002), pp. 43–64

p. 256   234. *a criminology journal*   Gaetan Gatian de Clérambault, *Passion érotique des étoffes chez la femme* (Paris: Le Seuil, 2002)

p. 257   235. *on the escalator*   Terry Eagleton, *Literary Theory* (Oxford: Blackwell, 1983), p. 7

p. 257   236. *nor a rapist*   Cf. the case of Zuma, in which he was accused and exonerated of rape. See, for example, *The Guardian*, 9 May 2006

p. 258   237. *make the language evolve*   Elisabeth Roudinesco, *Jacques Lacan* (Paris: Fayard, 1993), pp. 49–50

p. 259   238. *given way to psychosis*   ElisabethRoudinesco, *A History of Psychoanalysis in France* (London: Free Association Books, 1990), pp. 114–15

p. 260   239. *earned a good living*   *Le Journal*, 19 Apr. 1931, quoted in ibid., p. 57

p. 261   240. *delusions of grandeur*   Jacques Lacan, *De la psychose paranoïaque dans ses rapports avec la personnalite* (Paris: Le Seuil, 1975), p. 158. For the full case, see 151ff.

p. 264   241. *made her special*   According to later revelations, it seems that Marguerite bore the same name as an earlier child who had died before her parents' eyes when her party frock had caught fire. The mother had never fully recovered

p. 266   242. *doesn't want her home*   Lacan, *De la psychose paranoïaque*, p. 234

p. 266   243. *theme of persecution*   Ibid., p. 261

p. 266   244. *in a closed clinic*   Ibid., pp. 279–80

p. 270   245. *or some say eighty-nine*   The full story is told in Francis Dupré, *La 'solution' du passage à l'acte: le double crime des soeurs Papin* (Toulouse: Eres, 2003)

10   Mother and Child pp. 272–300

p. 273   246. *proportionately significant numbers*   See Appignanesi and Forrester, *Freud's Women*, for a fuller discussion of all this, and also for a fuller picture of Hermine Hug-Hellmuth.

p. 273   247. *6.5 per cent of doctors*   Eli Zaretsky, *Secrets of the Soul* (New York: Knopf, 2004), p. 195

p. 274   248. *of healthy children*   *SE* XX, pp. 69–70

p. 275   249. *development of character*   Melanie Klein, 'The Development of a Child', *International Journal of Psycho-Analysis* 4 (1923), pp. 419–74; see pp. 419–20

p. 276   250. *troubling and intelligible*   For a fine analysis of what becoming psychological means, see Nicholas Rose, 'Power and Subjectivity', available at http://www.academyanalyticarts.org/rose1.htm

p. 277   251. *to its integrity* Anna Freud, *The Ego and the Mechanisms of Defence*, trans. Cecil Baines from 1937 edn (London: Hogarth Press and the International Psychoanalytic Library, 1968), p. 4

p. 278   252. *anxiety in children*   Anna Freud, 'Reports on the Hampstead Nurseries 1939–1945', *Writings*, vol. III (New York: International Universities Press, 1966–81), p. 169

p. 278   253. *hard to bear*   Ibid., p. 189

p. 280   254. *bright imaginative eyes*   Virginia Woolf, *The Diaries*, vol. V, *1936–41* (London: Hogarth Press, 1984), p. 209

p. 281   255. *tolerating real deprivations*   Melanie Klein, 'The Psychological Principles of Infant Analysis', *International Journal of Psycho-Analysis* 8 (1927), pp. 25–37; see pp. 25–6.

p. 282   256. *by internal persecutors*   Melanie Klein, 'A Contribution to the Theory of Anxiety and Guilt', *International Journal of Psycho-Analysis* 49 (1948), pp. 114–23; see p. 116

p. 282   257. *fear of death*   Ibid., p. 117

p. 284   258. *made babies interesting*   Adam Phillips, *D. W. Winnicott* (London: Fontana Modern Masters, 1988)

p. 285   259. *considered as a couple*   For biographical information I am indebted to Masud R. Khan, introduction to *Through Paediatrics to Psychoanalysis* (London: Hogarth Press, 1978); Phillips, *D. W. Winnicott*; and F. Robert Rodman, MD, *Winnicott*, (Cambridge, Mass. Perseus, 2003)

p. 287   260. *without his being aware*   Quoted by Zaretsky, *Secrets of the Soul*, pp. 174–5

p. 288   261. *early mothering*   D.W. Winnicott, 'Primitive Emotional Development' (1945), in *Through Paediatrics to Psychoanalysis*, pp. 145–56

p. 289   262. *playing for time*   D.W. Winnicott, 'Primary Maternal Preoccupation'(1956), in ibid., pp. 304–5

p. 289   263. *gets lost this way*   Anna Freud, letter to J.C. Hill, 21 Oct 1974, quoted in Elisabeth Young-Bruehl, *Anna Freud* (London: Macmillan, 1988), p. 457

p. 290   264. *Gabrielle the Piggle*   D.W. Winnicott, *The Piggle* (London: Hogarth Press, 1978), pp. 5–7

p. 291   265. *fact of development itself*   Ibid., p. 4

p. 292   266. *makes everything black*   Ibid., p. 119

p. 293   267. *childhood questions*   Ibid., p. 74

p. 294   268. *on his child patient*   Pearl King and Eric Rayncr, 'John Bowlby', *IJP* 74 (1993), pp. 1823–8; see p. 1824

p. 294   269. *things in her child* J. Bowlby, 'The Influence of Early Environment in the Development of Neurosis and Neurotic Character', *IPJ* 21 (1940), pp. 154–78; see p. 175

p. 295   270. *post-war displacement*   Denise Riley, *War in the Nursery* (London: Virago, 1983), p. 98

p. 295   271. *preventive mental hygiene*   John Bowlby, *Maternal Care and Mental Health* (Geneva: World Health Organization, 1951), pp. 13–14 and passim

p. 296   272. *parents was recommended*   John Bowlby, 'Citation Classic: Bowlby J. Maternal care and mental health: a report prepared on behalf of the World Health Organization as a contribution to the United Nations programme for the welfare of homeless children' (Geneva: World Health Organization, 1951), in *Current Contents* 50 (15 Nov. 1986)

p. 296   273. *no-one else will do*   Riley, *War in the Nursery*, pp. 100–1.

p. 296   274. *for economic provision*   Bowlby, *Maternal Care and Mental Health*, p. 24

p. 298   275. *enacted in the transference*   King and Rayner, 'John Bowlby', p. 1827

p. 299   276. *fear of domination*   D.W. Winnicott, 'The Mother's Contribution to Society' (1957), republished in Clare Winnicott, Ray Shepherd, Madeleine Davis (eds), *Home Is Where We Start From* (London: Penguin Books, 1986), p. 125

11   Shrink for Life pp. 301–345

p. 302   277. *ever critical analytic profession*   Stephen Farber and Mark Green, *Hollywood on the Couch* (New York: Morrow, 1993)

p. 302   278. *arrived in America*   In his work in progress, *The Freudian Century*, John Forrester gives this figure as 130, though the number grows significantly if lay analysts, who didn't join American psychoanalytic societies, are included

p. 302   279. *vocational success* Hale, *The Rise and Crisis of Psychoanalysis in the United States*, p. 299

p. 303   280. *feelings of guilt*   Quoted in ibid., p. 278

p. 303   281. *suicide and delinquency* These statistics and the following ones come from ibid., pp. 246–8, and Zaretsky, *Secrets of the Soul*, pp. 280–1

p. 304   282. *of the talking cure*   Hale, *The Rise and Crisis of Psychoanalysis in the United States*, p. 289. Hale also notes that there were only 1400 practising analysts across the world in 1957, perhaps 14,000 people in analysis, and no more than 100,000 who had completed treatment. This nonetheless means that the USA had 67 per cent of the world's analysts

p. 304   283. *psychiatry and criminology*   Ibid., p. 286

p. 306   284. *insufficiency and unhappiness*   Edward Strecker, *Their Mothers' Sons* (New York, Philadelphia: Lippincott, 1946), pp. 52–9 and 31ff,. quoted in Betty Friedan, *The Feminine Mystique* (New York: Dell, 1963), pp. 162–4

p. 309   285. *accept the premises*   See, for example, Brenda Webster, *The Last Good Freudian* (New York: Holmes & Meier, 2000)

p. 309   286. *increasingly clinging*   Hale, *The Rise and Crisis of Psychoanalyis in the United States*, pp. 259–62

p. 311   287. *dispayed autistic features*   Lauren Slater, *Opening Skinner's Box* (London: Bloomsbury, 2004), pp. 133–56

p. 313   288. *shrinks were always there*   Quoted by Farber and Green, *Holllywood on the Couch*, p. 75

p. 317   289. *damn right I'm not*   Hannah Green, *I Never Promised You a Rose Garden*, reprinted from 1964 Victor Gollancz edn (London: Pan Books, 1991), pp. 141–2

p. 318   290. *level you are capable*   Ibid., pp. 10, 101

p. 318   291. *own self-enclosed world*   See Fromm-Reichmann, 'Psychotherapy and Schizophrenia', *American Journal of Psychiatry* 111 (Dec. 1954), p. 412; and Hale, *The Rise and Crisis of Psychoanalysis in the United States*, pp. 266–70

p. 319   292. *could afford them*   Alfred H. Stanton and Morris Schwartz, *The Mental Hospital* (New York: Basic Books, 1954), cited by Hale, *The Rise and Crisis of Psychoanalysis in the United States*, p. 269

p. 319   293. *rather than poems*   Quoted in Showalter, *The Female Malady*, p. 216

p. 323   294. *effect in some cases*   A recent figure from *Mind* puts this beneficial effect at 37 per cent of the patients given ECT

p. 323   295. *depression and schizophrenia*   Shorter, *A History of Psychiatry*, pp. 218–24

p. 324   296. *felt Father: why not*   Karen V. Kulik (ed.), *The Journals of Sylvia Plath 1950–1962* (London: Faber & Faber, 2000), pp. 201, 204

p. 325   297. *most out of it*   Ibid., pp. 429ff.

p. 326   298. *best do with it*   Ibid., p. 435

p. 326   299. *intellectual rapport*   Ibid., p. 495

p. 327   300. *mind disintegrating again*   Diane Middlebrook, *Her Husband* (London: Bloomsbury, 2003), p. 207

p. 328   301. *of the clergy*   Norman Holland, at http://www.lists.ufl.edu/cgi-bin/wa?A2=ind0012c&L=psyart&P=758

p. 329   302. *new flowering life*   Kalik, *The Journals of Sylvia Plath*, pp. 513–14

p. 330   303. *and others echo*   Truman Capote, 'A Beautiful Child,' in *Music for Chameleons* (London: Hamish Hamilton, 1981), pp. 206–22; also Sarah Churchwell, *The Many Lives of Marilyn Monroe* (London: Granta, 2004) and 'To Aristophanes and Back', *Time Magazine*, 14 May1956

p. 331   304. *wouldn't go away*   'To Aristophanes and Back', *Time Magazine*, 14 May1956

p. 332   305. *reporter in an interview*   Laura Miller, 'Norma Jeane', *New York Times*, 2 April 2002; see also Churchwell, *The Many Lives of Marilyn Monroe*

p. 333   306. *back into herself*   Donald Spoto, *Marilyn Monroe: The Biography* (London: Chatto & Windus, 1993), p. 475

p. 334   307. *how to love*   Arthur Miller, *After the Fall* (London: Secker & Warburg, 1965), pp. 122–3

p. 334   308. *too Freudian*   Susan Strasberg, *Marilyn and Me* (New York: Warner Books, 1992)

p. 335   309. *conscious memory*   Eric R. Kandel's autobiographical Nobel Prize speech available at http://nobelprize.org/nobel_prizes/medicine/laureates/2000/kandel-autobio.html

p. 336   310. *Kris's death*   Webster, *The Last Good Freudian*, pp. 47–8

p. 337   311. *which is not sleep*   Quoted in Farber and Green, *Hollywood on the Couch*, p. 93

p. 338   312. *concept of herself*   Anthony Summers, *The Secret Lives of Marilyn Monroe* (New York: Macmillan, 1986), p. 382

p. 338   313. *he's not for me*   Quoted in Churchwell, *The Many Lives of Marilyn Monroe*, p. 267

p. 338   314. *womankind in herself*   Ibid., p. 268

p. 339   315. *but I did*   Quoted in Farber and Green, *Hollywood on the Couch*, p. 94, and in the letter (cited on p. 000) to Greenson

p. 340   316. *building techniques*   Ralph R. Greenson, 'Transference: Freud or Klein', *International Journal of Psycho-Analysis* 55 (1974), pp. 37–48

p. 341   317. *anxiety or bad luck*   Ralph R. Greenson, *Explorations in Psychoanalysis* (New York: International Universities Press, 1978)

p. 342   318. *sweet, wholesome way* Farber and Green, *Hollywood on the Couch*, p. 103

p. 343   319. *said they preferred*   Appignanesi and Forrester, *Freud's Women*, from the Foreword to the revised edn (London: Phoenix, 2005) pp. xxii–xxiii

p. 344   320. *way of living* Quoted in Albert J. Solnit, 'Ralph R. Greenson – 1911–1979', *Psychoanalytic Quarterly* 49 (1980), pp. 512–16

PART 4

12   Rebels pp. 347–377

p. 349   321. *patient Maya*   R.D. Laing and A. Esterson, *Sanity, Madness and the Family* (London: Penguin Books, 1970), pp. 34–5 (1st edn, 1974)

p. 350   322. *by medical research*   Thomas S. Szasz, 'The Myth of Mental Illness', *American Psychologist* 15 (1960), pp. 113–18

p. 353   323. *first admission*   Andrew Scull, *Madhouse* (Yale and London: Yale University Press, 2005), pp. 241–5, 294–6

p. 353   324. *experiment showed*   David L. Rosenhan, 'On Being Sane in Insane Places', *Science* 179 (Jan. 1973), pp. 250–8

p. 356   325. *not be trusted*   R.D. Laing and A. Esterson, *Sanity, Madness and the Family* (London: Penguin Books, 1970), pp. 42–3

p. 357   326. *anybody's mind*   Ibid., pp. 127–8

p. 357   327. *long as you live*   L. Bernikow, *The American Women's Almanac. An Inspiring and Irreverent Women's History* (New York: Berkeley Books, 1997), pp. 153–4

p. 358   328. *Anne Sexton*   See Diane Middlebrook's fine biography, *Anne Sexton* (London: Virago, 1991)

p. 361   329. *is brought in*   R.D. Laing, *Wisdom, Madness and Folly* (London: Macmillan, 1985), p. 3

p. 361   330. *understand the patient*   R.D. Laing, *The Divided Self* (London: Penguin Books, 1965), pp. 29–31

p. 361   331. *from your writings*   Letter of 27 Apr. 1958, cited in F. Robert Rodman, MD, *Winnicott* (Cambridge, Mass.: Perseus, 2003), p. 243

p. 362   332. *have to interview*   J. Clay, *R. D. Laing: A Divided Self* (London: Sceptre, 1997), p. 70

p. 363   333. *of our age*   Ibid., p. 100

p. 365   334. *returned reason*   David Healy, *The Anti-Depressant Era* (Harvard: Harvard University Press, 1998), pp. 58–9

p. 365   335. *things of the past*   Shorter, *A History of Psychiatry*, pp. 249–50

p. 366   336. *educational system*   From an unpublished lecture by John Forrester

p. 366   337. *depression and withdrawal*   Showalter, *The Female Malady*, p. 236

p. 367   338. *array of possibilities*   B. Mullan, *Mad to be Normal: Conversations with R.D. Laing* (London: Free Association Books, 1995), p. 326

p. 368   339. *the female patient*   Showalter, *The Female Malady*, p. 247

p. 369   340. *of the phallus*   Simone de Beauvoir, *The Second Sex* (London: Picador edn, 1988), p. 80 and passim

p. 370   341. *fine volcanic ash*   Friedan, *The Feminine Mystique*, pp. 114–15

p. 370   342. *off her nut*   See Kate Millett, 'Sexual Politics' (1968), available at http://www.marxists.org/subject/women/authors/millett-kate/sexual-politics.htm

p. 371   343. *men exceed women*   Phyllis Chesler, *Women and Madness* (New York: Doubleday, 1972), pp. 150–69, 284–99

p. 373   344. *consciousness-raising*   Juliet Mitchell, *Women's Estate* (London: Penguin, 1971), p. 60, and (below) p. 61

p. 374   345. *the patient's needs*   S.A. Shapiro, 'The History of Feminism and Interpersonal Psychoanalysis', *Contemporary Psychoanalysis* 38 (2002), pp. 213–56

p. 376   346. *where the action is*   'Psychiatry on the Couch', cover story, *Time Magazine*, 2 Apr. 1979

p. 376   347. *audiences of two thousand*   John Leo, 'A Therapist in Every Corner', *Time Magazine*, 23 Dec. 1985

13   Body Madness pp. 378–404

p. 378   348. *or did not eat*   Grace Bowman, 'My Years of Living Dangerously', *Independent*, 28 Feb. 2006, p. 40–1

p. 380   349. *in America and Europe*   J.C. Seidell and K.M. Flegal, 'Assessing obesity: Classification and Epidemiology', *British Medical Bulletin* 53 (1997), pp. 238–52; and *Journal of the American Medical Association* 272 (1994), pp. 205–11

p. 380   350. *300 pounds (136 kilos)*   Ian Hacking, 'Kinds of People: Moving Targets', British Academy Lecture, 11 Apr. 2006 (Web version), pp. 10–11; and American Sports Data, 'US Population Dangerously Overweight', available at http://www.americansportsdata.com/weightstats.asp

p. 380   351. *total identity*   Ian Hacking, 'Making up People', *London Review of Books*, 17 Aug. 2006, pp. 23–5

p. 380   352. *and social life*   http://www.rcplondon.ac.uk/news/news.asp?PR_id=201

p. 380   353. *fast food industry*   Sander L. Gilman , 'Obesity, the Jews and Psychoanalysis', in *History of Psychiatry* 17:1, no. 65 (Mar. 2006), pp. 55–65; see p. 56

p. 381   354. *time and place*   Richard A. Gordon, *Eating Disorders*, 2nd edn (London: Blackwell, 2000), pp. 6–13

p. 382   355. *rather than contact*   Maud Ellmann, *The Hunger Artists* (London: Virago, 1992), p. 14

p. 383   356. *altar of cuisine*   See, for example, Bill Buford's masterly *Heat* (London: Jonathan Cape, 2006)

p. 384   357. *of eating disorders*   'Mental illness benefit claims up', *BBC News*, 1 Feb. 2007

p. 385   358. *excess of resistance*   Charles Lasègue, 'De l'Anorexie hystérique', *Archives Générales de médecine* (Apr. 1873), quoted by Joan Brumberg, *Fasting Girls: The History of Anorexia Nervosa* (New York: Vintage, 2000), pp. 128–9

p. 386   359. *all sexual satisfaction*   *SE* XII, p. 182

p. 386   360. *enough milk*   *SE* XXI, p. 234

p. 386   361. *an insatiable need*   For a brilliant account see Ellman, *The Hunger Artists*

p. 387   362. *hysterical anorexia*   See 'On Psychotherapy', *SE* VII, pp. 257–68; see p. 264

p. 388 363. *curable conditions* Gilman, 'Obesity, the Jews and Psychoanalysis', pp. 63–5

p. 388 364. *with the world* Susie Orbach, *Fat Is a Feminist Issue* (London: Paddington Press, 1978), p. 11

p. 389 365. *have been fat* Germaine Greer, *The Female Eunuch* (London: Granada, 1971), pp. 14, 33

p. 389 366. *and eating disorders* Jessica S. Ruffolo, Katharine A. Phillips, William Menard, Christina Fay and Risa B. Weisberg, 'Comorbidity of Body Dysmorphic Disorder and Eating Disorders', *International Journal of Eating Disorders*, vol. 39, issue 1 (Oct. 2006) pp. 11–19

p. 390 367. *the age of nine* Marya Hornbacher, *Wasted* (London: Flamingo, 1998), pp. 6–7

p. 391 368. *contain herself* Ibid., p. 22–5

p. 394 369. *dimensions in her head* Ibid., p. 170

p. 395 370. *acceptability of their bodies* Susie Orbach, *Hunger Strike* (London: Penguin Books, 1993), p. 59

p. 395 371. *don't need anymore* Ibid., pp. 71–2

p. 396 372. *a masculine one* See Marilyn Lawrence, 'Body, Mother, Mind', *International Journal of Psycho-Analysis* 83 (2002), pp. 837–50, for a discussion of the many positions analysts have taken on the origins of anorexia

p. 396 373. *points of starvation* Gordon, *Eating Disorders*, pp. 32–5

p. 396 374. *their abused sexuality* Anna Motz, *The Psychology of Female Violence* (London: Brunner-Routledge, 2001), pp. 153–9 and passim; preface by Estela Welldon

p. 397 375. *characteristic of the illness* Lawrence, 'Body, Mother, Mind', p. 839

p. 400 376. *lack of responsibility* H. Bruch, 'Four Decades of Eating Disorders', in David Garner and Paul Garfinkel (eds), *Handbook of Psychotherapy for Anorexia Nervosa and Bulimia* (New York/London: Guilford Press, 1985), p. 12

p. 400 377. *a call for help* Robert Lindner, *The Fifty-Minute Hour* (London: Free Association Books, 1986), 1st edn 1955, pp. 115–16

p. 401 378. *body is inescapable* Hornbacher, *Wasted*, p. 93

p. 401 379. *abuse features* See Gordon, *Eating Disorders*, pp. 37–50

p. 403 380. *bingeing and purging* Ibid., pp. 47–8

14 Abuse pp. 405–447

p. 405 381. *rape in another's* Freud, 'The Aetiology of Hysteria', *SE* III, pp. 187–221; see pp. 200–1

p. 406 382. *from 1920 to 1986* Theodore Shapiro, MD, 'The Reality of Trauma', *Contemporary Psychoanalysis* 31 (1995), pp. 451–8

p. 408   383. *men and women*   Noreen Connell and Cassandra Wilson (eds), *Rape: The First Sourcebook for Women* (New York: New American Library, 1974), available at http://www.americancivilrightsreview.com/docs-nyradicalfeministsrapemanifesto1971.htm

p. 410   384. *insults during quarrels*   Wendy McElroy, 'The New Mythology of Rape', at http://www.wendymcelroy.com/rape.htm

p. 410   385. *their latent hatred*   'Interview with Alice Miller', trans. by Simon Worrall, at http://www.alice-miller.com/interviews_en.php?page=1

p. 410   386. *rid of it*   Alice Miller, 'The Essential Role of an Enlightened Witness in Society', at http://www.alice-miller.com/index_en.php?page=2

p. 411   387. *new kind of person*   Ian Hacking, 'The Making and Molding of Child Abuse', *Critical Inquiry* vol. 17, no. 2 (Winter 1991), p. 260

p. 412   388. *was still climbing*   Ed Magnuson, 'Child Abuse: The Ultimate Betrayal', *Time Magazine*, 5 Sept. 1983

p. 412   389. *numbers may be greater*   Ellen Bass and Louise Thornton, *I Never Told Anyone* (New York: Harper & Row, 1983), pp. 24–5

p. 414   390. *their secrets intact*   Judith Herman, *Trauma and Recovery* (London: HarperCollins, 1992), p. 110

p. 415   391. *is creeping in*   Hacking, 'The Making and Molding of Child Abuse', pp. 259–60

p. 415   392. *like a victim*   Ellen Bass and Laura Davis, *The Courage to Heal*, pp. 35–9

p. 416   393. *and seek help*   'Incest Comes Out of the Dark', *Time Magazine*, 7 Oct. 1991

p. 417   394. *by him at five*   'Lies of the Mind', *Time Magazine*, 29 Nov. 1993

p. 418   395. *damned his research*   See Andrew Scull's *Madhouse* for this full story

p. 419   396. *them out psychically*   J. Laplanche and J.-B. Pontalis, *The Language of Psycho-analysis* (London: Hogarth Press and the Institute of Psychoanalysis, 1973), pp. 465–9.

p. 420   397. *or went blank*   Phyllis Greenacre, 'The Prepuberty Trauma in Girls', *Psychoanalytic Quarterly* 19 (1950), pp. 298–317; see p. 301

p. 422   398. *theory and treatment*   M.O. Tsaltas, 'Changes in the Treatment of Abused Children', *Journal of the American Academy of Psychoanalysis* 22 (1994), pp. 533–43

p. 424   399. *consulting room*   Shapiro, 'The History of Feminism and Interpersonal Psychoanalysis', pp. 223ff.

p. 425   400. *damage inflicted*   Helena Kennedy, *Eve was Framed* (New York: Vintage, 2005), p. 142

p. 426   401. *psychologically abused*   Herman, *Trauma and Recovery*, p. 118

p. 426   402. *denial of women's reality*   Ibid., p. 14

p. 426   403. *rule their own homes*   Ibid., pp. 2–3

p. 426   404. *after-effects of war*   See Allan Young, *The Harmony of Illusions* (New Jersey: Princeton University Press, 1997)

p. 427   405. *from its effects*   G. Davis and N. Breslau, 'Are Women at Greater Risk for PTSD than Men?', at http://www.healthyplace.com/Com munities/anxiety/women_ptsd.asp

p. 429   406. *idealize or denigrate*   Herman, *Trauma and Recovery*, p. 111

p. 430   407. *simply emulated*   See Hacking, 'Making up People', p. 23, for a summary version of these arguments

p. 431   408. *had been made*   Hacking, *Rewriting the Soul*, pp. 42–3

p. 431   409. *multiple personality*   Richard Ofshe and Ethan Watters, *Making Monsters: False Memories, Psychotherapy and Sexual Hysteria* (London: André Deutsch, 1995), p. 206

p. 432   410. *not do or say?*   Quoted in ibid., pp. 210–11, from F.W. Putnam, *Diagnosis and Treatment of Multiple Personality Disorder* (New York: Guilford, 1989), pp. 79, 90

p. 432   411. *taken the drink*   Jill Smolowe, 'The 21 Faces of Sarah', *Time* magazine 12 Nov. 1990

p. 433   412. *unavailable to singletons*   http://www.angelworld.org/

p. 433   413. *than one personality*   Quoted in Hacking, *Rewriting the Soul*, p. 18

p. 433   414. *turned it into a habit*   'Understanding Dissociative Disorders', at MIND, http://www.mind.org.uk/Information/Booklets/Understand ing/Understanding+dissociative+disorders.htm

p. 434   415. *child sexual abuse*   M. Target, 'The Recovered Memories Controversy', *International Journal of Psycho-Analysis* 79 (1998), pp. 1015–8; see p. 1015

p. 434   416. *perceive and protect*   Howard B. Levine, 'Recovered Memories of Trauma', *International Journal of Psychoanalysis* 79 (1998), pp. 187–90

p. 434   417. *present unconscious*   Target, 'The Recovered Memories Controversy', p. 1020, with a reference to Joseph and Anne Marie Sandler

p. 436   418. *neurotransmitter systems*   Peter D. Kramer, *Listening to Prozac* (London: Fourth Estate, 1994), pp. 119–21

p. 436   419. *after the abuse*   Ibid., p. 118

p. 438   420. *sufferers is high*   Bessel van der Kolk, 'Post Traumatic Therapy in the Age of Neuroscience, *Psychoanalytic Dialogues* 12 (2002), pp. 381–92

p. 438   421. *training or education*   Sally Satel, MD, 'Bread and Shelter, Yes, Psychiatrists No', *New York Times*, 29 Mar. 2005

p. 442   422. *psychiatric services*   Anna Motz, *The Psychology of Female Violence*, pp. 117–21

p. 443   423. *their imprisonment*   *Independent*, 2 Aug. 2006, p. 12

p. 444   424. *from acting violently*   *Lancet*, vol. 358 (8 Dec. 2001)

p. 445   425. *furious rebellion*   Herman, *Trauma and Recovery*, pp. 124–5

p. 446   426. *and her children*   National Institute for Mental Health in England, 'The Personality Disorder Capabilities Framework', Department of Health, 2005

p. 447   427. *high blood pressure*   See http://www.nimh.nih.gov/publicat/#7

                        15   Drugs pp. 448–475

p. 448   428. *external appearance*   Karl Menninger, *The Vital Balance* (New York: Viking, 1963), p. 2

p. 449   429. *another prescription drug*   http://www.benzo.org.uk/jegshock.htm

p. 450   430. *overreliance on drugs*   'Psychiatry on the Couch', cover story, *Time Magazine*, 2 Apr. 1979

p. 451   431. *constitute malpractice*   Shorter, *A History of Psychiatry*, pp. 309–10

p. 451   432. *biochemical practice*   For a brilliant analysis see T.M. Luhrman, *Of Two Minds* (New York: Knopf, 2000)

p. 451   433. *year as a sedative*   Shorter, *A History of Psychiatry*, pp. 201–3

p. 452   434. *year of its sale*   Healy, *The Creation of Psychopharmacology* (Harvard: Harvard University Press, 2001), p. 225 and passim

p. 453   435. *committed by women*   Home Office, 'Statistics on Women and the Criminal Justice System, 2003', p. 3, available at http://www.homeoffice.gov.uk/rds/pdfs2/s95women03.pdf

p. 456   436. *appearance of normalcy*   Elizabeth Wurtzel, *Prozac Nation* (London: Quartet Books, 1995), pp. 263–4

p. 457   437. *trials in psychiatry*   Healy, *The Creation of Psychopharmacology*, pp. 47–9

p. 457   438. *has a blackout effect*   Elizabeth Wurtzel, 'Shrug Drug that Saved My Life', *Guardian*, 21 Jan. 1999

p. 457   439. *the enemy's roof*   Lauren Slater, *Prozac Diary* (London: Hamish Hamilton, 1999), pp. 4–5

p. 459   440. *learning from it all*   Kay Redfield Jamison, *An Unquiet Mind* (London: Picador, 1996), p. 88

p. 459   441. *themselves on the child*   Lauren Slater, 'Parents Help Babies Learn Lessons of Love', *Deseret News*, 27 Mar. 2003

p. 461   442. *to gloomy thoughts*   Berrios and Porter, *A History of Clinical Psychiatry*, p. 386

p. 462   443. *and so dangerous*   'Mourning and Melancholia', *SE* XIV, pp. 251–2

p. 462   444. *difficulty sleeping*   Shorter, *History of Psychiatry*, p. 291

p. 463   445. *post-traumatic stress disorder* Royal College of Psychiatrists, 'Antidepressants', at http://www.rcpsych.ac.uk/mentalhealthinformation/mentalhealthproblems/depression/antidepressants.aspx

p. 464   446. *depressive by another*   Alix Smegel, 'The Dictionary of Disorders', *New Yorker*, 3 Jan. 2005, pp. 56–63; see p. 57

p. 464   447. *from that disorder*   Ibid., p. 58

p. 467   448. *pharmaceutical companies undertake*   See Healy, *The Anti-Depressant Era and Psychopharmacology*

p. 470   449. *their depression return*   Peta Bee, 'Seven Exercises That Heal', *Guardian*, 26 Aug. 2006

p. 471   450. *non-human intervention*   Wurtzel, 'Shrug Drug that Saved My life'

p. 471   451. *research and development*   Joan E. Gadzby, 'Some Shocking Facts on Prescription Drugs', at http://www.benzo.org.uk/jegshock.htm

p. 471   452. *slightly fallen off*   Based on the Ofsen study of 4400 Medicaid records in 1999–2000 reported in the *New York Times*

Epilogue pp. 477–484

p. 479   453. *drastic hormonal shifts*   Fiona Shaw, *Out of Me* (London: Viking, 1997), p. 42

p. 480   454. *erased the questions*   Ibid., pp. 85–6

p. 480   455. *go to a therapist*   See http://www.ynhh.org/healthlink/womens/womens_8_03.html for recent work in the USA on women's positive responses to psychotherapy for post-partum depression

p. 480   456. *therapy they wanted*   Healthcare Commission report, 29 Sept. 2006

p. 481   457. *and fare worse*   See Peter Fonagy et al., *What Works for Whom* (New York: Guilford Press, 2003); for a review of evaluations with control groups, see also: 'Medscape', http://www.medscape.com/viewarticle/457724_2

p. 482   458. *such a study*   Rolf Sandell, Johan Blomberg, Anna Lazar, Jan Carlsson, Jeanette Broberg and Johan Schubert , 'Varieties of Long-Term Outcome Among Patients in Psychoanalysis and Long-Term Psychotherapy: A Review of Findings in the Stockholm Outcome of Psychoanalysis and Psychotherapy Project (STOPPP)', *International Journal of Psycho-Analysis* 81 (2000), pp. 921–42; see pp. 921–33

p. 482   459. *and official records*   Ibid., pp. 922–3

p. 483   460. *has been found here*   Peter Fonagy and Mary Target, 'The History and Current Status of Outcome Research at the Anna Freud Centre', *Psychoanalytic Study of the Child* 57 (2002), pp. 27–60

p. 483   461. *emotions and minds*   See Darlian Leader and David Corfield, *Why Do People Get Ill?* (London: Hamish Hamilton, 2006), for a fascinating account of relations between the mind and body in illness

SELECT BIBLIOGRAPHY

For reasons of space, this bibliography only includes key texts. Many of the eighteenth- and nineteenth-century sources are now available in digitized form from Project Gutenberg and other Internet sites. These are listed in the endnotes, as are most of the journals and articles I have consulted.

Adelon, Alibert, Barbier, Bayle et al. (eds), *Dictionnaire des sciences médicales par une société de médecins et de chirurgien*, 60 vols (Paris: C.L.F. Pancoucke 1812–1822)

Andrews, Jonathan, and Digby, Anne (eds), *Sex and Seduction, Class and Custody: Perspectives on Gender and Class in the History of British and Irish Psychiatry* (Amsterdam: Rodopi, 2004)

Appignanesi, Lisa, and Forrester, John, *Freud's Women* (London: Weidenfeld & Nicolson, 1992, new edition, Phoenix, 2005)

Bair, Deirdre, *Jung: A Biography* (New York/London: Little Brown, 2004)

Bass, Ellen, and Thornton, Louise, *I Never Told Anyone* (New York: Harper & Row, 1983)

Battie, William, *A Treatise on Madness and Remarks on Dr Battie's Treatise on Madness by John Monroe*, reprinted from the 1758 edition with an introduction by R. Hunter and I. Macalpine (London: Dawsons of Pall Mall, 1962)

Bell, Quentin, *Virginia Woolf* (London: Hogarth, 1982)

Bernikow, L., *The American Women's Almanac. An Inspiring and Irreverent Women's History* (New York: Berkeley Books, 1997)

Berrios, German, and Porter, Roy (eds), *A History of Clinical Psychiatry* (London: Athlone Press, 1995)

Bleuler, Eugen, *Dementia Praecox or The Group of Schizophrenias*, trans. Joseph Zinkin (New York: International Universities Press, 1955)

Bloch, Ivan, *The Sexual Life of Our Times in its Relation to Modern Civilization* (London: Rebman, 1910)

Bourneville, D.M., and Regnard, P., *Iconographie photographique de la Salpêtrière*, 3 vols (Paris: Progrès Médical, 1876–7)

Bowlby, John, 'Maternal Care and Mental Health' (Geneva: World Health

Organization, 1952)

Attachment and Loss, 3 vols (London: Penguin Books, 1991)

Burrows, George Man, *Commentaries on the Causes, Forms, Symptoms and Treatment, Moral and Medical, of Insanity* (London: Underwood, 1828)

Burton, Sarah, *A Double Life* (London: Penguin Books, 2004)

Bynum, W.F., Porter, Roy, and Shepherd, Michael (eds), *Anatomy of Madness,* 2 vols (London: Tavistock, 1985)

Capote, Truman, 'A Beautiful Child', in *Music for Chameleons* (London: Hamish Hamilton, 1981)

Carroy, Jacqueline, *Hypnose, Suggestion et Psychologie* (Paris: Presse Universitaire de France, 1991)

Cartenuto, Aldo (ed.), *A Secret Symmetry* (London: Routledge & Kegan Paul 1984)

—— *Clinical Lectures on the Diseases of the Nervous System,* ed. Ruth Harris (London: Routledge, 1990)

Charcot, J.M. *The Clinician: The Tuesday Lessons,* trans. with commentary by Christopher G. Goetz (New York: Raven Press, 1987)

—— and Richer, Paul, *Les démoniaques dans l'art* (Paris: Macula, 1984)

Chesler, Phyllis, *Women and Madness* (New York: Doubleday, 1972)

Cheyne, George, *The English Malady: Or, a Treatise of Nervous Diseases of All Kinds,* ed. and with an introduction by Roy Porter (London: Routledge/Tavistock, 1991)

Churchwell, Sarah, *The Many Lives of Marilyn Monroe* (London: Granta, 2004)

Clay, John, *R.D. Laing: A Divided Self* (London: Hodder & Stoughton, 1996)

Coleridge, Samuel Taylor, *Poems,* ed. John Beer (London: Dent, 1974)

Collins, Wilkie, *The Woman in White* (Oxford: OUP, 1991)

Connell, Noreen, and Wilson, Cassandra (eds), *Rape: The First Sourcebook for Women* (New York: New American Library, 1974)

Craig, Maurice, *Nerve Exhaustion* (London: J. & A. Churchill, 1922)

Cullen, William, *Clinical lectures, delivered in the years 1765 and 1766, by William Cullen, M.D . . . Taken in short-hand by a gentleman who attended* (London, 1797)

De Beauvoir, Simone, *The Second Sex,* trans. and ed. H.M. Parshley (London: Picador, 1988)

Decker, Hannah, *Freud in Germany* (New York: International Universities Press, 1977)

De Clérambault, Gaetan Gatian, *L'Erotomanie* (Paris: Le Seuil, 2002)

—— *Passion érotique des étoffes chez la femme* (Paris: Le Seuil, 2002)

Didi-Huberman, Georges, *Invention de l'hystérie* (Paris: Macula, 1982)

Dupré, Francis, *La 'solution' du passage à l'acte: le double crime des soeurs Papin* (Toulouse: Eres, 2003)

Ellenberger, H.F., *The Discovery of the Unconscious* (London: Allen Lane, 1970)

——— 'The Story of Hélène Preiswerk', *History of Psychiatry*, vol. 2, part 1, no. 5 (Mar. 1991)

Ellmann, Maud, *The Hunger Artists* (London: Virago, 1992)

Esquirol, J.E.D., *Des Maladies Mentales* (Paris: Baillière, 1838)

Farber, Stephen, and Green, Mark, *Hollywood on the Couch* (New York: Morrow, 1993)

Fitzgerald, F. Scott, *Tender Is the Night*, preface by Malcolm Cowley (London: Penguin Books, 1988)

——— *Correspondence of F. Scott Fitzgerald*, ed. Matthew J. Bruccoli and Margaret M. Duggan (London: Bloomsbury, 2002)

——— and Fitzgerald, Zelda, *Dear Scott, Dearest Zelda: The Love Letters of F. Scott and Zelda Fitzgerald*, ed. Jackson R. Bryer and Cathy W. Barks (London: Bloomsbury, 2002)

——— *Save Me the Waltz* (London: Vintage Classics, 2001)

——— *The Collected Writings*, ed. Matthew Bruccoli (New York: Collier, 1992)

Flournoy, Théodore, *From India to the Planet Mars*, ed. and introduced by Sonu Shamdasani (New Jersey, Princeton University Press, 1994)

——— *The Letters of William James and Théodore Flournoy*, ed. R.C. Le Clair (Madison: University of Wisconsin Press, 1966)

Foss, Arthur, and Trick, Kerith, *St Andrew's Hospital, Northampton: The First 150 Years* (Cambridge: Granta Editions, 1989)

Foucault, Michel, *Madness and Civilization*, trans. Richard Howard (London: Random House, 1965)

——— *The Birth of the Clinic*, trans. A.M. Sheridan Smith (London: Tavistock, 1973)

——— *Interviews and Other Writings, 1977–1984* (London: Routledge, 1988)

Freud, Anna, *The Ego and the Mechanisms of Defence. Writings*, vol. II (New York: International Universities Press, 1966)

——— *The Writings of Anna Freud*, vol I–VIII (New York: International Universities Press, 1966–81)

——— *Infants without Families. Reports on the Hampstead Nurseries 1939–1945, Writings*, vol. III (New York: International Universities Press, 1973)

Freud, Sigmund, *The Standard Edition of the Complete Psychological Works of Sigmund Freud*, 24 vols, ed. James Strachey in collaboration with Anna Freud, assisted by Alix Strachey and Alan Tyson (London: Hogarth Press and Institute of Psycho-analysis, 1953–74)

The Freud–Jung letters, ed. William McGuire,; trans. Ralph Manheim and R.F.C. Hull, 1979 (Princeton: Princeton University Press, 1974)

Friedan, Betty, *The Feminine Mystique* (New York: Dell, 1963)

Fromm-Reichmann, F., 'Psychoanalytic and General Dynamic Conceptions of Theory and of Therapy – Differences and Similarities', *Journal of the American*

Psychoanalytic Association 2 (1954), pp. 711–21

—— 'Psychotherapy and Schizophrenia', *American Journal of Psychiatry* 111 (Dec. 1954)

Gamwell, Lynn, and Tomes, Nancy, *Madness in America* (Ithaca: Cornell University Press, 1995)

Garner, David, and Garfinkel, Paul, (eds), *Handbook of Psychotherapy for Anorexia Nervosa and Bulimia* (New York/London: Guilford Press, 1985)

—— *Discussions médico-legales sur la folie ou l'alienation mentale* (Paris: 1826),

Georget, Etienne-Jean, *De la physiologie du système nerveux* (Paris: 1821)

Gilman, Sander L., *Seeing the Insane* (Lincoln: University of Nebraska Press, 1996)

—— 'Obesity, the Jews and Psychoanalysis', *History of Psychiatry* 17(1), no. 65 (Mar. 2006), pp. 55–65

Goldman, Arnold I., 'Sex and the Emergence of Sexuality', *Critical Inquiry* vol. 14, no. 1 (Fall 1987)

Goldstein, Jan, *Console and Classify* (Cambridge: CUP, 1987)

Gordon, Richard A., *Eating Disorders*, 2nd edn (London: Blackwell, 2000)

Green, Hannah, *I Never Promised You a Rose Garden* (London: Pan Books, 1991)

Greenacre, Phyllis, 'The Prepuberty Trauma in Girls', *Psychoanalytic Quarterly* 19:190 (1950), pp. 298–317

Greenson, Ralph R., *The Technique and Practice of Psychoanalysis* (London: Hogarth Press, 1973)

—— *Explorations in Psychoanalysis* (New York: International Universities Press, 1978)

Greer, Germaine, *The Female Eunuch* (London: Granada, 1971)

Grosskurth, Phyllis, *Melanie Klein* (London: Hodder & Stoughton, 1986)

Hacking, Ian, 'The Making and Molding of Child Abuse', *Critical Inquiry*, vol. 17, no. 2 (Winter 1991)

—— *Rewriting the Soul* (New Jersey: Princeton University Press, 1995)

—— *The Social Construction of What?* (Cambridge, Mass./London: Harvard University Press, 1998)

—— 'Kinds of People: Moving Targets', British Academy Lecture, 11 Apr. 2006 (Web version)

—— 'Making up People', *London Review of Books*, vol. 28, no. 16, (17 Aug. 2006), pp. 23–5

Hale Jr, Nathan G., *The Rise and Crisis of Psychoanalysis in the United States* (New York/Oxford: OUP, 1995)

Healy, David, *The Anti-Depressant Era and Psychopharmacology* (Cambridge, Mass./London: Harvard University Press, 1997)

—— *The Creation of Psychopharmacology* (Cambridge, Mass./London: Harvard University Press, 2001)

Herman, Judith Lewis, *Trauma and Recovery* (London: HarperCollins, 1992)

Hornbacher, Marya, *Wasted* (London: Flamingo, 1998)

Hunter, Richard, and Macalpine, Ida, *Three Hundred Years of Psychiatry 1535–1860* (Oxford: OUP, 1963)

Huysmans, Joris-Karl, *A Rebours*, trans. Robert Baldick (London: Penguin Books, 1966)

James, Alice, *The Diary of Alice James* (London: R. Hart-Davis, 1965)

—— *The Death and Letters of Alice James*, ed. Ruth Bernard Yeazell (Berkeley, Calif./London: University of California Press, 1981)

James, Henry, *The Complete Letters*, eds. Pierre A. Walker and Greg W. Zacharias (Lincoln: University of Nebraska Press, 2006)

James, William, *Principles of Psychology*, 3 vols, (Cambridge, Mass./London: Harvard University Press, 1981)

James, William, and Flournoy, Théodore, *The Letters of William James and Théodore Flournoy*, ed. R.C. Le Clair (Madison: University of Wisconsin Press, 1966)

Jamison, Kay Redfield, *An Unquiet Mind* (London: Picador, 1996)

Janet, Pierre, *L'automatisme psychologique* (Paris: Alcan, 1889)

Jones, Ernest, *Sigmund Freud, Life and Work*, 3 vols (New York: Basic Books, 1953–57)

Jung, C.G., *The Collected Works of C.G. Jung*, ed. Sir Herbert Read, Michael Fordham and Gerhard Adler, trans. R.F.C. Hull (London: Routledge & Kegan Paul, vol. III, 1960; vol. IV, 1961; vol. V, 1967; vol. IX, 1959)

—— *Memories, Dreams and Recollections*, recorded by Amelia Jaffe, trans. Richard and Clara Winston (New York: Pantheon, 1963)

—— 'Ulysses: A Monologue,' in *The Spirit in Man, Art and Literature* (London: Routledge & Kegan Paul, 1971)

Kerr, John, *A Most Dangerous Method* (London: Sinclair-Stevenson, 1994)

Khan, Masud R., *Through Paediatrics to Psychoanalysis* (London: Hogarth Press, 1978)

Klein, Melanie, 'The Development of a Child', 4 (1923), pp. 419–74)

—— 'The Psychological Principles of Infant Analysis', *Analysis* 8 (1927), pp. 25–37

—— 'A Contribution to the Theory of Anxiety and Guilt', *International Journal of Psycho-Analysis* 49 (1948), pp. 114–23

—— *Envy and Gratitude and other works, 1946–1963* (London: Hogarth Press and the Institute of Psycho-Analysis, 1975)

—— *Love, Guilt and Reparation and other works, 1921-1945* (London: Virago, 1988)

Kraepelin, Emil, *One Hundred Years of Psychiatry*, trans. Wade Baskin (London: Peter Owen, 1962)

—— *Lectures on Clinical Psychiatry*, facsimile of 1904 edn, ed. Thomas Johnstone, introduction by Oskar Diethelm (New York: Hafner Publishing Co., 1968)

—— *Dementia Praecox and Paraphrenia*, trans. R.M. Barclay (New York: R.E. Krieger, 1981, facsimile of 1919 edn)

Krafft-Ebing, Richard von, *Text-book of Insanity Based on Clinical Observations*, trans.

Charles Gilbert Chaddock (Philadelphia, 1904)

Kramer, Peter D., *Listening to Prozac* (London: Fourth Estate, 1994)

Lacan, Jacques, *De la psychose paranoiaque dans ses rapports avec la personnalité* (Paris: Le Seuil, 1975)

Laing, R.D., *The Divided Self* (London: Penguin Books, 1965)

Laing, R.D., and Esterson, A., *Sanity, Madness and the Family* (London: Tavistock, 1964; Penguin Books, 1970)

Lamb, Charles, *The Last Essays of Elia* (London, Oxford: OUP, 1929)

—— *The Letters of Charles Lamb*, 2 vols (London: J.M. Dent, 1935)

—— *The Letters of Charles and Mary Lamb*, ed. Edwin W. Marrs Jr, (Ithaca/London: Cornell University Press, 1975)

—— and Lamb, Mary, *Books for Children*, ed. E.V. Lucas (London: Methuen, 1903) Also available online at Project Gutenberg

J. Laplanche and J.-B. Pontalis, *The Language of Psycho-analysis* (London: Hogarth Press and Institute of Psychoanalysis, 1973)

Lasègue, Charles, 'De l'anorexie hystérique', *Archives Générales de médecine* (April, 1873)

Lawrence, Marilyn, 'Body, Mother, Mind', *International Journal of Psycho-Analysis* 83 (2002), pp. 837–50

Laycock, Thomas, *Mind and Brain*, 2 vols (London: Marshall Simpkin, 1860)

Lee, Hermione, *Virginia Woolf* (London: Chatto & Windus, 1996)

Levine, Howard B., 'Recovered Memories of Trauma', 79 (1998), pp. 187–90

Leys, Ruth, *Trauma* (Chicago: University of Chicago Press, 2000)

Lindner, Robert, *The Fifty-Minute Hour* (London: Free Association Books, 1986)

Locke, John, *An Essay Concerning Human Understanding* (London: Everyman, 1961)

Lothane, Z., 'In Defense of Sabina Spielrein', *International Forum of Psycho-Analysis* 5 (1996), pp. 203–17

Luhrman, T.M., *Of Two Minds* (New York: Knopf, 2000)

Masson, Jeffrey, *Against Therapy* (London: Collins, 1989)

Maudsley, Henry, *Body and Will* (London: Kegan Paul, Trench, 1883)

Medico-Psychological Association, *Handbook for the Instruction of Attendants on the Insane, Prepared by a Sub-Committee of the Medico-Psychological Association* (London: Baillière & Co., 1884)

Menninger, Karl, *The Vital Balance* (New York: Viking, 1963)

Micale, Mark, *Approaching Hysteria* (New Jersey: Princeton University Press, 1995)

—— and Porter, Roy (eds), *Discovering the History of Psychiatry* (Oxford: OUP, 1994)

Middlebrook, Diane, *Anne Sexton* (London: Virago, 1991)

—— *Her Husband* (London: Bloomsbury, 2003)

Milford, Nancy, *Zelda* (New York: Avon, 1970)

Mill, J.S., *The Subjection of Women* (London: Longmans, 1869)

Miller, Arthur, *After the Fall* (London: Secker & Warburg, 1965)

Mitchell, Juliet, *Women's Estate* (Harmondsworth: Penguin Books, 1971)

—— *Psychoanalysis and Feminism* (Harmondsworth: Penguin Books, 1975)

Mitchell, S. Weir, *Lectures on the Diseases of the Nervous System, Especially in Women* 2nd edn. (Philadelphia: Henry C. Lea's Son & Co., 1885)

—— *Westways* (New York: Century Co., 1913)

Motz, Anna, *The Psychology of Female Violence* (London: Brunner-Routledge, 2001)

Moynihan, Ray, 'The Marketing of a Disease: Female Sexual Dysfunction', *British Medical Journal*, 326 (2003): pp. 45–7

Mullan, B., *Mad to be Normal: Conversations with R.D. Laing* (London: Free Association Books 1995)

Noble, Joan Russell (ed.), *Recollections of Virginia Woolf* (London: Peter Owen, 1972)

Ofshe, Richard, and Watters, Ethan, *Making Monsters: False Memories, Psychotherapy and Sexual Hysteria* (London: André Deutsch, 1995)

Oppenheim, Janet, *The Other World* (Cambridge: CUP, 1985)

—— *Shattered Nerves* (New York: Oxford University Press, 1991)

Orbach, Susie, *Fat Is a Feminist Issue* (London: Paddington Press, 1978)

—— *Hunger Strike* (London: Penguin Books, 1993)

Parry-Jones, W.L., *The Trade in Lunacy: A Study of Private Madhouses in England in the Eighteenth and Nineteenth Centuries* (London: Routledge & Kegan Paul, 1972)

Phillips, Adam, *D.W. Winnicott* (London: Fontana Modern Masters, 1988)

Pinel, Philippe, *Nosographie philosophique* (Paris: J.A.B. Rosson, 1810)

Plath, Sylvia, *The Journals of Sylvia Plath 1950–1962*, ed. Karen V. Kulik (London: Faber & Faber, 2000)

Porter, Roy, *Mind Forg'd Manacles* (London: Penguin Books, 1990)

Prince, Morton, 'Sexual Perversion or Vice? A Pathological and Therapeutic Inquiry' (1898)

—— *The Dissociation of a Personality* (Cambridge: CUP, 1905)

Putnam, F.W., *Diagnosis and Treatment of Multiple Personality Disorder* (New York: Guilford, 1989)

Rapp, Dean, 'The Early Discovery of Freud by the British General Educated Public, 1912–1919', *The Society for the Social History of Medicine*, 1990

Rieff, Philip, *Freud: The Mind of the Moralist* (London: Gollancz, 1960)

—— *The Triumph of the Therapeutic: Uses of Faith after Freud* (London: Chatto & Windus, 1966)

Riley, Denise, *War in the Nursery* (London: Virago, 1983)

Rodman, MD, F. Robert, *Winnicott* (Cambridge, Mass: Perseus, 2003)

Roudinesco, Elisabeth, *Histoire de la Psychanalyse en France*, 2 vols (Paris: Le Seuil, 1986)

—— *Jacques Lacan and Co., A History of Psychoanalysis in France*, trans. Jeffrey

Mehlman (London: Free Association Books, 1990)

—— *Théroigne de Méricourt*, trans. Martin Thom (London: Verso, 1991)

—— *Jacques Lacan* (Paris: Fayard, 1993)

Rouy, Hersilie, *Mémoires d'une aliénée* (Paris: Paul Ollendorff, 1883)

Scull, Andrew, *Social Order, Mental Disorder* (Berkeley: University of California Press, 1989)

—— *Madhouse* (Yale and London: Yale University Press, 2005)

Shloss, Carol Loeb, *Lucia Joyce: To Dance in the Wake* (London: Bloomsbury, 2004)

Shorter, Edward, *From Paralysis to Fatigue* (New York: Free Press, 1992)

—— *A History of Psychiatry* (New York: John Wiley & Sons, 1997)

Showalter, Elaine, *The Female Malady* (London: Virago, 1985)

—— *Hystories: Hysterical Epidemics and Modern Media* (New York: Columbia University Press, 1997)

Slater, Lauren, *Prozac Diary* (London: Hamish Hamilton, 1999)

—— *Opening Skinner's Box* (London: Bloomsbury, 2004)

Spoto, Donald, *Marilyn Monroe: The Biography* (London: Chatto & Windus, 1993)

Strasberg, Susan, *Marilyn and Me* (New York: Warner Books, 1992)

Strecker, Edward, *Their Mothers' Sons* (New York, Philadelphia: Lippincott, 1946)

Strouse, Jean, *Alice James* (London: Cape, 1981)

Sullivan, Harry Stack, 'The Modified Psychoanalytic Treatment of Schizophrenia', *American Journal of Psychiatry* 11 (1930), pp. 519–49

Summers, Anthony, *The Secret Lives of Marilyn Monroe* (New York: Macmillan, 1986)

Szasz, Thomas S., *The Myth of Mental Illness* (New York: Hoeber-Harper, 1961)

—— *Schizophrenia: The Sacred Symbol of Psychiatry* (New York, Basic Books, 1976)

Taine, H.A., *De L'intelligence* (1870)

Talfourd, Thomas Noon, *Final Memorials of Charles Lamb* (London: Moxon, 1850)

Tomes, Nancy, 'Feminist Histories of Psychiatry' in S. Micale and Roy Porter (eds), *Discovering the History of Psychiatry* (Oxford: OUP, 1994)

Torrey, E. Fuller, MD, and Miller, Judith, *The Invisible Plague* (New Jersey: Rutgers University Press, 2001)

Townsend, Howard, Winthrop, Bronson, and Gallatin, R. Horace (eds), *A Psychiatric Milestone: Bloomingdale Hospital Centenary, 1821–1921* (New York: Society of the New York Hospital, 1921),

Tuke, Samuel, *A Description of the Retreat* (1813; reprinted London: Dawsons, 1964)

Webster, Brenda, *The Last Good Freudian* (New York: Holmes & Meier, 2000)

Weininger, Otto, *Sex and Character* (New York: Putnam, 1907)

Winnicott, D.W., 'Primitive Emotional Development' (1945), in Masud R. Kahn (ed.), *Through Paediatrics to Psychoanalysis* (London: Hogarth Press, 1978)

—— *The Piggle* (London: Hogarth Press, 1978)

—— 'The Mother's Contribution to Society' (1957), republished in Winnicott, *Home is Where We Start From* (London: Penguin Books, 1986)

—— *Psycho-analytic Explorations*, ed. Claire Winnicott, Ray Shepherd, Madeleine Davis (Cambridge, Mass. 2000)

Winter, Alison, *Mesmerized* (Chicago/London, University of Chicago Press, 1998)

Wollstonecraft, Mary, *A Vindication of the Rights of Woman* (Boston: Peter Edes, 1792)

Woolf, Virginia, *The Diaries*, 5 vols (London: Hogarth Press, 1977–84)

—— *Mrs Dalloway* (London: Vintage, 2004)

Woolf, Leonard, *Letters of Leonard Woolf*, ed. Frederic Spotts (London: Bloomsbury, 1992)

—— *An Autobiography* (Oxford: Oxford University Press, 1980)

Wurtzel, Elizabeth, *Prozac Nation* (London: Quartet Books, 1995)

Young, Allan, *The Harmony of Illusions* (New Jersey: Princeton University Press, 1997)

Young-Bruehl, Elisabeth, *Anna Freud* (London: Macmillan, 1988)

Zaretsky, Eli, *Secrets of the Soul* (New York: Knopf, 2004)

Zulzer, W., *Klinisches Handbuch der Harn- und Sexualorgane* (Leipzig: F.C.W. Vogel, 1894)

INDEX